THE ANNOTATED®
Huckleberry Finn

"Mark Twain"
Samuel Langhorne Clemens
(1835–1910)

THE ANNOTATED®
Huckleberry Finn

Adventures of Huckleberry Finn
by Mark Twain (Samuel L. Clemens)

With an Introduction, Notes, and Bibliography by
MICHAEL PATRICK HEARN

Clarkson N. Potter, Inc./Publishers   New York
Distributed by Crown Publishers, Inc.

Publisher's Note

The text of *The Annotated® Huckleberry Finn* is reproduced from the first edition of *Adventures of Huckleberry Finn*, issued by Chatto & Windus, London, in 1884, which preceded by four months the first American edition, published by Charles L. Webster and Company, New York, in 1885. The British edition was set from the American galleys and contained all the illustrations by E. W. Kemble; it also corrected most typographical errors in the American text. Other misspellings have been silently changed in this edition.

The "Raft Chapter" in the Appendix is reprinted from the Chatto & Windus edition of *Life on the Mississippi*, 1883.

For
ADA FEAR FISK
M.P.H.

ACKNOWLEDGMENTS

Anyone who wishes to write about *Adventures of Huckleberry Finn* has a vast and rich tradition of critical and scholarly studies to consider. And I am no exception. My labors have been greatly lightened by the pioneering work of such scholars as Bernard DeVoto, Delancey Ferguson, and Dixon Wecter and by the biographies of Albert Bigelow Paine and Justin Kaplan. My efforts have also been greatly enriched by the perceptions made by Walter Blair in *Mark Twain and Huck Finn* (Berkeley and Los Angeles: University of California Press, 1960), perhaps the most thorough consideration of the book's composition and publication. Fortunately, Mark Twain himself preserved most of his working notes, galleys, and reading copies of his most famous novel; and his daughter, the late Clara Clemens Samossoud, in establishing a center for Mark Twain scholarship, deposited this priceless material in the Bancroft Library at the University of California, Berkeley. Throughout my work on *The Annotated Huckleberry Finn*, I have relied on the generosity of the staff of The Mark Twain Papers; I am indeed grateful in particular to the patience and encouragement of Victor Fischer, Robert H. Hirst, Henry Nash Smith, and the late Frederick Anderson. Previously unpublished materials by Mark Twain are copyright © 1981 by Edward J. Willi and Manufacturers Hanover Trust Company as trustees of the Mark Twain Foundation and are published with the permission of the University of California Press and Robert H. Hirst, General Editor of the Mark Twain Project in Berkeley, California; all citations of such work are identified by the notation (MTP). A principal concern of the directors of The Mark Twain Papers is the organization and publication of all of Twain's written work, and my research has depended heavily on the already completed volumes of the "approved text" issued by the University of California Press in collaboration with the Center of Textual Studies at the University of Iowa. I am also indebted to Henry H. Loos, curator of the Rare Book Room, Buffalo and Erie County Public Library, Buffalo, New York, for providing and granting permission to publish photographs (by Joseph Hryvniak) of pages of the manuscript of *Adventures of Huckleberry Finn*, and to the directors of the Berg Collection, The New York Public Library, Astor, Lenox and Tilden Foundations, for allowing me to quote from the letter from Twain to Walter Besant, February 22, 1898, in their collection. Harper & Row has generously granted permission to quote from the following works by Mark Twain: *Is Shakespeare Dead?* Copyright 1909 by The Mark Twain Company. Renewed 1936 by Clara Clemens Gabrilowitsch; *Mark Twain's Speeches*. Copyright 1910 by Harper & Row, Publishers, Inc. Renewed 1945 by Clara Clemens Samossoud; *Mark Twain's Notebook*, edited by Albert Bigelow Paine. Copyright 1935 by The Mark Twain Company. Renewed 1963 by Louise Paine Moore; *The Love Letters of Mark Twain*, edited by Dixon Wecter. Copyright 1947, 1949 by The Mark Twain Company; *The Autobiography of Mark Twain*, edited by Charles Neider. Copyright © 1959 by The Mark Twain Company. Copyright © 1959 by Charles Neider; and *Mark Twain: A Biography* by Albert Bigelow Paine. Copyright 1912 by Harper & Row, Publishers, Inc. Renewed 1940 by Dora L. Paine. Likewise, Professor William White Howells has kindly allowed me to quote from *My Mark Twain: Reminiscences and Criticisms* by William Dean Howells (New York and London: Harper & Bros., 1910). And, as always, I am grateful to the staffs of The New York Public Library and the Library of Congress for their kind and generous assistance throughout the research and writing of this study.

MICHAEL PATRICK HEARN

Library of Congress Cataloging in Publication Data

Twain, Mark, 1835–1910.
    The annotated Huckleberry Finn.

    Bibliography: p.
    I. Hearn, Michael Patrick. II. Title.
PS1305.A2H4 1981   813'.4   81-5904
                                      AACR2

ISBN: 0-517-530317

10 9 8 7 6 5 4 3 2 1
First Edition

CONTENTS

ΙNTRODUCTION

*"This is Huck Finn, a child of mine of
shady reputation. Be good to him for his
parent's sake."*

MARK TWAIN, IN A PRESENTATION COPY OF
Adventures of Huckleberry Finn [1]

MARK TWAIN once sarcastically defined a classic as "a
book which people praise and don't read." [2] However, his
Adventures of Huckleberry Finn is the exception to his rule: It
is a classic which is both praised and still read. It has also
been both condemned and banned. No other living work of
American literature has suffered so contradictory a history
as has the autobiography of Tom Sawyer's comrade. It has
been acknowledged a masterpiece; it has been called trash.
It has been marketed as a gift book for boys and girls; it has
been removed from the children's rooms of public libraries
across the country. It is required reading in most American
universities; it is banned from the curriculums of certain
city elementary and high school systems. Like Huckleberry
Finn himself during his famous journey down the Mississippi, the novel has seemed to be different things to many
people.

Its author never understood the controversy about
"Huck that abused child of nine who has had so much
unfair mud flung at him." [3] In July 1876 when he began the
novel, Twain considered "Huck Finn's Autobiography" to
be merely "a kind of companion" to the recently completed
The Adventures of Tom Sawyer. Twain had originally intend-

Mark Twain, 1885. *Courtesy the New York Historical
Society, New York City.*

1 From a note in the Mark Twain Papers, The
Bancroft Library, University of California at
Berkeley.

2 Aphorism from "Pudd'nhead Wilson's New Cal-
endar," Chapter 25, *Following the Equator* (1897).

3 In a letter to Joel Chandler Harris, November 29,
1885, Thomas H. English, *Mark Twain to Uncle
Remus* (Atlanta, Georgia: Emory University Library,
1953), p. 20.

William Dean Howells, 1875.

4 In a letter to William Dean Howells, July 5, 1875, *Mark Twain–Howells Letters*, Vol. I, edited by Henry Nash Smith, William M. Gibson, and Frederick Anderson (Cambridge, Massachusetts: Harvard University Press, 1960), p. 91.

5 In a letter to Howells, August 9, 1876, *Mark Twain–Howells Letters*, Vol. I, p. 144.

6 In Chapter 53 of *The Autobiography of Mark Twain*, edited by Charles Neider (New York: Harper & Row, 1959).

ed to carry the young hero of that novel into manhood, but, he wrote his literary confidant William Dean Howells, the novelist, "I believe it would be fatal to do it in any shape but autobiographically—like *Gil Blas*. I perhaps made a mistake in not writing it in the first person. If I went on, now, and took him into manhood, he would just be like all the one-horse men in literature and the reader would conceive a hearty contempt for him."[4] And in his "Conclusion" to *Tom Sawyer*, Twain left open the possibility of a sequel by suggesting that "some day it may seem worth while to take up the story of the younger ones again and see what sort of men and women they turned out to be." "By and by," he confided to Howells, "I shall take a boy of twelve and run him through life (in the first person) but not Tom Sawyer—he would not be a good character for it."

By August, Twain had found his proper spokesman. He wrote Howells that he had reluctantly begun "another boys' book—more to be at work than anything else. I have written 400 pages on it—therefore it is very nearly half done. It is Huck Finn's Autobiography."[5] The new novel developed directly from *Tom Sawyer*, from a final chapter that Howells advised Twain to delete, it being out of character with the rest of the story. Twain admitted to "the strong temptation to put Huck's life at the Widow's into detail, instead of generalizing it in a paragraph"; but he accepted his friend's suggestion to drop the passage, and then reworked it as the opening of the sequel. Soon the original scheme to run Huck Finn through life was abandoned; and Twain grew weary of his new effort. "I like it only tolerably well," he wrote Howells, "and may possibly pigeonhole or burn the ms. when it is done." Fortunately, he merely pigeonholed it; and over the next seven years, he intermittently pulled it out to work in additional episodes. While working on *Tom Sawyer*, Twain found that "a book is pretty sure to get tired along about the middle and refuse to go on with its work until its powers and its interest should have been refreshed by a rest and its depleted stock of raw materials reinforced by lapse of time."[6] The cause for this delay was simple: "My tank had run dry." However, after it had been neglected for two years, he took it out and reread the last chapter and now discovered that "when the tank runs dry you've only to leave it alone and it will fill up again in time. . . . There was plenty of material now and the book went on and finished itself without any trouble." And so too it was with *Huckleberry Finn*. "I haven't had such booming writing-days for many years," he wrote his family in July 1883 when his tank had refilled. "I am piling up manuscript in a really astonishing way. I believe I shall complete, in two months, a book which I have been going over for 7 years. This summer it is no more trouble to me to write than it is to lie."[7] By September the book was done; and Twain was so pleased with the final work that he proudly confessed, "Modesty compels me to say it's a rattling good one."[8]

The many years that covered the composition of *Huckleberry Finn* were perhaps the happiest and most productive of its author's troubled life. To the public, the famous author "Mark Twain" was as described by one twelve-year-old admirer: "He is Jolly; I imagine him to be a funny man . . . who always keeps every body laughing and who is happy as the Man in the Moon looks. . . . he makes so much money. . . . he is worth millions. . . . he has a beautiful wife and children. . . . he has everything a man could want."[9] This appraisal of the public man matches the impressions of Samuel Langhorne Clemens recorded by another child, his fourteen-year-old daughter Susy, in her 1885 biography, which she wrote in part as an answer to the popular image of her celebrated father. "We are a very happy family," she wrote. "We consist of Papa, Mamma, Jean, Clara, and me."[10] The adored and adoring eldest child described him with his "beautiful gray hair, not any too thick or any too long, but just right; a Roman nose, which greatly improves the beauty of his features; kind blue eyes and a small mustache. He has a wonderfully shaped head and profile. He has a very good figure. . . . All his features are perfect, except that he hasn't extraordinary teeth. His complexion is very fair. . . . He is a very good man and a very funny man. He *has* got a temper, but we all of us have in this family. He is the loveliest man I ever saw or hope to see—and oh, so absent-minded."

Olivia, Clara, Jean, Sam, and Susy Clemens on the porch of their **Hartford home, 1885.** *Courtesy the Mark Twain Papers, The Bancroft Library, University of California at Berkeley.*

7 In a letter to Jane Lampton Clemens and others, July 21, 1883, *Mark Twain's Letters*, Vol. I, edited by Albert Bigelow Paine (New York: Harper & Bros., 1935), p. 434.

8 In a letter to Andrew Chatto, September 1, 1883, quoted by Justin Kaplan, *Mr. Clemens and Mark Twain* (New York: Simon and Schuster, 1966), p. 251.

9 In a composition by David Watt Bowser, March 16, 1880, "Dear Master Wattie: The Mark Twain--David Watt Bowser Letters," edited by Pascal Covici, Jr., *Southwest Review* (Spring 1960), p. 106.

10 Quoted by Mark Twain in Chapter 40 of *Autobiography*. "The spelling is frequently desperate," Twain admitted of his daughter's biography, "but it was Susy's and it shall stand." And his wishes have been followed here.

Susy Clemens. *Courtesy the Mark Twain Papers, The Bancroft Library, University of California at Berkeley.*

Mark Twain, about 1880. *Courtesy the Library of Congress.*

The Clemens home in Hartford, Connecticut, 1885. *Courtesy the New-York Historical Society, New York City.*

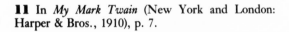

11 In *My Mark Twain* (New York and London: Harper & Bros., 1910), p. 7.

The Clemenses of Hartford, Connecticut, were indeed prosperous and content. They had settled in the booming, handsome state capital to be near his publishers as well as the circle of writers of Nook Farm, on the city's western edge. Here, where also lived Harriet Beecher Stowe, the author of *Uncle Tom's Cabin*, and Charles Dudley Warner, a newspaper editor who became coauthor of Twain's first novel *The Gilded Age* (1874), the Clemenses built a mansion Twain thought worthy of a successful author. Financed largely by the inheritance of his wealthy wife, the former Olivia L. Langdon of Elmira, New York, and his own profits from his best-selling books, the Mark Twain house reflected the former Mississippi riverboat pilot's personality as much as that of its architect. The most eccentric home in sedate Hartford, this nineteen-room, five-bath structure sported a porch shaped like a riverboat deck and a balcony like a pilot-house. The mansion's Gothic turrets and polychromatic bricks and roof tiles, and interiors designed by Louis Tiffany and "aesthetic" nursery wallpaper by Walter Crane reflected Mrs. Clemens's taste for what Howells defined as the currently fashionable "English violet order of architecture."**11** This bizarre, yet comfortable, combination of Mississippi steamboat and English castle took three years to complete, with further renovations and extensions in 1881; and in all, the Clemenses spent nearly $200,000 to buy the land and to build and furnish the main building and the carriage house.

Their residence was built as much for hospitality as

for show; and being conveniently situated between Boston and New York, the household entertained a steady stream of visitors traveling between the two major literary centers of the country. Such constant socializing and the general upkeep of the house (which required at least six servants) strained the family's finances; in one year the costs were as high as $100,000. "I have a badgered, harassed feeling, a good part of my time," Clemens wrote his mother in 1878. "It comes mainly of business responsibilities and annoyances. . . . There are other things also that help to consume my time and defeat my projects. Well, the consequence is, I cannot write a book at home. This cuts my income down."[12] In desperate attempts to economize, he took his family to Europe where he resolved to "budge no more until I shall have completed one of the half dozen books that lie begun, up stairs."

His study in Hartford was never the most convenient place to work: One reporter noted how the "floor was littered up with a confusion of newspapers, newspaper cuttings, books, children's toys, pipes, models of machinery, and cigar ends. Twain's method is to drop everything when he's done using it, but he will let nobody else interfere with the arrangements of his study."[13] And Twain's mind was as cluttered as his studio with new ideas and unfinished projects. With so many distractions at home, it is a wonder that he got any writing done. "Work?" he replied to a friend's question in 1881. "One *can't*, you know, to any purpose. I don't really get anything done worth speaking of, except during the three or four months that we are away in the Summer. I keep three or four books on the stocks all the time, but I seldom add a satisfactory chapter to one of them at home."[14] Nevertheless, during the seven years that *Huckleberry Finn* was "on the stocks," Twain produced *A Tramp Abroad* (1880), a record of his walking tour of Europe; *The Prince and the Pauper* (1882), another novel; and *Life on the Mississippi* (1883), partially a record of his recent return down the great river, which he had traveled as a young steamboat pilot before the Civil War.

It was not in Hartford but in Elmira that Twain did most of his writing. He admitted to an interviewer that this quiet upstate New York community "may be called, the home of *Huckleberry Finn* and other books of mine, for they were written here."[15] For years, the Clemenses spent their summers at Quarry Farm, the home of Olivia's sister, about three miles outside of Elmira and perched on a high hillside; it was a glorious summer camp for the girls and, for Livy, a needed refuge from the exhausting responsibilities of the Hartford house. Only in seclusion did Twain work best, and his sister-in-law thoughtfully built for him a lovely little studio, shaped like a pilot-house, that overlooked the countryside. "It is octagonal, with a peaked

12 In a letter to Jane Lampton Clemens, February 17, 1878, *Mark Twain's Letters*, Vol. I, pp. 319–320.

13 Quoted by Milton Meltzer in *Mark Twain Himself* (New York: Thomas Y. Crowell Co., 1960), p. 141.

14 In a letter to Charles Warren Stoddard, October 26, 1881, *Mark Twain's Letters*, Vol. I, p. 405.

15 In "A Day with Mark Twain" by Edwin J. Park, Chicago *Tribune*, September 19, 1886, p. 12.

Quarry Farm, Elmira, New York. *Courtesy the Mark Twain Papers, The Bancroft Library, University of California at Berkeley.*

Mark Twain returns to his study at Quarry Farm, 1903. *Courtesy the Library of Congress.*

16 In a letter to the Rev. Joseph and Mrs. Twichell, June 11, 1874, quoted by Meltzer, *Mark Twain Himself*, p. 146.

Olivia L. Clemens, 1885. *Courtesy the Mark Twain Papers, The Bancroft Library, University of California at Berkeley.*

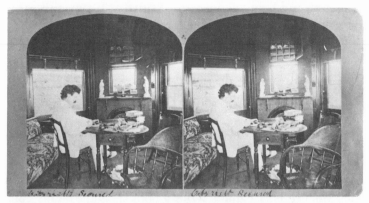

Mark Twain in his study at Quarry Farm, 1874. *Courtesy the Mark Twain Papers, The Bancroft Library, University of California at Berkeley.*

roof," he wrote friends, "each octagon filled with a spacious window, and it sits perched in complete isolation on top of an elevation that commands leagues of valley and city and retreating ranges of distant blue hills. It is a cosy nest, with just room in it for a sofa and a table and three or four chairs—and when the storms sweep down the remote valley and the lightning flashes above the hills below and the rain beats upon the roof over my head, imagine the luxury of it! . . . On hot days I spread the study wide open, anchor my papers with brickbats and write in the midst of hurricanes, clothed in the same thin linen we make shirts of."[16] But Twain did not spend all of his time at Quarry Farm writing. In her biography, Susy recorded his summer routine: "Papa rises about ½ past 7 in the morning, breakfasts at eight, writes, plays tennis with Clara and me and tries to make the donkey go . . . ; does varius things in P.M., and in the evening plays tennis with Clara and me and amuses Jean and the donkey." And during that productive summer that saw the completion of *Huckleberry Finn*, Twain was as much preoccupied with the possibilities of manufacturing a pair of grape scissors invented by Howells's father, marketing a history game Twain had created to amuse his daughters, and preparing a play or two with Howells as with the writing of his greatest book. Evidently the author was unaware of what he had accomplished in the new story.

Immediately he turned over the script to his "faithful, judicious and painstaking editor," Olivia Clemens. "Ever since papa and mama were married," Susy wrote in the biography, "papa has written his books . . . and she has expergated them. Papa read *Huckleberry Finn* to us in manuscript . . . , and then he would leave parts of it for mama to expergate, while he went off to the study to work, and sometimes Clara and I would be sitting with mama while she was looking the manuscript over, and I remember so well . . . one part perticularly which was perfectly fascinating it was so terrible, that Clara and I used to delight in and oh, with what despair we saw mama turn down the leaf on which it was written, we thought the book would be almost ruined without it. But we generally come to think as mama did."[17] Clemens was not above a little perverse teasing of his intrepid editor. "For my own entertainment and to enjoy the protests of the children," he confessed in Chapter 41 of his *Autobiography*, "I often abused my editor's innocent confidence. I often interlarded remarks of a studied and felicitously atrocious character purposely to achieve the children's brief delight and then see the remorseless pencil do its fatal work. I often joined my supplications to the children's for mercy . . . and pretended to be in earnest. They were deceived and so was their mother. . . . But it was very delightful and I could not resist the temptation. . . . Then I privately struck the passage out myself."

Much has been made of Mrs. Clemens's "expergating" of her husband's work. Van Wyck Brooks in *The Ordeal of Mark Twain* (1920, p. 116) went so far as to accuse Twain of having compromised his artistic integrity through his wife's attempt "to turn Caliban into a gentleman." Olivia Langdon's upbringing was far removed from that of Sam Clemens: A semi-invalid from the age of sixteen, she had been raised in a genteel and respectable home where piety, comfort, and morality were valued; her sheltered life knew none of the roughness and violence native to the American Southwest before the Civil War. But the lovesick Clemens yearned to do anything for his beloved. He was willing to swear off liquor and tobacco just for her sake, and, he admitted, "not that I believed there was the faintest *reason* in the matter, but just as I would deprive myself of sugar in my coffee if she wished it, or quit wearing socks if she thought them immoral."[18] As further proof of his devotion, he promised her mother that he would try to "earn enough money some way or other, to buy a remunerative share in a newspaper of high standing, and then instruct and elevate and civilize the public through its columns, and my wife (to be) will superintend the domestic economy, furnish ideas and sense, erase improprieties from the manuscript, and read proof."[19]

One of the habits that she could not abide was his swearing. "All through the first ten years of my married life," he continued in Chapter 41 of the *Autobiography*, "I kept a constant and discreet watch upon my tongue while in the house, and went outside and to a distance when circumstances were too much for me and I was obliged to seek relief. I prized my wife's respect and approval above all the rest of the human race's respect and approval." But Mrs. Clemens succeeded no better in reforming her hus-

17 Quoted by Meltzer, pp. 138 and 139.

18 In a letter to Twichell, quoted by Meltzer, p. 144. "Papa uses very strong language," Susy Clemens noted in her biography (in Chapter 41 of his *Autobiography*), "but I have an idea not nearly so strong as when he first married mamma."

19 In a letter to Mrs. Jervis Langdon, February 13, 1869, *The Love Letters of Mark Twain*, edited by Dixon Wecter (New York: Harper & Bros., 1949), p. 67.

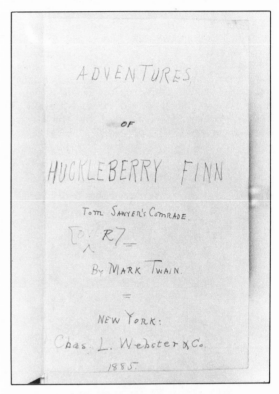

Title page of the manuscript of *Adventures of Huckleberry Finn*, 1885. *Courtesy the Buffalo and Erie County Public Library, Buffalo, New York.*

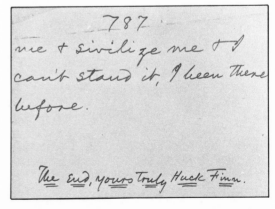

The final page of the manuscript of *Adventures of Huckleberry Finn*. *Courtesy the Buffalo and Erie County Public Library, Buffalo, New York.*

20 In "Mark Twain: An Inquiry," *North American Review* (February 1901), p. 314. For example, he once delivered a humorous lecture on the joys of onanism at the Stomach Club; and his notorious Elizabethan parody *1601* (in which the queen, Francis Bacon, Sir Walter Raleigh, and other notables of the English court discuss such indelicate subjects as who "did breake wind" in the royal presence) was composed to entertain Twichell, a Congregational minister, and it has since become an underground classic of ribaldry.

21 In a letter to Samuel L. Clemens, January 8, 1886, *Letters of Richard Watson Gilder*, edited by Rosamund Gilder (Boston and New York: Houghton Mifflin, 1916), pp. 398–399. Gilder included the following excerpts in *The Century:* "An Adventure of Huckleberry Finn: With An Account of the Famous Grangerford-Shepherdson Feud" (December 1884), pp. 268–278; "Jim's Investments, and King Sollermun" (January 1885), pp. 456–458; and "Royalty on the Mississippi: As Chronicled by Huckleberry Finn" (February 1885), pp. 544–567.

Richard Watson Gilder. *Courtesy the Library of Congress.*

band than did the Widow Douglas in "sivilizing" Huck Finn. "His profanity," Howells explained in *My Mark Twain* (p. 76), "was the heritage of his boyhood and young manhood in social conditions and under the duress of exigencies in which everybody swore about as impersonally as he smoked." It was a part of his nature; it could be arrested but never completely erased from his character.

Twain was generally open-minded about criticism. "If you wanted a thing changed," Howells recalled in *My Mark Twain* (p. 19), "very good, he changed it; if you suggested that a word or a sentence or a paragraph had better be struck out, very good, he struck it out." And Twain relied as much on Howells's as on Mrs. Clemens's opinions of his work; and oddly, Howells could be as much of a prude as Mrs. Clemens. Even though he and Clemens "were natives of the same vast Mississippi Valley; and Missouri was not so far from Ohio," Howells was shocked by his friend's ribaldry. "Throughout my long acquaintanceship with him," Howells wrote in *My Mark Twain* (pp. 3–4), "his graphic touch was always allowing itself a freedom which I cannot bring my fainter pencil to illustrate. He had the Southwestern, the Lincolnian, the Elizabethan breadth of parlance, which I suppose one ought not to call coarse without calling one's self prudish; and I was often hiding away in discreet holes and corners the letters in which he had loosed his bold fancy to stoop on rank suggestion; I could not bear to burn them, and I could not, after the first reading, quite bear to look at them." Twain could be uninhibitedly vulgar; and Howells once admitted that Twain's "humor was not for most women."[20] And not for all men either. However, the reticent Howells found nothing in the proofs of *Huckleberry Finn* so offensive that it needed to be struck out.

But not so Richard Watson Gilder, the editor of *The Century.* In the three excerpts from *Huckleberry Finn* that were serialized in the magazine before the novel's publication, Gilder deleted references to nakedness, offensive smells, and the blowing of noses; such a phrase as "both of them took on like they'd lost the twelve apostles" was suppressed, perhaps for being too blasphemous. Under Gilder's blue pencil, "such a sweat" became "such a hurry," "wet cloth" became "shroud." He thus left nothing in the text which might make Miss Watson blush. "Mr. Clemens has great faults," the cautious editor explained; "at times he is inartistically and indefensibly coarse . . . there is much of his writing which we would not print for a miscellaneous audience. If you should ever carefully compare the chapters of *Huckleberry Finn*, as we printed them, with the same as they appear in the book, you will see the most decided difference. These extracts were carefully edited for a magazine audience with his full consent."[21] And yet Gilder was astute enough to recognize the novel's considerable artistic value and also catholic enough in his tastes to include "Royalty on the Mississippi," the final excerpt from *Huckleberry Finn*, in the same issue as his serializations of Howells's *The Rise of Silas Lapham* and Henry James's *The Bostonians*. [22]

There is little evidence to support the popular assumption that, but for Mrs. Clemens, Mark Twain might have been a nineteenth-century Henry Miller or J. D. Salinger. As DeLancey Ferguson was the first to point out, in "Huck Finn Aborning" (*The Colophon*, Spring 1938), of the hundreds of changes within what remains of the holograph manuscript of *Huckleberry Finn*, none significantly alters the initial character of the story. What Mrs. Clemens changed in the cause of propriety is minimal. [23] Some improprieties were certainly carelessnesses, but others were apparently thrown in by Clemens merely to tease his wife.

Even in the relatively uninhibited *Huckleberry Finn*, Twain was ever conscious of what was appropriate and inappropriate to contemporary literature. In private he might revel in "the frank indelicacies of speech permissible among ladies and gentlemen in . . . ancient time," but in print he defended the current taste: "Many of the terms used in the most matter-of-fact way by . . . the first ladies and gentlemen in the land would have made a Comanche blush. Indelicacy is too mild a term to convey the idea. However, I had read *Tom Jones* and *Roderick Random*, and other books of that kind, and knew that the highest and first ladies and gentlemen in England had remained little or no cleaner in their talk, and in the morals and conduct which such talk implies, clear . . . into our own nineteenth century—in which century, broadly speaking, the earliest samples of the real lady and real gentleman discoverable in English history—or in European history . . . may be said to have made their appearance." [24] Even profane Clemens acknowledged limitations to strong speech: He did not approve of swearing before ladies and children. [25] He also recognized that "in certain trying circumstances, desperate circumstances, urgent circumstances, profanity furnishes a relief denied even to prayer." [26] However, only once in the manuscript of *Huckleberry Finn* did he insist on his original phrase: In Chapter 23 when Jim cries "de Lord God Almighty" on realizing what he has done to his little girl, Twain wrote in the margin, "This expression shall not be changed."

Suggestion is an important element of humor, and Twain knew exactly how far he could go in implying vulgarity. [27] In *Huckleberry Finn*, he cuts the boy short, in Chapter 14, just before he can say "hawking and spitting," and, in Chapter 23, before Huck dare describe in detail the king's phallic costume. When Twain did have to resort to "damned" for accuracy, it was always printed "d——d";

[22] "As an accessory of literature," Bernard DeVoto argued in *Mark Twain's America* (Boston and New York: Houghton Mifflin, 1932), p. 308, "American journalism attained its highest reach in the February or Midwinter number of the *Century Magazine* of 1885."

[23] Blasphemies were tempered: "Damn" became "dern," or "blame"; "Judas Iscariot" is merely "Judas," "as mild as a Sunday School" now "as mild as goose milk," and a character turns "up towards the sky" rather than "towards the throne." Some indelicacies were excised: "Iron-rust and spit" was changed to "iron-rust and tears," and the comment that a conscience "Takes up more room than all the rest of a person's bowels" was dropped. See Bernard DeVoto, *Mark Twain at Work* (Cambridge, Mass.: Harvard University Press, 1942), pp. 82–84.

[24] In Chapter 54 of *Autobiography*; in Chapter 4 of *A Connecticut Yankee in King Arthur's Court* (1889).

[25] Clemens could be as prudish as Lewis Carroll, who once proposed a bowdlerized edition of Shakespeare that might be suitable for little girls. "It pains me to think of your reading that book just as it is," Clemens warned his fiancée in a letter of March 1, 1869, about *Don Quixote*. "You are as pure as snow, and I would have you always so—untainted, untouched even by the impure thoughts of others. . . . Read nothing that is not *perfectly* pure . . . but neither it nor Shakespeare are proper books for virgins to read until some hand has culled them of their grossness" (*The Love Letters of Mark Twain*, p. 76).

[26] Quoted by Mrs. Thomas Bailey Aldrich, *Crowding Memories* (Boston and New York: Houghton Mifflin, 1916), pp. 150–151.

[27] Twain devised ingenious ways to imply profanity without actually having to use it. In Chapter 4 of *Roughing It* (1872), Twain digressed when someone is called "you son of a skunk": "No, I forget—skunk was not the word; it seems to me it was still stronger than that; I know it was, in fact. . . . However, it is no matter—probably it was too strong for print, anyway." In Chapter 22 of *A Connecticut Yankee in King Arthur's Court*, Sir Madok yells, "Blank-blank-blank him!"; in Chapter 27, the Yankee delivers "a hair-lifting soul-scorching thirteen-jointed insult." Also, in Chapter 13 of that novel, when describing the outrages inflicted upon the freeman by the noble of the Middle Ages, Twain continued that "if a freeman's daughter—but no, that last infamy of monarchical government is unprintable." The sounds may not be the same, but the sense is there.

28 Quoted by Meltzer, *Mark Twain Himself*, p. 194.

29 In a letter to Howells, quoted by Kaplan, *Mr. Clemens and Mark Twain*, p. 62.

Charles L. Webster. *Courtesy the Mark Twain Papers, The Bancroft Library, University of California at Berkeley.*

but there was no need to use that word in *Huckleberry Finn*, for Twain was a master of the euphemism. In his purported *The True Adventures of Huckleberry Finn* (1970), John Seelye has given all the precise profanity, but what is gained in the hero's describing the wildest part of the king's outfit as "a lit candle that was stuck upright in his ass"? The voice of the narrator, and so the tone of the novel, is so distorted by these "improvements" that Seelye has violated the integrity of Twain's original. Maybe Sam Clemens swore, but it is not in Huck Finn's nature as drawn in *Huckleberry Finn* to use profanity. Good-hearted Huck is uncomfortable around people who swear, such as his pap as well as the man on the ferry landing in Chapter 7; the boy does have his bad habits, but swearing is not one of them. Clearly, men who are blasphemous are to be scorned, not admired. Heaven and Hell are ever present to superstitious Huck, and only in a moment of overwhelming emotional crisis, in Chapter 31, does the boy vow to "*go to hell.*" Twain knew exactly what he was doing in suppressing common profanities by replacing them with colorful local, and sometimes ingenious, euphemisms. Only the most uncompromising of critics would prefer to exchange one of Huck's "derns" or "blames" for a single good "goddam."

On completion of the manuscript in September 1883, Twain cautiously considered the best way to publish *Huckleberry Finn*. His reputation as a best-selling author was established with his first commissioned book, *The Innocents Abroad* (1869); and its extraordinary sale of 100,000 copies in two years was accomplished by the American Publishing Company of Hartford, the most aggressive of subscription houses, which marketed their wares not in bookstores but door-to-door by an army of "broken-down clergymen, maiden ladies, grass widows, and college students" across the country.[28] Within a decade, works by Mark Twain, "the people's author," were as common to rural parlors as the family Bible and Webster's Dictionary. However, convinced that he had been swindled by the American Publishing Company, Twain broke with that firm in 1881 and gave his next book, *The Prince and the Pauper*, to a reputable Boston publisher. Unfortunately, although the reviews were laudatory, the sales were disastrous. For Twain, "Anything but subscription publishing is printing for private circulation."[29] The publisher pleaded with him to let him try again, and Twain gave him *Life on the Mississippi*, which was manufactured at the author's expense and sold by subscription. But sales of *Life on the Mississippi* were no better than those of *The Prince and the Pauper*.

The only answer was for Twain to publish *Huckleberry Finn* himself. In early 1884, he set up his nephew-in-law in a couple of offices in New York and, by May, established

"Some Uses for Electricity." Cartoon by E. W. Kemble, *Life*, March 13, 1884. *Courtesy the Library of Congress.*

Charles L. Webster and Company. The young backwoodsman had already proved himself to Twain to be capable and energetic in straightening out some of his uncle's business problems; but Webster knew nothing of the subscription business, so Twain employed another gentleman who had long been in the trade to teach Webster all he knew about book canvassing. Naïvely, the author believed that these two men, a secretary and a clerk, plus his capital, both literary and financial, were all that were needed to run a profitable publishing house.

An important feature of a subscription book was that, because it generally cost more than a regular trade book and thus the salesman had to offer the buyer more for his money, it had to be filled with pictures. Initially the publishers considered "a *very* cheap man" named Hooper to illustrate *Huckleberry Finn*. However, Twain enjoyed a cartoon of "the applying of electrical protectors to doorknobs, door-mats, etc., and electrical hurriers to messengers, waiters, etc." which had recently appeared in *Life*, the humor weekly; and in late March, he wrote Webster that he wanted the artist responsible for that drawing for his new book. **30** But Edward Windsor Kemble (1861–1933) was not cheap; although he had been illustrating professionally for only two years, Kemble was so in demand as a

Edward Windsor Kemble. *Courtesy the Art Division, The New York Public Library, Astor, Lenox, and Tilden Foundations.*

30 According to a note in *Mark Twain's Letters to His Publishers*, edited by Hamlin Hill (Berkeley and Los Angeles: University of California Press, 1967), p. 174; in a letter to Charles L. Webster, March 31, 1884, *Mark Twain, Business Man*, edited by Samuel Charles Webster (Boston: Little Brown and Co., 1946), p. 246. Unless otherwise stated, all further references to correspondence with Webster are from the latter work.

Self-caricature of E. W. Kemble at work on his illustrations for *Adventures of Huckleberry Finn*, from a letter, May 1, 1884. *Courtesy the Library of Congress.*

31 Twain may have known the artist's father, Edward Cleveland Kemble, the founder of the *Alta California*, for which Twain was a traveling correspondent and in which first appeared the series of letters which became *The Innocents Abroad*.

32 Quoted in his obituary in the New York *Times*, September 20, 1933.

33 In a letter to Dan Beard, quoted by Albert Bigelow Paine, *Mark Twain: A Biography*, Vol. II (New York and London, Harper & Bros., 1912), p. 888.

cartoonist that he charged $1,200 for his first book commission, to make 175 pen-and-ink drawings for *Huckleberry Finn*. Born in Sacramento, California,[31] Kemble studied for only a year at the Art Students League in New York. "I don't know what good it did," he later admitted, "for no one ever looked at what I drew."[32] Consequently, Kemble was largely self-taught. Undaunted by this lack of training, he secured a job as staff cartoonist on the New York *Daily Graphic* in 1881; and when *Life* was founded in 1883, Kemble was one of its early contributors.

Kemble never met with Twain to discuss his drawings for the new novel. "I am not going to tell you what to draw," Twain later told another of his artists. "If a man comes to me and says, 'Mr. Clemens, I want you to write me a story,' I'll write it for him; but if he undertakes to tell me what to write, I'll say, 'Go hire a typewriter.'"[33] But Twain was not above letting an illustrator know what *not* to draw. Kemble communicated directly with Webster, and the publisher kept the author informed of every step of the artist's progress. Then, if anything displeased Twain, Webster reported it back to Kemble.

Because the book had to be ready for the vital Christmas season of 1884, Kemble immediately set to work. Unfortunately, he was soon delayed. "I cannot have many of the illustrations finished until the latter part of next week," he wrote Webster on May 1, "as we all have the moving craze and are experiencing such little delights as eating our meals off the mantle piece, bathing in a coal scuttle behind a screen, etc., etc. I have tried to work but cannot make it go." The artist appended to his note a sketch of "a faint idea of my condition." In spite of the circumstances, Kemble did deliver the first batch of drawings as promised; but evidently he had hurried his work. Twain was not pleased with the results. "Some of the pictures are good," he wrote Webster on May 24, "but none of them are very *very* good. The faces are generally ugly, and wrenched into over-expression amounting sometimes to distortion. As a rule (though not always) the people in the pictures are forbidding and repulsive. Reduction will modify them, no doubt, but it can hardly make them pleasant folk to look at." The cover sketch for the "book-back" was "all right and good, and will answer; although the boy's mouth is a trifle more Irishy than necessary." However, Kemble depicted only what he found in the text; indeed, many of the people in *Huckleberry Finn* are forbidding and repulsive, but letter-perfect accuracy was not what Twain expected from the illustrations. "An artist shouldn't follow a book too literally, perhaps," he explained to Webster; "if this be the necessary result. And mind you, much of the drawing in these pictures is careless and bad."

Kemble worked with several disadvantages. Not only

was his home disrupted and he evidently never had the complete manuscript to refer to,[34] but also he used the same model for all the novel's many characters. The New York City boy who posed for Huck himself doubled for every one else, from Mrs. Judith Loftus to the "late Dauphin."[35] Certain problems in the sketches may be traced to Kemble's having to interpret rather than to copy the characterizations. Even for Huck Finn, the young model was not perfect: "He was a bit tall for the ideal boy," Kemble admitted, "but I could jam him down a few pegs in my drawing." But Twain found even this characterization wanting. "The frontispiece has the usual blemish—an ugly, ill-drawn face," the author complained to his publisher. "Huck Finn is an exceedingly good-hearted boy, and should carry a good and good-looking face."

Twain was as hesitant with Kemble's illustrations as he was with his own text. Certain subjects could not be depicted: Although Huck admits in Chapter 19 that "we was always naked, day and night," Kemble never portrays the boy and the slave nude; and Twain suppressed Kemble's drawing of the "lecherous old rascal kissing the girl at the campmeeting" in Chapter 20, because, Twain told Webster on June 11, "The subject won't *bear* illustrating. It is a disgusting thing, and pictures are sure to tell the truth about it too plainly." Again, suggestion was important, in the illustrations as well as the text. Only reluctantly did Twain say, "The pictures will *do*—they will just barely do—and that is the best I can say for them." He approved them apparently because the publisher needed sample drawings for their agents' canvassing books, bound prospectuses made up of representative chapters and their appropriate illustrations with strips of the various available bindings laid in the front and blank ruled pages at the back for orders; these had to be ready no later than midsummer, for Twain demanded a prepublication sale of 40,000 copies before he would issue the book at holiday time. The author did have faith in Kemble's abilities. He warned Webster, "Don't dishearten the artist—show him where he has *improved*, rather than where he has failed and punch him up to improve more." Happily, on receipt of more illustrations, Twain proudly wrote Webster on June 11, "I *knew* Kemble had it *in* him, if he would only modify his violences and come down to careful, painstaking work. This batch of pictures is most rattling good. They please me exceedingly."

Because *Huckleberry Finn* was advertised as "a companion to *The Adventures of Tom Sawyer*," Kemble was expected to follow the general design of True W. Williams's illustrations in the previous novel. At first glance, the two books with their myriads of spot line drawings darting in and out of the type do look alike, but the differences between Williams's and Kemble's art are greater than their sim-

Huckleberry Finn. Illustration by True W. Williams, *The Adventures of Tom Sawyer*, 1876.

34 This situation is suggested by a letter from Kemble to Webster, June 2, 1884, quoted by Beverly R. David in "The Pictorial *Huckleberry Finn:* Mark Twain and His Illustrator, E. W. Kemble" (*American Quarterly*, October 1979, p. 33) in which the artist asked the publisher to "send me the manuscript from XIII Chapter on . . . as these are illustrations here which are described minutely and I'm afraid to touch them without the reading matter to refer to." Kemble also apparently worked from the uncorrected manuscript, rather than from galleys, because there are details in his drawings which are not in the published book; for example, the two Phelps children depicted in the illustration in Chapter 32 are described in the manuscript but not in the book.

35 For the king, the young model "wore an old frock coat and padded his waistline with towels until he assumed the proper rotundity. Then he would mimic the sordid old reprobate and twist his boyish face into the most outlandish expressions. If I could have drawn the grimaces as they were," Kemble continued in "Illustrating *Huckleberry Finn*" (*The Colophon*, February 1930), "I would have had a convulsing collection of comics, but these would not have jibed with the text and I was forced to forgo them."

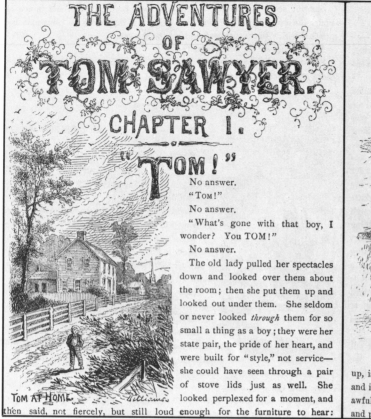

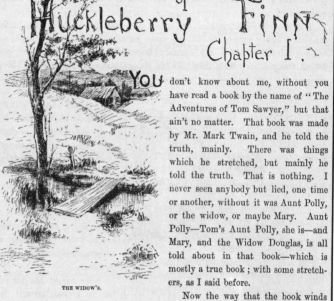

Left: Opening page, with illustration by True W. Williams, *The Adventures of Tom Sawyer*, 1876. **Right:** Opening page, with illustration by E. W. Kemble, the first American edition of *Adventures of Huckleberry Finn*, 1885.

36 In an unmailed letter, September 8, 1887, *Mark Twain's Letters*, Vol. II, p. 477.

ilarities. Kemble was clearly the better of the two draftsmen, but the pictures in *Tom Sawyer* are certainly prettier than those in *Huckleberry Finn*. Williams, as much as the author himself, idealized "St. Petersburg," Clemens's boyhood home Hannibal, Missouri; the artist captured the slightly sentimental view of childhood immortalized in what Twain called "simply a hymn, put into prose form to give it a worldly air."**36** The abrupt change in atmosphere within the same locale is established in the opening illustration of each novel: In the first, Tom Sawyer's humble home looks like a mansion; in the second, the Widow Douglas's mansion looks like any other backwoods dwelling. Kemble was less self-consciously a stylist than was Williams, and his strong, matter-of-fact drawings are free of the sweet fussiness of his predecessor's designs. Even when drawing violences such as the murder of Dr. Robinson, Williams emphasized the romance, the melodrama of the event; but in the shooting of Old Boggs by Colonel Sherburn, Kemble depicted the crime as coolly, as distantly, as Huck describes it.

But Kemble was by profession a cartoonist, and so

humor was essential to his drawings for *Huckleberry Finn*. What is most remarkable about these illustrations is the way the artist extended even the minor comedy that was merely suggested in the text: With tongue firmly in cheek, Kemble literally interpreted some ignorant absurdity, whether it concerned Solomon and his million wives, the king as Juliet, or Hannah with the mumps, mentioned only in passing by some character in the story. Further levity came from the captions, written, like the running heads, by the publisher; particularly effective are Webster's sardonic puns, such as "Falling from Grace" in Chapter 5 and "A Dead Head" in Chapter 22.

Also in his illustrations for *Huckleberry Finn*, Kemble proved himself an American master of humorous characterization. He was not strictly a caricaturist; his comedy came from the situation to be illustrated rather than from any stylistic trick he might employ. Whatever he may have lacked in technical grace (and some of his pictures are badly drawn), Kemble shared with the greatest illustrators the ability to give even the minor individual in a text his own distinct visual personality; just as Twain in a few sentences could suggest a fully rounded character, so too could Kemble depict with a few strokes of his pen that same whole personage. Kemble may have initially relied somewhat on Williams's depictions in *Tom Sawyer*, but he made the characters his own in his drawings for *Huckleberry Finn*. Kemble's designs now are as much a part of *Huckleberry Finn* as John Tenniel's wood engravings are of *Alice in Wonderland*; and although *Huckleberry Finn* has been re-illustrated innumerable times,[37] no other artist has de-

[37] The majority of newly illustrated editions of *Huckleberry Finn*, generally gift books for boys and girls, have been undistinguished. The most encouraging artist for the great American novel was Norman Rockwell; however, although he was perfect for the companion *Tom Sawyer*, the *Saturday Evening Post* illustrator, in his coy designs for the 1940 Heritage Press edition, failed to capture the bitter satire of Twain's classic. Thomas Hart Benton, in his athletic and energetic drawings for the 1942 Limited Editions Club edition, was tougher than Rockwell; but Benton's burlesque is more obvious than Kemble's. Of the more recent editions, only those by the contemporary masters Edward Ardizzone (1961) and Warren Chappell (1978) are memorable.

From time to time, Kemble returned to his first success to make new pictures for the story. In 1899 he provided four pen-and-wash illustrations for the reprint in the standard "Autograph Edition" of Mark Twain's collected works; and for a special Mark Twain number of the colored comic section "The Funny Side" of the New York *World* (December 10, 1899), Kemble contributed three new pen-and-ink sketches of incidents from Twain's greatest novel. One of the artist's last drawings was made for the 1933 Limited Editions Club edition: When the publisher, George Macy, learned that the original illustrator of *Huckleberry Finn* lived nearby, in Ridgefield, Connecticut, he asked Kemble to add something to the new edition, and the artist provided a picture of Huck, Tom, and Jim reading the famous story of their Mississippi travels. All of these supplemental illustrations are reprinted for the first time in this edition.

Jim and Huckleberry Finn. Lithograph of a detail of the mural in the Missouri State Capitol by Thomas Hart Benton.

38 Not all of Kemble's collaborators cared for his work. "For a man who has no conception whatever of human nature," Harris complained, "Kemble does very well. But he is too dog-goned flip to suit me." Harris disapproved of the dependence upon stock characters, such as those used by Kemble in his cartoons. "Neither fiction nor illustrative art," argued the author of *Uncle Remus*, "has any business with types. It must address itself to life, to the essence of life, which is character, which is individuality." See "Visions of the South: Joel Chandler Harris and His Illustrators" by Beverly R. David, *American Literary Realism* (Summer 1976), pp. 198–199. And Twain came to share Harris's disappointment with Kemble as an illustrator. He regretted the "blackboard outlines and charcoal sketches" in *Mark Twain's Library of Humor* (1888): "If Kemble illustrations for my last book were handed me today, I would understand how tiresome to me the sameness would get to be, when distributed through a whole book, and I would put them promptly in the fire" (in a note to *Mark Twain's Letters to His Publishers*, p. 254).

picted pious Miss Watson, drunken Pap Finn, the blubbering king and the bombastic duke, and all the others, as convincingly as did Twain's original illustrator. And Huck Finn himself is remembered as much for Kemble's image of the good-hearted boy as for Twain's description.

Even before the book was published, Kemble was recognized for his significant contribution to *Huckleberry Finn*. "We are not only indebted to you for a good chapter for our next number," Gilder told Twain in November, "but are profoundly indebted to you for unearthing a gem of an artist for us. As soon as we saw Kemble's pictures in your proofs, we recognized the fact that that was a find for us and so we went for him and we've got him. He is going to New Orleans for us to illustrate a long article." *Huckleberry Finn* made Kemble's reputation as one of the most admired of American illustrators of the late nineteenth century; it also determined the course of the rest of his career. Ironically, although he had never been farther south than Sandy Hook when he made the drawings for Twain's novel, through this book Kemble became famous for his depiction of the rural South; and then, whenever an editor such as Gilder needed an artist for a piece about that part of the country, he turned first to Kemble. Kemble was so in demand that, in addition to *Century, Harper's, Collier's, St. Nicholas*, and other major magazines competed for Kemble to illustrate work by such popular Southern writers as Joel Chandler Harris, George W. Cable, and Thomas Nelson Page. [38] Kemble did visit the South and filled his sketchbooks with sensitive studies of black life; these drawings were particularly helpful for his fine illustrations for *Uncle Tom's Cabin* (1892). However, he earned his widest popularity at the century's end for his unfortunate caricatures "Kemble's Coons" and "Blackberries," and consequently his present reputation has suffered for these dated stereotypes. *Huckleberry Finn* may have made Kemble's career, but he found time to illustrate only one other book prepared by Twain and published by Webster, *Mark Twain's Library of Humor*.

About the time *Huckleberry Finn* was going to press, Twain hastily inserted another plate in the already well illustrated book. That summer he had posed for a portrait bust by his protégé Karl Gerhardt, whose studies in Paris the author had subsidized since 1881; and Twain had the piece photographed for an extra plate in the front of the book to advertise the young man's skill as a sculptor. Thus the book clumsily contains two frontispieces, and the photogravure of the plaster bust is out of character with Kemble's clean, crisp pen-and-ink portrait of grinning Huck Finn. So carelessly was the plate printed that it exists in many varying states, and so it has been, since the

Mark Twain and George W. Cable on their public reading tour, 1884–1885. *Courtesy the New-York Historical Society, New York City.*

Bust of Mark Twain by Karl Gerhardt, 1884. Photogravure from *Adventures of Huckleberry Finn,* 1885.

book's publication, a bibliographic thorn in the side of the collector or librarian.

When the book finally went to the printers in the fall of 1884, all concerned were hopeful for a prodigious success. Despite the nation's recent economic crisis, orders for *Huckleberry Finn* were coming in steadily from all across the country. Twain too had been hit by the panic of 1884; and to correct some recent financial setbacks, he decided to "stump the Union" on a four-month public reading tour. He took as his partner the Southern novelist George Washington Cable, whom Twain had first heard read his work in Atlanta in 1882 when Twain was gathering material for *Life on the Mississippi.* Initially, Twain envisioned an ambitious series of traveling lectures by such

George W. Cable and Mark Twain. Caricature by
Thomas Nast, Thanksgiving, 1884. *Courtesy the
Library of Congress.*

39 Quoted by Meltzer, *Mark Twain Himself*, p. 188.

major contemporary men of letters as William Dean
Howells, Charles Dudley Warner, Thomas Bailey Aldrich, and Joel Chandler Harris; but it was just as well that
no one except Cable accompanied Twain on the long tour.
With only ten days off for Christmas holidays with their
families, Twain and Cable were on the road from November 5, 1884, through February 18, 1885, journeying 10,000
miles through seventy cities from Washington, D.C., to
Toronto, and as far west as Minnesota. Predictably, the
trip was exhausting and the lecturers got on each other's
nerves, but it did have its diversions: The two spent
Thanksgiving at the home of Thomas Nast, the *Harper's
Weekly* cartoonist; and in January, they visited Hannibal,
of which Clemens wrote his wife, "You can never imagine
the infinite great deeps of pathos that have rolled their tides
over me. I shall never see another such day. I have carried
my heart in my mouth for twenty-four hours."[39] Twain
was also moved by his audiences' enjoyment of his readings; nevertheless, the tour was such a strain that (according to Chapter 46 of his *Autobiography*) he "resolved at the
time that I would never rob the public from the platform
again unless driven to it by pecuniary compulsions."

Not only were "The 'Mark Twain'–Cable Readings" a
financial success, but they also proved to be excellent
advertising for the new novel, for Twain often read from
"advance sheets" of *Huckleberry Finn*. At first he was
distressed with his presentation. "Written things are not
for speech," he explained in Chapter 35 of the *Autobiography;* "their form is literary; they are stiff, inflexible and
will not lend themselves to happy and effective delivery
with the tongue . . . ; they have to be limbered up, collo-
quialized and turned into common forms of premeditated
talk." After a week on the road, he put the books aside and
memorized the passages; and "in delivering them from the
platform they soon transformed themselves into flexible
talk, with all their obstructing precisenesses and formalities
gone out of them." But even the selections from *Huckleberry
Finn* (generally "King Sollermun" from Chapter 14, or
"Huck Finn and Tom Sawyer's Brilliant Achievement"
from the conclusion), which were written in colloquial
speech, required revision to be read from the platform; the
advance proof sheets which Twain followed on his lecture
tour (now in The Mark Twain Papers, The Bancroft Library, University of California, Berkeley) are littered with
pencil alterations. Similarly, eleven years later, when the
"pecuniary compulsions" came and he had to lecture around
the world, Twain heavily annotated his copy of the 1893
reprinting of the 1885 Tauchnitz edition of *Huckleberry
Finn* (also in The Mark Twain Papers) with further revi-
sions for his platform readings. Although most of these

changes were merely for greater clarity when recited and for more precision in the humor, others show Twain's rethinking of certain crucial passages of the novel; significant reworkings of the story for his public readings are discussed in the notes to this edition.

Another strain on the tour with Cable was Twain's growing anxiety over the new novel's publication. When he took to the road, Twain believed that Webster had everything under control; but, just as the tour got under way, an unanticipated problem halted the book's production. While Webster was in San Francisco on business, an agent showed him an odd detail in one of the illustrations in the canvassing book: In "Who do you reckon it is?" (prophetically beneath the running head "In a Dilemma") of Chapter 33, something now was protruding from Uncle Silas's trousers like an erect penis. Webster immediately returned to New York and offered a $500 reward for the apprehension and conviction of the person responsible for the obscene alteration of the engraving. He also demanded that each agent now remove the offensive page from every copy of the prospectus or face immediate dismissal; and all released copies of the finished book were recalled for correction of the unsightly error. "The book was examined by W. D. Howells, Mr. Clemens, the proofreader and myself," Webster told a reporter in the New York *Herald* (November 29, 1884). "Nothing improper was discovered. . . . By the punch of an awl or graver, the illustration became an immoral one. But 250 copies left the office . . . before the mistake was discovered. Had the first edition been run off our loss would have been $250,000. Had the mistake not been discovered, Mr. Clemens' credit for decency and morality would have been destroyed." The only answer was to excise the offending page and tip in a corrected leaf. "This cost me plenty," J. J. Little, the printer, later admitted; but so competently did the firm handle the problem that no known copies of the first edition survive with the obscene plate. The initial investment was saved, but the Christmas market was lost; the American edition was not officially released until February 18, 1885. Also, despite the author's efforts to rid his book of all apparent improprieties, the widely reprinted item about the obscene engraving tainted the novel's reputation long before its official publication.

While on the road, Twain kept his eye on the book's progress. On December 10, the publication date of the London edition of *Huckleberry Finn* issued by Chatto & Windus, Twain went to Toronto where he remained from noon to 5:00 P.M., so that he was legally "domiciled" on British soil when Webster applied for foreign copyright in the author's name.[40] Still inexperienced as his own pub-

40 See Walter Blair, *Mark Twain and Huck Finn* (Berkeley and Los Angeles: University of California Press, 1960), p. 367.

41 The New York *World* attacked the book not once but twice: On March 2, it condemned *Huckleberry Finn* as "cheap and pernicious stuff"; and on March 18, it noted "what can be said of a man of Mr. Clemens's wit, ability, and position deliberately imposing upon the unoffending public a piece of careless hackwork in which a few good things are dropped amid a mass of rubbish." But Twain planned some form of revenge, by filling his notebook with reports of murders, rapes, suicides, and other sensational news printed in a single issue of the *World*, April 9, 1885; this material he gathered for an uncompleted article, questioning the integrity of this paper's editors. "In a week," he wrote, "they spread a full *Huck* before 1,000,000 families—4,000,000 a month they say. The same bulk is furnished to more than 50,000,000 people by that paper in a year—while 100,000,000 have read H.F. and forgotten him. *Moral*. If you want to rear a family just right for sweet and pure society here and Paradise hereafter, banish Huck Finn from the home circle and introduce the N.Y. *World* in his place."

Twain was a bit paranoid about his critics. He suspected that the attack in the Boston *Advertiser* was a personal vendetta against some indiscreet story the humorist had told about its editor in private: "The severest censor has been the Boston *Advertiser*. . . . He is merely taking what he imagines is legitimate revenge upon me for what was simply and solely an accident. I had the misfortune to catch him in a situation which will not bear describing. He probably thinks I have told that thing all around. It is an error. I have never told it, except to one man, and he came so near absolutely dying with laughter that I judged it best to take no more chances with that narrative."

And Twain was not above thinking of some appropriate punishment to one of his critics such as an "accident in a sitz-bath with a steel-trap to the editor of the Springfield *Republican*." See *Mark Twain's Notebooks and Journals*, Vol. III, edited by Robert Park Browning, Michael B. Frank, and Lin Salamo (Berkeley and Los Angeles: University of California Press, 1979), pp. 128, 130, 132, and 135–136.

lisher, Twain suddenly realized on February 10 that he and Webster had neglected to send review copies in time for the magazines: "How in *hell* we overlooked that unspeakably important detail, utterly beats my time." Consequently, the only major notice to appear in a national magazine at the book's publication was T. S. Perry's favorable review in *The Century;* and the newspapers generally ignored the new Mark Twain work. True, critics generally considered subscription books as inferior literature and unworthy of serious notice by the press. Nevertheless, Twain was disheartened by the lack of critical recognition of *Huckleberry Finn*. "Huck is a *good* book," he reassured his publisher on February 14, "and I am working intelligently and *hard* and if it don't sell, it won't be your fault or mine but the extreme hard times. It *shall* sell however."

Twain was feeling defensive also because of several damning notices of the novel. The Boston *Advertiser* attacked it for its irreverence; the Boston *Transcript* found it "so flat, as well as coarse, that nobody wants to read it after a taste in the *Century*." "It is time," the Springfield *Republican* editorialized, "that this influential pseudonym should cease to carry into homes and libraries unworthy productions. Mr. Clemens is a genuine and powerful humorist, with a bitter vein of satire on the weaknesses of humanity which is sometimes wholesome, sometimes only grotesque, but in certain of his works degenerates into a gross trifling with every fine feeling. The trouble with Mr. Clemens is that he has no reliable sense of propriety." To this paper, *Tom Sawyer* and *Huckleberry Finn* "are no better than the dime novels which flood the blood-and-thunder reading population. Mr. Clemens has made them smarter, for he has an inexhaustible fund of 'quips and cranks and wanton wiles,' and his literary skill is, of course, superior; but their moral level is low, and their perusal cannot be anything less than harmful."**41** Perhaps the most vicious review appeared in *Life* (March 12, 1885); Robert Bridges found nothing else in the book suitable for boys and girls. He sarcastically noted that "a very refined and delicate piece of narration by Huck Finn, describing his venerable and dilapidated 'pap' as afflicted with delirium tremens, rolling over and over, . . . is especially suited to amuse children on long, rainy afternoons"; and "an elevating and laughable description of how Huck killed a pig, smeared its blood on an axe and mixed in a little of his own hair, and then ran off, setting up a job on the old man and the community, and leading them to believe him murdered . . . can be repeated by any smart boy for the amusement of his fond parents."

But Twain was more hurt than actually harmed by such ugly appraisals of his work. In spite of the bad reviews, the book was selling so briskly that already by March 16, Twain could boast to Webster, "Huck certainly *is* a success, and from the standpoint of my own requirement." However, Twain wrote a public answer to his critics and instructed Webster to include in future editions of *Huckleberry Finn* "Prefatory Remark":

Huckleberry Finn is not an imaginary person. He still lives; or rather, *they* still live; for Huckleberry Finn is two persons in one—namely, the author's two uncles, the present editors of the Boston *Advertiser* and the Springfield *Republican*. In character, language, clothing, education, instinct, and origin, he is the painstakingly and truthfully drawn photograph and counterpart of these two gentlemen as they were in the time of their boyhood, forty years ago. The book has been most carefully and conscientiously done, and is exactly true to the originals, in even the minutest particulars, with but one exception, and that a trifling one: this boy's language has been toned down and softened, here and there, in deference to the taste of a more modern and fastidious day. [42]

However, discreet Mrs. Clemens forbade its publication.

The controversy of *Huckleberry Finn* was further fueled in March when the book was banned by the committee of the Public Library of Concord, Massachusetts. One member told the Boston *Transcript* that "while he does not wish to call it immoral, he thinks it contains but little humor, and that of a very coarse type. He considers it the veriest trash." The librarian and other members concurred, "characterizing it as rough, coarse and inelegant, dealing with a series of experiences not elevating, the whole book being more suited to the slums than to intelligent, respectable people." Perhaps the best summary of the community's opinion was that given by one of Concord's most prominent citizens, Louisa May Alcott, the author of *Little Women:* "If Mr. Clemens cannot think of something better to tell our pure-minded lads and lasses, he had best stop writing for them." [43] The story was dutifully reported in such papers as the Boston *Transcript* and the Springfield *Republican;* and *Life* gloated on April 9, 1885 (p. 202), "It is a pleasure to note that the Concord Library Committee agrees with *Life*'s estimate of Mark Twain's 'blood-curdling humor,' and have banished *Huckleberry Finn* to limbo."

Twain, however, although infuriated, was not worried by this new assault. On March 18, he wrote Webster, "The Committee of the Public Library of Concord, Mass., have given us a rattling tip-top puff which will go into every paper in the country. . . . That will sell 25,000 copies for us sure." The ban did not trouble him because, he argued in a letter released to the press on April 1, "It

[42] In a letter to Webster, April 4, 1885, *Mark Twain's Letters to His Publishers*, p. 188.

[43] Quoted by Kaplan, *Mr. Clemens and Mark Twain*, p. 268. Twain was not one of Alcott's admirers either: He wrote *The Gilded Age* in part as an answer to such popular contemporary novels as her *Little Women*.

The Concord Free Public Library.

44 In a letter to Webster, March 18, 1885, and one to the Concord Free Trade Club, April 1, 1885, in the New York *World* (quoted by Webster, *Mark Twain, Business Man*, p. 319). *Mark Twain's Letters*, Vol. II, pp. 252–253; also a letter of 1907, *Mark Twain: A Biography*, Vol. III, p. 1280.

45 Quoted by Kaplan, *Mr. Clemens and Mark Twain*, p. 269.

46 In a letter to his sister, April 15, 1885, quoted by Webster, *Mark Twain, Business Man*, p. 317.

47 In a letter to Harris, November 29, 1885, English, *Mark Twain to Uncle Remus*, p. 20.

will deter other libraries from buying the book, and you are doubtless aware that one book in a public library, prevents the sale of a sure ten and a possible hundred of its mates; and secondly, it will cause the purchasers of the book to read it out of curiosity, instead of merely intending to do so, after the usual way of the world and library committees, and then they will discover, to my great advantage and their own indignant disappointment that there is nothing objectionable in the book after all." As to the book's being immoral, he retorted, "The truth is that when a library expels a book of mine and leaves an un-expurgated Bible around where unprotected youth and age can get hold of it, the deep unconscious irony of it delights me and doesn't anger me."[44] Irony was rife that season: While the local library was banning *Huckleberry Finn*, the Concord Free Trade Club was electing its author an honorary member. Twain smugly admitted that this honor endorsed him "to associate with certain gentlemen whom even the moral icebergs of the Concord library committee are bound to respect."[45] Even bad press can be good publicity. "Those idiots in Concord are not a court of last resort," Twain, still smarting from the ban, wrote in his notebook on April 15, "and I am not disturbed by their moral gymnastics. No other book of mine has sold so many copies within 2 months after issue as this one has done."[46] He was further comforted by the sale of 51,000 copies of *Huckleberry Finn* within the first fourteen months of pub-lication.

And Twain did have his defenders. "I know that some of the professional critics will not agree with me," wrote Joel Chandler Harris, the author of *Uncle Remus*, in *The Critic* (November 28, 1885), "but there is not in our fictive literature a more wholesome book than *Huckleberry Finn*. It is history, it is romance, it is life. Here we behold human character stripped of all tiresome details; we see people growing and living; we laugh at their humor, share their griefs; and, in the midst of it all, behold we are taught the lessons of honesty, justice and mercy." Twain was deeply touched by his friend's kind words for Huck Finn. "Somehow, *I* can't help believing in him," Twain con-fessed to Harris, "and it's a great refreshment to my faith to have a man back me up who has been where such boys live."[47] And when a superintendent of schools angrily wrote *The Century* that the excerpts from *Huckleberry Finn* were "destitute of a single redeeming quality" and "hardly worth a place in the columns of the average county newspaper which never assumes any literary airs," Gilder replied, "At least, as a picture of the life which he describes, his *Century* sketches are of decided force and worth. Mark Twain is not a giber at religion or morality.

He is a good citizen and believes in the best things."

But how little even his friends understood him. Mark Twain was not merely a local colorist: He was indeed "a giber at religion and morality." "I cannot call to mind a single instance where I have ever been irreverent," he quipped in *Is Shakespeare Dead?* (1909) "except towards the things which were sacred to other people." In *Huckleberry Finn*, in the battle between the young hero's heart and his conscience, Twain describes his own struggle with his fundamentalist upbringing; in Huck Finn, he created the natural man, unfettered by most conventions, who must in the end run off to the wilderness to escape being "sivilized." "All the details of 'civilization' are legitimate matters for jeering," Twain believed. "It is made up of about three tenths of reality and sincerity, and seven tenths of wind and humbug."[48] *Huckleberry Finn* is indeed, as Lionel Trilling explained in *The Liberal Imagination* (1950, p. 112), "a subversive book—no one who reads thoughtfully the dialectic of Huck's moral crisis will ever again be wholly able to accept without some question and some irony the assumptions of the respectable morality by which he lives."

Not even Clemens's family was in complete sympathy with *Huckleberry Finn*. Susy in particular was distressed when someone wrote her father, "I enjoyed *Huckleberry Finn* immensely and am glad to see that you have returned to your old style." "That enoyed me," she wrote in her biography (in Chapter 41 of his *Autobiography*), "that enoyed me greatly, because it trobles me to have so few know papa, I mean realy know him, they think of Mark Twain as a humorist joking at everything." What the child demanded from her father was a more self-consciously serious work which would "reveal something of his kind sympathetic nature." Susy was likely paraphrasing her mother's opinions; as Howells noted in *My Mark Twain* (p. 48), Mrs. Clemens too wished her famous husband "to be known not only for the wild and boundless humor that was in him but for the beauty and tenderness and 'natural piety.'" And Susy was likely expressing as much the family's opinion as her own when she argued that *The Prince and the Pauper*, not *Huckleberry Finn*, was her father's finest effort: "The book is full of lovely charming ideas, and oh the language! It is perfect."

Susy Clemens was raised within the conventions upheld by the Concord Public Library committee. *The Prince and the Pauper* could have sat safely upon the library's shelf, for it was everything *Huckleberry Finn* was not: A refined historical romance larded with elegant archaic English phrases and anchored by an obviously moral scrutiny of the men and manners of sixteenth-century

Susy, Olivia, Clara, and Jean Clemens on the porch of their Hartford home, 1884. *Courtesy the Library of Congress.*

48 Quoted by Blair, *Mark Twain and Huck Finn*, p. 339.

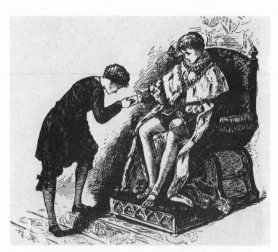

Tom Canty and Edward Tudor. Illustration by Frank T. Merrill, *The Prince and the Pauper*, 1882.

49 Quoted by C. Merton Babcock, "Mark Twain, Mencken and 'The Higher Goofyism,'" *American Quarterly* (Winter 1964), p. 593.

50 In "Mark Twain," *The Century* (September 1882), p. 781.

Britain. Concord, perhaps even more than Boston, was the great defender of New England's genteel traditions. It was the home of Emerson and Thoreau; and so it is ironic that Huck Finn, in his decision to "go to hell," should have offended the residents of the home of American "civil disobedience." However, his censors were apparently more concerned with the style and the spirit of a work of literature than with its intellectual content. Ever since the American Revolution, Yankee writers had suffered from an inferiority complex; in its youth, American literature did not have the grand traditions of Europe on which to build its reputation, and, unfortunately, written American English (unlike its spoken counterpart) became generally more formal and artificial than its British model. What was most admired in New England was the more self-consciously learned, or "bookish," prose. Then there came the self-made Mark Twain, the first important American novelist born west of the Mississippi. "Of all the literary men I have known," Howells wrote in *My Mark Twain* (p. 17), "he was the most unliterary in his make and manner. . . . he used English in all its alien derivations as if it were native to his own air, as if it had come up out of American, out of Missourian ground." The conventional critics did not know what to make of Twain's method and so generally failed to recognize this truly original voice crying out of the West.

Those who did accept local color only reluctantly and only when written by James Russell Lowell found Twain's bad grammar and slang merely coarse and inelegant; there was nothing quaint about Huck Finn's colloquialisms. Sadly, his critics studied surface and not substance. To them, dialect was suitable only for humorous writing, and then as now, the literary world, E. B. White has observed, "decorates its serious writers with laurel and its wags with Brussels sprouts." [49] Comic writing was generally considered an inferior form of literature; the critics agreed with Howells that American humorists "formerly chose the wrong in public matters; they were on the side of slavery, of drunkenness, or irreligion; the friends of civilization were their prey; their spirit was thoroughly vulgar and base." [50] But, at least to Howells, Twain deviated from other comic writers: "There is still sufficient flippancy and brutality in it; but there is no longer the stupid and monkeyish cruelty of motive and intention which once disgraced and insulted us."

Perhaps what most enraged the critics against American humor was its lack of earnestness; it did not elevate, it merely entertained. Twain, however, had a purpose in his levity. "I have always preached," he explained in Chapter 55 of his *Autobiography*. "If the humor came of its own accord and uninvited I have allowed it a place in my sermon, but I was not writing the sermon for the sake of the humor." And his secular preaching was not aimed to such as the Concord Public Library committee. "I have never tried in even one single little instance, to help cultivate the cultivated classes," he wrote in 1889. "I was not equipped for it, either by native gifts or training. And . . . honestly, I never cared what became of the cultured classes; they could go to the theater and the opera, they had no use for me and the melodeon."[51] Instead, Twain "always hunted for the bigger game—the masses." Surely such a popular writer was not worthy of serious critical consideration? How could one so widely read be a true artist?

Another problem with *Huckleberry Finn* was that, as Louisa May Alcott indicated, the novel was universally considered just another boy's book. The publishers encouraged this image by advertising it as uniform with *Tom Sawyer*; but even that novel, Twain said, "is *not* a boy's book, at all. It will only be read by adults. It is only written for adults." But Howells thought otherwise: "It's altogether the best boy's story I ever read. . . . But I think you ought to treat it explicitly *as* a boy's story. Grown-ups will enjoy it just as much if you do; and if you should put it forth as a study of boy character from the grown-up point of view, you'd give the wrong key to it." Only half-heartedly did Twain give in to his advisors: "Mrs. Clemens decides with you," he wrote Howells, "that the book should issue as a book for boys, pure and simple—and so do I. It is surely the correct idea."[52] However, so that his initial purpose should not be lost, Twain somewhat apologized in the preface, "Although my book is intended mainly for the entertainment of boys and girls, I hope it will not be shunned by men and women on that account, for part of my plan has been to try to pleasantly remind adults of what they once were themselves."

Tom Sawyer belongs to the sub-genre of "the bad boy's book."[53] This tradition in nineteenth-century American literature was largely founded by Thomas Bailey Aldrich's *The Story of a Bad Boy* (1870), a rambling series of thinly disguised autobiographical sketches told by "Tom Bailey." "I call my story the story of a bad boy," Aldrich explained, "partly to distinguish myself from those faultless young gentlemen who generally figure in narratives of this kind, and partly because I really was *not* a cherub. I may truthfully say I was an amiable, impulsive lad, blessed with fine digestive powers, and no hypocrite. . . . In short, I was a real human boy, such as you may meet anywhere in New England, and no more like the impossible boy in a story-book than a sound orange is like one that has been sucked

51 In a letter to Andrew Lang, 1889, *Mark Twain's Letters*, Vol. II, pp. 527–528.

52 In a letter to Howells, July 5, 1875, *Mark Twain–Howells Letters*, p. 91; in a letter to Clemens, November 21, 1875, pp. 110–111, and one to Howells, November 23, 1875, p. 112.

Illustration by Sol Eytinge, Jr., *The Story of a Bad Boy* by Thomas Bailey Aldrich, 1869. *Courtesy the Library of Congress.*

"Story of the Bad Little Boy." Illustration by True W. Williams, *Mark Twain's Sketches, New and Old*, 1875.

Tom Sawyer. Frontispiece by True W. Williams, *The Adventures of Tom Sawyer*, 1876.

53 See Joseph Hinz, "Huck and Pluck: 'Bad' Boys in American Fiction," *The South Atlantic Quarterly* (January 1952), pp. 120–129.

54 Parallels between *Tom Sawyer* and *The Story of a Bad Boy* are discussed by Blair in *Mark Twain and Huck Finn* (pp. 64–65) and in the introduction and explanatory notes in *The Adventures of Tom Sawyer; Tom Sawyer Abroad; Tom Sawyer, Detective*, edited by John C. Gerber, Paul Baender, and Terry Firkins (Berkeley and Los Angeles: University of California Press, 1980).

55 George W. Peck in his preface to *Peck's Bad Boy and His Pa* (Chicago: C. B. Beach, 1883).

56 Twain was familiar with *A Bad Boy's Diary:* On September 19, 1882, he told Webster to take legal action against its publishers. "They are using my name," the author complained about this originally anonymous work, "to sell stuff which I never wrote. I would not be the author of that witless stuff . . . for a million dollars." Apparently the publishers had implied in their advertising that *A Bad Boy's Diary* was by the author of *Tom Sawyer*.

dry." Although Howells found in Tom Bailey "a new thing . . . in American literature, an absolute novelty," others besides Aldrich had already explored the "bad boy" in fiction; for example, Benjamin Penhollow Shillaber introduced a mischievous foster child named Ike in *Life and Sayings of Mrs. Partington* (1854), and Twain had parodied the countless Sunday-school tracts about disobedient little boys who came to suffer for their sins, in "Story of the Bad Boy Who Didn't Come to Grief" (*Alta California*, December 23, 1865). Of his friend's *The Story of a Bad Boy*, Twain confessed that he just could not admire the volume much. Then perhaps he wrote *Tom Sawyer* in part to correct what he thought were Aldrich's misconceptions of the boy mind. [54]

Although initially a financial failure and ignored by most critics as just another subscription book, *Tom Sawyer* was championed by Howells in *The Atlantic Monthly* (May 1876, p. 621) as "a wonderful study of the boy-mind which inhabits a world quite distinct from that in which he is bodily present with his elders, and in this lies its quiet charm and its universality, for boy nature, however human nature varies, is the same everywhere." To Howells, Tom Sawyer was the archetypal boy: "He is mischievous, but not vicious; . . . he is not a downright liar, except upon terms of after shame and remorse that make his falsehood bitter to him. He is cruel, as all children are, but chiefly because he is ignorant; he is not mean, but there are definite bounds to his generosity. . . . In a word, he is a boy, and merely and exactly an ordinary boy on the moral side."

The reviewers may have overlooked Twain's hymn to boyhood, but not so his fellow writers. Soon it must have seemed, if one believes that literature is only a mirror held up to life, that the "Bad Boy" was indeed "located in every city, village and country hamlet throughout the land. He is wide awake, full of vinegar, and is ready to crawl under the canvas of a circus or repeat a hundred verses of the New Testament in Sunday School. He knows where every melon patch in the neighborhood is located, and at what hours the dog is chained up. He will tie an oyster can to a dog's tail to give the dog exercise, or will fight at the drop of the hat to protect the smaller boy or a school girl." [55] While Aldrich's book continued to encourage such dreary burlesques as *A Bad Boy's Diary* (1880) and other "Bad Boy" books by "Walter T. Gray" (Metta Victoria Victor) [56] as well as *Peck's Bad Boy and His Pa* (1883) and its sequels by George W. Peck, Twain's novel was succeeded by such obvious imitations as these autobiographical tales of regional boyhoods: *Being a Boy* (1878) by Charles Dudley Warner; *Ike Partington* (1879) by B. P. Shillaber; and *The Hoosier Schoolboy* (1883) by Edward Eggleston. Perhaps the one most indebted to *Tom Sawyer* was William Dean Howells's *A Boy's Town* (1890).[57] But such bloodless, sentimentalized accounts of a boy's paradise lost obviously appealed more to adults than to their children.

And then there was *Huckleberry Finn*. In its uncompromising scrutiny of a society long past, where everyone was either a scoundrel or a fool, the sequel declared that the idyll of *Tom Sawyer* was over. Naked Huck Finn on the river raft shocked a public that would be ready by year's end to embrace Frances Hodgson Burnett's Little Lord Fauntleroy in golden ringlets, lace collar, and velvet suit. Huck Finn was of an order lower than even that of "bad boy" Tom Sawyer, but not merely class prejudice had expelled Twain's waif from respectable parlors. Other street arabs had been introduced in the boys' books of Horatio Alger, Jr., and "James Otis" (James Otis Kaler) without any great public outcry. However, these shoe shines and newsboys were characterized by thrift, cheerfulness, and industry in their "rags to riches" stories. But Huck Finn does not trade in his rags for respectability: Instead, he follows the dictates of his own boy heart rather

Illustration by True W. Williams, *Peck's Bad Boy and His Pa* by George W. Peck, 1893 edition. *Courtesy the Library of Congress.*

57 This idealized recollection of childhood in the Ohio River valley at the same time Sam Clemens was growing up in Hannibal, Missouri, even has its own version of Huck Finn, the "juvenile pariah of the village": The protagonist's "closest friend was a boy who was probably never willingly at school in his life, and who had no more relish of literature or learning in him than the open fields, or the warm air of an early spring day. . . . He was like a piece of the genial earth, with no more hint of tailoring or spinning in him; willing for anything, but passive and without force or aim. He lived in a belated log cabin that stood . . . on the river-bank." (in "Other Boys").

Illustration by Reginald Birch, *Little Lord Fauntleroy* by Frances Hodgson Burnett, *St. Nicholas* Magazine, April 1886. *Courtesy the Library of Congress.*

Pictorial half-title page from *Ragged Dick* by Horatio Alger, 1867. *Courtesy the Library of Congress.*

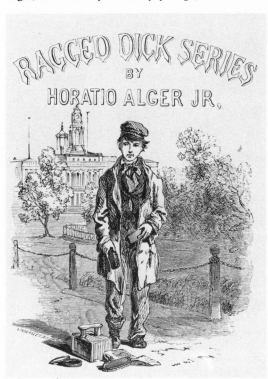

Frontispiece from *Little Men* by Louisa May Alcott, 1871. *Courtesy the Library of Congress.*

Illustration by Thomas Nast, *Hans Brinker or the Silver Skates* by Mary Mapes Dodge, 1865. *Courtesy the Library of Congress.*

58 In his introduction to the 1950 edition of *Huckleberry Finn* published in London by The Cresset Press and in New York by Chanticleer Press.

59 In a letter to Mary Fairbanks, quoted by Blair, *Mark Twain and Huck Finn*, p. 236.

than the demands of a corrupt society by his vowing "to go to hell" rather than to betray Miss Watson's Jim. As T. S. Eliot observed,[58] there is no more solitary figure in fiction than good-hearted Huck Finn.

Even if Huck is, as Brander Matthews argued in his notice in *The Saturday Review* (London, January 31, 1885, p.153), "neither a girl in boy's clothes like many of the modern heroes of juvenile fiction, nor is he a 'little man,' a full-grown man cut down; he is a boy, just a boy, only a boy," there was much more in the novel to threaten even the most liberal of late nineteenth-century households. Its vivid descriptions of family feuds and lynchings and its thirteen corpses littered throughout the story like snags in the Mississippi were strong meat for babes weaned on *Hans Brinker* and *Little Men*. Twain's violences were the stuff of dime novels, the comic books of their day, so eagerly read by adventure-seeking boys like Tom Sawyer; their Indian attacks and street gang fights anticipated the more sensational events of *Huckleberry Finn*. *Tom Sawyer* too contains grisly details such as Doc Robinson's murder and Injun Joe's threat to slit the Widow Douglas's nostrils like a sow's; but the melodrama of this boys' book is tempered by such famous scenes as the whitewashing of Aunt Polly's fence, Tom and Becky's schoolyard romance, and the bucolic exile on Jackson's Island. However, in having the ignorant boy tell his own story in his own words in his own time, Twain left no place in *Huckleberry Finn* for such nostalgic reveries.

Those comic and pastoral interludes which are in Huck Finn's autobiography were introduced for a specific dialectical function to contrast and thus to strengthen the horrific events. At work on *A Tramp Abroad*, Twain developed a specific satiric device which served him well in later fiction. He explained to a friend that the burlesque "Gambetta Duel" of Chapter 7 of *A Tramp Abroad* "will follow a perfectly serious description of five very bloody student duels which I witnessed in Heidelberg one day—a description which simply *describes* the terrific spectacle, with no jests interlarded and no comments added. The contrasts between that chapter and the next one (the Gambetta duel) will be silent but eloquent comment."[59] However, in *Huckleberry Finn*, Twain reversed the order of these two forms of contrasting descriptions, the straight and the comic, and the effect here is even more devastating than in the former book. In Chapter 17, Huck's petty thefts are followed by an encounter with murderous river pirates on a sinking steamboat; in Chapter 19, the boy's description of the blissful life on the Mississippi River acts as an ironic introduction to the ugly frauds perpetrated by the king and the duke; and in Chapter 21, the duke's burlesque of the existential "Hamlet's Soliloquy" is a brilliant contrast to the cold-blooded killing of Boggs by Sherburn. But the most powerful example of this dialectic in *Huckleberry Finn* is the juxtaposition of the boy's enraptured description of the absurd, hypocritically furnished Grangerford house in Chapter 17 with the straightforward account of the carnage left by the feud in the subsequent chapter. Surely such bitter irony would have been wasted in a book just for boys.

If Twain had indeed intended his novel for children, as his critics maintained, then certainly it would have been more logical to publish excerpts from *Huckleberry Finn* in *St. Nicholas* rather than in *The Century*. Evidently, even Twain came in time to think like his public about the book. In his notebook for July 1898, he jotted an idea for a story "Creatures of Fiction" in which Mother Goose, Hans Brinker, Tom Bailey, Uncle Remus's Little Boy, Mowgli the Jungle Boy, the Prince and the Pauper, and other prominent figures in juvenile literature are joined in some unnamed storybook land by Tom Sawyer and Huck Finn.[60] Although that tale was never written, this winsome picture of Tom and Huck as classic children's book characters persists, and particularly to people who have never read Twain's novel.[61] However true this popular image may be to *Tom Sawyer*, it is false to *Huckleberry Finn*. Likely Twain felt that if *Huckleberry Finn* was good enough to be read to his darling daughters, then surely it was suitable for any other girls or boys; and not even the censors could keep the novel completely out of the reach of children. The author was vindicated in his battle with the critics when Webster gave him a year after its publication a check for $54,500 as his royalty for *Huckleberry Finn*.

Huckleberry Finn (Mickey Rooney) in the M-G-M film *The Adventures of Huckleberry Finn*, 1939. © 1939 Loew's Incorporated. Copyright renewed 1966 by Metro-Goldwyn-Mayer Inc.

60 See *Mark Twain's Hannibal, Huck and Tom*, p. 13.

61 For example, James Joyce. While working on *Finnegans Wake*, the Irish author asked his brother's stepson to make some notes on *Huckleberry Finn* for use in the new novel. "I need to know something about it," Joyce wrote on August 8, 1937. "I never read it and have nobody to read it to me and it takes too much time with all I am doing" (*Selected Letters of James Joyce*, edited by Richard Ellmann, New York: The Viking Press, 1975, p. 387). Obviously the river and the raft appealed to the novelist as appropriate symbols for his dream novel. However, the stepson apparently did not do as Joyce asked; the references to Twain, Tom, and Huck in *Finnegans Wake* are more suggestive of *Tom Sawyer* than of *Huckleberry Finn*.

Screenwriters, too, have struggled with *Huckleberry Finn*. They generally have tried to transform *Huckleberry Finn* into *Tom Sawyer*; indeed, many of the adaptations of the second story have absorbed incidents from the earlier book. There have been five Hollywood productions: 1920, Paramount, a silent film with Lewis Sargent ("Huck Finn"), Gordon

Above: Jim (George Reed), doctor, Huck (Lewis Sargent), Tom (Gordon Griffith) in the Paramount silent film *Huckleberry Finn*, 1920. Below: Huck (Junior Durkin), Sid Sawyer (Jackie Searl), teacher in the Paramount film *Huckleberry Finn*, 1931. *Courtesy the Billy Rose Collection, The New York Public Library at Lincoln Center, Astor, Lenox, and Tilden Foundations.*

Griffith ("Tom Sawyer"), and George Reed ("Jim"); 1931, Paramount, with Junior Durkin ("Huck"), Jackie Coogan ("Tom"), Mitzi Green ("Becky Thatcher"), and Jackie Searl ("Sid Sawyer"); 1939, M-G-M, with Mickey Rooney ("Huck"), Rex Ingram ("Jim"), Walter Connolly ("The King"), and William Frawley ("The Duke"); 1960, M-G-M, with Samuel Goldwyn, Jr., a Technicolor production with four songs by Alan Jay Lerner and Burton Lane, with Eddie Hodges ("Huck"), Archie Moore ("Jim"), Tony Randall ("The King"), and Buster Keaton, Andy Devine, Judy Canova, Sterling Holloway, and John Carradine; and 1974, United Artists–Reader's Digest, with a script and ten songs by Richard M. and Robert B. Sherman, with Jeff East ("Huck"), Paul Winfield ("Jim"), Harvey Corman ("The King"), and David Wayne ("The Duke"). There was also a 1973 Russian film, directed by Georgii Daneliya, with Roma Modyanov ("Huck") and Felix Immokuede ("Jim"). Television, too, has tackled *Huckleberry Finn*, as in the 1955 production with Charles Taylor ("Huck"), Thomas Mitchell ("The King"), and John Carradine ("The Duke"); the 1957 U.S. Steel Hour version with Jimmy Boyd ("Huck"), Earle Hym ("Jim"), Basil Rathbone ("The King"), Jack Carson ("The Duke"), and Florence Henderson ("Mary Jane Wilks"); and the 1975 ABC special, with Ron Howard ("Huck"), Donny Most ("Tom"), Antonio Fargas ("Jim"), and Howard's father, mother, and brother all in the cast. Also, in 1952, M-G-M announced (but never produced) a Technicolor musical, with Dean Stockwell ("Huck"), Gene Kelly ("The King"), Danny Kaye ("The Duke"), and Margaret O'Brien ("Mary Jane Wilks"); and in 1969, Universal purchased the rights to the uncompleted "Huck Finn and Tom Sawyer among the Indians."

As yet, the definitive version has not been produced on the screen. Southern California just cannot approximate the Mississippi Valley, and the casts have been generally uninspired. The scripts have shown little respect for Twain's original and have concentrated on the initial flight of the fugitives and the episodes with the king and the duke. The 1974 United Artists–Reader's Digest film courageously included the Grangerford-Shepherdson feud, but its effect was lost in the singing and dancing of the rest of the film; also, Paul Winfield was closer to Nat Turner than to Twain's Jim. Generally, these films have soft-pedaled Twain's bitter satire with light comedy. None has done justice to Twain's epic of the Mississippi River. See also note 67.

Jim (Archie Moore) and Huck (Eddie Hodges) in the M-G-M–Samuel Goldwyn, Jr., Technicolor production *The Adventures of Huckleberry Finn*, 1960. © *1960 Loew's Incorporated and Formosa Productions, Inc.*

Huck (Jeff East) and Jim (Paul Winfield) in the Reader's Digest-United Artists musical film *The Adventures of Huckleberry Finn*, 1974. © *1974 United Artists Corporation. All rights reserved.*

"Once more I experienced a rebirth," he confessed in Chapter 46 of his *Autobiography*. "I have been born again more times than anybody except Krishna." Or Huck Finn.

Even when the critics abandoned the boy, Twain remained faithful to poor abused Huck. Not all the adventures of Huckleberry Finn made it into *Adventures of Huckleberry Finn*. Even before the book went to press, Twain began a sequel describing Tom and Huck's "howling adventures amongst the Indians, over in the Territory." During the summers between 1884 and 1889, he worked on "Huck Finn and Tom Sawyer among the Indians" and went so far as to have what he had completed set in type; then he stopped. The problem was that once the boys have discovered four pegs in the ground and a bloody scrap of the girl's gown in an abandoned Indian camp, Twain did not know how to handle the implication that the abducted heroine has been bound and gang-raped by her captors. [62] Other ideas for further adventures were inspired by the journey back to Hannibal in January 1885, by the "slathers of ancient friends, and such worlds of talk, and such deep enjoyment of it!" [63] He thought of having Tom and Huck steal a ride on a steamboat all the way down the river to New Orleans; Tom's brother Sid and Jim's little scarlet-fever daughter were to be in it, as well as an old liar who was to tell impossible tales about his world travels. Twain also considered "a kind of Huck Finn narrative—let him ship as cabin boy and another boy as cub pilot—and so put the great river and its bygone ways into history in form of a story." And he wrote in his 1885 notebook his desire to "put Huck and Tom and Jim through my Missouri campaign, and give a chapter to the *Century*. Union soldier accosts Tom and says his name is U. S. Grant." [64] But of all these notes, only the latter became a finished tale, and as the straight autobiographical "Private History of a Campaign that Failed," it appeared in *The Century* (December 1885) and was illustrated by Kemble.

Not until 1893 did Twain finally publish another Tom Sawyer story. He had become friendly with Mary Mapes Dodge, the author of *Hans Brinker* and the editor of *St. Nicholas*, the most prestigious children's magazine of its day; and when she asked him for a book to serialize in her monthly, he immediately began *Tom Sawyer Abroad*. He needed the money, and because "the humor flows as easily as the adventures and surprises," [65] he finished the tale in about two months. And there was no question that it, unlike *Huckleberry Finn*, was written for boys and girls; he admitted, "I tried to leave all the improprieties all out; if I didn't Mrs. Dodge can scissor them out." Twain even thought that should *Tom Sawyer Abroad* prove successful, then he could easily turn out a long line of Tom Sawyer travel books by just "adding 'Africa,' 'England,' 'Germany,' etc., to the title page of each successive volume of the series," in the manner of such popular boys' adventure stories as those about Horace Scudder's Bodleys, Hezekiah Butterworth's Zig-Zag Club, and Charles Asbury's Young Yachters and the Knockabout Club, all undistinguished fiction but best-sellers in their day. Twain, however, was not willing to limit the appeal of *Tom Sawyer Abroad* to children; he coyly advertised the book as suitable for any boy from eight to eighty. "I conceive that the right way to write a story for boys," he argued, "is to write so that it will not only interest boys but will strongly interest *any man who has ever been a boy*. That immensely *enlarges the audience*." Mrs. Dodge serialized the book in *St. Nicholas*, November 1893 through April 1894, with pictures by Dan

[62] See "Huck Finn and Tom Sawyer among the Indians," *Mark Twain's Hannibal, Huck and Tom*, edited by Walter Blair (Berkeley and Los Angeles: University of California Press, 1969). This story should not be confused with Clement Wood's *More Adventures of Huckleberry Finn* (New York and Cleveland: World, 1940), which is a completely original novel about the boys' travels in the Indian Territory.

[63] In a letter to Olivia L. Clemens, January 14, 1885, *The Love Letters of Mark Twain*, p. 228.

[64] In *Mark Twain's Notebooks and Journals*, Vol. III, pp. 88–91 and 105.

[65] In a letter of August 10, 1892, quoted in *The Adventures of Tom Sawyer, Tom Sawyer Abroad, Tom Sawyer, Detective*, p. 246. Most of this discussion was gleaned from the introduction to *Tom Sawyer Abroad* in that volume, pp. 241–250. See also O. M. Brack, Jr., "Mark Twain in Knee Pants: The Expurgation of *Tom Sawyer Abroad*," *Proof 2* (1972), pp. 145–151.

Tom, Huck, and Jim. Illustration by Dan Beard, *Tom Sawyer Abroad*, *St. Nicholas* Magazine, February 1894. *Courtesy the Library of Congress.*

Huck, Tom, and Aunt Polly. Illustration by A. B. Frost, "Tom Sawyer, Detective," *Harper's Monthly,* August 1896. *Courtesy the Library of Congress.*

66 At a party in Paris, Twain had been told the story of Sören Jenson Quist and adapted what he had heard into "Tom Sawyer, Detective." Unfortunately, he did not realize that the version the woman related was actually a paraphrasing of a fictionalized account of a true story, from the novel *The Minister of Veilby* (1829) by Steen Steenson Blicher. Twain's carelessness in failing to check his source resulted in his being accused of plagiarism by Valdemar Thorensen, in "Mark Twain og Blicher," *Maaneds-Magasinet* (1909). See the introduction to "Tom Sawyer, Detective," *The Adventures of Tom Sawyer; Tom Sawyer Abroad; Tom Sawyer, Detective,* pp. 348–349.

Beard, the illustrator of *A Connecticut Yankee in King Arthur's Court* (1889) and *The American Claimant* (1892); and only after she had "scissored out" what she thought improper for a juvenile audience. Not even fussy Gilder was as cautious as this lady editor: Drunkenness, death, and religious slurs were not allowed; Tom and Huck could not sweat, slobber, or even sicken in her respectable journal.

Her emasculation of Twain's story did nothing for the already puerile narrative. Just as "Huck Finn and Tom Sawyer among the Indians" attacked James Fenimore Cooper's romantic ideal of the Indian as the "noble savage," *Tom Sawyer Abroad* burlesqued Jules Verne's *Five Weeks in a Balloon;* but so absurd are Tom, Huck, and Jim's encounters with lions and Arabs, so unlikely the new locales for the Missouri boys, that *Tom Sawyer Abroad* is no better than one of Tom's "stretchers." Even Twain recognized how flat was the writing, how hopeless the tale: Without warning, he arbitrarily ended the intended world-tour in a balloon in mid-journey.

Having played with Jules Verne's science fiction in *Tom Sawyer Abroad,* Twain capitalized on the current rage for the Sherlock Holmes stories in "Tom Sawyer, Detective," published in *Harper's Monthly,* August and September 1896, illustrated by A. B. Frost. Again he was cautious about his audience; he said the new tale "is really written for grown folk, though I expect young folk to read it, too." However, this mystery which transferred the story of a Danish pastor of the seventeenth century who had been falsely accused and executed for the murder of his servant **66** to the banks of the Mississippi of the 1840s had little to recommend it to children besides the encouraging opportunity of having Huck play Dr. Watson to Tom's Sherlock Holmes, much as he was Sancho Panza to his comrade's Don Quixote in *Huckleberry Finn.* Unfortunately, such works as *Tom Sawyer Abroad* and "Tom Sawyer, Detective" fail, because, in injudiciously trying to capitalize on currently popular forms, Twain forced his distinctive characters into genres to which they were not compatible.

The collapse of his publishing house and the bankruptcy caused by his disastrous investments in an impractical typesetting machine in the 1890s forced Twain to try desperately to revive the old success of *Huckleberry Finn* by reshaping the famous Mississippi material into some new profitable form. He even sold the dramatic rights of the novel to Klaw & Erlanger, the producers who brought *Ben Hur* to the stage; but their musical of *Huckleberry Finn* with its singing and dancing Tom and Huck bore little resemblance to the Twain original. **67** Fragments survive for other Tom and Huck stories, and the most ambitious of these was "Tom Sawyer's Conspiracy." **68** In this man-

CAST OF CHARACTERS.

Huckleberry Finn, known as "Huck"......................Arthur Dunn
Tom Sawyer, Huck's Pal.....................................Jack Slavin
Joe Harper, the Cry Baby...........................Master Jack Ryan
Ben Rogers, the Smart Aleck............................James Devlin
Billy Fisher, known as "Fatty".................Master Archie Anderson
Sid Sawyer, the tattle-tale........................Master Webb Raum
Judge Thatcher.......................................Charles W. Stokes
Mr. Walters...Samuel Reed
The Duke..............⎰ Two Crooks ⎱..............Chas. Stanley
The Dauphin..........⎱   ⎰..............Wm. Sampson
Mr. Doughton......................................W. C. Kelley
Silas Finn, Huck's father..............................A. T. Earnest
Hannibal Johnson, known as " No 'count Johnson".........E. J. Connelly
Mr. Lawrence.....................................Robert Harold
Jim, a negro slave..................................Charles K. French
Pete, a negro boy......................................H. Van Cleve

Program Continued

Johnnie Russell.....................................Hughie Flaherty
Amy Lawrence...Flora Parker
Becky Thatcher, the Judge's niece....................Leonie Darmon
Mary Ann..Julie A. Herne
Aunt Polly...Marie Bingham
Widow Douglass...Mrs. Weston
Palmyra..........⎰ Reception Committee of Ladies ⎱....Virginia Ross
Agatha..........⎱ Temperance Union. ⎰....Lizette LeBaron
Cresy...........⎰   ⎱..........Jane Dara
Mrs. Lawrence.......................................Mabelle de Rham

Playmates of Huck and Tom.
Members of the Temperance Union and Villagers.

Program Continued

Act I—Scene I—REAR OF AUNT POLLY'S HOME,

Musical Numbers—A—Entrance of Pierrots (Galop). B—Pierrot Dance. C—"I want to be a drummer in the Band." (Words by Matt. C. Woodward. Music by Silvio Heine)—Mr. Dunn, assisted by the Misses Beatrice Walsh, Lillian Rice, Edna McClure, Florence Carette, Nellie Harris, Lucille de Mendz, Angie Wiemars, Louise Elton, Lola Merrill, Babe Adams, Sallie Bergere, May O'Neill, Norine Williams, Geraldine Royal, Sadie Haynes, Edith Williams, Mabel Mordaunt. D—Stanton, the Giant Rooster. E—"When Little Tommy Sawyer saw The Circus." (Words by Matt. C. Woodward, Music by Ben. M Jerome) Mr. Slavin.

Scene II—THE OLD HAUNTED HOUSE, EVENING SAME DAY.
Musical Number—Serenade, "Good night, Lucindy."—Mr. Slavin and full Chorus.

Act II—Scene I—THE PICNIC GROUNDS, NOON, NEXT DAY.

Musical Numbers—Opening Chorus. The Temperance Union Band. Quartette "Courting".—Misses Parker and Darmon, Messrs. Dunn and Slavin. A—Children's Temperance Glee. B—Madrigal. A—Chorus of Flower Girls. B—Song—"The Sunflower and the Violet."—Miss Flora Parker and Chorus.

Act III—Scene I—McDOWELL'S CAVE, EVENING SAME DAY.

Musical Numbers—Opening Chorus and Tarantella. "Oh, Isn't It Fine to be Robbers." Specialties. "Animal's Convention." (Words and Music by Cole and Johnson)—Charles K. French and Chorus.

Scene II—COURT HOUSE SQUARE, NEXT MORNING.
Locale of Scenes and time of action, St. Petersburg, Mo. (now known as (Hannibal) sixty years ago.

From the program for the Klaw & Erlanger musical production of *Huckleberry Finn* by Mark Twain and Arthur Lee, 1902. *Courtesy the Billy Rose Collection, The New York Public Library at Lincoln Center, Astor, Lenox, and Tilden Foundations.*

Amy Lawrence (Flora Parker) and chorus singing "The Sunflower and the Violet" in the Klaw & Erlanger musical production of *Huckleberry Finn*, 1902. *Courtesy the Billy Rose Collection, The New York Public Library at Lincoln Center, Astor, Lenox, and Tilden Foundations.*

uscript, Twain returned to the experiences of his boyhood, to the constant fear of abolitionist "nigger stealers" near Hannibal during the 1840s; but Twain weakened the drama with his now overused courtroom climax in which Tom exposes the murderers. Obviously, the author recognized how hackneyed the story had become; except for

67 Although credited as coauthored by Mark Twain, the play *Huckleberry Finn* was largely the work of Arthur Lee, a Southern writer. The three-act production was notable less for its plot than for its elaborate scenes, including the whitewashing of Aunt Polly's fence, the raid on a temperance meeting by Tom Sawyer's Gang, a swimming-hole sequence, and a boy's circus with Tom Sawyer as ringmaster. Huck and Tom were played by adults, Arthur Dunn and Jack Slavin; to balance Tom's romance with Becky Thatcher, Amy Lawrence was introduced as Huck's love interest. The weak plot revolved around the suspicion that Huck and his father "Silas Finn" are responsible for all the recent burglaries in the town; and only after the girls have been kidnapped by the thieves and rescued by Tom and Huck are the real criminals exposed. The play opened at Parson's Theatre in Hartford on November 11, 1902, and then went on the road; it never played Broadway. In 1951, Joshua Logan announced a Broadway musical "Huck and Jim," with book by Maxwell Anderson and music by Kurt Weill, to be directed by Reuben Mamoulian; when the original composer died, Frank Loesser was signed to provide the songs, but nothing came of this project (beyond five songs by Weill and Anderson), perhaps because of the proposed but never produced M-G-M movie musical.

68 This unfinished story as well as a fragment for a tale about Tom Sawyer's impersonation of Lord Nelson for the other St. Petersburg boys, and "Doughface," a fictional recounting by Huck Finn of an incident from Clemens's boyhood when a high-spirited girl so frightened a superstitious old woman that the lady went mad, are included in *Mark Twain's Hannibal, Huck and Tom*.

69 In a letter to Olivia L. Clemens, quoted by George Sanderlin, *Mark Twain: As Others Saw Him* (New York: Coward, McCann & Geoghegan, Inc., 1978), p. 59. "It is an odious world," he wrote his wife on August 29, 1896, "a horrible world—it is Hell; the true one, not the lying invention of the superstitious; and we have come to it from elsewhere to expiate our sins" (*Mark Twain's Letters*, Vol. II, p. 328).

70 "Mark Twain's *The Mysterious Stranger, A Romance*, as published in 1916," William M. Gibson prefaced the 1969 University of California Press edition, "is an editorial fraud perpetuated by Twain's official biographer and literary executor, Albert Bigelow Paine, and Frederick A. Duneka of Harper & Brothers publishing company." Gibson has restored the various drafts of Twain's manuscript, as they were originally written, in the text of 1969.

71 In a notebook entry, November 1898, reprinted by Gibson in *The Mysterious Stranger* (1969), p. 428.

apparently giving some of its details (such as having the duke and the king the villains) to the scenarist of the *Huckleberry Finn* play, he abandoned the manuscript.

During the last decades of his life, Twain had increasing difficulty in finishing manuscripts or novels. Much of his writing became mere therapy, not intended to be published or even completed. Even more painful than his financial disasters was the sudden death of his beloved daughter Susy, at age twenty-four, of spinal meningitis, in August 1896. Her father could not bear even to live in the house where she died, and so the Hartford home was closed and eventually sold. When Susy died, he angrily wrote her mother, "You want me to believe it is a judicious, a charitable God that runs this world. Why, I could run it better myself."[69] The same bitterness inspired his last major work, *The Mysterious Stranger* (1916).[70]

The original concept for his chronicle of Young Satan little resembled the published form. Indeed, in the earliest version of what became *The Mysterious Stranger*, Satan, Jr., did not live in "Eseldorf" (Assville), Austria, in 1409, but was a chum of Tom Sawyer and Huck Finn in "Petersburg" in the 1840s. "He was always doing miracles," Twain noted; "his pals knew they were miracles, the others thought them mysteries. . . . He is a good little devil; but swears, and breaks the Sabbath."[71] Among the proposed incidents in this late "bad boy" book was the devil's conquest of the school bully, his romance with the town tomboy "Hellfire Hotchkiss," and his showing Tom and Huck around Hell one Sunday. The fragment that survives is a cross between an allegory and a parody of *Tom Sawyer*; and, only slowly, after a couple of false starts, Twain reformed this burlesque into the nihilistic fable *The Mysterious Stranger*.

The pessimism of Twain's later life is found everywhere in his late writing. Although eventually out of debt, he also lost both Jean and Livy before his death in 1910. He came to believe, as he wrote in *The Mysterious Stranger*, "There is no God, no universe, no human race, no earthly life, no heaven, no hell. It is all a dream—a grotesque and foolish dream. Nothing exists but you. And you are but a *thought*—a vagrant thought, a useless thought, a homeless thought, wandering forlorn among the empty eternities!" Still, to the public at large, Mark Twain even in his sad last years remained the jolly humorist, the famous creator of Tom Sawyer and Huck Finn, always ready to give some bright quip to the papers. But his bitterest remarks about the "damned human race" he generally reserved only for private circulation.

About the time his financial troubles began, Twain told Rudyard Kipling that he might resurrect Tom Sawyer and hang him. "Don't!" the other writer protested. "He isn't your property any more. He belongs to us."[72] Nevertheless, Twain wrote in his notebook, in March 1891, the scheme for another book: "Huck comes back, 60 years old, from nobody knows where—and crazy. Thinks he is a boy again, and scans always every face for Tom and Becky, etc. Tom comes at last from . . . wandering the world and tends Huck, and together they talk the old times, both are desolate, life has been a failure, all that was lovable, all that was beautiful is under the mold. They die together."[73] This idea was revived briefly, in 1902, when Twain revisited Hannibal for the last time. When the University of Missouri invited him to receive an honorary degree at the June commencement, the trip west was the perfect opportunity for him to go home to gather more material for a new book. The journey back deeply moved the sixty-six-year-old author: He talked with old friends and reporters and stood in "the door of the old house I lived in when I whitewashed the fence 53 years ago . . . was photographed, with a crowd looking on"; and when he spoke before a local club about his boyhood, he broke into tears when talking about his mother.[74] He made notes for a story of "50 Years Later": "The Cold Spring—Jim has gone home—they can't find him—all railway tracks."[75] Apparently, this story was to be in two parts, the old times of Tom Sawyer's Gang and the failure of their lives on their reunion a half century later. Twain referred to such a story in Chapter 53 of his *Autobiography:* "Huck Finn was the teller of the story and of course Tom Sawyer and Jim were the heroes of it."[76] He wrote about 38,000 words of it; but, he confessed, "I believed that that trio had done work enough in this world and were entitled to a permanent rest," and so Twain "destroyed it for fear I might some day finish it."

Although Twain never recaptured the brilliance of *Huckleberry Finn* in any other work about Tom and Huck, the original sold handsomely into the twentieth century.[77] Generally regarded a classic boys' book by America's greatest humorist, *Huckleberry Finn* continued to offend librarians and teachers. The ban of the book from public institutions increased rapidly across the country; when it was removed from the children's room of the Brooklyn Public Library, Twain gave his most eloquent defense of his work in a sarcastic letter to one of the library's administrators: "I wrote *Tom Sawyer* and *Huck Finn* for adults exclusively, and it always distresses me when I find that boys and girls have been allowed access to them. The mind that becomes soiled in youth can never again be washed clean. I know this by my own experience, and to this day I cherish an unappeasable bitterness against the unfaithful guardians of my youth, who not only permitted but compelled me to read the unexpurgated Bible through before I

Mark Twain returns to his boyhood home, Hannibal, Missouri, 1902. *Courtesy the Library of Congress.*

72 Quoted by Sanderlin, *Mark Twain: As Others Saw Him,* p. 60.

73 In an entry, March 1891, *Mark Twain's Notebooks and Journals,* Vol. III, p. 606.

74 See Meltzer, *Mark Twain Himself,* p. 233; and *Mark Twain's Hannibal, Huck and Tom,* p. 17.

75 Quoted by Blair in introduction to *Mark Twain's Hannibal, Huck and Tom,* p. 17.

76 Howells hazily recollected in *My Mark Twain* (p. 90) that, although Twain later denied it, Twain had shown Howells a few chapters of a story "laid in a Missouri town, and the characters such as he had known in boyhood." Their letters suggest that the incomplete work was evidently the half-finished novel mentioned in Chapter 53 of Twain's *Autobiography.* See also *Mark Twain's Hannibal, Huck and Tom,* pp. 18–20.

77 According to Blair in *Mark Twain and Huck Finn* (p. 371), by 1960, more than 10 million copies of *Huckleberry Finn* had been sold. This estimate does not include the number of foreign editions, in at least thirty different languages, which have been sold since 1885.

78 Quoted by Paine, *Mark Twain: A Biography*, Vol. III, pp. 1280–1281. "I have no love for children's literature," Clemens wrote his brother on March 15, 1871, because Clemens had never seen any example "that I thought was worth the ink it was written with" (quoted in a note to *The Adventures of Tom Sawyer, Tom Sawyer Abroad, Tom Sawyer, Detective*, p. 8). He was likely referring to the pious books he read when a child; his own *Tom Sawyer* did much to reform juvenile literature. "Three of our libraries have thrown *Huckleberry Finn* out as being an unclean book," he complained. "Next they will be wanting an expurgated Bible." Twain believed, "All indecent books are forbidden by law, except the Bible. Yet it corrupts more young people than all the others put together. For 400 years the Bible has been soiling the minds of Protestant children of both sexes. No individual of them has ever escaped. They have all reveled in the salacious passages secretly" (quoted by Caroline Thomas Harnsberger, *Mark Twain's View of Religion*, Evanston, Ill.: The Schiori Press, 1961, p. 11).

79 In the New York *Times*, September 12, 1957; and an Associated Press dispatch, June 30, 1976, quoted by Sanderlin, *Mark Twain: As Others Saw Him*, pp. 151 and 159. "In attempting to be sensitive to the feelings of some of their constituents," the Illinois division of the American Civil Liberties Union responded to the latest censors, "they have seriously undermined their greater obligation to academic freedom." The prejudice against *Huckleberry Finn* persists in the trade, as in the establishment of the Huckleberry Finn Pin Award, given by the editor of *School Library Journal* to the worst written children's book of the year. "When first encountered in *The Adventures of Tom Sawyer*," Lillian H. Gerhardt has explained her reasoning for this prize, "Huckleberry Finn was illiterate and inclined to stay so." To her, Huck Finn was one of the most famous young illiterates in American fiction, and so it was appropriate to award the pin in his name to "the sorts of fiction, nonfiction, and picture books that ill-serve the limited reading time of young people and are so poorly conceived or presented that they prevent rather than extend the pleasure and profit to be had in reading."

was 15 years old. None can do that and ever draw a clear, sweet breath again this side of the grave. . . . Most honestly do I wish I could say a softening word or two in defense of Huck's character, . . . but really . . . it is no better than those of Solomon, David, and the rest of the sacred brotherhood." Twain concluded with an ironic request, "If there is an unexpurgated Bible in the Children's Department, won't you please . . . remove *Tom* and *Huck* from that questionable company?"[78]

How little times change. Although the politics may differ, the results are the same: *Huckleberry Finn* remains banned around the country. In September 1957, the New York City Board of Education barred the novel from the approved textbook lists in the elementary and junior high schools because Twain's indictment of the Slave South had been called "racially offensive" by the N.A.A.C.P. and the Urban League; likewise, in June 1976, it was removed from high school required reading lists in Illinois because of its use of the word "nigger."[79] Likely Twain would have been amused by the greatest irony in the *Huckleberry Finn* controversy: His worst critics have been liberals.

But by his death, Twain felt vindicated for his work. The University of Missouri gave him an honorary degree in literature; Yale University gave him two; and none of these titles pleased the self-taught backwoodsman more than the Doctor of Letters conferred upon him by Oxford University. "Privately I am quite well aware," he wrote in 1907, in Chapter 73 of his *Autobiography*, "that for a generation I have been as widely celebrated a literary person as America has ever produced, and I am also privately aware that in my own peculiar line I have stood at the head of my guild during all that time, with none to dispute the place with me." Oddly the English appreciated the American writer more readily than did his own countrymen. Robert Louis Stevenson, who wrote *Treasure Island*, was a great admirer of *Huckleberry Finn* and told its author that he had read it four times "and am quite ready to begin again tomorrow." Rudyard Kipling idolized "the great and God-like Clemens." "He is the biggest man you have on your side of the water by a damn sight, and don't you forget it," the author of *The Jungle Book* and *Kim* wrote a friend. "Cervantes was a relation of his." Even William Morris, who should have been offended by *A Connecticut Yankee in King Arthur's Court*, was, according to George Bernard Shaw, "an incurable Huckfinomaniac"; Morris assured his Irish friend that Twain was "a greater master of English" than even Thackeray. Shaw himself believed that "Mark Twain is the greatest American writer"; and the playwright wrote the Missouri sage that "the future historian of America will find your works as indispensable to him as a French historian finds the political tracts of Voltaire."[80]

The American critics were more reserved in their praise than the British and generally concurred with Fred Lewis Pattee's evaluation in *A History of American Literature Since 1870* (1915) that the Mark Twain who would survive would be "the romancer, who in his boyhood had dreamed by the great river, and who later caught the romance of a period in American life." *Tom Sawyer* and *Huckleberry Finn* were worth remembering for their historical accuracy, and thus began the institutionalization of Mark Twain as a national treasure, like the Declaration of Independence or the Washington Monument. Soon his hometown became a shrine where one could visit the actual homes of fictional characters. Still, Twain could not as yet be considered a serious literary artist in the same brotherhood as Emerson, Longfellow, Lowell, and Holmes; even Howells was then more admired as a man of letters than Twain. But Howells knew the truth, as he wrote in *My Mark Twain* (p. 101); "Emerson, Longfellow, Lowell, Holmes—I knew them all and all the rest of our sages, poets, seers, critics, humorists; they were like one another and like other literary men; but Clemens was sole, incomparable, the Lincoln of our literature."

The literary canonization of Mark Twain produced its heretics; and after World War I, when his reputation was ready for revision, it was generally acknowledged by the modernists that Twain's work was overrated. While the defenders of the nineteenth-century genteel tradition chastised him for his lack of restraint, the social Freudian critics of the Roaring Twenties, led by Van Wyck Brooks in *The Ordeal of Mark Twain*, attacked him for not going far enough.[81] And to William Faulkner, the author of *Huckleberry Finn* was "a hack writer who would not have been considered fourth rate in Europe, who tricked out a few of the old proven 'sure fire' literary skeletons with sufficient local color to intrigue the superficial and the lazy."

As before, Twain had his defenders as well as his detractors. "I have long wondered," Sherwood Anderson wrote a friend, "why Mark Twain, with Whitman, has not been placed where I have always believed he belonged— among the two or three really great American artists."[82] However, Twain did not undergo a substantial critical revival until after he was extravagantly praised by Anderson's most famous disciple, Ernest Hemingway. "All modern American literature comes from one book by Mark Twain called *Huckleberry Finn*," he declared in *Green Hills of Africa* (1935, p. 22). "All American writing comes from that. There was nothing before. There has been nothing as good since."

80 Stevenson quoted by Meltzer, *Mark Twain Himself*, pp. 179 and 277; Kipling and Shaw by Sanderlin, *Mark Twain: As Others Saw Him*, pp. 115 and 117–118. Also Stevenson told Brander Matthews in *The Tocsin of Revolt and Other Essays* (New York: Scribners, 1922), p. 268, that he believed *Huckleberry Finn* superior to *Tom Sawyer*, "not only because it was richer in matter more artistically presented, but also and especially because it had more of the morality which must ever be the support of the noblest fiction."

81 Although he recognized the humorist as a man of truly great talent, who might have been one of the world's great satiric masters if he had not been overpowered by the spirit of America, Upton Sinclair concluded in *Mammonart* (1925, pp. 328–329) that Twain was "the most repressed personality, the most completely cowed, shamed, and tormented great man in the history of letters." "Convention," complained Theodore Dreiser in "Mark the Double Twain" (*The English Journal*, October 1935, p. 626), "convention, the dross of a worthless and meaningless current opinion—this was the thing that restrained him." Lewis Mumford in *The Golden Day* (1926, pp. 176–179) accused Twain of being "afraid of his imagination" and of accepting "the values that surrounded him, and since they were not central human values—and he was too honest not to realize this—he stored up, secretly, the bile of despair."

82 Quoted by Sanderlin, *Mark Twain: As Others Saw Him*, pp. 129 and 125.

83 In his introduction to the 1948 edition published by Holt, Rinehart and Winston.

84 Quoted by Sanderlin, *Mark Twain: As Others Saw Him*, p. 89. Too often these studies reveal more about their particular author's preoccupations than anything pertinent about Twain's art. For example, Charles E. May has explored the "latent sexuality" of the novel in "Literary Masters and Masturbators: Sexuality, Fantasy, and Reality in *Huckleberry Finn*," *Literature and Psychology* (No. 2, 1978), pp. 85–92. Even more notorious than this psychoanalytic interpretation is Leslie Fiedler's essay, "Come Back to the Raft Again, Huck Honey," in *An End to Innocence* (1955): Perhaps there is evidence to make a case for an illicit affair between Ishmael and his savage Queequeg in *Moby Dick*, but Fiedler's unconvincing gropings for proof of an implicit homosexual liaison between Huck Finn and Jim on their Mississippi raft are irrelevant to *Huckleberry Finn*.

85 In *Is Shakespeare Dead?* (New York and London: Harper & Bros., 1909), p. 39.

86 In "Mark Twain," *The Century* (September 1882), p. 780.

Sam Clemens, printer's apprentice, 1850. *Courtesy the Mark Twain Papers, The Bancroft Library, University of California at Berkeley.*

Hemingway's approval coincided conveniently with the centenary of Clemens's birth, and now *Huckleberry Finn* became fashionable among critics and scholars. T. S. Eliot read it for the first time (it had been forbidden him by his parents when he was a boy in St. Louis) and pronounced it a masterpiece; likewise, Lionel Trilling recognized the novel as "one of the world's great books and one of the central documents of American culture." [83] Even Faulkner came to admit in an interview in *The Paris Review* (Spring 1956, p. 46) that Sherwood Anderson was "the father of my generation of American writers and the tradition which our successors will carry on. . . . Dreiser is his older brother and Mark Twain the father of them both."

Since World War II, so much has been written about *Huckleberry Finn* that this vast critical literature is almost an academic industry unto itself. The book has been debated and reinterpreted according to every current literary trend, so much so that one would hardly think that anything new could possibly be said about it. Unfortunately, not all of Twain's critics have kept in mind his sane advice, "Don't explain your author, read him right and he explains himself." [84] One writer, John Seelye, has even attempted to rewrite Twain's story according to all the best authorities as *The True Adventures of Huckleberry Finn;* sadly, Seelye is a better scholar than novelist, and his book lacks the spirit of Twain's original. Twain would have appreciated the irony in the recent revival of academic interest in his book. "I believe," he bitterly wrote in Chapter 55 of his *Autobiography*, "that the trade of critic in literature, music and the drama is the most degraded of all trades and that it has no real value—certainly no large value. . . . However, let it go. It is the will of God that we must have critics and missionaries and congressmen and humorists, and we must bear the burden."

While the writers of the 1920s stressed the author's life in their arguments, the New Critics have tried to analyze *Huckleberry Finn* purely as literature. However, the finest of his fiction is autobiographical, so one cannot divorce the life of Samuel Clemens from the art of Mark Twain. "Experience is an author's most valuable asset," he argued; "experience is the thing that puts the muscle and the breath and the warm blood into the book he writes." [85] Although some of the people and places described in *Huckleberry Finn* were gleaned from Clemens's years as a journeyman printer and as a riverboat pilot, many more were a recalling and reshaping of his boyhood in Hannibal, what Howells called "a loafing, out-at-the-elbows, down-at-the-heels, slave-owning Mississippi River town" before the Civil War. [86] "I confine myself to life with which I am familiar with when pretending to portray life," Twain explained in a letter of 1890. "But I confined myself to that boy-life on the Mississippi because that had a peculiar charm for me, and not because I was not familiar with other phases of life. . . . *Now* then: as the most valuable capital, or culture, or education usable in the building of novels is personal experience, I ought to be well-equipped for the trade." However, he appended to the letter, "And yet I can't get away from the boyhood period and write novels, because *capital* is not sufficient by itself and I lack the other essential; interest in handling the men and experience of later life."[87] Invention was never enough for Twain. "If you attempt to create a wholly imaginary incident, adventure or situation," he warned in a notebook entry of the late 1880s, "you will go astray and the artificiality of the thing will be detectable, but if you found on a *fact* in your personal experience it is as an acorn, a root, and every created adornment that grows up out of it, and spreads its foliage and blossom to the sun will seem reality, not inventions."[88] However, the writer who thinks he is actually inventing nevertheless draws from some forgotten experience. And it was as true with characters as with situations. "I don't believe an author . . . ever lived, who created a character," Twain told a reporter on the Portland *Oregonian* (August 11, 1895). "It was always drawn from his recollections of someone he had known. Something, like a composite photograph, an author's presentation of a character may possibly be from the blending of more than two or more real characters in his recollection. But, even when he is making no attempt to draw his character from life . . . , he is yet drawing unconsciously from memory."

In a sense, *Huckleberry Finn* was a summation and crystallization of not only the author's experience but of his earlier work as well. "It was a book," Bernard DeVoto argued in *Mark Twain's America* (p. 311), that Twain "was foreordained to write: it brought harmoniously to a focus everything that had a basic reality in his mind." His other books may be seen as mere apprentice work in preparation of his one masterpiece, *Huckleberry Finn.*[89] But what distinguishes *Huckleberry Finn* from what came before and after is the voice of the narrator. One need only compare three descriptions of a sunrise on the river—in *Tom Sawyer, Life on the Mississippi,* and *Huckleberry Finn*—to see how much was gained by having the ignorant boy speak for himself.[90] In Chapter 14 of *Tom Sawyer,* Tom awakens on Jackson's Island: "It was the cool gray dawn, and there was a delicious sense of repose and peace in the deep pervading calm and silence of the woods. Not a leaf stirred; not a sound obtruded upon great Nature's meditations. . . . Now, far away in the woods a bird called; another answered. . . . Gradually the cool dim gray of the morning whitened, and as gradually sounds multiplied and life manifested itself. The marvel of Nature shaking off sleep

87 In a letter quoted by Bernard DeVoto in *The Portable Mark Twain* (New York: Viking, 1946), pp. 9 and 773–775.

88 In *Mark Twain's Notebook,* edited by Albert Bigelow Paine (New York and London: Harper & Bros., 1935), pp. 192–193.

89 The opening and closing chapters are reworkings of *Tom Sawyer;* the Grangerford parlor is "The House Beautiful" and the feud the same as that between the Darnells and the Watsons, of *Life on the Mississippi;* Bricksville is Obedstown, Tennessee, of *The Gilded Age;* the king's and the duke's false histories parody Miles Hendon's usurped title and property and the mistaken identities of Tom and Huck echo those of Prince Edward and Tom Canty in *The Prince and the Pauper;* even the novel's form, a travelogue which describes the men and manners of a picturesque part of the world, is related to *The Innocents Abroad, A Tramp Abroad,* and *Life on the Mississippi.*

90 Suggested by Leo Marx in "The Pilot and the Passenger: Landscape Conventions and the Style of *Huckleberry Finn,*" *American Literature* (May 1956), pp. 129–146.

The Mississippi River north of Hannibal, Missouri, 1902. *Courtesy the Mark Twain Papers, The Bancroft Library, University of California at Berkeley.*

and going to work unfolded itself to the musing boy . . . now long lances of sunlight pierced down through the dense foliage far and near." This description is almost embarrassingly poor; not only is the writing hackneyed and cliché-ridden, but the imagery is so imprecise, the effects so artificial, that it was clearly invented in the studio, with aid of some books, and without regard to an actual sunrise. The strain to be poetic in the evocation of Nature only adds to the two-dimensionality. Since nothing reveals what the boy perceives in the scene, its props remain as dead as those of a stage set.

In Chapter 30 of *Life on the Mississippi*, Twain recalled a summer sunrise: "First, there is the eloquence of silence. . . . Next, there is the haunting sense of loneliness, isolation, remoteness from the worry and bustle of the world. The dawn creeps in stealthily; the solid walls of black forest soften to gray, and vast stretches of the river open up and reveal themselves; the water is glass-smooth, gives off spectral little wreaths of white mist; there is not the faintest breath of wind, nor stir of leaf. . . . Then a bird pipes up, another follows, and soon the pipings develop into a jubilant riot of music. . . . You have the intense green of the massed and crowded foliage near by; . . . upon the next projecting cape, a mile off or more, the tint has lightened to the tender young green of spring; the cape beyond that one has almost lost color, and the furthest one, miles away under the horizon, sleeps upon the water a mere dim vapor, and hardly separable from the sky above it and about it. . . . and when the sun gets well up, and distributes a pink flush here and a powder of gold yonder and a purple haze where it will yield the best effect, you grant that you have seen something that is worth remembering." But this description is no more convincing than that in *Tom Sawyer*. Perhaps Twain was working from notes of a recent landscape, or more likely from a print. Again the poetics muddle the imagery, and consequently the static picture no more suggests an actual sunrise than does an inferior painting or a Polaroid snapshot.

In Chapter 19 of *Huckleberry Finn*, Huck watches the sun rise: "Not a sound anywheres—perfectly still—just like the whole world was asleep . . . bull-frogs a-cluttering, maybe. The first thing to see, looking away over the water, was a kind of dull line—that was the woods on t'other side . . . then a pale place in the sky; then more paleness, spreading around; then the river softened up, away off, and warn't black any more, but gray . . . and you see the mist curl up off of the water, and the east reddens up, and the river . . . ; then the nice breeze springs up, and comes fanning you from over there, so cool and fresh, and sweet to smell, on account of the woods and the flowers . . . and next you've got the full day, and everything smiling in the sun, and the song-birds just going it!" Superficially this passage describes the same scene as those in *Tom Sawyer* or *Life on the Mississippi:* The stillness, the gray dawn, the birds. Yet it is so much more vivid than its predecessors, because Huck, unlike the previous narrators, reacts to and shapes the event; there is nothing abstract, nothing artificial, nothing self-consciously poetic in the language, and yet it has the lilt and rhythm of verse. All the boy's senses are employed to depict the process of the sun's rising. By comparison, the picture of the sunrise in *Life on the Mississippi* is as flat as a chromo.

Twain succeeds beautifully in his artifice that this is actually how such a boy would speak. Remarkably, he was also able to sustain at least seven different forms of American English throughout the story. The vast range of these varying dialects alone is impressive: Twain seems at much at ease with the Missouri slave lingo and the duke and the king's extravagant gibberish as with the ordinary "Pike County" idiom of the narrator.[91] Rarely does Huck fall out of character—as in Chapter 22 when Colonel Sherburn quells the Bricksville mob. In spite of the deliberate care taken in the novel's composition, one of the principal powers within the vivid style of *Huckleberry Finn* is how deceptively effortless the writing appears. Indeed so expertly did Twain tune Huck's distinctive voice that it is, as DeVoto in *Mark Twain's America* (p. 318) argued, "a sensitive, subtle, and versatile instrument—capable of every effect it is called upon to manage." To Dwight Macdonald ("Mark Twain: An Unsentimental Journey," *The New Yorker*, April 9, 1960, p. 174), Twain here "was able to raise the vernacular to a great style." Huck's voice in its particular lyricism avoids "the gaudiness and inane phraseology of many modern writers" of which William Wordsworth stripped contemporary poetry through his *Lyrical Ballads* (1798); nearly a century later, Huck's colloquial description of the sunrise on the Mississippi climaxed the nineteenth-century American attempt through local color to emulate the Wordsworthian principle of inventing a contemporary style from "a selection of the real language of men in a state of vivid sensation." In effect, as T. S. Eliot suggested, Mark Twain, through Huck Finn, brought the language up to date.

However, Twain's mastery of dialect does not fully account for the greatness of the style of *Huckleberry Finn*. Actually, although he may have been (as Eliot stated) the first author to use natural speech through the entirety of a novel, Samuel L. Clemens as "Mark Twain" wrote within a rich tradition of American humor. His was preceded by such once-famous *noms de plume* as "Artemus Ward" (Charles Farrar Browne), "Josh Billings" (Henry Wheeler Shaw), and "Petroleum V. Nasby" (David Ross Locke).

[91] And there was no carelessness in such work. "What is known as 'dialect' writing," he argued in "The Contributor's Cover: A Boston Girl" (*The Atlantic Monthly*, June 1880, p. 850), "looks simple and easy, but it is not. It is exceedingly difficult; it has rarely been done well. A man not born to write dialect cannot learn how to write it correctly. It is a gift." Twain perfected his art, as he explained to Howells, September 20, 1874, "by talking and talking and *talking* till it sounds right" (*Mark Twain–Howells Letters*, Vol. I, p. 26). Even from the platform, Twain revised his dialect in *Huckleberry Finn* because, he admitted in "The Art of Composition" (in *Life as I See It*, edited by Charles Neider, New York: Harper & Row, 1977, p. 228), "the difference between the *almost right* word and the *right* word is really a large matter—'tis the difference between the lightning-bug and the lightning."

Josh Billings, Mark Twain, and Petroleum V. Nasby, 1869. *Courtesy the Library of Congress.*

92 In "Theoretical and Practical Morals," a talk delivered in London, on July 8, 1899, *Mark Twain's Speeches* (New York: Harper & Bros., 1910), p. 131.

93 Twain had long admired the writing style of children. "They write simply and naturally," he wrote in "A Complaint about Correspondents" (San Francisco *Californian*, March 24, 1866), "and without straining for effect. They tell all they know and then stop. They seldom deal in abstractions or moral homilies. Consequently their epistles are brief; but, treating as they do of familiar scenes and persons, always entertaining." Twain was impressed also with a letter of another young admirer. "I notice," Twain wrote Wattie Bowser, March 20, 1880, "that you use plain, simple language, short words, and brief sentences. That is the way to write English—it is the modern way, and the best way. Stick to it; don't let fluff and flowers and verbosity creep in. When you catch an adjective, kill it. No, I don't mean that utterly, but kill the most of them—then the rest will be valuable. They weaken when they are close together, they give strength when they are wide apart. An adjective-habit, or a wordy, diffuse, or flowery habit, once fastened on a person, is as hard to get rid of as any other vice" (quoted by Covici, Jr., "Dear Master Wattie," *Southwest Review*, pp. 108–109). Although Twain himself did violate this sound advice in his other books, he followed it generally throughout *Huckleberry Finn*.

94 "Aurora Borealis" (Capt. Alphonso Wetmore), "The Beaver Hunter," Franklin, *Missouri Intelligencer*, October 29, 1822.

These comic writers formed a school of seemingly illiterate backwoodsmen whose common sense exposed the stupidities of contemporary life; and also, as in the manner of Huck Finn, each spoke in his natural idiom. However, Twain, unlike his colleagues, did not indulge (as Howells argued in "Mark Twain," *The Century*, September 1882, p. 781), "in literary attitude, in labored dictionary funning, in affected quaintness, in dreary dramatization, in artificial 'dialect.'"

But Twain stands head and shoulders above such writers as Nasby and Billings as much for his purpose as for his prose style. "Humor is only a fragrance, a decoration," Twain explained in Chapter 55 of his *Autobiography*. "Often it is merely an odd trick of speech and of spelling, as in the case of Ward and Billings and Nasby . . . , and presently the fashion passes and the fame along with it." For the work to survive, it must teach and preach as well as amuse. "The proper office of humor," Twain wryly explained, "is to reflect, to put you in a pensive mood of deep thought, to make you think of your sins."[92] With these ambitious intentions, Twain transformed mere humor into enduring satire.

Twain went even further than his predecessors in making his speaker a boy rather than a grown man.[93] And Huck Finn is not just any boy. He is the ignorant, semiliterate son of the town drunk. He is from the lowest level of St. Petersburg society, and yet he (like his Hannibal prototype) is the only really independent person in the community. Therefore, unlike Tom Sawyer, he owes nothing to anyone. He can thus tell the whole truth denied to Tom Sawyer. Through his ignorance, his lack of "sivilizing," he views the world through the clear eyes of the true innocent. Huck Finn is an American version of the Romantic ideal of the divine fool. He is Twain's wild boy of Aveyron, Twain's Kaspar Hauser.

He is also related to certain folk heroes of the Southwest. He is a descendant of Mike Fink, the Mississippi River boatman, so suspicious of progress that he kept moving west to stay ahead of civilization; he is a cousin of Mike Shuck, "a white-headed, hardy urchin, whom nobody claimed kin to, and who disclaimed connexion with all mankind," who too fled to the wilderness.[94] Indeed, there is much of Shuck and Fink in Huck Finn. The boy is (like Hank Morgan in Chapter 39 of *A Connecticut Yankee in King Arthur's Court*) "the champion of hard, unsentimental common-sense and reason."[95] Whether describing the carnage left by the Grangerford-Shepherdson feud, or the killing of Boggs by Sherburn, the boy records the horrible events free of any sentimental or intellectual elaboration. Here he merely observes, he does not judge. He does break down at the end of Chapter 18 on discovering the corpse of his murdered companion, but he pulls back on describing the aftermath: "I ain't agoing to tell *all* that happened—it would make me sick again if I was to do that. . . . I ain't ever going to get shut of them—lots of times I dream about them." What is most chilling in this passage is what is merely implied. Unlike Twain in his other work, Huck never digresses into diatribes: In Chapter 38 of *Life on the Mississippi*, Twain gave a factual account of an interior similar to the Grangerford parlor in Chapter 17 of *Huckleberry Finn*, but this sarcastic account of "The House Beautiful" lacks the subtle irony of Huck's version; the criticism of the vulgarity of a typical Southern household of the time is sharper in the second primarily because the ignorant boy so admires the Grangerford decor. As Walter Besant suggested in "My Favorite Novelist and His Best Book" (*Munsey's Magazine*, February 1898), the novel is so often unconsciously humorous because the narrator so infrequently sees the comedy in anything.

But Huck does give his opinions of the stupidities and cruelties as the journey progresses, particularly after Boggs's murder. Evidently all the horrible events that plagued his dreams have been playing on the boy's subconscious; he recognizes the king and the duke for the frauds they are; he later condemns the mob's tarring and feathering of these two scoundrels. "It was a dreadful thing to see," Huck says. "Human beings *can* be awful cruel to one another." Huck himself has one major flaw: A conscience deformed by his having been raised in slave society. Under the tutelage of his shiftless father, Huck believes that even in his poverty he is better than any Negro, either slave or free.

Ironically, the boy's companion down the river is Miss Watson's Jim, a fugitive slave, and this unfortunate soul, like Huck, has had much unfair mud flung at him. Ralph Ellison perhaps made the strongest case against this character. "Twain fitted Jim into the outlines of the minstrel tradition," he argued in "The Negro Writer in America" (*Partisan Review*, Spring 1958, p. 215), "and it is from behind this stereotype mask that we see Jim's dignity and human capacity—and Twain's complexity—emerge." When introduced, Jim is indeed just another superstitious "nigger," the butt of Tom Sawyer's practical jokes. Only slowly do Jim's dignity and human capacity emerge, all the time testing and conquering Huck's prejudices against the man's race. His very presence in the novel questions the validity of American republicanism in its allowing such a pernicious institution as slavery to thrive in the South and the Southwest. Just as Jim becomes the albatross around Huck's neck, so too was slavery the persistent shame upon Western democracy.

Particularly offensive to Twain's critics are the min-

95 Huck views society in much the way Mrs. Trollope did in her American journal of the 1830s. According to Twain, she "spoke of this civilization in plain terms—plain and unsugared, but honest and without malice, and without hate. Her voice rises to indignation, sometimes, but the object justifies the attitude—being slavery, rowdyism, 'chivalrous' assassinations, sham godliness, and several other devilishnesses which would be as hateful to you, now, as they were to her then." She shared with Twain's character "the prejudices of a humane spirit against inhumanities; of an honest nature against humbug; . . . of a right heart against unright speech and deed" (in a suppressed passage from *Life on the Mississippi*, New York: Limited Editions Club, 1944, pp. 392).

96 Quoted by Paine, *Mark Twain: A Biography*, Vol. II, p. 1096.

Huckleberry Finn, Jim, and Tom Sawyer. Drawing by E. W. Kemble, 1932. *Courtesy the Limited Editions Club.*

strel show exchanges between Jim as "Mr. Bones," the comic, and Huck as "Mr. Interlocator," the straight man. However, one must read between the lines of these deceptively light debates; in each instance, Jim wins the argument through his good common sense. In effect, Jim is the black descendant of Ward, Billings, and the other humorists. For example, in Chapter 14, Jim may miss the original lesson of Solomon and the baby, but he makes a plea for the humane treatment of all children. Jim may be illiterate, but he is not ignorant. He knows all the signs and ways of the river; and he acts as protector, as an "elder brother," to Huck, just as Miles Hendon served Edward Tudor in *The Prince and the Pauper.*

Ellison further objected that "Jim's friendship for Huck comes across as that of a boy for another boy rather than as the friendship of an adult for a junior." Twain portrayed Jim according to his own experience, from slaves he had known in childhood and servants of his later years. Unfortunately, in the slave country, one of the most effective ways of making the Black male subservient was to keep him in a childlike state by breaking his pride and stripping him of all responsibilities except manual labor and procreation. Although not the current ideal, Jim is true to his period. And Twain did not think it a tragedy to remain a boy. He himself never really grew up: His wife's pet name for Clemens was "Youth," and Howells noted in *My Mark Twain* (p. 5), "He was a youth to the end of his days, the heart of a boy with the head of a sage; the heart of a good boy, or a bad boy, but always a willful boy, and willfulest to show himself out at every time for just the boy he was." Therefore, for this man who longed to go back to the days when he was fourteen and then drown, Jim is, if anything, all the more admirable for remaining childlike. The only one who is universally kind to Huck is Jim, the boy's peer on the river.

The raft is a great equalizer. Huck admits in Chapter 19 that "what you want, above all things, on a raft, is for everybody to be satisfied, and feel right and kind towards the others." And only on the river can such harmony be found. Conflicts arise only when the fugitives come ashore or encounter men on the water. To Huck and Jim, Hell is other people. Their constant threat is civilization, what Twain called "a shoddy, poor thing and full of cruelties, vanities, and arrogancies, meannesses, and hypocrisies."**96** Every one they meet wants either to imprison or to steal Huck's "nigger"; whenever the boy goes ashore and leaves Jim alone, the man must be either tied up or disguised. When the king and the duke invade their raft, they introduce aristocracy on the river and make Huck a servant and Jim a slave again. Nothing civilization provides is worthwhile. Its religion teaches brotherly love, and yet such good churchgoers as the Grangerfords and the Shepherdsons slaughter one another; preachers such as Uncle Silas own slaves. Close family ties lead to the stupidities of the Grangerford-Shepherdson feud. And the slave system reveals all the ugliest qualities of men.

During the 1840s, the period of the novel, American culture was in transition. The Mississippi River valley was still in its prenatal state, largely a Jeffersonian agrarian society untouched by the Industrial Revolution, still free of railroads; even steam power was then but a marvelous toy. Nevertheless, in *Huckleberry Finn*, progress invades the American Eden: In the form of a steamship, it wrecks Huck's raft. Another threat to harmony on the river is greed. The progress Twain felt the nineteenth century had achieved was primarily in materialities.[97] To Twain, the corruption of the Mississippi Valley came with the California Gold Rush of 1849. Before that craze, Twain believed, "'Rich' men were not worshipped, and not envied. They were not arrogant, nor assertive, nor tyrannical, nor exigent."[98] It was the California movement with its "get-rich-quick" schemes which "begat the lust for money which is the rule today, and the hardness and cynicism which is the spirit of today." Although not mentioned specifically in the text, 1849 (when Sam Clemens, like Huck Finn, was fourteen) may indeed be the date of *Huckleberry Finn*. The lust for money begins to taint life on the river with the introduction of the shiftless king and duke, two professional swindlers, who sell Jim for "forty dirty dollars."

Huck's only defense against this civilization is to lie and to steal. "Whenever Huck is caught in a close place and is forced to explain," Twain prefaced the excerpt in the December 1884 *Century*, "the truth gets well crippled before he gets through." Paradoxically, although he vows in the novel's first paragraph to tell the truth, Huck Finn is an incurable liar. At every stop along the river, he takes on a new alias; and he succeeds so effortlessly in outwitting others on the water and the shore by appealing to their cowardice, vanity, cruelty, and greed. "All men are liars," Twain argued, "partial or hiders of facts, half tellers of truth, shirks, moral sneaks. When a merely honest man appears he is a comet—his fame is eternal—needs no genius, no talent—mere honesty."[99] Therefore Huck was no better than anyone else, certainly no better than those two professional deceivers, the king and the duke. However, the boy never lies or steals for self-gain, only for self-preservation. And he never deceives himself: In his struggles with his unrelenting conscience, he follows the honest dictates of his heart.

From the river the story draws its strengths and its weaknesses. A common complaint against *Huckleberry Finn* is that as a novel it is as formless as the mighty Mississippi

[97] "Prodigious acquisitions," Twain argued in a letter to Twichell, March 14, 1905, "were made in things which add to the comfort of many and make life harder for as many more. . . . Money is the supreme ideal—all others take tenth place. . . . Money-lust has always existed, but not in the history of the world was it ever a craze, a madness, until your time and mine. This lust will rot these nations; it has made them hard, sordid, ungentle, dishonest, oppressive" (*Mark Twain's Letters*, Vol. II, pp. 769–770).

[98] In "Villagers of 1840–3" in *Mark Twain's Hannibal, Huck and Tom*, p. 35.

[99] In *Mark Twain's Notebook* (1935), p. 181.

100 See DeVoto, *Mark Twain at Work*, p. 66.

101 To Matthews, in *The Tocsin of Revolt*, p. 267; Matthews too noticed that *Huckleberry Finn* shared with *Gil Blas* "an unheroic hero who is not the chief actor in the chief episodes he sets forth and who is often little more than a recording spectator, before whose tolerant eyes the panorama of human vicissitude is unrolled." Obviously Matthews was referring to the Grangerford-Shepherdson feud and Old Boggs's murder in Twain's novel. See also Charles E. Metzger, "*The Adventures of Huckleberry Finn* as Picaresque," *The Midwest Quarterly* (April 1964), pp. 249–256.

102 The development of the novel's composition has been described in detail by Blair in *Mark Twain and Huck Finn*, which suggested the substance of this argument.

itself. Despite the author's warning that "any persons attempting to find a plot in it will be shot," many critics have deplored the book's apparent lack of design. "Mark Twain was always the divine amateur," Arnold Bennett complained in *The Bookman* in 1910. "He had no notion of construction, and very little power of self-criticism." Indeed, *Huckleberry Finn* is, as T. S. Eliot noted, "not a book where the author knows, from the beginning, what is going to happen." This observation is supported by Twain's working notes for the novel which included such an absurd idea as having Huck escape the circus on the back of an elephant.[100] Twain was an intuitive writer; he composed, Howells explained in *My Mark Twain* (p. 17), "as he thought, and as all men think, without sequence, without an eye to what went before or should come after."

Twain admitted that his novel was in part inspired by *Gil Blas* (1715). Although he did acknowledge that he never actually read the Lesage book,[101] he was nevertheless acquainted with it and other picaresque novels such as *Tom Jones* and *Roderick Random*. Huck Finn may be seen as a *pícaro*, or "rogue, roguish wanderer," a type developed in eighteenth-century Spanish literature as the antithesis of the medieval hero. While the courtly knight is of noble birth and character, the *pícaro* is of low degree and immoral by conventional standards; the hero's adventures are a quest for something admirable, the *pícaro*'s an escape, often from the law. Whereas the medieval knight is generally characterized by superhuman strength and ideals, the rogue is usually physically weak and must survive on his wits through deception, stealth, and theft. A picaresque novel such as *Huckleberry Finn* is also generally told in the first person, has an episodic plot, and satirizes several levels of society. In *Huckleberry Finn*, Twain replaced the road of the picaresque novel with the Mississippi; and in so doing, he abandoned all semblance of a motive, a moral, and a plot. Nevertheless, what was sacrificed in an incoherent construction was gained in the introduction of a series of repetitions and variations on a set of contrasting and intersecting themes.

The inconsistencies and other problems within the narrative may be traced in part to the fits and starts the novel suffered during its composition.[102] Just as Huck's adventures are a series of deaths and rebirths on the river, the manuscript went through several reincarnations of its own. The early chapters do pick up where *Tom Sawyer* left off, but they also introduce reasons for Huck's flight down the river. Slowly the boy learns to reject St. Petersburg's religion, morality, and law as he flees the Widow Douglas and Pap Finn. Huck must say "good-bye to all that," fully to escape his past; and only through his "death" can he be truly free. The plot is further complicated by the entrance of the runaway slave: He is necessary as the boy's protector, and he instigates adventures not merely by his prophesies but also by his mere presence on the river. He and Huck must escape to the free states by way of Cairo; but in Chapter 16, when the raft is lost and Jim with it, Twain suddenly stopped. Surely he had no interest in taking the two up the Ohio River into territory with which he was not familiar; he had to send them farther south, but in having them miss Cairo, he made the chance for Jim's escape less likely the deeper they traveled into slave country. He just did not know what to do next.

Several years later, he returned briefly to the story to add the Grangerford-Shepherdson feud. This interlude introduced a new purpose for the text: Twain would satirize the various classes of Southern society. He now filled his notebook with ideas for subsequent chapters taken from such typical rural scenes as country cotillions, candy-pullings, house-raisings, quiltings, and horse-trades. This new development in the plot provided an opportunity for charting Huck's moral growth through encounters with the spiritual decay of all levels of this culture. However, the writing did not pick up again until Twain conceived the king and the duke who can introduce Huck as a servant to various classes of the South.

Before composing this part of the novel, Twain had been reading collections of Southern humor of the period for consideration in his proposed *Mark Twain's Library of Humor* (not published until 1888); this book was to be an American imitation of William E. Burton's *Cyclopedia of Wit and Humor* (1858), selected from such rural sketches as Johnson J. Hooper's *Adventures of Captain Simon Suggs* (1858), William Tappan Thompson's *Chronicles of Pineville* (1853), and Richard Malcolm Johnston's *Dukesborough Tales* (1871).[103] One of the common comic types of such literature was the shifty confidence man, and Twain expanded him into the false king and duke. "In attempting to represent some character which he cannot recall, which he thinks he draws from what he thinks is his imagination," Twain confessed to the interviewer from the Portland *Oregonian*, "an author may often fall into the error of copying in part a character already drawn by another, a character which impressed itself upon his memory from some book. . . . We mortals can't create, we only copy." Similarly, he borrowed incidents as well as characters from other fiction, including several from the books he read for his *Library of Humor*. "Mark Twain had a very good memory," an acquaintance quipped, "and that's where he gets most of his best stories."[104] Although the least admiring critic might consider it nothing but a soft name for

103 According to *Mark Twain's Notebooks and Journals*, Vol. II, pp. 361–362.

104 Quoted by Matthews, *The Tocsin of Revolt*, p. 268.

105 Quoted by Blair, *Mark Twain and Huck Finn*, p. 60.

106 In a letter to Olivia L. Clemens, May 17, 1882, *Mark Twain's Letters*, Vol. I, p. 419.

107 Hemingway so disliked this portion of the novel that he suspected that "the last few Chapters of it were just tacked on to finish it off by Howells or somebody" (in a letter to Ernest Walsh, January 2, 1926, *Ernest Hemingway Selected Letters*, edited by Carlos Baker, New York: Charles Scribner's Sons, 1981, p. 188).

108 In a letter of September 19, 1979.

109 In a letter to Olivia L. Clemens, December 28, 1884, *The Love Letters of Mark Twain*, p. 223.

"stealing," Twain did not think such "borrowing" from others' literature to be plagiarism. After all, he explained, "Shakespeare took other people's quartz and extracted gold from it—it was a nearly valueless commodity before."[105]

His trip back down the river for *Life on the Mississippi* also reinvigorated the writing of *Huckleberry Finn*. Not only did it revive many memories for Clemens, but the many contemporary accounts of Mississippi life which he had to read for the journey also refreshed his memory. The journey was a revelation: "The world which I knew in its blossoming youth," he wrote Livy from Hannibal, "is old and bowed and melancholy, now; its soft cheeks are leathery and wrinkled, the fire is gone out of its eyes, and the spring from its step. It will be dust and ashes when I come again."[106] This disillusionment as well as the realization that the good old days were not so good after all further transformed the character of the novel.

When he returned to Hartford, Twain at first did not know what to do with the novel, whether to publish it or even to complete it. Pressured by the publisher to pad *Life on the Mississippi*, the author threw in "The Raft Chapter" from Chapter 16 of the work in progress. Twain had intended to restore it to the novel; but when Webster objected to any old material in the new book, the author did not restore it to its proper place in *Huckleberry Finn*. "The Raft Chapter," as it appeared in *Life on the Mississippi* in 1882, is reprinted in the appendix of this edition.

The last chapters, the "evasion" on the Phelps farm, were written during Twain's final burst of inspiration for the novel, but how inspired the episode actually is still troubles the critics. In *Mark Twain at Work* (p. 92), DeVoto said that there was "no more abrupt or more chilling descent" in the whole range of the English novel than of Tom Sawyer's attempt to free Jim. Even Hemingway advised, "You must stop where Nigger Jim is stolen from the boys. That is the real end. The rest is just cheating."[107] Nevertheless, others have found it highly amusing. "It is, of course, broad burlesque unlike the rest of the book," Daniel P. Mannix, the writer, has explained. "Still, I remember reading it as a boy and laughing so hard I had to get up and pace the room."[108] Even in Twain's day, responses to this section were mixed. The author himself was so proud of Tom Sawyer's brilliant achievement that he read it aloud on his 1884–1885 lecture tour. Twain exclaimed in a letter to his wife that the piece was "the biggest card I've got in my whole repertoire. I always thought so. It went a-booming; and Cable's praises are not merely loud, they are boisterous. Says its literary quality is high and fine—and great; its truth to boy nature unchallengeable; its humor constant and delightful; and its dramatic close full of stir, and boom and *go*."[109] But other dramatizations, as well as Seelye's *The True Adeventures of Huckleberry Finn*, have wisely evaded the "evasion."

Certainly it goes on too long. It does seem mere padding at times: There had been complaints against *Tom Sawyer* that it was too slim for a proper subscription book, and perhaps Twain did not wish to repeat the problem in *Huckleberry Finn*. Also, the unnecessarily cruel treatment of Jim involving snakes and rats and whatever else Tom can dream up is out of character with the rest of the novel; Leo Marx in "Mr. Eliot, Mr. Trilling, and *Huckleberry Finn*" (*The American Scholar*, Autumn 1953) has suggested that the boys' abuse of the slave compromises the total integrity of the novel. In other aspects, the conclusion is related to what preceded it; and perhaps, as Eliot argued, "it is right that the mood of the end of the book should bring us back to the beginning." The ending appropriately revives the contrast between romantic Tom Sawyer and sensible Huck Finn. Also, throughout the novel, Huck wonders how Tom might handle a close situation; Tom finally gets his chance at the end—and he fails dismally. The "evasion" serves one other important function in the story by giving Jim an opportunity through his loyalty to wounded Tom to prove his humanity to the public at large.

The principal concern of the conclusion was to continue Twain's attack upon the romantic mentality which he felt corrupted Southern society not merely in the 1840s but also persisted into the 1880s. He thought "the most insidious manipulator of the imagination" to be "the felicitously written romance." In "International Copyright" (*The Century*, February 1886), Twain complained that these novels "fill the imagination with an unhealthy fascination for foreign life, with its dukes and earls and kings, its fuss and feathers, its graceful immoralities, its sugar-coated injustices and oppressions." Tom Sawyer has fallen under the evil influence of such romances, not only *The Count of Monte Cristo* and *The Man in the Iron Mask* but also the indiscreet memoirs of several of the most notorious roués in European history, Casanova, Cellini, and Baron von Trenck; and to free Jim he devises an absurd scheme based upon this literature. Huck does protest Tom's foolishness, but he is silenced in much the way the duke is censored during the Wilks fraud. Another of Tom's favorite authors, Sir Walter Scott, was one whom Twain most detested. "Lord, it's all so juvenile!" Twain decried Scott's fiction on May 4, 1903. "And oh, the poverty of invention! Not poverty in inventing situations, but poverty in furnishing reasons for them. Sir Walter . . . elaborates, and elaborates, and elaborates, til if you live to get to it you don't believe it when it happens."[110] Unfortunately, Twain in his travesty followed his model too closely: He likewise elaborates, and elaborates, and elaborates until the situa-

[110] In a letter to Brander Matthews, May 4, 1903, *Mark Twain's Letters*, Vol. II, p. 738.

111 Despite its being written in at least seven different Southern dialects of the early nineteenth century, *Huckleberry Finn* has indeed become an international classic. Soon after its publication in England and the United States, translations were available in Danish (1885), Dutch (1885), Swedish (1885), French (1886), and Russian (1888); and today the Huckleberry Finn Collection of the Buffalo and Erie County Public Library houses almost 75 foreign editions in 27 different languages.

tion is no longer plausible. Unlike the rest of the novel, the "evasion" is artificial. "Where he lacked the support of the solid fact and had to rely on his own fantastic imagination," Brander Matthews said of Twain in *The Tocsin of Revolt* (p. 270), "his whimsicality was likely to betray him disastrously. . . . He needed to have the sustaining solidity of the concrete fact, which he could deal with at will, bringing out its humor, its latent beauty, and its human significance." Perhaps the "evasion" so disappoints, as do "Huck Finn and Tom Sawyer among the Indians," *Tom Sawyer Abroad*, and "Tom Sawyer, Detective," because the humor derives primarily from literature and not from life.

For parody to succeed, the reader must be familiar with what is being burlesqued. Nearly a century has passed since *Huckleberry Finn* was published, and even at that date, the life it portrayed was already part of the nation's dead past. *The Annotated Huckleberry Finn* attempts not only to recall what has been forgotten but also to clarify the elusive subtleties within Mark Twain's great fiction. The customs, the language, the law, even the terrain have changed. But people never change. *Huckleberry Finn* is indeed a vivid picture of a time and a place long gone, but it is not merely the great American novel. **111** It survives as a major work of world literature for its distinctive art and its individual moral character. Mark Twain endures for what Howells in *My Mark Twain* (p. 13) called "the self-lawed genius of a man who will be remembered with the great humorists of all time, with Cervantes, with Swift, or with any others worthy his company; none of them was his equal in humanity."

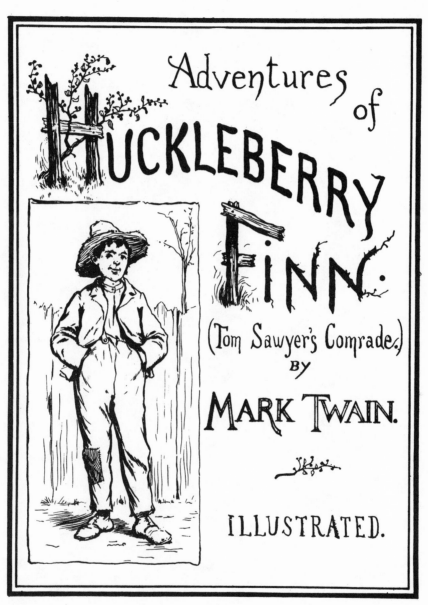

Cover of the first American edition of *Adventures of Huckleberry Finn*, 1885.

E·W·Kemble
·1884·

Frontispiece of the first American edition of *Adventures of Huckleberry Finn*, 1885.

ADVENTURES

OF

HUCKLEBERRY FINN

(TOM SAWYER'S COMRADE).

SCENE: THE MISSISSIPPI VALLEY.
TIME: FORTY TO FIFTY YEARS AGO.

BY

MARK TWAIN.

WITH ONE HUNDRED AND SEVENTY-FOUR ILLUSTRATIONS.

NEW YORK:
CHARLES L. WEBSTER AND COMPANY.
1885.

Title page of the first American edition of *Adventures of Huckleberry Finn*, 1885.

Map of the area covered in the novel, drawn by Charles Dibner, *Tom Sawyer and Huckleberry Finn*, 1943. "Everyman's Library." *Courtesy Elsevier-Dutton Publishing Co., Inc.*

EXPLANATORY.

IN this book a number of dialects are used, to wit: the **1**
Missouri negro dialect; the extremest form of the backwoods
South-Western dialect; the ordinary "Pike-County" dialect; **2**
and four modified varieties of this last. The shadings have not **3**
been done in a hap-hazard fashion, or by guess-work; but
pains-takingly, and with the trustworthy guidance and support
of personal familiarity with these several forms of speech.

I make this explanation for the reason that without it many
readers would suppose that all these characters were trying to
talk alike and not succeeding.

THE AUTHOR.

NOTICE.   4

PERSONS attempting to find a motive in this narrative will be prosecuted;
persons attempting to find a moral in it will be banished; persons attempting to find a plot in it will be shot.

BY ORDER OF THE AUTHOR

PER G. G., CHIEF OF ORDNANCE.   **5**

1 *In this book a number of dialects are used.* David Carkeet in "The Dialects in *Huckleberry Finn*" (*American Literature*, November 1979, pp. 315–332) has distinguished the various dialects spoken by characters in the novel as (1) Missouri Negro: Jim and the other slaves; (2) backwoods Southwestern: the Grangerfords in Chapters 17 and 18, and the various townspeople of Arkansas; (3) the "ordinary Pike County": Huckleberry Finn, Tom Sawyer, Ben Rogers, Pap Finn, Judith Loftus in Chapter 11, and Aunt Polly; and (4) four variants of modified "Pike County": (*a*) the robbers on the *Walter Scott* in Chapter 13; (*b*) the king; (*c*) the Bricksville loafers; and (*d*) Aunt Sally and Uncle Silas Phelps and their neighbors.

2 *"Pike-County."* The original home of the "Piker," a stock character in Western folk balladry of the 1850s, usually a Missourian or any other "squatter" who went West during the Gold Rush. The vogue for original "Pike County ballads" written in the squatter dialect began in 1871 with the publication of John Hay's collection; it was soon followed by Bret Harte's "Plain Language from Truthful James" and other verses. In an open letter to *Harper's Weekly* (October 21, 1905, p. 1530), Twain corrected the common assumption that Harte, and not his friend Hay, was the legitimate father of the genre.

3 *The shadings have not been done in a haphazard fashion, or by guess-work.* Edgar Lee Masters did not agree: The author of *Spoon River Anthology* (1915) grew up in Petersburg, Illinois, in the same boy lingo as Sam Clemens of Hannibal, Missouri; and Masters argued in *Mark Twain: A Portrait* (1938, pp. 130–131) that Huck should have said "feller" not "fellow," "ter-backer" not "tobacco," "et" not "eat." Nevertheless, most readers agree with James Dickey, in his introduction to the 1979 New American Library edition, that *Adventures of Huckleberry Finn* "is the only book I have ever read which used dialect in a manner not offensive to me."

4 *NOTICE.* Robert Bridges, in his review of the novel in *Life* (February 26, 1885, p. 119), accurately characterized this "Notice" as "a nice little artifice to scare off the critics—a kind of 'trespassers on these grounds will be dealt with according to the law.'"

5 *G. G.* Apparently General Ulysses S. Grant (1822–1885), commander of the Union Army during the Civil War and former President of the United States, whose memoirs Twain was then arranging for publication.

1 *Huckleberry Finn.* Huckleberries are a kind of blueberry and were then commonly considered a particularly inferior fruit. They are not native to Missouri. Samuel Clemens first encountered the fruit in Hartford, Connecticut, where he saw some children gathering them. "They are a new beverage to me," he admitted in "Morality and Huckleberries" (*Alta California*, September 6, 1868). "They are excellent. I had always thought a huckleberry was something like a turnip. On the contrary, they are no larger than buckshot. They are better than buckshot, though, and more digestible."

His hero's surname derived from Jimmy Finn, the town drunkard of Hannibal. "There was something about the name 'Finn' that suited," Twain admitted to an interviewer in the Portland *Sunday Oregonian* (August 11, 1895), "and 'Huck Finn' was all that was needed to somehow describe another kind of a boy than 'Tom Sawyer,' a boy of lower extraction or degree. Now, 'Arthur Van de Vanter Montague' would have sounded ridiculous, applied to characters like either 'Tom Sawyer' or 'Huck Finn.'"

In Chapter 6 of *Tom Sawyer* (1876), Twain introduced his most famous character: "Huckleberry was cordially hated and dreaded by all the mothers of the town, because he was idle, and lawless, and vulgar and bad—and because all their children admired him so, and delighted in his forbidden society, and wished they dared to be like him. . . . Huckleberry was always dressed in the cast-off clothes of full-grown men, and they were in perennial bloom and fluttering with rags. . . . Huckleberry came and went, at his own free will. He slept on door-steps in fine weather and in empty hogsheads in wet; he did not have to go to school or to church, or call any

56

The Adventures of Huckleberry Finn

Chapter I.

1

2

YOU don't know about me, without you have read a book by the name of "The Adventures of Tom Sawyer," but that ain't no matter. That book was made by Mr. Mark Twain, and he told the truth, mainly. There was things which he stretched, but mainly he told the truth. That is nothing. I never seen anybody but lied, one time or another, without it was Aunt Polly, or the widow, or maybe Mary. Aunt Polly—Tom's Aunt Polly, she is—and

3

THE WIDOW'S.

4 Mary, and the Widow Douglas, is all told about in that book—which is mostly a true book; with some stretchers, as I said before.

Now the way that the book winds up, is this: Tom and me found the money that the robbers hid in the cave, and it made us rich. We got six thousand dollars apiece—all gold. It was an awful sight of money when it was piled up. Well, Judge Thatcher, he took it and put it out at interest, and it fetched us a dollar a day apiece, all the year round—more than a body could tell what to do with. The Widow Douglas,

The home of Tom Blankenship, Hannibal, Missouri.
Courtesy the Mark Twain Papers, The Bancroft Library, University of California at Berkeley.

being master or obey anybody; he could go fishing or swimming when and where he chose, and stay as long as it suited him; nobody forbade him to fight; he could sit up as late as he pleased; he was always the first boy that went barefoot in the spring and the last to resume leather in the fall; he never had to wash, nor put on clean clothes; he could swear wonderfully. In a word, everything that goes to make life precious, that boy had. So thought every harassed, hampered, respectable boy in St. Petersburg."

Huck Finn, the abandoned son of the town drunkard, "the juvenile pariah of the village," was considerably lower in class than Tom Sawyer; Tom is switched by the schoolmaster for just stopping to talk to Huckleberry Finn. As another character admits in Chapter 29, "Huckleberry Finn! It ain't a name to open many doors, I judge!" Of course, his status changes when the boy is adopted by the Widow Douglas.

"Huck Finn is drawn from life," Twain wrote in his preface to *Tom Sawyer*, and the model for the character was Clemens's boyhood friend Tom Blankenship (who was five years older than Clemens). He described the boy's family in his notes on Hannibal (published in *Mark Twain's Hannibal, Huck and Tom*, edited by Walter Blair, 1969, p. 31): "The parents paupers and drunkards, the girls charged with prostitution—not proven. Tom, a kindly young heathen. . . . These children were never sent to school or church. Played out and disappeared." In Chapter 14 of *The Autobiography of Mark Twain* (edited by Charles Neider, 1959), Twain further described his old friend as "ignorant, unwashed, insufficiently fed; but he had a good heart as ever any boy had. . . . He was the only really independent person—man or boy—in the community, and by consequence he was tranquilly and continuously happy and was envied by the rest of us. . . . And as his society was forbidden us by our parents the prohibition trebled and quadrupled its value, and therefore we sought and got more of his society than of any other boy's." So well executed was the portrait of his old Hannibal companion that when his sister had read a few pages of the novel to their mother, Mrs. Clemens exclaimed, "Why, that's Tom Blankenship!" (Samuel Charles Webster, *Mark Twain, Business Man*, 1946, p. 265). What happened to Tom Blankenship is not known. Twain said in his *Autobiography* that he had heard that Tom "was justice of the peace in a remote village in Montana and was a good citizen and greatly respected"; however, another of Tom's boyhood companions told Clifton Johnson (*Highways and Byways of the Mississippi Valley*, 1906, p. 162) that when Tom left town it was to go to the penitentiary. Maybe Twain was only hoping that Tom Blankenship was a bad little boy who prospered. In his scenario for "Tom Sawyer: A Drama," deposited for copyright July 21, 1875 (and reprinted in *Mark Twain's Hannibal, Huck and Tom*, 1969, p. 245), Twain slyly noted, "Fifty Years Later—General Sawyer, Bishop Finn."

E. W. Kemble based his characterization on a New York City boy named Cort Morris. The two had met around 1878, at the New York Athletic Club Boathouse, where the boy ran errands for and fished with the artist. "Being a nimrod and fisherman just like Huck, landed me the job which lasted from May 1st to October 1st, 1884," Morris recalled in "The Model for Huck Finn" (*Mark Twain Quarterly*, Summer-Fall, 1938, p. 23). "And was I gloriously interested in being Huckleberry Finn? No, but in the $4.00 a week. Yes, tremendously. . . . Huckleberry Finn was not known at that time. He was not established, nobody knew him or ever heard of him." "He was always grinning," the artist wrote of his model in "Illustrating Huckleberry Finn" (*The Colophon*, February 1930), "and one side of his cheek was usually well padded with a 'sour ball' or a huge wad of molasses taffy. Throwing his wool cap and muslin-covered schoolbooks on a lounge, he would ask what was wanted at this session. I would designate the character." At first Twain was disappointed with Kemble's interpretation (he thought Huck Finn looked too "Irishy"); but he eventually came to admire his illustrator's contribution to the novel.

2 *"The Adventures of Tom Sawyer."* Many of the introductory incidents in this sequel are reworkings of material in the earlier novel. Even before completing *Tom Sawyer*, Twain (as he confided to William Dean Howells) already was planning to describe in detail Huck's life at the Widow Douglas's.

3 *Mary.* Tom Sawyer's cousin, the only member of his family who is fully sympathetic toward the boy; she appears briefly in Chapter 8 of *Huckleberry Finn.*

4 *the Widow Douglas.* Huckleberry Finn's foster mother, described in *Tom Sawyer* as a "fair, smart,

Mary and the Widow Douglas. Illustrations by True W. Williams, *The Adventures of Tom Sawyer*, **1876.**

and forty, generous, good-hearted soul and well-to-do." Because she was once kind to him, the boy warns her of Injun Joe's threat to "slit her nostrils . . . notch her ears like a sow" as payment back to her dead husband, a justice of the peace, who once had the thief publicly horsewhipped. In gratitude for his heroism, she opened her heart and home to the outcast Huck. However, she is less affectionately portrayed in *Huckleberry Finn* than in the earlier work. The Widow Douglas was based on Mrs. Richard Holliday of Hannibal: "Lived on Holiday's Hill. Well off. Fond of having parties of young people. Widow. Old, but anxious to marry" (*Mark Twain's Hannibal, Huck and Tom*, pp. 30–31).

5 *my sugar-hogshead.* A large barrel, used to contain a ship's cargo of sugar. In *Tom Sawyer*, Huck lives "among some old empty hogsheads behind the abandoned slaughterhouse."

6 *and feel all cramped up.* In his copy of the edition printed by B. Tauchnitz of Leipzig in 1893 which he used for his public readings (now in the Mark Twain Papers, University of California at Berkeley), Twain expanded on this image by adding a particularly sharp simile: "They make you feel all cramped up and uncomfortable, like a bee that's busted through a spider's web and wisht he'd gone *around*" (MTP).

7 *Moses and the "Bulrushers."* Clearly the widow wishes Huck to identify her with the Pharaoh's daughter who befriended the baby Moses. This casual reference to Exodus 2: 3–10 establishes a central theme of the novel: Like Moses who freed the Israelites from bondage, so too does Huckleberry Finn aid a Southern slave in his flight from his master. Both outlawed boys escape by a river: Moses in an ark of bulrushes along the Nile, Huck by a raft down the Mississippi. And both are wards of women of the upper class, the slave-owning class: Moses by the Pharaoh's daughter, and Huck by the Widow Douglas. Ironically, although he led his people to freedom, Moses provided for slavery among the Israelites in Exodus 21; and it was this holy ordinance which was so often referred to by the Southern slave owners of Huck's time as proof that God sanctioned their system of servitude.

In "Annie and Huck: A Note on *The Adventures of Huckleberry Finn*" (*American Literature*, May 1967, pp. 207–214), Horst H. Kruse suggested that Twain was likely recalling the religious instruction he received from his nine-year-old niece Annie. "She used to try to teach me lessons from the Bible," Clemens wrote his mother on April 2, 1862, "but I never could understand them. Doesn't she remember telling me the story of Moses, one Sunday, last Spring, and how hard she tried to explain it and simplify it so that I could understand it—but I *couldn't*? And how she said it was strange that while her ma and her grandma and her uncle Orion could understand anything in the world, I was so dull I couldn't understand the 'ea-siest thing'?"

she took me for her son, and allowed she would sivilize me; but it was rough living in the house all the time, considering how dismal regular and decent the widow was in all her ways; and so when I couldn't stand it no longer, I lit out. I got **5** into my old rags and my sugar-hogshead again, and was free and satisfied. But Tom Sawyer he hunted me up and said he was going to start a band of robbers, and I might join if I would go back to the widow and be respectable. So I went back.

The widow she cried over me, and called me a poor lost lamb, and she called me a lot of other names, too, but she never meant no harm by it. She put me in them new clothes again, **6** and I couldn't do nothing but sweat and sweat, and feel all cramped up. Well, then, the old thing commenced again. The widow rung a bell for supper, and you had to come to time. When you got to the table you couldn't go right to eating, but you had to wait for the widow to tuck down her head and grumble a little over the victuals, though there warn't really anything the matter with them. That is, nothing only everything was cooked by itself. In a barrel of odds and ends it is different; things get mixed up, and the juice kind of swaps around, and the things go better.

After supper she got out her book and learned me about **7** Moses and the "Bulrushers;" and I was in a sweat to find out

LEARNING ABOUT MOSES AND THE "BULRUSHERS."

all about him; but by-and-by she let it out that Moses had been dead a considerable long time; so then I didn't care no more about him; because I don't take no stock in dead people.

Pretty soon I wanted to smoke, and asked the widow to let me. But she wouldn't. She said it was a mean practice and wasn't clean, and I must try to not do it any more. That is just the way with some people. They get down on a thing when they don't know nothing about it. Here she was a bothering about Moses, which was no kin to her, and no use to anybody, being gone, you see, yet finding a power of fault with me for doing a thing that had some good in it. And she took **8** snuff too; of course that was all right, because she done it herself.

Frontispiece from *Life and Sayings of Mrs. Partington* by B. P. Shillaber, 1854.

Miss Watson

Her sister, Miss Watson, a tolerable slim old maid, with **9** goggles on, had just come to live with her, and took a set at **10** me now, with a spelling book. She worked me middling hard **11** for about an hour, and then the widow made her ease up. I couldn't stood it much longer. Then for an hour it was deadly dull, and I was fidgety. Miss Watson would say, "Don't put your feet up there, Huckleberry;" and "don't scrunch up like that, Huckleberry—set up straight;" and pretty soon she would say, "Don't gap and stretch like that, Huckleberry— **12** why don't you try to behave?" Then she told me all about the bad place, and I said I wished I was there. She got mad, **13** then, but I didn't mean no harm. All I wanted was to go somewheres; all I wanted was a change, I warn't particular. She said it was wicked to say what I said; said she wouldn't say it for the whole world; *she* was going to live so as to go to the good place. Well, I couldn't see no advantage in going where she was going, so I made up my mind I wouldn't try for it. But I never said so, because it would only make trouble, and wouldn't do no good.

Now she had got a start, and she went on and told me all

8 *And she took snuff too.* In this part of the country, it was proper for women and girls of all classes and ages to take snuff; men and boys generally smoked or chewed their tobacco. "Some people take it in snuff," Benjamin Penhallow Shillaber explained in "Tobacco" in *Knitting-Work* (1859, p. 380), "by holding the snuff between the thumb and finger, and drawing it up into the nose. This is an exciting operation with elderly females, and it is interesting to watch its effects when the nose is fully charged and primed, before it sneezes off." In the Widow Douglas's chastisement of Huck for smoking, Twain was likely recalling another episode by Shillaber, "Mrs. Partington on Tobacco," in *Life and Sayings of Mrs. Partington* (1854, p. 285), in which the old woman, after dipping into her snuff box, decries "the body and soul destroying nature of the weed" and then stops "a moment to lecture Ike who was enjoying a sugar cigar upon the front door-step." Twain and Shillaber were friends; Shillaber's Boston paper *The Carpet-Bag* was the first journal outside of Hannibal to publish Clemens's work. Also, Shillaber's Mrs. Partington and Ike, her foster son, were sources for Twain's Aunt Polly and Tom Sawyer. See Walter Blair, *Mark Twain and Huck Finn*, 1960, pp. 62–63.

9 *Miss Watson.* The model for this spinster was Mary Ann Newcomb, a teacher in Hannibal who had her meals with the Clemenses; Sam described her later as "a Calvinist, devoutly pious," and "You could not tell her breast from her back if she had her head up a stovepipe hole" (quoted by Blair, *Mark Twain and Huck Finn*, p. 106).

10 *took a set.* Took a turn.

11 *a spelling book.* In *Tom Sawyer*, Huck does not attend school with the other boys. He is so illiterate, that in Chapter 10 when they sign their oath to "keep mum" about the murder of Dr. Robinson, Tom must show Huck "how to make an H and F."

12 *gap and stretch.* Yawn and stretch.

13 *the bad place.* Miss Watson is so pious that she cannot say the word Hell—nor can she say Heaven (the "good place").

14 *She said all a body would have to do there was to go around all day long with a harp and sing for ever and ever.* Miss Watson describes the popular Protestant view of Paradise. Huck's resistance to this vision of Eternity was shared by Old Taggart in *History of the Big Bonanza* (1876, pp. 368–369), by "Dan De Quille," Twain's friend William Wright. On his deathbed, Old Taggart confesses to the Deacon Dudley that he would not feel at home in Heaven. "I'm surprised, my good friend," replies the deacon, "to hear that you don't want to be one of that heavenly band that sit before the throne, playing on golden harps, and singing praises forever and forever!" "Me play on a harp, Deacon?" says Old Taggart, smiling. "It's all nonsense to talk about me playin' a harp. I tell you plainly, Deacon, that I don't want to go among the musicians up there. It wouldn't suit me!"

Twain no more looked forward to such an afterlife than did Huck or Old Taggart. "The Presbyterian hell is all misery," he complained in "Reflections on the Sabbath" (*The Golden Era*, March 18, 1866); "the heaven all happiness—nothing to do." In "Letters from the Earth," 1909 (in *What Is Man?*, edited by Paul Baender, 1973, p. 409), Twain attacked what he thought were the stupidities in Miss Watson's fundamentalist vision of Paradise: "In man's heaven *everybody sings!* . . . the man who did not sing on earth, . . . is able to do it there. This universal singing is not casual, not occasional, not relieved by intervals of quiet, it goes on, all day long, and every day, during a stretch of twelve hours. . . . The singing is of hymns alone. Nay, it is of *one* hymn alone. The words are always the same, in number they are only about a dozen, there is no rhyme, there is no poetry; 'Hosannah, hosannah, hosannah, Lord God of Sabaoth, 'rah! 'rah! 'rah!—ssht!—boom! . . . a-a-ah!'

"Meantime, *every person* is playing on a harp—those millions and millions! whereas not more than twenty in the thousand of them could play an instrument in the earth, or ever *wanted* to."

The most elaborate of Twain's burlesques of the "pearly gate" concept of the afterlife was *Extract from Captain Stormfield's Visit to Heaven* (1909); but by the time this book was published, few Protestants still held Miss Watson's simplistic vision of the "World to Come."

15 *the niggers.* The slaves. When Missouri (originally part of the Louisiana Purchase) was admitted to the Union in 1820, by the infamous Missouri Compromise, slavery was preserved there but forever prohibited in territory north of lat. 36° 30' N. "In my schoolboy days," Twain confessed in Chapter 2 of his *Autobiography*, "I had no aversion to slavery. I was not aware that there was anything wrong about it. No one arraigned it in my hearing; the local papers said nothing against it; the local pulpit taught us that God approved it . . . ; if the slaves themselves had an aversion to slavery they were wise and said nothing. In Hannibal we seldom saw a slave misused."

Twain also had no aversion to using the word "nigger," then the universal Southern term for a slave. As Arthur G. Pettit has argued in "Mark Twain and the Negro, 1867–1869" (*The Journal of Negro History*, April 1971, pp. 88–96), Clemens only gradually learned to use other expressions such as "colored" or "Negro." However, Huckleberry Finn

14 about the good place. She said all a body would have to do there was to go around all day long with a harp and sing for ever and ever. So I didn't think much of it. But I never said so. I asked her if she reckoned Tom Sawyer would go there, and she said, not by a considerable sight. I was glad about that, because I wanted him and me to be together.

Miss Watson she kept pecking at me, and it got tiresome **15** and lonesome. By-and-by they fetched the niggers in and **16** had prayers, and then everybody was off to bed. I went up to my room with a piece of candle and put it on the table. Then I set down in a chair by the window and tried to think of some- **17** thing cheerful, but it warn't no use. I felt so lonesome I most wished I was dead. The stars was shining, and the leaves **18** rustled in the woods ever so mournful; and I heard an owl, **19** away off, who-whooing about somebody that was dead, and a **20** whippowill and a dog crying about somebody that was going to die; and the wind was trying to whisper something to me and I couldn't make out what it was, and so it made the cold shivers run over me. Then away out in the woods I heard that kind of a sound that a ghost makes when it wants to tell about something that's on its mind and can't make itself understood, and so can't rest easy in its grave and has to go about that way every night grieving. I got so downhearted and scared, I did **21** wish I had some company. Pretty soon a spider went crawling up my shoulder, and I flipped it off and it lit in the candle; and before I could budge it was all shriveled up. I didn't need anybody to tell me that that was an awful bad sign and would fetch me some bad luck, so I was scared and most shook the **22** clothes off of me. I got up and turned around in my tracks

HUCK STEALING AWAY.

would have used the word common to his time and to his class. When *Tom Sawyer Abroad* was serialized in *St. Nicholas* (November 1893 through April 1894), Mary Mapes Dodge, the magazine's editor, in trying to soften any improprieties, replaced "nigger" with "darky," but this alteration hardly solved the problem. *Huckleberry Finn* remains banned in parts of the country solely for the narrator's use of "nigger."

16 *prayers*. Many god-fearing slave-owners believed their servants' religious instruction to be their responsibility. The more pious among them might have both morning and evening prayers, but generally their slaves were allowed to attend only the latter services, after their day's work was done.

17 *I felt so lonesome I most wished I was dead.* The same sentiments are expressed by Tom Sawyer in Chapter 9 of *Tom Sawyer*, just before he and Huck run off to the graveyard; also, each boy recognizes many of the same "signs" of the night. In the opening of "Tom Sawyer, Detective" (1896), Huck defined these feelings as "spring fever": which "sets him to sighing and saddening around, and there's something the matter with him, he don't know what. But anyway, he gets out by himself and mopes and thinks; and mostly he hunts for a lonesome place high up on the hill in the edge of the woods and sets there and looks away off on the big Mississippi down there a-reaching miles and miles around the points where the timber looks smoky and dim it's so far off and still, and everything's so solemn it seems like everybody you've loved is dead and gone and you most wish you was dead and gone too, and done with it all."

These sentiments are the first indication of the boy's great preoccupation with death. Perhaps an important reason for Huck's excessive morbidity was the high infant mortality rate of the Mississippi Valley at this time. "One quarter of the children born," Dixon Wecter in *Sam Clemens of Hannibal* (1952, p. 80) quoted the Hannibal *Gazette* of June 3, 1847, "die before they are one year old; one half die before they are twenty-one, and not one quarter reach the age of forty." Few families were free of the death of children; a brother of Sam Clemens, Pleasants Hannibal Clemens, died at three months, another brother Benjamin at ten years, and a sister Margaret at nine years.

18 *an owl . . . who-whooing about somebody that was dead.* Being a bird of the night with a mournful hoot, the owl since antiquity is said to have the power to predict the death of a loved one. Pliny called it "the funeral bird of the night," Edmund Spenser in *The Faerie Queene* called it "death's dreadful messenger." "A screech owl flapping its wings against the windows of a sick person's chamber, or screeching at them," explained Frances Grose in *A Provincial Glossary* (1787), "portends the same." "My First Call in the Swamp," a sketch in *Odd Leaves from the Life of a Louisiana "Swamp Doctor"* (1846, p. 154) by "Madison Tensas" (Henry Clay Lewis), plays with the folk belief, "The screech-owl has hollered, and she is boun' to die—it's a sure sign, and can't fail!" And Uncle Remus tells the little boy in Joel Chandler Harris's *Uncle Remus, His Songs and Sayings* (1880, p. 133), "Squinch-owl holler ev'ry time he see a witch." In his preface to *Tom Sawyer*, Twain explained,

"The odd superstitions touched upon were all prevalent among children and slaves in the West at the period of this story." In Chapter 9 of that novel, Tom and Huck confirmed this statement by acknowledging that they learned one of their "signs" from the slaves, "and they know all about these kinds of things." However, most of these superstitions were learned from their white masters; as Daniel G. Hoffman has argued in "Black Magic—and White—in *Huckleberry Finn*" (*Form and Fable in American Literature*, 1961, pp. 317–342), the majority of these "signs" are of European, and not of African, origin.

19 *a whippowill.* Or "whip-poor-will," the popular name in the United States and Canada for a species of goat-sucker, which has a low, plaintive call. In Chapter 10 of *Tom Sawyer*, Twain played with a common superstition of this bird: Huck tells Tom that, two weeks earlier, at a friend's house, "a whippowill come in and lit on the bannisters and sung," but "there ain't anybody dead there yet."

20 *a dog crying about somebody that was going to die.* An ancient superstition in Europe and parts of the Near East that, according to Grose in *A Provincial Glossary*, dogs "have the faculty of seeing spirits . . . they usually shew signs of terror by whining and creeping to their masters for protection"; and the howling of a dog is a certain sign that some member of the family is going to die. The death of Maximus is said to have been predicted by the baying of dogs; in Book XV of *The Odyssey*, the dogs of Eumaeus are terrified by the presence of Minerva. As a boy in the Ohio River valley, William Dean Howells, as he recounts in *A Boy's Town* (1890), was familiar with this omen: "He shuddered when he heard a dog howling in the night, for that was a sign that somebody was going to die"; and in discussing witches in his book of songs and sayings (p. 133), Uncle Remus warned that "w'en you hear de dog howlin' in de middle er de night, one un um's mighty ap' ter be prowlin' 'roun'." Likewise in Chapter 10 of *Tom Sawyer*, Huck mentions that "they say a stray dog come howling around Johnny Miller's house, 'bout midnight, as much as two weeks ago," but "there ain't anybody dead there yet." Although these superstitions had proven to be ineffectual in the earlier novel, Huck here is not so ready to deny his pagan beliefs as he does Miss Watson's Sunday-school teachings.

21 *a spider.* A spider seen in the evening is said to signify peace, but to kill it is thought to be a bad omen. A common English nursery rhyme is:

> *If you wish to live and thrive*
> *Let the spider walk alive.*

22 *I . . . turned around in my tracks three times and crossed my breast every time.* Nearly every culture has a ritual that must be performed in threes to ward off evil spirits; crossing one's breast is equivalent to making the sign of the cross, the symbol of Christ, and doing it three times invokes the protection of the Holy Trinity.

23 *I tied up a little lock of my hair with a thread to keep witches away.* "Niggers tie wool up with thread," Twain wrote in his *Notebooks and Journals* (Vol. I, 1975, p. 160), "to keep witches from riding them." Clemens learned this custom from "Aunt" Hannah, a slave owned by his uncle. "Whenever witches were around," he recalled in Chapter 2 of his *Autobiography*, "she tied up the remnant of her wool in little tufts, with white thread, and this promptly made the witches impotent." Similarly, Nat, Jim's "nigger," in Chapter 34 of *Huckleberry Finn* wears his hair "all tied up in little bunches with thread. That was to keep witches off." And like so many of these superstitions mentioned by Huck, this one is of European origin. See also Chapter 2, note 4.

24 *lost a horse-shoe that you've found, instead of nailing it up over the door.* It is good luck to find a horse-shoe, bad luck to lose it. In Chapter 3 of *Pudd'nhead Wilson* (1894), Roxy, the slave, totes "along a hoss-shoe to keep off de witch-work." It is said that when a witch spies a horseshoe nailed over a door, she must ride every road that the horseshoe has traveled, and by that time, it will be morning, when her evil powers cease. Although it dates from antiquity, the superstition in England is credited to St. Dunstan, the patron saint of goldsmiths: He drove the Devil off with hot pincers, and ever since then, evil spirits avoid any place in Britain where a horseshoe is hung.

25 *I heard a twig snap.* One of the devices most frequently mentioned in James Fenimore Cooper's romantic Indian tales, and most despised by Mark Twain, was the introduction of a character by the sound of a twig's snapping. Twain complained in "Fenimore Cooper's Literary Offenses" (*North American Review*, July 1895, pp. 1–12) that his predecessor "prized his dry twig above all the rest of his effects, and worked it the hardest. It is a restful chapter in any book of his when somebody doesn't step on a broken twig and alarm all the reds and the whites for two hundred yards around. . . . In fact, the Leatherstocking Series ought to have been called the Broken Twig Series." Then why did Twain himself use it here? Roger B. Bailey in *The Explicator* (No. 2, September 1967) has argued that this device is a particularly apt way of introducing Tom Sawyer, a descendant of Cooper's romantic heroes, into *Huckleberry Finn*. It is a good contrast to Huck's tripping over a root in the next chapter, what Twain obviously considered one of "a hundred handier things to step on" than a broken twig. Therefore, early in the novel Twain had already implied the distinction between romantic Tom Sawyer and pragmatic Huckleberry Finn.

26 *I could just barely hear a "me-yow! me-yow!" down there. . . . and sure enough there was Tom Sawyer waiting for me.* This is the same signal Huck used to call Tom to his window, in Chapter 9 of *Tom Sawyer*. The roles of the character have been reversed: In the first novel Huck inaugurates the adventures, in the second Tom is the instigator.

23 three times and crossed my breast every time ; and then I tied up a little lock of my hair with a thread to keep witches away.

24 But I hadn't no confidence. You do that when you've lost a horse-shoe that you've found, instead of nailing it up over the door, but I hadn't ever heard anybody say it was any way to keep off bad luck when you'd killed a spider.

I set down again, a-shaking all over, and got out my pipe for a smoke ; for the house was all as still as death, now, and so the widow wouldn't know. Well, after a long time I heard the clock away off in the town go boom—boom—boom—twelve

25 licks—and all still again—stiller than ever. Pretty soon I heard a twig snap, down in the dark amongst the trees—some-

26 thing was a-stirring. I set still and listened. Directly I could just barely hear a " *me-yow ! me-yow !* " down there. That was good ! Says I, " *me-yow ! me-yow !* " as soft as I could, and then I put out the light and scrambled out of the window on to the shed. Then I slipped down to the ground and crawled in amongst the trees, and sure enough there was Tom Sawyer waiting for me.

Chapter II.

THEY TIP-TOED ALONG.

WE went tip-toeing along a path amongst the trees back towards the end of the widow's garden, stooping down so as the branches wouldn't scrape our heads. When we was passing by the kitchen I fell over a root and made a noise. We scrouched down and laid still. Miss Watson's big nigger, named Jim, was setting in the kitchen door; we could see him pretty clear, because there was a light behind him. He got up and stretched his neck out about a minute, listening. Then he says:

"Who dah?"

He listened some more; then he come tip-toeing down and stood right between us; we could a touched him, nearly. Well, likely it was minutes and minutes that there warn't a sound, and we all there so close together. There was a place on my ankle that

1 *Miss Watson's . . . Jim.* In Chapter 9 of *Pudd'nhead Wilson*, Roxy informs her son that he, a Southern slave, "ain't *got* no fambly name, beca'se niggers don't *have* 'em!" In a note to Chapter 10 of *Tom Sawyer*, Twain discussed an oddity of this custom: Miss Watson's slave named Jim is spoken of as "Miss Watson's Jim," but a son or a dog of that name would be "Jim Watson." (Ironically, emancipated slaves often took the surname of their former masters as their "family" name.) But royalty are no better than slaves: In talking about "that old humpbacked" Richard III in Chapter 25 of *Tom Sawyer*, Tom tells Huck, "Kings don't have any but a given name." "Well, if they like it, Tom, all right," Huck replies; "but I don't want to be a king and have only just a given name, like a nigger."

Twain admitted in Chapter 2 of his *Autobiography* that Miss Watson's Jim was in part based on Uncle Dan'l, "a faithful and affectionate good friend, ally and advisor . . . , a middle-aged slave whose head was the best one in the Negro quarter, whose sympathies were wide and warm and whose heart was honest and simple and knew no guile. . . . I have not seen him for more than half a century and yet spiritually I have had his welcome company a good part of that time and have staged him in books under his own name and as 'Jim,' and I carted him all around—to Hannibal, down the Mississippi on a raft and even across the Desert of Sahara in a balloon—and he has endured it all with the patience and friendliness and loyalty which were his birthright. It was on the farm [of Clemens's Uncle John A. Quarles; see Chapter 32, note 2] that I got my strong liking for his race and my appreciation of certain of its fine qualities. . . . The black face is as welcome to me now as it was then." Uncle Dan'l also appears briefly in *The Gilded Age* (1874), as the forty-year-old

63

John Lewis and Mark Twain, 1903.
Courtesy the Library of Congress.

JIM!

slave of Squire Hawkins. Certain qualities of Jim's character have been traced also to Uncle Ned, the old slave owned by the Clemenses of Hannibal; John Lewis, the handyman on the Quarry Farm in Elmira, New York, where Clemens's family spent their summers; and George Griffin, Clemens's butler in Hartford, Connecticut, described by his master as "handsome, . . . well-built, shrewd, wise, polite, always good-natured, cheerful to gaiety, honest, religious, a cautious truth-speaker, devoted friend to the family, champion of its interests." See Arthur G. Pettit's *Mark Twain and the South*, 1974, pp. 95–106.

Miss Watson's Jim is not to be confused with another Jim, "the small colored boy" who cuts wood and totes water for Aunt Polly in *Tom Sawyer*. This character was based on Sandy, a young slave whom the Clemenses had hired from a man in Hannibal during Sam's childhood. See *Autobiography*, Chapters 2 and 9.

2 *the quality*. "At the social summit stood the 'quality,'" Twain explained in his uncompleted "Indiantown," 1899 (published in *Which Was the Dream?*, 1967, p. 157). "The word was used by the commoner folk of the South and the Southwest, and was the equivalent of 'aristocracy.'"

3 *Tom . . . wanted to tie Jim to the tree for fun; but I said no*. Huck is less likely to play such a trick on a "nigger" than is Tom. It is not a part of Huck's character. In Chapter 28 of *Tom Sawyer*, Huck defines his ambiguous relationship with another slave, Ben Rogers's father's Uncle Jake: "I tote water for Uncle Jake whenever he wants me to, and any time I ask him he gives me a little something to eat if he can spare it. That's a mighty good nigger, Tom. He likes me, becuz I don't ever act as if I was above him. Sometimes, I've set right down and eat *with* him. But you needn't tell that. A body's got to do things when he's awful hungry he wouldn't want to do as a steady thing." These paradoxical feelings of affection and disdain toward Uncle Jack anticipate the boy's attitudes toward Miss Watson's Jim.

got to itching; but I dasn't scratch it; and then my ear begun to itch; and next my back, right between my shoulders. Seemed like I'd die if I couldn't scratch. Well, I've noticed **2** that thing plenty of times since. If you are with the quality, or at a funeral, or trying to go to sleep when you ain't sleepy— if you are anywheres where it won't do for you to scratch, why you will itch all over in upwards of a thousand places. Pretty soon Jim says:

"Say—who is you? Whar is you? Dog my cats ef I didn' hear sumf'n. Well, I knows what I's gwyne to do. I's gwyne to set down here and listen tell I hears it agin."

So he set down on the ground betwixt me and Tom. He leaned his back up against a tree, and stretched his legs out till one of them most touched one of mine. My nose begun to itch. It itched till the tears come into my eyes. But I dasn't scratch. Then it begun to itch on the inside. Next I got to itching underneath. I didn't know how I was going to set still. This miserableness went on as much as six or seven minutes; but it seemed a sight longer than that. I was itching in eleven different places now. I reckoned I couldn't stand it more'n a minute longer, but I set my teeth hard and got ready to try. Just then Jim begun to breathe heavy; next he begun to snore—and then I was pretty soon comfortable again.

Tom he made a sign to me—kind of a little noise with his mouth—and we went creeping away on our hands and knees. **3** When we was ten foot off, Tom whispered to me and wanted to tie Jim to the tree for fun; but I said no; he might wake and make a disturbance, and then they'd find out I warn't in. Then Tom said he hadn't got candles enough, and he would slip in the kitchen and get some more. I didn't want him to try. I said Jim might wake up and come. But Tom wanted to resk it; so we slid in there and got three candles, and Tom laid five cents on the table for pay. Then we got out, and I was in a sweat to get away; but nothing would do Tom but he must crawl to where Jim was, on his hands and knees, and play something on him. I waited, and it seemed a good while, everything was so still and lonesome.

As soon as Tom was back, we cut along the path, around the garden fence, and by-and-by fetched up on the steep top of the hill the other side of the house. Tom said he slipped Jim's hat off of his head and hung it on a limb right over him, and Jim stirred a little, but he didn't wake. Afterwards Jim **4** said the witches bewitched him and put him in a trance, and rode him all over the State, and then set him under the trees again and hung his hat on a limb to show who done it. And next time Jim told it he said they rode him down to New **5** Orleans; and after that, every time he told it he spread it more and more, till by-and-by he said they rode him all over the world, and tired him most to death, and his back was all over saddle-boils. Jim was monstrous proud about it, and he got so he wouldn't hardly notice the other niggers. Niggers would come miles to hear Jim tell about it, and he was more looked up to than any nigger in that country. Strange niggers would stand with their mouths open and look him all over, same as if he was a wonder. Niggers is always talking about **6** witches in the dark by the kitchen fire; but whenever one was talking and letting on to know all about such things, Jim would happen in and say, "Hm! What you know 'bout witches?" and that nigger was corked up and had to take a back seat. Jim always kept that five-center piece around his **7** neck with a string, and said it was a charm the devil give to **8** him with his own hands and told him he could cure anybody with it and fetch witches whenever he wanted to, just by saying something to it; but he never told what it was he said to it. Niggers would come from all around there and give Jim anything they had, just for a sight of that five-center piece; but they wouldn't touch it, because the devil had had his hands on it. Jim was most ruined, for a servant, because he got so stuck up on account of having seen the devil and been rode by witches.

Well, when Tom and me got to the edge of the hill-top, we looked away down into the village and could see three or four **9** lights twinkling, where there was sick folks, maybe; and the stars over us was sparkling ever so fine; and down by the village was the river, a whole mile broad, and awful still and grand. We went down the hill and found Jo Harper, and Ben Rogers, and two or three more of the boys, hid in the old tan-yard. So we unhitched a skiff and pulled down the river two **10** mile and a half, to the big scar on the hillside, and went ashore. **11**

4 *Jim said the witches . . . rode him all over the State.* A common superstition among Southern slaves, apparently of European origin. Proofs that one had been ridden by witches were feeling "down and out" the next morning; sores on the sides of the mouth (supposedly the result of witches' bridling); and "witch's stirrups," tangles in the hair. Being ridden by witches was also thought to be a common cause of nightmares.

5 *next time Jim . . . said they rode him down to New Orleans.* In Missouri, slaves were generally house servants or worked the fields side by side with their masters, and thus they were relatively well treated by their owners; but in the Deep South, many toiled on the plantations as field hands under the supervision of cruel overseers. Many tales of how plantation slaves were beaten, overworked, chained, disfigured, and sometimes killed, traveled up the river, and nothing was more feared by those in the border states than to be sold South. So Jim's statement that witches rode him down to New Orleans, the point farthest south in the slave states, is equivalent to his saying that he was taken to Hell. See Chapter 8, note 21.

6 *Niggers is always talking about witches in the dark by the kitchen fire.* It was in Uncle Dan'l's kitchen that young Sam Clemens first heard similar tales, "the white and black children grouped on the hearth, with the firelight playing on their faces and the shadows flickering upon the walls, clear back toward the cavernous gloom of the rear, and I can hear Uncle Dan'l telling the immortal tales which Uncle Remus Harris was to gather into his books and charm the world with, by and by; and I can feel again the creepy joy which quivered through me when the time for the ghost story of the 'Golden Arm' [retold in "How to Tell a Story," *The Youth's Companion*, October 3, 1895] was reached—and the sense of regret, too, which came over me, for it was always the last story of the evening" (*Autobiography*, Chapter 4).

7 *five-center piece.* There were no nickels at this time; they were not minted until after the Civil War.

8 *it was a charm the devil give to him with his own hands.* Coins (usually silver) were worn by Southern slaves as protection against hoodoo, or evil magic. In Chapter 35 of *Uncle Tom's Cabin* (1852), Harriet Beecher Stowe described a similar witch's talisman— silver dollars worn by slaves around the neck with black string which "keeps 'em from feelin' when they's flogged." Obviously the potency of Jim's charm derives from its having been touched by the Devil.

9 *the village.* Hannibal, Missouri, the little riverside town where Samuel Clemens lived from his third to his seventeenth year; and renamed by Twain in *Tom Sawyer* "St. Petersburg"—literally "Heaven." Certainly this name was appropriate for the locale of that novel, what he called his "hymn to boyhood." Also, he may have had in mind his slightly scandalous reference to the town in his burlesque verse "To Miss Katie of H——l [or 'Hell']," that he published in his

Hannibal, Missouri. Illustration by Henry Lewis, *Das illustrirte Mississippithal*, 1857. *Courtesy the Rare Book Room, the Library of Congress.*

brother's paper, the Hannibal *Journal* (May 6, 1853). Many early American settlements had religious names, particularly that of the Devil. "This personage," Twain commented in a suppressed passage from *Life on the Mississippi* (published in the 1944 Limited Editions Club edition, p. 390), "gets a shade too much of this sort of compliment—not along the Mississippi alone, but all over the country." Similarly, Charles Dickens sarcastically named the dismal little town along the Mississippi visited by his hero in *Martin Chuzzlewit* (1844) "Eden." See Chapter 15, note 1.

10 *a skiff.* A flat-bottomed open boat.

11 *the big scar on the hillside.* A large, bare place on the side of a hill.

12 *Tom Sawyer's Gang.* The immediate inspiration for this band of robbers was, as explained in Chapter 33 of *Tom Sawyer*, Injun Joe and his cohorts. However, the breadth of Tom's ambitions for his gang are comparable with those of John A. Murrell, the notorious land pirate of the Mississippi Valley. He is mentioned in passing in Chapter 26 of *Tom Sawyer* and in the working notes for *Huckleberry Finn*, and Twain described "Murrell's Gang" in detail in Chapter 29 of *Life on the Mississippi* as "a colossal combination of robbers, horsethieves, Negro-stealers, and counterfeiters engaged in business along the river some fifty or sixty years ago."

13 *hacked a cross in their breasts.* Obviously Tom has been reading Robert Montgomery Bird's *Nick of the Woods* (1837) in which an evil spirit called "Jabbenainosay" (the Spirit-that-walks) by the Indians and "Nick of the Woods" by the white settlers leaves its victims with "a knife cut, or a brace of 'um, over the ribs in the shape of a cross."

14 *a cross . . . which was the sign of the band.* This too has been borrowed from Injun Joe: In Chapter 33 of *Tom Sawyer*, Tom and Huck find the robber's gold buried beneath a cross carved into the wall of the cave. See Chapter 4, note 3.

We went to a clump of bushes, and Tom made everybody swear to keep the secret, and then showed them a hole in the hill, right in the thickest part of the bushes. Then we lit the candles and crawled in on our hands and knees. We went about two hundred yards, and then the cave opened up. Tom poked about amongst the passages and pretty soon ducked under a wall where you wouldn't a noticed that there was a hole. We went along a narrow place and got into a kind of room, all damp and sweaty and cold, and there we stopped. Tom says:

TOM SAWYER'S BAND OF ROBBERS.

12 "Now we'll start this band of robbers and call it Tom Sawyer's Gang. Everybody that wants to join has got to take an oath, and write his name in blood."

Everybody was willing. So Tom got out a sheet of paper that he had wrote the oath on, and read it. It swore every boy to stick to the band, and never tell any of the secrets; and if anybody done anything to any boy in the band, whichever boy was ordered to kill that person and his family must do it, and he mustn't eat and he mustn't sleep till he had killed them

13,14 and hacked a cross in their breasts, which was the sign of the

15 band. And nobody that didn't belong to the band could use that mark, and if he did he must be sued; and if he done it again he must be killed. And if anybody that belonged to the band told the secrets, he must have his throat cut, and then have his carcass burnt up and the ashes scattered all around, and his name blotted off of the list with blood and never mentioned again by the gang, but have a curse put on it and be forgot, for ever.

Everybody said it was a real beautiful oath, and asked Tom if he got it out of his own head. He said, some of it, but the

16 rest was out of pirate books, and robber books, and every gang

17 that was high-toned had it.

18 Some thought it would be good to kill the *families* of boys that told the secrets. Tom said it was a good idea, so he took a pencil and wrote it in. Then Ben Rogers says:

"Here's Huck Finn, he hain't got no family—what you **19** going to do 'bout him?"

"Well, hain't he got a father?" says Tom Sawyer.

"Yes, he's got a father, but you can't never find him, these days. He used to lay drunk with the hogs in the tanyard, but he hain't been seen in these parts for a year or more."

They talked it over, and they was going to rule me out, because they said every boy must have a family or somebody to kill, or else it wouldn't be fair and square for the others. Well, nobody could think of anything to do—everybody was stumped, and set still. I was most ready to cry; but all at once I thought of a way, and so I offered them Miss Watson— **20** they could kill her. Everybody said:

"Oh, she'll do, she'll do. That's all right. Huck can come in."

Then they all stuck a pin in their fingers to get blood to sign with, and I made my mark on the paper.

"Now," says Ben Rogers, "what's the line of business of **21** this Gang?"

"Nothing only robbery and murder," Tom said.

"But who are we going to rob? houses—or cattle—or——"

"Stuff! stealing cattle and such things ain't robbery, it's burglary," says Tom Sawyer. "We ain't burglars. That ain't no sort of style. We are highwaymen. We stop stages and carriages on the road, with masks on, and kill the people and take their watches and money."

"Must we always kill the people?"

"Oh, certainly. It's best. Some authorities think different, but mostly it's considered best to kill them. Except some that you bring to the cave here and keep them till they're ransomed."

"Ransomed? What's that?" **22**

"I don't know. But that's what they do. I've seen it in **23** books; and so of course that's what we've got to do."

"But how can we do it if we don't know what it is?"

"Why blame it all, we've *got* to do it. Don't I tell you it's **24** in the books? Do you want to go to doing different from what's in the books, and get things all muddled up?"

"Oh, that's all very fine to *say*, Tom Sawyer, but how in the nation are these fellows going to be ransomed if we don't **25** know how to do it to them? that's the thing *I* want to get at. Now what do you *reckon* it is?"

"Well, I don't know. But per'aps if we keep them till they're ransomed, it means that we keep them till they're dead."

"Now, that's something *like*. That'll answer. Why couldn't you said that before? We'll keep them till they're ransomed to death—and a bothersome lot they'll be, too, eating up everything and always trying to get loose."

"How you talk, Ben Rogers. How can they get loose when there's a guard over them, ready to shoot them down if they move a peg?"

15 *nobody that didn't belong to the band could use that mark, and if he did he must be sued.* Just like a trademark? Clemens had just recently registered "Mark Twain" as a trademark; and this little joke may have been intended as a warning to anyone who might try to "pirate" his work.

16 *pirate books, and robber books.* In addition to popular histories of Murrell's gang and Bird's *Nick of the Woods*, the most likely books Tom has been reading are the "dime novels" written by "Ned Buntline" (Edward Zane Carroll Judson). His *The Black Avenger; or, The Fiend of Blood* (1847) had given Tom his alias as the pirate chief in Chapter 8 of *Tom Sawyer.* Just the titles (such as *The Last Days of Callao; or, The Doomed City of Sin!* 1847; and *The King of the Sea; A Tale of the Fearless and Free,* 1847) of these pirate and robber books insured each to be "a story of thrilling scenes, daring deeds and stirring times," or "a tale of love, strife and chivalry." Judson continued to grind out these lurid adventure novels throughout the century, but he eventually turned from pirates and highway robbers to Western heroes; he was largely responsible for creating the legends of "Wild Bill" Hickok and "Buffalo Bill" Cody.

When Twain was writing *Huckleberry Finn,* there was a national movement against the distribution of "dime novels" to impressionable young readers. According to *The Innocent Eye* by Albert E. Stone, Jr. (1961), the most notorious juvenile delinquent of the age, Jesse Pomeroy, a fourteen-year-old newsboy accused of murdering three children and of torturing many others, admitted to being "inspired" by dime novels. Twain, of course, was in part burlesquing such fiction for children in his novel; and yet not every one recognized the humor. For example, the Springfield *Republican* found *Tom Sawyer* and *Huckleberry Finn* no better than sensationalistic dime novels. Consequently, Twain's books were banned from libraries across the country.

17 *high-toned.* Aristocratic, stylish.

18 *Some thought it would be good to kill the* families *of boys that told the secrets.* Such wisdom from the mouths of babes! Such vendettas were the common stuff of popular nineteenth-century fiction. As a boy in Hannibal, Sam Clemens was enthralled by a carpenter's tales of how "he had killed his victims in every quarter of the globe, and that these victims were always named Lynch" in revenge for the murder of his sweetheart by a "base hireling" named Archibald Lynch; the boy was crestfallen when he learned that this self-proclaimed murderer of thirty human beings was a fraud. See *Life on the Mississippi,* Chapter 55.

19 *Huck Finn . . . hain't got no family—what you going to do 'bout him?* Huckleberry Finn is an outcast even among his supposed peers; this statement can only reinforce his feeling of loneliness described in the previous chapter. However, Tom Blankenship, the real Huck Finn, was a leader of the Hannibal boys. See Dixon Wecter, *Sam Clemens of Hannibal,* 1952, p. 149.

20 *I offered them Miss Watson—they could kill her.* Not only is this comment a splendid joke, but it also sets up Miss Watson as an antagonist to Pap Finn.

21 *"Now . . . what's the line of business of this Gang?"* This exchange is largely a rephrasing of Tom's discussion with Huck about his proposed Gang in Chapter 33 of *Tom Sawyer*.

22 *"Ransomed? . . . I don't know."* Tom has a short memory: In Chapter 33 of *Tom Sawyer*, he told Huck that a ransom is "money. You make them raise all they can, off'n their friends; and after you've kept them a year, if it ain't raised then you kill them. That's the general way."

23 *I've seen it in books; and so of course that's what we've got to do.* Tom Sawyer is one of those trusting, naïve souls who believe that just because he has seen it in print, it must be true. Because he does not trust to either instinct or experience, he cannot distinguish fact from fiction. See also Chapter 3, note 17.

24 *blame.* Euphemism for "damn"—from "blasphemous."

25 *the nation.* Euphemism for "damnation."

26 *Kill the women? No—nobody ever saw anything in the books like that.* In the dime novels Tom has read, even the criminals followed a chivalrous code. "The heroes of these young people—even the pirates—were moved by lofty impulses," Twain recalled in discussing the character of the literature read in Hannibal during the 1840s; "they waded in blood, in the distant fields of war and adventure and upon the pirate deck, to rescue the helpless, not to make money; they spent their blood and made their self-sacrifice for 'honor's' sake, not to capture a giant fortune; they married for love, not for money and position. It was an intensely sentimental age, but it took no sordid form" (*Mark Twain's Hannibal, Huck and Tom*, p. 35).

27 *Little Tommy Barnes . . . cried, and said he wanted to go home to his ma, and didn't want to be a robber any more.* Tom's dreams of glory are undercut by this reminder that his band is only a group of children, and no real threat to society. After all, "boys will be boys." "A boy hardly knows what harm is," Howells explained in Chapter 18 of *A Boy's Town*, "and he does it mostly without realizing that it hurts. He cannot invent anything, he can only imitate; and it is easier to imitate evil than good." Then their play must be an accurate reflection of adult society; they can be only as good as their parents are.

In Chapter 31 of *A Connecticut Yankee in King Arthur's Court*, Twain described how far such a band of "innocent" children might go in imitating their elders: "A small mob of half-naked boys and girls came tearing out of the woods, scared and shrieking. The eldest among them were not more than twelve or fourteen years old. They implored help, but they were so beside themselves that we couldn't make out

"A guard. Well, that *is* good. So somebody's got to set up all night and never get any sleep, just so as to watch them. I think that's foolishness. Why can't a body take a club and ransom them as soon as they get here?"

"Because it ain't in the books so—that's why. Now Ben Rogers, do you want to do things regular, or don't you?—that's the idea. Don't you reckon that the people that made the books knows what's the correct thing to do? Do you reckon *you* can learn 'em anything? Not by a good deal. No, sir, we'll just go on and ransom them in the regular way."

"All right. I don't mind; but I say it's a fool way, anyhow. Say—do we kill the women, too?"

"Well, Ben Rogers, if I was as ignorant as you I wouldn't **26** let on. Kill the women? No—nobody ever saw anything in the books like that. You fetch them to the cave, and you're always as polite as pie to them; and by-and-by they fall in love with you and never want to go home any more."

"Well, if that s the way, I'm agreed, but I don't take no stock in it. Mighty soon we'll have the cave so cluttered up with women, and fellows waiting to be ransomed, that there won't be no place for the robbers. But go ahead, I ain't got nothing to say."

27 Little Tommy Barnes was asleep, now, and when they waked him up he was scared, and cried, and said he wanted to go home to his ma, and didn't want to be a robber any more.

So they all made fun of him, and called him cry-baby, and that made him mad, and he said he would go straight and tell all the secrets. But Tom give him five cents to keep quiet, and said we would all go home and meet next week and rob somebody and kill some people.

Ben Rogers said he couldn't get out much, only Sundays, **28** and so he wanted to begin next Sunday; but all the boys said it would be wicked to do it on Sunday, and that settled the thing. They agreed to get together and fix a day as soon as they could, and then we elected Tom Sawyer first captain and Jo Harper second captain of the Gang, and so started home.

29 I clumb up the shed and crept into my window just before day was breaking. My new clothes was all greased up and clayey, and I was dog-tired.

HUCK CREEPS INTO HIS WINDOW.

what the matter was. However, we plunged into the wood, they scurrying in the lead, and the trouble was quickly revealed: they had hanged a little fellow with a bark rope, and he was kicking and struggling, in the process of choking to death. We rescued him, and fetched him around." Many of the crimes Tom wishes his gang to commit are effectively carried out by adults later in the novel. Thus the boy's absurd fantasies accurately anticipate the violent realities of his own culture encountered by Huck ironically during his flight from civilization.

28 *all the boys said it would be wicked to do it on Sunday.* Samuel Clemens was brought up a good Presbyterian, and it was considered sacreligious to do anything on Sunday. "We didn't break the Sabbath often enough to signify—once a week perhaps," he facetiously recalled in an address printed in *Mark Twain's Speeches* (1910, p. 371). Clemens never did reconcile himself to this taboo. "God runs his worldly business," he once complained, "just the same on Sundays as on weekdays, but if you break the Sabbath we get damned for it" (quoted by Caroline Thomas Harnsberger, *Mark Twain's View of Religion*, 1961, p. 6).

29 *I . . . crept into my window.* Notice that Kemble's tailpiece is an exact mirror image of that of "Huck Stealing Away" in Chapter 1. John Tenniel drew a similar pair of pictures to illustrate Chapter 1 of Lewis Carroll's *Through the Looking Glass* (1872), which were likely known to the American artist.

1 *Miss Watson . . . took me in the closet and prayed.* Miss Watson, a fundamentalist, has literally interpreted Matthew 6:6: "But thou, when thou prayest, enter into thy closet." Similarly, in Chapter 30 of *The Prince and the Pauper*, Tom Canty as King Edward VI is so offended by the grimly holy Lady Mary that he commands her "to go to her closet, and beseech God to take away the stone that was in her breast, and give her a human heart."

2 *She told me to pray every day, and whatever I asked for I would get it. But it warn't so.* The young Sam Clemens was more successful with such childish experiments with answered prayers than was Huckleberry Finn. As he recalled in Chapter 8 of the *Autobiography*, his teacher Mrs. Horr once lectured on the text, "Ask and ye shall receive" (Matthew 7:7), and she reassured the children that "whosoever prayed for a thing with earnestness and strong desire need not doubt that his prayer would be answered. . . . I prayed for gingerbread. Margaret Kooneman, who was the baker's daughter, brought a slab of gingerbread to school every morning; she had always kept it out of sight before but when I finished my prayer and glanced up, there it was in easy reach and she was looking the other way. In all my life I believe I never enjoyed an answer to my prayer more than I enjoyed that one; and I was a convert, too. I had no ends of wants and they had always remained unsatisfied up to that time, but I meant to supply them and extend them now that I had found out how to do it." However, this was the only prayer of his that was ever answered.

3 *Miss Watson . . . said I was a fool. She never told me why, and I couldn't make it out no way.* Miss Watson is

CHAPTER III

WELL, I got a good going-over in the morning, from old Miss Watson, on account of my clothes; but the widow she didn't scold, but only cleaned off the grease and clay, and looked so sorry that I thought I would behave a while if I could. Then Miss Watson she took me in the closet and prayed, but nothing come of it. She told me to pray every day, and whatever I asked for I would get it. But it warn't so. I tried it. Once I got a fish-line, but no hooks. It warn't any good to me without hooks. I tried for the hooks three or four times, but somehow I couldn't make it work. By-and-by, one day, I asked Miss Watson to try for me, but she said I was a fool. She never told me why, and I couldn't make it out no way.

I set down, one time, back in the woods, and had a long think about it. I says to myself, if a body can get anything they pray for, why don't Deacon Winn get back the money he lost on pork? Why can't the widow get back her silver snuff-box that was stole? Why can't Miss Watson fat up? No, says I to myself, there ain't nothing in it. I went and told the

MISS WATSON'S LECTURE.

widow about it, and she said the thing a body could get by praying for it was " spiritual gifts." This was too many for me, but she told me what she meant—I must help other people, and do everything I could for other people, and look out for them all the time, and never think about myself. This was including Miss Watson, as I took it. I went out in the woods and turned it over in my mind a long time, but I couldn't see no advantage about it—except for the other people—so at last I reckoned I wouldn't worry about it any more, but just let it go. Sometimes the widow would take me one side and talk about Providence in a way to make a body's mouth water ; but maybe next day Miss Watson would take hold and knock it all down again. I judged I could see that there was two Providences, and a poor chap would stand considerable **4** show with the widow's Providence, but if Miss Watson's got him there warn't no help for him any more. I thought it all out, and reckoned I would belong to the widow's, if he wanted me, though I couldn't make out how he was agoing to be any better off then than what he was before, seeing I was so ignorant and so kind of low-down and ornery.

Pap he hadn't been seen for more than a year, and that was comfortable for me ; I didn't want to see him no more. He used to always whale me when he was sober and could get his hands on me ; though I used to take to the woods most of the time when he was around. Well, about this time he was found in the river drowned, about twelve mile above town, so people said. They judged it was him, anyway ; said this drowned man was just his size, and was ragged, and had uncommon long hair —which was all like pap—but they couldn't make nothing out of the face, because it had been in the water so long it warn't much like a face at all. They said he was floating on his back in the water. They took him and buried him on the bank. But I warn't comfortable long, because I happened to think of something. I knowed mighty well that a drownded man don't **5** float on his back, but on his face. So I knowed, then, that this warn't pap, but a woman dressed up in a man's clothes. So I was uncomfortable again. I judged the old man would turn **6** up again by-and-by, though I wished he wouldn't.

We played robbers now and then about a month, and then I resigned. All the boys did. We hadn't robbed nobody, we hadn't killed any people, but only just pretended. We used to hop out of the woods and go charging down on hog-drovers and women in carts taking garden stuff to market, but we never hived any of them. Tom Sawyer called the hogs " ingots," and **7** he called the turnips and stuff " julery," and we would go to the cave and pow-wow over what we had done and how many people **8** we had killed and marked. But I couldn't see no profit in it. **9** One time Tom sent a boy to run about town with a blazing **10** stick, which he called a slogan (which was the sign for the Gang to get together), and then he said he had got secret news by his spies that next day a whole parcel of Spanish merchants and rich A-rabs was going to camp in Cave Hollow with two **11**

constantly using her limited erudition to put down ignorant Huck. Twain had no sympathy for such false attitudes of superiority. He agreed with a friend named Macfarlane who said that "man's intellect was a brutal addition to him and degraded him to a rank far below the plane of the other animals, and that there was never a man who did not use his intellect daily all his life to advantage himself at other people's expense" ("Macfarlane," 1896, in *What Is Man?*, 1973, p. 78). See also note 24, this chapter, and Chapter 14, note 8.

4 *two Providences.* In "The Two Providences" (*College English*, January 1950, pp. 188–195), Edgar M. Branch has argued that the Widow Douglas's morality is intuitive and based upon example, Miss Watson's conventional and derived from fear. The widow encourages the unselfish aid to others through "good works" while her sister is merely selfish in her dread of "the bad place." Also, Blair in *Mark Twain and Huck Finn* (pp. 135–136) has pointed to the similarity between Huck's internal debate and W.E.H. Lecky's theory of two fundamentally opposed groups of moralists in his *History of European Morals from Augustus to Charlemagne* (1869), a two-volume work admired by Twain. Lecky defined the first to be "the stoical, the intuitive, the independent, and the sentimental," the second "the epicurean, the inductive, the utilitarian, or the selfish." "The moralists of the former school," he continued, "believe that we have a natural power of perceiving that some qualities such as benevolence, chastity, or veracity, are better than others, and that we ought to cultivate them, and to repress their opposites. . . . The moralist of the opposite school . . . maintains that we have by nature absolutely no knowledge of merit and demerit, of the comparative excellence of our feelings and actions, and that we derive these notions solely from observation of the course . . . which is conducive to human happiness. That which makes actions good is, that they increase the happiness or diminish the pains of mankind." According to Blair, Clemens underscored certain other passages in the book in which Lecky applied his theory to the Greek philosophers: The Stoics abstained from sin "not through fear of punishment" but "from the desire and obligation of what is just and good," while the general populace followed another order, for the Greek word for superstition signified "fear of gods" or daemons; and "the philosophers sometimes represented the vulgar as shuddering at the thought of death, through dread of certain endless sufferings to which it would lead them."

According to Lecky's theory, Huck's thinking is muddled: He exhibits both selfish and unselfish reasons for his choosing one philosophy over the other. Arguably, no matter what he does in seeking either the Widow's or Miss Watson's Providence, Huck does so selfishly. "From his cradle to his grave," Twain explained in *What Is Man?* (1973, p. 136), "a man never does a single thing which has any *first and foremost* object but one—to secure peace of mind, spiritual comfort, for *himself*." However, Huck's philosophy is never neatly worked out. His actions generally follow the simple morality defined by another country boy, Nicodemus Dodge, in

Chapter 20 of *A Tramp Abroad:* "I think 't if a feller he'ps another feller when he's in trouble, and don't cuss, and don't do no mean things, nur noth'n' he ain' no business to do, and don't spell the Saviour's name with a little g, he ain't runnin' no resks—he's about as saift as if he b'longed to a church."

5 *a drownded man don't float on his back, but on his face. . . . this warn't pap, but a woman dressed up in a man's clothes.* "You will always find the body of a drowned woman floating face up," reported Harry Middleton Hyatt in *Folk-Lore from Adams County, Illinois* (1965, p. 697); "the body of a drowned man, face down. Although these positions are occasionally reversed in some sayings, this is the general belief—they are the normal positions of coitus."

6 *I judged the old man would turn up again by-and-by.* Huck made a similar prediction in Chapter 25 of *Tom Sawyer,* when he and Tom contemplated what they might do should they discover buried treasure: "Pap would come back to thish-yer town some day and get his claws on it." Many of the attitudes of Huck and of Tom in this chapter of *Huckleberry Finn* are reworkings of those in that chapter of *Tom Sawyer.*

7 *hived.* Robbed.

8 *pow-wow.* Discuss, usually noisily; an Indian word originally applied to feasts, dances, and other public doings, preliminary to a hunt, a council, or a war expedition.

9 *marked.* Highwaymen often "marked," or scarred, their victims, so (Twain noted in the margin of his public reading copy of the 1893 Tauchnitz edition) "they'd know who *done* it—and we'd get a reputation" (MTP). The most famous example of this custom is the "Z" slashed on the enemies of Johnston McCulley's "Zorro."

10 *Tom sent a boy to run about town with a blazing stick, which he called a slogan (which was the sign for the Gang to get together).* Leo Marx has suggested in his notes to the 1967 Bobbs-Merrill edition that Tom has confused two passages from the work of Sir Walter Scott: In *The Lay of the Last Minstrel* (Canto Fourth, xxvii), slogan is used in its earliest meaning as a Scottish warcry; in *The Lady of the Lake* (Canto Third), the "fiery cross" was carried throughout the countryside to call the clans together. For Twain's opinions of Scott's work, see Chapter 13, note 7.

11 *Cave Hollow.* In Chapter 15 of his *Autobiography,* Twain identified this term as "Missourian for 'valley.'"

12 *"sumter" mules.* "Sumpter," or pack, mules; appropriately Tom adopts an archaic, eighteenth-century spelling of the word, obviously found in the boy's eclectic reading.

13 *lay in ambuscade.* Another archaic phrase, for "lay in ambush."

14 *slick up.* Colloquial for polish, from to "sleek."

12 hundred elephants, and six hundred camels, and over a thousand "sumter" mules, all loaded down with di'monds, and they **13** didn't have only a guard of four hundred soldiers, and so we would lay in ambuscade, as he called it, and kill the lot and **14** scoop the things. He said we must slick up our swords and guns, and get ready. He never could go after even a turnip-cart but he must have the swords and guns all scoured up for it; though they was only lath and broom-sticks, and you might scour at them till you rotted, and then they warn't worth a mouthful of ashes more than what they was before. I didn't believe we could lick such a crowd of Spaniards and A-rabs, but I wanted to see the camels and elephants, so I was on hand next day, Saturday, in the ambuscade; and when we got the word, we rushed out of the woods and down the hill. But there warn't no Spaniards and A-rabs, and there warn't no camels nor no elephants. It warn't anything but a Sunday-**15** school picnic, and only a primer-class at that. We busted it

THE ROBBERS DISPERSED.

up, and chased the children up the hollow; but we never got anything but some doughnuts and jam, though Ben Rogers **16** got a rag doll, and Jo Harper got a hymn-book and a tract; and then the teacher charged in and made us drop everything and cut. I didn't see no di'monds, and I told Tom Sawyer so. He said there was loads of them there, anyway; and he said there was A-rabs there, too, and elephants and things. I said, why couldn't we see them, then? He said if I warn't so **17** ignorant, but had read a book called "Don Quixote," I would

know without asking. He said it was all done by enchantment.
He said there was hundreds of soldiers there, and elephants
and treasure, and so on, but we had enemies which he called
magicians, and they had turned the whole thing into an infant
Sunday school, just out of spite. I said all right, then the
thing for us to do was to go for the magicians. Tom Sawyer
said I was a numskull.

"Why," says he, "a magician could call up a lot of genies,
and they would hash you up like nothing before you could say **18**
Jack Robinson. They are as tall as a tree and as big around **19**
as a church."

"Well," I says, "s'pose we got some genies to help *us*—
can't we lick the other crowd then ? "

"How you going to get them ? "

"I don't know. How do *they* get them ? "

"Why, they rub an old tin lamp or an iron ring, and then **20**
the genies come tearing in, with the thunder and lightning a-
ripping around and the smoke a-rolling, and everything they're
told to do they up and do it. They don't think nothing of
pulling a shot tower up by the roots, and belting a Sunday **21, 22**
school superintendent over the head with it—or any other man."

"Who makes them tear around so ? "

"Why, whoever rubs the lamp or the ring. They belong
to whoever rubs the lamp or the ring, and they've got to do
whatever he says. If he tells them to build a palace forty
miles long, out of di'monds, and fill it full of chewing gum, or
whatever you want, and fetch an emperor's daughter from **23**
China for you to marry, they've got to do it—and they've got
to do it before sun-up next morning, too. And more—they've

RUBBING THE LAMP.

15 *a primer-class.* A reading class, the youngest
group of schoolchildren, now equivalent to a kinder-
garten.

16 *a tract.* Likely some pious pamphlet, issued by
the American Tract Society. This prolific publisher
equipped Sunday schools with booklets of short
stories of religious instruction which were given as
reward to boys and girls for regular attendance,
punctuality, good conduct, and success in exams.
These cheap publications were the most common
literature known to backwoods children at this time.

17 *"Don Quixote."* Tom is recalling Chapter 18 of
Part I of the Cervantes novel, wherein the don
explains to his servant Sancho Panza, after they have
been driven off by an irate herdsman, that his mortal
enemy, a magician, has transformed an army of
knights into a flock of sheep. Tom is a literalist:
Because he reads for story only, he cannot distinguish burlesque from true romance. Several critics
have noted the similarities between bookish Tom
Sawyer and Don Quixote, and between matter-of-
fact Huckleberry Finn and Sancho Panza.

Twain admired *Don Quixote*—but with certain
reservations. When recommending it to his wife-to-
be Olivia Langdon, Clemens insisted that he should
expurgate it for her perusal: *"Don Quixote* is one of the
most exquisite books that was ever written, and to
lose it from the world's literature would be as the
wresting of a constellation from the symmetry and
perfection of the firmament—but neither it nor
Shakespeare are proper books for virgins to read until
some hand has culled them of their grossness"
(quoted by Dixon Wecter in *The Love Letters of Mark
Twain*, 1949, pp. 76–77). A less prudish Twain
further praised the novel in Chapter 46 of *Life on the
Mississippi* for its having "swept the world's admiration for the medieval chivalry-silliness out of exis-
tence"; however, he lamented, Sir Walter Scott's
Ivanhoe restored it.

Tom's Quixotean raid on the Sunday-school class
is only one of Twain's attacks upon such romantic
deceptions in his fiction. Another important instance
is in Chapter 20 of *A Connecticut Yankee in King
Arthur's Court* in which Hank Morgan plays Sancho
Panza to the Don Quixote of the Demoiselle Ali-
sande la Carteloise, "Sandy." The lady gets him to
take her on a quest to a castle where, she says, three
ogres have imprisoned her mistress and forty-four
other princesses; but when they arrive at the object of
their search, it turns out to be nothing but a pigsty.
And even then Sandy is convinced that the castle
must now be under a wicked enchantment. Morgan
pities the girl, but her kissing and caressing the hogs
and addressing them as princesses is too much for the
Connecticut Yankee. "I was ashamed of her," he
admits (just like Huck Finn at the end of Chapter 24),
"ashamed of the human race."

18 *before you could say Jack Robinson.* This expression,
common in both the United States and Great Britain,
derives from the last line of a popular song, "And he
was off before he could say Jack Robinson." This old
gentleman, when calling on friends, had the habit of
disappearing before even his name was announced.

19 *as big around as a church.* Churches were often the most impressive structures in these rural towns, occasionally large enough to hold the entire population of a settlement.

20 *they rub an old tin lamp or an iron ring, and then the genies come tearing in.* Tom is referring to "Aladdin and His Wonderful Lamp" in *The Arabian Nights*. In this episode Twain is likely describing himself as a boy. "He used to tell us tales," a childhood friend recalled Sam Clemens to Clifton Johnson (*Highways and Byways of the Mississippi Valley*, p. 181), "and we loved to listen to him. His father had a book—*The Arabian Nights*—that no one else had in town, and Sam would get us boys together of evenings and tell us stories from that book, and we was glad to listen as long as he'd talk." When Harper & Bros. asked several men of letters and other prominent public figures to suggest selections for their edition of *Favorite Fairy Tales* (1907), Mark Twain chose "Aladdin and His Wonderful Lamp." See also Chapter 40, note 6.

21 *a shot tower.* A tall, round tower where buckshot is made; molten lead is dropped from the top and forms in spherical balls when it falls into a tank of cold water below.

Saint Louis shot tower. *Courtesy the Library of Congress.*

22 *a Sunday school superintendent.* Such a gentleman was among the most intimidating of adults to small-town boys, because he was often held up to a child as a model of respect and an example of impeccable character. Similarly, in "A Little Pilgrim" in *Whilomville Stories* (1900), Stephen Crane characterizes the "ideal Sunday-School superintendent" as "one who had never felt hunger or thirst or the wound of the challenge of dishonor."

got to waltz that palace around over the country wherever you want it, you understand."

"Well," says I, "I think they are a pack of flatheads for not keeping the palace themselves 'stead of fooling them away like that. And what's more—if I was one of them I would see **24** a man in Jericho before I would drop my business and come to him for the rubbing of an old tin lamp."

"How you talk, Huck Finn. Why, you'd *have* to come when he rubbed it, whether you wanted to or not."

"What, and I as high as a tree and as big as a church? All right, then; I *would* come; but I lay I'd make that man climb the highest tree there was in the country."

25 "Shucks, it ain't no use to talk to you, Huck Finn. You **26** don't seem to know anything, somehow—perfect sap-head."

I thought all this over for two or three days, and then I reckoned I would see if there was anything in it. I got an old tin lamp and an iron ring and went out in the woods and **27** rubbed and rubbed till I sweat like an Injun, calculating to build a palace and sell it; but it warn't no use, none of the genies come. So then I judged that all that stuff was only just one of Tom Sawyer's lies. I reckoned he believed in the **28** A-rabs and the elephants, but as for me I think different. It had all the marks of a Sunday school.

23 *an emperor's daughter from China*. It should be noted that, although the tales of *The Arabian Nights* are of Persian origin, the story of Aladdin takes place in ancient China.

24 *Jericho*. Euphemism for Hell; "to see a man in Jericho" is "to see him damned." Actually, the phrase derives from II Samuel 10:1–5: In suspecting David's servants of being spies, Hanun seizes them and has their beards cut off; on their return in disgrace, David sends them to stay in Jericho until their beards have grown back. In his public reading copy of the 1893 Tauchnitz edition, Twain replaced this term with "Halifax" (MTP), another euphemism for Hell; this expression dates from the sixteenth century when Halifax, England, was notorious for its thieves and other criminals.

25 *it ain't no use to talk to you, Huck Finn. You don't seem to know anything, somehow*. In *Tom Sawyer Abroad*, Huck is less tolerant than in the earlier novel of Tom's tossing his erudition in his face. In Chapter 1, when Tom asks him if he knows what a crusade is, Huck retorts, "No . . . I don't. And I don't care, nuther. I've lived till now and done without it, and had my health, too. But as soon as you tell me, I'll know, and that's soon enough. I don't see no use in finding out things and clogging my head up with them when I mayn't ever have any occasion for them." Unlike bookish Tom, Huck has no interest in knowledge for its own sake; it must have some practical application to be of worth to him.

In Chapter 13 of *Tom Sawyer Abroad*, in another parody of *The Arabian Nights*, Huck ponders whether it is knowledge or instinct which determines Tom's delusions. While in Egypt, Tom believes that he has found the locale of a famous house described in the famous Persian stories; however, all that he has discovered is a single brick. Huck is baffled as to how Tom can be certain he has located the fabled house. "Is it knowledge or instink?" Huck wonders; "it's my opinion that some of it is knowledge but the main bulk of it is instink." To test his friend's claim, Huck puts "another brick considerable like it in its place, and he didn't know no difference—but there was no difference, you see. . . . Instink tells him where the exact *place* is for the brick to be in, and so he recognizes it by the place it's in, not by the look of the brick. If it was knowledge, not instink, he would know the brick again by the look of it the next time he seen it—which he didn't. So it shows that for all the brag you hear about knowledge being such a wonderful thing, instink is worth forty of it for real

unerringness." Here, as throughout *Huckleberry Finn*, pragmatic Huck prefers the proven to the theoretical; and again he will trust his own heart rather than what he may learn elsewhere.

Huck is a descendant of the anti-intellectual backwoodsman common to Southern and Southwestern literature. "Well," Simon Suggs explains in Johnson Jones Hooper's *Adventures of Captain Simon Suggs* (1846, pp. 53–54), "mother-wit kin beat book-larnin', at *any* game! . . . Human natur' and the human family is *my* books, and I've never seed many but what I could hold my own with. . . . Books ain't fitten for nothin' but jist to give to children goin' to school, to keep 'em outen mischief." Just like Huck Finn, Mark Twain seemed to share this contempt for "book-larnin'." "The most valuable capital or culture or education usable in the building of novels is personal experience," he wrote in a letter of 1891 (*Letters*, Vol. II, p. 543). "I surely have the equipment, a wide culture, and all of it real, none of it artificial, for I don't know anything about books." However, just a glance at his many references to other literature in this chapter of *Huckleberry Finn* reveals how widely read Clemens actually was.

26 *sap-head*. A fool, referring to the sap or soft wood in timber; Tom's evaluation of Huck Finn confirms Miss Watson's opinion, made earlier in the chapter.

27 *sweat like an Injun*. As noted in John S. Farmer's *Americanisms Old and New* (1889), California Indian tribes were famous for their "sweat-houses," "half a religious temple, . . . half a sanitary asylum," where braves sweltered all night by smothered fires and in the morning plunged, still perspiring, into ice-cold water.

28 *It had all the marks of a Sunday school*. Thus Tom's boyish fantasies are no different than Miss Watson's religious teachings. While identifying Tom's thinking with Miss Watson's morality, Huck in experimenting with his friend's arguments reinforces his decision to follow the Widow Douglas's Providence. In an address delivered in London on July 8, 1899 (in *Mark Twain's Speeches*, 1910, p. 132), he distinguished between theoretical and practical morals, between those of Miss Watson and those of the Widow Douglas: "Theoretical morals are the sort you get on your mother's knee, in good books, and from the pulpit. You gather them in your head, and not in your heart; they are theory without practice." Only through his actions, in practicing what he preaches, can Huck develop his own set of practical morals.

Chapter IV.

1 *At first I hated the school.* And well he might, if one is to believe Twain's bitter recollection of a typical school of the period in Chapter 5 of *The Gilded Age:* "a place where tender young humanity devoted itself for eight to ten hours a day to learning incomprehensible rubbish by heart out of books and reciting it by rote, like parrots; so that a finished education consisted simply of a permanent headache and the ability to read without stopping to spell the words or take breath." He was likely reporting his own experiences at J. D. Dawson's school in Hannibal, described so vividly as that of Mr. Dobbins in *Tom Sawyer*. It was a time when strict discipline was administered; nearly every school master or marm was quick to use the hickory stick on a disobedient pupil. Perhaps no other child hated school more than did young Sam Clemens. "And we know papa played 'Hookey' all the time," Susy Clemens recorded in her biography (quoted in Chapter 41 of the *Autobiography*. "And how readily would papa pretend to be dying so as not to have to go to school!" He so despised it that, when his mother summoned him to his father's deathbed, the boy begged, "I will promise anything, if you won't make me go to school! Anything!" (quoted by Albert Bigelow Paine, *Mark Twain: A Biography*, Vol. I, 1912, p. 75).

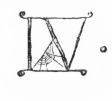

!!!!!

WELL, three or four months run along, and it was well into the winter, now. I had been to school most all the time, and could spell, and read, and write just a little, and could say the multiplication table up to six times seven is thirty-five, and I don't reckon I could ever get any further than that if I was to live for ever. I don't take no stock in mathematics, anyway.

1   At first I hated the school, but by-and-by I got so I could stand it. Whenever I got uncommon tired I played hookey, and the hiding I got next day done me good and cheered me up. So the longer I went to school the easier it got to be. I was getting sort of used to the widow's ways, too, and they warn't so raspy on me. Living in a house, and sleeping in a bed, pulled on me pretty tight, mostly, but before the cold weather I used to slide out and sleep in the woods, sometimes, and so that was a rest to me. I liked the old ways best, but I was getting so I liked the new ones, too, a little bit. The widow said I was coming along slow but sure, and doing very satisfactory. She said she warn't ashamed of me.

One morning I happened to turn over the salt-cellar at **2** breakfast. I reached for some of it as quick as I could, to throw over my left shoulder and keep off the bad luck, but Miss Watson was in ahead of me, and crossed me off. She says, " Take your hands away, Huckleberry—what a mess you are always making!" The widow put in a good word for me, but that warn't going to keep off the bad luck, I knowed that well enough. I started out, after breakfast, feeling worried and shaky, and wondering where it was going to fall on me, and what it was going to be. There is ways to keep off some kinds of bad luck, but this wasn't one of them kind; so I never tried to do anything, but just poked along low-spirited and on the watch-out.

I went down the front garden and clumb over the stile, where you go through the high board fence. There was an inch of new snow on the ground, and I seen somebody's tracks. They had come up from the quarry and stood around the stile a while, and then went on around the garden fence. It was funny they hadn't come in, after standing around so. I couldn't make it out. It was very curious, somehow. I was going to follow around, but I stooped down to look at the tracks first. I didn't notice anything at first, but next I did. There was a cross in the left boot-heel made with big nails, to **3** keep off the devil.

I was up in a second and shinning down the hill. I looked over my shoulder every now and then, but I didn't see nobody. I was at Judge Thatcher's as quick as I could get there. He said :

" Why, my boy, you are all out of breath. Did you come for your interest ? "

" No, sir," I says ; " is there some for me ? "

" Oh, yes, a half-yearly is in, last night. Over a hundred and fifty dollars. Quite a fortune for you. You better let me invest it along with your six thousand, because if you take it you'll spend it."

" No, sir," I says, " I don't want to spend it. I don't want it at all—nor the six thousand, nuther. I want you to take it ; I want to give it to you—the six thousand and all."

He looked surprised. He couldn't seem to make it out. He says :

" Why, what can you mean, my boy ? "

I says, " Don't you ask me no questions about it, please. You'll take it—won't you ? "

He says :

" Well, I'm puzzled. Is something the matter ? "

" Please take it," says I, " and don't ask me nothing—then **4** I won't have to tell no lies."

2 *I happened to turn over the salt-cellar at breakfast. I reached for some of it as quick as I could, to throw over my left shoulder and keep off the bad luck.* "To scatter salt, by overturning the vessel in which it is contained, is very unlucky," explained Frances Grose in *A Provincial Glossary*, "and portends quarreling with a friend, or fracture of a bone, sprain, or other bodily misfortune. Indeed this may in some measure be averted, by throwing it over one's head." When salt was precious, it was given as a token of friendship; when spilled, it came to be known as an omen of a rift between friends. It is also believed that the Devil lingers on the left side of the body and watches at the table to cause mischief; the spilling of salt thus gives him a cause to provoke a quarrel, unless one throws it over the left shoulder to hit him in the eye. This superstition is apparent in Leonardo da Vinci's fresco of "The Last Supper," in which salt spilled on the table points to Judas Iscariot.

3 *There was a cross in the left boot-heel made with big nails, to keep off the devil.* The cross, the symbol of Christ, is a common protection against demons. Tom Sawyer repeats this belief in Chapter 33 of *Tom Sawyer*: "Looky-here, Huck. . . . Injun Joe's ghost ain't a-going to come around where ther's a cross!" Nails were used, because iron was said to be a protection against witches and other evil spirits.

4 *don't ask me nothing—then I won't have to tell no lies.* Huck is trying to remember the old English proverb, "Ask me no questions and I'll tell you no lies" (as in Oliver Goldsmith's *She Stoops to Conquer*, 1773, Act III, scene i).

5 *Miss Watson's . . . Jim, had a hair-ball as big as your fist, which had been took out of the fourth stomach of an ox, and he used to do magic with it.* A cow licks her hair which goes down in the left side of the pouch and forms a ball; and it was believed that such a hair-ball could not only tell the future but also be used to bewitch others. Since ancient times, visceral objects have been thought to possess soothsaying powers; and, although divination with a hair-ball is said to be a voodoo practice (and one of the few examples of Jim's "magic" which is of African origin), it is also a tradition native to Germany.

JUDGE THATCHER SURPRISED.

He studied a while, and then he says:

"Oho-o. I think I see. You want to *sell* all your property to me—not give it. That's the correct idea."

Then he wrote something on a paper and read it over, and says:

"There—you see it says 'for a consideration.' That means I have bought it of you and paid you for it. Here's a dollar for you. Now, you sign it."

So I signed it, and left.

5   Miss Watson's nigger, Jim, had a hair-ball as big as your fist, which had been took out of the fourth stomach of an ox, and he used to do magic with it. He said there was a spirit inside of it, and it knowed everything. So I went to him that night and told him pap was here again, for I found his tracks in the snow. What I wanted to know, was, what he was going to do, and was he going to stay? Jim got out his hair-ball, and said something over it, and then he held it up and dropped it on the floor. It fell pretty solid, and only rolled about an inch. Jim tried it again, and then another time, and it acted just the same. Jim got down on his knees and put his ear against it and listened. But it warn't no use; he said it wouldn't talk. He said sometimes it wouldn't talk without money. I told him I had an old slick counterfeit quarter that warn't no good because the brass showed through the silver a little, and it wouldn't pass nohow, even if the brass didn't show, because it was so slick it felt greasy, and so that would tell on it every time. (I reckoned I wouldn't say nothing about the dollar I got from the judge.) I said it was pretty bad money, but maybe the hair-ball would take it, because maybe it wouldn't know the difference. Jim smelt it, and bit it, and rubbed it, and said he would manage so the hair-ball would think it was good. He said he would split open a raw Irish potato and stick the quarter in between and keep it there **6** all night, and next morning you couldn't see no brass, and it **7** wouldn't feel greasy no more, and so anybody in town would take it in a minute, let alone a hair-ball. Well, I knowed a potato would do that, before, but I had forgot it.

JIM LISTENING.

Jim put the quarter under the hair-ball and got down and listened again. This time he said the hair-ball was all right. He said it would tell my whole fortune if I wanted it to. I says, go on. So the hair-ball talked to Jim, and Jim told it to me. He says:

"Yo' ole father doan' know, yit, what he's a-gwyne to do. Sometimes he spec he'll go 'way, en den agin he spec he'll **8** stay. De bes' way is to res' easy en let de ole man take his own way. Dey's two angels hoverin' roun' 'bout him. One uv **9** 'em is white en shiny, en t'other one is black. De white one gits him to go right, a little while, den de black one sail in en bust it all up. A body can't tell, yit, which one gwyne to fetch him at de las'. But you is all right. You gwyne to have considable trouble in yo' life, en considable joy. Sometimes you gwyne to git hurt, en sometimes you gwyne to git sick; but every time you's gwyne to git well agin. Dey's two gals flyin' 'bout you in yo' life. One uv 'em's light en t'other one is dark. One is rich en t'other is po'. You's gwyne to marry de po' one fust en de rich one by-en-by. You want to keep 'way fum de water as much as you kin, en don't run no resk, 'kase it's down **10** in de bills dat you's gwyne to git hung." **11**

When I lit my candle and went up to my room that night, there set pap, his own self! **12**

6 *Irish potato.* Term used in the South to distinguish the white potato from the sweet potato. Discovered in Peru and imported first to Spain, the potato was introduced into Ireland by Sir Walter Raleigh in 1610, and it quickly became the staple crop of the people; however, not until the nineteenth century was it widely accepted elsewhere as a food.

7 *next morning you couldn't see no brass, and it wouldn't feel greasy no more.* Oddly enough, the white of the potato can indeed clean the tarnish off brass.

8 *Sometimes he spec he'll go 'way, en den agin he spec he'll stay.* Twain, of course, is playing with the duplicity of fortune-tellers. By nature a skeptic, Twain nevertheless frequently subjected himself to palmists and phrenologists, but in each instance, he concealed his identity; and astonishingly, as he explained in Chapter 13 of his *Autobiography*, they all concurred that "the evidence that I do not possess the sense of humor is overwhelming, satisfying, convincing, incontrovertible—and at last I believe it myself."

9 *Dey's two angels hoverin' roun' 'bout him. . . . De white one gits him to go right, a little while, den de black one sail in en bust it all up.* There was a common superstition in Europe and the United States that every person has two angels, one good and one bad, influencing his actions. Twain, however, tended to correlate this belief with paganism, here as followed by the black slave, and in "Huck Finn and Tom Sawyer among the Indians" as by the Indians: ". . . the Injuns hadn't only but two Gods, a good one and a bad one, and they never paid no attention to the good one, nor ever prayed to him or worried about him at all, but only tried their level best to flatter up the bad god and keep on the good side of him; because the good one loved them and wouldn't ever think of doing them any harm, and so there warn't any occasion to be bothering him with prayers and things, because he was always doing the very best he could for them, anyway, and prayers couldn't better it; but all the trouble come from the bad god, who was setting up nights to think up ways to bring them bad luck and bust up all their plans, and never fooled away a chance to do them all the harm he could; and so the sensible thing was to keep praying and fussing around him all the time, and get him to let up" (*Mark Twain's Hannibal, Huck and Tom*, 1969, p. 120).

Samuel Clemens was brought up on the Presbyterian catechism, which declared that there was one God the Almighty who decided all, both the good and the bad. No matter what happened, whether it were a blessing or a disaster, it was an act of divine Providence. But Clemens never did accept this concept of a single omnipotent godhead. "To trust the God of the Bible," he complained, "is to trust an irascible, vindictive, fierce and ever fickle and changeful master." See Harnsberger, *Mark Twain's View of Religion*, p. 20.

10 *it's down in de bills.* Leo Marx explained this phrase in his notes to the 1967 Bobbs-Merrill edition: "Written down in the specifications (bills, as in phrase, fill the bill); thus, foreordained."

11 *you's gwyne to git hung*. Jim's nebulous prophesy may be a take-off of the old saying, "He that is born to be hanged shall never be drowned." Twain told Paine (*Mark Twain: A Biography*, Vol. I, p. 35) that a pet motto of his mother was, "People born to be hanged are safe in water."

12 *pap*. Based in part on Jimmy Finn, the town drunkard of Hannibal, Missouri, who "slept in the deserted tanyard with the hogs" (*Autobiography*, Chapter 14), Pap Finn is also the stereotype of the "squatter," or "poor white trash." "Lank, lean, angular, and bony," Daniel Robinson Hundley contemptuously described him in Chapter 7 of *Social Relations in Our Southern States* (1860); "sallow complexion, awkward manners, and a natural stupidity or dullness of intellect that almost surpasses belief." Preferring the wilderness to civilization, squatters "build their pine-pole cabins among the sterile sand hills, or in the very heart of the dismal solitude of the burr-oak or pine barrens." Like Pap Finn, they are superstitious, "being firm believers in witches and hobgoblins; likewise old-time spiritualists, or . . . believers in fortune-telling after the ancient modes—such as palm-reading, card-cutting, or the revelations of coffee-grounds left in the bottom of the cup after the fluid has been drained off." But their worst characteristic was their drunkenness: "Too lazy to distill honest peach or apple brandy, like the industrious yeomanry, they prefer to tramp to the nearest groggery with a gallon-jug on their shoulders, which they get filled with 'bust-head,' 'rot-gut,' or some other equally poisonous abomination; and then tramp home again, reeling as they trudge along, and laughing idiotically, or shouting like mad in a glorious state of beastly intoxication." "All they seem to care for, is, to live from hand to mouth," Hundley continued his evaluation; "to get drunk, provided they can do so without having to trudge too far after their liquor; to shoot for beef; to hunt; . . . to vote at elections; to eat and to sleep; to lounge in the sunshine of a bright summer's day, and to bask in the warmth of a roaring wood fire, when the summer days are over." Surely there is much of Pap in his son Huckleberry Finn.

Little more is said about the man in *Tom Sawyer*. However, Twain had originally intended to introduce Pap Finn as Injun Joe's partner in grave-robbing; it was not until he had finished much of the manuscript that Twain replaced him with Muff Potter. Pap Finn was obviously the prototype for that other town drunkard, Si Higgins ("He was a monument of rags and dirt; he was the profanest man in town; he had bleary eyes, and a nose like a mildewed cauliflower; he slept with the hogs in an abandoned tan-yard"), of "Autobiography of a Damned Fool," a novel Twain began in 1877 soon after he had pigeonholed the manuscript of *Huckleberry Finn*, and in turn abandoned later when he lost interest in it. See *Mark Twain's Satires and Burlesques*, 1968, p. 152.

Chapter V.

I HAD shut the door to. Then I turned around, and there he was. I used to be scared of him all the time, he tanned me so much. I reckoned I was scared now, too; but in a minute I see I was mistaken. That is, after the first jolt, as you may say, when my breath sort of hitched —he being so unexpected; but right away after, I see I warn't scared of him worth bothering about.

He was most fifty, and he looked it. His hair was long and tangled and greasy, and hung down, and you could see his eyes shining through like he was behind vines. It was all black, no gray; so was his long, mixed-up whiskers. There warn't no color in his face, where his face showed; it was white; not like another man's white, but a white to make a body sick, a white to make a body's flesh crawl—a tree-toad white, a fish-belly white. As for his clothes—just rags, that

" PAP."

1 *it was white*. By emphasizing Pap Finn's complexion, Twain contrasts the old man with Miss Watson's Jim. In presenting the nobility of one race through Jim in opposition to the degradation of another in Pap Finn, Twain argues that one cannot judge a person's character by the color of his skin. Also, it is possible that of the two spirits described by Jim in his prophecy, the black one may be good, the white one evil, for Huck Finn.

2 *an old black slouch.* A soft felt hat with a broad floppy brim.

3 *a big-bug.* A "big shot," a person of consequence, used contemptuously.

4 *put on . . . frills.* Have affectations in manners. Their purpose is merely ornamental, for "style," for, as Tom observes in Chapter 5 of *Tom Sawyer Abroad*, "They don't put ruffles on a shirt to help keep a person warm, do they?"

5 *You think you're better'n your father, now, don't you, because he can't?* This was before mandatory universal primary education in Missouri, so Pap Finn was never required to learn to read and write; there were no free public schools in Hannibal then, so Huck has attended classes only because the Widow Douglas paid for them.
Blair in *Mark Twain and Huck Finn* (p. 128) has pointed to the similarities between the way pap abuses Huck and Jerry Cruncher's treatment of his son in Dickens's *A Tale of Two Cities* (1859). Edward Tudor (in the clothes of Tom Canty), too, is treated cruelly by John Canty in Twain's *The Prince and the Pauper* (1882).

6 *put in her shovel.* Or "put in one's oar"; take an active interest in a matter.

was all. He had one ankle resting on t'other knee; the boot on that foot was busted, and two of his toes stuck through, and he worked them now and then. His hat was laying on **2** the floor; an old black slouch with the top caved in, like a lid.

I stood a-looking at him; he set there a-looking at me,

HUCK AND HIS FATHER.

with his chair tilted back a little. I set the candle down. I noticed the window was up; so he had clumb in by the shed. He kept a-looking me all over. By-and-by he says:

"Starchy clothes—very. You think you're a good deal of **3** a big-bug, *don't* you?"

"Maybe I am, maybe I ain't," I says.

"Don't you give me none o' your lip," says he. "You've **4** put on considerble many frills since I been away. I'll take you down a peg before I get done with you. You're educated, **5** too, they say; can read and write. You think you're better'n your father, now, don't you, because he can't? *I'll* take it out of you. Who told you you might meddle with such hifalut'n foolishness, hey?—who told you you could?"

"The widow. She told me."

6 "The widow, hey?—and who told the widow she could put in her shovel about a thing that ain't none of her business?"

"Nobody never told her."

"Well, I'll learn her how to meddle. And looky here— you drop that school, you hear? I'll learn people to bring up a boy to put on airs over his own father and let on to be better'n what *he* is. You lemme catch you fooling around that school again, you hear? Your mother couldn't read, and she couldn't write, nuther, before she died. None of the family couldn't, before *they* died. *I* can't; and here you're a-swelling yourself up like this. I ain't the man to stand it—you hear? Say — lemme hear you read."

I took up a book and begun something about General

Washington and the wars. When I'd read about a half minute, he fetched the book a whack with his hand and knocked it across the house. He says:

"It's so. You can do it. I had my doubts when you told me. Now looky here; you stop that putting on frills. I won't have it. I'll lay for you, my smarty; and if I catch you about **7** that school I'll tan you good. First you know you'll get religion, too. I never see such a son."

He took up a little blue and yaller picture of some cows and a boy, and says:

"What's this?"

"It's something they give me for learning my lessons good." **8**

He tore it up, and says:

"I'll give you something better—I'll give you a cowhide." **9**

He set there a-mumbling and a-growling a minute, and then he says:

"*Ain't* you a sweet-scented dandy, though? A bed; and bedclothes; and a look'n-glass; and a piece of carpet on the floor—and your own father got to sleep with the hogs in the tanyard. I never see such a son. I bet I'll take some o' these frills out o' you before I'm done with you. Why, there ain't no end to your airs—they say you're rich. Hey?—how's that?"

"They lie—that's how."

"Looky here—mind how you talk to me; I'm a-standing about all I can stand, now—so don't gimme no sass. I've been in town two days, and I hain't heard nothing but about you bein' rich. I heard about it away down the river, too. That's why I come. You git me that money to-morrow—I want it."

"I hain't got no money."

"It's a lie. Judge Thatcher's got it. You git it. I want it."

"I hain't got no money, I tell you. You ask Judge Thatcher; he'll tell you the same."

"All right. I'll ask him; and I'll make him pungle, too, **10** or I'll know the reason why. Say—how much you got in your pocket? I want it."

"I hain't got only a dollar, and I want that to ——"

"It don't make no difference what you want it for—you just shell it out."

He took it and bit it to see if it was good, and then he said he was going down town to get some whisky; said he hadn't had a drink all day. When he had got out on the shed, he put his head in again, and cussed me for putting on frills and trying to be better than him; and when I reckoned he was gone, he came back and put his head in again, and told me to mind about that school, because he was going to lay for me and lick me if I didn't drop that.

Next day he was drunk, and he went to Judge Thatcher's and bullyragged him and tried to make him give up the **11** money, but he couldn't, and then he swore he'd make the law force him.

The judge and the widow went to law to get the court to

7 *I'll lay for you.* I'll lie in wait for you, I'll ambush you.

8 *It's something they give me for learning my lessons good.* Called a "reward of merit," a cheaply and gaudily printed picture with a blank space across it for the child's name. Evidently his lessons have not stuck: In saying he has learned them "good" rather than "well," Huck makes a classic error of the illiterate.

9 *give you a cowhide.* Give you a whipping; a cowhide was a strong hide whip, often used on slaves.

10 *pungle.* Pay, hand over (usually money), from Spanish *pongálo:* out with it, let's have it.

11 *bullyragged.* Vehemently badgered, scolded.

12 *the new judge said he was agoing to make a man of him.* Twain admitted in Chapter 14 of his *Autobiography* that his father, Justice John M. Clemens, once tried to reform Jimmy Finn, the town drunkard; he did not succeed. In a letter to the *Alta Californian* (May 26, 1867), Twain described how the temperance people "made much of Jimmy Finn—dressed him up in new clothes, and had him out to breakfast and to dinner, and so forth, and showed him off as a living curiosity—a shining example of the power of temperance doctrines when earnestly and eloquently set forth . . . , but Jimmy Finn couldn't stand it. He got remorseful of his liberty; and then he got melancholy from thinking about it so much; and after that, he got. . . . awfully drunk in the chief citizen's house, and the next morning the house was as if the swine had tarried in it." Although outraged, these total abstainers from alcoholic drink did not give up: They "rallied and reformed Jim once more, but in an evil hour temptation came upon him and he sold his body to a doctor for a quart of whiskey, and that ended all his earthly troubles. He drank it all in one sitting, and his soul went to its long account and his body went to Dr. Grant."

13 *just old pie to him.* As pleasant to him as could be. Pie, then a luxury, referred to anything particularly good.

14 *There's a hand that was the hand of a hog.* This confession is a reminder that Pap Finn usually slept with the hogs in the tanyard.

take me away from him and let one of them be my guardian; but it was a new judge that had just come, and he didn't know the old man; so he said courts mustn't interfere and separate families if they could help it; said he'd druther not take a child away from its father. So Judge Thatcher and the widow had to quit on the business.

That pleased the old man till he couldn't rest. He said he'd cowhide me till I was black and blue if I didn't raise some money for him. I borrowed three dollars from Judge Thatcher, and pap took it and got drunk and went a-blowing around and cussing and whooping and carrying on; and he kept it up all over town, with a tin pan, till most midnight; then they jailed him, and next day they had him before court, and jailed him again for a week. But he said *he* was satisfied; said he was boss of his son, and he'd make it warm for *him.*

12 When he got out the new judge said he was agoing to make a man of him. So he took him to his own house, and dressed him up clean and nice, and had him to breakfast and dinner **13** and supper with the family, and was just old pie to him, so to speak. And after supper he talked to him about temperance and such things till the old man cried, and said he'd been a fool, and fooled away his life; but now he was agoing to turn over a new leaf and be a man nobody wouldn't be ashamed of, and he hoped the judge would help him and not look down on him. The judge said he could hug him for them words; so *he* cried, and his wife she cried again; pap said he'd been a man that had always been misunderstood before, and the judge said he believed it. The old man said that what a man wanted that was down, was sympathy; and the judge said it was so; so they cried again. And when it was bedtime, the old man rose up and held out his hand, and says:

"Look at it, gentlemen, and ladies all; take ahold of it; **14** shake it. There's a hand that was the hand of a hog; but it

REFORMING THE DRUNKARD.

ain't so no more; it's the hand of a man that's started in on a new life, and 'll die before he'll go back. You mark them words—don't forget I said them. It's a clean hand now; shake it—don't be afeard."

So they shook it, one after the other, all around, and cried. The judge's wife she kissed it. Then the old man he signed a **15** pledge—made his mark. The judge said it was the holiest time on record, or something like that. Then they tucked the old man into a beautiful room, which was the spare room, and in the night sometime he got powerful thirsty and clumb out on to the porch-roof and slid down a stanchion and traded his new coat for a jug of forty-rod, and clumb back again and had **16** a good old time; and towards daylight he crawled out again, drunk as a fiddler, and rolled off the porch and broke his left arm in two places and was most froze to death when somebody found him after sun-up. And when they come to look at that spare room, they had to take soundings before they could navi- **17** gate it.

The judge he felt kind of sore. He said he reckoned a body could reform the ole man with a shot-gun, maybe, but he didn't know no other way.

15 *the old man . . . signed a pledge.* Converts to the Temperance Movement generally signed written oaths to abstain from all intoxicating beverages.

16 *forty-rod.* Cheap whiskey, so strong that it was warranted to kill a man, like a rifle, at forty rods.

17 *they had to take soundings before they could navigate it.* Riverboat slang, here meaning to proceed cautiously. Chapter 12 of *Life on the Mississippi* gives a detailed description of a "sounding": While the ship is tied up in a shallow crossing, the pilot not on watch takes some of the crew in a yawl to hunt the deepest water; and once found, the pilot "sounds" its depth by measuring it with a pole ten or twelve feet long, so the pilot on watch can navigate the boat safely into the deep water beyond.

FALLING FROM GRACE.

Chapter VI.

WELL, pretty soon the old man was up and around again, and then he went for Judge Thatcher in the courts to make him give up that money, and he went for me, too, for not stopping school. He catched me a couple of times and thrashed me, but I went to school just the same, and dodged him or out-run him most of the time. I didn't want to go to school much, before, but I reckoned I'd go now to spite pap. That law trial was a slow business; appeared like they warn't ever going to get started on it; so every now and then I'd borrow two or three dollars off of the judge for him, to keep from getting a cowhiding. Every time he got money he got drunk; and every time he got drunk he raised Cain around town; and every time he raised Cain he got jailed. He was just suited—this kind of thing was right in his line.

GETTING OUT OF THE WAY.

He got to hanging around the widow's too much, and so **1** she told him at last, that if he didn't quit using around there she would make trouble for him. Well, *wasn't* he mad? He

1 *if he didn't quit using around there*. If he didn't stop hanging around there.

86

said he would show who was Huck Finn's boss. So he watched out for me one day in the spring, and catched me, and took me up the river about three mile, in a skiff, and crossed over **2** to the Illinois shore where it was woody and there warn't no houses but an old log hut in a place where the timber was so thick you couldn't find it if you didn't know where it was.

He kept me with him all the time, and I never got a chance to run off. We lived in that old cabin, and he always locked the door and put the key under his head, nights. He had a gun which he had stole, I reckon, and we fished and hunted, and that was what we lived on. Every little while he locked me in and went down to the store, three miles to the ferry, and traded fish and game for whisky and fetched it home and got drunk and had a good time, and licked me. The widow she found out where I was by-and-by, and she sent a man over to try to get hold of me, but pap drove him off with the gun, and it warn't long after that till I was used to being where I was, and liked it, all but the cowhide part.

It was kind of lazy and jolly, laying off comfortable all day, smoking and fishing, and no books nor study. Two months or

SOLID COMFORT.

more run along, and my clothes got to be all rags and dirt, and I didn't see how I'd ever got to like it so well at the widow's, where you had to wash, and eat on a plate, and comb up, and **3** go to bed and get up regular, and be for ever bothering over a book and have old Miss Watson pecking at you all the time. I didn't want to go back no more. I had stopped cussing, because the widow didn't like it; but now I took to it again because pap hadn't no objections. It was pretty good times up in the woods there, take it all around.

But by-and-by pap got too handy with his hick'ry, and I **4** couldn't stand it. I was all over welts. He got to going away so much, too, and locking me in. Once he locked me in and was gone three days. It was dreadful lonesome. I judged he

2 *crossed over to the Illinois shore*. That side of the Mississippi River was out of the jurisdiction of "St. Petersburg" (Hannibal), Missouri.

3 *comb up*. Make oneself neat, spruce up.

4 *too handy with his hick'ry*. Too quick to administer a beating; children were then often whipped by their parents and teachers with the hickory stick.

5 *allowed*. Or "'lowed," meaning "guessed" in the Northern and Middle States, "reckoned" in the South; it has no kinship to the usual meaning of "allowed."

6 *a considerable parcel of people*. A particularly large number of people.

7 *I reckoned I wouldn't stay on hand till he got that chance*. Huck, who has so easily shed the widow's influences, has so quickly regressed to his old ways; and although he prefers the freedom of the wilderness to the confines of the "sivilizing" town, Huck decides to run away only when his life is threatened. He has now denied the guardianship of both the widow and his father.

8 *an old book and two newspapers for wadding*. At this time, paper was often made of rags and could be used in the packing of powder and shot in rifles.

9 *tow*. Rope made from broken strands of flax or hemp.

had got drowned and I wasn't ever going to get out any more. I was scared. I made up my mind I would fix up some way to leave there. I had tried to get out of that cabin many a time, but I couldn't find no way. There warn't a window to it big enough for a dog to get through. I couldn't get up the chimbly, it was too narrow. The door was thick solid oak slabs. Pap was pretty careful not to leave a knife or anything in the cabin when he was away; I reckon I had hunted the place over as much as a hundred times; well, I was most all the time at it, because it was about the only way to put in the time. But this time I found something at last; I found an old rusty wood-saw without any handle; it was laid in between a rafter and the clapboards of the roof. I greased it up and went to work. There was an old horse-blanket nailed against the logs at the far end of the cabin behind the table, to keep the wind from blowing through the chinks and putting the candle out. I got under the table and raised the blanket and went to work to saw a section of the big bottom log out, big enough to let me through. Well, it was a good long job, but I was getting towards the end of it when I heard pap's gun in the woods. I got rid of the signs of my work, and dropped the blanket and hid my saw, and pretty soon pap come in.

Pap warn't in a good humor—so he was his natural self. He said he was down to town, and everything was going wrong. His lawyer said he reckoned he would win his lawsuit and get the money, if they ever got started on the trial; but then there was ways to put it off a long time, and Judge Thatcher

5 knowed how to do it. And he said people allowed there'd be another trial to get me away from him and give me to the widow for my guardian, and they guessed it would win, this time. This shook me up considerable, because I didn't want to go back to the widow's any more and be so cramped up, and sivilized, as they called it. Then the old man got to cussing, and cussed everything and everybody he could think of, and then cussed them all over again to make sure he hadn't skipped any, and after that he polished off with a kind of a general cuss

6 all round, including a considerable parcel of people which he didn't know the names of, and so called them what's-his-name, when he got to them, and went right along with his cussing.

He said he would like to see the widow get me. He said he would watch out, and if they tried to come any such game on him he knowed of a place six or seven mile off, to stow me in, where they might hunt till they dropped and they couldn't find me. That made me pretty uneasy again, but only for a

7 minute; I reckoned I wouldn't stay on hand till he got that chance.

The old man made me go to the skiff and fetch the things he had got. There was a fifty-pound sack of corn meal, and a side of bacon, ammunition, and a four-gallon jug of whisky,

8 and an old book and two newspapers for wadding, besides some

9 tow. I toted up a load, and went back and set down on the bow of the skiff to rest. I thought it all over, and I reckoned

THINKING IT OVER.

10 *A body would a thought he was Adam, he was just all mud*. Huck is making a joke of Genesis 1:8 which tells how God created Adam out of the dust of the earth.

11 *The law backs that old Judge Thatcher up and helps him to keep me out o' my property*. At this time, under the law, a child's property belonged to his parents, but because he suspected pap's return, Huck wisely transferred it to Judge Thatcher's keeping.

I would walk off with the gun and some lines, and take to the woods when I run away. I guessed I wouldn't stay in one place, but just tramp right across the country, mostly night times, and hunt and fish to keep alive, and so get so far away that the old man nor the widow couldn't ever find me any more. I judged I would saw out and leave that night if pap got drunk enough, and I reckoned he would. I got so full of it I didn't notice how long I was staying, till the old man hollered and asked me whether I was asleep or drownded.

I got the things all up to the cabin, and then it was about dark. While I was cooking supper the old man took a swig or two and got sort of warmed up, and went to ripping again. He had been drunk over in town, and laid in the gutter all night, and he was a sight to look at. A body would a thought **10** he was Adam, he was just all mud. Whenever his liquor begun to work, he most always went for the govment. This time he says:

"Call this a govment! why, just look at it and see what it's like. Here's the law a-standing ready to take a man's son away from him—a man's own son, which he has had all the trouble and all the anxiety and all the expense of raising. Yes, just as that man has got that son raised at last, and ready to go to work and begin to do suthin' for *him* and give him a rest, the law up and goes for him. And they call *that* govment! That ain't all, nuther. The law backs that old Judge Thatcher up and **11** helps him to keep me out o' my property. Here's what the law does. The law takes a man worth six thousand dollars and upards, and jams him into an old trap of a cabin like this, and lets him go round in clothes that ain't fitten for a hog. They call that govment! A man can't get his rights in a govment

12 *Says I, for two cents I'd leave the blamed country and never come anear it agin.* Pap Finn expresses the arrogance of democracy. Why anyone should care whether or not he leaves the country never occurs to him, because he is convinced that he is just as important as any other citizen. Twain apparently agreed with Frederick Marryat's evaluation of the failure of the American republic. The Englishman argued that New World democracy took the power out of a few of the aristocracy and put it into the morally corrupt crowd which led to "the total extinction, or if not extinction, absolute bondage, of the aristocracy of the country, both politically and as well as socially." "There was an aristocracy at the time of the independence—not an aristocracy of title, but a much superior one," he continued in Chapter 14 of the second series of his American diaries (1840, p. 149); "an aristocracy of great, powerful, and leading men, who were looked up to and imitated; . . . but although a portion of it remains, it may be said to have been almost altogether smothered, and in society it no longer exists." Clemens identified with this American nobility; he was a descendant of the First Families of Virginia. "I am an aristocrat (in the aristocracy of the mind of achievement)," he wrote on the flyleaf of his copy of Sarah Grand's *The Heavenly Twins* (Item 195 in *Catalogue of the Library and Manuscripts of Samuel L. Clemens*, 1911), "and from my Viscountship look reverently up at all earls, marquises and dukes above me, and superciliously down upon the barons, baronets, and knights below me." He had little sympathy for the popular opinion. "Whenever you find that you are on the side of the majority," he wrote in his *Notebook* (1935, p. 393), "it is time to reform—(or to pause and reflect)."

13 *like my head was shoved up through a jint o' stove-pipe.* In Chapter 10, Huck makes the same jocular simile when he puts on the sun-bonnet.

14 *There was a free nigger there, from Ohio.* Slavery was abolished in Ohio when it became a state in 1803. In the 1840s, free Negroes did reside in Hannibal, but then only under severe restrictions. According to Donald H. Welsh in "Sam Clemens' Hannibal, 1836–1838" (*Midcontinent American Studies Journal*, Spring 1962, p. 38), a city ordinance stated that no free Negro or mulatto could remain within the town without first securing a license from the mayor, and that to receive this permit he must have shown evidence of good moral character and behavior; then he had to pay $5 annually for the use of the city, as well as give a maximum bond of $1,000 for his good conduct. Also, any unlicensed Negro without proof of freedom could be jailed as a runaway. Obviously the only free Negroes who could reside in the town had to be of both the social and financial status of this college professor.

15 *a mulatter, most as white as a white man.* Being "persons of color," mulattoes under Southern law were equal to Negroes. In his advance sheets of the novel which he used in preparing his 1884–1885 lecture tour (and which are now in the Mark Twain Papers in the University of California at Berkeley), Twain enriched the humor of this statement by

like this. Sometimes I've a mighty notion to just leave the country for good and all. Yes, and I *told* 'em so; I told old Thatcher so to his face. Lots of 'em heard me, and can tell **12** what I said. Says I, for two cents I'd leave the blamed country and never come anear it agin. Them's the very words. I says, look at my hat—if you call it a hat—but the lid raises up and the rest of it goes down till it's below my chin, and then it ain't **13** rightly a hat at all, but more like my head was shoved up through a jint o' stove-pipe. Look at it, says I—such a hat for me to wear—one of the wealthiest men in this town, if I could git my rights.

"Oh, yes, this is a wonderful govment, wonderful. Why, **14,15** looky here. There was a free nigger there, from Ohio; a mulatter, most as white as a white man. He had the whitest shirt on you ever see, too, and the shiniest hat; and there ain't a man in that town that's got as fine clothes as what he had; and he had a gold watch and chain, and a silver-headed **16** cane—the awfullest old grey-headed nabob in the State. And **17** what do you think? they said he was a p'fessor in a college, and could talk all kinds of languages, and knowed everything. And that ain't the wust. They said he could *vote*, when he **18** was at home. Well, that let me out. Thinks I, what is the country a-coming to? It was 'lection day, and I was just about to go and vote, myself, if I warn't too drunk to get there; but when they told me there was a State in this country where they'd let that nigger vote, I drawed out. I says I'll never vote agin. Them's the very words I said; they all heard me; and the country may rot for all me—I'll never vote agin as long as I live. And to see the cool way of that nigger—why, he wouldn't a give me the road if I hadn't shoved him out o' the way. I says to the people, why ain't this nigger put up at auction and sold?—that's what I want to know. And what do **19** you reckon they said? Why, they said he couldn't be sold till he'd been in the State six months, and he hadn't been there that long yet. There, now—that's a specimen. They call that a govment that can't sell a free nigger till he's been in the State six months. Here's a govment that calls itself a govment, and lets on to be a govment, and thinks it is a govment, and yet's got to set stock-still for six whole months before it can take ahold of a prowling, thieving, infernal, white-shirted free nigger, and——"

Pap was agoing on so, he never noticed where his old limber **20** legs was taking him to, so he went head over heels over the **21** tub of salt pork, and barked both shins, and the rest of his speech was all the hottest kind of language—mostly hove at the nigger and the govment, though he give the tubs some, too, all along, here and there. He hopped around the cabin considerable, first on one leg and then on the other, holding first one shin and then the other one, and at last he let out with his left foot all of a sudden and fetched the tub a rattling kick. But it warn't good judgment, because that was the boot that had a couple of his toes leaking out of the front end of it;

changing it to "most as white as I'd be—if I was washed" (MTP). Again Twain is attacking the absurdity of judging a person's character by his color and his appearance.

16 *nabob.* A prominent member of the community.

A nabob. Illustration from *Roughing It*, 1872.

17 *they said he was a p'fessor in a college. . . . And that ain't the wust. They said he could* vote, *when he was at home.* Pap Finn expresses the then commonly held view throughout the South that not all men were created equal and thus they did not all deserve the same rights under the law. Twain, however, believed that intelligence, and not race, should determine one's right to vote. In his lecture "Universal Suffrage," delivered on February 15, 1875 (and discussed by Blair in *Mark Twain and Huck Finn*, p. 132), Twain disapproved of equating the vote of "a consummate scoundrel" with that of "a president, a bishop, a college professor, a merchant prince." In his study of Utopia, the article "The Curious Republic of Gondour" (*The Atlantic Monthly*, October 1875), Twain agreed that universal suffrage, giving "every citizen, however poor or ignorant," one vote, should be preserved, "but if a man possessed a good common-school education and no money, he had two votes; a high school education gave him four; if he had property likewise, to the value of three thousand *sacos*, he wielded one more vote; for every fifty thousand sacos a man added to his property, he was entitled to another vote; a university education entitled a man to nine votes, even if he owned no property." Twain suffered from the nineteenth-century misassumption that wealth and education were the natural rewards of superior intelligence. Therefore, in Gondour, "learning being more prevalent and more easily acquired than riches, educated men became a wholesome check upon wealthy men, since they could outvote them. Learning goes usually with uprightness, broad views, and humanity; so the

learned voters, possessing the balance of power, became the vigilant and efficient protectors of the great lower rank of society." Thus, one is to suppose that the mulatto college professor is more worthy of his right to vote than is Pap Finn. Unfortunately, Twain suffers from the same twisted reasoning as does Pap: While the squatter hates the gentleman from Ohio for his race, the writer admires him for his social achievement. Neither has judged him by the quality of his character.

18 *Thinks I, what is the country a-coming to?* But why does Pap Finn so hate this man? Why is he, a poor white, so in favor of slavery, which does not benefit him? "That this sentiment should exist among slave-owners," Twain explained in an 1895 notebook entry (quoted by Philip S. Foner, *Mark Twain: Social Critic*, 1958, pp. 206–207), "is comprehensible—there were good commercial reasons for it—but that it should exist and did exist among the paupers, the loafers, the rag-tag and bobtail of the community, and in a passionate and uncompromising form, is not in our remote day realizable. It seemed natural enough that Huck and his father the worthless loafer should feel it and approve it, though it now seems absurd." Twain's argument was that training was at fault here. Surely, as indicated by the boy's detached, uneditorialized recording of all his father's absurd remarks in this chapter, Huck has learned his attitudes toward slaves largely from Pap Finn. "It shows," Twain continued, "that that strange thing, the conscience—the unerring monitor—can be trained to approve any wild thing you *want* it to approve if you begin its education early and stick to it."

However, Twain does not recognize that the poor freemen did have reason for their resentment of their "inferiors," even if this animosity was largely caused by the white slave-owners. Ironically, because a slave was considered valuable property, he was generally treated to certain courtesies not available to other laborers. Because nothing was invested in the Irish and German immigrants, they were considered expendable (see Chapter 32, note 12). For example, at least on the steamboats, the heavier labor was often given to the immigrants while the slaves were rarely overworked, generally well fed, had limited hours, and were treated when ill or injured. Consequently, some slaves were contemptuous of their fellow white workers; "poor white trash" is said to be a term the slaves applied to their "inferiors." Such animosity between groups who do not benefit from the system and who therefore should be working together to fight its injustice persists so long as those in power provide privileges to one faction while denying them to others.

A final paradox of Pap Finn's class toward the slave was (as Twain argued in Chapter 30 of *A Connecticut Yankee in King Arthur's Court*) that "the 'poor whites' of our South who were always despised, and frequently insulted, by the slave-lords around them, and who owed their base condition simply to the presence of slavery in their midst, were yet pusillanimously ready to side with the slave-lords in all political moves for the upholding and perpetuating of slavery, and did also finally shoulder their muskets and pour out their lives in an effort to prevent the destruction of the very institution which degraded them. And there was only one redeeming feature connected with that pitiful piece of history . . . that secretly the 'poor white' did detest the slave-lord, and did feel his own shame."

19 *they said he couldn't be sold till he'd been in the State six months.* The Missouri constitution of 1820 provided that it was the responsibility of the legislature to pass laws preventing free Negroes and mulattoes from entering the state. The common assumption throughout the slave states was that the appearance of such freemen would incite the slaves to overthrow their masters. The Missouri Code of 1825 stated that any Negro traveler, even a citizen of another state and with proof of his freedom, was prohibited to stay in the state for more than six months. "De law ken sell me now," says the freed Roxy in Chapter 16 of *Pudd'nhead Wilson*, "if dey tell me to leave de State in six months en I don't go." By February 16, 1847, the law was changed to say, "No free negro or mulatto shall, under any pretext, emigrate to this State, from any other State or territory."

20 *he went head over heels over the tub of salt pork.* Twain may be reminding the reader that Pap Finn slept with the hogs in the tanyard and implying that his provisions, such as the salt pork, were stolen. However, in the advance sheets for his lecture tour, Twain wrote an entirely new incident here: ". . . so he went head over heels into a vat of molasses and was most drowned. We fished him out and stood him up: It was the first time I ever see him stuck. He couldn't say a word. Just stood there and dripped—stood there and looked oncomfortable. I never see a man look so on [comfortable] over a little thing. . . ." (MTP).

"To be stuck" was a colloquial expression for "to be speechless," making the burlesque here even more outrageous than in the original. Throughout this entire section, Pap has been anything but speechless in his incessant diatribe against "the nigger and the govment."

21 *barked both shins.* Scraped the skin off both shins.

22 *delirium tremens.* Commonly called "D.T.'s," hallucinations with loss of muscular control, peculiar to heavy drinkers. Twain revealed in Chapter 56 of *Life on the Mississippi* that the man's namesake, Jimmy Finn, "died a natural death in a tan vat, of a combination of delirium tremens and spontaneous combustion."

23 *snakes.* A common hallucination of heavy drinkers; a synonym for delirium tremens is "seeing snakes."

RAISING A HOWL.

so now he raised a howl that fairly made a body's hair raise, and down he went in the dirt, and rolled there, and held his toes; and the cussing he done then laid over anything he had ever done previous. He said so his own self, afterwards. He had heard old Sowberry Hagan in his best days, and he said it laid over him, too; but I reckon that was sort of piling it on, maybe.

After supper pap took the jug, and said he had enough

22 whisky there for two drunks and one delirium tremens. That was always his word. I judged he would be blind drunk in about an hour, and then I would steal the key, or saw myself out, one or t'other. He drank and drank, and tumbled down on his blankets, by-and-by; but luck didn't run my way. He didn't go sound asleep, but was uneasy. He groaned, and moaned, and thrashed around this way and that, for a long time. At last I got so sleepy I couldn't keep my eyes open, all I could do, and so before I knowed what I was about I was sound asleep, and the candle burning.

I don't know how long I was asleep, but all of a sudden there was an awful scream and I was up. There was pap, looking wild and skipping around every which way and yelling

23 about snakes. He said they was crawling up his legs; and then he would give a jump and scream, and say one had bit him on the cheek—but I couldn't see no snakes. He started and run round and round the cabin hollering "take him off! take him off! he's biting me on the neck!" I never see a man look so wild in the eyes. Pretty soon he was all fagged out, and fell down panting; then he rolled over and over, wonderful fast, kicking things every which way, and striking and grabbing at the air with his hands, and screaming, and saying there was devils ahold of him. He wore out, by-and-by, and laid still a while, moaning. Then he laid stiller, and didn't make a sound. I could hear the owls and the wolves, away off in the woods and it seemed terrible still. He was laying over by the corner. By-and-by he raised up, part way, and listened, with his head to one side. He says very low:

" Tramp—tramp—tramp; that's the dead; tramp—tramp —tramp; they're coming after me; but I won't go— Oh, they're here! don't touch me—don't! hands off—they're cold; let go— Oh, let a poor devil alone! "

Then he went down on all fours and crawled off begging them to let him alone, and he rolled himself up in his blanket and wallowed in under the old pine table, still a-begging; and then he went to crying. I could hear him through the blanket.

By-and-by he rolled out and jumped up on his feet looking wild, and he see me and went for me. He chased me round and round the place with a clasp-knife, calling me the Angel of Death, **24,25** and saying he would kill me, and then I couldn't come for him no more. I begged, and told him I was only Huck, but he laughed *such* a screechy laugh, and roared and cussed, and kept on chasing me up. Once when I turned short and dodged under his arm he made a grab and got me by the jacket between my shoulders, and I thought I was gone; but I slid out of the jacket quick as lightning, and saved myself. Pretty soon he was all tired out, and dropped down with his back against the door, and said he would rest a minute and then kill me. He put his knife under him, and said he would sleep and get strong, and then he would see who was who.

So he dozed off, pretty soon. By-and-by I got the old split- **26** bottom chair and clumb up, as easy as I could, not to make any noise, and got down the gun. I slipped the ramrod down it to make sure it was loaded, and then I laid it across the turnip barrel, pointing towards pap, and set down behind it to wait for him to stir. And how slow and still the time did drag along.

24 *a clasp-knife.* A knife with a large blade that folds into the handle.

25 *the Angel of Death.* It was believed in this part of the country that once this spirit has appeared before someone, he will soon die. Although Pap Finn has earlier berated his son's possibly "getting religion," he nevertheless has a sense of Heaven and Hell. This seems to be an example of there being "no atheists in a foxhole."

26 *split-bottom chair.* Splint-bottomed chair, a home-made chair with a cane seat.

1 *palavering.* Jabbering, from the Spanish term *palabra*, "words."

CHAPTER VII.

"GIT UP."

Git up! what you 'bout!"

I opened my eyes and looked around, trying to make out where I was. It was after sun-up, and I had been sound asleep. Pap was standing over me, looking sour—and sick, too. He says—

"What you doin' with this gun?"

I judged he didn't know nothing about what he had been doing, so I says:

"Somebody tried to get in, so I was laying for him."

"Why didn't you roust me out?"

"Well, I tried to, but I couldn't; I couldn't budge you."

1 "Well, all right. Don't stand there palavering all day, but out with you and see if there's a fish on the lines for breakfast. I'll be along in a minute."

He unlocked the door and I cleared out, up the river bank. I noticed some pieces of limbs and such things floating down, and a sprinkling of bark; so I knowed the river had begun to rise. I reckoned I would have great times, now, if I was over at the town. The June rise used to be always luck for me; **2** because as soon as that rise begins, here comes cord-wood float- **3** ing down, and pieces of log rafts—sometimes a dozen logs together; so all you have to do is to catch them and sell them to the wood yards and the sawmill.

I went along up the bank with one eye out for pap and t'other one out for what the rise might fetch along. Well, all at once, here comes a canoe; just a beauty, too, about thirteen or fourteen foot long, riding high like a duck. I shot head first off of the bank, like a frog, clothes and all on, and struck out for the canoe. I just expected there'd be somebody laying down in it, because people often done that to fool folks, and when a chap had pulled a skiff out most to it they'd raise up and laugh at him. But it warn't so this time. It was a drift-canoe, sure enough, and I clumb in and paddled her ashore. Thinks I, the old man will be glad when he sees this—she's worth ten dollars. But when I got to shore pap wasn't in sight yet, and as I was running her into a little creek like a gully, all hung over with vines and willows, I struck another idea; I judged I'd hide her good, and then, stead of taking to the woods when I run off, I'd go down the river about fifty mile and camp in one place for good, and not have such a rough time tramping on foot.

It was pretty close to the shanty, and I thought I heard the old man coming, all the time; but I got her hid; and then I out and looked around a bunch of willows, and there was the old man down the path apiece just drawing a bead on **4** a bird with his gun. So he hadn't seen anything.

THE SHANTY.

When he got along, I was hard at it taking up a " trot " **5** line. He abused me a little for being so slow, but I told him I fell in the river and that was what made me so long. I knowed he would see I was wet, and then he would be asking questions. We got five cat-fish off of the lines and went home.

2 *June rise.* The spring flooding of the river, when (Twain explained in "Indiantown" in *Which Was the Dream?*, p. 154) "the snows melted in the mountains at the head waters of the mighty Missouri river some thousands of miles to the north and west and delivered the results into the Mississippi."

The Mississippi River at low water.

The same scene during the June rise. Illustrations from *Harper's Monthly*, December 1855.

3 *cord-wood.* Wood for fuel; a cord is a stack, eight feet long by four feet high, each billet of the pile being four feet wide.

Illustration from *Harper's Monthly*, December 1855.

4 *drawing a bead on a bird with his gun.* Taking aim at the bird, by gradually raising the front sight, or "bead," to a level with the hindsight of the rifle.

5 *a "trot" line.* "A very long fishing-line attached to the shore at one end and permanently anchored in the water at the other. Little gangs or branch lines are attached to it at frequent intervals, and each of these has a hook at the end of it. Usually the line is examined every day by drawing a boat along under the line, which passes over the boat and falls back into the water. The fish are thus removed from the hooks, which are baited again" (Edward Eggleston in a note to the 1890 edition of *The Hoosier School-Boy*, p. 83).

A "trot" line. Illustration from *Every Saturday*, September 30, 1871. *Courtesy the Library of Congress.*

While we laid off, after breakfast, to sleep up, both of us being about wore out, I got to thinking that if I could fix up some way to keep pap and the widow from trying to follow me, it would be a certainer thing than trusting to luck to get far enough off before they missed me; you see, all kinds of things might happen. Well, I didn't see no way for a while, but by-and-by pap raised up a minute, to drink another barrel of water, and he says:

"Another time a man comes a-prowling round here, you roust me out, you hear? That man warn't here for no good. I'd a shot him. Next time, you roust me out, you hear?"

Then he dropped down and went to sleep again—but what he had been saying give me the very idea I wanted. I says to myself, I can fix it now so nobody won't think of following me.

About twelve o'clock we turned out and went along up the bank. The river was coming up pretty fast, and lots of driftwood going by on the rise. By-and-by, along comes part of a log raft—nine logs fast together. We went out with the skiff and towed it ashore. Then we had dinner. Anybody but pap would a waited and seen the day through, so as to catch more stuff; but that warn't pap's style. Nine logs was enough for one time; he must shove right over to town and sell. So he locked me in and took the skiff and started off towing the raft about half-past three. I judged he wouldn't come back that night. I waited till I reckoned he had got a good start, then I out with my saw and went to work on that log again. Before he was t'other side of the river I was out of the hole; him and his raft was just a speck on the water away off yonder.

I took the sack of corn meal and took it to where the canoe was hid, and shoved the vines and branches apart and put it in; then I done the same with the side of bacon; then the whisky jug; I took all the coffee and sugar there was, and all the ammunition; I took the wadding; I took the bucket and gourd, I took a dipper and a tin cup, and my old saw and two blankets, and the skillet and the coffee-pot. I took fish-lines and matches and other things—everything that was worth a cent. I cleaned out the place. I wanted an axe, but there wasn't any, only the one out at the wood pile, and I knowed why I was going to leave that. I fetched out the gun, and now I was done.

I had wore the ground a good deal, crawling out of the hole and dragging out so many things. So I fixed that as good as I could from the outside by scattering dust on the place, which covered up the smoothness and the sawdust. Then I fixed the piece of log back into its place, and put two rocks under it and one against it to hold it there,—for it was bent up at that place, and didn't quite touch ground. If you stood four or five foot away and didn't know it was sawed, you wouldn't ever notice it; and besides, this was the back of the cabin and it warn't likely anybody would go fooling around there.

It was all grass clear to the canoe; so I hadn't left a track.

I followed around to see. I stood on the bank and looked out over the river. All safe. So I took the gun and went up a piece into the woods and was hunting around for some birds, when I see a wild pig; hogs soon went wild in them bottoms **6** after they had got away from the prairie farms. I shot this fellow and took him into camp.

SHOOTING THE PIG.

I took the axe and smashed in the door. I beat it and hacked it considerable, a-doing it. I fetched the pig in and took him back nearly to the table and hacked into his throat with the axe, and laid him down on the ground to bleed—I say ground, because it *was* ground—hard packed, and no boards. Well, next I took an old sack and put a lot of big rocks in it,— all I could drag—and I started it from the pig and dragged it to the door and through the woods down to the river and dumped it in, and down it sunk, out of sight. You could easy see that something had been dragged over the ground. I did wish Tom **7** Sawyer was there, I knowed he would take an interest in this kind of business, and throw in the fancy touches. Nobody could spread himself like Tom Sawyer in such a thing as that. **8**

Well, last I pulled out some of my hair, and bloodied the axe good, and stuck it on the back side, and slung the axe in the corner. Then I took up the pig and held him to my breast with my jacket (so he couldn't drip) till I got a good piece below the house and then dumped him into the river. Now I thought of something else. So I went and got the bag of meal and my old saw out of the canoe and fetched them to the house. I took the bag to where it used to stand, and ripped a hole in the bottom of it with the saw, for there warn't no knives and forks on the place—pap done everything with his clasp-knife, about the cooking. Then I carried the sack about a hundred yards across the grass and through the willows east of the house, to a shallow lake that was five miles wide and full of rushes—and ducks too,

6 *bottoms.* Or "bottomlands," Western term for the rich flatlands along the banks of rivers.

7 *I did wish Tom Sawyer was there.* Although he had earlier in Chapter 3 rejected his friend's wild fantasies, Huck nevertheless venerates Tom in much the same manner that Tom envied Huck in *Tom Sawyer.* Nevertheless, practical Huck has proven that he is perfectly capable of thinking for himself without the aid of Tom's "fancy touches."

8 *spread himself.* Exert or display oneself ostentatiously.

9 *a slough*. A comparatively narrow stretch of back-water; a sluggish channel or inlet.

10 *they'll . . . drag the river for me*. "At the end of two or more lines," Hyatt described this procedure in *Folk-Lore of Adams County, Illinois* (p. 696), "grapnel or similar hooks are attached, and these are sometimes weighted by pieces of iron pipe slipped through the lines."

11 *They won't ever hunt the river for anything but my dead carcass*. This is the first of Huck's "deaths."

12 *Jackson's Island*. The refuge of Tom Sawyer's gang of "pirates" in Chapters 13–16 of *Tom Sawyer*; appropriately, Huck returns to the scene of his previous escape from "sivilization" when he and his companions were thought dead. This place was Glassock's Island, a deserted spot on the river opposite Hannibal, which has since been eroded away by the Mississippi. For Twain, it remained a mythical asylum from the strains of life. He confessed to Walter Besant on February 22, 1898 (in a letter now in the Berg Collection of the New York Public Library), "I suppose we all have a Jackson's Island somewhere, and dream of it when we are tired."

13 *the easy water*. "Not much current," Twain noted in Chapter 9 of *Life on the Mississippi*.

9 you might say, in the season. There was a slough or a creek leading out of it on the other side, that went miles away, I don't know where, but it didn't go to the river. The meal sifted out and made a little track all the way to the lake. I dropped pap's whetstone there too, so as to look like it had been done by accident. Then I tied up the rip in the meal sack with a string, so it wouldn't leak no more, and took it and my saw to the canoe again.

It was about dark, now; so I dropped the canoe down the river under some willows that hung over the bank, and waited for the moon to rise. I made fast to a willow; then I took a bite to eat, and by-and-by laid down in the canoe to smoke a **10** pipe and lay out a plan. I says to myself, they'll follow the track of that sackful of rocks to the shore and then drag the river for me. And they'll follow that meal track to the lake and go browsing down the creek that leads out of it to find the **11** robbers that killed me and took the things. They won't ever hunt the river for anything but my dead carcass. They'll soon get tired of that, and won't bother no more about me. All right; I can stop anywhere I want to. Jackson's Island is good enough for me; I know that island pretty well, and nobody ever comes there. And then I can paddle over to town, nights, **12** and slink around and pick up things I want. Jackson's Island's the place.

I was pretty tired, and the first thing I knowed, I was asleep. When I woke up I didn't know where I was, for a minute. I set up and looked around, a little scared. Then I remembered. The river looked miles and miles across. The moon was so bright I could a counted the drift logs that went a slipping along, black and still, hundreds of yards out from shore. Everything was dead quiet, and it looked late, and *smelt* late. You know what I mean—I don't know the words to put it in.

I took a good gap and a stretch, and was just going to unhitch and start, when I heard a sound away over the water. I listened. Pretty soon I made it out. It was that dull kind of a regular sound that comes from oars working in rowlocks when it's a still night. I peeped out through the willow branches, and there it was—a skiff, away across the water. I couldn't tell how many was in it. It kept a-coming, and when it was abreast of me I see there warn't but one man in it. Thinks I, maybe it's pap, though I warn't expecting him. He dropped below me, with the current, and by-and-by he come a-swinging **13** up shore in the easy water, and he went by so close I could a reached out the gun and touched him. Well, it *was* pap, sure enough—and sober, too, by the way he laid to his oars.

I didn't lose no time. The next minute I was a-spinning down stream soft but quick in the shade of the bank. I made two mile and a half, and then struck out a quarter of a mile or more towards the middle of the river, because pretty soon I would be passing the ferry landing and people might see me and hail me. I got out amongst the drift-wood and then laid

14 *the dead water.* Calm, without any current.

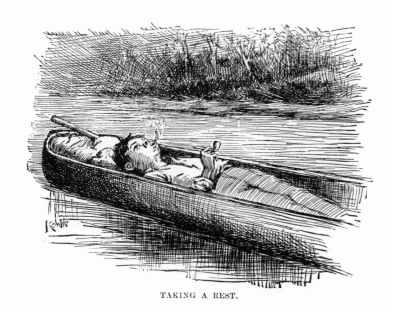

TAKING A REST.

down in the bottom of the canoe and let her float. I laid there and had a good rest and a smoke out of my pipe, looking away into the sky, not a cloud in it. The sky looks ever so deep when you lay down on your back in the moonshine; I never knowed it before. And how far a body can hear on the water such nights! I heard people talking at the ferry landing. I heard what they said, too, every word of it. One man said it was getting towards the long days and the short nights, now. T'other one said *this* warn't one of the short ones, he reckoned —and then they laughed, and he said it over again, and they laughed again; then they waked up another fellow and told him, and laughed, but he didn't laugh; he ripped out something brisk and said let him alone. The first fellow said he 'lowed to tell it to his old woman—she would think it was pretty good; but he said that warn't nothing to some things he had said in his time. I heard one man say it was nearly three o'clock, and he hoped daylight wouldn't wait more than about a week longer. After that, the talk got further and further away, and I couldn't make out the words any more, but I could hear the mumble; and now and then a laugh, too, but it seemed a long ways off.

I was away below the ferry now. I rose up and there was Jackson's Island, about two mile and a half down stream, heavy-timbered and standing up out of the middle of the river, big and dark and solid, like a steamboat without any lights. There warn't any signs of the bar at the head—it was all under water now.

It didn't take me long to get there. I shot past the head at a ripping rate, the current was so swift, and then I got into the dead water and landed on the side towards the Illinois **14** shore. I run the canoe into a deep dent in the bank that I knowed about; I had to part the willow branches to get in; and when I made fast nobody could a seen the canoe from the outside.

15 *stabboard*. Or "starboard," the right-hand side of
the vessel.

I went up and set down on a log at the head of the island
and looked out on the big river and the black driftwood, and
away over to the town, three mile away, where there was three
or four lights twinkling. A monstrous big lumber raft was
about a mile up stream, coming along down, with a lantern in
the middle of it. I watched it come creeping down, and when
it was most abreast of where I stood I heard a man say, " Stern
15 oars, there! heave her head to stabboard ! " I heard that just
as plain as if the man was by my side.

There was a little gray in the sky, now; so I stepped into
the woods and laid down for a nap before breakfast.

Chapter VIII.

IN THE WOODS.

The sun was up so high when I waked, that I judged it was after eight o'clock. I laid there in the grass and the cool shade, thinking about things and feeling rested and ruther comfortable and satisfied. I could see the sun out at one or two holes, but mostly it was big trees all about, and gloomy in there amongst them. There was freckled places on the ground where the light sifted down through the leaves, and the freckled places swapped about a little, showing there was a little breeze up there. A couple of squirrels set on a limb and jabbered at me very friendly.

I was powerful lazy and comfortable—didn't want to get up and cook breakfast. Well, I was dozing off again, when I thinks I hears a deep sound of "boom!" away up the river. I rouses up and rests on my elbow and listens; pretty soon I hears it again. I hopped up and went and looked out at a hole in the leaves, and I see a bunch of smoke laying on the water a long ways up—about abreast the ferry. And there was the ferry-boat full of people, floating along down. I knowed what was the matter, now. "Boom!" I see the white smoke squirt out of the ferry-boat's side. You see, they was firing cannon **1** over the water, trying to make my carcass come to the top.

1 *they was firing cannon over the water, trying to make my carcass come to the top.* It was a common British superstition that the concussion from the explosion would break the gall bladder, thus causing the body to float. Once when he was thought to be drowned, young Sam Clemens witnessed a similar scene as the townspeople of Hannibal fired cannon over the water to raise him to the surface. "I jumped overboard from the ferryboat in the middle of the river that stormy day to get my hat," he recalled in a letter of February 6, 1870 (*Mark Twain's Letters to Will Bowen*, 1941, p. 19), "and swam two or three miles after it (and *got* it), while all the town collected on the wharf and for an hour or so looked out across . . . toward where people said Sam Clemens was last seen before he went down." Twain repeated this incident in Chapter 14 of *Tom Sawyer* when Huck, Tom, and Joe Harper have run off to Jackson's Island to play pirates.

Evidently it was a foregone conclusion along the river that if someone were missing, he obviously had drowned and sunk to the bottom. "There was a foolish superstition of some little prevalence in that day," Twain explained in a note to Chapter 27 of *Life on the Mississippi*, "that the Mississippi would neither buoy up a swimmer, nor permit a drowned person's body to rise to the surface."

The search for the drowned. Illustration by True W. Williams, *The Adventures of Tom Sawyer*, 1876.

2 *they always put quicksilver in loaves of bread and float them off because they always go right to the drownded carcass and stop there.* There was another British superstition that a hollowed-out loaf of bread, filled with mercury (which is insoluble in water) and which has been blessed, would float above where the body lay. H. M. Belden in "Scyld Scefing and Huck Finn" (*Modern Language Notes*, May 1918, p. 315) traced this practice to an ancient British rite of divinition by shield, sheaf, and candle: "It is precisely the bread, the staff of life, the modern representative of the medieval sheaf, by which the divination is wrought. The quicksilver in place of the candle seems to be the case of metallurgy displacing medieval devotion." However, in Chapter 14 of *Tom Sawyer*, Tom argues that it is the blessing, not the bread, which makes it work: "'Oh, it ain't the bread so much,' said Tom; 'I reckon it's mostly what they *say* over it before they start it out.' 'But they don't say anything over it,' said Huck. 'I've seen 'em, and they don't.' 'Well, that's funny,' said Tom. 'But maybe they say it to themselves. Of *course* they do. Anybody might know that.' The other boys agreed that there was reason in what Tom said, because an ignorant lump of bread, uninstructed by an incantation, could not be expected to act very intelligently when sent upon an errand of such gravity."

Most likely the bread received its blessing on land, probably with benefit of clergy.

3 *A big double loaf come along, and I . . . set my teeth in.* Apparently Twain is playing with Ecclesiastes 11:1: "Cast thy bread upon the waters: for thou shalt find it after many days." This reference is more evident in a passage in his notes for the novel which did not make it into the final book: "And bread cast *returns*—which it don't and can't, less'n you heave it up-stream—you cast your bread downstream once, and see. It can't stem the current; so, it can't come back no more. But the widow she didn't know no better than to believe it, and it warn't my business to correct my betters. There's a heap of ignorance like that, around" (quoted by DeVoto, *Mark Twain at Work*, p. 75). Possibly this observation was intended as an alternate lesson to the Widow Douglas's instruction of Moses and the bullrushes to foreshadow this floating of the bread filled with quicksilver.

I was pretty hungry, but it warn't going to do for me to start a fire, because they might see the smoke. So I set there and watched the cannon-smoke and listened to the boom. The river was a mile wide, there, and it always looks pretty on a summer morning—so I was having a good enough time seeing

WATCHING THE BOAT.

them hunt for my remainders, if I only had a bite to eat. **2** Well, then I happened to think how they always put quicksilver in loaves of bread and float them off because they always go right to the drownded carcass and stop there. So says I, I'll keep a look-out, and if any of them's floating around after me, I'll give them a show. I changed to the Illinois edge of the island to see what luck I could have, and I warn't disappointed. **3** A big double loaf come along, and I most got it, with a long stick, but my foot slipped and she floated out further. Of course I was where the current set in the closest to the shore—I knowed enough for that. But by-and-by along comes another one, and this time I won. I took out the plug and shook out the little dab of quicksilver, and set my teeth in. It was **4, 5** "baker's bread"—what the quality eat—none of your low-down corn-pone.

I got a good place amongst the leaves, and set there on a log, munching the bread and watching the ferry-boat, and very well satisfied. And then something struck me. I says, now I reckon the widow or the parson or somebody prayed that this bread would find me, and here it has gone and done it. So there ain't no doubt but there is something in that thing.

That is, there's something in it when a body like the widow or the parson prays, but it don't work for me, and I reckon it don't work for only just the right kind.

I lit a pipe and had a good long smoke and went on watching. The ferry-boat was floating with the current, and I allowed I'd have a chance to see who was aboard when she come along, because she would come in close, where the bread did. When she'd got pretty well along down towards me, I put out my pipe and went to where I fished out the bread, and laid down behind a log on the bank in a little open place. Where the log forked I could peep through.

By-and-by she come along, and she drifted in so close that they could a run out a plank and walked ashore. Most every-body was on the boat. Pap, and Judge Thatcher, and Bessie Thatcher, and Jo Harper, and Tom Sawyer, and his old Aunt Polly, and Sid and Mary, and plenty more. Everybody was talking about the murder, but the captain broke in and says:

"Look sharp, now; the current sets in the closest here, and maybe he's washed ashore and got tangled amongst the brush at the water's edge. I hope so, anyway."

I didn't hope so. They all crowded up and leaned over the rails, nearly in my face, and kept still, watching with all their might. I could see them first-rate, but they couldn't see me. Then the captain sung out:

"Stand away!" and the cannon let off such a blast right before me that it made me deef with the noise and pretty near blind with the smoke, and I judged I was gone. If they'd a had some bullets in, I reckon they'd a got the corpse they was after. Well, I see I warn't hurt, thanks to goodness. The boat floated on and went out of sight around the shoulder of the island. I could hear the booming, now and then, further and further off, and by-and-by after an hour, I didn't hear it no more. The island was three mile long. I judged they had got to the foot, and was giving it up. But they didn't yet a-while. They turned around the foot of the island and started up the channel on the Missouri side, under steam, and booming once in a while as they went. I crossed over to that side and watched them. When they got abreast the head of the island they quit shooting and dropped over to the Missouri shore and **8** went home to the town.

I knowed I was all right now. Nobody else would come a-hunting after me. I got my traps out of the canoe and made **9** me a nice camp in the thick woods. I made a kind of a tent out of my blankets to put my things under so the rain couldn't get at them. I catched a cat-fish and haggled him open with my saw, and towards sundown I started my camp fire and had supper. Then I set out a line to catch some fish for breakfast.

When it was dark I set by my camp fire smoking, and feeling pretty satisfied; but by-and-by it got sort of lonesome, and so I went and set on the bank and listened to the currents washing along, and counted the stars and drift-logs and rafts

4 *"baker's bread."* Or "store-bought bread," made from white wheat flour, then a luxury.

5 *your low-down corn-pone.* Corn meal mixed with a tablespoon of salt and water, then baked in a skillet or small oven. This Indian dish (*pone* is Indian for corn) was particularly meager fare. "Corn pone . . . , a very good thing of its kind for ostriches," complained Frederick L. Olmstead in *The Cotton Kingdom* (1861), "is not bread."

6 *Most everybody was on the boat.* Actually, almost the entire cast of *Tom Sawyer*. Huck seems to be sym-bolically saying goodbye to his past, both to St. Petersburg and to the former novel.

7 *Bessie Thatcher.* Confused, Twain scribbled in his notes for the novel, "'Bessie' or 'Becky'?" (quoted by DeVoto, *Mark Twain at Work*, p. 74). Carelessly, he did not bother to check *Tom Sawyer* in which Becky Thatcher is introduced as Tom Sawyer's childhood sweetheart. But no matter: Huck Finn would not necessarily have known the girl well, and he could easily have gotten her name wrong. Similarly, he misspells "Joe Harper."

Becky Thatcher. Illustration by True W. Williams, *The Adventures of Tom Sawyer*, 1876.

8 *they . . . went home to the town.* Originally, Twain intended to include Huck's "reflections upon the satisfaction of being a guest at one's own funeral and with such prime refreshments furnished free" (quoted by DeVoto, *Mark Twain at Work*, p. 74); but he dropped the idea, evidently because it is too similar to incidents in Chapter 17 of *Tom Sawyer*.

9 *traps.* Trappings, belongings.

10 *summer-grapes.* North American wild grape.

11 *They would all come handy by-and-by.* Evidently Huck intended to hide out on the island for quite some time.

12 *all of a sudden I bounded right on to the ashes of a camp fire that was still smoking.* Huck's fears on discovering the traces of other human life on his deserted island were apparently based on Daniel Defoe's *Robinson Crusoe* (1719); the hero describes similar feelings to Huck's on his discovery of "the print of a man's naked foot on the shore" of *his* island: "I stood like one thunder-struck . . . ; I listened, I looked round me, I could hear nothing, nor see . . . no other impression but that one. . . . But after inumerable fluttering thoughts, like a man perfectly confused and out of my self, I came home to my fortification, not feeling, as we say, the ground I went on, but terrify'd to the last degree, looking behind me at every two or three steps, mistaking every bush and tree, and fancying every stump at a distance to be a man; nor is it possible to describe how many various shapes affrighted imagination represented things to me in, how many wild ideas were found every moment in my fancy, and what strange unaccountable whimsies came into my thoughts by the way." See also Chapter 9, note 15.

Robinson Crusoe finds the footprint in the sand. Illustration by George Cruikshank, *The Life and Adventures of Robinson Crusoe*, 1831.

13 *there warn't much sand in my craw.* I didn't have much courage left.

that come down, and then went to bed; there ain't no better way to put in time when you are lonesome; you can't stay so, you soon get over it.

And so for three days and nights. No difference—just the same thing. But the next day I went exploring around down through the island. I was boss of it; it all belonged to me, so to say, and I wanted to know all about it; but mainly I wanted to put in the time. I found plenty strawberries, ripe and **10** prime; and green summer-grapes, and green razberries; and **11** the green blackberries was just beginning to show. They would all come handy by-and-by, I judged.

Well, I went fooling along in the deep woods till I judged I warn't far from the foot of the island. I had my gun along, but I hadn't shot nothing; it was for protection; thought I would kill some game nigh home. About this time I mighty near stepped on a good-sized snake, and it went sliding off through the grass and flowers, and I after it, trying to get a **12** shot at it. I clipped along, and all of a sudden I bounded

DISCOVERING THE CAMP FIRE.

right on to the ashes of a camp fire that was still smoking.

My heart jumped up amongst my lungs. I never waited for to look further, but uncocked my gun and went sneaking back on my tip-toes as fast as ever I could. Every now and then I stopped a second, amongst the thick leaves, and listened; but my breath come so hard I couldn't hear nothing else. I slunk along another piece further, then listened again; and so on, and so on; if I see a stump, I took it for a man; if I trod on a stick and broke it, it made me feel like a person had cut one of my breaths in two and I only got half, and the short half, too.

13   When I got to camp I warn't feeling very brash, there warn't much sand in my craw; but I says, this ain't no time to be fooling around. So I got all my traps into my canoe again so as to have them out of sight, and I put out the fire and scattered the ashes around to look like an old last year's camp, and then clumb a tree.

I reckon I was up in the tree two hours; but I didn't see nothing, I didn't hear nothing—I only *thought* I heard and seen as much as a thousand things. Well, I couldn't stay up there for ever; so at last I got down, but I kept in the thick woods and on the look-out all the time. All I could get to eat was berries and what was left over from breakfast.

By the time it was night I was pretty hungry. So when it was good and dark, I slid out from shore before moonrise and paddled over to the Illinois bank—about a quarter of a mile. I went out in the woods and cooked a supper, and I had about made up my mind I would stay there all night, when I hear a *plunkety-plunk, plunkety-plunk*, and says to myself, horses coming; and next I hear people's voices. I got everything into the canoe as quick as I could, and then went creeping through the woods to see what I could find out. I hadn't got far when I hear a man say:

"We better camp here, if we can find a good place; the horses is about beat out. Let's look around."

I didn't wait, but shoved out and paddled away easy. I tied up in the old place, and reckoned I would sleep in the canoe.

I didn't sleep much. I couldn't, somehow, for thinking. And every time I waked up I thought somebody had me by the neck. So the sleep didn't do me no good. By-and-by I says to myself, I can't live this way; I'm agoing to find out who it is that's here on the island with me; I'll find it out or bust. Well, I felt better, right off.

So I took my paddle and slid out from shore just a step or two, and then let the canoe drop along down amongst the shadows. The moon was shining, and outside of the shadows it made it most as light as day. I poked along well on to an hour, everything still as rocks and sound asleep. Well, by this time I was most down to the foot of the island. A little ripply, cool breeze begun to blow, and that was as good as saying the night was about done. I give her a turn with the paddle and brung her nose to shore; then I got my gun and slipped out and into the edge of the woods. I set down there on a log and looked out through the leaves. I see the moon go off watch and the darkness begin to blanket the river. But in a little while I see a pale streak over the tree-tops, and knowed the day was coming. So I took my gun and slipped off towards where I had run across that camp fire, stopping every minute or two to listen. But I hadn't no luck, somehow; I couldn't seem to find the place. But by-and-by, sure enough, I catched a glimpse of fire, away through the trees. I went for it, cautious and slow. By-and-by I was close enough to have a look, and there laid a man on the ground. It most give me the fan-tods. **14** He had a blanket around his head, and his head was nearly in the fire. I set there behind a clump of bushes, in about six foot of him, and kept my eyes on him steady. It was getting

14 *the fan-tods*. The fidgets.

"He bounced up and stared at me." Illustration by
E. W. Kemble, New York *World*, December 10,
1899.

15 *I hain't ever done no harm to a ghos'. . . . You go en
git in de river agin, whah you b'longs.* Because they had
not been properly buried with benefit of clergy,
ghosts of the unrecovered bodies of the drowned
were said to be restless and wander up and down the
banks of the river. "The Ancients believed that
Charon was not permitted to ferry over Ghosts of
unburied persons," Grose explained in *A Provincial
Glossary*, "but that they wandered up and down the
banks of the river Styx for an hundred years."

16 *truck*. Stuff, here market produce, "garden-
truck" or "market-truck."

JIM AND THE GHOST.

gray daylight, now. Pretty soon he gapped, and stretched
himself, and hove off the blanket, and it was Miss Watson's
Jim! I bet I was glad to see him. I says:

"Hello, Jim!" and skipped out.

He bounced up and stared at me wild. Then he drops
down on his knees, and puts his hands together and says:

15   "Doan' hurt me—don't! I hain't ever done no harm to a
ghos'. I awluz liked dead people, en done all I could for 'em.
You go en git in de river agin, whah you b'longs, en doan' do
nuffn to Ole Jim, 'at 'uz awluz yo' fren'."

Well, I warn't long making him understand I warn't dead.
I was ever so glad to see Jim. I warn't lonesome, now. I told
him I warn't afraid of *him* telling the people where I was. I
talked along, but he only set there and looked at me; never
said nothing. Then I says:

"It's good daylight. Le's get breakfast. Make up your
camp fire good."

"What's de use er makin' up de camp fire to cook strawbries en sich truck? But you got a gun, hain't you? Den we
kin git sumfn' better den strawbries."

16   "Strawberries and such truck," I says. "Is that what you
live on?"

"I couldn' git nuffn' else," he says.

"Why, how long you been on the island, Jim?"

"I come heah de night arter you's killed."

"What, all that time?"

"Yes-indeedy."

"And ain't you had nothing but that kind of rubbage to
eat?"

"No, sah—nuffn' else."

"Well, you must be most starved, ain't you?"

"I reck'n I could eat a hoss. I think I could. How long
you ben on de islan'?"

"Since the night I got killed."

"No! W'y, what has you lived on? But you got a gun?
Oh, yes, you got a gun. Dat's good. Now you kill sumfn' en
I'll make up de fire."

So we went over to where the canoe was, and while he built

a fire in a grassy open place amongst the trees, I fetched meal and bacon and coffee, and coffee-pot and frying-pan, and sugar and tin cups, and the nigger was set back considerable, because he reckoned it was all done with witchcraft. I catched a good big cat-fish, too, and Jim cleaned him with his knife, and fried him.

When breakfast was ready, we lolled on the grass and eat it smoking hot; Jim laid it in with all his might, for he was most about starved. Then when we had got pretty well stuffed, we laid off and lazied.

By-and-by Jim says:

"But looky here, Huck, who wuz it dat 'uz killed in dat shanty, ef it warn't you?"

Then I told him the whole thing, and he said it was smart. He said Tom Sawyer couldn't get up no better plan than what **17** I had. Then I says:

"How do you come to be here, Jim, and how'd you get here?"

He looked pretty uneasy, and didn't say nothing for a minute. Then he says:

"Maybe I better not tell."

"Why, Jim?"

"Well, dey's reasons. But you wouldn' tell on me ef I 'uz to tell you, would you, Huck?"

"Blamed if I would, Jim."

"Well, I b'lieve you, Huck. I—I run off."

"Jim!"

"But mind, you said you wouldn't tell—you know you said you wouldn't tell, Huck."

"Well, I did. I said I wouldn't, and I'll stick to it. Honest **18,19** injun I will. People would call me a low down Ablitionist and **20** despise me for keeping mum—but that don't make no difference. I ain't agoing to tell, and I ain't agoing back there anyways. So now, le's know all about it."

"Well, you see, its 'uz dis way. Ole Missus—dat's Miss Watson—she pecks on me all de time, en treats me pooty rough, but she awluz said she wouldn' sell me down to Orleans. But **21** I noticed dey wuz a nigger trader roun' de place considerable, **22** lately, en I begin to git oneasy. Well, one night I creeps to de do', pooty late, en de do' warn't quite shet, en I hear ole missus tell de widder she gwyne to sell me down to Orleans, but she didn' want to, but she could git eight hund'd dollars **23** for me, en it 'uz sich a big stack o' money she couldn' resis'. De widder she try to git her to say she wouldn' do it, but I never waited to hear de res'. I lit out mighty quick, I tell you.

"I tuck out en shin down de hill en 'spec to steal a skift 'long de sho' som'ers 'bove de town, but dey wuz people a-stirrin' yit, so I hid in de ole tumble-down cooper shop on de bank to wait for everybody to go 'way. Well, I wuz dah all night. Dey wuz somebody roun' all de time. 'Long 'bout six in de mawnin', skifts begin to go by, en 'bout eight er nine

17 *He said Tom Sawyer couldn't get up no better plan than what I had.* Jim shares Huck's veneration for his friend's ingenuity.

18 *I said I wouldn't, and I'll stick to it.* It was not Tom Blankenship, Twain's model for Huckleberry Finn, but rather his big brother Benson whose history is recalled in Huck's promise not to tell on Jim. According to Wecter's *Sam Clemens of Hannibal* (1952, p. 148), in the summer of 1847, ignoring a posted reward of $50 and possible conviction for aiding a fugitive, Bence befriended a runaway slave whom he came across while fishing off an island opposite Hannibal, Missouri, in Pike County, Illinois. For days, he brought food and remained silent about the man's hideout; however, some woodchoppers flushed out the slave, and he disappeared in the swamp. The Hannibal *Journal* reported on August 9: "While some of our citizens were fishing a few days since on the Sny Island, they discovered in what is called Bird Slough the body of a negro man. On examination of the body, they found it to answer the description of a negro recently advertised in handbills as a runaway from Neriam Todd, of Howard County. . . . The body when found was much mutilated." Among "our citizens" was the young Sam Clemens: Twain told Paine (*Biography*, Vol. I, p. 64) that he and some friends had been exploring the area, likely for berries or pecans, and had been pushing some dirt aside when suddenly rose the man about half length out of the water. Terrified that the dead man was after them, the boys tore back to the town.

19 *Honest* injun. Originally a sarcastic allusion to the Indians purported propensity for thievery, this term was transformed by the myth of "the noble savage," as popularized by such novelists as Chateaubriand and James Fenimore Cooper. In "Huck Finn and Tom Sawyer among the Indians" (*Mark Twain's Hannibal, Huck and Tom*, p. 94), Tom Sawyer, who has been reading such fictions, tells Huck the white man's view of the "Injun": "They're the noblest human beings that's ever been in the world. . . . if an Injun tells you a thing, you can bet on it every time for the petrified fact; because you can't get an Injun to lie, he would cut his tongue out first. If you trust to a white man's honor, you better look out; but you trust to an Injun's honor, and nothing in the world can make him betray you—he would die first, and be glad to. An Injun is *all* honor. It's what they're *made* of." Twain, however, did not concur with Tom's opinion: Soon after the boy makes this statement, a band of settlers are massacred by the Indians whom they have trusted.

20 *People would call me a low down Ablitionist and despise me for keeping mum.* The growth of the Abolitionist Movement in the 1830s called for the total abolition of human slavery and by any means possible, regardless of political results or of constitutional loyalty to slave-holders. "In those old slave-holding days," Twain wrote in his notebook in 1895 (quoted by Foner, *Mark Twain; Social Critic*, p. 206), "the whole community was agreed as to one thing—the awful sacredness of slave property. To steal a horse or a cow was a low crime, but to help a hunted slave, or feed him or shelter him, or hide him, or comfort

Abolitionists in jail in Palmyra, Missouri, 1841.
Courtesy the Library of Congress.

him, in his trouble, his terrors, his despair, or
hesitate to promptly betray him to the slave-catcher
when opportunity offered was a much baser crime,
and carried with it a stain, a moral smirch which
nothing could wipe away." Clemens said that when
he was ten years old, he saw the execution of Robert
Hardy, an abolitionist, in Marion City, a small town
near Hannibal. "People came for miles around to see
the hanging," Twain recalled (quoted by DeVoto in
Mark Twain's America, 1932, p. 64), "they brought
cakes and cider, also the women and children, and
made a picnic of the matter. It was the largest crowd
the village had ever seen. The rope that hanged
Hardy was eagerly bought up, in inch samples, for
everybody wanted a momento of the memorable
event." (However, as Frank H. Sosey has proven in
"Palmyra and Its Historical Environment," *The Missouri Historical Review*, April 1929, pp. 361–362, no
such hanging of Richard Hardy occurred in Palmyra;
either it happened somewhere else or Twain made up
the incident.)

21 *sell me down to Orleans.* "That selling to the south
is set before the negro from childhood as the last
severity of punishment," Harriet Beecher Stowe
explained in Chapter 10 of *Uncle Tom's Cabin*. "The
threat that terrifies more than whipping or torture of
any kind is the threat of being sent down river. We
have ourselves heard this feeling expressed by them,
and seen the unaffected horror with which they will
sit in their gossiping hours, and tell frightful stories
of that 'down river.'" Because Missouri slaves were
primarily household or familial servants, they feared
the horrors said to be suffered by fieldhands on the
large, overseered Southern plantations. "It was the
mild domestic slavery," Twain described the system

Sold South. *Courtesy the Library of Congress.*

every skift dat went 'long wuz talkin' 'bout how yo' pap come
over to de town en say you's killed. Dese las' skifts wuz full o'
ladies en genlmen agoin' over for to see de place. Sometimes
dey'd pull up at de sho' en take a res' b'fo' dey started acrost,
so by de talk I got to know all 'bout de killin'. I 'uz powerful
sorry you's killed, Huck, but I ain't no mo', now.

"I laid dah under de shavins all day. I 'uz hungry, but I
warn't afeared; bekase I knowed ole missus en de widder wuz
24 goin' to start to de camp-meetn' right arter breakfas' en be
gone all day, en dey knows I goes off wid de cattle 'bout daylight, so dey wouldn' 'spec to see me roun' de place, en so dey
wouldn' miss me tell arter dark in de evenin'. De yuther
servants wouldn' miss me, kase dey'd shin out en take holiday,
soon as de ole folks 'uz out'n de way.

"Well, when it come dark I tuck out up de river road, en
went 'bout two mile er more to whah dey warn't no houses. I'd
made up my mine 'bout what I's agwyne to do. You see ef I
kep' on tryin' to git away afoot, de dogs 'ud track me; ef I
stole a skift to cross over, dey'd miss dat skift, you see, en
dey'd know 'bout whah I'd lan' on de yuther side en whah to
pick up my track. So I says, a raff is what I's arter; it doan'
make no track.

"I see a light a-comin' roun' de p'int, bymeby, so I wade' in
en shove' a log ahead o' me, en swum more'n half-way acrost de
river, en got in 'mongst de drift-wood, en kep' my head down
low, en kinder swum agin de current tell de raff come along.
Den I swum to de stern uv it, en tuck aholt. It clouded up
en 'uz pooty dark for a little while. So I clumb up en laid down
on de planks. De men 'uz all 'way yonder in de middle, whah
de lantern wuz. De river wuz arisin' en dey wuz a good current;
so I reck'n'd 'at by fo' in de mawnin' I'd be twenty-five mile
25 down de river, en den I'd slip in, jis' b'fo' daylight, en swim
asho' en take to de woods on de Illinoi side.

"But I didn' have no luck. When we 'uz mos' down to de
head er de islan', a man begin to come aft wid de lantern. I
see it warn't no use fer to wait, so I slid overboard, en struck
out fer de islan'. Well, I had a notion I could lan' mos' any-
whers, but I couldn't—bank too bluff. I 'uz mos' to de foot er
de islan' b'fo' I foun' a good place. I went into de woods en
jedged I wouldn' fool wid raffs no mo', long as dey move de
26 lantern roun' so. I had my pipe en a plug er dog-leg, en some
matches in my cap, en dey warn't wet, so I 'uz all right."

"And so you ain't had no meat nor bread to eat all this
time? Why didn't you get mud-turkles?"

"How you gwyne to git'm? You can't slip up on um en
grab um; en how's a body gwyne to hit um wid a rock? How
could a body do it in de night? en I warn't gwyne to show
mysef on de bank in de daytime."

"Well, that's so. You've had to keep in de woods all the
time, of course. Did you hear 'em shooting the cannon?"

"Oh, yes. I knowed dey was arter you. I see um go by
heah; watched um thoo de bushes."

Some young birds come along, flying a yard or two at a

time and lighting.   Jim said it was a sign it was going to rain.
He said it was a sign when young chickens flew that way, and **27**
so he reckoned it was the same way when young birds done it.
I was going to catch some of them, but Jim wouldn't let me.
He said it was death.   He said his father lay mighty sick once,
and some of them catched a bird, and his old granny said his **28**
father would die, and he did.

And Jim said you musn't count the things you are going to **29**
cook for dinner, because that would bring bad luck.   The same
if you shook the tablecloth after sundown.   And he said if a **30**
man owned a bee-hive, and that man died, the bees must be
told about it before sun-up next morning, or else the bees
would all weaken down and quit work and die.   Jim said bees **31**
wouldn't sting idiots; but I didn't believe that, because I had
tried them lots of times myself, and they wouldn't sting
me.

I had heard about some of these things before, but not all
of them.   Jim knowed all kinds of signs.   He said he knowed
most everything.   I said it looked to me like all the signs was
about bad luck, and so I asked him if there warn't any good-
luck signs.   He says:

"Mighty few—an' *dey* ain' no use to a body.   What you **32**
want to know when good luck's a-comin' for? want to keep it
off?"   And he said: "Ef you's got hairy arms en a hairy **33**
breas', it's a sign dat you's agwyne to be rich.   Well, dey's
some use in a sign like dat, 'kase it's so fur ahead.   You see,
maybe you's got to be po' a long time fust, en so you might git
discourage' en kill yo'self 'f you didn' know by de sign dat you
gwyne to be rich bymeby."

"Have you got hairy arms and a hairy breast, Jim?"

"What's de use to axe dat question? don' you see I has?"

"Well, are you rich?"

"No, but I been rich wunst, and gwyne to be rich agin. **34**
Wunst I had foteen dollars, but I tuck to speculat'n', en got
busted out."

"What did you speculate in, Jim?"

"Well, fust I tackled stock?"

"What kind of stock?"

"Why, live stock.   Cattle, you know.   I put ten dollars in
a cow.   But I ain' gwyne to resk no mo' money in stock.   De
cow up 'n' died on my han's."

"So you lost the ten dollars."

"No, I didn' lose it all.   I on'y los' 'bout nine of it.   I sole
de hide en taller for a dollar en ten cents." **35**

"You had five dollars and ten cents left.   Did you speculate
any more?"

"Yes.   You know dat one-laigged nigger dat b'longs to old
Misto Bradish? well, he sot up a bank, en say anybody dat put **36**
in a dollar would git fo' dollars mo' at de en' er de year.
Well, all de niggers went in, but dey didn' have much.   I wuz
de on'y one dat had much.   So I stuck out for mo' dan fo'
dollars, en I said 'f I didn' git it I'd start a bank mysef.   Well
o' course dat nigger want' to keep me out er de business,

in Hannibal, "not the brutal plantation article. Cruelties were very rare and exceedingly and wholesomely
unpopular. . . . If the threat to sell an incorrigible
slave 'down the river' would not reform him, nothing
would—his case was past cure" (*Autobiography*, Chapter 7). In a sense, Jim's nightmare in Chapter 2 has
come true; as Twain noted in Chapter 2 of *Pudd'nhead
Wilson*, the threat of slaves' being sold down the river
"was equivalent to condemning them to hell!"

22 *a nigger trader.* "The 'nigger trader' was loathed
by everybody," Twain explained in Chapter 7 of his
Autobiography. "He was regarded as a sort of human
devil who bought and conveyed poor helpless creatures to hell—for to our whites and blacks alike the
Southern plantation was simply hell; no milder name
could describe it." See note 36.

23 *she didn' want to, but she could git eight hund'd dollars
for me, en it 'uz sich a big stack o' money she couldn' resis'.*
Although the threat was common, actually to sell a
slave "down the river" was frowned upon by the
upper classes of Missouri. Around 1840, a male slave
brought between $500 and $600 on the slave market.
This price is confirmed by Twain in Chapter 54 of
Life on the Mississippi in which he said that a black
family "in my time . . . would have been worth not
less than five hundred dollars apiece." With the
abolition of the importation of African slaves into the
United States in 1808 and the increase in production
of cotton with the invention of the cotton gin, the
interstate traffic of slave-trading greatly increased;
and by 1860, the same slave could demand a price of
$1,300. Obviously Miss Watson's sole motivation to
sell Jim is greed. Occasionally, even the leading
citizens of Hannibal (including Judge John M. Clemens; see Chapter 31, note 9) did sell slaves "down the
river."

24 *de camp-meetn'.* A congress held in the open air or
under tents in the wilderness, usually for religious
services and chiefly among the Methodists; sometimes these meetings went on for several weeks. See
Chapter 20.

25 *I'd slip in . . . en swim asho' en take to de woods on de
Illinoi side.* Abolitionists from Illinois often raided the
Missouri side of the Mississippi. "They are as thick
down there in the bottoms," one woman in Palmyra,
Missouri, described the abolitionists of Quincy, Illinois, "as maggots in a dead horse, watching for
slaves." Possibly Twain was recalling the case in
Marion City in 1841 when three abolitionist "libera-
tors" tried to convince a couple of slaves to escape
across the river with them to Canada and freedom.
However, perhaps because slaves were often told that
their worst enemies were abolitionists and reminded
of how Murrell's Gang deceived slaves into selling
them "down the river," the servants told their masters, and the three men were captured. Although
they were threatened with being lynched, the abolitionists were finally tried (Judge Clemens was on the
jury) and sentenced to twelve years imprisonment at
hard labor. They were released before their term
expired, and one of them, George Thompson, wrote
an impassioned account of the failed plot, the trial,

and the imprisonment in *Prison Life and Reflections* (1847).

Several critics have complained with DeVoto in *Mark Twain at Work* (p. 54) about Twain's "lordly disregard of the fact that Jim . . . could have reached free soil by simply paddling to the Illinois shore from Jackson's Island." However, others have defended Jim's (and Twain's) reasoning. Although Illinois was technically a free state, it did not automatically recognize a runaway a free man: It was separated from slave states only by the Mississippi and Ohio rivers; and in support of the Fugitive Slave Law, Illinois legislation considered any Negro without freedom papers as subject to arrest and, upon conviction, to a system of indentured labor. "Rewards were offered for runaways," DeLancey Ferguson retorted in *The Explicator* (No. 42, April 1946); "capturing and returning them was a profitable business. Jim would have had a much better chance of staying free had he entered free soil at a remote point, instead of right opposite the place where the alarm had already been raised." And Jim has already given a plausible explanation why he has not paddled over to the Illinois side: There is the danger of being tracked by dogs and of the tracing of the stolen skiff, that would be avoided by taking a raft; and he also already attempted to cross, but had no luck in his efforts.

26 *a plug er dog-leg.* A tightly twisted stick of a cheap tobacco.

27 *it was a sign when young chickens flew that way.* A common superstition in this part of the country warned that when chickens flocked together, it was going to rain.

28 *his old granny said his father would die, and he did.* Jim may be referring to the superstition that if a bird entered the home of a sick person and died, then the ailing individual would die too.

29 *you mustn't count the things you are going to cook for dinner.* This superstition was common to both blacks and whites in this area of the United States. Counting was often associated with bad luck: One should not count stars, cars in a funeral cortège, followers to a funeral, or the graves in a churchyard.

30 *if a man owned a bee-hive, and that man died, the bees must be told about it before sun-up next morning, or else the bees would all . . . die.* A common European superstition; in ancient Greece and Rome, bees were said to be the messengers of the gods. "A remarkable custom, brought from the Old Country, formerly prevailed in the rural districts of New England," John Greenleaf Whittier prefaced his poem "Telling the Bees" (1858). "On the death of a member of the family, the bees were at once informed of the event, and their hives dressed in mourning. This ceremonial was supposed to be necessary to prevent the swarms from leaving their hives and seeking a new home." Eugene Field of Missouri, too, used this superstition in his poem "Telling the Bees" (1893).

31 *bees wouldn't sting idiots; but I didn't believe that, because I had tried them lots of times myself, and they wouldn't sting me.* The handicapped were once believed to be "God's Poor" and thus were blessed by Him. Twain made a similar joke in Chapter 26 of his *Autobiography:* "The proverb says that Providence protects children and idiots. This is really true. I know it because I have tested it."

32 *What you want to know when good luck's a-comin' for? want to keep it off?* Obviously, Jim agrees with an Indian belief that one need only concern oneself with bad spirits. See Chapter 4, note 9.

33 *Ef you's got hairy arms en a hairy breas', it's a sign dat you's agwyne to be rich.* This omen of eventual prosperity (also common in parts of Great Britain) argued that a person with a hairy body would always have money. Perhaps it originally referred to the Queen of Sheba, who was said to have legs as hairy as those of an ape; and so it was also believed that a hairy woman would marry a rich man.

34 *I been rich wunst. . . . Wunst I had foteen dollars, but I tuck to speculat'n, en got busted out.* Jim's investments were inspired by a similar exchange between a Piute guide named Captain Juan and "Dan De Quille," Twain's friend William Wright who recorded the discussion in *History of the Big Bonanza* (1870, pp. 272–273), his recollections of the California Gold Rush. "I was pretty well off once," Captain Juan explains; "I had *fifty dollars*." Wright continues: "And what became of all this wealth?"

"Me burst all to smash!"

"Well, that was bad. In kind of speculation?"

"Me not understand spectoolation. What you call um spectoolation?"

"Well, it's when you . . . plant your money in some speculation to get more money."

"Yes; well, me make one bad plant."

Unlike Jim, Captain Juan lost his money to a demanding Spanish wife who throws him out when he runs out of cash. In transforming Wright's ignorant Indian into a sort of "Mr. Bones," the comic of the traditional minstrel show, Twain plays with the conflict between the non-white and the American culture, a theme common to nineteenth-century humor. However, Twain greatly improves on Wright's original by using it as an ironic introduction of certain paradoxes in the slave system which treated men merely as capital.

35 *taller.* Tallow, the cow's fat.

36 *Misto Bradish.* In the uncompleted "Tom Sawyer's Conspiracy," 1897 (published in *Mark Twain's Hannibal, Huck and Tom,* 1969, p. 216), Huck reveals that Tom Sawyer has discovered that Bat Bradish, "a nigger trader in a little small way," was "at the bottom of it the time old Miss Watson come so near selling Jim down the river and Jim heard about it and run away and me and him floated down to Arkansaw on the raft. It was Bradish that persuaded her to sell Jim and give him the job of doing it for her." When Mister Bradish is murdered, the freed Jim is falsely arrested for the crime and accused of doing it in revenge for his betrayal by this "nigger trader."

MISTO BRADISH'S NIGGER.

bekase he say dey warn't business 'nough for two banks, so he say I could put in my five dollars en he pay me thirty-five at de en' er de year.

"So I done it. Den I reck'n'd I'd inves' de thirty-five dollars right off en keep things a-movin'. Dey wuz a nigger name' Bob, dat had ketched a wood-flat, en his marster didn' **37, 38** know it; en I bought it off'n him en told him to take de thirty-five dollars when de en' er de year come; but some-body stole de wood-flat dat night, en nex' day de one-laigged nigger say de bank 's busted. So dey didn' none uv us git no money."

"What did you do with the ten cents, Jim?"

"Well, I uz gwyne to spen' it, but I had a dream, en de dream tole me to give it to a nigger name' Balum—Balum's **39** Ass dey call him for short, he's one er dem chuckle-heads, you **40** know. But he's lucky, dey say, en I see I warn't lucky. De dream say let Balum inves' de ten cents en he'd make a raise for me. Well, Balum he tuck de money, en when he wuz in church he hear de preacher say dat whoever give to de po' len' **41** to de Lord, en boun' to git his money back a hund'd times. So Balum he tuck en give de ten cents to de po', en laid low to see what wuz gwyne to come of it."

"Well, what did come of it, Jim?"

"Nuffn' never come of it. I couldn' manage to k'leck dat money no way; en Balum he couldn'. I ain't gwyne to len' no mo' money 'dout I see de security. Boun' to git yo' money back a hund'd times, de preacher says! Ef I could git de ten *cents* back, I'd call it squah, en be glad er de chanst."

"Well, it's all right, anyway, Jim, long as you're going to be rich again some time or other."

"Yes—en I's rich now, come to look at it. I owns mysef, en I's wuth eight hund'd dollars. I wisht I had de money, I **42** wouldn' want no mo'."

37 *a wood-flat*. A raft or flat-bottomed boat for transporting timber.

38 *en his marster didn' know it*. By law, a slave could not hold property; whatever he might find automatically became his owner's.

39 *Balum's Ass*. In Numbers 22: 7–35, God sends Balaam, the Lord's prophet, to curse the Israelites; but on the journey, he fails to see the avenging angel in his path. His ass, however, protects his master by turning away, and for his faithfulness, the beast is punished. Suddenly the ass speaks to Balaam who then is allowed to see the Lord's messenger before him. Of course, Twain is burlesquing Jim's abilities as a seer (and he does prove to be a prophet in Chapter 10). Perhaps because of the slightly off-color name, Balaam's Ass was occasionally introduced into Southwestern humor; for example, Twain said in his *Burlesque Autobiography* (1871) that one of his ances-tors was Balaam's Ass; and in Chapter 31 of *The Gilded Age* introduces the Reverend Orson Balaam, a pompous ass who exploits the Indians. And in *The Innocents Abroad* (Vol. II, Chapters 16 and 17), Twain described the absurdity of visiting a fountain in Figia, Syria, said to have once refreshed Balaam's Ass, "the patron saint of all pilgrims like us." Possibly Joel Chandler Harris had in mind this episode of *Huckleberry Finn* when he named an abused slave "Balaam" in *Balaam and His Master and Other Sketches and Stories* (1891).

40 *he's one er dem chuckle-heads. . . . But he's lucky, dey say*. As mentioned in note 31, fools are believed to be blessed by God.

41 *de preacher say dat whoever give to de po' len' to de Lord, en boun' to git his money back a hund'd times*. Jim's preacher repeats much the same teaching that Miss Watson lectured to Huck at the opening of Chapter 3; as Jim and Huck make similar conclusions about such religious investments, Twain has established an affinity between the boy and the slave in the way in which each thinks.

42 *I wisht I had de money, I wouldn' want no mo'*. Twain was particularly fond of the foregoing episode (which was evidently an afterthought to the novel); he often included it in his public reading tours. However, the humorist had some difficulty with the "punch line." When serialized with part of Chapter 14 in "Jim's Investments, and King Sollermun" (*The Century*, January 1885), it concluded with a new observation: "But live stock's too resky, Huck;—I wisht I had de eight hund'ed dollars en somebody had de nigger." And in his reading copy of the Tauchnitz edition, he amended it to read, "I wisht I had de money, cuz niggers is might resky property" (MTP).

Chapter IX.

EXPLORING THE CAVE.

I WANTED to go and look at a place right about the middle of the island, that I'd found when I was exploring ; so we started, and soon got to it, because the island was only three miles long and a quarter of a mile wide.

This place was a tolerable long steep hill or ridge, about forty foot high. We had a rough time getting to the top, the sides was so steep and the bushes so thick. We tramped and clumb around all over it, and by-and-by found a good big cavern in the rock, most up to the top on the side towards Illinois. The cavern was as big as two or three rooms bunched together, and Jim could stand up straight in it. It was cool in there. Jim was for putting our traps in there, right away, but I said we didn't want to be climbing up and down there all the time.

Jim said if we had the canoe hid in a good place, and had all the traps in the cavern, we could rush there if anybody was to come to the island, and they would never find us without dogs. And besides, he said them little birds had said it was going to rain, and did I want the things to get wet ?

112

So we went back and got the canoe and paddled up abreast the cavern, and lugged all the traps up there. Then we hunted up a place close by to hide the canoe in, amongst the thick willows. We took some fish off of the lines and set them again, and begun to get ready for dinner.

The door of the cavern was big enough to roll a hogshead in, and on one side of the door the floor stuck out a little bit and was flat and a good place to build a fire on. So we built it there and cooked dinner.

We spread the blankets inside for a carpet, and eat our dinner in there. We put all the other things handy at the back of the cavern. Pretty soon it darkened up and begun to

1 *a perfect ripper of a gust.* An especially powerful gust.

2 *as bright as glory . . . ; dark as sin.* Huck may have resisted the Widow Douglas's and Miss Watson's Sunday-school teachings, but his similes here nevertheless reflect the boy's deep unconscious religious sense.

3 *you wouldn't a ben here, 'f it hadn't a ben for Jim.* This is only the first of many times the slave helps the boy during his flight from civilization. Although he may be just a "nigger" to Huck, Jim possesses considerable common sense; and although he too is a fugitive, the slave remains the boy's protector during their journey down the river and he (like Miles Hendon to Edward in *The Prince and the Pauper*) acts as an elder brother to Huck.

IN THE CAVE.

thunder and lighten; so the birds was right about it. Directly it begun to rain, and it rained like all fury, too, and I never see the wind blow so. It was one of these regular summer storms. It would get so dark that it looked all blue-black outside, and lovely; and the rain would thrash along by so thick that the trees off a little ways looked dim and spider-webby; and here would come a blast of wind that would bend the trees down and turn up the pale underside of the leaves; and then a **1** perfect ripper of a gust would follow along and set the branches to tossing their arms as if they was just wild; and next, when it was just about the bluest and blackest—*fst!* it was as bright **2** as glory and you'd have a little glimpse of tree tops a-plunging about, away off yonder in the storm, hundreds of yards further than you could see before; dark as sin again in a second, and now you'd hear the thunder let go with an awful crash and then go rumbling, grumbling, tumbling down the sky towards the under side of the world, like rolling empty barrels downstairs, where it's long stairs and they bounce a good deal, you know.

"Jim, this is nice," I says. "I wouldn't want to be nowhere else but here. Pass me along another hunk of fish and some hot corn-bread."

"Well, you wouldn't a ben here, 'f it hadn't a ben for Jim. **3** You'd a ben down dah in de woods widout any dinner, en gittin'

4 *We could a had pets enough if we'd wanted them.* The flood has made friends of creatures that otherwise would be natural antagonists. Only the intrusion of civilization in the form of a floating house disrupts this delicate balance. In "Man's Place in the Animal World," 1896 (in *What Is Man?*, 1973, p. 85), Twain discussed a similar situation: "In truth, man is incurably foolish. Simple things which the other animals easily learn, he is incapable of learning. . . . In an hour I taught a cat and a dog to be friends. I put them in a cage. In another hour I taught them to be friends with a rabbit. In the course of two days I was able to add a fox, a goose, a squirrel and some doves. Finally a monkey. They lived together in peace; even affectionately." However, not so with man, for, to Twain, "man's heart was the only bad heart in the animal kingdom." He agreed with a gentleman named Macfarlane, a Scotsman Clemens said he met during his youth in Cincinnati, who argued that "man was the only animal capable of feeling malice, envy, vindictiveness, vengefulness, hatred, selfishness, the only animal that loved drunkenness, almost the only animal that could endure personal uncleanliness and a filthy habitation . . . the sole animal that robs, persecutes, oppresses, and kills members of his own immediate tribe, the sole animal that steals and enslaves the members of *any* tribe" ("Macfarlane," 1896, *What Is Man?* 1973, p. 78). And symbols of these human characteristics may be found in the floating house. The seemingly gratuitous adventure, being the boy and the slave's first encounter with civilization outside the village, introduces an important underlying theme: What is Man?

5 *saw-logs.* Logs, split on one side and with the bark still on them, cut into the proper length for boards, before being taken to the mill to be sawed.

6 *all over the walls was the ignorantest kind of words and pictures, made with charcoal.* This detail is reminiscent of that in another thief's den, that of the late Tom Sheppard, described in Chapter 1 of William Harrison Ainsworth's *Jack Sheppard* (1839), a novel Twain owned and enjoyed: "The bare walls were scored all over with grotesque designs, the chief of which represented Nebuchadnezzer. The rest were hieroglyphic characters, executed in red chalk and charcoal." Likely, Twain is emphasizing that this dwelling is so poor that its inhabitants cannot even afford a cheap print to decorate the walls. However, Thomas Hart Benton in his illustration of this scene in the 1942 Limited Editions Club edition (as did John Seelye in *The True Adventures of Huckleberry Finn*, 1970) interpreted "ignorantest kind of words" as such common profanities as "shit," "piss," and "fuck."

mos' drownded, too, dat you would, honey. Chickens knows when its gwyne to rain, en so do de birds, chile."

The river went on raising and raising for ten or twelve days, till at last it was over the banks. The water was three or four foot deep on the island in the low places and on the Illinois bottom. On that side it was a good many miles wide; but on the Missouri side it was the same old distance across—a half a mile—because the Missouri shore was just a wall of high bluffs.

Daytimes we paddled all over the island in the canoe. It was mighty cool and shady in the deep woods even if the sun was blazing outside. We went winding in and out amongst the trees; and sometimes the vines hung so thick we had to back away and go some other way. Well, on every old broken-down tree you could see rabbits, and snakes, and such things; and when the island had been overflowed a day or two, they got so tame, on account of being hungry, that you could paddle right up and put your hand on them if you wanted to; but not the snakes and turtles—they would slide off in the water. The

4 ridge our cavern was in was full of them. We could a had pets enough if we'd wanted them.

One night we catched a little section of a lumber raft—nice pine planks. It was twelve foot wide and about fifteen or sixteen foot long, and the top stood above water six or seven

5 inches, a solid level floor. We could see saw-logs go by in the daylight, sometimes, but we let them go; we didn't show ourselves in daylight.

Another night, when we was up at the head of the island, just before daylight, here comes a frame house down, on the west side. She was a two-storey, and tilted over, considerable. We paddled out and got aboard—clumb in at an upstairs window. But it was too dark to see yet, so we made the canoe fast and set in her to wait for daylight.

The light begun to come before we got to the foot of the island. Then we looked in at the window. We could make out a bed, and a table, and two old chairs, and lots of things around about on the floor; and there was clothes hanging against the wall. There was something laying on the floor in the far corner that looked like a man. So Jim says:

"Hello, you!"

But it didn't budge. So I hollered again, and then Jim says:

"De man ain't asleep—he's dead. You hold still—I'll go en see."

He went and bent down and looked, and says:

"It's a dead man. Yes, indeedy; naked, too. He's ben shot in de back. I reck'n he's ben dead two er three days. Come in, Huck, but doan' look at his face—it's too gashly."

I didn't look at him at all. Jim throwed some old rags over him, but he needn't done it; I didn't want to see him. There was heaps of old greasy cards scattered around over the floor, and old whisky bottles, and a couple of masks made out of black cloth; and all over the walls was the ignorantest kind of words and

6 cloth; and all over the walls was the ignorantest kind of words and

JIM SEES A DEAD MAN.

pictures, made with charcoal. There was two old dirty calico **7**
dresses, and a sun-bonnet, and some women's under-clothes, hang- **8**
ing against the wall, and some men's clothing, too. We put the
lot into the canoe; it might come good. There was a boy's
old speckled straw hat on the floor; I took that too. And
there was a bottle that had had milk in it; and it had a rag
stopper for a baby to suck. We would a took the bottle, but
it was broke. There was a seedy old chest, and an old hair **9**
trunk with the hinges broke. They stood open, but there
warn't nothing left in them that was any account. The way
things was scattered about, we reckoned the people left in a
hurry and warn't fixed so as to carry off most of their stuff.

We got an old tin lantern, and a butcher knife without any
handle, and a bran-new Barlow knife worth two bits in any **10,11**
store, and a lot of tallow candles, and a tin candlestick, and a
gourd, and a tin cup, and a ratty old bed-quilt off the bed, and
a reticule with needles and pins and beeswax and buttons and **12,13**
thread and all such truck in it, and a hatchet and some nails,
and a fish-line as thick as my little finger, with some monstrous
hooks on it, and a roll of buckskin, and a leather dog-collar,
and a horse-shoe, and some vials of medicine that didn't have
no label on them; and just as we was leaving I found a tolerable good curry-comb, and Jim he found a ratty old fiddle-bow, **14**
and a wooden leg. The straps was broke off of it, but barring
that, it was a good enough leg, though it was too long for me
and not long enough for Jim, and we couldn't find the other
one, though we hunted all around.

And so, take it all around, we made a good haul. When **15**
we was ready to shove off, we was a quarter of a mile below the
island, and it was pretty broad day; so I made Jim lay down
in the canoe and cover up with the quilt, because if he set up,
people could tell he was a nigger a good ways off. I paddled
over to the Illinois shore, and drifted down most a half a mile
doing it. I crept up the dead water under the bank, and
hadn't no accidents and didn't see nobody. We got home all
safe.

7 *calico.* Brightly printed cotton cloth, coarser than
muslin.

8 *some women's under-clothes, hanging against the wall,
and some men's clothing too.* These details suggested to
V. S. Pritchett in "Current Literature" (*The New
Statesman and Nation*, August 2, 1941, p. 113) that
this frame house was "evidently some sort of
brothel."

9 *hair trunk.* A trunk made from the untanned hide,
still with the hair on it. This rather ugly article was
occasionally the brunt of Twain's jokes. For example,
in Chapter 17 of *A Tramp Abroad*, in complaining
about how slow German "slow freight" was, Twain
noted, "The hair on my trunk was soft and thick and
youthful, when I got it ready for shipment in
Hamburg. It was baldheaded when it reached Hei-
delburg."

10 *Barlow knife.* A jack-knife with only one blade,
named after its eighteenth-century English inventor
Russell Barlowe.

11 *two bits.* Twenty-five cents. This unit of American currency is based on the Spanish milled dollar of
eight *reals*, or "bits," known as "pieces of eight."

12 *a reticule.* A handbag, here a sewing bag. In *Mark
Twain: A Portrait* (p. 130), Masters complained that
this word was uncharacteristic of a boy of Huck
Finn's class and region, and that he should have said
something like "one of them things they keep needles
in, ratacoul or something."

13 *beeswax.* Used by seamstresses to wax their
thread.

14 *curry-comb.* A metal comb, generally used for
grooming horses; here evidently referring to the
musical instrument made by placing a piece of paper
over the teeth and blowing through it. See Chapter
38, note 11.

15 *And so, take it all around, we made a good haul.*
T. S. Eliot was particularly impressed by this
passage. "This is the sort of list that a boy reader
should pore over with delight," the poet wrote in his
introduction to a 1950 edition of *Huckleberry Finn*;
"but the paragraph performs other functions of
which the boy reader would be unaware. It provides
the right counterpoise to the horror of the wrecked
house and the corpse; it has a grim precision which
tells the reader all he needs to know about the way of
life of the human derelicts who had used the house;
and (especially the wooden leg, and the fruitless
search for its mate) reminds us at the right moment of
the kinship of mind and sympathy between the boy
outcast from society and the negro fugitive from the
injustice of society."

Twain's inventory of what Huck and Jim found in
the floating house is reminiscent of Defoe's exhaus-
tive description of what Robinson Crusoe salvaged
from the shipwreck to help sustain him on his
deserted island.

1 *Jim . . . said a man that warn't buried was more likely to go a-ha'nting around than one that was planted and comfortable.* It was commonly believed that the spirit of a dead person cannot rest in peace until it has been properly burried in hallowed ground.

2 *an old blanket overcoat.* Or "wrap-rascal," a cheap coat common to itinerants of the West, made from a heavy blanket and often with the stripe of the border of the original blanket crossing various parts of the garment; it often served two functions, as a coat during the day and as a blanket at night. Apparently this one is pocketless, for silver has been sewn in its lining.

A blanket overcoat. Illustration by F.O.C. Darley, *Adventures of Captain Simon Suggs* by Johnson Jones Hooper, 1846.

Chapter X.

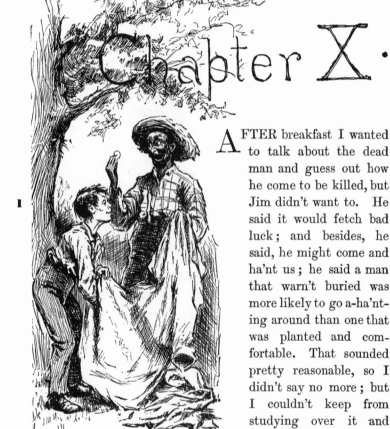

THEY FOUND EIGHT DOLLARS.

AFTER breakfast I wanted to talk about the dead man and guess out how he come to be killed, but Jim didn't want to. He said it would fetch bad luck; and besides, he said, he might come and ha'nt us; he said a man that warn't buried was more likely to *go a-ha'nt*ing around than one that was planted and comfortable. That sounded pretty reasonable, so I didn't say no more; but I couldn't keep from studying over it and wishing. I knowed who shot the man, and what they done it for.

We rummaged the clothes we'd got, and found eight dollars in silver sewed up in the lining of an old blanket overcoat. Jim said he reckoned the people in that house stole the coat, because if they'd a knowed the money was there they wouldn't a left it. I said I reckoned they killed him, too; but Jim didn't want to talk about that. I says:

"Now you think it's bad luck; but what did you say when I fetched in the snake-skin that I found on the top of the ridge day before yesterday?   You said it was the worst bad luck in **3** the world to touch a snake-skin with my hands.   Well, here's your bad luck!   We've raked in all this truck and eight dollars besides.   I wish we could have some bad luck like this every day, Jim."

"Never you mind, honey, never you mind.   Don't you git too peart.   It's a-comin'.   Mind I tell you, it's a-comin'." **4**

It did come, too.   It was a Tuesday that we had that talk. Well, after dinner Friday, we was laying around in the grass at the upper end of the ridge, and got out of tobacco.   I went to the cavern to get some, and found a rattlesnake in there.   I killed him, and curled him up on the foot of Jim's blanket, ever so natural, thinking there'd be some fun when Jim found him there.   Well, by night I forgot all about the snake, and when Jim flung himself down on the blanket while I struck a light, the snake's mate was there, and bit him.

He jumped up yelling, and the first thing the light showed was the varmint curled up and ready for another spring.   I laid him out in a second with a stick, and Jim grabbed pap's **5** whisky jug and begun to pour it down.

He was barefooted, and the snake bit him right on the **6** heel.   That all comes of my being such a fool as to not remember that wherever you leave a dead snake its mate always comes there and curls around it.   Jim told me to chop off the **7** snake's head and throw it away, and then skin the body and roast a piece of it.   I done it, and he eat it and said it would

3 *You said it was the worst bad luck in the world to touch a snake-skin with my hands.* One common superstition of this part of the country, said to originate with the Indians, warned that he who touched a snakeskin would be bitten by one within three days. Aunty Cord, a former Southern slave who was the cook at Quarry Farm in Elmira, New York, told the Clemens children that "snakes must be killed on sight, even the harmless ones; and the discoverer of a sloughed snake-skin lying in the road was in for all kinds of calamities" (quoted by Pettit, *Mark Twain and the South*, pp. 53–54). However, Southern slaves also used snakeskins as protection against evil spirits and in the treatment of such ills as rheumatism, headache, and fits.

4 *peart.* Also spelled "peert," fresh, smart.

5 *Jim grabbed pap's whisky jug and begun to pour it down.* It was commonly believed that whiskey could cure snakebite, but this practice could have proven to be actually dangerous to the victim: Whiskey dilates the blood vessels and therefore can facilitate the flow of venom rather than slow it down.

6 *the snake bit him right on the heel.* Twain may be referring to the superstition that rattlesnakes strike only below the knee; in Chapter 13 of *The Gilded Age*, Charles Dudley Warner described how an Easterner buys leather top boots that came above his knees, "a perfect protection against prairie rattle-snakes, which never strike above the knee."

7 *Jim told me to chop off the snake's head and throw it away, and then skin the body and roast a piece of it. I done it, and he eat it and said it would help cure him.* These common folk remedies for snakebite apparently derived from the medical theory of *similia similibus curantur*, like cures like.

JIM AND THE SNAKE.

8 *He made me take off the rattles and tie them around his wrist, too. He said that that would help.* The custom of wearing a necklace or bracelet of rattlesnake rattles to cure or to ward off various ills, including snakebite, originated with Southern slaves. In Chapter 16 of *Tom Sawyer*, Tom, in throwing off his trousers to take a swim, "had kicked his string of rattlesnake rattles off his ankle, and he wondered how he had escaped cramp so long without the protection of this mysterious charm."

9 *I've always reckoned that looking at the new moon over your left shoulder is one of the carelessest and foolishest things a body can do.* To view the new moon over the right shoulder was said to be good luck, but to view it over the left was believed to be fatal.

10 *Old Hank Bunker . . . got drunk and fell off of the shot tower and spread himself out so that he was just a kind of a layer . . . ; and they slid him edgeways between two barn doors for a coffin, and buried him so.* The sad fate of reckless Hank Bunker is a typical example of the extravagantly violent slapstick, once common to Southwestern humor, which survives in contemporary comic strips and animated cartoons. Twain was fond of this sort of comedy and inserted examples of it into his earlier writing. Hank Bunker's tragedy is reminiscent of that of William Wheeler (described in Chapter 53 of *Roughing It*, 1872) who "got nipped by the machinery in a carpet factory and went through in less than a quarter of a minute; his widder bought the piece of carpet that had his remains wove in, and people come a hundred mile to 'tend the funeral. There was fourteen yards in the piece. She wouldn't let them roll him up, but planted him just so—full length. . . . and let him stand up, same as a monument. And they nailed a sign to it and put on it": Sacred to the Memory of Fourteen Yards of Three-Ply Carpet Containing All That Was Mortal of William Wheeler.

8 help cure him. He made me take off the rattles and tie them around his wrist, too. He said that that would help. Then I slid out quiet and throwed the snakes clear away amongst the bushes; for I warn't going to let Jim find out it was all my fault, not if I could help it.

Jim sucked and sucked at the jug, and now and then he got out of his head and pitched around and yelled; but every time he come to himself he went to sucking at the jug again. His foot swelled up pretty big, and so did his leg; but by-and-by the drunk begun to come, and so I judged he was all right; but I'd druther been bit with a snake than pap's whisky.

Jim was laid up for four days and nights. Then the swelling was all gone and he was around again. I made up my mind I wouldn't ever take aholt of a snake-skin again with my hands, now that I see what had come of it. Jim said he reckoned I would believe him next time. And he said that handling a snake-skin was such awful bad luck that maybe we hadn't got to the end of it yet. He said he druther see the new moon over his left shoulder as much as a thousand times than take up a snake-skin in his hand. Well, I was getting to feel that **9** way myself, though I've always reckoned that looking at the new moon over your left shoulder is one of the carelessest and **10** foolishest things a body can do. Old Hank Bunker done it once, and bragged about it; and in less than two years he got drunk and fell off of the shot tower and spread himself out so that he was just a kind of a layer, as you may say; and they slid him edgeways between two barn doors for a coffin, and buried him so, so they say, but I didn't see it Pap told me.

OLD HANK BUNKER.

But anyway, it all come of looking at the moon that way, like a fool.

Well, the days went along, and the river went down between its banks again; and about the first thing we done was **11** to bait one of the big hooks with a skinned rabbit and set it, and catch a cat-fish that was as big as a man, being six foot two inches long, and weighed over two hundred pounds. We couldn't handle him, of course; he would a flung us into Illinois. We just set there and watched him rip and tear around till he drownded. We found a brass button in his stomach, and a round ball, and lots of rubbage. We split the ball open with the hatchet, and there was a spool in it. Jim said he'd had it there a long time, to coat it over so and make a ball of it. It was as big a fish as was ever catched in the Mississippi, I reckon. Jim said he hadn't ever seen a bigger one. He would a been worth a good deal over at the village. They peddle out such a fish as that by the pound in the market house there; everybody buys some of him; his meat's as white as snow and makes a good fry.

Next morning I said it was getting slow and dull, and I wanted to get a stirring up, some way. I said I reckoned I would slip over the river and find out what was going on. Jim liked that notion; but he said I must go in the dark and look sharp. Then he studied it over and said, Couldn't I put on some of them old things and dress up like a girl? That was a good notion, too. So we shortened up one of the calico gowns and I turned up my trowser-legs to my knees and got

"A FAIR FIT."

into it. Jim hitched it behind with the hooks, and it was a fair fit. I put on the sun-bonnet and tied it under my chin, and then for a body to look in and see my face was like looking down a joint of stove-pipe. Jim said nobody would know me,

11 *we . . . catch a cat-fish that was as big as a man, being six foot two inches long, and weighed over two hundred pounds.* One would think this was just another "fish story," except that Twain admitted in Chapter 2 of *Life on the Mississippi,* "I have seen a Mississippi catfish that was more than six feet long and weighed two hundred and fifty pounds."

"I practiced around all day." Illustration by E. W. Kemble, "Autograph Edition," 1899.

12 *you couldn't start a face in that town that I didn't know*. You couldn't introduce me to anyone in that town that I didn't know.

even in the daytime, hardly.   I practiced around all day to get the hang of the things, and by-and-by I could do pretty well in them, only Jim said I didn't walk like a girl; and he said I must quit pulling up my gown to get at my britches pocket. I took notice, and done better.

I started up the Illinois shore in the canoe just after dark.

I started across to the town from a little below the ferry landing, and the drift of the current fetched me in at the bottom of the town.   I tied up and started along the bank. There was a light burning in a little shanty that hadn't been lived in for a long time, and I wondered who had took up quarters there.   I slipped up and peeped in at the window. There was a woman about forty year old in there, knitting by a candle that was on a pine table.   I didn't know her face; **12** she was a stranger, for you couldn't start a face in that town that I didn't know.   Now this was lucky, because I was weakening; I was getting afraid I had come; people might know my voice and find me out.   But if this woman had been in such a little town two days she could tell me all I wanted to know; so I knocked at the door, and made up my mind I wouldn't forget I was a girl.

Chapter XI

"COME in," says the woman, and I did. She says:

"Take a cheer."

I done it. She looked me all over with her little shiny eyes, and says:

"What might your name be?"

"Sarah Williams."

"Where 'bouts do you live? In this neighborhood?"

"No'm. In Hookerville, seven mile below. I've walked all the way, and I'm all tired out."

"COME IN."

"Hungry, too, I reckon. I'll find you something."

"No'm, I ain't hungry. I was so hungry I had to stop two mile below here at a farm; so I ain't hungry no more. It's what makes me so late. My mother's down sick, and out of money and everything, and I come to tell my uncle Abner Moore. He lives at the upper end of the town, she says. I hain't ever been here before. Do you know him?"

1 *Hookerville.* Saverton, Missouri, a small town seven miles south of Hannibal.

2 *a right smart chance of people.* A particularly great number of people. "No phrase of the . . . Southwestern dialect is such a stumbling block to the outsider as *right smart*," Eggleston explained in the 1913 annotated edition of *The Hoosier Schoolmaster* (p. 71). "The writer from the North or East will generally use it wrongly. Mrs. Stowe says, 'I sold right smart of eggs,' but the Hoosier woman as I knew her would have said 'a right smart lot of eggs' or 'a right smart of eggs,' using the article and understanding the noun. A farmer omitting the preposition boasts of having 'raised right smart corn' this year. No expression could have a more vague sense than this."

3 *He'll never know how nigh he come to getting lynched.* Vigilanteism, known as "Lynch law," was widespread throughout the South and the Southwest at the time. "I believe it originated in one of the Southern States," Charles Augustus Murray explained in Chapter 5, Vol. II, of *Travels in North America* (1839), "where a body of farmers, unable to bring some depredators to justice, according to legal form, chose one of their number, named Lynch, judge; from the rest they selected a jury, and from this self-constituted court they issued and enforced sundry whippings, and other punishments. During the last few years the settlements in the Mississippi valley have increased so fast, that the number of law-courts have been found too few and dilatory; and the inhabitants have, in many places assembled together, assumed the sovereign authority of the law, appointed a judge Lynch and a jury from among themselves, and have punished, and frequently hanged, those brought before them." Originally, "lynching" referred to any punishment executed by these courts, but the term soon became synonymous with "hanging." In a chapter on Southern violence that was suppressed from *Life on the Mississippi* (but published in the 1944 Limited Editions Club edition, p. 414), Twain argued that the chief cause of such lawlessness was that "it is not the rule for courts to hang murderers. . . . Their juries fail to convict, even in the clearest cases. That is not agreeable to the public, as is shown by the fact that very frequently such a miscarriage of justice so rouses the people that they rise, in a passion, and break into the jail, drag out their man and lynch him. . . . But this hundred or two hundred men usually do this act of public justice with masks on. They go to their given work with clear consciences, but with their faces disguised. They know that the law will not meddle with them—otherwise, at least, than by empty form—and they know that the community will applaud their act."

And lynching was only one form of lawlessness said to be common to the South and Southwest. Frederick Marryat wrote in Chapter 8 of the second of his diaries in America (1840): "Never, perhaps, in the records of nations was there an instance of a century of such unvarying and unmitigated crime as is to be collected from the history of the turbulent and blood-stained Mississippi." Understandably, Twain

"No; but I don't know everybody yet. I haven't lived here quite two weeks. It's a considerable ways to the upper end of the town. You better stay here all night. Take off your bonnet."

"No," I says, "I'll rest awhile, I reckon, and go on. I ain't afeard of the dark."

She said she wouldn't let me go by myself, but her husband would be in by-and-by, maybe in a hour and a half, and she'd send him along with me. Then she got to talking about her husband, and about her relations up the river, and her relations down the river, and about how much better off they used to was, and how they didn't know but they'd made a mistake coming to our town, instead of letting well alone—and so on and so on, till I was afeard *I* had made a mistake coming to her to find out what was going on in the town; but by-and-by she dropped on to pap and the murder, and then I was pretty willing to let her clatter right along. She told about me and Tom Sawyer finding the six thousand dollars (only she got it ten) and all about pap and what a hard lot he was, and what a hard lot I was, and at last she got down to where I was murdered. I says:

1   "Who done it? We've heard considerable about these goings on, down in Hookerville, but we don't know who 'twas that killed Huck Finn."

2   "Well, I reckon there's a right smart chance of people *here* that'd like to know who killed him. Some thinks old Finn done it himself."

"No—is that so?"

3   "Most everybody thought it at first. He'll never know how nigh he come to getting lynched. But before night they changed around and judged it was done by a runaway nigger named Jim."

"Why he——"

I stopped. I reckoned I better keep still. She run on, and never noticed I had put in at all.

"The nigger run off the very night Huck Finn was killed.

4 So there's a reward out for him—three hundred dollars. And there's a reward out for old Finn too—two hundred dollars. You see, he come to town the morning after the murder, and told about it, and was out with 'em on the ferry-boat hunt, and right away after he up and left. Before night they wanted to lynch him, but he was gone, you see. Well, next day they

5 found out the nigger was gone; they found out he hadn't ben seen sence ten o'clock the night the murder was done. So then they put it on him, you see, and while they was full of it, next

6 day back comes old Finn and went boo-hooing to Judge Thatcher to get money to hunt for the nigger all over Illinois with. The judge give him some, and that evening he got drunk and was around till after midnight with a couple of mighty hard looking strangers, and then went off with them. Well, he hain't come back sence, and they ain't looking for him back till this thing blows over a little, for people thinks now that he killed his boy and fixed things so folks would think robbers done it, and then he'd get Huck's money without having to bother a long time with a lawsuit. People do say he warn't any too good to do it. Oh, he's sly, I reckon. If he don't come back for a year, he'll be all right. You can't prove anything on him, you know; everything will be quieted down then, and he'll walk into Huck's money as easy as nothing."

"Yes, I reckon so, 'm. I don't see nothing in the way of it. Has everybody quit thinking the nigger done it?"

"Oh, no, not everybody. A good many thinks he done it. But they'll get the nigger pretty soon, now, and maybe they can scare it out of him."

"Why, are they after him yet?"

"Well, you're innocent, ain't you! Does three hundred dollars lay round every day for people to pick up? Some folks thinks the nigger ain't far from here. I'm one of them—but I hain't talked it around. A few days ago I was talking with an old couple that lives next door in the log shanty, and they happened to say hardly anybody ever goes to that island over yonder that they call Jackson's Island. Don't anybody live there? says I. No, nobody, says they. I didn't say any more, but I done some thinking. I was pretty near certain I'd seen smoke over there, about the head of the island, a day or two before that, so I says to myself, like as not that nigger's hiding over there; anyway, says I, it's worth the trouble to give the place a hunt. I hain't seen any smoke sence, so I reckon maybe he's gone, if it was him; but husband's going over to see—him and another man. He was gone up the river; but he got back to-day and I told him as soon as he got here two hours ago."

"HIM AND ANOTHER MAN."

was defensive toward this prejudice. "It is imagined in the North," he wrote in the suppressed passage (p. 413), "that the South is one vast and gory murderfield, and that every man goes armed, and has at one time or another taken a neighbor's life. . . . There is a superstition, current everywhere, that the Southern temper is peculiarly hot; whereas, in truth, the temper of the average Southerner is not hotter than that of the average Northerner." And yet even so quiet a town as St. Petersburg could easily turn ugly when its citizens take the law into their own hands. For example, as recounted by Thompson in his memoirs (mentioned in Chapter 8, note 25), during the abolitionists' trial, a mob was organized in Palmyra and "had erected our gallows, provided ropes, blackened their faces, and ever ready to take us at a moment's notice, in case we were acquitted, and hang us on the spot!" (p. 91). Reconstruction did nothing to correct the situation. "The social condition of the State is worse than we have ever known it," a contemporary article in a Louisville, Kentucky, paper was quoted by Twain in the suppressed chapter (p. 415). "Murders are more frequent, punishment is lighter, pardons more numerous, and abuses more flagrant than at any period within our recollection, dating back fifteen years." And consequently lynching was widely revived. Surely, Twain in his numerous references to lynchings and other violent social punishments throughout *Huckleberry Finn* was as much speaking about his own time as recollecting the evils of the past.

4 *So there's a reward out for him—three hundred dollars. And there's a reward out for old Finn too—two hundred dollars.* Although each is accused of the same crime, Jim, who is valuable property, has a higher bounty on his head than does the derelict Pap Finn.

5 *he hadn't ben seen sence ten o'clock.* Because the curfew for slaves was at nine o'clock at night in Hannibal, it took only about an hour for Jim's disappearance to be noticed.

6 *Finn . . . went boo-hooing . . . to get money to hunt for the nigger all over Illinois with.* According to the Fugitive Slave Act of 1850, runaways could be pursued into free soil.

7 *Some calls me Sarah, some calls me Mary.* Twain was caught in a similarly tight situation while traveling through Europe when a woman acknowledged him and yet he did not remember her. In Chapter 25 of *A Tramp Abroad*, he described how she plied him with questions, for each of which he invented some answer. She begins: "'. . . And what a pretty little thing his child was! . . . What *was* that name? I can't call it to mind.'

"It appeared to me that the ice was getting pretty thin here. . . . I thought I might risk a name for it and trust to luck. Therefore I said:

"'I called that one Thomas Henry.'

"She said musingly:

"'That is very singular . . . very singular.'"

She then went on to other topics and still Twain did not know what she was talking about, and yet he persisted in the pretense of recognizing her. Finally she said: "'But there is one thing that is ever so puzzling to me.'

"'Why, what is that?'

"'That dead child's name. What did you say it was?'

"Here was another balmy place to be in. I had forgotten the child's name. . . . However, I had to pretend to know anyway, so I said:

"'Joseph Williams.'

"The youth at my side corrected me and said:

"'No, Thomas Henry.'

"I thanked him. . . . 'Thomas Henry—yes, Thomas Henry was the poor child's name. I named him for Thomas—er—Thomas Carlyle, the great author, you know—and Henry—er—er—Henry the Eighth. The parents were very grateful to have a child named Thomas Henry.'

"'That makes it more singular than ever,' murmured my beautiful friend.

"'Does it? Why?'

"'Because when the parents speak of that child now they always call it Susan Amelia.'"

I had got so uneasy I couldn't set still. I had to do something with my hands; so I took up a needle off of the table and went to threading it. My hands shook, and I was making a bad job of it. When the woman stopped talking, I looked up, and she was looking at me pretty curious, and smiling a little. I put down the needle and thread and let on to be interested—and I was, too—and says:

"Three hundred dollars is a power of money. I wish my mother could get it. Is your husband going over there to-night?"

"Oh, yes. He went up town with the man I was telling you of, to get a boat and see if they could borrow another gun. They'll go over after midnight."

"Couldn't they see better if they was to wait till daytime?"

"Yes. And couldn't the nigger see better, too? After midnight he'll likely be asleep, and they can slip around through the woods and hunt up his camp fire all the better for the dark, if he's got one."

"I didn't think of that."

The woman kept looking at me pretty curious, and I didn't feel a bit comfortable. Pretty soon she says:

"What did you say your name was, honey?"

"M—Mary Williams."

Somehow it didn't seem to me that I said it was Mary before, so I didn't look up; seemed to me I said it was Sarah; so I felt sort of cornered, and was afeared maybe I was looking it, too. I wished the woman would say something more; the longer she set still, the uneasier I was. But now she says:

"Honey, I thought you said it was Sarah when you first come in?"

"Oh, yes'm, I did. Sarah Mary Williams. Sarah's my first name. Some calls me Sarah, some calls me Mary."

"Oh, that's the way of it?"

"Yes'm."

I was feeling better, then, but I wished I was out of there, anyway. I couldn't look up yet.

Well, the woman fell to talking about how hard times was, and how poor they had to live, and how the rats was as free as if they owned the place, and so forth, and so on, and then I got easy again. She was right about the rats. You'd see one stick his nose out of a hole in the corner every little while. She said she had to have things handy to throw at them when she was alone, or they wouldn't give her no peace. She showed me a bar of lead, twisted up into a knot, and said she was a good shot with it generly, but she'd wrenched her arm a day or two ago, and didn't know whether she could throw true, now. But she watched for a chance, and directly she banged away at a rat, but she missed him wide, and said "Ouch!" it hurt her arm so. Then she told me to try for the next one. I wanted to be getting away before the old man got back, but of course I didn't let on. I got the thing, and the first rat that showed his nose I let drive, and if he'd a stayed where he was he'd a been a tolerable sick rat. She said that that was first-rate, and she reckoned I would hive the next one. She went and got the lump of lead and fetched it back and brought along a hank of yarn, which she wanted me to help her with. I held up my two hands and she put the hank over them and went on talking about her and her husband's matters. But she broke off to say:

"Keep your eye on the rats. You better have the lead in your lap, handy."

So she dropped the lump into my lap, just at that moment, and I clapped my legs together on it and she went on talking. But only about a minute. Then she took off the hank and looked me straight in the face, but very pleasant, and says:

"Come, now—what's your real name?"

"Wh-what, mum?"

"What's your real name? Is it Bill, or Tom, or Bob?—or what is it?"

I reckon I shook like a leaf, and I didn't know hardly what to do. But I says:

"Please to don't poke fun at a poor girl like me, mum. If I'm in the way, here, I'll——"

"No, you won't. Set down and stay where you are. I ain't going to hurt you, and I ain't going to tell on you, nuther. You just tell me your secret, and trust me. I'll keep it; and what's more, I'll help you. So'll my old man, if you want him to. You see, you're a runaway 'prentice—that's all. It ain't anything. There ain't any harm in it. You've been treated bad, and you made up your mind to cut. Bless you, child, I wouldn't tell on you. Tell me all about it, now—that's a good boy."

So I said it wouldn't be no use to try to play it any longer, and I would just make a clean breast and tell her everything, but she mustn't go back on her promise. Then I told her my **8** father and mother was dead, and the law had bound me out to a mean old farmer in the country thirty mile back from the river, and he treated me so bad I couldn't stand it no longer; he went away to be gone a couple of days, and so I took my chance and stole some of his daughter's old clothes, and cleared out, and I had been three nights coming the thirty miles; I travelled nights, and hid day-times and slept, and the bag of bread and meat I carried from home lasted me all the way and I had a plenty. I said I believed my uncle Abner Moore would take care of me, and so that was why I struck out for this town of Goshen. **9**

"Goshen, child? This ain't Goshen. This is St. Petersburg. Goshen's ten mile further up the river. Who told you this was Goshen?"

"Why, a man I met at day-break this morning, just as I was going to turn into the woods for my regular sleep. He told me when the roads forked I must take the right hand, and five mile would fetch me to Goshen."

8 *I told her my father and mother was dead, and the law had bound me out to a mean old farmer.* A male orphan, being a ward of the state, could by law be bound as an apprentice from the age of fourteen until he reached twenty-one years of age.

9 *Goshen.* The biblical Land of Plenty, a fitting name for a town in the same area as "St. Petersburg"; here possibly Marion City, Missouri.

10 *hocus me.* Play a trick on me; from "hoax" or "hocus-pocus."

11 *hold the needle still and poke the thread at it—that's the way a woman most always does; but a man always does t'other way.* And yet Miles Hendon does it exactly the opposite way in Chapter 13 of *The Prince and the Pauper:* "He did as men have always done, and probably always will do, to the end of time—held the needle still, and tried to thrust the thread through the eye, which is the opposite of a woman's way." Obviously Twain himself was not sure which was the true "woman's way."

"He was drunk I reckon. He told you just exactly wrong."

"Well, he did act like he was drunk, but it ain't no matter now. I got to be moving along. I'll fetch Goshen before daylight."

"Hold on a minute. I'll put you up a snack to eat. You might want it."

SHE PUTS UP A SNACK.

So she put me up a snack, and says:

"Say—when a cow's laying down, which end of her gets up first? Answer up prompt, now—don't stop to study over it. Which end gets up first?"

"The hind end, mum."

"Well, then, a horse?"

"The for'rard end, mum."

"Which side of a tree does the most moss grow on?"

"North side."

"If fifteen cows is browsing on a hillside, how many of them eats with their heads pointed the same direction?"

"The whole fifteen, mum."

"Well, I reckon you *have* lived in the country. I thought **10** maybe you was trying to hocus me again. What's your real name, now?"

"George Peters, mum."

"Well, try to remember it, George. Don't forget and tell me it's Elexander before you go, and then get out by saying it's George-Elexander when I catch you. And don't go about women in that old calico. You do a girl tolerable poor, but you might fool men, maybe. Bless you, child, when you set out to thread a needle, don't hold the thread still and fetch the **11** needle up to it; hold the needle still and poke the thread at it—that's the way a woman most always does; but a man always does t'other way. And when you throw at a rat or anything, hitch yourself up a tip-toe, and fetch your hand up over your head as awkard as you can, and miss your rat about six or seven foot. Throw stiff-armed from the shoulder, like there was a pivot there for it to turn on—like a girl; not from the wrist and elbow, with your arm out to one side, like a boy. And mind you, when a girl tries to catch anything in her lap, **12** she throws her knees apart; she don't clap them together, the way you did when you catched the lump of lead. Why, I spotted you for a boy when you was threading the needle; and I contrived the other things just to make certain. Now trot **13** along to your uncle, Sarah Mary Williams George Elexander Peters, and if you get into trouble you send word to Mrs. Judith Loftus, which is me, and I'll do what I can to get you out of it. Keep the river road, all the way, and next time you tramp, take shoes and socks with you. The river road's a rocky **14** one, and your feet'll be in a condition when you get to Goshen, I reckon."

I went up the bank about fifty yards, and then I doubled on my tracks and slipped back to where my canoe was, a good piece below the house. I jumped in and was off in a hurry. I went up stream far enough to make the head of the island, and then started across. I took off the sun-bonnet, for I didn't want no blinders on, then. When I was about the middle, I **15** hear the clock begin to strike; so I stops and listens; the sound come faint over the water, but clear—eleven. When I struck the head of the island I never waited to blow, though I was most winded, but I shoved right into the timber where my old camp used to be, and started a good fire there on a high-and-dry spot.

Then I jumped in the canoe and dug out for our place a mile and a half below, as hard as I could go. I landed, and slopped through the timber and up the ridge and into the

"HUMP YOURSELF."

12 *when a girl tries to catch anything in her lap, she throws her knees apart; she don't clap them together*. Blair in *Mark Twain and Huck Finn* (p. 400) has noted a similar incident in George Payne Ramsford James's forgotten romance *One in a Thousand* (1836): A woman, disguised as a page, is unmasked by a guard when he throws a knife in her lap and she spreads her legs to catch it. And Phillip H. Highfill, Jr., in *Mark Twain Journal* (Fall 1961, p. 6) acknowledged as a possible source for Mrs. Judith Loftus's trick "The Two Thieves," an anecdote included in Edmund H. Barker's *Literary Anecdotes and Contemporary Reminiscences* (Vol. I, 1852, p. 282): "Two thieves, disguised as country-girls, obtained admittance at a farmhouse, which they intended to rob. In the course of the evening, the farmer began to entertain suspicion of their sex. To settle the point, he tossed into their laps the shells of some nuts he had been cracking. The pretended females immediately closed their knees to prevent the shells from falling through, forgetting that women never do so because, their petticoats accomplish that purpose for them. The farmer secretly left the house and returned with assistance to capture his deceitful guests."

However, the most likely inspiration for this episode appears in Charles Reade's *The Cloister and the Hearth* (1861), a romance set in Rome in the age of Lorenzo de Medici, which Twain greatly admired. In Chapter 63, two ladies, jealous of the attention lavished on a stranger introduced as "Marcia," conspire against the creature:

"Signora, do you love almonds?"
The speaker had a lapful of them.
"Yes, I love them; when I can get them," said Marcia, pettishly, and eying the fruit with ill-concealed desire; "but yours is not the hand to give me any, I trow."
"You are much mistook," said the other. "Here, catch!"
And suddenly threw a double handful into Marcia's lap.
Marcia brought her knees together by an irresistible instinct.
"Aha! you are caught, my lad," cried she of the nuts. "'Tis a man; or a boy. A woman still parteth her knees to catch the nuts the surer in her apron; but a man closeth his for fear they shall fall between his hose. . . ."

13 *I contrived the other things just to make certain*. Mrs. Judith Loftus is one of several clever housewives in Twain's fiction who, in their cunning interrogations of boys, owe something to Shillaber's Mrs. Partington (see Chapter 1, note 8) and to Jane Clemens, the author's mother. Of course the most famous of these characters is Tom Sawyer's Aunt Polly. "Like many other simple-hearted souls," Twain described her in Chapter 1 of *Tom Sawyer*, "it was her pet vanity to believe she was endowed with a talent for dark and mysterious diplomacy, and she loved to contemplate her most transparent devices as marvels of low cunning."

This "pet vanity" is shared by a kind-hearted farmwife who befriends the fugitive Edward in Chapter 19 of *The Prince and the Pauper*. Curious about the strange boy's origins, she "set herself to contriving devices to surprise the boy into betraying his real secret." But unlike Judith Loftus, this woman fails; she suspects him to be a cow-boy, a shepherd, a servant, or an apprentice, but never the truth that he is the real king of England.

14 *The river road's a rocky one . . . to Goshen.* An unintended pun? A common religious cliché is that it is a long and rocky road to Heaven. Note that Huck characteristically takes the opposite route.

15 *blinders.* Or blinkers; flaps on a horse's bridle to prevent it from seeing objects at its sides. Twain is reminding the reader that the sun-bonnet so hid Huck's face that to see it "was like looking down a joint of stove-pipe."

16 *hump yourself.* "Be sharp!," "Look alive!"

cavern. There Jim laid, sound asleep on the ground. I roused him out and says:

16   "Git up and hump yourself, Jim! There ain't a minute to lose. They're after us!"

Jim never asked no questions, he never said a word; but the way he worked for the next half an hour showed about how he was scared. By that time everything we had in the world was on our raft and she was ready to be shoved out from the willow cove where she was hid. We put out the camp fire at the cavern the first thing, and didn't show a candle outside after that.

I took the canoe out from shore a little piece and took a look, but if there was a boat around I couldn't see it, for stars and shadows ain't good to see by. Then we got out the raft and slipped along down in the shade, past the foot of the island dead still, never saying a word.

ON THE RAFT.

Chapter XII.

I must a been close on to one o'clock when we got below the island at last, and the raft did seem to go mighty slow. If a boat was to come along, we was going to take to the canoe and break for the Illinois shore; and it was well a boat didn't come, for we hadn't ever thought to put the gun into the canoe, or a fishing-line or anything to eat. We was in ruther too much of a sweat to think of so many things. It warn't good judgment to put *everything* on the raft.

If the men went to the island, I just expect they found the camp fire I built, and watched it all night for Jim to come. Anyways, they stayed away from us, and if my building the fire never fooled them it warn't no fault of mine. I played it as low-down on them as I could.

When the first streak of day begun to show, we tied up to a tow-head in a big bend on the Illinois side, and hacked off [1] cotton-wood branches with the hatchet and covered up the raft with them so she looked like there had been a cave-in in the bank there. A tow-head is a sand-bar that has cotton-woods on it as thick as harrow-teeth. [2]

We had mountains on the Missouri shore and heavy timber on the Illinois side, and the channel was down the Missouri

1 *a tow-head.* "'Tow-head' means infant, an infant island, a growing island" (*Mark Twain's Notebook*, 1935, p. 161).

2 *as thick as harrow-teeth.* As numerous as the blades on a peg-toothed cultivating machine.

3 *up-bound steamboats.* Steamboats heading upstream.

4 *a snag.* Large trees or their branches which are torn out along the river banks and carried along by the floods until they are covered with sand and other refuse, and remain fixed in the water with one end pointing upward, creating a danger to navigation; these obstructions caused the most frequent damage to steamboats, flatboats, and other vessels along the Mississippi.

Snags. Illustration from *Harper's Monthly*, December 1855.

5 *a "crossing."* A place in the river where steamboats, seeking the safest current, cross from one side to the other.

6 *they used to say there was twenty or thirty thousand people in St. Louis.* In Chapter 22 of *Life on the Mississippi*, Twain quotes Marryat's 1839 American diary and confirms that the population of St. Louis at about this time was 20,000.

St. Louis, Missouri. Illustration by J. C. Wild, *The Valley of the Mississippi* by J. E. Thomas, 1842.
Courtesy the General Research and Humanities Division, The New York Public Library, Astor, Lenox, and Tilden Foundations.

shore at that place, so we warn't afraid of anybody running across us. We laid there all day and watched the rafts and
3 steamboats spin down the Missouri shore, and up-bound steamboats fight the big river in the middle. I told Jim all about the time I had jabbering with that woman; and Jim said she was a smart one, and if she was to start after us herself *she* wouldn't set down and watch a camp fire—no, sir, she'd fetch a dog. Well, then, I said, why couldn't she tell her husband to fetch a dog? Jim said he bet she did think of it by the time the men was ready to start, and he believed they must a gone up town to get a dog, and so they lost all that time, or else we wouldn't be here on a tow-head sixteen or seventeen mile below the village—no, indeedy, we would be in that same old town again. So I said I didn't care what was the reason they didn't get us, as long as they didn't.

When it was beginning to come on dark, we poked our heads out of the cottonwood thicket and looked up, and down, and across; nothing in sight; so Jim took up some of the top planks of the raft and built a snug wigwam to get under in blazing weather and rainy, and to keep the things dry. Jim made a floor for the wigwam, and raised it a foot or more above the level of the raft, so now the blankets and all the traps was out of the reach of steamboat waves. Right in the middle of the wigwam we made a layer of dirt about five or six inches deep with a frame around it for to hold it to its place; this was to build a fire on in sloppy weather or chilly; the wigwam would keep it from being seen. We made an extra steering
4 oar, too, because one of the others might get broke, on a snag or something. We fixed up a short forked stick to hang the old lantern on; because we must always light the lantern whenever we see a steamboat coming down stream, to keep from getting run over; but we wouldn't have to light it for
5 up-stream boats unless we see we was in what they call a "crossing;" for the river was pretty high yet, very low banks being still a little under water; so up-bound boats didn't always run the channel, but hunted easy water.

This second night we run between seven and eight hours, with a current that was making over four mile an hour. We catched fish, and talked, and we took a swim now and then to keep off sleepiness. It was kind of solemn, drifting down the big still river, laying on our backs looking up at the stars, and we didn't ever feel like talking loud, and it warn't often that we laughed, only a little kind of a low chuckle. We had mighty good weather, as a general thing, and nothing ever happened to us at all, that night, nor the next, nor the next.

Every night we passed towns, some of them away up on black hillsides, nothing but just a shiny bed of lights, not a house could you see. The fifth night we passed St. Louis, and it was
6 like the whole world lit up. In St. Petersburg they used to say there was twenty or thirty thousand people in St. Louis, but I never believed it till I see that wonderful spread of lights at two o'clock that still night. There warn't a sound there; everybody was asleep.

HE SOMETIMES LIFTED A CHICKEN.

Every night, now, I used to slip ashore, towards ten o'clock, at some little village, and buy ten or fifteen cents' worth of meal or bacon or other stuff to eat; and sometimes I lifted a chicken that warn't roosting comfortable, and took him along. Pap always said, take a chicken when you get a chance, because if you don't want him yourself you can easy find somebody that does, and a good deed ain't ever forgot. I never see pap when he didn't want the chicken himself, but that is what he used to say, anyway.

Mornings, before daylight, I slipped into corn-fields and borrowed a watermelon, or a mushmelon, or a punkin, or some **7** new corn, or things of that kind. Pap always said it warn't no **8** harm to borrow things, if you was meaning to pay them back, sometime; but the widow said it warn't anything but a soft name for stealing, and no decent body would do it. Jim said he reckoned the widow was partly right and pap was partly right; so the best way would be for us to pick out two or three things from the list and say we wouldn't borrow them any more —then he reckoned it wouldn't be no harm to borrow the others. So we talked it over all one night, drifting along down the river, trying to make up our minds whether to drop the watermelons, or the cantelopes, or the mushmelons, or what. But towards daylight we got it all settled satisfactory, and concluded to drop crabapples and p'simmons. We warn't feeling **9** just right before that, but it was all comfortable now. I was glad the way it came out, too, because crabapples ain't ever good, and the p'simmons wouldn't be ripe for two or three months yet.

We shot a water-fowl, now and then, that got up too early in the morning or didn't go to bed early enough in the evening. Take it all around, we lived pretty high.

7 *mushmelon.* Muskmelon.

8 *Pap always said it warn't no harm to borrow things, . . . but the widow said it warn't anything but a soft name for stealing.* Along the river, the theft of edibles was not considered stealing, but the taking of money was. It was widely assumed that it was one's right to take whatever was needed to feed oneself—if one could get away with it. "'Stole' is a strong word," Twain commented about his own theft of a watermelon when a boy, in a talk on "Morals and Memory" at Barnard College, March 7, 1906 (in *Mark Twain's Speeches,* 1910, p. 228). "Stole? Stole? No, I don't mean that. It was the first time I ever withdrew a watermelon. It was the first time I ever *extracted* a watermelon. That is exactly the word I want— 'extracted.' It is definite. It is precise."

As Fred W. Lorch found in his research for "A Note on Tom Blankenship" (*American Literature,* November 1940, pp. 351–353), the real Huckleberry Finn was notorious for his petty thefts. The Hannibal *Daily Messenger* reported on April 21, 1861, that Tom Blankenship was charged with stealing turkeys and sentenced to thirty days in the county jail; and as soon as he was released, he stole some onions from a garden on the Sunday night. "What is it that Tom wouldn't steal?" asked the *Daily Messenger* on June 4. "We expect next to hear of his 'cabbaging' all the garden vegetables in town, after which he will probably go out in the country and 'hook' a few wheat and oat fields." So great was Tom's reputation as a thief that he seemed to be the obvious suspect when anything was stolen in Hannibal. On June 12, the paper reported in "Wholesale Thievery" on the current increase in stealing in Hannibal when two horses, a large lot of bacon, a six-gallon jug of butter, a washtubful of clothes, a large quantity of sugar, ten gallons of molasses, and some chickens were missing. "Tom Blankenship must have concluded to make another descent," the *Daily Messenger* sarcastically speculated, "and effectually clean out the Bay; or at least the surplus products of the inhabitants." Such evidence would suggest that Tom Blankenship did indeed leave the town to go to the penitentiary as mentioned in Chapter 1, note 1.

9 *p'simmons.* Persimmons, orange-colored fruit, the American date-plum, common in Missouri and the South; although astringent when unripe, it was particularly popular with slaves who brewed "persimmon beer."

A Mississippi steamboat. *Courtesy the Library of Congress.*

10 *chimbly-guy.* Chimney-guy, a steel cable used to fix and hold a smokestack in place.

11 *a chair by the big bell, with an old slouch hat hanging on the back of it.* Obviously the pilot was away from his watch, which appears to have caused the wreck of the steamboat.

12 *let blame' well alone, as de good book says.* Actually the maxim, "Let well enough alone," is not biblical; it has been traced as far back as 161 B.C., to Terence's *Phormio* in which, even then, it is referred to as an "old saying." It was a common device in Southern and Southwestern humor to credit any old proverb to the Bible (or to Shakespeare).

13 *the texas.* The officers' quarters, comprising the upper deck of a river steamer, with the pilot-house located before or on top. Farmer's *Americanisms* explained that this open deck was originally "frequented by the personal friends of the pilot, . . . men of great daring, . . . and expert in the use of the bowie-knife and pistol, but as little desirable as the first settlers in the Republic of Texas, which attracted all the lawless and desperate characters of the Union"; and thus its name came from these characters. However, the most common theory for the origin of this term is that the cabins of Mississippi riverboats were often named for the states (see note 15), and in the 1840s, after Texas had entered the Union, the largest of the rooms became known as "the texas."

Kemble was unfamiliar with this term: Twain wrote the publishers on June 25, 1884, that "on the pilot-house of that steamboat-wreck the artist has put *Texas*—having been misled by some of Huck's remarks about the boat's 'texas'—a thing which is a part of *every* boat. That word had better be removed from that pilot-house—that is where a boat's *name* is put, and that particular boat's name was Walter Scott, I think" (quoted by Webster, *Mark Twain, Business Man*, p. 262). And the correction was made on the illustration on p. 140.

The fifth night below St. Louis we had a big storm after midnight, with a power of thunder and lightning, and the rain poured down in a solid sheet. We stayed in the wigwam and let the raft take care of itself. When the lightning glared out we could see a big straight river ahead, and high rocky bluffs on both sides. By-and-by says I, "Hel-*lo*, Jim, looky yonder!" It was a steamboat that had killed herself on a rock. We was drifting straight down for her. The lightning showed her very distinct. She was leaning over, with part of her upper deck **10** above water, and you could see every little chimbly-guy clean **11** and clear, and a chair by the big bell, with an old slouch hat hanging on the back of it when the flashes come.

Well, it being away in the night, and stormy, and all so mysterious-like, I felt just the way any other boy would a felt when I see that wreck laying there so mournful and lonesome in the middle of the river. I wanted to get aboard of her and slink around a little, and see what there was there. So I says:

"Le's land on her, Jim."

But Jim was dead against it, at first. He says:

"I doan' want to go fool'n 'long er no wrack. We's doin' **12** blame' well, en we better let blame' well alone, as de good book says. Like as not dey's a watchman on dat wrack."

"Watchman your grandmother!" I says; "there ain't **13,14** nothing to watch but the texas and the pilot-house; and do you reckon anybody's going to resk his life for a texas and a pilot-house such a night as this, when it's likely to break up and wash off down the river any minute?" Jim couldn't say nothing to that, so he didn't try. "And besides," I says, "we might borrow something worth haying, out of the captain's **15** stateroom. Seegars, *I* bet you—and cost five cents apiece, solid **16** cash. Steamboat captains is always rich, and gets sixty dollars a month, and *they* don't care a cent what a thing costs, you know, long as they want it. Stick a candle in your pocket; I can't rest, Jim, till we give her a rummaging. Do you reckon **17** Tom Sawyer would ever go by this thing? Not for pie, he wouldn't. He'd call it an adventure—that's what he'd call it; and he'd land on that wreck if it was his last act. And wouldn't he throw style into it?—wouldn't he spread himself, nor nothing? Why, you'd think it was Christopher C'lumbus discovering Kingdom-Come. I wish Tom Sawyer *was* here."

Jim he grumbled a little, but give in. He said we mustn't talk any more than we could help, and then talk mighty low. The lightning showed us the wreck again, just in time, and we fetched the stabboard derrick, and made fast there.

The deck was high out, here. We went sneaking down the **18** slope of it to labboard, in the dark, towards the texas, feeling our way slow with our feet, and spreading our hands out to **19** fend off the guys, for it was so dark we couldn't see no sign of them. Pretty soon we struck the forward end of the skylight, and clumb on to it; and the next step fetched us in front of the captain's door, which was open, and by Jimminy, away down through the texas hall we see a light! and all in the same second we seemed to hear low voices in yonder!

Jim whispered and said he was feeling powerful sick, and told me to come along. I says, all right; and was going to start for the raft; but just then I heard a voice wail out and say:

"Oh, please don't boys: I swear I won't ever tell!"

Another voice said, pretty loud:

"It's a lie, Jim Turner. You've acted this way before. You always want more'n your share of the truck, and you've always got it, too, because you've swore 't if you didn't you'd tell. But this time you've said it jest one time too many. You're the meanest, treacherousest hound in this country."

By this time Jim was gone for the raft. I was just a-biling **20** with curiosity; and I says to myself, Tom Sawyer wouldn't back out now, and so I won't either; I'm agoing to see what's going on here. So I dropped on my hands and knees, in the little passage, and crept aft in the dark, till there warn't but about one stateroom betwixt me and the cross-hall of the texas. Then, in there I see a man stretched on the floor and tied hand and foot, and two men standing over him, and one of them had a dim lantern in his hand, and the other one had a pistol. This one kept pointing the pistol at the man's head on the floor and saying—

"I'd *like* to! And I orter, too, a mean skunk!"

The man on the floor would shrivel up, and say: "Oh, please don't, Bill—I hain't ever goin' to tell."

And every time he said that, the man with the lantern would laugh, and say:

"'Deed you *ain't*! You never said no truer thing 'n that, you bet you." And once he said: "Hear him beg! and yit if we hadn't got the best of him and tied him, he'd a killed us both. And what *for*? Jist for noth'n. Jist because we stood on our *rights*—that's what for. But I lay you ain't agoin' to threaten nobody anymore, Jim Turner. Put *up* that pistol, Bill."

Bill says:

" PLEASE DON'T, BILL."

14 *do you reckon anybody's going to resk his life for a texas and a pilot-house such a night as this, when it's likely to break up and wash off down the river any minute?* Huck frequently displays an extensive knowledge of river wisdom, reflecting that learned by Sam Clemens when a pilot on the Mississippi.

15 *stateroom*. An individual sleeping room on a passenger steamer, originally named for the states of the Union. The earliest riverboats contained only a large cabin for men and a smaller one for women; but about 1817, Henry M. Shreve, captain of the steamboat *Washington*, broke these up into smaller rooms for individual passengers, naming them after the various states. Captain Isaiah Sellers, another pilot (and the author of a newspaper column that the young Sam Clemens burlesqued), is credited with having given the term "stateroom" to the cabins.

16 *Steamboat captains . . . gets sixty dollars a month.* Apparently Huck is underestimating a captain's salary, because, Twain recalled in Chapter 4 of *Life on the Mississippi*, just "the pilot, even in those days of trivial wages, had a princely salary—from a hundred and fifty to two hundred and fifty dollars a month, and no board to pay." Obviously sixty dollars is "a princely salary" to destitute Huck.

17 *Not for pie*. Not for anything. See Chapter 6, note 13.

18 *labboard*. Larboard, the port, or left, side of the boat, looking toward the bows. "The term 'larboard,'" Twain noted in Chapter 12 of *Life on the Mississippi*, "is never used at sea, now, to signify the left hand; but was always used on the river in my time."

19 *the guys*. The ropes fastened aloft for hoisting or dropping cargo.

20 *a-biling*. Boiling.

21 *crawfished*. Crawled backward, like a crawfish.

22 *treed*. Literally, to be chased up a tree, but here merely cornered.

23 *he'll turn State's evidence*. To avoid criminal prosecution himself, the third thief may make a deal with the state prosecutor to testify in court against his partners.

24 *to go court'n around after a halter*. To risk getting hanged. Packard recognizes that the only punishment for shooting and killing a man, even another thief, is public execution.

25 *it ain't good sense, it ain't good morals*. By allowing his selfish interests to shape what he says is a moral decision, Packard follows the same line of thinking that Huck used earlier in the chapter when he rationalized his stealing only the good fruit and leaving the bad and the unripe.

" I don't want to, Jake Packard. I'm for killin' him—and didn't he kill old Hatfield jist the same way—and don't he deserve it ? "

" But I don't *want* him killed, and I've got my reasons for it."

" Bless yo' heart for them words, Jake Packard ! I'll never forgit you, long's I live ! " says the man on the floor, sort of blubbering.

Packard didn't take no notice of that, but hung up his lantern on a nail, and started towards where I was, there in the
21 dark, and motioned Bill to come. I crawfished as fast as I could, about two yards, but the boat slanted so that I couldn't make very good time ; so to keep from getting run over and catched I crawled into a stateroom on the upper side. The man come a-pawing along in the dark, and when Packard got to my stateroom, he says :

" Here—come in here."

And in he came, and Bill after him. But before they got in, I was up in the upper berth, cornered, and sorry I come. Then they stood there, with their hands on the ledge of the berth, and talked. I couldn't see them, but I could tell where they was, by the whisky they'd been having. I was glad I didn't drink whisky ; but it wouldn't made much difference, anyway, because
22 most of the time they couldn't a treed me because I didn't breathe. I was too scared. And besides, a body *couldn't* breathe, and hear such talk. They talked low and earnest. Bill wanted to kill Turner. He says :

" He's said he'll tell, and he will. If we was to give both our shares to him *now*, it wouldn't make no difference after the
23 row, and the way we've served him. Shore's you're born, he'll turn State's evidence ; now you hear *me*. I'm for putting him out of his troubles."

" So'm I," says Packard, very quiet.

" Blame it, I'd sorter begun to think you wasn't. Well, then, that's all right. Le's go and do it."

" Hold on a minute ; I ain't had my say yit. You listen to me. Shooting's good, but there's quieter ways if the thing's
24 *got* to be done. But what *I* say, is this ; it ain't good sense to go court'n around after a halter, if you can git at what you're up to in some way that's jist as good and at the same time don't bring you into no resks. Ain't that so ? "

" You bet it is. But how you goin' to manage it this time ? "

" Well, my idea is this ; we'll rustle around and gether up whatever pickins we've overlooked in the staterooms, and shove for shore and hide the truck. Then we'll wait. Now I say it ain't agoin' to be more 'n two hours befo' this wrack breaks up and washes off down the river. See ? He'll be drownded, and won't have nobody to blame for it but his own self. I reckon that's a considerble sight better'n killin' of him. I'm unfavour-
25 able to killin' a man as long as you can git around it ; it ain't good sense, it ain't good morals. Ain't I right ? "

" Yes—I reck'n you are. But s'pose she *don't* break up and wash off ? "

"IT AIN'T GOOD MORALS."

26 *"Well, we can wait the two hours, anyway, and see, can't we?"* In the manuscript, Bill had other plans for Jim Turner: *"Then, if the thing don't work, it'll still be long enough befo' daylight, and we'll come back and do the next best thing—tie a rock to him and dump him into the river"* (quoted by DeLancey Ferguson, "Huck Finn Aborning," *The Colophon,* Spring 1938, p. 177). They then gag him, but he works it free, and his cries call them back, just as Huck and Jim are making their getaway. Twain dropped this passage before the book went to press, apparently because, Ferguson argued, "it merely complicated the action without intensifying it."

27 *coarse whisper.* Or "stage whisper," speaking low but also clearly and distinctly.

28 *there's a gang of murderers in yonder.* These thieves' crimes trivialize Huck's stealing, earlier in the chapter.

"Well, we can wait the two hours, anyway, and see, can't **26** we?"

"All right, then; come along."

So they started, and I lit out, all in a cold sweat, and scrambled forward. It was dark as pitch there; but I said in a kind of coarse whisper, "Jim!" and he answered up, right at **27** my elbow, with a sort of moan, and I says:

"Quick, Jim, it ain't no time for fooling around and moaning; there's a gang of murderers in yonder, and if we don't hunt **28** up their boat and set her drifting down the river so these fellows can't get away from the wreck, there's one of 'em going to be in a bad fix. But if we find their boat we can put *all* of 'em in a bad fix—for the Sheriff 'll get 'em. Quick—hurry! I'll hunt the labboard side, you hunt the stabboard. You start at the raft, and——"

"Oh! my lordy, lordy! *Raf'?* Dey ain' no raf' no mo', she done broke loose en gone!—'en here we is!"

"OH! LORDY, LORDY!"

1 *sentimentering*. Sentimentalizing.

2 *scrabbled*. Scrambled.

Chapter XIII.

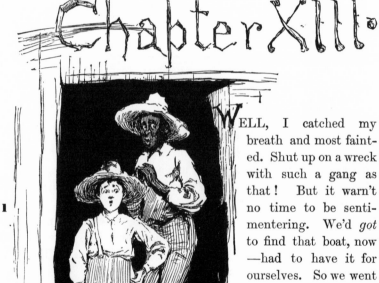

IN A FIX.

WELL, I catched my breath and most fainted. Shut up on a wreck with such a gang as that! But it warn't no time to be sentimentering. We'd *got* to find that boat, now —had to have it for ourselves. So we went a-quaking and shaking down the stabboard side, and slow work it was, too—seemed a week before we got to the stern. No sign of a boat. Jim said he didn't believe he could go any further—so scared he hadn't hardly any strength left, he said. But I said come on, if we get left on this wreck, we are in a fix, sure. So on we prowled, again. We struck for the stern of the texas, and found it, and then scrabbled along forwards on the skylight, hanging on from shutter to shutter, for the edge of the skylight was in the water. When we got pretty close to the crosshall door, there was the skiff, sure enough! I could just barely see her. I felt ever so thankful. In another second I would a been aboard of her; but just then the door opened. One of

136

the men stuck his head out, only about a couple of foot from me, and I thought I was gone; but he jerked it in again, and says:

"Heave that blame lantern out o' sight, Bill!"

He flung a bag of something into the boat, and then got in himself, and set down. It was Packard. Then Bill *he* come out and got in. Packard says, in a low voice:

"All ready—shove off!"

I couldn't hardly hang on to the shutters, I was so weak. But Bill says:

"Hold on—'d you go through him?"

"No. Didn't you?"

"No. So he's got his share o' the cash, yet."

"Well, then, come along—no use to take truck and leave money."

"Say—won't he suspicion what we're up to?"

"Maybe he won't. But we got to have it anyway. Come along."

So they got out and went in.

The door slammed to, because it was on the careened side; and in a half second I was in the boat, and Jim come a tumbling after me. I out with my knife and cut the rope, and away we went!

We didn't touch an oar, and we didn' speak nor whisper, nor hardly even breathe. We went gliding swift along, dead silent, past the tip of the paddle-box, and past the stern; then in a second or two more we was a hundred yards below the wreck, and the darkness soaked her up, every last sign of her, and we was safe, and knowed it

When we was three or four hundred yards down stream, we see the lantern show like a little spark at the texas door, for a second, and we knowed by that the rascals had missed their boat, and was beginning to understand that they was in just as much trouble, now, as Jim Turner was.

Then Jim manned the oars, and we took out after our raft. Now was the first time that I begun to worry about the men— I reckon I hadn't had time to before. I begun to think how dreadful it was, even for murderers, to be in such a fix. I says to myself, there ain't no telling but I might come to be a murderer myself, yet, and then how would *I* like it? So says I to Jim:

"The first light we see, we'll land a hundred yards below it or above it, in a place where it's a good hiding-place for you and the skiff, and then I'll go and fix up some kind of a yarn, **3** and get somebody to go for that gang and get them out of their scrape, so they can be hung when their time comes."

But that idea was a failure; for pretty soon it begun to storm again, and this time worse than ever. The rain poured down, and never a light showed; everybody in bed, I reckon. We boomed along down the river, watching for lights and watching for our raft. After a long time the rain let up, but the clouds staid, and the lightning kept whimpering, and

3 *I'll . . . get somebody to go for that gang and get them out of their scrape, so they can be hung when their time comes*. Apparently another example of Twain's playing with the maxim, "He that is born to be hanged shall never drown." See Chapter 4, note 11.

4 *the jackstaff*. A short staff, usually set upon the bowsprit or at the bow of a ship, on which the "jack," or flag, is hoisted.

5 *the bitts*. Posts with ropes strung between and fastened in pairs above the deck, to which lines or cables can be secured.

by-and-by a flash showed us a black thing ahead, floating, and we made for it.

It was the raft, and mighty glad was we to get aboard of it again. We seen a light, now, away down to the right, on shore. So I said I would go for it. The skiff was half full of plunder which that gang had stole, there on the wreck. We hustled it on to the raft in a pile, and I told Jim to float along down, and show a light when he judged he had gone about two mile, and keep it burning till I come; then I manned my oars and shoved for the light. As I got down towards it, three or four more showed—up on a hillside. It was a village. I closed in above the shore-light, and laid on my oars and floated.

4 As I went by, I see it was a lantern hanging on the jackstaff of a double-hull ferry-boat. I skimmed around for the watchman, a-wondering whereabouts he slept; and by-and-by I found him

5 roosting on the bitts, forward, with his head down between his knees. I give his shoulder two or three little shoves, and begun to cry.

He stirred up, in a kind of a startlish way; but when he see it was only me, he took a good gap and stretch, and then he says:

"Hello, what's up? Don't cry, bub. What's the trouble?"

"HELLO, WHAT'S UP?"

I says:

"Pap, and mam, and sis, and——"

Then I broke down. He says:

"Oh, dang it, now, *don't* take on so, we all has to have our troubles and this'n 'll come out all right. What's the matter with 'em?"

"They're—they're—are you the watchman of the boat?"

"Yes," he says, kind of pretty-well-satisfied like. "I'm the captain and the owner, and the mate, and the pilot, and watchman, and head deck-hand: and sometimes I'm the freight and passengers. I ain't as rich as old Jim Hornback, and I can't be so blame' generous and good to Tom, Dick, and Harry as what he is, and slam around money the way he does; but I've told him a many a time 't I wouldn't trade places with him; for, says I, a sailor's life's the life for me, and I'm derned if *I'd* live two mile out o' town, where there ain't nothing ever goin' on, not for all his spondulicks and as much more on top **6** of it. Says I——"

I broke in and says:

"They're in an awful peck of trouble, and——"

"*Who* is?"

"Why, pap, and mam, and sis, and Miss Hooker; and if you'd take your ferry-boat and go up there——"

"Up where? Where are they?"

"On the wreck."

"What wreck?"

"Why, there ain't but one."

"What, you don't mean the *Walter Scott?*" **7**

"Yes."

"Good land! what are they doin' *there*, for gracious sakes?"

"Well, they didn't go there a-purpose."

"I bet they didn't! Why, great goodness, there ain't no chance for 'em if they don't get off mighty quick! Why, how in the nation did they ever git into such a scrape?"

"Easy enough. Miss Hooker was a-visiting, up there to the town——"

"Yes, Booth's Landing—go on."

"She was a-visiting, there at Booth's Landing, and just in the edge of the evening she started over with her nigger woman in the horse-ferry, to stay all night at her friend's **8** house, Miss What-you-may-call-her, I disremember her name, and they lost their steering-oar, and swung around and went a-floating down, stern-first, about two mile, and saddle-baggsed **9** on the wreck, and the ferry man and the nigger woman and the horses was all lost, but Miss Hooker she made a grab and got aboard the wreck. Well, about an hour after dark, we come along down in our trading-scow, and it was so dark we didn't **10** notice the wreck till we was right on it; and so *we* saddle-baggsed; but all of us was saved but Bill Whipple—and oh, he *was* the best cretur!—I most wish't it had been me, I do."

"My George! It's the beatenest thing I ever struck. And **11** *then* what did you all do?"

"Well, we hollered and took on, but it's so wide there, we couldn't make nobody hear. So pap said somebody got to get ashore and get help somehow. I was the only one that could swim, so I made a dash for it, and Miss Hooker she said if I didn't strike help sooner, come here and hunt up her uncle, and he'd fix the thing. I made the land about a mile below, and been fooling along ever since, trying to get people to do something, but they said, 'What, in such a night and such a current? there ain't no sense it; go for the steam-ferry.' Now if you'll go, and——"

6 *spondulicks*. Or "spondulix," cash, money.

7 *the* Walter Scott. According to *Merchant Steam Vessels of the United States 1807–1868*, compiled by William M. Lytle and edited by Forrest R. Holdcamper (1952), a side-wheeler named *Walter Scott*, whose home port was New Orleans, traveled up and down the Mississippi from 1829 until it was "lost" in 1838. Several other steamships of the period were named for characters (such as *Ivanhoe* and *Lady of the Lake*) in Scott's popular romances and poems. Appropriately Twain names the floundering ship after this writer; Twain hated Scott's fiction and contended in "Enchantments and Enchanters" (Chapter 46 of *Life on the Mississippi*) that the novelist "sets the world in love with dreams and phantoms; with decayed and swinish forms of religion; with decayed and degraded systems of government; with the sillinesses and emptinesses, sham grandeurs, sham gauds, and sham chivalries of a brainless and worthless long-vanished society. He did measureless harm; more real and lasting harm, perhaps, than any other individual that ever wrote. Most of the world has now outlived a good part of these harms . . .; but in our South they flourish pretty forcefully still. . . . Sir Walter had so large a hand in making Southern character, as it existed before the war, that he is in great measure responsible for the war." Twain further argued that it was the residue of this "Sir Walter disease" which had kept the South from progressing after the Civil War. In Chapter 4 of *The American Claimant* (1892), Twain continues his attack upon the "Walter Scott disease" by inventing Rowena-Ivanhoe College, "the selectest and most aristocratic seat of learning for young ladies in our country. . . . Castellated college-buildings—towers and turrets and an imitation moat—and everything about the place named out of Sir Walter Scott's books and redolent of royalty and state and style," and where the girls "don't learn a blessed thing . . . but showy rubbish and un-American pretentiousness." The accuracy of Twain's accusations have been considered by Hamilton James Eckenrode in "Sir Walter Scott and the South," *The North American Review*, October 1917, pp. 595–603; Grace Warren Ludlam in "Sir Walter Scott and His

Walter Scott. *Courtesy the Library of Congress.*

Literary Rivals in the Old South," *American Literature*, Vol. 2, 1930–1931, pp. 256–276; and G. Harrison Orians in "Walter Scott, Mark Twain, and the Civil War," *The South Atlantic Quarterly*, October 1941, pp. 342–359.

8 *the horse-ferry*. A ferry which carried horses and carriages across the water.

A horse-ferry. Illustration from *Emerson's Magazine and Putnam's Monthly*, October 1857. *Courtesy the Library of Congress.*

9 *saddle-baggsed*. Caught on the wreck and doubled around it like a saddle-bag.

10 *trading-scow*. Riverboat for carrying cargo.

11 *My George! . . . By Jackson*. These interjections perhaps suggest to Huck the alias he uses in Chapter 17.

12 *to dart you out*. To send you forth.

13 *rapscallions and dead beats is the kind the widow and good people takes the most interest in*. The widow and the others evidently are believers in the parable of the prodigal son, Luke 15:11–32, who is of more concern to the parent than the obedient child.

"By Jackson, I'd *like* to, and blame it I don't know but I will; but who in the 'dingnations agoin' to *pay* for it? Do you reckon your pap——"

"Why, *that's* all right. Miss Hooker she told me, *particular*, that her uncle Hornback——"

"Great guns! is *he* her uncle? Looky here, you break for that light over yonder-way, and turn out west when you git there, and about a quarter of a mile out you'll come to the tavern; tell 'em to dart you out to Jim Hornback's and he'll foot the bill. And don't you fool around any, because he'll wan't to know the news. Tell him I'll have his niece all safe before he can get to town. Hump yourself, now; I'm agoing up around the corner here, to roust out my engineer."

I struck for the light, but as soon as he turned the corner I went back and got into my skiff and baled her out and then pulled up shore in the easy water about six hundred yards, and tucked myself in among some woodboats; for I couldn't rest easy till I could see the ferry-boat start. But take it all around, I was feeling ruther comfortable on accounts of taking all this trouble for that gang, for not many would a done it. I wished the widow knowed about it. I judged she would be proud of me for helping these rapscallions, because rapscallions and dead beats is the kind the widow and good people takes the most interest in.

Well, before long, here comes the wreck, dim and dusky,

THE WRECK.

sliding along down! A kind of cold shiver went through me, and then I struck out for her. She was very deep, and I see in a minute there warn't much chance for anybody being alive in her. I pulled all around her and hollered a little, but there wasn't any answer; all dead still. I felt a little bit heavy-hearted about the gang, but not much, for I reckoned if they could stand it, I could.

Then here comes the ferry-boat; so I shoved for the middle

of the river on a long down-stream slant; and when I judged
I was out of eye-reach, I laid on my oars, and looked back and
see her go and smell around the wreck for Miss Hooker's
remainders, because the captain would know her uncle Hornback would want them; and then pretty soon the ferry-boat
give it up and went for shore, and I laid into my work and
went a-booming down the river.

It did seem a powerful long time before Jim's light showed
up; and when it did show, it looked like it was a thousand
mile off. By the time I got there the sky was beginning to
get a little gray in the east; so we struck for an island, and
hid the raft, and sunk the skiff, and turned in and slept like
dead people.

WE TURNED IN AND SLEPT.

Chapter XIV

1 *We hadn't ever been this rich before, in neither of our lives.* And yet Huckleberry Finn is worth six thousand dollars, at least on paper. Because he has had so little experience with money, the boy defines wealth in the accumulation of objects and not in the relative abstract of capital. "Money, in truth, is almost a perfectly unknown commodity in their midst," Hundley in *Social Relations in Our Southern States* (p. 262) explained the poor white trash attitude toward currency, "and nearly all of their trafficking is carried on by means of barter alone. . . . Dollars and dimes, . . . they never bother their brains any great deal about."

TURNING OVER THE TRUCK.

BY-and-by, when we got up, we turned over the truck the gang had stole off of the wreck, and found boots, and blankets, and clothes, and all sorts of other things, and a lot of books, and a spyglass, and three boxes of seegars. We hadn't ever been this rich before, in neither of our lives. The seegars was prime. We laid off all the afternoon in the woods talking, and me reading the books, and having a general good time. I told Jim all about what happened inside the wreck, and at the ferry-boat; and I said these kinds of things was adventures; but he said he didn't want no more adventures. He said that when I went in the texas, and he crawled back to get on the raft and found her gone, he nearly died; because he judged it was all up with *him*, anyway it could be fixed; for if he didn't get saved he would get drownded; and if he did get saved, whoever saved him would send him back home so as to get the reward, and then Miss Watson would sell him South, sure. Well, he was right; he was most always right; he had an uncommon level head, for a nigger.

I read considerable to Jim about kings, and dukes, and **2** earls, and such, and how gaudy they dressed, and how much style they put on, and called each other your majesty, and your grace, and your lordship, and so on, 'stead of mister; and Jim's eyes bugged out, and he was interested. He says:

"I didn't know dey was so many un um. I hain't hearn 'bout none un um, skasely, but ole King Sollermun, onless you **3** counts dem kings dat's in a pack er k'yards. How much do a king git?"

"Get?" I says; "why, they get a thousand dollars a month if they want it; they can have just as much as they want; everything belongs to them."

"*Ain't* dat gay? En what dey got to do, Huck?"

"*They* don't do nothing! Why, how you talk. They just set around."

"No--is dat so?"

"Of course it is. They just set around. Except maybe when there's a war; then they go to the war. But other times they just lazy around; or go hawking—just hawking and sp— **4** Sh!—d' you hear a noise?"

We skipped out and looked; but it warn't nothing but the flutter of a steamboat's wheel, away down coming around the point; so we come back.

"Yes," says I, "and other times, when things is dull, they fuss with the parlyment; and if everybody don't go just so he whacks their heads off. But mostly they hang round the harem." **5**

"Roun' de which?"

"Harem."

"What's de harem?"

"The place where he keep his wives. Don't you know about the harem? Solomon had one; he had about a million **6** wives."

SOLOMON AND HIS MILLION WIVES.

2 *I read considerable to Jim about kings, and dukes, and earls.* Twain was particularly fond of the ensuing discussion of royalty, an apparent afterthought he added to the novel to prepare the boy and the slave for the entrance of the duke and the king in Chapter 19. Twain revised this chapter as "Advance sheets from *The Adventures of Huckleberry Finn,*" part of his 1884–1885 lecture tour with George W. Cable; later he combined this episode with the Balum's Ass exchange of Chapter 8 as "Jim's Investments, and King Sollermun" as a prepublication excerpt in *The Century* (January 1885).

3 *ole King Sollermun.* King Solomon of Israel, considered in his day to be the wisest man in the world, and whose reign is described in the First Book of Kings.

This comic discourse between a slave and a white is reminiscent of the discussion between Uncle Dan'l and Clay Hawkins in Chapter 3 of *The Gilded Age* about "he-brew" and "she-brew chil'en" in the fiery furnace (Daniel 3:1–30).

4 *hawking and sp——.* "Hawking and spitting," a common vulgar British expression for noisily clearing the throat of phlegm; the interruption of the steamboat leaves one to think Huck is referring to falconry. In his reading copy of the 1893 Tauchnitz edition, Twain revised, and thus weakened, his joke by adding "hawking or hogging or whatever it is" (MTP).

5 *they hang round the harem.* Twain originally wrote that kings "wallow" around the harem, but this word was thought too suggestive and struck out of the manuscript.

6 *Solomon . . . had about a million wives.* According to the Bible, King Solomon, a lover of women and the supposed author of the erotic "Song of Solomon," had seven hundred wives who were princesses, and another three hundred concubines. Many of these women were not Jews, and because the Lord had forbidden Israelites from marrying women of other faiths, these unions ultimately led to the downfall of Solomon's kingdom. There are countless jokes in American humor describing the obvious troubles Solomon suffered in having so many wives.

7 *a biler-factry.* Robert L. Ramsay and Frances Guthrie Emberson in "A Mark Twain Lexicon" (*University of Missouri Studies*, January 1, 1938) explained that Twain used "boiler factory" as "a synonym for noise or pandemonium."

8 *because the widow she told me so, her own self.* Surprisingly Huck now defends the religious instruction he had scorned in previous chapters. Like Miss Watson, he is using religion to keep a social "inferior" in his place. This episode may seem at first glance gratuitous to the story, but it does repeat an important theme of the novel, that one's morality must come naturally from within oneself and not from some abstract set of values.

9 *Does you know 'bout dat chile dat he 'uz gwyne to chop in two?* According to I Kings 3:16–28, two harlots came before Solomon, each claiming that the other was the mother of a child who had died in the night. When he threatened to have the other, the living baby, cut in two so that each might have a half, the true mother revealed herself by offering to give the child to the other woman if its life were spared. Twain may have introduced this lesson here as a comment on the custody battle between Pap Finn and the Widow Douglas over Huckleberry Finn.

10 *gumption.* Common sense.

" Why, yes, dat's so; I—I'd done forgot it. A harem's a bo'd'n-house, I reck'n. Mos' likely dey has rackety times in de nussery. En I reck'n de wives quarrels considable; en dat 'crease de racket. Yit dey say Sollermun de wises' man dat ever live'. I doan' take no stock in dat. Bekase why: would a wise man want to live in de mids' er sich a blimblammin' all de time? No—'deed he wouldn't. A wise man 'ud take en **7** buil' a biler-factry; en den he could shet *down* de biler-factry when he want to res'."

8 "Well, but he *was* the wisest man, anyway; because the widow she told me so, her own self."

" I doan k'yer what de widder say, he *warn't* no wise man, nuther. He had some er de dad-fetchedes' ways I ever see. **9** Does you know 'bout dat chile dat he 'uz gwyne to chop in two?"

THE STORY OF " SOLLERMUN."

" Yes, the widow told me all about it."

" *Well*, den! Warn' dat de beatenes' notion in de worl'? You jes' take en look at it a minute. Dah's de stump, dah—dat's one er de women; heah's you—dat's de yuther one; I's Sollermun; en dish-yer dollar bill's de chile. Bofe un you claims it. What does I do? Does I shin aroun' mongs' de neighbours en fine out which un you de bill *do* b'long to, en han' it over to de right one, all safe en soun', de way dat any-**10** body dat had any gumption would? No—I take en whack de bill in *two*, en give half un it to you, en de yuther half to de yuther woman. Dat's de way Sollermun was gwyne to do wid de chile. Now I want to ast you: what's de use er dat half a bill?—can't buy noth'n wid it. En what use is a half a chile? I would'n give a dern for a million un um."

" But hang it, Jim, you've clean missed the point—blame it, you've missed it a thousand mile."

" Who? Me? Go 'long. Doan' talk to *me* 'bout yo' pints. I reck'n I knows sense when I sees it; en dey ain' no sense in sich doin's as dat. De 'spute warn't 'bout a half a chile, de 'spute was 'bout a whole chile ; en de man dat think he kin settle a 'spute 'bout a whole chile wid a half a chile, doan' know enough to come in out'n de rain. Doan' talk to me 'bout Sollermun, Huck, I knows him by de back." **11**

"But I tell you you don't get the point."

"Blame de pint ! I reck'n I knows what I knows. En mine you, de *real* pint is down furder—it's down deeper. It lays in de way Sollermun was raised. You take a man dat's **12** got on'y one er two chillen ; is dat man gwyne to be waseful o' chillen ? No, he ain't ; he can't 'ford it. *He* know how to value 'em. But you take a man dat's got 'bout five million chillen runnin' roun' de house, en it's diffunt. *He* as soon chop a chile in two as a cat. Dey's plenty mo'. A chile er two, mo' er less, warn't no consekens to Sollermun, dad fetch him !"

I never see such a nigger. If he got a notion in his head once, there warn't no getting it out again. He was the most down on Solomon of any nigger I ever see. So I went to talking about other kings, and let Solomon slide. I told about Louis Sixteenth that got his head cut off in France long time ago ; and about his little boy the dolphin, that would a been a **13** king, but they took and shut him up in jail, and some say he died there.

"Po' little chap."

"But some says he got out and got away, and come to America."

"Dat's good ! But he'll be pooty lonesome—dey ain' no kings here, is dey, Huck ?"

"No."

"Den he cain't git no situation. What he gwyne to do ?"

"Well, I don't know. Some of them gets on the police, **14** and some of them learns people how to talk French."

"Why, Huck, doan' de French people talk de same way we does ?"

"*No*, Jim ; you couldn't understand a word they said—not **15** a single word."

"Well, now, I be ding-busted ! How do dat come ?"

"*I* don't know ; but it's so. I got some of their jabber out of a book. S'pose a man was to come to you and say *Polly-voo-* **16** *franzy*—what would you think ?"

"I wouldn' think nuff'n ; I'd take en bust him over de **17** head. Dad is, if he warn't white. I wouldn't 'low no nigger to call me dat."

"Shucks, it ain't calling you anything. It's only saying do you know how to talk French."

"Well, den, why couldn't he *say* it ?"

"Why, he *is* a-saying it. That's a Frenchman's *way* of saying it."

"Well, it's a blame' ridicklous way, en I doan' want to hear no mo' 'bout it. Dey ain' no sense in it."

"Looky here, Jim ; does a cat talk like we do ?"

"No, a cat don't."

11 *I knows him by de back.* I know him to the backbone, all through ; in Chapter 28 of *Following the Equator* (1897), Twain identified this phrase as gambling slang.

12 *You take a man dat's got on'y one er two chillen.* Jim, for example ; the fugitive slave is expressing his love for his own children. See also Chapter 16, note 11 ; and Chapter 23, note 13.

13 *the dolphin . . . some says he got out and got away, and come to America.* The Dauphin, Louis Charles (1785–1795), survived the execution of his father Louis XVI and his mother Marie Antoinette to die of scrofula in prison. However, the mysterious circumstances of his burial gave rise to the legend that he escaped (just as Anastasia, the daughter of Czar Nicholas and Czarina Alexandra, survived the Russian Revolution) ; and at least thirty-five imposters are known to have claimed the throne of France. So wide was the speculation that even a monthly *Revue historique de la question Louis XVIII* was founded, in 1905. And several of the claimants did come to the United States. See Chapter 19, note 36.

Louis Charles, the Dauphin. *Courtesy the Library of Congress.*

14 *Some of them gets on the police.* Huck is obviously thinking of Napoleon III who (as Twain explained in *The Innocents Abroad*, Vol. I, Chapter 13), when sent into exile, "associated with the common herd in America, and . . . kept his faithful watch and walked his weary beat a common policeman of London" before he returned to his homeland as President of France through a *coup d'état.*

Napoleon III. Illustration from *The Innocents Abroad*, 1869.

15 *you couldn't understand a word they said.* Twain himself struggled all his life with foreign languages, which were frequently the subjects for his jokes; he had particular difficulty with French, what he called in Chapter 68 of his *Autobiography* "plainly a language likely to fail a person at the crucial moment."

16 Polly-voo franzy. *Parlez-vous français?:* Do you speak French?

17 *I'd take en bust him over de head. Dad is, if he warn't white.* Jim amends his statement, because, according to Missouri law, any slave who lifted his hand against any person not a Negro or a mulatto unless "wantonly assaulted" was liable to receive a maximum sentence of thirty lashes.

18 *you can't learn a nigger to argue.* Huck's sentiments have changed from the sympathy of the earlier part of the chapter when he praised Jim for having "an uncommon level head, for a nigger." His attitude remains ambiguous, drifting toward admiration and then reverting back to contempt.

" Well, does a cow ? "

" No, a cow don't, nuther."

" Does a cat talk like a cow, or a cow talk like a cat ? "

" No, dey don't."

" It's natural and right for 'em to talk different from each other, ain't it ? "

" 'Course."

" And ain't it natural and right for a cat and a cow to talk different from *us* ? "

" Why, mos' sholy it is."

" Well, then, why ain't it natural and right for a *Frenchman* to talk different from us ?   You answer me that."

" Is a cat a man, Huck ? "

" No."

" Well, den, dey ain't no sense in a cat talkin' like a man. Is a cow a man ?—er is a cow a cat ? "

" No, she ain't either of them."

" Well, den, she ain't got no business to talk like either one er the yuther of 'em.   Is a Frenchman a man ? "

" Yes."

" *Well,* den ! Dad blame it, why doan' he *talk* like a man? You answer me *dat !* "

18   I see it warn't no use wasting words—you can't learn a nigger to argue.   So I quit.

Chapter XV.

WE judged that three nights more would fetch us to Cairo,[1] at the bottom **1** of Illinois, where the Ohio River comes in, and that was what we was after. We **2** would sell the raft and get on a steamboat and go way up the Ohio amongst the free States, and then be **3** out of trouble.

Well, the second night a fog begun to come on, and we made for a tow-head to tie to, for it wouldn't do to try to run in fog;

"WE WOULD SELL THE RAFT."

but when I paddled ahead in the canoe, with the line, to make fast, there warn't anything but little saplings to tie to. I passed the line around one of them right on the edge of the **4** cut bank, but there was a stiff current, and the raft come booming down so lively she tore it out by the roots and away she went. I see the fog closing down, and it made me so sick and scared I couldn't budge for most a half a minute it seemed to me—and then there warn't no raft in sight; you couldn't see twenty yards. I jumped into the canoe and run back to

1 *Cairo*. Pronounced "Kay-ro," a settlement in Illinois at the junction of the Ohio and Mississippi rivers. As recalled in Chapter 12 of *American Notes* (1842), Charles Dickens found Cairo "a spot so much more desolate than any we had yet beheld, that the forlornest places we had passed, were, in comparison with it, full of interest. At the junction of the two rivers, on ground so flat and low and marshy, that at certain seasons of the year it is inundated to the house-tops, lies a breeding-ground of fever, ague, and death. . . . A dismal swamp, on which the half-built houses rot away: cleared here and there for the space of a few yards; and teeming, then, with rank unwholesome vegetation, in whose baleful shade the wretched wanderers who are tempted hither, droop, and die, and lay their bones; the hateful Mississippi circling and eddying before it, and turning off upon

Cairo, Illinois. Illustration by Henry Lewis, *Das illustrirte Mississippithal*, 1857. *Courtesy the Rare Book Room, the Library of Congress.*

its southern course a slimy monster hideous to behold; a hotbed of disease, an ugly sepulchre, a grave uncheered by any gleam of promise, a place without one single quality, in earth or air or water, to commend it." Dismal Cairo inspired "Eden," the miserable American settlement in *Martin Chuzzlewit*.

2 *We would sell the raft . . . and go way up the Ohio.* Those who traveled down the river on flatboats or rafts, to return upstream, usually had to sell their crafts to get passage on up-bound steamboats.

3 *then be out of trouble.* The fugitives have had to change their plans: Because pro-slavery elements dominated the southern section of Illinois in the 1840s, the farther South Huck and Jim travel, the more dangerous their escape becomes. However, even if Jim does escape to the free states, he will not legally be a freeman. The fugitive slave laws provided that a runaway anywhere in the United States was subject to arrest. Harriet Beecher Stowe recalled in the 1881 introduction to *Uncle Tom's Cabin* that even in free Massachusetts there were day to day reports of "the terror and despair which the law had occasioned to industrious, worthy colored people who had from time to time escaped to Boston. . . . She heard of families broken up and fleeing in the dead of winter to the frozen shores of Canada. But what seemed to her more inexplicable, more dreadful, was the apparent apathy of the Christian world of the free North to these proceedings. The pulpits that denounced them were exceptions; the voices raised to remonstrate few and far between. In New England, as at the West, professed abolitionists were a small, despised, unfashionable band, whose constant remonstrances from year to year had been disregarded as the voices of impracticable fanatics." Jim's only hope for complete freedom is to escape to Canada through the Underground Railway. However, in the subsequent chapter Twain abandoned the plan to escape north.

4 *the cut bank.* A precipitous hillside, formed by the river's cutting into it.

the stern and grabbed the paddle and set her back a stroke. But she didn't come. I was in such a hurry I hadn't untied her. I got up and tried to untie her, but I was so excited my hands shook so I couldn't hardly do anything with them.

As soon as I got started I took out after the raft, hot and heavy, right down the tow-head. That was all right as far as it went, but the tow-head warn't sixty yards long, and the minute I flew by the foot of it I shot out into the solid white fog, and hadn't no more idea which way I was going than a dead man.

Thinks I, it won't do to paddle; first I know I'll run into the bank or a tow-head or something; I got to set still and float, and yet it's mighty fidgety business to have to hold your hands still at such a time. I whooped and listened. Away down there, somewheres, I hears a small whoop, and up comes my spirits. I went tearing after it, listening sharp to hear it again. The next time it come, I see I warn't heading for it but heading away to the right of it. And the next time, I was heading away to the left of it—and not gaining on it much, either, for I was flying around, this way and that and t'other, but it was going straight ahead all the time.

I did wish the fool would think to beat a tin pan, and beat it all the time, but he never did, and it was the still places between the whoops that was making the trouble for me. Well, I fought along, and directly I hears the whoop *behind* me. I was tangled good, now. That was somebody else's whoop, or else I was turned around.

I throwed the paddle down. I heard the whoop again; it was behind me yet, but in a different place; it kept coming, and kept changing its place, and I kept answering, till by-and-by it was in front of me again and I knowed the current had swung the canoe's head down stream and I was all right, if that was Jim and not some other raftsman hollering. I couldn't tell nothing about voices in a fog, for nothing don't look natural nor sound natural in a fog.

The whooping went on, and in about a minute I come a booming down on a cut bank with smoky ghosts of big trees on it, and the current throwed me off to the left and shot by, amongst a lot of snags that fairly roared, the current was tearing by them so swift.

In another second or two it was solid white and still again. I set perfectly still, then, listening to my heart thump, and I reckon I didn't draw a breath while it thumped a hundred.

I just give up, then. I knowed what the matter was. That cut bank was an island, and Jim had gone down t'other side of it. It warn't no tow-head, that you could float by in ten minutes. It had the big timber of a regular island; it might be five or six mile long and more than a half a mile wide.

I kept quiet, with my ears cocked, about fifteen minutes, I reckon. I was floating along, of course, four or five mile an hour; but you don't ever think of that. No, you *feel* like you

AMONG THE SNAGS.

5 *a Jack-o-lantern*. Huck is referring not to the Halloween lamp made of a hollowed-out pumpkin with a candle in it but to a variant of the "will-o-the wisp," an elusive light made by ignited methane gas or by sulphurated hydrogen from clumps of bacteria, suspended over bodies of water at night and said to be carried by evil spirits.

are laying dead still on the water; and if a little glimpse of a snag slips by, you don't think to yourself how fast *you're* going, but you catch your breath and think, my! how that snag's tearing along. If you think it ain't dismal and lonesome out in a fog that way, by yourself, in the night, you try it once— you'll see.

Next, for about a half an hour, I whoops now and then; at last I hears the answer a long ways off, and tries to follow it, but I couldn't do it, and directly I judged I'd got into a nest of tow-heads, for I had little dim glimpses of them on both sides of me, sometimes just a narrow channel between; and some that I couldn't see, I knowed was there, because I'd hear the wash of the current against the old dead brush and trash that hung over the banks. Well, I warn't long losing the whoops, down amongst the tow-heads; and I only tried to chase them a little while, anyway, because it was worse than chasing a Jack-o-lantern. You never knowed a sound dodge **5** around so, and swap places so quick and so much.

I had to claw away from the bank pretty lively, four or five times, to keep from knocking the islands out of the river; and so I judged the raft must be butting into the bank every now and then, or else it would get further ahead and clear out of hearing—it was floating a little faster than what I was.

Well, I seemed to be in the open river again, by-and-by, but I couldn't hear no sign of a whoop nowheres. I reckoned Jim had fetched up on a snag, maybe, and it was all up with him. I was good and tired, so I laid down in the canoe and said I wouldn't bother no more. I didn't want to go to sleep, of course; but I was so sleepy I couldn't help it; so I thought I would take just one little cat-nap.

But I reckon it was more than a cat-nap, for when I waked up the stars was shining bright, the fog was all gone, and I was spinning down a big bend stern first. First I didn't know where I was; I thought I was dreaming; and when things

6 *you ain' dead—you ain' drownded—you's back agin?*
The second of Huck's "deaths" and "resurrections."
Huck's malicious joke is like that played by Hank
on the gullible Pike in *History of the Big Bonanza*
(pp. 547–555) by "Dan De Quille," William Wright.
To get even with Pike, Hank and some friends fabri-
cate an Indian attack so convincing that Pike rushes
down the canyon "at the speed of an antelope." The
next morning, the others come upon him in the
town, now telling everyone about the terrible fight
with the Indians. Certain that he had left them for
dead, Pike is understandably startled when he sees
his companions arrive unharmed. They then confess
that they had seen no Indians and that Pike must
have been dreaming. Reluctant at first, Pike is finally
convinced that, yes, it was all a dream, "sartain and
sure . . . jist the same as bein' wide awake!" De
Quille concluded, "Pike continued to tell his dream
for some years, constantly adding new matter, till at
last it was a wonderful yarn." And although the
others tried once to tell him the whole truth of the
affair, Pike refused to believe it, for, "Do you think
. . . I was fool enough to believe that sich things
actually happened? No, it was all a dream from fust
to last, and the biggest and plainest dream I ever
had!"

Even though the two yarns follow the same
scheme, they differ significantly in each perpetrator's
motivation: De Quille introduced the possibility of
its being only a dream in part to protect Pike from the
suspicious and potentially violent crowd; Huck's
only purpose is to play some practical joke on a
"nigger" by taking advantage of the slave's deep
affection and concern for the boy. But Jim is not so
easily fooled as Pike. See also note 12.

begun to come back to me, they seemed to come up dim out
of last week.

It was a monstrous big river here, with the tallest and the
thickest kind of timber on both banks; just a solid wall, as
well as I could see, by the stars. I looked away down stream,
and seen a black speck on the water. I took out after it; but
when I got to it it warn't nothing but a couple of saw-logs
made fast together. Then I see another speck, and chased
that; then another, and this time I was right. It was the
raft.

When I got to it Jim was sitting there with his head down

ASLEEP ON THE RAFT.

between his knees, asleep, with his right arm hanging over the
steering oar. The other oar was smashed off, and the raft was
littered up with leaves and branches and dirt. So she's had a
rough time.

I made fast and laid down under Jim's nose on the raft,
and begun to gap, and stretch my fists out against Jim, and
says:

"Hello, Jim, have I been asleep? Why didn't you stir
me up?"

6 "Goodness gracious, is dat you, Huck? En you ain' dead
—you ain' drownded—you's back agin? It's too good for true,
honey, it's too good for true. Lemme look at you, chile,
lemme feel o' you. No, you ain' dead! you's back agin', live
en soun', jis de same ole Huck—de same ole Huck, thanks to
goodness!"

"What's the matter with you, Jim? You been a drinking?"

"Drinkin'? Has I ben a drinkin'? Has I had a chance
to be a drinkin'?"

"Well, then, what makes you talk so wild?"

"How does I talk wild?"

"*How?* why, hain't you been talking about my coming
back, and all that stuff, as if I'd been gone away?"

"Huck—Huck Finn, you look me in de eye; look me in de eye. *Hain't* you ben gone away?"

"Gone away? Why, what in the nation do you mean? *I* hain't been gone anywheres. Where would I go to?"

"Well, looky here, boss, dey's sumf'n wrong, dey is. Is I *me*, or who *is* I? Is I heah, or whah *is* I? Now dat's what I wants to know?"

"Well, I think you're here, plain enough, but I think you're a tangle-headed old fool, Jim."

"I is, is I? Well you answer me dis. Didn't you tote out de line in de canoe, fer to make fas' to de tow-head?"

"No, I didn't. What tow-head? I hain't seen no tow-head."

"You hain't seen no tow-head? Looky here—didn't de line pull loose en de raf' go a hummin' down de river, en leave you en de canoe behine in de fog?"

"What fog?"

"Why *de* fog. De fog dat's ben aroun' all night. En didn't you whoop, en didn't I whoop, tell we got mix' up in de islands en one un us got los' en t'other one was jis' as good as los', 'kase he didn' know whah he wuz? En didn't I bust up agin a lot er dem islands en have a turrible time en mos' git drownded? Now ain' dat so, boss—ain't it so? You answer me dat."

"Well, this is too many for me, Jim. I hain't seen no fog, nor no islands, nor no troubles, nor nothing. I been setting here talking with you all night till you went to sleep about ten minutes ago, and I reckon I done the same. You couldn't a got drunk in that time, so of course you've been dreaming."

"Dad fetch it, how is I gwyne to dream all dat in ten minutes?" **7**

"Well, hang it all, you did dream it, because there didn't any of it happen."

"But Huck, it's all jis' as plain to me as——"

"It don't make no difference how plain it is, there ain't nothing in it. I know, because I've been here all the time."

Jim didn't say nothing for about five minutes, but set there studying over it. Then he says:

"Well, den, I reck'n I did dream it, Huck; but dog my cats ef it ain't de powerfullest dream I ever see. En I hain't ever had no dream b'fo' dat's tired me like dis one."

"Oh, well, that's all right, because a dream does tire a body like everything, sometimes. But this one was a staving dream **8** —tell me all about it, Jim."

So Jim went to work and told me the whole thing right through, just as it happened, only he painted it up considerable. Then he said he must start in and "'terpret" it, because it was sent for a warning. He said the first tow-head stood for **9** a man that would try to do us some good, but the current was another man that would get us away from him. The whoops was warnings that would come to us every now and then, and if we didn't try hard to make out to understand them they'd

7 *how is I gwyne to dream all dat in ten minutes?* Actually, the duration of time is so distorted in dreams that one can experience a long string of events in what seems to be a relatively short period.

8 *staving*. Fine, strong, vivid.

9 *it was sent for a warning*. Although the interpretation which follows at first resembles the duplicity of Jim's earlier prophecy with the hairball (see Chapter 4, note 7), the boy and the slave indeed do encounter many "quarrelsome people and all kinds of mean folks" farther down the river.

The Ohio River. *Courtesy the Library of Congress.*

10 *the big clear river.* The Ohio River: Unlike the muddy lower Mississippi, the Ohio is a clear river.

11 *trash is what people is dat puts dirt on de head er dey fren's en makes 'em ashamed.* Jim calls Huck by the most contemptuous term slaves had for white men— "white trash."

12 *It made me feel so mean.* So too did Dan De Quille suffer such guilt after Pike, terrified, dashed down into the canyon and out of sight. "For my part," he admitted in *History of the Big Bonanza* (pp. 551–552), "now that the fun was all over, I began to feel quite miserable over the whole affair. . . . I firmly resolved never to take part in another affair of the kind." However, De Quille worried that Pike might have been hurt when he did not return after his mad flight into the canyon. Huck learns a more devastating moral lesson than that of De Quille: Jim's demonstration of his dignity has aroused an awakening of Huck's conscience. Earlier, in Chapter 10, when Huck lay the rattlesnake in Jim's bed and its mate bit Jim, the boy learned that the slave felt pain just like anyone else; in this chapter, he realizes that Jim has emotions like himself. However, when he killed the rattler and threw the skin away, Huck was protecting himself from further upsetting Jim. The first instance of Huck's feeling guilt toward his treatment of the slave is here when Jim admonishes him for acting like "trash."

13 *humble myself to a nigger.* Huck has performed what must have been the most degrading thing for a white man to do for a slave. Now Huck and Jim are equals.

T. S. Eliot in his 1950 introduction to the novel pointed to a meaning in this passage which is often overlooked. "What is obvious, in it," he explained, "is the pathos and dignity of Jim, and this is moving enough; but what I find still more disturbing, and still more unusual in literature, is the pathos and dignity of the boy, when reminded so humbly and humiliatingly, that his position in the world is not that of other boys, entitled from time to time to a practical joke; but that he must bear, and bear alone, the responsibility of a man."

just take us into bad luck, 'stead of keeping us out of it. The lot of tow-heads was troubles we was going to get into with quarrelsome people and all kinds of mean folks, but if we minded our business and didn't talk back and aggravate them, **10** we would pull through and get out of the fog and into the big clear **river**, which was the free States, and wouldn't have no more trouble.

It had clouded up pretty dark just after I got on to the raft, but it was clearing up again, now.

"Oh, well, that's all interpreted well enough, as far as it goes, Jim," I says; "but what does *these* things stand for?"

It was the leaves and rubbish on the raft, and the smashed oar. You could see them first rate, now.

Jim looked at the trash, and then looked at me, and back at the trash again. He had got the dream fixed so strong in his head that he couldn't seem to shake it loose and get the facts back into its place again, right away. But when he did get the thing straightened around, he looked at me steady, without ever smiling, and says:

"What do dey stan' for? I's gwyne to tell you. When I got all wore out wid work, en wid de callin' for you, en went to sleep, my heart wuz mos' broke bekase you wuz los', en I didn' k'yer no mo' what become er me en de raf'. En when I wake up en fine you back agin', all safe en soun', de tears come en I could a got down on my knees en kiss' yo' foot I's so thankful. En all you wuz thinkin 'bout wuz how you could make a fool uv ole Jim wid a lie. Dat truck dah is *trash*; en **11** trash is what people is dat puts dirt on de head er dey fren's en makes 'em ashamed."

Then he got up slow, and walked to the wigwam, and went in there, without saying anything but that. But that was **12** enough. It made me feel so mean I could almost kissed *his* foot to get him to take it back.

It was fifteen minutes before I could work myself up to go **13** and humble myself to a nigger—but I done it, and I warn't ever sorry for it afterwards, neither. I didn't do him no more mean tricks, and I wouldn't done that one· if I'd a knowed it would make him feel that way.

Chapter XVI

"IT AMOUNTED TO SOMETHING BEING A RAFTSMAN."

WE slept most all day, and started out at night, a little ways behind a monstrous long raft that was as long going by as a procession. She had four long **1** sweeps at each end, so we judged she carried as many as thirty men, likely. She had five big wigwams aboard, wide apart, and an open camp fire in the middle, and a tall flag-pole at each end. There was a power of style about her. It *amounted* to something being a raftsman on such a craft as that.

We went drifting down into a big bend, and the night clouded up and got hot. The river was very wide, and was walled with solid timber on both sides; you couldn't see a break in it hardly ever, or a light. We talked about Cairo, and wondered whether we would know it when we got to it. I said likely we wouldn't, because I had heard say there warn't but about a dozen houses there, and if they didn't happen to

1 *long sweeps.* Especially long oars, used to propel or to steer the craft.

2 *Jim said if the two big rivers joined together there, that would show.* Because one is a clear river and the other a muddy one, Twain explained in "The Raft Chapter," a deleted section of *Huckleberry Finn*, published in Chapter 3 of *Life on the Mississippi* "Ohio water didn't like to mix with Mississippi water. . . . if you take the Mississippi on a rise when the Ohio is low, you'll find a wide band of clear water all the way down the east side of the Mississippi for a hundred mile down shore and past the line, it is all thick and yaller the rest of the way across." See Appendix.

3 *pap . . . was a green hand at the business.* With some scorn toward his real father, Huck always describes the "pap" of his yarns as unskilled and ineffectual.

4 *Jim thought it was a good idea, so we took a smoke on it and waited.* It was here that "The Raft Chapter" appeared in the manuscript, completed in 1876. Having pigeonholed *Huckleberry Finn* several years before, Twain decided to include the episode in *Life on the Mississippi* when he was expanding and padding his magazine articles, "Old Times on the Mississippi," into a subscription book. However, when he finally finished the novel, Twain intended to return "The Raft Chapter" to its original place; but Charles L. Webster, the publisher, wrote him that he found the new book "so *much* larger than Tom Sawyer, would it not be better to omit that old Mississippi matter? I think it would improve it." Disregarding George W. Cable's suggestion that it be left in the novel, Twain agreed with Webster in a letter of April 22, 1884, "Yes, I think the raft chapter can be left wholly out, by heaving in a paragraph to say Huck visited the raft to find out how far it might be to Cairo, but got no satisfaction. Even *this* is not necessary unless that raft-visit is referred to later in the book. I think it is, but am not certain" (quoted by Webster, *Mark Twain, Business Man*, pp. 249–250). And *this* was not necessary; the text was not altered. Although DeVoto returned the deleted episode to its original place in the 1944 Limited Editions Club edition, in this edition, "The Raft Chapter" has been reprinted as an Appendix.

5 *the slave country.* Cairo was the point farthest south in free soil along the Mississippi; the farther downstream Jim and Huck travel, the deeper into slave country they will be.

6 *no more show.* No further opportunity, not another chance.

7 *lightning-bugs.* Fireflies.

8 *my conscience.* Believing that "in a crucial moral emergency a sound heart is a safer guide than an ill-trained conscience," Twain prefaced an 1895 reading of this episode by acknowledging Huck's moral struggle as an example in which "a sound heart and a deformed conscience come into collision and conscience suffers defeat" (quoted by Blair, *Mark Twain and Huck Finn*, p. 143). By identifying the sound heart with one's natural responses in this conflict and the deformed conscience with conventional morality,

have them lit up, how was we going to know we was passing a **2** town? Jim said if the two big rivers joined together there, that would show. But I said maybe we might think we was passing the foot of an island and coming into the same old river again. That disturbed Jim—and me too. So the question was, what to do? I said, paddle ashore the first time a **3** light showed, and tell them pap was behind, coming along with a trading-scow, and was a green hand at the business, and **4** wanted to know how far it was to Cairo. Jim thought it was a good idea, so we took a smoke on it and waited.

There warn't nothing to do, now, but to look out sharp for the town, and not pass it without seeing it. He said he'd be mighty sure to see it, because he'd be a free man the minute **5** he seen it, but if he missed it he'd be in the slave country **6** again and no more show for freedom. Every little while he jumps up and says:

"Dah she is!"

7 But it warn't. It was Jack-o-lanterns, or lightning-bugs; so he set down again, and went to watching, same as before. Jim said it made him all over trembly and feverish to be so close to freedom. Well, I can tell you it made me all over trembly and feverish, too, to hear him, because I begun to get it through my head that he *was* most free—and who was to **8** blame for it? Why, *me*. I couldn't get that out of my conscience, no how nor no way. It got to troubling me so I couldn't rest; I couldn't stay still in one place. It hadn't ever come home to me before, what this thing was that I was doing. But now it did; and it staid with me, and scorched me more and more. I tried to make out to myself that *I* warn't to blame, because *I* didn't run Jim off from his rightful owner; but it warn't no use, conscience up and says, every time, "But you knowed he was running for his freedom, and you could a paddled ashore and told somebody." That was so—I couldn't get around that, no way. That was where it pinched. Conscience says to me, "What had poor Miss Watson done to you, that you could see her nigger go off right under your eyes and never say one single word? What did that poor old woman do to **9** you, that you could treat her so mean? Why, she tried to learn you your book, she tried to learn you your manners, she tried to be good to you every way she knowed how. *That's* what she done."

I got to feeling so mean and so miserable I most wished I was dead. I fidgeted up and down the raft, abusing myself to myself, and Jim was fidgeting up and down past me. We neither of us could keep still. Every time he danced around and says, "Dah's Cairo!" it went though me like a shot, and I thought if it *was* Cairo I reckoned I would die of miserableness.

Jim talked out loud all the time while I was talking to myself. He was saying how the first thing he would do when he **10** got to a free State he would go to saving up money and never spend a single cent, and when he got enough he would buy his wife, which was owned on a farm close to where Miss Watson lived ; and then they would both work to buy the two children, **11** and if their master wouldn't sell them, they'd get an Ab'litionist **12** to go and steal them.

It most froze me to hear such talk. He wouldn't ever dared to talk such talk in his life before. Just see what a difference it made in him the minute he judged he was about free. It was according to the old saying, "Give a nigger an **13** inch and he'll take an ell." Thinks I, this is what comes of my not thinking. Here was this nigger which I had as good as helped to run away, coming right out flat-footed and saying he would steal his children—children that belonged to a man I didn't even know ; a man that hadn't ever done me no harm.

I was sorry to hear Jim say that, it was such a lowering of him. My conscience got to stirring me up hotter than ever, until at last I says to it, "Let up on me—it ain't too late, yet—I'll paddle ashore at the first light, and tell." I felt easy, and happy, and light as a feather, right off. All my troubles was gone. I went to looking out sharp for a light, and sort of singing to myself. By-and-by one showed. Jim sings out :

"We's safe, Huck, we's safe ! Jump up and crack yo' heels, dat's de good ole Cairo at las', I jis knows it ! "

I says :

"I'll take the canoe and go see, Jim. It mightn't be, you know."

He jumped and got the canoe ready, and put his old coat **14** in the bottom for me to set on, and give me the paddle ; and as I shoved off, he says :

" Pooty soon I'll be a-shout'n for joy, en I'll say, it's all on accounts o' Huck ; I's a free man, en I couldn't ever ben free ef it hadn' ben for Huck ; Huck done it. Jim won't ever forgit you, Huck ; you's de bes' fren' Jim's ever had ; en you's de *only* fren' ole Jim's got now."

I was paddling off, all in a sweat to tell on him ; but when he says this, it seemed to kind of take the tuck all out of me. **15** I went along slow then, and I warn't right down certain whether I was glad I started or whether I warn't. When I was fifty yards off, Jim says :

" Dah you goes, de ole true Huck ; de on'y white genlman dat ever kep' his promise to ole Jim."

Well, I just felt sick. But I says, I *got* to do it—I can't get *out* of it. Right then, along comes a skiff with two men in it, with guns, and they stopped and I stopped. One of them says :

" What's that, yonder ? "

" A piece of a raft," I says.

" Do you belong on it ? "

" Yes, sir."

" Any men on it ? "

" Only one, sir."

" Well, there's five niggers run off to-night, up yonder above

Twain has reintroduced the choice between the Widow Douglas's "Providence" and that of Miss Watson as discussed in Chapter 3, note 4. As Jim and Huck head closer to Cairo, the boy is confronted with the first crisis in which to test these arguments; before this episode, all questions of morality were merely theoretical.

In *What Is Man?* (1973), Twain suggests that the struggle is between temperament, the disposition one is born with, and the conscience, "that independent Sovereign, that insolent absolute Monarch inside of a man who is the man's Master" (pp. 140–141). Huck is plagued by this "mysterious autocrat, lodged in a man, which compels the man to content its desires. It may be called the Master Passion—the hunger for Self-Approval. . . . It is indifferent to the man's good; it never concerns itself about anything but the satisfying of its own desires" (p. 206). The conscience can be trained to accept certain things. "From the cradle to the grave, during all his waking hours," Twain continued in *What Is Man?* (p. 161), "the human being is under training. In the very first rank of his trainers stands *association*. It is his human environment which influences his mind and his feelings, furnishes him his ideals, and sets him on his road and keeps him in it. If he leave that road he will find himself shunned by the people whom he most loves and esteems, and whose approval he most values." Huck has already suffered from this disapproval by helping the slave to run away. Training can make the conscience "prefer things which will be for the man's good, but it will prefer them only because it will content *it* better than other things would." It has no reason: "In *all* cases it seeks a *spiritual* contentment, let the *means* be what they may." Only the temperament can keep it in line, because "its desires are determined by the man's temperament—and it is lord over that." Thus Huck's conscience suffers another defeat in this particular battle.

Huck's oversensitive conscience was shared by Mark Twain. "Mine was a trained Presbyterian conscience," he explained in Chapter 9 of his *Autobiography*, "and knew but one duty—to hurt and harry its slave upon all pretexts and on all occasions, particularly when there was no sense nor reason in it." "All the consciences *I* have ever heard of," Twain admitted in "The Facts Concerning the Recent Carnival of Crime in Connecticut," (published in *The Atlantic Monthly*, June 1876, pp. 641–650, one month before he began writing *Huckleberry Finn*), "were nagging, badgering, fault-finding, execrable savages! Yes; and always in a sweat about some poor little insignificant trifle or other—destruction catch the lot of them, *I* say! I would trade mine for the small-pox and seven kinds of consumption, and be glad of the chance." Thus Twain agreed with Lecky's argument in his *History of European Morals* that the conscience is indeed "the cause of more pain than pleasure. Its reproaches are felt more than its approval."

9 *she tried to learn you . . . your manners.* In his public reading copy of the 1893 Tauchnitz edition, Twain inserted an even more sarcastic comment: "she tried to learn you to be a Christian" (MTP). Huck's conscience is so malicious that it tries to make him feel guilty for things Miss Watson had done which he had earlier despised, things which went against his temperament.

10 *he would go to saving up money . . . and when he got enough he would buy his wife.* Because legally they were merely chattel, families could be and frequently were broken up according to the whims of their masters. "Don't you know a slave can't be married?" George reminds his wife in Chapter 3 of *Uncle Tom's Cabin* when his master sells him down the river. "There is no law in this country for that; I can't hold you for my wife if he [the master] chooses to part us."

11 *they would both work to buy the two children.* The children of slaves belonged to the mother's, and not the father's, owner. This law was derived from the rights of the slave as defined by Moses, that former Egyptian slave, in Exodus 21:24: "If a master has given him a wife, and she have borne him sons or daughters; the wife and her children shall be her master's, and he shall go out by himself."

A slave father sold away from his family. Illustration from The Child's Anti-Slavery Book, 1859. *Courtesy the Rare Book Room, the Library of Congress.*

12 *if their master wouldn't sell them, they'd get an Ab'litionist to go and steal them.* Twain never resolved this situation in *Huckleberry Finn*. However, in the uncompleted "Tom Sawyer's Conspiracy," 1898 (in *Mark Twain's Hannibal, Huck and Tom,* 1969, p. 163), "the Widow was hiring Jim for wages so he could buy his wife and children's freedom some time or other"; and, in a typewritten fragment in the Mark Twain Papers at the University of California at Berkeley, Tom and Huck present Jim with his wife and child (Twain had apparently forgotten that Jim had both a daughter and a son), with a bill of sale for $550 pinned to the woman's breast reading, "The Property of our Old Jim—Christmas gift from Tom and Huck" (MTP).

13 *the old saying, "Give a nigger an inch and he'll take an ell."* The current American version is "give a man an inch and he'll take a mile." This common English proverb has been traced back as far as the sixteenth century.

the head of the bend. Is your man white or black?"

I didn't answer up prompt. I tried to, but the words wouldn't come. I tried, for a second or two, to brace up and out with it, but I warn't man enough—hadn't the spunk of a rabbit. I see I was weakening; so I just give up trying, and up and says:

"He's white."

"I reckon we'll go and see for ourselves."

"I wish you would," says I, "because it's pap that's there, and maybe you'd help me tow the raft ashore where the light is. He's sick—and so is mam and Mary Ann."

"Oh, the devil! we're in a hurry, boy. But I s'pose we've got to. Come—buckle to your paddle, and let's get along."

I buckled to my paddle and they laid to their oars. When we had made a stroke or two, I says:

"Pap'll be mighty much obleeged to you, I can tell you. Everybody goes away when I want them to help me tow the raft ashore, and I can't do it by myself."

"Well, that's infernal mean. Odd, too. Say, boy, what's the matter with your father?"

"It's the—a—the—well, it ain't anything much."

They stopped pulling. It warn't but a mighty ways to the raft, now. One says:

"Boy, that's a lie. What *is* the matter with your pap? Answer up square, now, and it'll be the better for you."

" BOY, THAT'S A LIE."

" I will, sir, I will, honest—but don't leave us, please. It's the—the—gentlemen, if you'll only pull ahead, and let me heave you the head-line, you won't have to come a-near the raft—please do."

"Set her back John, set her back!" says one. They backed water. "Keep away, boy—keep to looard. Confound it, I just expect the wind has blowed it to us. Your pap's got the small-pox, and you know it precious well. Why didn't you come out and say so? Do you want to spread it all over?"

"Well," says I, a-blubbering, "I've told everybody before, and then they just went away and left us."

"Poor devil, there's something in that. We are right down sorry for you, but we—well, hang it, we don't want the small-pox, you see. Look here, I'll tell you what to do. Don't you try to land by yourself, or you'll smash everything to pieces. You float along down about twenty miles and you'll come to a town on the left-hand side of the river. It will be long after sun-up, then, and when you ask for help, you tell them your folks are all down with chills and fever. Don't be a fool again, and let people guess what is the matter. Now we're trying to **24** do you a kindness; so you just put twenty miles between us, that's a good boy. It wouldn't do any good to land yonder where the light is—it's only a wood-yard. Say—I reckon **25, 26** your father's poor, and I'm bound to say he's in pretty hard luck. Here—I'll put a twenty dollar gold piece on this board, and you get it when it floats by. I feel mighty mean to leave you, but my kingdom! it won't do to fool with small-pox, don't you see?"

"Hold on, Parker," says the other man, "here's a twenty to put on the board for me. Good-bye, boy, you do as Mr. Parker told you, and you'll be all right."

"That's so, my boy—good-bye, good-bye. If you see any runaway niggers, you get help and nab them, and you can make some money by it."

"Good-bye, sir," says I, "I won't let no runaway niggers get by me if I can help it."

They went off and I got aboard the raft, feeling bad and low, because I knowed very well I had done wrong, and I see it warn't no use for me to try to learn to do right; a body that don't get *started* right when he's little, ain't got no show—when the pinch comes there ain't nothing to back him up and keep him to his work, and so he gets beat. Then I thought a minute, and says to myself, hold on,—s'pose you'd a done right and give Jim up; would you felt better than what you do now? No, says I, I'd feel bad—I'd feel just the same way I do now. Well, then, **27** says I, what's the use you learning to do right, when it's troublesome to do right and ain't no trouble to do wrong, and the wages is just the same? I was stuck. I couldn't answer that. So I reckoned I wouldn't bother no more about it, but **28** after this always do whichever come handiest at the time.

I went into the wigwam; Jim warn't there. I looked all around; he warn't anywhere. I says:

"Jim!"

"Here I is, Huck. Is dey out o' sight yit? Don't talk loud."

He was in the river, under the stern oar, with just his nose out. I told him they was out of sight, so he come aboard. He says:

"I was a-listenin' to all de talk, en I slips into de river en was gwyne to shove for sho' if dey come aboard. Den I was gwyne to swim to de raf' agin when dey was gone. But lawsy,

14 *He . . . put his old coat in the bottom for me to set on.* An unnecessarily chivalrous act for Jim, which could only further grate on Huck's conscience.

15 *take the tuck all out of me.* Deflate me.

16 *I see I was weakening.* In his public reading copy of the 1893 Tauchnitz edition, Twain explained exactly what finally broke Huck's courage: While the slave-hunter demands, "Come, answer up—is he white or black?" the frustrated boy hears the voice across the water, saying, "De good ole Huck, de good ole Huck!" (MTP).

17 *buckle.* Begin paddling in earnest.

18 *they laid to their oars.* They came to a halt.

19 *lie.* "You always got to do that," Huck comments in Twain's reading copy of the 1893 Tauchnitz edition, "when you get in a close place. Facts ain't no good when a person is crowded" (MTP).

20 *the head-line.* A line fastening the head of a vessel to the shore.

21 *They backed water.* They retreated.

22 *looard.* The editors of the 1962 Houghton Mifflin edition explained in their notes that the term *leeward* "means in the direction toward which the wind blows; as contrasted with *windward* the direction from which it blows. If Huck stays to leeward of the men, the wind cannot carry contagion to them."

23 *Your pap's got the small-pox, and you know it precious well.* Claude R. Flory in "Huck, Sam and the Small-Pox" (*Mark Twain Journal*, Winter 1964–1965, pp. 1–2, 8) has suggested that Twain was inspired by a similar "dodge" in Harriet Beecher Stowe's dialect collection *Sam Lawson's Oldtown Fireside Stories* (1872): "They had a putty bad name, them Hokums. . . . Why, they got to owin' two dollars to Joe Gidger for butcher's meat . . . ; but he couldn't never get it out o' him. 'Member once Joe walked clean up to the cranberry-pond arter that 'are two dollars; but Mother Hokum she see him comin'. . . . She says to Hokum, 'Get into bed old man, quick, and let me tell the story,' says she. So she covered him up; and when Gidger come in she come up to him, and says she, 'Why, Mr. Gidger, I'm jist ashamed to see ye: why, Mr. Hokum was jest a comin' down to pay ye that 'are money last week, but ye see he was took down with the small-pox'—Joe didn't hear no more: he just turned round, and he streaked it out that 'are door with his coat-tails flyin' out straight ahind him; and old Mother Hokum she jest stood at the window holdin' her sides and laughin' fit to split, to see him run. That 'are's jest a sample o' the ways them Hokums cut up."

24 *we're trying to do you a kindness.* Even these slave-hunters have some redeeming human qualities. "The great mass of Southerners, both in town and country," Twain explained in a suppressed passage of *Life on the Mississippi* (published in the 1944 Limited Editions Club edition, pp. 412–413), "are neighborly, friendly, hospitable, peaceable, and have an aversion to disagreements and embroilments; they belong to the church, and they frequent it; they are Sabbath-observers; they are promise-keepers; they are honorable and upright in their dealings; where their prejudices are not at the front, they are just, and they like to see justice done; they are able to reason, and they reason." Only in their upholding of the institution of slavery were they different from other men. Ironically, although these two gentlemen feel some concern for Huck's "family's" sad fate, they show no compassion for the injustices done to slaves.

25 *it's only a wood-yard.* A wood-yard was a rude settlement, which existed primarily as a spot for steamboats to stop and "wood up" with fuel.

A wood-yard. Illustration from *Emerson's Magazine and Putnam's Monthly*, October 1857. *Courtesy the Library of Congress.*

26 *I reckon your father's poor, and . . . he's in pretty hard luck. . . . I'll put a twenty dollar gold piece on this board, and you get it when it floats by.* To assuage his conscience the slave-hunter vainly offers money to help the doomed family. Twenty dollars in gold was a considerable sum in those days; obviously slave-hunting was a profitable business near Cairo, Illinois.

27 *I'd feel just the same way I do now.* "As far as I can see," Twain makes Huck say, in the margin of his reading copy of the 1893 Tauchnitz edition, "a conscience is put in you just to *object* to whatever you *do* do, don't make no difference what it *is*" (MTP).

28 *So I reckoned I wouldn't bother no more about it, but after this always do whichever come handiest at the time.* Rather than develop a moral code by which he would act in the future, Huck, like the slave-hunters, chooses to do whatever seems the most expedient. "He is a chameleon," Twain argued in *What Is Man?* (1973, p. 161); "by law of his nature he takes the color of the place of resort. The influences about him create his preferences, his aversions, his politics, his tastes, his morals, his religion. He creates none of these things for himself." However, Huck's heart conquers these influences, and because it (unlike

" HERE I IS, HUCK."

29 how you did fool 'em, Huck! Dat *wuz* de smartes' dodge! I tell you, chile, I 'speck it save' ole Jim—ole Jim ain't gwyne to forgit you for dat, honey."

Then we talked about the money. It was a pretty good **30** raise, twenty dollars apiece. Jim said we could take deck passage on a steamboat now, and the money would last us as far as we wanted to go in the free States. He said twenty mile more warn't far for the raft to go, but he wished we was already there.

Towards daybreak we tied up, and Jim was mighty particular about hiding the raft good. Then he worked all day fixing things in bundles, and getting all ready to quit rafting.

That night about ten we hove in sight of the lights of a town away down in a left hand bend.

I went off in the canoe, to ask about it. Pretty soon I found a man out in the river with a skiff, setting a trot-line. I ranged up and says:

" Mister, is that town Cairo? "

" Cairo? no. You must be a blame' fool."

" What town is it, mister? "

" If you want to know, go and find out. If you stay here botherin' around me for about half a minute longer, you'll get something you won't want."

I paddled to the raft. Jim was awful disappointed, but I said never mind, Cairo would be the next place, I reckoned.

We passed another town before daylight, and I was going out again; but it was high ground, so I didn't go. No high ground about Cairo, Jim said. I had forgot it. We laid up for the day, on a tow-head tolerably close to the left-hand bank. I begun to suspicion something. So did Jim. I says:

" Maybe we went by Cairo in the fog that night."

He says:

"Doan' less' talk about it, Huck. Po' niggers can't have no luck. I awluz 'spected dat rattle-snake skin warn't done wid its work."

"I wish I'd never seen that snake-skin, Jim —I do wish I'd never laid eyes on it."

"It ain't yo' fault, Huck; you didn' know. Don't you **31** blame yo'self 'bout it."

When it was daylight, here was the clear Ohio water in shore, sure enough, and outside was the old regular Muddy! **32** So it was all up with Cairo.

We talked it all over. It wouldn't do to take to the shore; we couldn't take the raft up the stream, of course. There warn't **33** no way but to wait for dark, and start back in the canoe and take the chances. So we slept all day amongst the cotton-wood thicket, so as to be fresh for the work, and when we went back to the raft about dark the canoe was gone!

We didn't say a word for a good while. There warn't anything to say. We both knowed well enough it was some more work of the rattle-snake skin; so what was the use to talk about it? It would only look like we was finding fault, and that would be bound to fetch more bad luck—and keep on fetching it, too, till we knowed enough to keep still.

By-and-by we talked about what we better do, and found there warn't no way but just to go along down with the raft till we got a chance to buy a canoe to go back in. We warn't going to borrow it when there warn't anybody around, the way pap would do, for that might set people after us.

So we shoved out, after dark, on the raft.

Anybody that don't believe yet, that it's foolishness to handle a snake-skin, after all that that snake-skin done for us, will believe it now, if they read on and see what more it done for us.

The place to buy canoes is off of rafts laying up at shore. But we didn't see no rafts laying up; so we went along during three hours and more. Well, the night got gray, and ruther thick, which is the next meanest thing to fog. You can't tell the shape of the river, and you can't see no distance. It got to be very late and still, and then along comes a steamboat up the river. We lit the lantern, and judged she would see it. Up-stream boats didn't generly come close to us; they go out and follow the bars and hunt for easy water under the reefs; but nights like this they bull right up the channel against the whole river.

We could hear her pounding along, but we didn't see her good till she was close. She aimed right for us. Often they do that and try to see how close they can come without touching; sometimes the wheel bites off a sweep, and then the pilot sticks his head out and laughs, and thinks he's mighty smart. Well, here she comes, and we said she was going to try to shave us; **34** but she didn't seem to be sheering off a bit. She was a big one, and she was coming in a hurry, too, looking like a black cloud

those of the slave-hunters) is good, what seems most expedient is also the only moral decision to follow.

29 *dodge*. Ingenuous contrivance.

30 *deck passage*. Steerage passage, the cheapest form of transport on a steamboat. "For every cabin passenger living in relative elegance of the upper deck on a typical Mississippi riverboat," the editors of the University of California edition of *The Adventures of Tom Sawyer; Tom Sawyer Abroad; Tom Sawyer, Detective* (1980) explained in a note to "Tom Sawyer, Detective" (p. 498), "there would be as many as four or five deck passengers crowded together below with no bed, no food other than what they brought aboard, no toilet facilities, often not even enough deck space on which to lie down. Deck passengers were not allowed on the upper deck except . . . to buy drinks at a carefully designated bar."

Deck passengers. Illustration from *Every Saturday*, September 2, 1871. *Courtesy the Library of Congress.*

31 *"It ain't yo' fault, Huck. . . . Don't you blame yo'self 'bout it."* But of course the rattlesnake *was* Huck's fault, and Jim's comment is just another thing to grate on his "deformed conscience."

32 *the old regular Muddy.* A popular name for the Mississippi River, describing its color and consistency.

33 *we couldn't take the raft up the stream, of course.* Unlike steamboats, rafts were not self-propelled; they were always at the mercy of the river.

34 *we said she was going to try to shave us.* "Shaving," or bringing one boat as close as possible along the side of another without touching, was a popular sport along the Mississippi, and it also was a frequent cause of accidents. In Chapter 6 of *Life on the Mississippi*, Twain recalled an order he was given when a cub pilot to "shave those steamboats as close as you'd peel an apple": "I took the wheel, and my heartbeat fluttered up into the hundreds; for it seemed to me that we were about to scrape the side off every ship in the line, we were so close. I held my breath and began to claw the boat away from the danger; and I had my own opinion of the pilot who had known no better than to get us into such peril, but I was too wise to express it. In half a minute I had a wide margin of safety intervening between the *Paul Jones* and the ships; and within ten seconds more I was set aside in disgrace, and Mr. Bixby was going into

"Shaving" a riverboat. Illustration from *Emerson's Magazine and Putnam's Monthly*, October 1857. *Courtesy the Library of Congress.*

danger again and flaying me alive with abuse of my cowardice. I was stung, but I was obliged to admire the easy confidence with which my chief loafed from side to side of his wheel, and trimmed the ships so closely that disaster seemed ceaselessly imminent." Apparently, the expression "a close shave" came from this practice.

35 *the left-hand shore.* Although one of the original publisher's running heads in the next chapter reads "The Farm in Arkansas," Huck has actually swum ashore in Kentucky.

36 *a big old-fashioned double log house.* "It consisted of two separate cots, or wings, standing a little distance apart, but united by a common roof; which thus afforded shelter to the open hall, or passage, between them; while the roof being continued also from the eaves, both before and behind, in pent-house fashion, it allowed space for wide porches, in which, and in the open passage, the summer traveller, resting in such a cabin, will always find the most agreeable quarters" (Bird, *Nick of the Woods*, Vol. II, Chapter 1).

with rows of glow-worms around it; but all of a sudden she bulged out, big and scary, with a long row of wide-open furnace doors shining like red-hot teeth, and her monstrous bows and guards hanging right over us. There was a yell at us, and a jingling of bells to stop the engines, a pow-wow of cussing, and whistling of steam—and as Jim went overboard on one side and I on the other, she come smashing straight through the raft.

I dived—and I aimed to find the bottom, too, for a thirty-foot wheel had got to go over me, and I wanted it to have plenty of room. I could always stay under water a minute; this time I reckon I staid under water a minute and a half. Then I bounced for the top in a hurry, for I was nearly busting. I popped out to my arm-pits and blowed the water out of my nose, and puffed a bit. Of course there was a booming current; and of course that boat started her engines again ten seconds after she stopped them, for they never cared much for raftsmen; so now she was churning along up the river, out of sight in the thick weather, though I could hear her.

I sung out for Jim about a dozen times, but I didn't get any answer; so I grabbed a plank that touched me while I was "treading water," and struck out for shore, shoving it ahead of me. But I made out to see that the drift of the current was
35 towards the left-hand shore, which meant that I was in a crossing; so I changed off and went that way.

It was one of these long, slanting, two-mile crossings; so I was a good long time in getting over. I made a safe landing, and clum up the bank. I couldn't see but a little ways, but I

CLIMBING UP THE BANK.

went poking along over rough ground for a quarter of a mile or
36 more, and then I run across a big old-fashioned double log house before I noticed it. I was going to rush by and get away, but a lot of dogs jumped out and went to howling and barking at me, and I knowed better than to move another peg.

Chap. XVII.

In about half a minute somebody spoke out of a window, without putting his head out, and says:

"Be done, boys! Who's there?"

I says:

"It's me."

"Who's me?"

"George Jackson, sir."

"What do you want?"

"I don't want nothing, sir. I only want to go along by, but the dogs won't let me."

"WHO'S THERE?"

"What are you prowling around here this time of night, for—hey?"

"I warn't prowling around, sir; I fell overboard off of the steamboat."

"Oh, you did, did you? Strike a light there, somebody. What did you say your name was?"

"George Jackson, sir. I'm only a boy."

"Look here; if you're telling the truth, you needn't be afraid—nobody 'll hurt you. But don't try to budge; stand right where you are. Rouse out Bob and Tom, some of you,

1 "*George Jackson, sir.*" In Chapter 49 of *Life on the Mississippi*, Twain used a similar alias—"George Johnson."

2 *two young women which I couldn't see right well*. Because, as Twain's reading copy of the 1893 Tauchnitz edition notes, "they was bundled up in quilts, anyway" (MTP).

3 *rag carpet*. Homemade rug of strips of cloth knitted or sewn together; these carpets were the standard kind used throughout Missouri and the South by backwoods people of modest means.

and fetch the guns. George Jackson, is there anybody with you?"

"No, sir, nobody."

I heard the people stirring around in the house, now, and see a light. The man sung out:

"Snatch that light away, Betsy, you old fool—ain't you got any sense? Put it on the floor behind the front door. Bob, if you and Tom are ready, take your places."

"All ready."

"Now, George Jackson, do you know the Shepherdsons?"

"No, sir—I never heard of them."

"Well, that may be so, and it mayn't. Now, all ready. Step forward, George Jackson. And mind, don't you hurry— come mighty slow. If there's anybody with you, let him keep back—if he shows himself he'll be shot. Come along, now. Come slow; push the door open, yourself—just enough to squeeze in, d' you hear?"

I didn't hurry, I couldn't if I'd a wanted to. I took one slow step at a time, and there warn't a sound, only I thought I could hear my heart. The dogs were as still as the humans, but they followed a little behind me. When I got to the three log door-steps, I heard them unlocking and unbarring and unbolting. I put my hand on the door and pushed it a little and a little more, till somebody said, "There, that's enough—put your head in." I done it, but I judged they would take it off.

The candle was on the floor, and there they all was, looking at me, and me at them, for about a quarter of a minute. Three big men with guns pointed at me, which made me wince, I tell you; the oldest, gray and about sixty, the other two thirty or more—all of them fine and handsome—and the sweetest old **2** gray-headed lady, and back of her two young women which I couldn't see right well. The old gentleman says:

"There—I reckon it's all right. Come in."

As soon as I was in, the old gentleman he locked the door and barred it and bolted it, and told the young men to come in with their guns, and they all went in a big parlour that had a **3** new rag carpet on the floor, and got together in a corner that was out of range of the front windows—there warn't none on the side. They held the candle, and took a good look at me, and all said, "Why *he* ain't a Shepherdson—no, there ain't any Shepherdson about him." Then the old man said he hoped I wouldn't mind being searched for arms, because he didn't mean no harm by it—it was only to make sure. So he didn't pry into my pockets, but only felt outside with his hands, and said it was all right. He told me to make myself easy and at home, and tell all about myself; but the old lady says:

"Why bless you, Saul, the poor thing's as wet as he can be; and don't you reckon it may be he's hungry?"

"True for you, Rachel—I forgot."

So the old lady says:

"Betsy" (this was a nigger woman), "you fly around and get him something to eat, as quick as you can, poor thing; and one of you girls go and wake up Buck and tell him— Oh, here he is himself. Buck, take this little stranger and get the wet clothes off from him and dress him up in some of yours that's dry."

Buck looked about as old as me—thirteen or fourteen or **4** along there, though he was a little bigger than me. He hadn't **5** on anything but a shirt, and he was very frowsy-headed. He come in gaping and digging one fist into his eyes, and he was dragging a gun along with the other one. He says:

"Ain't they no Shepherdsons around?"

They said, no, 'twas a false alarm.

"Well," he says, "if they'd a ben some, I reckon I'd a got one."

They all laughed, and Bob says:

"BUCK."

"Why, Buck, they might have scalped us all, you've been so slow in coming."

"Well, nobody come after me, and it ain't right. I'm always kep' down; I don't get no show."

"Never mind, Buck, my boy," says the old man, "you'll have show enough, all in good time, don't you fret about that. Go 'long with you now, and do as your mother told you."

When we got upstairs to his room, he got me a coarse shirt and a roundabout and pants of his, and I put them on. While **6** I was at it he asked me what my name was, but before I could tell him, he started to telling me about a blue jay and a young rabbit he had catched in the woods day before yesterday, and he asked me where Moses was when the candle went out. I **7** said I didn't know; I hadn't heard about it before, no way.

"Well, guess," he says.

4 *Buck looked about as old as me—thirteen or fourteen or along there*. Twain wrote in his notes for the novel that Huck is "a boy of 14."

In Chapter 11 of his *Autobiography*, Twain referred to fourteen or fifteen as "the age which a boy is willing to endure all things, suffer all things short of death by fire, if thereby he may be conspicuous and show off before the public." That age had been the happiest time of Twain's life. "Those were pleasant days," he confessed to a childhood friend on June 6, 1900 (*Mark Twain's Letters to Will Bowen*, p. 27); "none since have been so pleasant, none so well worth living over again. For the romance of life is the only part of it that is overwhelmingly valuable, and romance dies with youth. After that, life is a drudge, and indeed a sham. A sham, and likewise a failure. . . . I should greatly like to re-live my youth, and then get drowned. I should like to call back Will Bowen and John Garth and the others, and live the life, and be as we were, and make holiday until 15, then all drown together."

5 *He hadn't on anything but a shirt*. "Not much of a shirt—couldn't tell it from a *lampshade*" (MTP), Twain appended his reading copy of the 1893 Tauchnitz edition.

6 *a roundabout*. A short, close jacket.

7 *he asked me where Moses was when the candle went out*. This common riddle also inspired a popular "serio-comic song" by John Stamford, "Where Was Moses When the Lights Went Out?" (1878), beginning:

When I was but a child, I used to go to bed at eight each night,
The nurse-girl to frighten me when she put out the light,
She'd talk of ghosts and goblins in a very awful way,
She'd then put out the candle, and to me she used to say

Chorus
Where was Moses when the lights went out?
Where was Moses, what was he about?
Now, my little man, tell me if you can,
Where was Moses when the lights went out?

8 *Say, how long are you going to stay here?* This barrage of questions, littered with non sequiturs and un-solicited information, is reminiscent of a soliloquy delivered by one of the Sellers twins in Chapter 7 of *The Gilded Age:* "She was my great-grandmother—and George's too; wasn't she, father! *You* never saw her, but Sis has seen her, when Sis was a baby—didn't you, Sis! Sis has seen her most a hundred times. She was awful deef—she's dead now. Ain't she, father! . . . It's our clock, now—and it's got wheels inside of it, and a thing that flutters every time she strikes—don't it, father! Great-grandmother died before hardly any of us was born—she was an Old-School Baptist and had warts all over her—you ask father if she didn't. She had an uncle once that was bald-headed and used to have fits; he wasn't *our* uncle, I don't know what he was to us—some kin or another I reckon—father's seen him a thousand times—hain't you, father? We used to have a calf that et apples and just chawed up dishrags like nothing, and if you stay here you'll see lots of funerals—won't he, Sis! Did you ever see a house afire? *I* have! . . ."

The passage is effective in introducing Buck as a typical and likable little boy. It only makes his fate in Chapter 18 even the more tragic.

9 *they don't have no school now.* Because, according to Chapter 7, it is June.

10 *old hoss.* A corruption of "horse," an affectionate, colloquial nickname used by Buck to make Huck feel at home.

11 *cob pipes.* Light, durable tobacco pipes, the bowls made out of corn-cobs; Twain himself was fond of these pipes, and he often had himself photographed smoking one.

12 *G-o-r-g-e J-a-x-o-n.* In his reading copy of the 1893 Tauchnitz edition, Twain further milked the phonetic humor of Buck's misspelling: "G-o-r-j-e G-a-x-o-n!" (MTP).

13 *slouch.* Poor, indifferent, ineffectual; but when used in the negative as "no slouch," it is high praise.

" How'm I going to guess," says I, "when I never heard tell about it before? "

" But you can guess, can't you?   It's just as easy."

" *Which* candle? " I says.

" Why, any candle," he says.

" I don't know where he was," says I; "where was he? "

" Why, he was in the *dark!*   That's where he was! "

" Well, if you knowed where he was, what did you ask me for ? "

8   " Why, blame it, it's a riddle, don't you see? Say, how long are you going to stay here? You got to stay always.

9 We can just have booming times—they don't have no school now. Do you own a dog? I've got a dog—and he'll go in the river and bring out chips that you throw in. Do you like to comb up, Sundays, and all that kind of foolishness? You bet I don't, but ma she makes me. Confound these old britches, I reckon I'd better put 'em on, but I'd ruther not, it's

10 so warm. Are you all ready? All right—come along, old hoss."

Cold corn-pone, cold corn-beef, butter and butter-milk—that is what they had for me down there, and there ain't nothing better that ever I've come across yet. Buck and his ma and

11 all of them smoked cob pipes, except the nigger woman, which was gone, and the two young women. They all smoked and talked, and I eat and talked. The young women had quilts around them, and their hair down their backs. They all asked me questions, and I told them how pap and me and all the family was living on a little farm down at the bottom of Arkansaw, and my sister Mary Ann run off and got married and never was heard of no more, and Bill went to hunt them and he warn't heard of no more, and Tom and Mort died, and then there warn't nobody but just me and pap left, and he was just trimmed down to nothing, on account of his troubles; so when he died I took what there was left, because the farm didn't belong to us, and started up the river, deck passage, and fell overboard; and that was how I come to be here. So they said I could have a home there as long as I wanted it. Then it was most daylight, and everybody went to bed, and I went to bed with Buck, and when I waked up in the morning, drat it all, I had forgot what my name was. So I laid there about an hour trying to think, and when Buck waked up, I says:

" Can you spell, Buck ? "

" Yes," he says.

" I bet you can't spell my name," says I.

" I bet you what you dare I can," says he.

" All right," says I, " go ahead."

12   " G-o-r-g-e J-a-x-o-n—there now," he says.

" Well," says I, " you done it, but I didn't think you could.

13 It ain't no slouch of a name to spell—right off without studying."

I set it down, private, because somebody might want *me* to spell it, next, and so I wanted to be handy with it and rattle it off like I was used to it.

It was a mighty nice family, and a mighty nice house, too. **14** I hadn't seen no house out in the country before that was so nice and had so much style. It didn't have an iron latch on the front door, nor a wooden one with a buckskin string, but a brass knob to turn, the same as houses in a town. There warn't no bed in the parlor, not a sign of a bed; but heaps of parlours in towns has beds in them. There was a big fireplace that was bricked on the bottom, and the bricks was kept clean and red by pouring water on them and scrubbing them with another brick; sometimes they washed them over with red water-paint that they call Spanish-brown, same as they do in town. They had big brass dog-irons that could hold up a saw- **15** log. There was a clock on the middle of the mantel-piece, **16** with a picture of a town painted on the bottom half of the glass front, and a round place in the middle of it for the sun, and you could see the pendulum swing behind it. It was beautiful to hear that clock tick; and sometimes when one of these **17** peddlers had been along and scoured her up and got her in good shape, she would start in and strike a hundred and fifty before she got tuckered out. They wouldn't took any money for her.

Well, there was a big outlandish parrot on each side of the **18** clock, made out of something like chalk, and painted up gaudy. By one of the parrots was a cat made of crockery, and a crockery dog by the other; and when you pressed down on them they squeaked, but didn't open their mouths nor look different nor interested. They squeaked through underneath. There was a couple of big wild-turkey-wing fans spread out behind those things. On a table in the middle of the room was a kind of a lovely crockery basket that had apples and oranges and peaches **19** and grapes piled up in it, which was much redder and yellower and prettier than real ones is, but they warn't real because you could see where pieces had got chipped off and showed the white chalk or whatever it was, underneath.

This table had a cover made out of beautiful oil-cloth, with **20** a red and blue spread-eagle painted on it, and a painted border all around. It come all the way from Philadelphia, they said. **21** There was some books too, piled up perfectly exact, on each **22** corner of the table. One was a big family Bible, full of pic- tures. One was "Pilgrim's Progress," about a man that left **23** his family it didn't say why. I read considerable in it now and then. The statements was interesting, but tough. Another was "Friendship's Offering," full of beautiful stuff and poetry; **24** but I didn't read the poetry. Another was Henry Clay's **25** Speeches, and another was Dr. Gunn's Family Medicine, which **26** told you all about what to do if a body was sick or dead. There was a Hymn Book, and a lot of other books. And there was nice split-bottom chairs, and perfectly sound, too—not bagged down in the middle and busted, like an old basket.

They had pictures hung on the walls—mainly Washingtons and Lafayettes, and battles, and Highland Marys, and one **27**

"The House Beautiful." Illustration from *Life on the Mississippi*, 1883.

14 *a mighty nice house*. The prototype for the Grangerford mansion is the house Squire Hawkins erected with his new fortune, described in Chapter 5 of *The Gilded Age*: "Hawkins even built a new house, made it two full stories high. . . . Hawkins fitted out his house with 'store' furniture from St. Louis, and the fame of its magnificence went abroad in the land. Even the parlor carpet was from St. Louis—though the other rooms were clothed in the 'rag' carpeting of the country. . . . His oil-cloth window-curtains had noble pictures on them of castles such as had never been seen anywhere in the world but on window-curtains."

The Grangerford and Hawkins homesteads are typical examples of "The House Beautiful" of this region, as described in Chapter 38 of *Life on the Mississippi:*

"Every town and village along that vast stretch of double river frontage had a best dwelling, . . . the home of its wealthiest and most conspicuous citizen. It is easy to describe it: . . . iron knocker; brass door knob—discolored, for lack of polishing. Within, an uncarpeted hall, of planed boards; opening out of it, a parlor, fifteen feet by fifteen . . .; ingrain carpet; mahogany center-table; lamp on it, with green paper shade—standing on a gridiron, so to speak, made of high-colored yarns, by the young ladies of the house, and called a lamp mat; several books, piled and disposed, with cast-iron exactness, according to the inherited and unchangeable plan; among them, . . . *Friendship's Offering*, and *Affection's Wreath*, with their sappy inanities illustrated in die-away mezzotints; . . . maybe *Ivanhoe;* also *Album*, full of original 'poetry' of Thou-hast-wounded-the-spirit-that-loved-thee breed; two or three goody-goody works . . .;

current number of the chaste and innocuous *Godey's Lady's Book* with painted fashion plate of wax-figure women with mouths all alike—lips and eyelids the same size. . . . On each end of the wooden mantel, over the fireplace, a large basket of peaches and other fruits, natural size, all double in plaster, rudely, or in wax, and painted to resemble the originals—which they don't. Over middle of mantel, engraving—Washington Crossing the Delaware; on the wall by the door, copy of it done in thunder-and-lightning crewels by one of the young ladies—work of art which would have made Washington hesitate about crossing. . . . Piano—kettle in disguise—with music, bound and unbound, piled on it, and on a stand near by: 'Battle of Prague'; 'Bird Waltz'; 'Arkansas Traveler'; . . . 'The Last Link is Broken'; . . . 'Go Forget Me, Why Should Sorrow o'er that Brow a Shadow Fling'; . . . and spread open on the rack, where the plaintive singer has left it, *Ro*-holl on, silver *moo*-hoon, guide the *tra*vel-lerr his *way*, etc. . . . Framed in black moldings on the wall, other works of art, conceived and committed on the premises, by the young ladies; being grim black-and-white crayons; landscapes, mostly: lake, solitary sailboat, petrified clouds, pre-geological trees on shore, anthracite precipice; name of criminal conspicuous in the corner. . . . Other bric-a-brac: . . . painted toy dog, seated upon bellows attachment—drops its under jaw and squeaks when pressed upon. . . . Bracketed over whatnot—place of special sacredness—an outrage in water color, done by the young niece that came on a visit long ago, and died. Pity, too; for she might have repented of this in time. Horsehair chairs, horsehair sofa which keeps sliding from under you. Window shades, of oil stuff, with milkmaids and ruined castles stencilled on them in fierce colors."

15 *dog-irons.* Andirons, where one rested one's "dogs," or feet.

16 *a clock . . . with a picture of a town painted on the bottom half of the glass front.* Likely a variation of the Terry clock, named for its inventor Eli Terry (1772–1852): an inexpensive clock with a glass front which was painted on the inside, popular from 1815 until 1840.

17 *sometimes . . ., she would start in and strike a hundred and fifty before she got tuckered out.* This peculiarity is similar to a characteristic of the Sellers clock in Chapter 7 of *The Gilded Age:* "Remarkable clock!" Col. Sellers says. "Ah . . . she's beginning again! Nineteen, twenty, twenty-one, twenty-two, twen—ah, that's all. . . . Now just listen at that. She'll strike a hundred and fifty, now, without stopping,—you'll see. There ain't another clock like that in Christendom." None, except the Grangerford clock.

18 *a big outlandish parrot . . ., made out of something like chalk.* Although actually made of plaster of Paris, such figurines were commonly called "chalkware" because, when rubbed against a surface, they left marks like that made by a piece of chalk. These cheap models of fruit, cats, dogs, birds, and other animals were popular American imitations of Staffordshire

pottery and were manufactured and sold in the backwoods by itinerants.

19 *apples and oranges and peaches and grapes piled up . . . which was much redder and yellower and prettier than real ones is, but they warn't real.* The furnishings of a home reflect the character of the family who dwells within it; and in this house, where the bricks are painted redder than they actually are, where the fancy clock cannot tell the correct time, where the crockery is fake china and the imitation fruit is not as fine as it is painted, artifice is evidently highly treasured. Here live people who are not as noble as their manners and their wealth suggest.

20 *This table had a cover made out of beautiful oil-cloth, with a red and blue spread-eagle painted on it.* This display, sporting the emblem of the Union, serves as a shrine to the tastes of a typical American family of the South at the time. Each detail in Huck's meticulous description of the house's decor adds to the satire in much the same way that details enhance the artist's pictorial statement in a political cartoon.

A spread eagle on the American National Seal.
Courtesy the Library of Congress.

21 *It come all the way from Philadelphia, they said.* This oil-cloth is an example of what Richard Malcolm Johnson called in "Samuel Hele, Esq." (in Joseph G. Baldwin's *The Flush Times on the Mississippi*, 1853, p. 290) "the Southern propensity of getting everything from abroad," from Yankeedom, "as if, as in the case of wines, the process of importing added to the value." Likewise, wealthy Yankees import products from Europe, West Coasters from the East, not so much because the local article is inferior to the foreign, but because the extravagance and the expense of carting it by land, sea, or air gives the purchaser a certain preeminence in the community.

22 *some books.* Huck's selection from the Grangerford library serves the same function as the books left by Twain's bed by a porter in Chapter 30, Part II, of *The Innocents Abroad:* It covers "the whole range of legitimate literature"—theology, romance, poetry, law, and medicine. The titles perfectly reflect the religious, social, and political character of this part of the country. Being "piled up perfectly exact, on each corner of the table," these volumes were evidently placed in the parlor merely as decoration.

23 *"Pilgrim's Progress."* One of the most popular books ever published, Bunyan's 1678 Calvinist allegory was one of the books routinely found in rural American homes of the period. Twain recognized the book's appeal when he subtitled his first subscription book, *The Innocents Abroad*, "The New Pilgrim's Progress"; and, as he wrote somewhat sarcastically in his *Notebook* (1935, p. 192), he once contemplated photographing people dressed as Christian, Simple, Sloth, Presumption, and the other characters of the novel in modern settings and believed that "this stereoptic panorama of Bunyan's *Pilgrim's Progress* could be exhibited in all countries at the same time and clear a fortune in a year."

24 *"Friendship's Offering."* One of a popular set of annuals, first published in England, designed as gifts for young ladies and filled with sentimental prints and literature. Its poetry often dwelled on grief and death.

25 *Henry Clay's Speeches.* Henry Clay (1777–1852), the popular congressman from Kentucky who unsuccessfully ran for the presidency and who was known as "the Great Pacificator" for his part in the formulation of the Missouri Compromise.

Henry Clay. *Courtesy the Library of Congress.*

26 *Dr. Gunn's Family Medicine.* This popular American household encyclopedia, originally titled *Domestic Medicine or Poor Man's Friend, in the House of Affliction, Pain and Sickness* (Knoxville, Tennessee,

1830), was also one of the few books owned by backwoods physicians (see *Odd Leaves from the Life of a Louisiana "Swamp Doctor"* by Lewis, p. 23). Leo Marx, in his notes to the 1967 Bobbs-Merrill edition of *Huckleberry Finn*, points to one chapter "On the Passions," "a combination of psychology, ethics, and advice to the lovelorn," as being particularly appropriate to the household of the amateur artist, Emmeline Grangerford.

27 *Highland Marys.* Popular prints of Mary Campbell, the first love of the Scottish poet Robert Burns; she was a fitting subject for sentimental verse and painting, because she died soon after she met the writer.

Highland Mary. Print by Sarony & Major, 1846. *Courtesy the Library of Congress.*

28 *"Signing the Declaration."* Usually prints after John Trumbull's painting then in the Rotunda of the United States Capitol. The Grangerfords properly decorate their home with symbols of the American Revolution. As slave-holders, however, they are as hypocritical in their politics as in their religion. They may be *patriotic* but not *democratic*.

"The Declaration of Independence." Print after John Trumbull by N. Currier, 1840s. *Courtesy the Library of Congress.*

29 *one of the daughters which was dead . . . when she was only fifteen years old.* The girl was not much older than Huck. See also Chapter 18, note 15.

30 *One was a woman in a slim black dress.* Huck describes a typical "mourning picture," with its tombstone, weeping willow, and stylish mourner, popular in America from the late eighteenth century until the Civil War; these folk paintings were generally the work of amateur lady artists who were encouraged to pursue the "female arts" to help beautify the wilderness.

A mourning picture. *Courtesy the Library of Congress.*

31 *scoop-shovel bonnet.* A descriptive turn of phrase, the actual term being "scoop bonnet."

32 *white slim ankles crossed about with black tape, and very wee black slippers, like a chisel.* In having Huck literally describe her ribbons as black tape and her

28 called "Signing the Declaration." There was some that they
29 called crayons, which one of the daughters which was dead made her own self when she was only fifteen years old. They was different from any pictures I ever see before; blacker,
30 mostly, than is common. One was a woman in a slim black dress, belted small under the arm-pits, with bulges like a cab-
31 bage in the middle of the sleeves, and a large black scoop-
32 shovel bonnet with a black veil, and white slim ankles crossed about with black tape, and very wee black slippers, like a chisel, and she was leaning pensive on a tombstone on her right elbow, under a weeping willow, and her other hand hanging down her side holding a white handkerchief and a reticule, and underneath the picture it said, "Shall I Never See Thee More Alas?" Another one was a young lady with her hair all combed up straight to the top of her head, and knotted there in front of a comb like a chair-back, and she was crying into a handkerchief and had a dead bird laying on its back in her other hand with
33 its heels up, and underneath the picture it said, "I Shall Never Hear Thy Sweet Chirrup More Alas!" There was one where a young lady was at a window looking up at the moon, and tears
34 running down her cheeks; and she had an open letter in one hand with black sealing-wax showing on one edge of it, and she was mashing a locket with a chain to it against her mouth, and underneath the picture it said, "And Art Thou Gone Yes Thou Art Gone Alas!" These was all nice pictures, I reckon, but I didn't somehow seem to take to them, because if ever I was down a little, they always give me the fan-tods. Everybody was sorry she died, because she had laid out a lot more of these pictures to do, and a body could see by what she had done what they had lost. But I reckoned, that with her disposition, she was having a better time in the grave-yard. She was at work on what they said was her greatest picture when she took sick, and every day and every night it was her prayer to be allowed
35 to live till she got it done, but she never got the chance. It
36 was a picture of a young woman in a long white gown, standing on the rail of a bridge all ready to jump off, with her hair all down her back, and looking up to the moon, with the tears running down her face, and she had two arms folded across her breast, and two arms stretched out in front, and two more reaching up towards the moon—and the idea was, to see which pair would look best and then scratch out all the other arms; but, as I was saying, she died before she got her mind
37 made up, and now they kept this picture over the head of the bed in her room, and every time her birthday come they hung flowers on it. Other times it was hid with a little curtain. The young woman in the picture had a kind of a nice sweet face, but there was so many arms it made her look too spidery, seemed to me.

38 　This young girl kept a scrap-book when she was alive, and used to paste obituaries and accidents and cases of patient suf-
39 fering in it out of the 'Presbyterian Observer,' and write poetry after them out of her own head. It was very good poetry.

"IT MADE HER LOOK SPIDERY."

This is what she wrote about a boy by the name of Stephen Dowling Bots that fell down a well and was drownded:

ODE TO STEPHEN DOWLING BOTS, DEC'D.   **40**

And did young Stephen sicken,
    And did young Stephen die?
And did the sad hearts thicken,
    And did the mourners cry?

No; such was not the fate of
    Young Stephen Dowling Bots;
Though sad hearts round him thickened,
    'Twas not from sickness' shots.

No whooping-cough did rack his frame,
    Nor measles drear, with spots:
Not these impaired the sacred name
    Of Stephen Dowling Bots.

Despised love struck not with woe
    That head of curly knots,
Nor stomach troubles laid him low,
    Young Stephen Dowling Bots.

Oh no. Then list with tearful eye,
    Whilst I his fate do tell.
His soul did from this cold world fly,
    By falling down a well.

They got him out and emptied him;
    Alas it was too late;
His spirit was gone for to sport aloft
    In the realms of the good and great.

If Emmeline Grangerford could make poetry like that **41**
before she was fourteen, there ain't no telling what she could

slippers as chisels, Twain sarcastically jibes at the naïveté of technique in such painting. In his opinions on art, Twain was a bit of a Philistine. During his European tour, Twain was wearied by all the museums crammed with works by the Old Masters. "Wherever you find a Raphael, a Rubens, a Michael Angelo, a Caracci, or a Da Vinci (and we see them every day)" he wrote in Chapter 19, Part I, of *The Innocents Abroad*, "you find artists copying them, and the copies are always the handsomest. Maybe the originals were handsome when they were new, but they are not now." He was unimpressed by Da Vinci's "The Last Supper": "The colors are dimmed with age; the countenances are scaled and marred, and nearly all expression is gone from them; the hair is a dead blur upon the wall, and there is no life in the eyes. Only the attitudes are certain. People come here from all parts of the world, and . . . stand entranced before it with bated breath and parted lips, and when they speak, it is only in the catchy ejaculations of rapture." But Twain saw nothing but a battered, scarred, stained and discolored picture on a wall. "It vexes me to hear people talk so glibly," he continued, "of 'feeling,' 'expression,' 'tone,' and those other easily-acquired and inexpensive technicalities of art that make such a fine show in conversations concerning pictures."

33 *"I Shall Never Hear Thy Sweet Chirrup More Alas!"* The false pity lavished on this dead bird becomes less ridiculous and more tragic when one learns of the carnage spread by the girl's family in the following chapter. There it becomes clear why she is so preoccupied with death.

34 *an open letter in one hand with black sealing-wax showing on one edge of it.* One sealed one's letters with black wax when in mourning.

35 *It was a picture of a young woman in a long white gown.* This description profoundly affected Grant Wood, the American painter, best known for his "American Gothic"; he found it a "revelation." "Having been born into a world of Victorian standards," he explained in "My Debt to Mark Twain" (*Mark Twain Quarterly*, Fall 1937, p. 14), "I had accepted and admired the ornate, the lugubrious, and the excessively sentimental naturally and without question. And this was my first intimation that there was something ridiculous about sentimentality." Certainly Wood, in his parodying of American popular taste in his paintings, has much in common with Twain.

36 *standing on the rail of a bridge all ready to jump off.* Is it possible that the artist was contemplating her own suicide?

37 *now they kept this picture over the head of the bed in her room, and every time her birthday come they hung flowers on it. Other times it was hid with a little curtain.* So sentimental are these people that they have made a small shrine to the memory of the dead daughter. However, all these feelings are as false as their painted bricks, phony Staffordshire china, and chalk fruit.

38 *a scrap-book.* Nineteenth-century American households commonly kept scrapbooks of obituaries of family, friends, and famous people.

39 *Presbyterian Observer.* An anachronism: According to *The National Union Catalogue*, this journal did not begin publication until 1872, twenty or thirty years after the time of the story.

40 *Ode to Stephen Dowling Bots, Dec'd.* Common abbreviation for "deceased." John R. Byers, Jr., in "Miss Emmeline Grangerford's Hymn Book" (*American Literature*, May 1971, pp. 259–263) has suggested that the "ode" is a parody of Isaac Watts's "Submission at the bleeding cross," first published as Hymn 311 in *Hymns and Spiritual Songs* (1707):

> *Alas! and did my Saviour bleed!*
> *And did my sovereign die:*
> *Did he devote that sacred head*
> *For such a worm as I?*

Another possible source is Watts's "The resurrection," Hymn 620:

> *And must this body die?*
> *This mortal frame decay?*
> *And must these active limbs of mine*
> *Lie mould'ring in the clay?*

Twain was greatly amused by what he called "Post-Mortem Poetry," common to American newspapers and magazines during the nineteenth century. The most popular volume of this genre was *The Sentimental Song Book* (1876) by Julia A. Moore (1847–1920), "The Sweet Singer of Michigan." Twain admitted in Chapter 36 of *Following the Equator* that her alarming verse has "in it the . . . subtle touch . . . that makes an intentionally humorous episode pathetic and an intentionally pathetic one funny." The majority of her "songs" concern child death, and the fates of the late Little Susan, Little Minnie, Little Charley Hades, and all the others are as pathetic as the sad history of Stephen Dowling Bots. Typical of these verses is "Little Andrew":

> *Andrew was a little infant,*
> *And his life was two years old;*
> *He was his parents' eldest boy,*
> *And he was drowned, I was told.*
> *His parents never more can see him*
> *In this world of grief and pain,*
> *And Oh! they will not forget him*
> *While on earth they do remain.*

> *On one bright and pleasant morning*
> *His uncle thought it would be nice*
> *To take his dear little nephew*
> *Down to play upon a raft,*
> *Where he was to work upon it,*
> *And this little child would company be—*
> *The raft the water rushed around it,*
> *Yet he the danger did not see.*

> *This little child knew no danger—*
> *Its little soul was free from sin—*
> *He was looking in the water,*
> *Where, alas, this child fell in.*

"THEY GOT HIM OUT AND EMPTIED HIM."

a done by-and-by. Buck said she could rattle off poetry like nothing. She didn't ever have to stop to think. He said she would slap down a line, and if she couldn't find anything to rhyme with it she would just scratch it out and slap down another one, and go ahead. She warn't particular, she could write about anything you choose to give her to write about, just so it was sadful. Every time a man died, or a woman died, or a child died, she would be on hand with her "tribute" before he was cold. She called them tributes. The neighbours said it was the doctor first, then Emmeline, then the undertaker —the undertaker never got in ahead of Emmeline but once, and then she hung fire on a rhyme for the dead person's name, which was Whistler. She warn't ever the same, after that; she never complained, but she kind of pined away and did not live long. Poor thing, many's the time I made myself go up to the little room that used to be hers and get out her poor old scrap-book and read in it when her pictures had been aggravating me and I had soured on her a little. I liked all that family, dead ones and all, and warn't going to let anything come between us. Poor Emmeline made poetry about all the dead people when she was alive, and it didn't seem right that there warn't nobody to make some about her, now she was gone; so I tried to sweat out a verse or two myself, but I couldn't seem to make it go, somehow. They kept Emmeline's room trim and nice and all the things fixed in it just the way she liked to have them when she was alive, and nobody ever slept there. The old lady took care of the room herself, though there was plenty of niggers, and she sewed there a good deal and read her Bible there, mostly.

Well, as I was saying about the parlor, there was beautiful curtains on the windows: white, with pictures painted on them, of castles with vines all down the walls, and cattle coming down to drink.   There was a little old piano, too, that had tin pans **44** in it, I reckon, and nothing was ever so lovely as to hear the young ladies sing, "The Last Link is Broken" and play "The **45, 46** Battle of Prague" on it.   The walls of all the rooms was plas- **47** tered, and most had carpets on the floors, and the whole house was whitewashed on the outside.

It was a double house, and the big open place betwixt them was roofed and floored, and sometimes the table was set there in the middle of the day, and it was a cool, comfortable place. Nothing couldn't be better.   And warn't the cooking good, and just bushels of it too!

THE HOUSE.

Julia A. Moore. *Courtesy the Library of Congress.*

Beneath the raft the water took him in,
  For the current was so strong,
And before they could rescue him
  He was drowned and was gone.

Oh! how sad were his kind parents
  When they saw their drowned child,
As they brought him from the water,
  It almost made their hair grow wild.
Oh! how mournful was the parting
  From that little infant son.
Friends, I pray you, all take warning,
  Be careful of your little ones.

There are fine examples of parodies of "mortuary poetry" in Midwestern and Southern literature; by Eugene Field, Bill Nye, John Phoenix and others. In *Out of the Hurly Burly* (1874, pp. 113–127) by "Max Adeler" (Charles Heber Clark), Col. Bangs asks a poet to write uplifting verses to accompany some newspaper obituaries. The results are as absurd as the "Ode to Stephen Dowling Bots," as in the following:

Willie had a purple monkey climbing on a yellow
  stick,
And when he sucked the paint all off it made him
  deathly sick;
And in his latest hours he clasped that monkey in his
  hand,
And bade good-bye to earth and went into a better
  land.

Oh! no more he'll shoot his sister with his little
  wooden gun;
And no more he'll twist the pussy's tail and make her
  yowl, for fun.
The pussy's tail now stands out straight; the gun is
  laid aside;
The monkey doesn't jump around since little Willie
  died.

But none of these parodies is as famous as Emmeline Grangerford's effort. In a letter published in *The Mark Twain Quarterly* (Winter 1936), A. E.

Housman confessed that "The inimitable ode to Stephen Dowling Bots is one of the poems I know by heart."

41 *Emmeline Grangerford.* This dead girl's name was possibly taken from "impressionist water color" of "a head of a beautiful young girl, life size—called Emmeline, because she looked just about like that." This was just one of various ornamental objects that stood on both sides of the Clemens chimneypiece and the mantel; at the opposite end from the portrait of "Emmeline" was a framed oil painting of a cat's head. "Every now and then," Twain recounted in Chapter 40 of his *Autobiography*, "the children required me to construct a romance—always impromptu—not a moment's preparation permitted—and into that romance I had to get all that bric-à-brac and the . . . pictures. I had to start always with the cat and finish with Emmeline." As these romances were always filled with violence and bloodshed, it seems appropriate that the dead Grangerford girl should take her name from the tribulated "Emmeline" on the Clemens library wall.

The parlor of the Clemens home in Hartford, Connecticut. *Courtesy the New-York Historical Society, New York City.*

42 *"tribute."* An encomium.

43 *hung fire.* Hesitated.

44 *a little old piano . . . that had tin pans in it.* "Perhaps the little old piano . . . really had tin pans in it," Joseph Slater explained in "Notes and Queries: Music at Col. Grangerford's" (*American Literature*, March 1949, p. 111). "Piano-makers of the early nineteenth century, responding to the programmatic demands of the battle-pieces and to the popularity of Turkish music and instruments, introduced devices for the production of a variety of unusual musical effects. Extra pedals were constructed which permitted the pianist to embellish his performance with the sound of cymbals, drums and bells."

45 *"The Last Link is Broken."* A popular song of "noble resignation," written by William Clifton, a composer of minstrel-songs, and published in 1840:

The last link is broken that bound me to thee,
And the words I have spoken have rendered me free;
That bright glance misleading on others may shine,
Those eyes smil'd unheeding when tears burst from mine,
If my love was deem'd boldness that error is o'er,
I've witnessed thy coldness and prize thee no more.

Refrain:
I have no lov'd lightly, I'll think on thee yet,
I'll pray for thee nightly till life's sun is set.

This song was popular with the young people of Hannibal during the 1840s. Twain recalled their tastes in some notes quoted in *Mark Twain's Hannibal, Huck and Tom* (1969, p. 34): "Songs tended to regrets for bygone days and vanished joys: Oft in the Stilly Night; Last Rose of Summer; The Last Link; Bonny Doon; Old Dog Tray; for the lady I love will soon be a bride; Gaily the Troubadour; Bright Alforata."

46 *"The Battle of Prague."* A crude musical composition by Franz Kotzwana, a Bohemian fiddler, in 1788, to commemorate the 1757 skirmish between the armies of Prussia and those of Austria. The score contains such novelties as three sharp staccato notes to represent "flying bullets" and a sobbing treble figure to imitate "cries of the wounded." In 1878, as he recorded in Chapter 32 of *A Tramp Abroad*, Twain was alarmed by a performance of it by an "Arkansaw" girl in the drawing-room of the Jungfrau Hotel in Interlaken: "Without any more preliminaries," Twain recorded, "she turned on all the horrors of the 'Battle of Prague,' that venerable shivaree, and waded chin deep in the blood of the slain. . . . The audience stood it with pretty fair grit for a while, but when the cannonade waxed hotter and fiercer, and the discord average rose to four in five, the procession began to move. A few stragglers held their ground ten minutes longer, but when the girl began to wring the true inwardness out of the 'cries of the wounded,' they struck their colors and retired in a kind of panic." It must certainly have been unsettling for anyone to hear the pensive "The Last Link is Broken" followed by this musical blitzkrieg.

47 *The walls of all the rooms was plastered.* This domestic detail was obviously unusual in the backwoods. In Chapter 1 of *The Gilded Age*, Twain recorded the following conversation between two citizens of Obedstown, East Tennessee: "'Si Higgins he's ben over to Kaintuck n' married a high-toned gal thar, outen the fust families, an' he's come back to the Forks with jist a hell's-mint o' whoop-jamboree notions, folk says. He's tuck and fixed up the ole house like they does in Kaintuck, he say. . . . He's tuck an gawmed it all over on the inside with plarsterin'.'"
"'What's plarsterin'!?'"
"'*I* dono. . . . Ole Mam Higgins, she tole me. She say she warn't gwyne to hang out in sich a dern hole like a hog. Says it's mud, or some sich kind o' nastness that sticks on n' kivers up everything. Plarsterin', Si calls it.'"

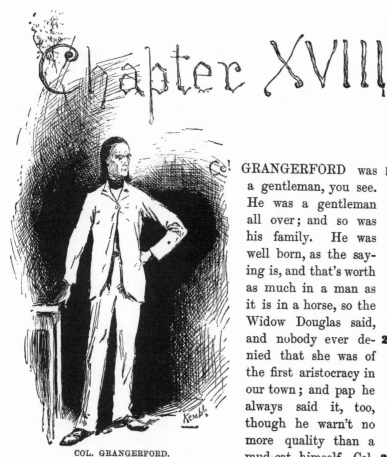

Chapter XVIII

Col. GRANGERFORD was **1** a gentleman, you see. He was a gentleman all over; and so was his family. He was well born, as the saying is, and that's worth as much in a man as it is in a horse, so the Widow Douglas said, and nobody ever de- **2** nied that she was of the first aristocracy in our town; and pap he always said it, too, though he warn't no more quality than a mud-cat, himself. Col. **3**

COL. GRANGERFORD.

Grangerford was very tall and very slim, and had a darkish-paly complexion, not a sign of red in it anywheres; he was clean-shaved every morning, all over his thin face, and he had the thinnest kind of lips, and the thinnest kind of nostrils, and a high nose, and heavy eyebrows, and the blackest kind of eyes, sunk so deep back that they seemed like they was looking out of caverns at you, as you may say. His forehead was high, and his hair was black and straight, and hung to his shoulders. His **4** hands was long and thin, and every day of his life he put on a clean shirt and a full suit from head to foot made out of linen

1 *Col. Grangerford was a gentleman.* A gentleman as defined by Sir Walter Scott's "maudlin Middle-Age romanticism." Twain complained in Chapter .46 of *Life on the Mississippi*, "It was Sir Walter who made every gentleman in the South a Major or a Colonel, or a General or a Judge, before the war; and it was he, also, who made these gentlemen value these bogus decorations. For it was he that created rank and caste down there, and also reverence for rank and caste, and pride and pleasure in them." And Hundley, however, in *Social Relations in Our Southern States* (p. 127), argued that it was not the influence of Sir Walter Scott but rather a "military fever" that inspired such affectations. The Southern Middle Class "are much given to a love of military titles, bestowed without regard to any sort of military service and upon all sorts of people. The young men, also, very much affect blue coats with brass buttons, and even sometimes sport veritable stripes down the legs of their pantaloons. To such an extent does the military fever rage in some localities, a stranger would conclude at least every other male citizen to be either 'Captain, or Co-lo-nel, or Knight at arms.'"

To those in Col. Grangerford's class, "gentleman" could only be determined by one's pedigree. Judge Griswold, the Southern gentleman of the uncompleted "Simon Wheeler, Detective," 1877–1878 (in *Mark Twain's Satires and Burlesques*, 1968, pp. 313–314) declared, "a man who came of gentle blood and fell to the ranks of scavengers and blacklegs, was still a gentleman and could not help it, since the word did not describe character but only birth; and a man who did not come of gentle blood might climb to the highest pinnacle of human grandeur but must still lack one thing—nothing could make him a gentleman; he might be called so by courtesy, but there an end."

But to Twain, it was not a question of birth but of character. "It seems to me," he explained in his "Laymen's Sermon," delivered at the New York YMCA on March 4, 1906 (in *Mark Twain's Speeches*, 1910, p. 138), "that if any man has just, merciful and kindly instincts he would be a gentleman, for he would need nothing else in the world." According to this definition, Col. Grangerford would not be a "gentleman," but Huckleberry Finn would be.

2 *nobody ever denied that she was of the first aristocracy in our town.* According to Chapter 5 of *Tom Sawyer*, the Widow Douglas (like Col. Grangerford) lives in the "best dwelling" of her village, a "hill mansion the only palace in the town, and the most hospitable and much the most lavish in the matter of festivities that St. Petersburg could boast."

3 *mud-cat.* Popular name of the yellow catfish, commonly considered an inferior species.

4 *his hair was black and straight.* Twain has forgotten that in the previous chapter he described Col. Grangerford as "gray and about sixty." Blair in *Mark Twain and Huck Finn* (p. 214) has suggested that this error resulted from Twain's rephrasing of a description of another Southern gentleman, Judge Griswold, in the uncompleted "Simon Wheeler, Detective" as that of Col. Grangerford: "'Judge' [Griswold] had never been on the bench; but that was no matter; he was the first citizen of the place, he was a man of great personal dignity, therefore no power in this world could have saved him from a title. He had been dubbed Major, then Colonel, then Squire; but gradually the community settled upon 'Judge,' and Judge he remained, after that.

"He was sixty years old; very tall, very spare, with a long, thin, smooth-shaven, intellectual face, and long black hair that lay close to his head, was kept to the rear by his ears as one keeps curtains back by brackets, and fell straight to his coat collar without a single tolerant kink or relenting curve. He had an eagle's beak and an eagle's eye. He was a Kentuckian by birth and rearing. . . . Judge Griswold's manners and carriage were of the courtly old-fashioned sort; he had never worked; he was a gentleman" (*Mark Twain's Satires and Burlesques*, p. 313).

There are other similarities between that aborted project and Huck's visit to the Grangerford homestead: "Simon Wheeler, Detective" describes the long-running feud between the Griswolds and the Burnsides which is reminiscent of that between the Grangerfords and the Shepherdsons; and the Burnsides have a "giddy and thoughtless, when . . . not sappy and sentimental" child named Hugh, who, like Emmeline Grangerford, is an amateur poet: "The world was hollow to him, then, and he was more than likely to shut himself up in his room and write some stuff about 'bruised hearts' or 'the despised and friendless,' and print it in one of the village journals under the impression that it was poetry" (p. 315).

5 *a liberty-pole.* A tall mast or staff with a Phrygian cap or some other symbol of liberty on top; one

so white it hurt your eyes to look at it; and on Sundays he wore a blue tail-coat with brass buttons on it. He carried a mahogany cane with a silver head to it. There warn't no frivolishness about him, not a bit, and he warn't ever loud. He was as kind as he could be—you could feel that, you know, and so you had confidence. Sometimes he smiled, and it was good **5,6** to see ; but when he straightened himself up like a liberty-pole, and the lightning begun to flicker out from under his eyebrows you wanted to climb a tree first, and find out what the matter was afterwards. He didn't ever have to tell anybody to mind their manners—everybody was always good-mannered where he was. Everybody loved to have him around, too ; he was sunshine most always—I mean he made it seem like good weather. When he turned into a cloud-bank it was awful dark for a half a minute and that was enough ; there wouldn't nothing go wrong again for a week.

When him and the old lady come down in the morning, all the family got up out of their chairs and give them good-day, and didn't set down again till they had set down. Then Tom and Bob went to the sideboard where the decanters was, and mixed a glass of bitters and handed it to him, and he held it in his hand and waited till Tom's and Bob's was mixed, and then **7** they bowed and said, " Our duty to you, sir, and madam ; " and *they* bowed the least bit in the world and said thank you, and **8** so they drank, all three, and Bob and Tom poured a spoonful of water on the sugar and the mite of whisky or apple brandy in the bottom of their tumblers, and give it to me and Buck, and we drank to the old people too.

Bob was the oldest, and Tom next. Tall, beautiful men with very broad shoulders and brown faces, and long black hair and black eyes. They dressed in white linen from head to foot, like the old gentleman, and wore broad Panama hats.

Then there was Miss Charlotte, she was twenty-five, and tall and proud and grand, but as good as she could be, when she warn't stirred up ; but when she was, she had a look that would make you wilt in your tracks, like her father. She was beautiful.

So was her sister, Miss Sophia, but it was a different kind. She was gentle and sweet, like a dove, and she was only twenty.

Each person had their own nigger to wait on them—Buck, too. My nigger had a monstrous easy time, because I warn't used to having anybody do anything for me, but Buck's was on the jump most of the time.

This was all there was of the family, now ; but there used to be more—three sons ; they got killed ; and Emmeline that died.

The old gentleman owned a lot of farms, and over a hundred niggers. Sometimes a stack of people would come there, horseback, from ten or fifteen mile around, and stay five or six days, and have such junketings round about and on the river, and dances and picnics in the woods, day-times, and balls at the house, nights. These people was mostly kin-folks of the family.

The men brought their guns with them. It was a handsome lot of quality, I tell you.

There was another clan of aristocracy around there—five or six families—mostly of the name of Shepherdson. They was as high-toned, and well born, and rich and grand, as the tribe of Grangerfords. The Shepherdsons and the Grangerfords used the same steamboat landing, which was about two mile above our house; so sometimes when I went up there with a lot of our folks I used to see a lot of the Shepherdsons there, on their fine horses.

One day Buck and me was away out in the woods, hunting, and heard a horse coming. We was crossing the road. Buck says:

"Quick! Jump for the woods!"

We done it, and then peeped down the woods through the leaves. Pretty soon a splendid young man come galloping down the road, setting his horse easy and looking like a soldier. He had his gun across his pommel. I had seen him before. It was young Harney Shepherdson. I heard Buck's gun go off at my ear, and Harney's hat tumbled off from his head. He

YOUNG HARNEY SHEPHERDSON.

grabbed his gun and rode straight to the place where we was hid. But we didn't wait. We started through the woods on a run. The woods warn't thick, so I looked over my shoulder, to dodge the bullet, and twice I seen Harney cover Buck with his gun; and then he rode away the way he come—to get his hat, I reckon, but I couldn't see. We never stopped running till we got home. The old gentleman's eyes blazed a minute—

would think this an ironic simile for this Southern aristocrat, except that here it is used to indicate merely "alone and erect."

6 *when . . . the lightning begun to flicker out from under his eyebrows you wanted to climb a tree first, and find out what the matter was afterwards.* Twain has described the typical "Southern Gentleman." "Besides being of faultless pedigree," Hundley explained in *Social Relations in Our Southern States* (p. 28), "the Southern Gentleman is usually possessed of an equally faultless physical development. His average height is about six feet, yet he is rarely gawky in his movements; or in the least clumsily put together; and his entire *physique* conveys to the mind an impression of firmness united to flexibility." But what Twain does (and Hundley does not) acknowledge is that the Southern Gentleman is usually short-tempered. Southern literature has many examples of these well-mannered aristocrats who are too quick to brutally defend a point of honor.

Blair in *Mark Twain and Huck Finn* (pp. 216–217) has pointed to Champ Effingham, Esquire, of John Esten Cooke's *The Virginia Comedians* (1854) and Col. Culpepper Starbottle of Bret Harte's *Gabriel Conroy* (1876). Frank Merriweather of John Pendleton Kennedy's *Swallow Barn; or, A Sojourn in the Old Dominion* (1832), too, is a kind and hospitable planter who is "always very touchy on a point of honor"; and like the Grangerfords, the Merriweathers have two daughters, the elder high-spirited, the younger sweet and gentle, and a thirteen-year-old son who is full of mischief. The most likely prototype for Col. Grangerford in contemporary literature was Peyton Beaumont of J. W. De Forest's *Kate Beaumont* (1872), a popular novel known to Twain which concerns (as Howells wrote in his *Atlantic Monthly* review, March 1872) "the high-tone Southern society . . . before the war . . . with slavery and chivalry, with hard drinking and easy shooting." Howells described the head of the household as "a quivering mass of affection for his own flesh and blood, an impersonation of the highest and stupidest family pride, his hot blood afire with constant cocktails and his life always in his hand for the resentment of an insult, an impatient parent and an impenitent homicide" (quoted by Blair, pp. 218–219). Howells's last remark refers to the Beaumonts' feud with the McAlisters. See also note 28.

7 *they bowed and said, "Our duty to you, sir, and madam;" and* they *bowed.* An odd, empty formality for an American backwoods family, a courtesy evidently inspired by Sir Walter Scott's chivalry.

8 *a spoonful of water on the sugar and the mite of whisky or apple brandy in the bottom of their tumblers.* An Old-Fashioned, said to be Twain's favorite cocktail.

9 *"I don't like that shooting from behind a bush."* Unlike his children, Col. Grangerford does not believe that all is fair in love and war.

10 *the corn-cribs.* Structures for drying corn; the air circulates through the open sides, either slats or latticework.

11 *the feud.* Such a vendetta, once common to Scottish clans, was known throughout the South before the Civil War; the most legendary of American blood-feuds was that between the Hatfields and the McCoys. The names of the families engaged in the Grangerford-Shepherdson conflict suggest the eternal struggle on the American frontier between the farmers and the herders; there is also a biblical prototype in the rivalry between Abel, a shepherd, and Cain, a granger, which resulted in the first murder in history, that between two brothers.

When asked by a correspondent whether "blood-feuds really existed in Arkansas" within the last fifty years as described in *Huckleberry Finn*, Twain replied on March 28, 1885 (in *Mark Twain's Notebooks and Journals*, Vol. II, 1975, pp. 568–569), "I came very near being an eye-witness of the general engagement detailed in the book. The details are historical and correct." Twain was referring to the troubles between one family who lived on the Kentucky side of the river and the other who lived on the Missouri side near New Madrid. In Chapter 26 of *Life on the Mississippi*, Twain described another feud, that between the Darnells and the Watsons along the Kentucky-Tennessee border, with similarities to that observed along the Kentucky-Missouri line. "In no part of the South," Twain wrote, "has the vendetta flourished more briskly, or held out longer between warring families," than in that area along the Ken-

Darnell vs. Watson. Illustration by A. B. Shute, *Life on the Mississippi*, 1883.

MISS CHARLOTTE.

t'was pleasure, mainly, I judged—then his face sort of smoothed down, and he says, kind of gentle:

9 "I don't like that shooting from behind a bush. Why didn't you step into the road, my boy?"

"The Shepherdsons don't, father. They always take advantage."

Miss Charlotte she held her head up like a queen while Buck was telling his tale, and her nostrils spread and her eyes snapped. The two young men looked dark, but never said nothing. Miss Sophia she turned pale, but the colour come back when she found the man warn't hurt.

10 Soon as I could get Buck down by the corn-cribs under the trees by ourselves, I says:

"Did you want to kill him, Buck?"

"Well, I bet I did."

"What did he do to you?"

"Him? He never done nothing to me."

"Well, then, what did you want to kill him for?"

11 "Why, nothing—only it's on account of the feud."

"What's a feud?"

12 "Why, where was you raised? Don't you know what a feud is?"

"Never heard of it before—tell me about it."

"Well," says Buck, "a feud is this way. A man has a quarrel with another man, and kills him; then that other man's brother kills *him*; then the other brothers, on both sides, goes for one another; then the *cousins* chip in—and by-and-by everybody's killed off, and there ain't no more feud. But it's kind of slow, and takes a long time."

"Has this one been going on long, Buck?"

"Well, I should *reckon!* it started thirty year ago, or som'ers along there. There was trouble 'bout something and then a lawsuit to settle it; and the suit went agin one of the men, and so he up and shot the man that won the suit—which he would naturally do, of course. Anybody would."

"What was the trouble about, Buck?—land?"

"I reckon maybe—I don't know."

"Well, who done the shooting?—was it a Grangerford or a Shepherdson?"

"Laws, how do *I* know? it was so long ago."

"Don't anybody know?"

"Oh, yes, pa knows, I reckon, and some of the other old folks; but they don't know now what the row was about in the first place."

"Has there been many killed, Buck?"

"Yes—right smart chance of funerals. But they don't always kill. Pa's got a few buck-shot in him; but he don't **13** mind it 'cuz he don't weigh much anyway. Bob's been carved up some with a bowie, and Tom's been hurt once or twice." **14**

"Has anybody been killed this year, Buck?"

"Yes, we got one and they got one. 'Bout three months ago, my cousin Bud, fourteen year old, was riding through the **15** woods, on t'other side of the river, and didn't have no weapon with him, which was blame' foolishness, and in a lonesome place he hears a horse a-coming behind him, and sees old Baldy Shepherdson a-linkin' after him with his gun in his hand and his white hair a-flying in the wind; and 'stead of jumping off and taking to the brush, Bud 'lowed he could outrun him; so they had it, nip and tuck, for five mile or more, the old man a- **16** gaining all the time; so at last Bud seen it warn't any use, so he stopped and faced around so as to have the bullet holes in front, you know, and the old man he rode up and shot him down. But he didn't git much chance to enjoy his luck, for inside of a week our folks laid *him* out."

"I reckon that old man was a coward, Buck."

"I reckon he *warn't* a coward. Not by a blame' sight. There **17** ain't a coward amongst them Shepherdsons—not a one. And there ain't no cowards amongst the Grangerfords, either. Why, that old man kep' up his end in a fight one day, for a half an hour, against three Grangerfords, and come out winner. They was all a-horseback; he lit off of his horse and got behind a little wood-pile, and kep' his horse before him to stop the bullets; but the Grangerfords staid on their horses and capered around the old man, and peppered away at him, and he peppered away at them. Him and his horse both went home pretty leaky and crippled, but the Grangerfords had to be *fetched* home—and one of 'em was dead, and another died the next day. No, sir, if a body's out hunting for cowards, he don't want to fool away any time amongst them Shephersons, becuz they don't breed any of that *kind*."

Next Sunday we all went to church, about three mile, **18** everybody a-horseback. The men took their guns along, so did

tucky-Tennessee border. "Nobody don't know what the first quarrel was about," Twain's companion on the riverboat tells him about the worst feud in that part of the country. "Some says it was about a horse or a cow—anyway, it was a little matter; the money in it wasn't of no consequence . . . both families was rich. . . . Rough words had been passed; and so, nothing but blood could fix it up after that. That horse or cow . . . cost sixty years of killing and crippling! Every year or so somebody was shot, on one side or the other; and as fast as one generation was laid out, their sons took up the feud and kept it a-going. And it's just as I say; they went on shooting each other year in and year out—making a kind of religion of it, you see—till they'd done forgot, long ago, what it was all about."

12 *where was you raised?* Aristocratic Buck puts down low-down Huck for his ignorance of the code of honor in this part of the country. Twain has introduced in Buck another example of how training corrupts youth.

13 *but he don't mind it 'cuz he don't weigh much anyway.* In his reading copy of the 1893 Tauchnitz edition, Twain added the comic aside, "It's just ballast" (MTP).

14 *a bowie.* This formidable weapon was a knife about a foot long in the blade, single-edged, very heavy, and with a sharp point; good either for cutting or stabbing, it was a common weapon of hunters and desperadoes in the Southern backwoods. Although said to be named for Jim Bowie, the famous Indian fighter, it was supposedly invented by his brother Rezin P. Bowie, as a hunting knife and not as a deadly weapon.

A bowie knife. Illustration by A. B. Frost, "Tom Sawyer, Detective," *Harper's Monthly*, September 1896. *Courtesy the Library of Congress.*

15 *my cousin Bud, fourteen year old.* This boy was the same age as Huck and Buck. "Men would shoot boys, boys would shoot men," Twain's companion reported on the Darnell-Watson feud in Chapter 26 of *Life on the Mississippi*. "A man shot a boy twelve years old—happened on him in the woods, and didn't give him no chance. If he *had* 'a' given him a chance, the boy'd 'a' shot *him*." Twain recalled a similar incident in his *Notebooks and Journals* (Vol. II, 1975, p. 568): "Once a boy 12 years old connected with the Kentucky family was riding thro the woods on the Missouri side. He was overtaken by a full-grown man and he shot that boy dead." By increasing Bud's age at the time of his death to that of Huck's present age, Twain indicates that his hero too will not live much longer if he does not escape these feuding families soon.

16 *nip and tuck*. Neck and neck.

17 *There ain't a coward amongst them Shepherdsons—not a one. And there ain't no cowards amongst the Grangerfords, either.* So far the feud has been between equals. Buck expresses a common flaw in Southern thinking of the period. "The two greatest causes of the present lawless state of society in the South," Marryat argued in Chapter 8 of his 1840 American diary, "are a mistaken notion of physical courage, and a total want of moral courage." These beliefs made such customs as duels and feuds respectable ways of settling difficulties throughout the South before the Civil War.

18 *Next Sunday we all went to church. . . . The Shepherdsons done the same.* So too the Darnells and the Watsons of *Life on the Mississippi*: "Both families belonged to the same church (everybody around here is religious); through all this fifty or sixty years' fuss, both tribes was there every Sunday, to worship. They lived each side of the line, and the church was at a landing called Compromise. Half the church and half the aisle was in Kentucky, the other half in Tennessee. Sundays you'd see the families drive up, all in their Sunday clothes, men, women, and children, and file up the aisle, and set down, quiet and orderly, one lot on the Tennessee side of the church and the other on the Kentucky side, and the men and boys would lean their guns up against the wall, handy, and then all hands would join in with the prayer and praise; though they say the man next the aisle didn't kneel down, along with the rest of the family; kind of stood guard."

19 *free grace*. The unmerited favor of God in disclosing to an individual the mystery of salvation.

20 *preforeordestination*. Huck has garbled two of the cardinal doctrines of Presbyterianism: predestination and foreordination. These principles argue that all things are already planned by God and consequently He has already decided who will receive salvation. One would think that the blood-feud would have damned their eternal souls, but being of "the first aristocracy," the Grangerfords and the Shepherdsons apparently are certain that they remain among God's elect. The "ornery" preaching only reinforces their immorality and hypocrisy.

21 *a puncheon floor*. A floor, Twain explained in Chapter 1 of his *Autobiography*, "made of logs whose upper surfaces have been chipped flat with the adz."

Buck, and kept them between their knees or stood them handy against the wall. The Shepherdsons done the same. It was pretty ornery preaching—all about brotherly love, and such-like tiresomeness; but everybody said it was a good sermon, and they all talked it over going home, and had such a powerful lot **19, 20** to say about faith, and good works, and free grace, and preforeordestination, and I don't know what all, that it did seem to me to be one of the roughest Sundays I had run across yet.

About an hour after dinner everybody was dozing around, some in their chairs and some in their rooms, and it got to be pretty dull. Buck and a dog was stretched out on the grass in the sun, sound asleep. I went up to our room, and judged I would take a nap myself. I found that sweet Miss Sophia standing in her door, which was next to ours, and she took me in her room and shut the door very soft, and asked me if I

"AND ASKED ME IF I LIKED HER."

liked her, and I said I did; and she asked me if I would do something for her and not tell anybody, and I said I would. Then she said she'd forgot her Testament, and left it in the seat at church, between two other books, and would I slip out quiet and go there and fetch it to her, and not say nothing to nobody. I said I would. So I slid out and slipped off up the road, and there warn't anybody at the church, except maybe a hog or two, for there warn't any lock on the door, and hogs **21** likes a puncheon floor in summer-time because it's cool. If **22** you notice, most folks don't go to church only when they've got to; but a hog is different.

Says I to myself something's up—it ain't natural for a girl to be in such a sweat about a Testament; so I give it a shake, and out drops a little piece of paper with " *Half-past-two* " wrote on it with a pencil. I ransacked it, but couldn't find anything else. I couldn't make anything out of that, so I put the paper in the book again, and when I got home and up-stairs, there was Miss Sophia in her door waiting for me. She pulled me in and shut the door; then she looked in the Testament till she found the paper, and as soon as she read it she looked glad; and before a body could think, she grabbed me and give me a squeeze, and said I was the best boy in the world, and not to tell anybody. She was mighty red in the face, for a minute, and her eyes lighted up, and it made her powerful pretty. I was a good deal astonished, but when I got my breath I asked her what the paper was about, and she asked me if I had read it, and I said "no," and she asked me if I could read writing, and I told her "No, only coarse-hand," and **23** then she said the paper warn't anything but a book-mark to keep her place, and I might go and play now.

I went off down to the river, studying over this thing, and pretty soon I noticed that my nigger was following along behind. When we was out of sight of the house, he looked back and around a second, and then comes a-running, and says :—

"Mars Jawge, if you'll come down into de swamp, I'll show you a whole stack o' water-moccasins." **24**

Thinks I, that's mighty curious; he said that yesterday. He oughter know a body don't love water-moccasins enough to go around hunting for them. What is he up to anyway? So I says—

"All right, trot ahead."

I followed a half a mile, then he struck out over the swamp and waded ankle deep as much as another half-mile. We come to a little flat piece of land which was dry and very thick with trees and bushes and vines, and he says—

"You shove right in dah, jist a few steps, Mars Jawge, dah's whah dey is. I's seed 'm befo', I don't k'yer to see 'em no mo'."

Then he slopped right along and went away, and pretty soon the trees hid him. I poked into the place a-ways, and come to a little open patch as big as a bedroom, all hung around with vines, and found a man laying there asleep—and by jings it was my old Jim!

I waked him up, and I reckoned it was going to be a grand surprise to him to see me again, but it warn't. He nearly cried, he was so glad, but he warn't surprised. Said he swum along behind me, that night, and heard me yell every time, but dasn't answer, because he didn't want nobody to pick *him* up, and take him into slavery again. Says he—

"I got hurt a little, en couldn't swim fas', so I wuz a con-sidable ways behine you, towards de las'; when you landed I reck'ned I could ketch up wid you on de lan' 'doubt havin' to shout at you, but when I see dat house I begin to go slow. I 'uz off too fur to hear what dey say to you—I wuz 'fraid o' de dogs—but when it 'uz all quiet agin, I knowed you's in de house, so I struck out for de woods to wait for day. Early in

The Grangerford-Shepherdson church is like the one Clemens remembered from his birthplace, Florida, Missouri: "The church was perched upon short sections of logs, which elevated it two or three feet from the ground. Hogs slept under there, and whenever dogs got after them during services the minister had to wait till the disturbance was over."

22 *Most folks don't go to church only when they've got to; but a hog is different.* Considering how much the sermon on brotherly love has affected the Grangerfords and the Shepherdsons, one must agree with Huck's observation that the hogs got more out of the church than did its congregation.

23 *coarse-hand.* Block letters, printing.

24 *water-moccasins.* A species of venomous crotaline snake, native to the South.

25 *I ben a-buyin' pots en pans en vittles.* Obviously, as another sign of the boy's accepting the slave as an equal on the raft, Huck has shared the money found in the blanket overcoat in Chapter 10 (and possibly the gold from the slave-hunters in Chapter 16) with Jim.

26 *jawin'.* Quarreling.

27 *He ain't ever told me you was here. . . . If anything happens, he ain't mixed up in it.* For self-preservation, the Southern slave, like Huck's Jack, was often skilled in the art of justifiable deception. When asked by his wife why there did not seem to be any honest slaves, Augustine St. Clare, himself a slave-owner, replies in Chapter 18 of *Uncle Tom's Cabin,* "From the mother's breast the colored child feels and sees that there are none but underhand ways open to it. It can get along no other way with its parents, its mistress, its young master and missie play-fellows. Cunning and deception become necessary, inevitable habits. It isn't fair to expect anything else of him. He ought not to be punished for it. As to honesty, the slave is kept in the dependent, semi-childish state, that there is no making him realize the rights of property, or feel that his master's goods are not his own, if he can get them. For my part, I don't see how they *can* be honest." See also Chapter 26, note 14.

de mawnin' some er de niggers come along, gwyne to de fields, en dey tuck me en showed me dis place, whah de dogs can't track me on accounts o' de water, en dey brings me truck to eat every night, en tells me how you's a gitt'n along."

" Why didn't you tell my Jack to fetch me here sooner, Jim ? "

25 " Well, 'twarn't no use to 'sturb you, Huck, tell we could do sumfn—but we's all right, now. I ben a-buyin' pots en pans en vittles, as I got a chanst, en a patchin' up de raf', nights, when——"

" *What* raft, Jim ? "

" Our ole raf'."

" You mean to say our old raft warn't smashed all to flinders ? "

" No, she warn't. She was tore up a good deal—one en' of her was—but dey warn't no great harm done, on'y our traps was mos' all los'. Ef we hadn' dive' so deep en swum so fur under water, en de night had'n ben so dark, en we warn't so sk'yerd, en ben sich punkin-heads, as de sayin' is, we'd a seed de raf'. But it's jis' as well we didn't, 'kase now she's all fixed up agin mos' as good as new, en we's got a new lot o' stuff, too, in de place o' what 'uz los'."

" Why, how did you get hold of the raft again, Jim—did you catch her ? "

" How I gwyne to ketch her, en I out in de woods ? No, some er de niggers foun' her ketched on a snag, along heah in **26** de ben', en dey hid her in a crick, 'mongst de willows, en dey wuz so much jawin' 'bout which un 'um she b'long to de mos', dat I come to heah 'bout it pooty soon, so I ups en settles de trouble by tellin' 'um she don't b'long to none uv um, but to you en me ; en I ast 'm if dey gwyne to grab a young white genlman's propaty, en git a hid'n for it ? Den I gin 'm ten cents apiece, en dey 'uz mighty well satisfied, en wisht some mo' raf's 'ud come along en make 'm rich agin. Dey's mighty good to me, dese niggers is, en whatever I wants 'm to do fur me, I doan' have to ast 'm twice, honey. Dat Jack's a good nigger, en pooty smart."

27 " Yes, he is. He ain't ever told me you was here ; told me to come, and he'd show me a lot of water-moccasins. If anything happens, *he* ain't mixed up in it. He can say he never seen us together, and it'll be the truth."

I don't want to talk much about the next day. I reckon I'll cut it pretty short. I waked up about dawn, and was agoing to turn over and go to sleep again, when I noticed how still it was—didn't seem to be anybody stirring. That warn't usual. Next I noticed that Buck was up and gone. Well, I gets up, a-wondering, and goes downstairs—nobody around ; everything as still as a mouse. Just the same outside ; thinks I, what does it mean ? Down by the wood-pile I comes across my Jack, and says :

" What's it all about ? "

Says he :

"Don't you know, Mars Jawge?"

"No," says I, "I don't."

"Well, den, Miss Sophia's run off! 'deed she has. She run **28** off in de night, sometime—nobody don't know jis' when—run off to git married to dat young Harney Shepherdson, you know —leastways, so dey 'spec. De fambly foun' it out, 'bout half an hour ago—maybe a little mo'—en' I *tell* you dey warn't no time los'. Sich another hurryin' up guns en hosses *you* never see! De women folks has gone for to stir up de relations, en ole Mars Saul en de boys tuck dey guns en rode up de river road for to try to ketch dat young man en kill him 'fo' he kin git acrost de river wid Miss Sophia. I reck'n dey's gwyne to be mighty rough times."

"Buck went off 'thout waking me up."

"Well, I reck'n he *did!* Dey warn't gwyne to mix you up in it. Mars Buck he loaded up his gun en 'lowed he's gwyne to fetch home a Shepherdson or bust. Well, dey'll be plenty un 'm dah, I reck'n, en you bet you he'll fetch one ef he gits a chanst."

I took up the river road as hard as I could put. By-and-by **29, 30** I begin to hear guns a good ways off. When I come in sight of the log store and the wood-pile where the steamboats land, I worked along under the trees and brush till I got to a good place, and then I clumb up into the forks of a cotton-wood that was out of reach, and watched. There was a wood-rank four **31** foot high, a little ways in front of the tree, and first I was going to hide behind that; but maybe it was luckier I didn't.

There was four or five men cavorting around on their horses in the open place before the log store, cussing and yelling, and trying to get at a couple of young chaps that was behind the wood-rank alongside of the steamboat landing—but they couldn't come it. Every time one of them showed himself on the river side of the wood-pile he got shot at. The two boys

"BEHIND THE WOOD PILE."

28 *Miss Sophia's run off . . . to git married to dat young Harney Shepherdson.* This backwoods version of *Romeo and Juliet* may have been suggested by the romance between the sweet younger sister Kate Beaumont and the young Frank McAlister, members of the two feuding families of De Forest's *Kate Beaumont.* See also Chapter 20, note 17.

29 *as hard as I could put.* As hard as I could run.

30 *By-and-by I begin to hear guns a good ways off.* The climax of the Grangerford-Shepherdson feud is an elaboration of an incident Twain recorded in his *Notebooks and Journals* (Vol. II, 1975, p. 568): "I was on a Memphis packet and at a landing we made on the Kentucky side there was a row. Don't remember as there was anybody hurt then; but shortly afterwards there was another row at that place and a youth of 19 belonging to the Missouri tribe had wandered over there. Half a dozen of that Kentucky tribe got after him. He dodged among the wood piles and answered their shots. Presently he jumped into the river and they followed on after and peppered him and he had to make for the shore. By that time he was about dead—did shortly die." Twain's riverboat companion recounts the same incident in Chapter 26 of *Life on the Mississippi;* but he could not recall if it concerned the Darnells and the Watsons, or another feud. "Years ago," he told Twain, "the Darnells was so thinned out that the old man and his two sons concluded they'd leave the country . . .; but the Watsons got wind of it; and they arrived just as the two young Darnells was walking up the companion-way with their wives on their arms. The fight begun then, and they never got no further—both of them killed. After that, old Darnell got into trouble with the man that run the ferry, and the ferryman got the worst of it—and died. But his friends shot old Darnell through and through—filled him full of bullets, and ended him."

The Darnell-Watson feud. Illustration by A. B. Shute, *Life on the Mississippi,* 1883.

31 *a wood-rank.* Or "wood-rick," a neatly stacked pile of timber, generally half a cord.

"Buck said his father and brothers ought to waited for their relations." Illustration by E. W. Kemble, "Autograph Edition," 1899.

32 *had the bulge*. Had the advantage, said to be mining slang.

33 *to get shut of*. To get rid of, to forget.

was squatting back to back behind the pile, so they could watch both ways.

By-and-by the men stopped cavorting around and yelling. They started riding towards the store; then up gets one of the boys, draws a steady bead over the wood-rank, and drops one of them out of his saddle. All the men jumped off of their horses and grabbed the hurt one and started to carry him to the store; and that minute the two boys started on the run. They got half-way to the tree I was in before the men noticed. Then the men see them, and jumped on their horses and took out after them. They gained on the boys, but it didn't do no good, the boys had too good a start; they got to the wood-pile that was **32** in front of my tree, and slipped in behind it, and so they had the bulge on the men again. One of the boys was Buck, and the other was a slim young chap about nineteen years old.

The men ripped around awhile, and then rode away. As soon as they was out of sight, I sung out to Buck and told him. He didn't know what to make of my voice coming out of the tree, at first. He was awful surprised. He told me to watch out sharp and let him know when the men came in sight again; said they was up to some devilment or other—wouldn't be gone long. I wished I was out of that tree, but I dasn't come down. Buck begun to cry and rip, and 'lowed that him and his cousin Joe (that was the other young chap) would make up for this day, yet. He said his father and his two brothers was killed, and two or three of the enemy. Said the Shepherdsons laid for them, in ambush. Buck said his father and brothers ought to waited for their relations—the Shepherdsons was too strong for them. I asked him what was become of young Harney and Miss Sophia. He said they'd got across the river and was safe. I was glad of that; but the way Buck did take on because he didn't manage to kill Harney that day he shot at him—I hain't ever heard anything like it.

All of a sudden, bang! bang! bang! goes three or four guns—the men had slipped around through the woods and come in from behind without their horses! The boys jumped for the river—both of them hurt—and as they swum down the current the men run along the bank shooting at them and singing out, "Kill them, kill them!" It made me so sick I most fell out of the tree. I ain't agoing to tell *all* that happened—it would make me sick again if I was to do that. I wished I hadn't ever come ashore that night, to see such things. I ain't ever going **33** to get shut of them—lots of times I dream about them.

I staid in the tree till it begun to get dark, afraid to come down. Sometimes I heard guns away off in the woods; and twice I seen little gangs of men gallop past the log store with guns; so I reckoned the trouble was still agoing on. I was mighty down-hearted; so I made up my mind I wouldn't ever go anear that house again, because I reckoned I was to blame, somehow. I judged that that piece of paper meant that Miss Sophia was to meet Harney somewheres at half-past two and run off; and I judged I ought to told her father about that paper and the curious way she acted, and then maybe he would a locked her up and this awful mess wouldn't ever happened.

When I got down out of the tree, I crept along down the river bank a piece, and found the two bodies laying in the edge of the water, and tugged at them till I got them ashore; then I covered up their faces, and got away as quick as I could. I cried a little when I was covering up Buck's face, for he was mighty good to me.

It was just dark, now. I never went near the house, but struck through the woods and made for the swamp. Jim warn't on his island, so I tramped off in a hurry for the crick, and crowded through the willows, red-hot to jump aboard and get out of that awful country—the raft was gone! My souls, but I was scared! I couldn't get my breath for most a minute. Then I raised a yell. A voice not twenty-five foot from me, says—

"Good lan'! is dat you, honey? Doan' make no noise."

It was Jim's voice—nothing ever sounded so good before. I run along the bank a piece and got aboard, and Jim he grabbed me and hugged me, he was so glad to see me. He says—

"Laws bless you, chile, I 'uz right down sho' you's dead agin. Jack's been heah, he say he reck'n you's ben shot, kase you didn' come home no mo'; so I's jes' dis minute a startin' de raf' down towards de mouf er de crick, so's to be all ready for to shove out en leave soon as Jack comes agin en tells me for certain you *is* dead. Lawsy, I's mighty glad to git you back agin, honey."

I says—

"All right—that's mighty good; they won't find me, and they'll think I've been killed, and floated down the river— **34** there's something up there that'll help them to think so—so don't you lose no time, Jim, but just shove off for the big **35** water as fast as ever you can."

I never felt easy till the raft was two mile below there and out in the middle of the Mississippi. Then we hung up our signal lantern, and judged that we was free and safe once more. I hadn't had a bite to eat since yesterday; so Jim he got out some corn-dodgers and butter-milk, and pork and cabbage, and **36** greens—there ain't nothing in the world so good, when it's **37** cooked right—and whilst I eat my supper we talked, and had a good time. I was powerful glad to get away from the feuds, and so was Jim to get away from the swamp. We said there warn't no home like a raft, after all. Other places do seem so cramped up and smothery, but a raft don't. You feel mighty free and easy and comfortable on a raft.

34 *they'll think I've been killed, and floated down the river.* The third of Huck's "deaths."

35 *the big water.* The Mississippi River, from the probable Indian etymology of the name.

36 *corn-dodgers.* Corn-meal cakes, baked until hard.

37 *greens.* Vegetables, usually boiled; often dandelion or beet leaves, or spinach.

1 *Here is the way we put in the time.* Here begins one of the most famous passages in *Huckleberry Finn*, the finest of the boy's descriptions of the power and the beauty of Nature as experienced on the journey down the river. Twain wrote a draft of this revery in a letter to a twelve-year-old boy. When David Bowser wrote Clemens on March 16, 1880, about a school project "to select some man among the living great ones, . . . with whom we would exchange place," he continued, "A few of us boys thought it would be a 'lark' to send our compositions to our favorites, and ask them if they would be willing to change with us, and if their fame, riches, honors, and glory had made them perfectly happy—in fact to ask them if they would 'be a boy again.'" Just the suggestion to "Be a boy again" sent Twain into a rapturously nostalgic mood. He wrote he would be a "cub pilot" along the Mississippi again. "Summer always," he wrote the boy; "the magnolias at Rifle Point always in bloom, so that the dreamy twilight should have the added charm of their perfume; the oleanders on the 'coast' always in bloom, likewise; the sugar cane always green . . .; the river always bankfull, so we could run all the chutes . . .; we should see the thick banks of young willows dipping their leaves into the currentless water, and we could thrash right along against them without any danger of hurting anything; . . . and I would have the trips long, and the stays in port short" (quoted by Pascal Covici, Jr., in "Dear Master Wattie," *Southwest Review*, Spring 1960, pp. 107–108). Likewise, Huck describes this endless summer along the Mississippi.

What Thomas Wolfe found most memorable in his fellow Southerner's fiction was "how that huge river moves itself—not like a shining golden serpent of the day—but how it drinks from out the continent—

Chapter XIX

HIDING DAY-TIMES.

1 TWO or three days and nights went by; I reckon I might say they swum by, they slid along so quiet and smooth and lovely. Here is the way we put in the time. It was a monstrous big river down there—sometimes a mile and a half wide; we run nights, and laid up and hid day-times; soon as night was most gone, we stopped navigating and tied up—nearly always in the dead water under a tow-head; and then cut young cotton-woods and willows and hid the raft with them. Then we set out the lines. Next we slid into the river and had a swim, so as to freshen up and cool off; then we set down on the sandy bottom where the water was about knee-deep, and watched the daylight come. Not a sound anywheres—perfectly still—just like the whole world was asleep, only sometimes the bull-frogs a-clattering, maybe. The first thing to see, looking away over the water, was a kind of dull line—that was the woods on t'other side—you couldn't make nothing else out; then a pale place in the sky; then more paleness, spreading around; then the river softened up, away off, and warn't black any more, but gray; you could see little dark spots drifting along, ever so far away—trading scows, and such things; and long black streaks—rafts; sometimes you could hear a sweep screaking; or jumbled up voices, it was so still, and sounds **2** come so far; and by-and-by you could see a streak on the water which you know by the look of the streak that there's a snag there in a swift current which breaks on it and makes that streak look that way; and you see the mist curl up off of the water, and the east reddens up, and the river, and you make out a log cabin in the edge of the woods, away on the bank on t'other side of the river, being a wood-yard, likely, and piled by them cheats so you can throw a dog through it any- **3** wheres; then the nice breeze springs up, and comes fanning you from over there, so cool and fresh, and sweet to smell, on account of the woods and the flowers; but sometimes not that way, because they've left dead fish laying around, gars, and **4** such, and they do get pretty rank; and next you've got the full day, and everything smiling in the sun, and the song-birds just going it!

A little smoke couldn't be noticed, now, so we would take some fish off of the lines and cook up a hot breakfast. And afterwards we would watch the lonesomeness of the river, and kind of lazy along, and by-and-by lazy off to sleep. Wake up, by-and-by, and look to see what done it, and maybe see a steamboat, coughing along up stream, so far off towards the other side you couldn't tell nothing about her only whether she was stern-wheel or side-wheel; then for about an hour there **5** wouldn't be nothing to hear nor nothing to see—just solid lonesomeness. Next you'd see a raft sliding by, away off yonder, and maybe a galoot on it chopping, because they're most always **6** doing it on a raft; you'd see the axe flash, and come down—you don't hear nothing; you see that axe go up again, and by the time it's above the man's head, then you hear the *k'chunk!*—it **7** had took all that time to come over the water. So we would put in the day, lazying around, listening to the stillness. Once there was a thick fog, and the rafts and things that went by was beating tin pans so the steamboats wouldn't run over them. A scow or a raft went by so close we could hear them talking and cussing and laughing—heard them plain; but we couldn't see no sign of them; it made you feel crawly, it was like spirits carrying on that way in the air. Jim said he believed it was spirits; but I says:

"No, spirits wouldn't say, ' dern the dern fog.' "

Soon as it was night, out we shoved; when we got her out to about the middle, we let her alone, and let her float where-ever the current wanted her to; then we lit the pipes, and dangled our legs in the water and talked about all kinds of things—we was always naked, day and night, whenever the **8** mosquitoes would let us—the new clothes Buck's folks made

moves forever like a mighty, dark and secret river of the night" (quoted by Elizabeth Evans, "Thomas Wolfe: Some Echoes from Mark Twain," *Mark Twain Journal*, Summer 1976, p. 5). "How" is the crucial word, for Twain, in his careful selection of vernacular expressions, presents the river as a living force. "Nothing is fixed, absolute or perfect," Leo Marx observed in "The Pilot and the Passenger: Landscape Conventions and the Style of *Huckleberry Finn*" (*American Literature*, May 1956, p. 139). "The passage gains immensely in verisimilitude from his repeated approximations: 'soon as the night was *most* gone,' '*nearly always* in the dead water,' 'a *kind* of dull line,' '*sometimes* you could hear'. . . . Nature too is in process: 'the daylight *come*,' 'paleness, *spreading* around,' 'river *softened* up,' 'mist *curl* up,' 'east *reddens* up'. . . ." The river does appear like some great god, passing on regardless of the struggles of men. "As with Conrad," T. S. Eliot wrote in his introduction to a 1950 edition, "we were continually reminded of the power and terror of Nature, and the isolation and feebleness of Man." This god's only sin is its indifference. "The Book of Nature," Twain wrote in his *Notebook* (1935, p. 360), "tells us distinctly that God cares not a rap for us—nor for any living creature. It tells us that His laws inflict pain and suffering and sorrow, but it does not say that this is done in order that He may get pleasure out of this misery."

But is Nature so terrible? Surely this passage serves as an idyllic interlude between the brutality of the Grangerfords and the introduction of the two scoundrels, the duke and the king. The trouble lies not with Nature but with Man. The boy makes vivid these recollections of his experiences along the river by offering a feast for all five senses: sight (the pale landscape); sound (bullfrogs' cluttering); smell (the sweet breezes); taste (the fish breakfast); and touch (swimming nude). Twain seems to suggest that man needs only to enjoy and stop fighting the river to comprehend its beauty and power. But those who inhabit the land remain ignorant.

Never even on the river are Huck and Jim completely free of civilization, no matter how primitive it may seem; the tranquility of life on the raft is disrupted only by the intrusion of men, by their cheating, their swearing, their killing. No matter how deceptively distant, the presence of men along the banks threatens the fugitives all throughout their otherwise idyllic journey down the river.

2 *screaking*. The sound of the sweep's ungreased hinge or axle.

3 *piled by them cheats so you can throw a dog through it anywheres*. As Leo Marx explained in his notes to the 1967 Bobbs-Merrill edition, stacks of wood were sold by volume, gaps included.

4 *gars*. Large hard-scaled fish with sharp teeth. They are not considered particularly edible; fishermen kill them generally because they are so rapacious. Because they have not slain them for food, the men have left the dead fish laying around to rot in the sunshine. "Of the entire brood," Twain noted in "The Character of Man," 1890 (in *What Is Man?*, 1973, p. 60), Man "is the only one—the solitary one—that possesses malice. That is the basest of all instincts, passions, vices—the most hateful. That one thing puts him below the rats, the grubs, the trichenae. He is the only creature that inflicts pain for sport, knowing it to *be* pain. . . . *All* creatures kill—there seems to be no exception; but of the whole list, man is the only one that kills for fun; he is the only one that kills in malice, the only one that kills for revenge."

5 *stern-wheel or side-wheel.* The shallow waters of the Western rivers were navigated by small steamboats with the wheel at the front instead of side-wheels which are used only on the larger steamers. The preference of one form over the other was evidently based on tradition and taste and not on practical technology; stern-wheelers were cheaper to build and cheaper to run, and yet they were less popular and used primarily for freight.

6 *a galoot on it chopping, because they're most always doing it on a raft.* A "galoot" now refers to an awkward, uncouth fellow; but Huck uses an earlier meaning, that of a young, unfledged sailor, a novice, usually given the menial work on a vessel.

7 *it had took all that time to come over the water.* An acoustic mirage: The sound was actually made when the ax hit the wood, but, because water distorts the speed of sound, it only seems that the "k'chunk" took a long time to cross the river to Huck.

8 *we was always naked, day and night.* In his *Notebook* (1935, p. 153), Twain once commented on the hypocrisy of nineteenth-century prudery: "If I print 'she was stark naked' and then proceed to describe her person in detail, what critic would not howl? Who would venture to leave the book on a parlor table? But the artist does this, and all ages gather around and look and talk and admire." But this double standard as to what was appropriate for art and not for literature took varying shapes: Victorian propriety forbade Kemble from following this detail in Twain's text in his illustrations; similarly Gilder

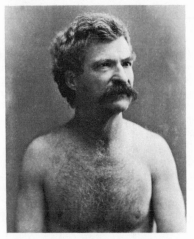

Mark Twain, about 1883. *Courtesy the Mark Twain Papers, The Bancroft Library, University of California at Berkeley.*

for me was too good to be comfortable, and besides I didn't go much on clothes, nohow.

Sometimes we'd have that whole river all to ourselves for the longest time. Yonder was the banks and the islands, across the water; and maybe a spark—which was a candle in a cabin window—and sometimes on the water you could see a spark or two—on a raft or a scow, you know; and maybe you could hear a fiddle or a song coming over from one of them crafts. It's lovely to live on a raft. We had the sky, up there, all speckled with stars, and we used to lay on our backs and look up at them, and discuss about whether they was made, or only just happened—Jim he allowed they was made, but I allowed they happened; I judged it would have took too long to *make* so many. Jim said the moon could a *laid* them; well, that looked kind of reasonable, so I didn't say nothing against it, because I've seen a frog lay most as many, so of course it could be done. We used to watch the stars that fell, too, and see them streak down. Jim allowed they'd got spoiled and was hove out of the nest.

Once or twice of a night we would see a steamboat slipping along in the dark, and now and then she would belch a whole world of sparks up out of her chimbleys, and they would rain down in the river and look awful pretty; then she would turn a corner and her lights would wink out and her pow-wow shut off and leave the river still again; and by-and-by her waves would get to us, a long time after she was gone, and joggle the raft a bit, and after that you wouldn't hear nothing for you couldn't tell how long, except maybe frogs or something.

After midnight the people on shore went to bed, and then for two or three hours the shores was black—no more sparks in the cabin windows. These sparks was our clock—the first one that showed again meant morning was coming, so we hunted a place to hide and tie up, right away.

9
10 One morning about day-break, I found a canoe and crossed over a chute to the main shore—it was only two hundred yards—and paddled about a mile up a crick amongst the cypress woods, to see if I couldn't get some berries. Just as I was passing a place where a kind of cow-path crossed the crick, here comes a couple of men tearing up the path as tight as they could foot it. I thought I was a goner, for whenever anybody was after anybody I judged it was *me*—or maybe Jim. I was about to dig out from there in a hurry, but they was pretty close to me then, and sung out and begged me to save their lives—said they hadn't been doing nothing, and was being chased for it—said there was men and dogs a-coming. They wanted to jump right in, but I says—

"Don't you do it. I don't hear the dogs and horses yet; you've got time to crowd through the brush and get up the crick a little ways; then you take to the water and wade down to me and get in—that'll throw the dogs off the scent."

They done it, and soon as they was aboard I lit out for our tow-head, and in about five or ten minutes we heard the dogs and the men away off, shouting. We heard them come along

"AND DOGS A-COMING."

towards the crick, but couldn't see them ; they seemed to stop and fool around a while ; then, as we got further and further away all the time, we couldn't hardly hear them at all ; by the time we had left a mile of woods behind us and struck the river, everything was quiet, and we paddled over to the tow-head and hid in the cotton-woods and was safe.

One of these fellows was about seventy, or upwards, and had a bald head and very gray whiskers.   He had an old battered-up slouch hat on, and a greasy blue woollen shirt, and ragged old blue jeans britches stuffed into his boot tops, and home-knit galluses—no, he only had one.   He had an old long-tailed blue jeans coat with slick brass buttons, flung over his arm, and both of them had big fat ratty-looking carpet-bags.

The other fellow was about thirty and dressed about as ornery.   After breakfast we all laid off and talked, and the first thing that come out was that these chaps didn't know one another.

"What got you into trouble?" says the baldhead to t'other chap.

"Well, I'd been selling an article to take the tartar off the teeth—and it does take it off, too, and generly the enamel along with it—but I staid about one night longer than I ought to, and was just in the act of sliding out when I ran across you on the trail this side of town, and you told me they were coming, and begged me to help you to get off.   So I told you I was expecting trouble myself and would scatter out *with* you. That's the whole yarn—what's yourn?"

"Well, I'd ben a-runnin' a little temperance revival thar, 'bout a week, and was the pet of the women-folks, big and little, for I was makin' it mighty warm for the rummies, I *tell* you, and takin' as much as five or six dollars a night—ten cents a

11
12
13
14
15

dropped all references to Huck and Jim's being naked on the river in the excerpt, "Royalty on the Mississippi: As Chronicled by Huckleberry Finn," (*The Century*, February 1885). Twain himself may have insisted that the artist not depict them nude; and yet True Williams drew Huck, Tom, and Joe Harper skinny-dipping on Jackson's Island in Chapter 14 of *Tom Sawyer*, and Huck was shown naked in the illustrations to "The Raft Chapter" in Chapter 3, as were the Hannibal boy bathers in Chapter 54 of *Life on the Mississippi*.

Privately Twain had no sympathy for such false morality. "The convention miscalled Modesty has no standard," he wrote in "Letters to the Earth," 1909 (in *What Is Man?*, 1973, p. 417), "and cannot have one, because it is opposed to nature and reason, and is therefore an artificiality and subject to anybody's whim, anybody's diseased caprice." Obviously Huck is speaking for the author when he says in Chapter 8 of *Tom Sawyer Abroad*, "Clothes is well enough in school, and in towns, and at balls, too, but there ain't no sense in them when there ain't no civilization nor other kinds of bothers and fussiness around." Certainly Clemens when a boy must have hated (and frequently broken) an 1845 Hannibal ordinance forbidding anyone from swimming naked within the town's perimeter from one hour before sunrise until one hour after sunset; violators were subject to fines. "Man, with his soiled mind, covers himself," Twain observed in "Man's Place in the Animal World," 1890 (in *What Is Man?*, p. 83). "He will not even enter a drawing room with his breast and back naked, so alive is he and his mates to indecent suggestion. . . . No—man is the Animal that Blushes. He is the only one that does it—or has occasion to."

9 *I found a canoe*. Twain had written "I took the canoe" in the manuscript, but an alert copy-editor noted that the boat had been lost when the raft had been broken up at the end of Chapter 16, and so the change was made in the galleys. Huck and Jim have evidently long since given up the plan to return north by canoe. Apparently Twain did not know exactly what to do with Jim: At one point in his notes, he wrote, "And Jim can be smuggled north on a ship?— no, a steamboat"; and at another place, "Jim has fever and is in concealment" (quoted by DeVoto, *Mark Twain at Work*, pp. 75 and 66). At this point in their journey deeper into slave country, the boy and the slave are at the mercy of the river.

10 *a chute*. A narrow passage between an island and the mainland, with a swift current and navigable only when the river is high enough; a French word. In Chapter 4 of *The Gilded Age*, Twain described a steamboat's entrance into such a waterway: "Sometimes she approached a solid wall of tall trees as if she meant to break through it, but all of a sudden a little crack would open just enough to admit her, and away she would go plowing through the 'chute' with just barely room enough between the island on one side and the mainland on the other."

11 *home-knit galluses—no, he only had one*. One suspender is all one needs to keep one's pants up, two are worn for "style" and would have suggested that this derelict was of a higher class than he actually is.

12 *carpet-bags*. The common luggage of the itinerant, being the cheapest and most convenient way of transporting one's goods while traveling; at one time they were actually made out of old, unwanted carpets. Consequently they became the common baggage of traveling salesmen, confidence men, and anyone else who had to move as swiftly as possible from place to place. Often these contained all the material goods their owners possessed in the world; and one who carried carpet-bags was generally considered as an outsider, having no house nor land nor shelter nor any property of any kind. Not surprisingly, Southerners named the Yankee speculators during the Reconstruction "carpet-baggers."

13 *an article to take the tartar off the teeth*. Joseph Jones in "The 'Duke's' Tooth-Powder Racket: A Note on *Huckleberry Finn*" (*Modern Language Notes*, November 1946, pp. 468–469) has quoted an article "Tooth Destroyers" (New York *Weekly*, August 24, 1871, p. 6) which describes exactly what line of business this gentleman was engaged in: "A boy is selected from a crowd gathered by the peddler's eloquence, and in an instant his teeth are cleansed. The staring spectators having thus seen a practical test of its virtue, purchase the tooth-powder, and use it on their own masticators until the acid and potash, of which it is composed, eats away the protecting enamel of the teeth rendering speedy decay certain." But once such a swindler was caught, he could get as much as a year in prison.

14 *a little temperance revival*. The old scoundrel has been lecturing on the evils of Demon rum and recruiting converts to the Temperance Movement by swearing off all intoxicating liquors. The Temperance Party, which argued that most social ills were the result of drinking and called for the outlawing of the manufacture and sale of all intoxicating liquors, grew tremendously in strength in the nineteenth century, its ranks consisting primarily of women.

15 *ten cents a head, children and niggers free*. A common admission price to a backwoods lecture of the time: Because the speech is supposedly educational, and the lecturer wishes to encourage the attendance of as many people (both adults and children) as possible, the young are admitted without charge; slaves were considered no different than children, they too being the white adults' property, and since their owners would not wish to leave them alone, they were also admitted free.

16 *tar and feather*. A common backwoods punishment: The offender is stripped bare, covered in tar and rolled in feathers, and then driven from the town in disgrace. The practice goes back as far as 1185 when Richard I of England approved it as a punishment for theft; in the seventeenth century, it was administered by English bishops as punishment for incontinent nuns and friars. It was a custom which came over with the early settlers, and was used in colonial days.

head, children and niggers free—and business a growin' all the time ; when somehow or another a little report got around, last night, that I had a way of puttin' in my time with a private jug, on the sly. A nigger rousted me out this mornin', and told me the people was getherin' on the quiet, with their dogs and horses, and they'd be along pretty soon and give me 'bout half an hour's start, and then run me down, if they could ; and **16,17** if they got me they'd tar and feather me and ride me on a rail, sure. I didn't wait for no breakfast—I warn't hungry."

"Old man," says the young one. " I reckon we might **18** double-team it together ; what do you think ? "

19   " I ain't undisposed. What's your line—mainly ? "

20,21   " Jour printer, by trade ; do a little in patent medicines ; **22,23** theatre-actor—tragedy, you know ; take a turn at mesmerism **24,25** and phrenology when there's a chance ; teach singing geography **26** school for a change ; sling a lecture, sometimes—oh, I do lots of things—most anything that comes handy, so it ain't work. What's your lay ? "

" I've done considerble in the doctoring way in my time. **27,28** Layin' on o' hands is my best holt—for cancer, and paralysis, **29** and sich things ; and I k'n tell a fortune pretty good, when I've **30** got somebody along to find out the facts for me. Preachin's my line, too ; and workin' camp-meetin's ; and missionaryin' around."

Nobody never said anything for a while ; then the young man hove a sigh and says—

" Alas ! "

" What 're you alassin' about ? " says the baldhead.

" To think I should have lived to be leading such a life, and be degraded down into such company." And he begun to wipe the corner of his eye with a rag.

" Dern your skin, ain't the company good enough for you ? " says the baldhead, pretty pert and uppish.

" Yes, it *is* good enough for me ; it's as good as I deserve ; for who fetched me so low, when I was so high ? *I* did myself. I don't blame *you*, gentlemen—far from it ; I don't blame anybody. I deserve it all. Let the cold world do its worst ; one thing I know—there's a grave somewhere for me. The world may go on just as its always done, and take everything from me —loved ones, property, everything—but it can't take that. Some day I'll lie down in it and forget it all, and my poor broken heart will be at rest." He went on a-wiping.

" Drot your pore broken heart," says the baldhead : " what are you heaving your pore broken heart at *us* f'r ? *We* hain't done nothing."

" No, I know you haven't. I ain't blaming you, gentlemen. I brought myself down—yes, I did it myself. It's right I should suffer—perfectly right—I don't make any moan."

" Brought you down from whar ? Whar was you brought down from ? "

" Ah, you would not believe me ; the world never believes —let it pass—'tis no matter. The secret of my birth——"

" The secret of your birth ? Do you mean to say——"

Tarring and feathering. Illustration by True W. Williams, *Mark Twain's Sketches, New and Old*, 1875.

17 *ride me on a rail*. "'Riding on a Rail' is an old custom," Walter Besant noted in "My Favorite Novelist and His Best Book" (*Munsey's Magazine*, February 1898, p. 662), "and originally Scandinavian. It was practiced in the north of England within the memory of man, but is now discontinued." Chadwick Hansen in "The Character of Jim in the Ending of *Huckleberry Finn*" (*The Massachusetts Review*, Autumn 1963, p. 63) has explained why the old fraud should be so terrified by the punishment: "A rail was made by splitting a log length-wise, and then splitting the halves, so that the fence-rail was wedge-shaped at the ends with a sharp and splintery edge. When a man was ridden on a rail, with nothing between his body and the rail but a coat of tar and feathers, there would be very little left of his groin, and chances were that he would lose at least part of his genitals as well."

18 *double-team it*. Work in concert, like a team of horses or oxen.

19 *What's your line—mainly?* The two gentlemen are by profession confidence or flim-flam men who deceive for profit. These roving frauds were stock characters in Midwestern and Southern literature, the finest examples being the hero of Johnson J. Hooper's *Adventures of Captain Simon Suggs* whose motto is "It is good to be a *shifty* man in a new country," and the protagonist of Herman Melville's *The Confidence-Man* (1857) who, like Twain's scoundrels, travels down the Mississippi in a series of disguises. The con-man was a new kind of thief, the old romantic desperado having been driven from the river by civilization. As Melville astutely noted in Chapter 1 of his novel, "In new countries, where the wolves are killed off, the foxes increase."

20 *jour printer*. Journeyman printer, one who works by the day at odd jobs and is not yet a master. In the talk "The Old-Fashioned Printer" delivered at the New York Typothetae Dinner on January 18, 1886 (in *Mark Twain's Speeches*, 1910, p. 185), Twain described the typical "tramping 'jour'" as one "who flitted by in the summer and tarried a day, with his wallet stuffed with one shirt and a hatful of handbills; for if he couldn't get any type to set he would do a temperance lecture. His way of life was simple, his needs not complex; all he wanted was plate and bed

and money enough to get drunk on, and he was satisfied." In his youth, Sam Clemens too had traveled the country as a tramp printer; however, he said that this young man was based on a journeyman printer Clemens knew in Virginia City, Nevada. Originally Twain had planned to have two printers in the novel to "deliver temp. lectures, teach dancing, elocution, feel heads, distribute tracts, preach, fiddle, doctor (quack)" (quoted by DeVoto, *Mark Twain at Work*, p. 66). The one who remained has all the qualities of another "jour printer" as described by John S. Robb in *Streaks of Squatter Life, and Far-West Scenes* (1847, p. 11): "intelligent, reckless, witty, improvident, competent, and unsteady."

21 *patent medicines*. Little federal legislation to protect the public from such bogus cure-alls existed during the nineteenth century; these medicinal frauds, usually no more than a mixture of alcohol and some flavoring, claimed to cure anything and everything from cold to cancer.

22 *theatre-actor*. At the time, acting was considered a disgraceful profession; theaters were said to be "moral pest-houses." "Church members did not attend shows out there in those days," Twain recalled his Hannibal boyhood in Chapter 12 of his *Autobiography*. Twain harbored no such prejudice against the profession.

A former circuit lecturer and a frustrated playwright, Twain had many theatrical friends. He even supported his secretary William Gillette (and against the young man's family's wishes) in his pursuit of an acting career; and Gillette did become a popular dramatist and actor, being the first to play "Sherlock Holmes." Twain was also one of the founders, with Edwin Booth, John Drew, and Joseph Jefferson, of The Players Club in New York City.

23 *mesmerism*. An early method of hypnotism, named for Franz Anton Mesmer (1734–1815). A follower of occultism and a firm believer in the astrological influence on human behavior, this German physician developed the theory of "animal magnetism" as the life force which affected human health. To cure nervous disorders through magnetism, he held seances in which patients sat around a vat of dilute sulfuric acid while holding hands or grasping bars of iron protruding from the solution. Denounced by the Viennese medical profession as a fraud, Mesmer fled to Paris where his sessions became fashionable; and although the French Academy (which included Antoine Lavoisier and Benjamin Franklin) called him a charlatan, his theories gained wide acceptance throughout Europe. The form of hypnotism known as "mesmerism" was actually developed by his disciple Count Maxine de Puységur. The practice eventually became a sideshow attraction and in this form was known throughout the United States before the Civil War. "These traveling 'Professors,' or many of them," Joseph M. Field noted in *The Drama in Pokerville* (1847, p. 129), "are charlatans, thus far, that they pretend to treat, *scientifically*, phenomena, the real nature of which they are entirely ignorant of; and the study of which they are, neither by education, habit, or *aim*, at all fitted for. They are charlatans, in that their superficial knowl-

Franz Anton Mesmer. *Courtesy the Library of Congress.*

edge of mere *effects* is simply made available in the shape of *exhibition;* and the success of the *show* being their first object, they may be suspected, perhaps, in some cases, of a little *management.*" Although no longer practiced, this pseudoscience is, however, credited with being a progenitor of modern psychotherapy.

An important event in Sam Clemens's boyhood was the arrival of the mesmerist in Hannibal. "Every night for three nights," he recollected in Chapter 11 of his *Autobiography,* "I sat in the row of candidates on the platform and held the magic disk in the palm of my hand and gazed at it and tried to get sleepy, but it was a failure." He was, however, envious of how the spell affected another of the candidates; and on the fourth night, he succumbed to the temptation to pretend to be sleepy while gazing at the whirling disk. "Straightaway came the professor," he wrote, "and made passes over my head and down my body and legs and arms, finishing each pass with a snap of

A mesmerist. Illustration by Farny, *A Boy's Town* by William Dean Howells, *Harper's Young People,* August 21, 1890. *Courtesy the Library of Congress.*

his fingers in the air to discharge the surplus electricity; then he began to 'draw' me with the disk, holding it in his fingers and telling me I could not take my eyes off it, try as I might; so I rose slowly, bent and gazing, and followed that disk all over the place, just as I had seen the others do. . . . Upon suggestion I fled from snakes, passed buckets at a fire, became excited over hot steamboat races, made love to imaginary girls and kissed them, fished from the platform and landed mud cats that outweighed me— and so on, all the customary marvels." Another part of the act had the professor make passes over the boy's body. "But I didn't wince," he confessed; "I only suffered and shed tears on the inside. . . . They would stick a pin in my arm and bear on it until they drove a third of its length in, and then be lost in wonder that by a mere exercise of will power the professor could turn my arm to iron and make it insensible to pain. Whereas it was not insensible at all; I was suffering agonies of pain." So convincing was this act that Clemens was never able to make his mother understand, even after he confessed every detail of the fraud, that he had only been pretending to be mesmerized. It was this performance that Twain recalled when he wrote in his notebook of the possibility of including in the novel "the mesmeric foolishness, with Huck (and the King) for performers" (quoted by DeVoto, *Mark Twain at Work,* p. 67).

24 *phrenology.* The pseudoscience of studying the contours of the skull to determine one's dispositions, characteristics, and talents. It was the ideology of Franz Joseph Gall (1758–1828), a Viennese doctor, who argued that the physical formation of the head was directly related to one's intellectual capacity, religious beliefs, and propensity to crime. Banned in Vienna as charlatanism, the movement spread across Europe to Great Britain and the United States. Here it was popularized in 1832 by Johann Kaspar Spurzheim; and soon many American parlors were decorated with plaster phrenological heads which doubled as sculptures. It eventually became a fortune-telling scheme run by con-men as a sideshow attraction.

Clemens was introduced to phrenology as well as mesmerism, growing up in Missouri. "One of the most frequent arrivals in our village of Hannibal was

Franz Joseph Gall. *Courtesy the Picture Collection, The New York Public Library, Astor, Lenox, and Tilden Foundations.*

the peripatetic phrenologist," he recalled in Chapter 13 of his *Autobiography*. "He gathered the people together and gave them a gratis lecture on the marvels of phrenology, then felt their bumps and made an estimate of the result, at twenty-five cents per head. . . . Phrenology found many a bump on a man's head and it labeled each bump with a formidable and outlandish name of its own." Clemens acquainted himself with the terminology of "the doctrine of temperaments" by reading George Sumner Weaver's *Lectures on Mental Science According to the Philosophy of Phrenology* (1852) and copied certain passages on "the physiology and general form of body and face, as indicating character" as they applied to his own features, into his notebook of 1855. When in London several years later, still fascinated and still a bit skeptical, Twain went under an assumed name to see Orson Fowler, then "the head of the phrenological industry." The writer subjected himself to a reading by the great Fowler himself, and he was amused by the findings until the phrenologist came upon one particular cavity: "He startled me by saying that the cavity represented the total absence of the sense of humor!" But three months later, when skeptical Twain returned to be examined under his own name, that cavity had miraculously disappeared and in its place was "the loftiest bump of humor he had ever encountered in his lifelong experience!" See also "Mark Twain, Phrenology, and the 'Temperaments': A Study of Pseudoscientific Influence" by Alan Gribben, *American Quarterly*, March 1972, pp. 45–68.

25 *teach singing geography school*. Singing and geography classes on the frontier were generally not taught by the local schoolmaster but by roving teachers.

26 *sling a lecture*. To deliver it with ease or rapidity.

27 *Layin' on o' hands*. "Faith healing" was commonly practiced in the backwoods, where there was a shortage of physicians. "When I was a boy," Twain wrote in "Christian Science," 1907 (*What Is Man?*, 1973, p. 232), "a farmer's wife who lived five miles from our village had great fame as a faith-doctor. . . . Sufferers came to her from all around, and she laid her hand upon them and said 'Have faith—it is all that is necessary,' and they went away well of their ailments. She was not a religious woman, and pretended to no occult powers. She said that the patient's faith in her did the work. Several times I saw her make immediate cures of severe tooth-aches. My mother was the patient."

Likewise, his wife benefitted from such a treatment. At sixteen, Olivia L. Langdon became an invalid as a result of a fall on the ice, and none of the prominent physicians brought to Elmira to treat her were of any help. Finally, her family sent for the famous Dr. Newton, denounced as a quack by the medical profession. When he came to her, Olivia could not even sit up without suffering nausea and exhaustion. After saying a short fervent prayer, he put an arm behind her shoulders and told her to sit up which she did without any discomfort. He then helped her stand and walk a few steps; but he then confessed that although she would never be cured, she would be able to walk at least one or two hundred

yards at a time for the rest of her life. "His charge was fifteen hundred dollars," Twain wrote in Chapter 36 of his *Autobiography*, "and it was easily worth a hundred thousand." Years later the writer met Dr. Newton and asked him what his secret was: "He said he didn't know but thought perhaps some subtle form of electricity proceeded from his body and wrought the cures."

Twain, however, did recognize the possible quackery in such treatments. Hank Morgan in Chapter 26 of *A Connecticut Yankee in King Arthur's Court* is particularly contemptuous of the ability of kings to cure the sick merely with their touch; it seems appropriate that the second of the two scoundrels in *Huckleberry Finn* should, like monarchy, be engaged in the laying on of hands. See note 36.

28 *bolt*. Hold, specialty.

29 *I k'n tell a fortune pretty good, when I've got somebody along to find out the facts for me*. Like the younger man's tooth powder and mesmerismic frauds, this trick requires a second party, if not the other con-artist, then a boy. Obviously both men anticipate some profit in keeping Huck around.

30 *Preachin's my line, too; and workin' camp-meetin's; and missionaryin' around*. On the sparsely populated frontier, the scarcity of ordained preachers required the clergy to travel widely from congregation to congregation; and from colonial days, parishioners were frequently swindled by false circuit riders. This old scoundrel plays on different human frailties than does his companion: The young man takes advantage of faith in current fads, the other of the faith in God and in one's fellow man. While the first profits on the baser instincts of man, on physical vanity, entertainment, and improvement, the other is the greater swindler in that he appeals to the higher aims, to spiritual vanity and religion.

Blair in *Mark Twain and Huck Finn* (pp. 274–277) has suggested that the religious fraud was in part based on Charles C. Duncan, the captain of the *Quaker City*, whom Twain thought a temperance hypocrite, "filled to the chin with sham godliness, and forever oozing and dripping false piety and pharasaical prayers"; but Robert P. Weeks in "The Captain, the Prophet, and the King" (*Mark Twain Journal*, Winter 1975–1976, pp. 9–12) has argued for another possible source as George J. Adams, whom Twain described (in *The Innocents Abroad*, Part II, Chapter 30) as "once an actor, then several other things, afterward a Mormon and a missionary, always an adventurer." The grandest of Adams's swindles was his having convinced about one hundred disciples, men, women, and children, many of them destitute, to leave New England to found a supposedly divinely inspired colony in the Holy Land. In Jaffa, the *Quaker City* took aboard about forty of Adams's weary pilgrims who had fled from the desert; they were "miserable enough in the first place, and they lay about the decks seasick all the voyage, which about completed their misery. . . , shamefully having been shamelessly hum-bugged by their prophet, they felt humiliated and unhappy." How little times change.

31 *By rights I am a duke!* Apparently the frontier was plagued with many American claimants to European titles. Clemens himself was said to be descended on his mother's side from the Earls of Durham. When a boy, he heard (as he recalled in Chapter 7 of his *Autobiography)* "the whole disastrous history of how the Lambton heir came to this country a hundred and fifty years or so ago, disgusted with that foolish fraud, hereditary aristocracy, and married, and shut himself away from the world in the remotenesses of the wilderness, and went to breeding ancestors of future American claimants, while at home in England he was given up as dead and his titles and estates turned over to his younger brother, usurper and personally responsible for the perverse and unseatable usurpers of our day."

The then "rightful Earl of Durham" was a distant cousin, Jesse Leather. Twain admitted that "all his time was taken up in trying to get me and others of the tribe to furnish him capital to fight his claim through the House of Lords with. He had all the documents, all the proofs; he knew he could win. And so he dreamed his life away, always in poverty, sometimes in actual want, and died at last, far from home, and was buried from a hospital by strangers who did not know that he was an earl, for he did not look it." Certainly something of that "earl" is in this "duke." So bombastic were Leather's letters that Twain toyed with the idea of getting him to write a book. "I think he'll write a gassy, extravagant, idiotic book that will be delicious reading," he confided to Howells in a letter of March 7, 1881 (quoted by Blair, *Mark Twain and Huck Finn*, p. 273), "for I've read some of his rot; and it is just the sort of windy stuff which a Kentucky tramp who has been choused out of an English earldom would write." Twain himself made further use of the Lambton history in *The American Claimant* (1892) in which Colonel Mulberry Sellers of *The Gilded Age* attempts to regain the earldom of Rossmore. Clemens did not sympathize with the Lambton nobles; he far preferred a Clemens ancestor "who *did* something; something which was very creditable to him and satisfactory to me, in that he was a member of the court that tried Charles I and delivered him over to the executioner."

Always fascinated and amused by the possibility, Twain introduced many claimants to usurped titles and property in his other books. There is the night watchman on the *Paul Jones*, described in Chapter 6 of *Life on the Mississippi*, who claims to be the son of an English nobleman; and at least one true heir, Miles Hendon of *The Prince and the Pauper*, who while fighting in Europe has been cheated out of his title, his estates, and his betrothed by his treacherous younger brother.

32 *the Duke of Bridgewater.* W. G. Gaffney, in "Mark Twain's 'Duke' and 'Dauphin'" (*Names*, September 1966, pp. 175–178) has identified the real Duke of Bridgewater. The American has not chosen just any title, but rather that of Francis Egerton (1736–1803), the third Duke of Bridgewater, said in his time to have been the richest man in the world. But what makes the American's claim even more outrageous was that Egerton died childless: Crushed by a thwarted love affair, he retired at age twenty-three

"Gentlemen," says the young man, very solemn, "I will **31** reveal it to you, for I feel I may have confidence in you. By rights I am a duke!"

"BY RIGHTS I AM A DUKE!"

Jim's eyes bugged out when he heard that; and I reckon mine did, too. Then the baldhead says: "No! you can't mean it?"

32 "Yes. My great-grandfather, eldest son of the Duke of Bridgewater, fled to this country about the end of the last century, to breathe the pure air of freedom; married here, and died, leaving a son, his own father dying about the same time. The second son of the late duke seized the title and estates— the infant real duke was ignored. I am the lineal descendant of that infant—I am the rightful Duke of Bridgewater; and here am I, forlorn, torn from my high estate, hunted of men, despised by the cold world, ragged, worn, heart-broken, and degraded to the companionship of felons on a raft!"

Jim pitied him ever so much, and so did I. We tried to comfort him, but he said it warn't much use, he couldn't be much comforted; said if we was a mind to acknowledge him, that would do him more good than most anything else; so we said we would, if he would tell us how. He said we ought to bow, when we spoke to him, and say "Your Grace," or "My Lord," or "Your Lordship"—and he wouldn't mind it if we called him plain "Bridgewater," which he said was a title, anyway, and not a name; and one of us ought to wait on him at dinner, and do any little thing for him he wanted done.

Well, that was all easy, so we done it. All through dinner Jim stood around and waited on him, and says, "Will yo' Grace have some o' dis, or some o' dat?" and so on, and a body could see it was mighty pleasing to him.

But the old man got pretty silent, by-and-by—didn't have much to say, and didn't look pretty comfortable over all that petting that was going on around that duke. He seemed to have something on his mind. So, along in the afternoon, he says:

"Looky here, Bilgewater," he says, "I'm nation sorry for **33, 34** you, but you ain't the only person that's had troubles like that."

"No?"

"No, you ain't. You ain't the only person that's ben snaked **35** down wrongfully out'n a high place."

"Alas!"

"No, you ain't the only person that's had a secret of his birth." And by jings, *he* begins to cry.

"Hold! What do you mean?"

"Bilgewater, kin I trust you?" says the old man, still sort of sobbing.

"To the bitter death!" He took the old man by the hand and squeezed it, and says, "The secret of your being: speak!"

"Bilgewater, I am the late Dauphin!" **36**

You bet you Jim and me stared, this time. Then the duke says:

"You are what?"

"Yes, my friend, it is too true—your eyes is lookin' at this very moment on the pore disappeared Dauphin, Looy the Seventeen, son of Looy the Sixteen and Marry Antonette."

"You! At your age! No! You mean you're the late **37, 38** Charlemagne; you must be six or seven hundred years old, at the very least."

"Trouble has done it, Bilgewater, trouble has done it; trouble has brung these gray hairs and this premature balditude. **39** Yes, gentlemen, you see before you, in blue jeans and misery, the wanderin', exiled, trampled-on, and sufferin' rightful King of France."

"I AM THE LATE DAUPHIN."

Francis Egerton, the Duke of Bridgewater. *Courtesy the Library of Congress.*

from London society to devote the remainder of his life to the care and improvement of his estates; he never again associated with women in any capacity, whether social or menial, and so great was his bitterness that he refused to have any woman-servant wait on him. Therefore he could not have had any sons, legitimate or bastard; he was the third, the last, and the only bachelor Duke of Bridgewater. Thus the American "duke" (and Twain as well) could make any ludicrous claim to the title and property without any fear of legal action by a true descendant of the great Duke of Bridgewater.

The title of Bridgewater did survive Egerton, but by British law it was demoted from "duke" to "earl" when passed on to his cousin; and even this disappeared, in 1829, when the eighth Earl of Bridgewater died in Paris. The last earl was almost as well known, in his day, as the great duke; this aristocrat was famous for his eccentricities (supposedly he never wore the same pair of boots twice, and he fed his many dogs at the great dining table of his ancestral home) as well as being the author of an odd collection of "family anecdotes"; amusing stories about the Earl of Bridgewater were frequently reprinted in anthologies of humor in both the United States and Great Britain. Likely Twain also had in mind this absurd earl when he created the duke.

33 *Bilgewater*. The disgustingly foul and noxious water which collects in the bottom of a ship's "bilge," or hull. As early as 1865, Twain used "Bilgewater" as a comic name (see the footnotes to *Mark Twain's Notebooks and Journals*, Vol. I, 1975, pp. 76–77). For example, there is a Colonel Bilgewater in Chapter 77 of *Roughing It*, and one of the indelicate courtiers of the off-color "Date 1601" (1882) is "Ye Duchess of Bilgewater, twenty-two yeres of age" who bears the distinction of having been "rog'red by four lords before she had a husband."

34 *nation sorry*. Extremely sorry, from "damnation."

35 *snaked down*. Dragged down.

36 *I am the late Dauphin!* A fine example of one-upmanship among scoundrels: Because the young man has claimed to be the true descendant of the once richest man in the world, the old swindler says that he is the rightful king of France. The legend that the son of Louis XVI did not die in prison and had escaped inspired several false claimants on the American frontier. Twain's likely source for such tales was a chapter in Horace W. Fuller's *Noted French Trials: Imposters and Adventurers* (1882), which described and debunked the stories of several of these phony dauphins. At least one of these bogus kings, the Duke of Normandy, came to the United States, in 1804. But perhaps the strangest of these stories was that of Eleazer Williams, the Iroquois, who was the son of a European father and an Indian mother, and bore a striking resemblance to Louis XVIII, Lord Palmerston; born a deafmute, Williams miraculously began to relate memories of the French court one day when struck on the head by a stone. Blair in *Mark Twain and Huck Finn* (pp. 278–279) has noted the similarity between the duke's bombastic style and that of Williams in his purported journal (quoted in *The Lost Prince*, 1853): "Is it true, that I am among the number, who are destined to . . . degradation—from a mighty power to a helpless prisoner of the state— from a palace to a prison and dungeon—to be exiled from one of the finest empires in Europe, and to be a wanderer in the wilds of America—from the society of the most polite and accomplished courtiers, to be associated with ignorant and degraded Indians."

John Ashmead has suggested in "A Possible Hannibal Source for Mark Twain's Dauphin" (*American Literature*, March 1962, pp. 105–107) that Clemens may have been familiar with an article "A Visit from Our Bourbon" in the Hannibal *Journal*, May 12, 1853, apparently reprinted from a Philadelphia paper, in which another of these American claimants, "Amininidab Fitz-Louis X Dolphin Borebon," was interviewed by the local press. This piece (which may have inspired Huck's use of "Dolphin" for the king) was only one of many American jibes at the possibility of a lost king of France.

Although he may claim to be of a higher rank than the younger man, the king is of a lower class than the duke. Using such words as "thar," "sich," and "k'n" and littering his talk with mild curses, the king's speech is a more extreme backwoods dialect than the duke's. The verbose duke has an extensive vocabulary, uses proper syntax, and throws about complex and effective phrases; the king is basically ignorant with a vague and limited vocabulary and resorts to clumsy double-talk and phony words when pressed into tight situations. Although less original, the king is nevertheless slyer than the duke. Obviously Twain is suggesting that kings are an inferior breed to even dukes. "There are shams and shams," he wrote in his *Notebook* (1935, p. 196); "there are frauds and frauds, but the transparentest of all is the sceptered one. We

Eleazer Williams. *Courtesy the Library of Congress.*

see monarchs meet and go through solemn ceremonies, farces, with straight countenances; but it is not possible to imagine them meeting in private and not laughing in each other's faces." Although in later years he was charmed by the queen of Rumania, the emperor of Austria, the emperor and empress of Germany, and certain other royalty, Twain generally could not "find anything durable in the aristocracy of birth and privilege—*it* turns my stomach" (quoted in Item 195, *Catalogue of the Library and Manuscripts of Samuel L. Clemens*). He wrote empassioned pamphlets denouncing what King Leopold of Belgium did in the Congo and what Czar Nicholas of Russia did to suppress the Revolution of 1905. Of all Twain's characters, the most contemptuous toward aristocracy was Hank Morgan, the Connecticut Yankee; and he was clearly speaking for the writer when he said, in Chapter 8, that "*any* kind of royalty, howsoever modified, *any* kind of aristocracy, howsoever pruned, is rightly an insult."

37 *At your age!* Had he lived, the dauphin would have been only in his mid-fifties.

38 *You mean you're the late Charlemagne!* The first great king of France who died in 814.

39 *trouble has brung these gray hairs and this premature balditude.* Extreme grief can turn one's hair gray; that of Marie Antoinette, the young queen of France and mother of the dauphin, turned white while in prison. Likewise, Byron in "The Prisoner of Chillon" noted:

> *My hair is gray, but not with years,*
> *Nor grew it white*
> *In a single night,*
> *As men's have grown from sudden fears.*

Well, he cried and took on so, that me and Jim didn't know hardly what to do, we was so sorry—and so glad and proud we'd got him with us, too. So we set in, like we done before with the duke, and tried to comfort *him*. But he said it warn't no use, nothing but to be dead and done with it all could do him any good; though he said it often made him feel easier and better for a while if people treated him according to his rights, **40** and got down on one knee to speak to him, and always called him "Your Majesty," and waited on him first at meals, and didn't set down in his presence till he asked them. So Jim and me set to majestying him, and doing this and that and t'other for him, and standing up till he told us we might set down. This done him heaps of good, and so he got cheerful and comfortable. But the duke kind of soured on him, and didn't look a bit satisfied with the way things was going; still, the king acted real friendly towards him, and said the duke's great-grandfather and all the other Dukes of Bilgewater was a good deal thought of by *his* father, and was allowed to come to the palace considerable; but the duke staid huffy a good while, till by-and-by the king says:

"Like as not we got to be together a blamed long time, on this h-yer raft, Bilgewater, and so what's the use o' your bein' sour? It'll only make things oncomfortable. It ain't my fault I warn't born a duke, it ain't your fault you warn't born a king—so what's the use to worry? Make the best o' things the way you find 'em, says I—that's my motto. This ain't no bad thing that we've struck here—plenty grub and an easy life—come, give us your hand, Duke, and less all be friends."

The duke done it, and Jim and me was pretty glad to see it. It took away all the uncomfortableness, and we felt mighty good over it, because it would a been a miserable business to have any unfriendliness on the raft; for what you want, above all things, on a raft, is for everybody to be satisfied, and feel right and kind towards the others.

It didn't take me long to make up my mind that these liars warn't no kings nor dukes, at all, but just low-down humbugs and frauds. But I never said nothing, never let on; kept it to myself; it's the best way; then you don't have no quarrels, and don't get into no trouble. If they wanted us to call them kings and dukes, I hadn't no objections, 'long as it would keep peace in the family; and it warn't no use to tell Jim, so I didn't tell him. If I never learnt nothing else out of pap I learnt that the best way to get along with his kind of people is to let them have their own way.

40 *if people . . . didn't set down in his presence till he asked them.* Twain found this courtesy due monarchs particularly loathsome: Hank Morgan contemptuously mentions it in Chapter 8 of *A Connecticut Yankee in King Arthur's Court;* and, in Chapter 12 of *The Prince and the Pauper,* when King Edward vows to grant in recognition of the man's service to him any privilege he wishes, Miles Hendon requests only that "I and my heirs; forever, *sit* in the presence of the majesty of England!"

ON THE RAFT.

1 *Pike County, in Missouri.* A county a little way down the river from Hannibal, the birthplace of the typical "wandering gypsy-like, Southern poor white." See Explanatory, note 2. The duke and the king could hardly be impressed with the boy's place of origin. "This person often lives with his family in a wagon," John Russell Bartlett reported on the "Piker" in his *Dictionary of Americanisms* (1877); "he is frequently a squatter on other people's lands; 'he owns a rifle, a lot of children and dogs, a wife, and, if he can read, a law-book,' said a lawyer . . .; he moves from place to place, as the humor seizes him, and is generally an injury to his neighbors. He will not work regularly; but he has a great tenacity of life, and is always ready for a law-suit." Unlike the romantic duke and king, practical Huck has invented a "yarn" that will fit his current circumstances; he admits to being a member of the lowest class of

Pike County in relation to Hannibal, Missouri. Sketch by Mark Twain, "The Private History of a Campaign that Failed," *The Century,* December 1885.

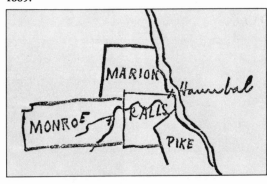

asked us considerable many questions; wanted to know what we covered up the raft that way for, and laid by in the day-time instead of running —was Jim a runaway nigger? Says I—

"Goodness sakes, would a runaway nigger run *south*?"

No, they allowed he wouldn't. I had to account for things some way, so I says:

"My folks was living in Pike County, in Missouri, where I was born, **2** and they all died off but me and pa and my brother Ike. Pa, he 'lowed he'd break up and go down and live with Uncle Ben, **3** who's got a little one-horse place on the river, forty-four mile below Orleans. Pa was pretty poor, and had some debts; so **4** when he'd squared up there warn't nothing left but sixteen dollars and our nigger, Jim. That warn't enough to take us fourteen hundred mile, deck passage nor no other way. Well, when the river rose, pa had a streak of luck one day; he ketched this piece of a raft; so we reckoned we'd go down to Orleans on it. Pa's luck didn't hold out; a steamboat run

196

over the forrard corner of the raft, one night, and we all went overboard and dove under the wheel; Jim and me come up, all right, but pa was drunk, and Ike was only four years old, so they never come up no more. Well, for the next day or two we had considerable trouble, because people was always coming out in skiffs and trying to take Jim away from me, saying they believed he was a runaway nigger. We don't run day-times no more, now; nights they don't bother us."

The duke says—

"Leave me alone to cipher out a way so we can run in the day-time if we want to. I'll think the thing over—I'll invent a plan that'll fix it. We'll let it alone for to-day, because of course we don't want to go by that town yonder in daylight—it mightn't be healthy."

Towards night it begun to darken up and look like rain: the heat lightning was squirting around, low down in the sky, and the leaves was beginning to shiver—it was going to be pretty ugly, it was easy to see that. So the duke and the king went to overhauling our wigwam, to see what the beds was like. My bed was a straw tick—better than Jim's, which was a corn-shuck **5** tick; there's always cobs around about in a shuck tick, and they poke into you and hurt; and when you roll over, the dry shucks sound like you was rolling over in a pile of dead leaves; it makes such a rustling that you wake up. Well, the duke **6** allowed he would take my bed; but the king allowed he wouldn't. He says—

"I should a reckoned the difference in rank would a sejested to you that a corn-shuck bed warn't just fitten for me to sleep on. Your Grace'll take the shuck bed yourself."

Jim and me was in a sweat again, for a minute, being afraid there was going to be some more trouble amongst them; so we was pretty glad when the duke says—

"'Tis my fate to be always ground into the mire under the iron heel of oppression. Misfortune has broken my once haughty spirit; I yield, I submit; 'tis my fate. I am alone in the world —let me suffer; I can bear it."

We got away as soon as it was good and dark. The king told us to stand well out towards the middle of the river, and not show a light till we got a long ways below the town. We come in sight of the little bunch of lights by-and-by—that was the town, you know—and slid by, about a half a mile out, all right. When we was three-quarters of a mile below, we hoisted up our signal lantern; and about ten o'clock it come on to rain and blow and thunder and lighten like everything; so the king told us to both stay on watch till the weather got better; then him and the duke crawled into the wigwam and turned in for the night. It was my watch below, till twelve, but I wouldn't a turned in, anyway, if I'd had a bed; because a body don't see such a storm as that every day in the week, not by a long sight. My souls, how the wind did scream along! And every second or two there'd come a glare that lit up the white-caps for half a mile around, and you'd see the islands looking dusty through

Southern society. Note also that in his story the boy uses certain extreme dialect words (such as "'lowed" and "ketched") not employed by him elsewhere, evidently to make his speech here more authentically that of a "Piker."

2 *my brother Ike.* Carkeet in "The Dialects in *Huckleberry Finn*" (pp. 325–326) has identified this as "the name of a forever undeveloped character in Pike County balladry, his sole claim to fame being his ability to rhyme with 'Pike.'" In Chapter 72 of Wright's *History of the Big Bonanza* (p. 547) appears the first stanza of the most famous traditional Pike County ballad, that of Joe Bowers:

> *My name it is Joe Bowers, I've got a brother Ike,*
> *I come from old Missouri, yes, all the way from Pike.*

3 *a little one-horse place.* A contemptuous term for a place so small and insignificant that one horse is all that is necessary to do all of its hauling and transporting.

4 *squared up.* Settled his debts.

5 *tick.* A mattress.

6 *the duke allowed he would take my bed; but the king allowed he wouldn't.* In this dispute over the fine distinction between the two rude beds, Twain again points to the pettiness of protocol among royalty in general.

7 *sockdolager.* In England "slogdollager," literally a knock-out blow, a "finisher"; said to be a perversion in spelling and pronunciation of "doxology" (see Chapter 25, note 6), which is sung at the close of a service as a signal of dismissal.

8 *the middle watch.* This was the watch (on moonlit nights) that Clemens himself preferred when a pilot on the Mississippi. "The middle watch in summer moonlit nights is a gracious time," he admitted to Wattie Bowser (in Covici, Jr. "Dear Master Wattie," pp. 107–108), "especially if the boat steers like a duck, and friends have staid up to keep one company, and sing, and smoke, and spin yarns, and blow the whistle when other boats are met."

9 *seven-up.* Also called "Old Sledge" or "All Fours," popular trumping game of the backwoods won by the first player to get seven "chalks," or points.

10 *"lay out a campaign."* Military slang, to plan a battle.

11 *"The celebrated Dr. Armand de Montalban, of Paris" would . . . "furnish charts of character at twenty-five cents apiece."* Because phrenology was particularly fashionable in Paris at the time and many of its disciples came to the United States to practice, the duke has appropriately taken a French alias. A phrenological chart was a large drawing of a subject's skull in profile, marked into sections like a map and labeled with human characteristics.

12 *the "world renowned Shakesperean tragedian, Garrick the Younger, of Drury Lane, London."* The duke has taken a British alias, and that of the most famous English actor of the late eighteenth century, because, as Twain explained in a suppressed passage in *Life on the Mississippi* (published in the 1944 Limited Editions Club edition, p. 406), "the stage was almost exclusively occupied by the English—very few native actors could 'draw.'" There was no real Garrick the Younger. See Chapter 21, note 8.

13 *like finding water and gold with a "divining rod."* In certain parts of the world it is believed that some people (said to be the members of the family with the most "devil" in them) inherit a sixth sense which enables them to discover where it is best to dig for water or gold. A "water witch," or "witch hazel professor," walks with a "divining rod," a crotched witch hazel stick, held in front of him; and wherever the point turns downward water or gold will be found. In an article, "A Big Thing," in the Buffalo *Express*, March 12, 1870 (quoted by Henry Duskis in *The Forgotten Works of Mark Twain*, 1963, p. 214), Twain described "how for four dreadful weeks I followed step by step in the track of a 'Professor' with a hazel stick in his hand—a 'divining-rod' which was to turn and tilt down and point to the gold whenever we came to any. But we never came to any, I suppose."

14 *"dissipating witch-spells."* Nervous disorders were once thought to be caused by witches, and "witch doctors" in the South were often called on to exorcise the demons from the afflicted by various folk cures.

the rain, and the trees thrashing around in the wind; then comes a *h-wack!*—bum! bum! bumble-umble-um-bum-bum-bum-bum—and the thunder would go rumbling and grumbling away, and quit—and then *rip* comes another flash and another

7 sockdolager. The waves most washed me off the raft, sometimes, but I hadn't any clothes on, and didn't mind. We didn't have no trouble about snags; the lightning was glaring and flittering around so constant that we could see them plenty soon enough to throw her head this way or that and miss them.

8 I had the middle watch, you know, but I was pretty sleepy by that time, so Jim he said he would stand the first half of it for me; he was always mighty good that way, Jim was. I crawled into the wigwam, but the king and the duke had their legs sprawled around so there warn't no show for me; so I laid outside—I didn't mind the rain, because it was warm, and the waves warn't running so high, now. About two they come up again, though, and Jim was going to call me, but he changed his mind because he reckoned they warn't high enough yet to do any harm; but he was mistaken about that, for pretty soon all of a sudden along comes a regular ripper, and washed me overboard. It most killed Jim a-laughing. He was the easiest nigger to laugh that ever was, anyway.

I took the watch, and Jim he laid down and snored away; and by-and-by the storm let up for good and all; and the first cabin-light that showed, I rousted him out and we slid the raft into hiding-quarters for the day.

The king got out an old ratty deck of cards, after breakfast, **9** and him and the duke played seven-up a while, five cents a **10** game. Then they got tired of it, and allowed they would "lay out a campaign," as they called it. The duke went down into his carpet-bag and fetched up a lot of little printed bills, and **11** read them out loud. One bill said "The celebrated Dr. Armand de Montalban, of Paris," would "lecture on the Science of Phrenology" at such and such a place, on the blank day of blank, at ten cents admission, and "furnish charts of character at twenty-five cents apiece." The duke said that was *him*. In **12** another bill he was the "world renowned Shaksperean tragedian, Garrick the Younger, of Drury Lane, London." In other bills he had a lot of other names and done other wonderful things, **13,14** like finding water and gold with a "divining rod," "dissipating witch-spells," and so on. By-and-by he says—

15 "But the histrionic muse is the darling. Have you ever trod the boards, Royalty?"

"No," says the king.

"You shall, then, before you're three days older, Fallen Grandeur," says the duke. "The first good town we come to, **16,17** we'll hire a hall and do the sword-fight in Richard III. and the balcony scene in Romeo and Juliet. How does that strike you?"

18 "I'm in, up to the hub, for anything that will pay, Bilgewater, but you see I don't know nothing about play-actn', and hain't ever seen much of it. I was too small when pap used to have 'em at the palace.   Do you reckon you can learn me ? "

"Easy ! "

"All right.   I'm jist a-freezn' for something fresh, anyway. **19**
Less commence, right away."

So the duke he told him all about who Romeo was, and who
Juliet was, and said he was used to being Romeo, so the king
could be Juliet.

THE KING AS JULIET.

"But if Juliet's such a young gal, duke, my peeled head **20**
and my white whiskers is goin' to look oncommon odd on her,
maybe."

"No, don't you worry—these country jakes won't ever think **21**
of that.   Besides, you know, you'll be in costume, and that
makes all the difference in the world ; Juliet's in a balcony,
enjoying the moonlight before she goes to bed, and she's got
on her night-gown and her ruffled night-cap.   Here are the
costumes for the parts."

He got out two or three curtain-calico suits, which he said **22**
was meedyevil armour for Richard III. and t'other chap, and a **23, 24**
long white cotton night-shirt and a ruffled night-cap to match.
The king was satisfied ; so the duke got out his book and read
the parts over in the most splendid spread-eagle way, prancing **25**
around and acting at the same time, to show how it had got to
be done ; then he give the book to the king and told him to get
his part by heart.

There was a little one-horse town about three mile down
the bend, and after dinner the duke said he had ciphered out
his idea about how to run in daylight without it being dangersome for Jim ; so he allowed he would go down to the town

15 *Have you ever trod the boards, Royalty?* Have you
ever acted in the theater; theatrical cliché, the
"boards" being the stage of a theater.

16 *the sword-fight in Richard III.* Act V, scene v, the
climax of Shakespeare's play. *Richard III* was one of
the most popular plays of American touring companies of the early nineteenth century; and in Chapter 51 of *Life on the Mississippi*, Twain recalled how,
when he was a schoolboy in Hannibal, "a couple of
young Englishmen came to the town and sojourned a
while; and one day they got themselves up in cheap
royal finery and did the Richard III swordfight with
maniac energy and prodigous powwow, in the presence of the village boys."

17 *the balcony scene in Romeo and Juliet.* Act II, scene
ii, perhaps the most famous love scene in English
literature. Appropriately in this part of the country
where the Grangerfords and the Shepherdsons have
slaughtered one another, the duke has decided to
perform scenes from two of the most famous plays
about family feuds, that between the Montagues and
Capulets in *Romeo and Juliet* and that between the
House of York and the House of Lancaster in *Richard
III*; and just like Sophia Grangerford and Harney
Shepherdson, King Henry VII and Elizabeth,
daughter of Edward IV, united the two feuding
families in England through their marriage.

18 *up to the hub.* Deeply, no further; when a vehicle
is stuck in the mud up to the hub of the wheels, it
cannot move.

19 *a-freezn' for something fresh.* Possessed with an
intense longing for something new to do.

20 *Juliet's such a young gal.* She is about Huck's age:
Lady Capulet tells the Nurse, "She's not fourteen"
(Act I, scene iii, line 12).

21 *No, don't you worry—these country jakes won't ever
think of that.* Wecter explained in *Sam Clemens of
Hannibal* (p. 186) that in this time (as in Shakespeare's
day) in this part of the country no woman could
appear on the stage; all feminine roles were played by
men. Certainly this was true of the Thespian Society
of Hannibal in which James Minor played "Romeo"
to Presley Lane's "Juliet"; by 1842, this troupe dis-
banded, supposedly because "the female impersona-
tors had too large beards to perform well."

22 *curtain-calico.* A particularly gaudily printed
cheap cloth.

23 *meedyevil armour for Richard III.* The War of the
Roses raged from 1455 to 1485; nineteenth-century
"Richards" generally wore chainmail rather than full
medieval armor.

24 *t'other chap.* "Richmond," or Henry, Earl of
Richmond, afterward King Henry VII.

25 *spread-eagle.* An extravagant, exaggerated, bombastic style of oratory, originally of a patriotic nature,
referring to the eagle, the national emblem.

26 *camp-meeting*. This particular congress is what was known as a "revival," an unusually sudden re-emergence of intense religious feeling, often evangelical in intent and spreading beyond the immediate community in its acquisition of new converts to its faith. Inspired by the Sermon on the Mount, these meetings were generally held out in the open so that they could include as many people as possible. In America, they originated in the early nineteenth century with the Presbyterians who migrated from North Carolina to Tennessee and Kentucky; later the Methodists adopted the camp-meeting for their revivals. These evangelists secured so many new church members, because in involving the community at large, they brought all its people directly and uninterruptedly under an intense concentration of religious instruction for several days in succession. The procedure survives in the work of certain modern religious sects and self-help groups.

A camp meeting. Illustration by A. Hervieu, *Domestic Manners of the Americans* by Mrs. Frances Trollope, 1832. *Courtesy the General Research and Humanities Division, The New York Public Library, Astor, Lenox, and Tilden Foundations.*

27 *We got there in about a half an hour.* Twain's fictional account that follows is reminiscent of Marryat's description of a camp-meeting the Englishman encountered and recorded in Chapter 32 of his 1839 American diary, a work Twain read and extensively quoted from in *Life on the Mississippi*: "About an acre and a half was surrounded on the four sides by cabins built up of rough boards, the whole area in the centre was fitted up with planks, laid about a foot from the ground, as seats. At one end, but not close to the cabins, was a raised stand, which served as a pulpit for the preachers, one of them praying, while five or six others sat down behind him on benches. . . . At a farther distance were all the wagons and other vehicles which had conveyed the people to the meeting, whilst hundreds of horses were tethered under the trees, and plentifully provided with forage. . . . Fires were burning in every direction: pots boiling, chickens roasting, hams seething; indeed there appeared to be no want of creature comforts.

". . . One of the preachers rose and gave out a hymn, which was sung by the congregation, amounting to about seven or eight hundred. . . . At last an elderly gentleman . . . knelt down in the center, and commenced a prayer . . .; then another burst out into prayer, and another followed him; then their voices became all confused together; and then were heard the more silvery tones of woman's supplica-

and fix that thing. The king allowed he would go too, and see if he couldn't strike something. We was out of coffee, so Jim said I better go along with them in the canoe and get some.

When we got there, there warn't nobody stirring; streets empty, and perfectly dead and still, like Sunday. We found a sick nigger sunning himself in a back yard, and he said everybody that warn't too young or too sick or too old was gone to **26** camp-meeting, about two mile back in the woods. The king got the directions, and allowed he'd go and work that camp-meeting for all it was worth, and I might go, too.

The duke said what he was after was a printing office. We found it; a little bit of a concern, up over a carpenter shop—carpenters and printers all gone to the meeting, and no doors locked. It was a dirty, littered-up place, and had ink marks, and handbills with pictures of horses and runaway niggers on them, all over the walls. The duke shed his coat and said he was all right, now. So me and the king lit out for the camp-meeting.

27 We got there in about a half an hour, fairly dripping, for it was a most awful hot day. There was as much as a thousand people there, from twenty mile around. The woods was full of teams and wagons, hitched everywheres, feeding out of the wagon troughs and stomping to keep off the flies. There was sheds made out of poles and roofed over with branches, where they had lemonade and gingerbread to sell, and piles of watermelons and green corn and such-like truck.

The preaching was going on under the same kinds of sheds, only they was bigger and held crowds of people. The benches was made out of outside slabs of logs, with holes bored in the round side to drive sticks into for legs. They didn't have no backs. The preachers had high platforms to stand on, at one end of the sheds. The women had on sun-bonnets; and some **28, 29** had linsey-woolsey frocks, some gingham ones, and a few of the **30** young ones had on calico. Some of the young men was barefooted, and some of the children didn't have on any clothes but **31** just a tow-linen shirt. Some of the old women was knitting, **32** and some of the young folks was courting on the sly.

33 The first shed we come to, the preacher was lining out a hymn. He lined out two lines, everybody sung it, and it was kind of grand to hear it, there was so many of them and they done it in such a rousing way; then he lined out two more for them to sing—and so on. The people woke up more and more, and sung louder and louder; and towards the end some begun to groan, and some begun to shout. Then the preacher begun to preach; and begun in earnest, too; and went weaving first to one side of the platform and then the other, and then a leaning down over the front of it, with his arms and his body going all the time, and shouting his words out with all his might; and every now and then he would hold up his Bible and spread it open, and kind of pass it around this way and that, shouting, **34** "It's the brazen serpent in the wilderness! Look upon it and live!" And people would shout out, "Glory!—A-a-*men!*"

"COURTING ON THE SLY."

And so he went on, and the people groaning and crying and saying amen:

"Oh, come to the mourners' bench! come, black with sin! **35, 36** (*amen!*) come, sick and sore! (*amen!*) come, lame and halt, and blind! (*amen!*) come, pore and needy, sunk in shame! (*a-a-men!*) come all that's worn, and soiled, and suffering!— come with a broken spirit! come with a contrite heart! come in your rags and sin and dirt! the waters that cleanse is free, the door of heaven stands open—oh, enter in and be at rest!" (*a-a-men! glory, glory hallelujah!*)

And so on. You couldn't make out what the preacher said, any more, on account of the shouting and crying. Folks got up, everywheres in the crowd, and worked their way, just by main strength, to the mourners' bench, with the tears running down their faces; and when all the mourners had got up there to the front benches in a crowd, they sung, and shouted, and flung themselves down on the straw, just crazy and wild.

Well, the first I knowed, the king got agoing; and you **37** could hear him over everybody; and next he went a-charging up on to the platform and the preacher he begged him to speak to the people, and he done it. He told them he was a pirate— been a pirate for thirty years, out in the Indian Ocean, and his crew was thinned out considerable, last spring, in a fight, and he was home now, to take out some fresh men, and thanks to goodness he'd been robbed last night, and put ashore off of a steamboat without a cent, and he was glad of it, it was the blessedest thing that ever happened to him, because he was a changed man now, and happy for the first time in his life; and

tion. As the din increased so did their enthusiasm; handkerchiefs were raised to bright eyes, and sobs were intermingled with prayers and ejaculations. . . . One young man clung to the form, crying 'Satan tears at me, but I will hold fast. Help—help, he drags me down!'" . . . when it was at its height, one of the preachers came in, and, raising his voice high, above the tumult, entreated the Lord to receive into his fold those who now repented and would fain return. . . . Groans, ejaculations, broken sobs, frantic motions and convulsions succeeded; some fell on their backs with their eyes closed, waving their hands with a slow motion, and crying out—'Glory, glory, glory!' I quitted the spot, and hastened into the forest, for the sight was too painful, too melancholy."

Marryat concluded that the camp-meeting hysteria arose from "a fever created by collision and contact, of the same nature as that which stimulates a mob to deeds of blood and horror. Gregarious animals are by nature inoffensive. The cruel and the savage live apart, and in solitude; but the gregarious, upheld and stimulated by each other, become formidable. So it is with man." Marryat's point is further proven by the incidents of Chapter 21.

The king's "working the camp-meeting" was apparently inspired by "The Captain Attends a Camp-Meeting," Chapter 10 of Johnson Jones Hooper's *Adventures of Captain Simon Suggs.* See notes 36 and 39.

28 *linsey-woolsey frocks.* Cheap dresses, made of a coarse homespun cloth, woven from a mixture of wool and flax or wool and cotton.

29 *gingham.* A cheap cotton cloth with the pattern woven in with colored threads.

30 *calico.* Twain distinguishes the classes of these women by their clothing. In Chapter 1 of *The Gilded Age,* he noted that the wearing of "tolerably fanciful patterns of *calico*" was "a fashion which prevails there to this day among those of the community who have tastes above the common level and are able to afford style."

31 *a tow-linen shirt.* A shirt made of coarse-spun linen cloth, generally the only clothing worn by both white and slave boys and girls of the backwoods. See Chapter 32, note 7.

32 *some of the young folks was courting on the sly.* Twain may be referring to the "bundling courtships" and the resulting "camp-meeting babies" caused by these congresses in the wilderness. In Chapter 32 of his 1839 *Diary in America,* Marryat noted how many people came as much as one hundred miles to attend camp-meetings just "to indulge in the licentiousness which, it is said, but too often follows, when night has thrown her veil over the scene." Anniversaries and other events were often marked according to camp-meetings; for example, if a boy was twelve years old, he might say he will be "twelve years old come next camp-meeting." This attitude may express how important these social gatherings were to the community, but it may also be a slightly sarcastic reference to when the child was conceived.

33 *the preacher was lining out a hymn.* At this time hymn books were scarce and costly, so the preacher had to read the verses aloud line by line so that the crowd could join in the song of praise.

34 *It's the brazen serpent in the wilderness!* The preacher is of course referring to Genesis 3:1–6, recording the Temptation of Adam and Eve in the Garden of Eden by the Devil in the form of a snake.

35 *the mourner's bench.* Or "anxious seat," front-row seats reserved for penitents who "mourn" for absolution of their sins.

36 *come, black with sin! . . . come, sick and sore!* John R. Byers, Jr., in "The Pokeville Preacher's Invitation in *Huckleberry Finn*" (*Mark Twain Journal*, Summer 1977, pp. 15–16) has suggested that the preacher is paraphrasing the hymn "Come Ye Sinners" by Joseph Hart (1712–1768), No. 118 of his *Hymns Composed on Various Subjects* (1759), which begins:

> *Come, ye sinners, poor and needy,*
> *Weak and wounded, sick and sore,*
> *Jesus ready stands to save you,*
> *Full of pity, love and pow'r*
> *He is able, He is able,*
> *He is willing, doubt no more.*

Other stanzas begin "Come, ye thirsty, come and welcome," and "Come, ye weary, heavy-laden." This straightforward proclamation of salvation by grace alone was one of the most popular of the old-fashioned camp-meeting "spirituals," being Hymn No. 2 in the American Methodist hymnal until 1849.

37 *Well, the first I knowed, the king got agoing.* So too does Simon Suggs, "the very 'chief of sinners' in that region," confess his sins with false tears in his eyes before the revival's congregation, but without resorting to any of the king's sillinesses. Hooper's swindler milks their sympathy by weeping that divine grace has aided him in his conquest of Satan who appeared to him as "the biggest, longest, rip-roarenest, blackest, scaliest . . . Allegator!" And like Twain's king, Suggs runs off with the church's collection. Of the two accounts, Hooper's is perhaps the sharper in its cynicism; but Twain's is more sarcastic in its opinion of society, in demonstrating how easily the Pokeville congregation is duped by the king's absurd yarn about converted pirates from the Indian Ocean.

38 *he was going . . . back to the Indian Ocean and put in the rest of his life trying to turn the pirates into the true path.* During the early nineteenth century, the Indian Ocean was infamous for its pirates; also, the growing influx of missionaries into this part of the world helped cause the Sepoy Rebellion in 1857 against foreign influence in India.

39 *Pokeville.* The name was possibly taken from Joseph M. Field's *The Drama in Pokerville*; it also suggests William Tappan Thompson's "Pineville," Georgia.

40 *the prettiest kind of girls, . . . he hugged and kissed as many as five or six times.* Kemble had originally depicted this incident, but Twain suppressed the

"A PIRATE FOR THIRTY YEARS."

38 poor as he was, he was going to start right off and work his way back to the Indian Ocean and put in the rest of his life trying to turn the pirates into the true path: for he could do it better than anybody else, being acquainted with all the pirate crews in that ocean; and though it would take him a long time to get there without money, he would get there anyway, and every time he convinced a pirate he would say to him, "Don't you thank me, don't you give me no credit, it all belongs to them **39** dear people in Pokeville camp-meeting, natural brothers and benefactors of the race—and that dear preacher there, the truest friend a pirate ever had!"

And then he busted into tears, and so did everybody. Then somebody sings out, "Take up a collection for him, take up a collection!" Well, a half a dozen made a jump to do it, but somebody sings out, "Let *him* pass the hat around!" Then everybody said it, the preacher too.

So the king went all through the crowd with his hat, swabbing his eyes, and blessing the people and praising them and thanking them for being so good to the poor pirates away off **40** there; and every little while the prettiest kind of girls, with the tears running down their cheeks, would up and ask him would he let them kiss him, for to remember him by; and he always done it; and some of them he hugged and kissed as many as five or six times—and he was invited to stay a week; and everybody wanted him to live in their houses, and said they'd think it was an honor; but he said as this was the last day of the camp-meeting he couldn't do no good, and besides he was in a sweat to get to the Indian Ocean right off and go to work on the pirates.

When we got back to the raft and he come to count up, he found he had collected eighty-seven dollars and seventy-five cents. And then he had fetched away a three-gallon jug of whisky, too, that he found under a wagon when we was starting home through the woods. The king said, take it all around, it laid over any day he'd ever put in in the missionarying line. He said it warn't no use talking, heathens don't amount to shucks, alongside of pirates, to work a camp-meeting with.

The duke was thinking *he'd* been doing pretty well, till the king come to show up, but after that he didn't think so so much. He had set up and printed off two little jobs for farmers, in that printing office—horse bills—and took the money, four dollars. And he had got in ten dollars' worth of advertisements for the paper, which he said he would put in for four dollars if they would pay in advance—so they done it. The price of the paper was two dollars a year, but he took in three subscriptions for half a dollar apiece on condition of them paying him in advance; they were going to pay in cord-wood and onions, **41** as usual, but he said he had just bought the concern and knocked down the price as low as he could afford it, and was going to run it for cash. He set up a little piece of poetry, **42** which he made, himself, out of his own head—three verses— kind of sweet and saddish—the name of it was, "Yes, crush, cold world, this breaking heart"—and he left that all set up and ready to print in the paper and didn't charge nothing for it. Well, he took in nine dollars and a half, and said he'd done a pretty square day's work for it.

Then he showed us another little job he'd printed and hadn't charged for, because it was for us. It had a picture of

ANOTHER LITTLE JOB.

drawing. "It is powerful good," Twain admitted to Webster about the picture of "the lecherous old rascal kissing the girl at the campmeeting" (quoted by Webster, *Mark Twain, Business Man*, p. 260), "but it mustn't go in—don't forget it. Let's not make *any* pictures of the camp-meeting. The subject won't *bear* illustrating. It is a disgusting thing, and pictures are sure to tell the truth about it too plainly." Gilder agreed: He dropped this passage when "Royalty on the Mississippi" appeared in *The Century*.

The king's lechery was evidently suggested by incidents in Hooper's "The Captain Attends a Camp-Meeting" in which a preacher's passions are aroused by the revival fever. Simon Suggs shrewdly sees through the hypocrisy, however, and comments, "'Wonder what's the reason these here preachers never hugs up the old, ugly women? Never seed one do it in my life—the sperrit never moves 'em that way! It's nater tho'; and . . . I judge ef I was a preacher, I should save the purtiest souls fust, myself!'" Although he does introduce sexual hysteria veiled as religious inspiration at the Pokeville camp-meeting, Twain judiciously limits the goatishness solely to the king; unlike Hooper, Twain evidently did not wish to unnecessarily offend the clergy. Besides which, even if he had introduced a rakish preacher as Hooper had, Livy likely would have penciled him out.

41 *they were going to pay in cord-wood and onions, as usual.* Cash was scarce in the backwoods at this time. Twain recalled in "The Old-Fashioned Printer" (in *Mark Twain's Speeches*, 1910, p. 183) that when he was a printer's apprentice in a newspaper office in Hannibal, "the town subscribers paid in groceries and the country ones in cabbages and cord-wood—when they paid at all, which was merely sometimes, and then we always stated the fact in the paper, and gave them a puff; and if we forgot it they stopped the paper."

42 *He set up a little piece of poetry, . . . the name of it was, "Yes, crush, cold world, this breaking heart."* Sentimental Hugh Burnside, the amateur poet of the uncompleted "Simon Wheeler, Detective" (*Mark Twain's Satires and Burlesques*, p. 360), composed an equally maudlin verse, the "ten-line deformity, christened 'The Crushed Heart's Farewell,' and leading off with this couplet":

Tho' chill be the desert and bleak its aspect,
Far kinder its storms than this cold world's neglect.

Young Sam Clemens himself was taken to writing such conventional love poetry, and three of his compositions, "The Heart's Lament," "Love Concealed," and "Separation," appeared in his brother Orion's newspaper, the Hannibal *Daily Journal*, and the last in the rival *Missouri Courier*, all within a week's time in May 1853. Typical of this ardent verse is the opening stanza of "The Heart's Lament":

I know thou wilt forget me,
For that fond soul of thine
Turns boldly from the passionate,
And ardent love of mine.
It may be, that thou deemest it

A light and simple thing,
To strike with bold and nervous arm,
The heart's lone mystic string.

Such deathless doggerel is worthy of Emmeline Grangerford, Hugh Burnside, and the duke. All the early Clemens verses are reprinted in *Early Tales and Sketches* (Vol. I, 1975, pp. 89–90, 94, and 101).

43 *St. Jacques' plantation, forty mile below New Orleans.* This notice provides for Huck and Jim's free passage all the way down the Mississippi to the fictitious Uncle Ben's place, forty-four miles below New Orleans.

44 *we must preserve the unities.* We must follow the rules; theatrical slang, the "unities" referring to the three rigid principles of Aristotelian dramatic composition as adopted and expanded by the French classical playwrights, limiting the Action, Time, and Place to one main event, occurring at one time and in one place.

a runaway nigger, with a bundle on a stick, over his shoulder, and "$200 reward" under it. The reading was all about Jim, **43** and just described him to a dot. It said he run away from St. Jacques' plantation, forty mile below New Orleans, last winter, and likely went north, and whoever would catch him and send him back, he could have the reward and expenses.

"Now," says the duke, "after to-night we can run in the daytime if we want to. Whenever we see anybody coming, we can tie Jim hand and foot with a rope, and lay him in the wigwam and show this handbill and say we captured him up the river, and were too poor to travel on a steamboat, so we got this little raft on credit from our friends and are going down to get the reward. Handcuffs and chains would look still better on Jim, but it wouldn't go well with the story of us being so poor. **44** Too much like jewellery. Ropes are the correct thing—we must preserve the unities, as we say on the boards."

We all said the duke was pretty smart, and there couldn't be no trouble about running daytimes. We judged we could make miles enough that night to get out of the reach of the pow-wow we reckoned the duke's work in the printing office was going to make in that little town—then we could boom right along, if we wanted to.

We laid low and kept still, and never shoved out till nearly ten o'clock; then we slid by, pretty wide away from the town, and didn't hoist our lantern till we was clear out of sight of it.

When Jim called me to take the watch at four in the morning, he says—

"Huck, does you reck'n we gwyne to run across any mo' kings on dis trip?"

"No," I says, "I reckon not."

"Well," says he, "dat's all right, den. I doan' mine one er two kings, but dat's enough. Dis one's powerful drunk, en de duke ain' much better."

I found Jim had been trying to get him to talk French, so he could hear what it was like; but he said he had been in this country so long, and had so much trouble, he'd forgot it.

Chapter XXI.

PRACTICING.

IT was after sun-up, now, but we went right on, and didn't tie up. The king and the duke turned out, by-and-by, looking pretty rusty; but after they'd jumped overboard and took a swim, it chippered them up a good deal. After breakfast the king he took a seat on a corner of the raft, and pulled off his boots and rolled up his britches, and let his legs dangle in the water, so as to be comfortable, and lit his pipe, and went to getting his Romeo and Juliet by heart. When he had got it pretty good, him and the duke begun to practise it together. The duke had to learn him over and over again, how to say every speech; and he made him sigh, and put his hand on his heart, and after while he said he done it pretty well; "only," he says, "you musn't bellow out *Romeo!* that way, like a bull—you must say it soft, and sick, and languishy, so—R–o–o–meo! that is the idea; for Juliet's a dear sweet mere child of a girl, you know, and she don't bray like a jackass."

"The king tripped and fell overboard." Illustration by E. W. Kemble, New York *World*, December 10, 1899.

1 *Capet.* Family name of the French dynasty which ruled from the Middle Ages. After his arrest, King Louis XVI was treated as a private citizen and was always addressed as Louis Capet.

2 *the Highland fling.* A spirited Scottish folk dance in which the performer stands on one foot, moving the other leg back and forward and keeping the arms stiffly posed.

The Highland fling. Print by Sarony & Major, 1846.
Courtesy the Library of Congress.

3 *the sailor's hornpipe.* Originally the "Herne-pipe," a spirited dance in honor of Herne, the pre-Saxon god of the harvest; but in the eighteenth century, it was introduced into the popular theater as a solo dance step in which the performer's arms imitate certain shipboard tasks, performed to the tune of a pipe. It and the Highland fling were generally danced between acts or scenes of a play; and as they were common to minstrel shows and other popular theater, they would hardly make the duke's Shakespearean performance a "first-class show."

4 *Then he strikes a most noble attitude, with one leg shoved forwards, and his arms stretched away up, and his head tilted back, looking up at the sky.* Huck describes the conventional pose of the melancholy Dane. The performances of such backwoods thespians was more a matter of exaggerated pose than of any acting ability: In Chapter 51 of *Life on the Mississippi,* Twain recalled his coming upon a country jake who had become so "stage-struck" that he left Hannibal to "trod the boards" in St. Louis. "He was standing musing on a street corner," Twain wrote, "with his right hand on his hip, the thumb of his left supporting his chin, face bowed and frowning, slouch hat pulled down over the forehead—imagining himself to be Othello or some such character, and imagining that the passing crowd marked his tragic bearing and were awe-struck." For thirty-four years, this man took walk-on parts, and only rarely did these include a line or two of dialogue; and "yet, poor devil, he had been patiently studying the part of Hamlet for more than thirty years, and he lived and died in the belief that some day he would be invited to play it!"

Well, next they got out a couple of long swords that the duke made out of oak laths, and begun to practise the swordfight—the duke called himself Richard III.; and the way they laid on, and pranced around the raft was grand to see. But by-and-by the king tripped and fell overboard, and after that they took a rest, and had a talk about all kinds of adventures they'd had in other times along the river.

After dinner, the duke says:

1 " Well, Capet, we'll want to make this a first-class show, you know, so I guess we'll add a little more to it. We want a little something to answer encores with, anyway."

" What's onkores, Bilgewater? "

The duke told him, and then says:

2,3 " I'll answer by doing the Highland fling or the sailor's hornpipe; and you—well, let me see—oh, I've got it—you can do Hamlet's soliloquy."

" Hamlet's which? "

" Hamlet's soliloquy, you know; the most celebrated thing in Shakespeare. Ah, it's sublime, sublime! Always fetches the house. I haven't got it in the book—I've only got one volume—but I reckon I can piece it out from memory. I'll just walk up and down a minute, and see if I can call it back from recollection's vaults."

So he went to marching up and down, thinking, and frowning horrible every now and then; then he would hoist up his eyebrows; next he would squeeze his hand on his forehead and stagger back and kind of moan; next he would sigh, and next he'd let on to drop a tear. It was beautiful to see him. By-
4 and-by he got it. He told us to give attention. Then he strikes a most noble attitude, with one leg shoved forwards, and his arms stretched away up, and his head tilted back, looking up at the sky; and then he begins to rip and rave and grit his teeth; and after that, all through his speech he howled, and spread around, and swelled up his chest, and just knocked the
5 spots out of any acting ever *I* see before. This is the speech—I learned it, easy enough, while he was learning it to the king:

To be, or not to be; that is the bare bodkin
That makes calamity of so long life;
For who would fardels bear, till Birnam Wood do come to Dunsinane,
But that the fear of something after death
Murders the innocent sleep,
Great nature's second course,
And makes us rather sling the arrows of outrageous fortune
Than fly to others that we know not of.
There's the respect must give us pause:
Wake Duncan with thy knocking! I would thou couldst;
For who would bear the whips and scorns of time,
The oppressor's wrong, the proud man's contumely,
The law's delay, and the quietus which his pangs might take,
In the dead waste and middle of the night, when churchyards yawn
In customary suits of solemn black,
But that the undiscovered country from whose bourne no traveler returns,
Breathes forth contagion on the world,
And thus the native hue of resolution, like the poor cat i' the adage,

5 *This is the speech.* Twain's burlesque of the most famous soliloquy in English drama is a hodgepodge of some of the most frequently quoted lines in *Hamlet* and *Macbeth* and one from *Richard III:* "And all the clouds that lowr'd on our house" (Act I, scene i, line 3). However, E. Bruce Kirkham has argued in "Huck and Hamlet" (*Mark Twain Journal,* Summer 1969, pp. 17–19) that the duke's fractured soliloquy is not so foolish as it sounds, and that its debate of whether to act or not to act reinforces the importance of the internal monologue as a dialectical device throughout the novel.

Huck Finn was not the only American of the time who was so easily impressed by such a phony *Hamlet:* In the manuscript of *Life on the Mississippi* (Limited Editions Club edition, 1944, pp. 404–405), Twain mentioned an Englishman's account of a performance in Pittsburgh in which "an English dramatic troupe played Hamlet there one night, in the regulation way, and played a burlesque of it the next night; but they didn't *tell* the audience that it was a burlesque; so the women-folk went on crying whilst the roaring, gigantic Ophelia cavorted hither and thither, scattering her carrots and cabbages around, in lieu of rosemary and rue."

"Mutilations of Shakespeare," DeVoto noted in *Mark Twain's America* (pp. 254–255), "can be met with everywhere in this literature but most often and most amusingly in the anecdotal recollections of Sol Smith." DeVoto (and Twain) may have been referring to the traveling troupes of amateur actors who with makeshift props and costumes garbled lines of selected scenes from Shakespeare such as *Richard III* (in *Sol Smith's Theatrical Apprenticeship,* 1845, pp. 61–62) and *Romeo and Juliet* (in *The Theatrical Journey-Work and Anecdotal Recollections of Sol Smith,* 1854, pp. 200–201). Leo Marx in his notes to the 1967 Bobbs-Merrill edition has described another possible source for Twain's thespians, a popular routine of bits of Shakespeare mixed with the antics of a circus clown by Dan Rice whom Clemens saw while a boy in Hannibal.

HAMLET'S SOLILOQUY.

Is sicklied o'er with care,
And all the clouds that lowered o'er our housetops,
With this regard their currents turn awry,
And lose the name of action.
'Tis a consummation devoutly to be wished.　But soft you, the fair Ophelia:
Ope not thy ponderous and marble jaws,
But get thee to a nunnery—go !

Well, the old man he liked that speech, and he mighty soon got it so he could do it first rate.　It seemed like he was just born for it ; and when he had his hand in and was excited, it was perfectly lovely the way he would rip and tear and rair up behind when he was getting it off.

The first chance we got, the duke he had some show bills printed ; and after that, for two or three days as we floated along, the raft was a most uncommon lively place, for there warn't nothing but sword-fighting and rehearsing—as the duke called it —going on all the time.　One morning, when we was pretty well down the State of Arkansaw, we come in sight of a little one-horse town in a big bend ; so we tied up about three-quarters of a mile above it, in the mouth of a crick which was shut in like a tunnel by the cypress trees, and all of us but Jim took the canoe and went down there to see if there was any chance in that place for our show.

We struck it mighty lucky ; there was going to be a circus there that afternoon, and the country people was already beginning to come in, in all kinds of old shackly wagons, and on

6 *Shaksperean Revival!!!* Twain may be punning on religious "revival," such as the camp-meeting in the last chapter; a theatrical "revival" is the restoration of a play to the stage, but the word is generally not applied to standard dramas such as Shakespeare's. "Shakspere" was not a colloquial but an accepted spelling of the Bard's name during the nineteenth century.

7 *The world renowned tragedians, David Garrick the younger . . . and Edmund Kean the elder.* David Garrick (1717–1779) was England's most famous actor of his day. He was also a producer and playwright; and he

David Garrick as Richard III. Print by William Hogarth. *Courtesy Prints Division, The New York Public Library, Astor, Lenox, and Tilden Foundations.*

Edmund Kean as Richard III, supporting the Drury Lane Theatre. Caricature by George Cruikshank, 1814.

horses. The circus would leave before night, so our show would have a pretty good chance. The duke he hired the court house, and we went around and stuck up our bills. They read like this :

6

Shaksperean Revival ! ! !

Wonderful Attraction !

For One Night Only !

7

The world renowned tragedians,

8

David Garrick the younger, of Drury Lane Theatre, London,
and
Edmund Kean the elder, of the Royal Haymarket Theatre, White-
chapel, Pudding Lane, Piccadilly, London, and the
Royal Continental Theatres, in their sublime
Shaksperean Spectacle entitled

The Balcony Scene
in
Romeo and Juliet ! ! !

Romeo.. Mr. Garrick
Juliet.. Mr. Kean

9

Assisted by the whole strength of the company !
New costumes, new scenery, new appointments !

Also :
The thrilling, masterly, and blood-curdling
Broad-sword conflict
In Richard III. ! ! !

Richard III... Mr. Garrick.
Richmond.. Mr. Kean.

also :
(by special request,)

Hamlet's Immortal Soliloquy ! !

By the Illustrious Kean !
Done by him 300 consecutive nights in Paris !

For One Night Only,

On account of imperative European engagements !
Admission 25 cents   children and servants, 10 cents.

10   Then we went loafing around the town. The stores and houses was most all old shackly dried-up frame concerns that hadn't ever been painted; they was set up three or four foot above ground on stilts, so as to be out of reach of the water when the river was overflowed. The houses had little gardens around them, but they didn't seem to raise hardly anything in **11** them but jimpson weeds, and sunflowers, and ash-piles, and old curled-up boots and shoes, and pieces of bottles, and rags, and played-out tin-ware. The fences was made of different **12** kinds of boards, nailed on at different times; and they leaned every which-way, and had gates that didn't generly have but one hinge—a leather one. Some of the fences had been white-washed, some time or another, but the duke said it was in C'lumbus's time, like enough. There was generly hogs in the garden, and people driving them out.

All the stores was along one street. They had white-domestic awnings in front, and the country people hitched their horses to the awning-posts. There was empty dry-goods boxes

Charles Kean as Richard III. *Courtesy the Picture Collection, The New York Public Library, Astor, Lenox, and Tilden Foundations.*

rewrote Shakespeare, such as adding a death scene to *Romeo and Juliet* and dropping the tragic fate of Ophelia from *Hamlet*. He also raised the English stage to respectability. He gained his first fame in 1741 in *Richard III*; and his farewell performance included scenes from *Hamlet* and *Richard III*.

Edmund Kean (1787?–1833) succeeded Garrick as England's greatest actor. Although his "Romeo" was thought laughable, Kean was famous for his "Richard III." His son, Charles John Kean (1811–1868), succeeded his father, but there was no Edmund Kean the younger; and David Garrick died childless. In calling himself "the younger" and his partner "the elder," titles usually given only to distinguished members of a family in the same profession, the duke is merely helping the frontier audience to distinguish between the two performers; he may also be making another joke on the king's age.

8 *Drury Lane Theatre, London, and . . . the Royal Haymarket Theatre, Whitechapel, Pudding Land, Piccadilly, London.* David Garrick made the Drury Lane Theatre the most famous playhouse in London; here he played "Hamlet" and "Romeo," and later Kean appeared as "Richard III." The Haymarket was another popular London theater of the time; Whitechapel, Pudding Lane, and Picadilly are various well-known parts of the city. So often did foreign acting companies traveling through the United States advertise as having played these famous English theaters, that it soon became something of a joke to be straight from an engagement at the Drury Lane Theatre or any other London house. Francis A. Durwige complained in "Newspaper Advertisements" (in *Stray Subjects*, 1848, p. 148) that "the theatre going man will find 'the small bill' . . . where he will believe, if he be sufficiently credulous, that all the characters down to the 'dummies,' are supported by gentlemen from the Royal Theatres of London . . . after many a brilliant triumph at Drury Lane."

9 *appointments.* Props.

10 *the town.* The name of the town, "Bricksville," is not revealed until Chapter 28; it is a particularly sarcastic name, because the town contains not a single brick building. There are several theories of exactly what town Twain was referring to when he described 'Bricksville,' Arkansas. It is similar to Hannibal, Missouri, as recollected in Chapter 4 of *Life on the Mississippi:* "the white town drowsing in the sunshine of a summer's morning; the streets empty, or pretty nearly so; one or two clerks sitting in front of the . . . stores, with their splint-bottomed chairs tilted back against the wall, chins on breasts, hats slouched over their faces, asleep—with shingle shavings enough around to show what broke them down; a sow and a litter of pigs loafing along the sidewalk, doing a good business in watermelon rinds and seeds."

It has also been suggested that Bricksville lies close to where Napoleon, Arkansas, once stood; like the fictional town, Napoleon was threatened by the constant gnawing of the river against its bank, and Twain reported in Chapter 32 of *Life on the Mississippi* that finally "the Arkansas River burst through it, tore it all to rags, and emptied it into the Mississippi! . . . Yes, it was an astonishing thing to see the Mississippi rolling between unpeopled shores and straight over the spot where I used to see a good big self-complacent town twenty years ago."

Obviously, rather than describing one specific settlement, Twain intended Bricksville as a typical community of the Mississippi Valley. It was perhaps in part based on another fictional town, in Georgia, described in "The Mystery Revealed" (Thompson's *Chronicles of Pineville*, pp. 59–60): "Pineville awoke from the quiet slumber of a starless night. The . . . dense fog still rested upon the earth, involving houses and horseblocks, shops and shanties, sign-posts and horse-racks, flower-gardens and duck-ponds, chimneys and fodder-stacks, objects conspicuous and objects out of sight, things elegant and things inelegant, (which in our villages are usually disposed in such pleasing contrast), in one general, indiscriminate obscurity. . . . The village swine were performing scavenger duty in the streets and yards . . . while a gang of vagabond goats were performing feats of agility about the court-house steps."

However, Huck Finn here, unlike either Twain or Thompson earlier, records only the foul aspects of a small river town.

11 *jimpson weeds, and sunflowers.* The Jimson or Jamestown weed (said to be first encountered at Jamestown, Virginia) is the thorn-apple, a particularly ugly, poisonous plant. In Chapter 20 of *A Tramp Abroad*, Twain described a neglected garden as "thickly grown with the bloomy and villainous 'jimpson' weed and its common friend the stately sunflower." The gardens of Bricksville can grow nothing else, obviously because their owners are too lazy to tend them.

12 *they . . . had gates that didn't generly have but one hinge—a leather one.* Because metal was scarce on the American frontier, rarely were nails or other iron used in constructing houses and other buildings; doors and gates usually had only leather or wooden latches and leather straps for the hinges. Surprisingly, although few buildings had metal locks on them, theft was largely unknown in this part of the country.

13 *loafers.* Twain describes in the Bricksville loafer the typical "Southern Bully." He was, as Hundley described in *Social Relations in Our Southern States* (pp. 223–224), "a swearing, tobacco-chewing, brandy drinking Bully, whose chief delight is to hang about the doors of groggeries and tavern tap-rooms, to fight chicken cocks, to play Old Sledge, or pitch-and-toss, chuck-a-luck, and the like, as well as to encourage dog-fights, and occasionally to get up a little raw-head-and-bloody-bones affair on his own account." And nowhere else was the Southern Bully in more abundance than in rough and uncivilized Arkansas: A popular joke of the time (reprinted in Shillaber's *Mrs. Partington's Carpet-Bag of Fun*, 1855, p. 174) related how a tall, Arkansas-meat-axe-looking man sent a porter to fetch his luggage, and when the porter asked him what it was, the fellow from Arkansas replied, "Why, three pistols, a pack of cards, a Bowie-knife, and one shirt. You'll find them all under my pillow." Twain too used this popular image of "Mr. Arkansas," "a stalwart ruffian . . . who carried two revolvers in his belt and a bowie knife projecting from his boot, and who was always suffering for a fight," in Chapter 31 of *Roughing It.*

An early version of these backwoods loafers are the citizens of Obedstown, East Tennessee, in Chapter 1 of *The Gilded Age.* "Some wore vests, but few wore coats," Twain explained. "Every individual arrived with his hands in his pockets; a hand came out occasionally for a purpose, but it always went back again after service . . .; many [dilapidated straw] hats were present. . . . every individual was either chewing natural tobacco prepared on his own premises or smoking the same in a corn-cob pipe. . . . But presently there was a dog-fight . . . the visitors slid off their perch like so many turtles and strode to the battle-field with an interest bordering on eagerness."

But Twain apparently based the Bricksville discourse on tobacco that follows in part on a similar dispute among the citizens of Pineville, Georgia, in Thompson's "The Mystery Revealed" in *Chronicles of Pineville* (pp. 60–61): "There was a dearth of news just at that time and conversation was dull. . . . Billy Wilder asked if anybody had any good tobacco; upon which Bob Echols pulled out a piece about the size of his hand . . . passed it on to Billy, after which it passed through divers other hands until the greater part found its way into the mouths of the bystanders, and not even the slightest moiety would have reached its owner again, had not some one on the outskirts of the crowd—who probably had a hole in his pocket—

Obedstown, Tennessee, loafers. Illustration by True W. Williams, *The Gilded Age*, 1874.

13 under the awnings, and loafers roosting on them all day long, whittling them with their Barlow knives ; and chawing tobacco. and gaping and yawning and stretching—a mighty ornery lot. They generly had on yellow straw hats most as wide as an umbrella, but didn't wear no coats nor waistcoats; they called one another Bill, and Buck, and Hank, and Joe, and Andy, and talked lazy and drawly, and used considerable many cuss-words. There was as many as one loafer leaning up against every awning-post, and he most always had his hands in his britches pockets, except when he fetched them out to lend a chaw of tobacco or scratch. What a body was hearing amongst them, all the time was—

" Gimme a chaw 'v tobacker, Hank."

" GIMME A CHAW.'

" Cain't—I hain't got but one chaw left. Ask Bill."

Maybe Bill he gives him a chaw ; maybe he lies and says he ain't got none. Some of them kinds of loafers never has a cent in the world, nor a chaw of tobacco of their own. They get all their chawing by borrowing—they say to a fellow, " I wisht you'd len' me a chaw, Jack, I jist this minute give Ben Thompson the last chaw I had "—which is a lie, pretty much every time; it don't fool nobody but a stranger; but Jack ain't no stranger, so he says—

" *You* give him a chaw, did you ? so did your sister's cat's grandmother. You pay me back the chaws you've awready

14 borry'd off'n me, Lafe Buckner, then I'll loan you one or two ton of it, and won't charge you no back intrust nuther."

" Well, I *did* pay you back some of it wunst."

" Yes, you did—'bout six chaws. You borry'd store tobacker and paid back nigger-head." **15**

Store tobacco is flat black plug, but these fellows mostly chaws the natural leaf twisted. When they borrow a chaw, they don't generly cut it off with a knife, but they set the plug in between their teeth, and gnaw with their teeth and tug at the plug with their hands till they get it in two—then sometimes the one that owns the tobacco looks mournful at it when it's handed back, and says, sarcastic—

" Here, gimme the *chaw*, and you take the *plug*." **16**

All the streets and lanes was just mud, they warn't nothing else *but* mud—mud as black as tar, and nigh about a foot deep in some places; and two or three inches deep in *all* the places. The hogs loafed and grunted around, everywheres. You'd see a muddy sow and a litter of pigs come lazying along the street and whollop herself right down in the way, where folks had to walk around her, and she'd stretch out, and shut her eyes, and wave her ears, whilst the pigs was milking her, and look as happy as if she was on salary. And pretty soon you'd hear a loafer sing out, " Hi! *so* boy! sick him, Tige!" and away the sow would go, squealing most horrible, with a dog or two swinging to each ear, and three or four dozen more a-coming; and then you would see all the loafers get up and watch the thing out of sight, and laugh at the fun and look grateful for the noise. Then they'd settle back again till there was a dog-fight. There couldn't anything wake them up all over, and make them happy all over, like a dog-fight—unless it might be putting turpentine on a stray dog and setting fire to him, or tying a **17** tin pan to his tail and see him run himself to death.

On the river front some of the houses was sticking out over the bank, and they was bowed and bent, and about ready to tumble in. The people had moved out of them. The bank was caved away under one corner of some others, and that corner was hanging over. People lived in them yet, but it was dangersome, because sometimes a strip of land as wide as a house caves in at a time. Sometimes a belt of land a quarter of a mile deep will start in and cave along and cave along till it all caves into the river in one summer. Such a town as that has to be always moving back, and back, and back, because the **18** river's always gnawing at it.

The nearer it got to noon that day, the thicker and thicker was the wagons and horses in the streets, and more coming all the time. Families fetched their dinners with them, from the country, and eat them in the wagons. There was considerable whisky drinking going on, and I seen three fights. By-and-by somebody sings out—

" Here comes old Boggs!—in from the country for his little old monthly drunk—here he comes, boys!"

All the loafers looked glad—I reckoned they was used to having fun out of Boggs. One of them says—

" Wonder who he's a gwyne to chaw up this time. If he'd a chawed up all the men he's ben a gwyne to chaw up in the

called out, 'Who's tobacco's this?' Bob owned the remnant, remarking that he '*bought* it at Harley's,' and conversation and expectoration became brisk and general." See also notes 14 and 16.

14 *I'll loan you one or two ton of it, and won't charge you no back intrust.* By suggesting that the only capital of this one-horse town is chewing tobacco, Twain emphasizes the blackness and filth of Bricksville. Few things were more revolting to European visitors than the American habit of spitting tobacco juice in public; Dickens and Mrs. Trollope were particularly offended by this custom. However, although the citizens of Obedstown in *The Gilded Age* are proficient in the art, Huck fails to mention any of the Bricksville chewers as expectorating. Perhaps Olivia (or Twain himself) thought that detail too vulgar. Nevertheless, although not stated, it is still understood exactly what habit the Bricksville loafers are engaged in.

15 *nigger-head.* A strong black plug tobacco, here apparently homemade and inferior to flat black plug.

16 "*Here, gimme the* chaw, *and you take the* plug." The "chaw" is the mouthful, the "plug" the stick of tobacco. Cecil D. Eby, Jr., in "Mark Twain's 'Plug' and 'Chaw': An Anecdotal Parallel" (*Mark Twain Journal*, Summer 1960, pp. 11 and 25) has discovered a similar joke recorded in August 1873 by David Hunter Strother ("Porte Crayon") in his Denver journal as an example of mining camp humor: "First loafer: 'Gimme a chaw of tobaccer, will ye?' The miner hands out his plug. Loafer helps himself. Miner says, 'Well, mister, if ye'll only gimme that chaw ye may keep the plug.'"

Although Twain did meet Strother in 1876, at the centennial celebration in Philadelphia, it is more likely that Twain learned the joke during his mining days in Nevada than through Strother.

17 *tying a tin pan to his tail and see him run himself to death.* Twain thought this common trick "a practical joke of sufficiently poor quality." In Chapter 4 of *A Connecticut Yankee in King Arthur's Court*, to demonstrate how lacking in wit and good humor was the court at Camelot, Hank Morgan describes how Sir Dinadan the Humorist "tied some metal mugs to a dog's tail and turned him loose, and he tore around the place in a frenzy of fright, with all the other dogs bellowing after him and battering and crashing against everything that came in their way and making altogether a chaos of confusion and a most deafening din and turmoil; at which every man and woman of the multitude laughed till the tears flowed, and some fell out of their chairs and wallowed on the floor in ecstasy. It was just like so many children." "When a person of mature age perpetrates a practical joke it is fair evidence," Twain noted in Chapter 10 of his *Autobiography*, "that he is weak in the head and hasn't enough heart to signify."

18 *the river's always gnawing at it.* The wearing away of the waterfront reinforces the town's indifference to its moral decay.

19 *he'd come to town to kill old Colonel Sherburn.* Here Twain has retold one of the most disturbing incidents of his childhood in Hannibal: the shooting of "Uncle Sam" Smarr by William Owsley, the first premeditated murder in the town's history. Wecter has reconstructed the events in *Sam Clemens of Hannibal* (pp. 106–109) largely through twenty-eight depositions Judge John M. Clemens, the justice of the peace, took from the various witnesses. Although when sober he was (as a neighbor testified) "as honest a man as any in the state," old Smarr "when drinking . . . was a little turbulent," and yet he was still not considered a dangerous man. However, when on a binge, Smarr ranted to everyone that Owsley was "a damned pickpocket . . . a damned son of a bitch . . . if he ever does cross my path I will kill him." Twain recalled in his notes on Hannibal citizens (published in *Mark Twain's Hannibal, Huck and Tom*, p. 36) that Owsley was a "prosperous merchant," somewhat of a dandy who "smoked fragrant cigars—regalias." However, Smarr believed that the gentleman had swindled a couple of his friends and should be whipped. Smarr's slander soon became insufferable to the merchant, and on January 24, 1845, he confronted Smarr, only a few steps from the Clemens home. A witness told Judge Clemens that Owsley called out, "'You Sam Smarr'—Mr. Smarr turned around, seeing Mr. Owsley in the act of drawing a pistol from his pocket, said Mr. Owsley don't fire, or something to that effect. Mr. Owsley was within about four paces of Mr. Smarr when he drew the pistol and fired twice in succession, after the second fire, Mr. Smarr fell, when Mr. Owsley turned on his heel and walked off. . . . Dr. Grant then came up and invited us to take him in to his store. . . . In about a half an hour from the time he was shot he expired." Another witness recalled that Smarr fell backward, while Owsley (just like Sherburn) kept his arm extended as he fired a second time.

20 *"Meat first, and spoon vittles to top off on."* Main course first, soup later.

last twenty year, he'd have considerble ruputation, now."

Another one says, "I wisht old Boggs 'd threaten me, 'cuz then I'd know I warn't gwyne to die for a thousan' year."

Boggs comes a-tearing along on his horse, whooping and yelling like an Injun, and singing out—

"Cler the track, thar. I'm on the waw-path, and the price uv coffins is a gwyne to raise."

A LITTLE MONTHLY DRUNK.

He was drunk, and weaving about in his saddle; he was over fifty year old, and had a very red face. Everybody yelled at him, and laughed at him, and sassed him, and he sassed back, and said he'd attend to them and lay them out in their regular turns, but he couldn't wait now, because he'd come to town to kill old Colonel Sherburn, and his motto was, "Meat first, and spoon vittles to top off on."

He see me, and rode up and says—

"Whar'd you come f'm, boy? You prepared to die?"

Then he rode on. I was scared; but a man says—

"He don't mean nothing; he's always a carryin' on like that, when he's drunk. He's the best-naturedest old fool in Arkansaw—never hurt nobody, drunk nor sober."

Boggs rode up before the biggest store in town and bent his head down so he could see under the curtain of the awning, and yells—

"Come out here, Sherburn! Come out and meet the man you've swindled. You're the houn' I'm after, and I'm a gwyne to have you, too!"

And so he went on, calling Sherburn everything he could lay his tongue to, and the whole street packed with people listening and laughing and going on. By-and-by a proud-looking man about fifty-five—and he was a heap the best-dressed man in that town, too—steps out of the store, and the crowd drops back on each side to let him come. He says to Boggs, mighty calm and slow—he says:

"I'm tired of this; but I'll endure it till one o'clock. Till one o'clock, mind—no longer.   If you open your mouth against **21** me only once, after that time, you can't travel so far but I will find you."

Then he turns and goes in. The crowd looked mighty sober; nobody stirred, and there warn't no more laughing. Boggs rode off blackguarding Sherburn as loud as he could yell, all down the street; and pretty soon back he comes and stops before the store, still keeping it up. Some men crowded around him and tried to get him to shut up, but he wouldn't; they told him it would be one o'clock in about fifteen minutes, and so he *must* go home—he must go right away. But it didn't do no good. He cussed away, with all his might, and throwed his hat down in the mud and rode over it, and pretty soon away he went a-raging down the street again, with his gray hair a-flying. Everybody that could get a chance at him tried their best to coax him off of his horse so they could lock him up and get him sober; but it warn't no use—up the street he would tear again, and give Sherburn another cussing. By-and-by somebody says:

"Go for his daughter!—quick, go for his daughter; sometimes he'll listen to her. If anybody can persuade him, she can."

So somebody started on a run. I walked down street a ways, and stopped. In about five or ten minutes, here comes Boggs again—but not on his horse. He was a-reeling across the street towards me, bareheaded, with a friend on both sides of him aholt of his arms and hurrying him along. He was quiet, and looked uneasy; and he warn't hanging back any, but was doing some of the hurrying himself. Somebody sings out—

"Boggs!"

I looked over there to see who said it, and it was that Colonel Sherburn. He was standing perfectly still in the street, and had a pistol raised in his right hand—not aiming it, but holding it out with the barrel tilted up towards the sky. The same second I see a young girl coming on the run, and two men with her. Boggs and the men turned round, to see who called him, and when they see the pistol the men jumped to one side, and the pistol barrel come down slow and steady to a level—both barrels cocked. Boggs throws up both of his hands, and says, "O Lord, don't shoot!" Bang! goes the first shot, and he staggers back clawing at the air—bang! goes the second one, and he tumbles backwards on to the ground, heavy and solid, with his arms spread out. That young girl screamed out, and comes rushing, and down she throws herself on her father, crying, and saying, "Oh, he's killed him, he's killed him!" The crowd closed up around them, and shouldered and jammed one another, with their necks stretched, trying to see, and people on the inside trying to shove them back, and shouting, "Back, back! give him air, give him air!"

Colonel Sherburn he tossed his pistol on to the ground, and turned around on his heels and walked off.

They took Boggs to a little drug store, the crowd pressing

21 *If you open your mouth against me only once, after that time, you can't travel so far but I will find you.* Such a threat was seen by Marryat in Chapter 22 of his 1839 diary as a peculiarly American problem. "Slander and detraction are the inseparable evils of a democracy," the Englishman argued; "and as neither the public nor private characters are spared, and the law is impotent to protect them, men have no other recourse than to defend their reputations with their lives, or to deter the defamer by the risk which he must incur." Consequently, on the American frontier, dueling and other lethal contests were the generally accepted means in settling questions of honor.

22 *They . . . put one large Bible under his head, and opened another one and spread it on his breast*. Here the "giver of life" is used to crush it out. It was the custom in this part of the country to place a Bible under the chin of the dead, but these people might have waited until Boggs had expired. "Bible on breast," Twain recalled Smarr's death in a note (quoted in Item 187 in *Catalogue of the Library and Manuscripts of Samuel L. Clemens*). "Gave him spiritual relief, no doubt, but must have crowded him physically." Although Wecter reported in *Sam Clemens of Hannibal* that no witness mentioned this detail in Judge Clemens's depositions, Twain confessed in Chapter 9 of his *Autobiography* how his dreams were troubled by "the grotesque closing picture—the great family Bible spread open on the profane old man's breast by some thoughtful idiot and rising and sinking to the labored breathings and adding the torture of its leaden weight to the dying struggles. . . . In all the throng of gaping and sympathetic onlookers there was not one with common sense enough to perceive that an anvil would have been in better taste there than the Bible, less open to sarcastic criticism and swifter in its atrocious work."

23 *scrouging*. Crowding, squeezing.

24 *other folks has their rights as well as you*. The crowd reacts as if the shooting were done merely for their pleasure. It would seem that the Bricksville mob take great delight in looking upon such human suffering, but, in "The United States of Lyncherdom" (in *A Pen Warmed-up in Hell*, edited by Frederick Anderson, 1972, p. 185), Twain argued that the reason for such a crowd's active interest in a horrible incident is because "each man is afraid of his neighbor's disapproval—a thing which, to the general run of the race, is more dreaded than wounds and death. When there is to be a lynching the people hitch up and come miles to see it, bringing their wives and children. Really to see it? No—they come only because they are afraid to stay at home, lest it be noticed and offensively commented upon."

25 *One long lanky man . . . marked out the places on the ground*. The reconstruction of the murder in all its gory details by this prominent citizen, possibly the justice of the peace, was likely inspired by a scene Twain witnessed in Europe (and described in Chapter 23 of *A Tramp Abroad*) when a boy fell down a steep hillside and a crowd then gathered: "All who had seen the catastrophe were describing it at once, and each trying to talk louder than his neighbor; and one youth of a superior genius ran a little up the hill, called attention, tripped, fell, rolled down among us, and thus triumphantly showed exactly how the thing had been done." Twain increases the bitterness of the satire by having a man, not a boy, perform such a reenactment in *Huckleberry Finn*.

around, just the same, and the whole town following, and I rushed and got a good place at the window, where I was close **22** to him and could see in. They laid him on the floor, and put one large Bible under his head, and opened another one and spread it on his breast—but they tore open his shirt first, and I seen where one of the bullets went in. He made about a dozen long gasps, his breast lifting the Bible up when he drawed in his breath, and letting it down again when he breathed it out

THE DEATH OF BOGGS.

—and after that he laid still; he was dead. Then they pulled his daughter away from him, screaming and crying, and took her off. She was about sixteen, and very sweet and gentle-looking, but awful pale and scared.

Well, pretty soon the whole town was there, squirming and **23** scrouging and pushing and shoving to get at the window and have a look, but people that had the places wouldn't give them up, and folks behind them was saying all the time, " Say, now, you've looked enough, you fellows; 'taint right and 'taint fair, for you to stay thar all the time, and never give nobody a **24** chance; other folks has their rights as well as you."

There was considerable jawing back, so I slid out, thinking maybe there was going to be trouble. The streets was full, and everybody was excited. Everybody that seen the shooting was telling how it happened, and there was a big crowd packed around each one of these fellows, stretching their necks and **25** listening. One long lanky man, with long hair and a big white fur stove-pipe hat on the back of his head, and a crooked-handled cane, marked out the places on the ground where Boggs stood, and where Sherburn stood, and the people following him around from one place to t'other and watching everything he done, and bobbing their heads to show they understood, and stooping a little, and resting their hands on their thighs to watch him mark the places on the ground with his cane; and then he stood up straight and stiff where Sherburn had stood, frowning and having his hat-brim down over his eyes, and sung out, "Boggs!" and then fetched his cane down slow to a dead level, and says "Bang!" staggered backwards, says "Bang!" again, and fell down flat on his back. The people that had seen the thing said he done it perfect; said it was just exactly the way it all happened. Then as much as a dozen people got out their bottles and treated him.

Well, by-and-by somebody said Sherburn ought to be **26** lynched. In about a minute everybody was saying it; so away they went, mad and yelling, and snatching down every clothes-line they come to, to do the hanging with.

26 *somebody said Sherburn ought to be lynched.* No such incident took place after the murder of Smarr by Owsley in Hannibal, but Twain may in part have recalled "The Mystery Revealed" in Thompson's *Chronicles of Pineville* (pp. 67–77) in which when a posse is formed to capture some suspected bank robbers, "in less than five minutes, all of Pineville was in commotion." Thompson observed, "There are always some one or two persons in every small community, who lead the mass, and, as when some avant-swine breaks through the barrier that circumscribes the wanderings of the herd, the balance are sure to rush impetuously through the same hole, so the multitude are certain to give unanimous assent to the opinions of those whose lead they are accustomed to follow." Twain shared this cynical opinion of the mob. "We are descreet sheep," Twain complained in "The Character of Man," 1885 (published in *What Is Man?*, 1973, p. 62); "we wait to see how the drove is going, and then go with the drove. We have two opinions: one private, which we are afraid to express; and another one—the one we use—which we force ourselves to wear to please Mrs. Grundy, until habit makes us comfortable in it, and the custom of defending it presently makes us love it, adore it, and forget how pitifully we came by it." Even good-hearted Huck Finn is momentarily carried away with the excitement of a lynching party and joins the mob on its way to Sherburn's home. However, the boy remains merely a spectator and not an active participant in the drama.

1 *bucks and wenches*. Young slave men and women.

2 *Sherburn's palings*. The erecting of a wooden fence around one's property was a mark of high social status in the backwoods; in Chapter 5 of *The Gilded Age*, one of the first things that Squire Hawkins does with his new wealth is to "put up the first 'paling' fence that had ever adorned the village; and he did not stop there, but whitewashed it."

1

SHERBURN STEPS OUT.

Chapter XXII

They swarmed up the street towards Sherburn's house, a-whooping and yelling and raging like Injuns, and everything had to clear the way or get run over and tromped to mush, and it was awful to see. Children was heeling it ahead of the mob, screaming and trying to get out of the way; and every window along the road was full of women's heads, and there was nigger boys in every tree, and bucks and wenches looking over every fence; and as soon as the mob would get nearly to them they would break and skaddle back out of reach. Lots of the women and girls was crying and taking on, scared most to death.

They swarmed up in front of Sherburn's palings as thick as they could jam together, and you couldn't hear yourself think for the noise. It was a little twenty-foot yard. Some sung out, "Tear down the fence! tear down the fence!" Then there was a racket of ripping and tearing and smashing, and down she goes, and the front wall of the crowd begins to roll in like a wave.

Just then Sherburn steps out on to the roof of his little front porch, with a double-barrel gun in his hand, and takes his stand perfectly calm and deliberate, not saying a word. The racket stopped, and the wave sucked back.

Sherburn never said a word—just stood there, looking down. The stillness was awful creepy and uncomfortable. Sherburn run his eye slow along the crowd; and wherever it struck, the people tried a little to outgaze him, but they couldn't; they dropped their eyes and looked sneaky. Then pretty soon Sherburn sort of laughed; not the pleasant kind, but the kind that **3** makes you feel like when you are eating bread that's got sand in it.

Then he says, slow and scornful:

"The idea of *you* lynching anybody! It's amusing. The idea of you thinking you had pluck enough to lynch a *man!* Because you're brave enough to tar and feather poor friendless **4** cast-out women that come along here, did that make you think you had grit enough to lay your hands on a *man?* Why, a *man's* safe in the hands of ten thousand of your kind—as long as it's daytime and you're not behind him.

"Do I know you? I know you clear through. I was born **5** and raised in the South, and I've lived in the North; so I **6** know the average all around. The average man's a coward. In the North he lets anybody walk over him that wants to, and goes home and prays for a humble spirit to bear it. In the **7** South one man, all by himself, has stopped a stage full of men, in the daytime, and robbed the lot. Your newspapers call you a brave people so much that you think you *are* braver than any other people—whereas you're just *as* brave, and no braver. Why don't your juries hang murderers? Because they're afraid **8** the man's friends will shoot them in the back, in the dark—and it's just what they *would* do.

"So they always acquit; and then a *man* goes in the night, with a hundred masked cowards at his back, and lynches the rascal. Your mistake is, that you didn't bring a man with you; that's one mistake, and the other is that you didn't come in the dark, and fetch your masks. You brought *part* of a man—Buck Harkness, there—and if you hadn't had him to start you, you'd a taken it out in blowing.

"You didn't want to come. The average man don't like trouble and danger. *You* don't like trouble and danger. But if only *half* a man—like Buck Harkness, there—shouts 'Lynch him, lynch him!' you're afraid to back down—afraid you'll be found out to be what you are—*cowards*—and so you raise a yell, and hang yourselves on to that half-a-man's coat tail, and come raging up here, swearing what big things you're going to do. The pitifulest thing out is a mob; that's what an army is —a mob; they don't fight with courage that's born in them, but with courage that's borrowed from their mass, and from their officers. But a mob without any *man* at the head of it, is *beneath* pitifulness. Now the thing for *you* to do, is to

3 *not the pleasant kind, but the kind that makes you feel like when you are eating bread that's got sand in it.* This excellent simile by this master of laughter was an afterthought; in the manuscript, Twain wrote the undistinguished phrase, "not the kind of laugh you hear at the circus, but the kind that's fitten for a funeral—the kind that makes you feel crawly" (Ferguson, "Huck Finn Aborning," p. 174). Certainly eating sand in one's bread would make one feel "crawly."

4 *poor friendless cast-out women that come along here.* Twain had added in the manuscript, "lowering themselves to your level to earn a bite of bitter bread to eat" (quoted by Wecter, *Sam Clemens of Hannibal,* p. 175); but the phrase was dropped, evidently because it made their profession, prostitution, too explicit.

5 *I was born and raised in the South, and I've lived in the North.* Like the author himself. "I am a border-ruffian from the State of Missouri," Twain boasted in a talk "Plymouth Rock and the Pilgrims," delivered in Philadelphia on December 22, 1881 (in *Mark Twain's Speeches,* 1910, pp. 19–20). "I am a Connecticut Yankee by adoption. In me, you have Missouri morals, Connecticut culture; this, gentlemen, is the combination which makes the perfect man." Sherburn's speech has been criticized for being the most conspicuous part of *Huckleberry Finn* where the narrator has dropped his idiom; here the author speaks for himself. Sherburn's tone is clearly that of Twain on Southern violence in the suppressed chapter of *Life on the Mississippi* (see Chapter 11, note 3) and in "The United States of Lyncherdom" (in *A Pen Warmed-up in Hell,* pp. 180–190).

6 *I know the average all around. The average man's a coward.* In the manuscript, Twain had written, "I know the average man of the country, and the average man of the world. The average man of the world is a coward" (quoted by Blair, *Mark Twain and Huck Finn,* p. 337); but this knowledge may have been true of Mark Twain, world-traveler, but not of Colonel Sherburn of the Arkansas backwoods, so the detail was deleted.

7 *In the South one man, all by himself, has stopped a stage full of men, in the daytime, and robbed the lot.* In lamenting the want of personal courage in the average man, in the suppressed chapter of *Life on the Mississippi* (published in the 1944 Limited Editions Club edition, p. 415), Twain mentioned a similar episode: "The other day in Kentucky, a single highwayman, revolver in hand, stopped a stagecoach and robbed the passengers, some of whom were armed—and he got away unharmed. The unaverage Kentuckian, being plucky, is not afraid to attack half a dozen average Kentuckians; and his bold enterprise succeeds—probably because the average Kentuckian is like the average of the human race, not plucky, but timid." Colonel Sherburn's speech here is largely a rephrasing of Twain's argument in the suppressed passage of *Life on the Mississippi:* "Now, in every community, North and South, there is one hot-head, or a dozen, or a hundred, according to the distribution of population; the rest of the community are quiet folk. What do these hot-heads amount to, in the North? Nothing. . . . Their heads never get so hot but that they retain cold sense enough to remind them that they are among a people who will not allow themselves to be walked over by their sort; a people who, although they will not insanely hang them upon suspicion and without trial, nor try them, convict them, and then let them go, but who will give them a fair and honest chance in the courts, and if conviction follow will punish them with imprisonment or the halter.

"In the South the case is very different. The one hot-head defies the hamlet. . . . Could he come North and be the terror of a town? Such a thing is impossible. Northern resolution, backing Northern law, was too much for even the 'Molly Maguires,' powerful, numerous, and desperate as was that devilish secret organization. But it could have lived a long life in the South; for there it is not the rule for courts to hang murderers" (pp. 113–114).

The original purpose of this chapter was to attack the idea of a "solid" South for a single political party. It was suppressed, probably because its conclusion surely would have offended Twain's Southern readers: "In one thing the average Northerner seems to be in a step in advance of the average Southerner, in that he bands himself with his timid fellows to support the law (at least in the matter of murder), protect judges, juries, and witnesses, and also to secure all citizens from personal danger and from obliquy or social ostracism on account of opinion, political or religious; whereas the average Southerners do not band themselves together in these high interests, but leave them to look out for themselves unsupported; the results being unpunished murder, against the popular approval, and the decay and destruction of independent thought and action in politics" (p. 415).

Colonel Sherburn, however, does not make regional distinctions; he calls the average man everywhere a moral coward. Each suffers from what Twain defined in "The United States of Lyncherdom" (*A Pen Warmed-up in Hell*, pp. 183–184) as "man's commonest weakness, his aversion to being unpleasantly conspicuous, pointed at, shunned, as being on the unpopular side."

8 *Why don't juries hang murderers? Because they're afraid the man's friends will shoot them in the back, in the dark.* It was also true of witnesses. "The other day in Kentucky," Twain wrote in the suppressed chapter of *Life on the Mississippi* (p. 414), "a witness testified against a young man in court, and got him fined for a violation of a law. The young man went home and got his shot gun and made short work of that witness. He did not invent that method of correcting witnesses; it had been used before, in the South. Perhaps this detail accounts for the reluctance of witnesses, there, to testify; and also the reluctance for juries to convict; and perhaps, also, for the disposition of lynchers to go to their grewsome labors disguised."

9 *droop your tails and go home and crawl in a hole.* Like other cowardly animals.

10 *The crowd washed back sudden, and then broke all*

9 droop your tails and go home and crawl in a hole. If any real lynching's going to be done, it will be done in the dark, Southern fashion; and when they come they'll bring their masks, and fetch a *man* along. Now *leave*—and take your half-a-man with you"—tossing his gun up across his left arm and cocking it, when he says this.

10 The crowd washed back sudden, and then broke all apart and went tearing off every which way, and Buck Harkness he heeled it after them, looking tolerable cheap. I could a staid, if I'd a wanted to, but I didn't want to.

I went to the circus, and loafed around the back side till **11** the watchman went by, and then dived in under the tent. I

12   A DEAD HEAD.

had my twenty-dollar gold piece and some other money, but I reckoned I better save it, because there ain't no telling how soon you are going to need it, away from home and amongst strangers, that way. You can't be too careful. I ain't opposed to spending money on circuses, when there ain't no other way, but there ain't no use in *wasting* it on them.

13 It was a real bully circus. It was the splendidest sight that ever was, when they all come riding in, two and two, a gentleman and lady, side by side, the men just in their drawers and under-shirts, and no shoes nor stirrups, and resting their hands on their thighs, easy and comfortable—there must a' been twenty of them—and every lady with a lovely complexion, and perfectly beautiful, and looking just like a gang of real sure-enough queens, and dressed in clothes that cost millions of dollars, and just littered with diamonds. It was a powerful fine sight; I never see anything so lovely. And then one by one they got up and stood, and went a-weaving around the ring so gentle and wavy and graceful, the men looking ever so tall and airy and straight, with their heads bobbing and skimming along, away up there under the tent-roof, and every lady's rose-leafy dress flapping soft and silky around her hips, and she looking like the most loveliest parasol.

And then faster and faster they went, all of them dancing,

first one foot stuck out in the air and then the other, the horses leaning more and more, and the ring-master going round and round the centre-pole, cracking his whip and shouting "hi!—hi!" and the clown cracking jokes behind him; and by-and-by all hands dropped the reins, and every lady put her knuckles on her hips and every gentleman folded his arms, and then how the horses did lean over and hump themselves! And so, one after the other they all skipped off into the ring, and made the sweetest bow I ever see, and then scampered out, and everybody clapped their hands and went just about wild.

Well, all through the circus they done the most astonishing things; and all the time that clown carried on so it most killed the people. The ring-master couldn't ever say a word to him but he was back at him quick as a wink with the funniest things a body ever said; and how he ever *could* think of so many of them, and so sudden and so pat, was what I couldn't noway understand. Why, I couldn't a thought of them in a year. And by-and-by a drunk man tried to get into the ring **14** —said he wanted to ride; said he could ride as well as anybody that ever was. They argued and tried to keep him out, but he wouldn't listen, and the whole show come to a standstill. Then the people begun to holler at him and make fun of him, and that made him mad, and he begun to rip and tear; so that stirred up the people, and a lot of men begun to pile down off of the benches and swarm towards the ring, saying, "Knock him down! throw him out!" and one or two women begun to scream. So, then, the ring-master he made a little speech, and said he hoped there wouldn't be no disturbance, and if the man would promise he wouldn't make no more trouble, he would let him ride, if he thought he could stay on the horse. So everybody laughed and said all right, and the man got on. The minute he was on, the horse begun to rip and tear and jump and cavort around, with two circus men hanging on to his bridle trying to hold him, and the drunk man hanging on to his neck, and his heels flying in the air every jump, and the whole crowd of people standing up shouting and laughing till the tears rolled down. And at last, sure enough, all the circus men could do, the horse broke loose, and away he went like the very nation, round and round the ring, **15** with that sot laying down on him and hanging to his neck, with first one leg hanging most to the ground on one side, and then t'other one on t'other side, and the people just crazy. It **16** warn't funny to me, though; I was all of a tremble to see his danger. But pretty soon he struggled up astraddle and grabbed the bridle, a-reeling this way and that; and the next minute he sprung up and dropped the bridle and stood! and the horse agoing like a house afire too. He just stood up there, a-sailing around as easy and comfortable as if he warn't ever drunk in his life—and then he begun to pull off his clothes and sling them. He shed them so thick they kind of clogged up the

apart and went tearing off every which way. A similar incident takes place in Chapter 11 of *Tom Sawyer*: "The villagers had a strong desire to tar-and-feather Injun Joe and ride him on a rail, for body-snatching, but so formidable was his character that nobody could be found who was willing to take the lead in the matter, so it was dropped."

Wecter reported in *Sam Clemens of Hannibal* (p. 108) that there was nothing in Judge Clemens's depositions indicating that Owsley had suppressed a mob, and the murderer was not brought to trial until more than a year after the shooting. He was acquitted. "His party brought him huzzaing in from Palmyra at midnight," Twain recalled in some notes (*Mark Twain's Hannibal, Huck and Tom*, p. 36). "But there was a cloud upon him—a social chill—and he presently moved away."

Without being specific, Twain recalled in "The United States of Lyncherdom" (*A Pen Warmed-up in Hell*, p. 186), "When I was a boy I saw a brave gentleman deride and insult a mob and drive it away." Twain evidently believed in the great man theory of history. "A Savonarola can quell and scatter a mob of lynchers with a mere glance of his eyes," Twain argued in "The United States of Lyncherdom" (p. 186), "for no mob has any sand in the presence of a man known to be splendidly brave. Besides, a lynching mob would *like* to be scattered, for of a certainty there are never ten men in it who would not prefer to be somewhere else—and would be, if they but had the courage to go."

Twain did consider a solution to such lawlessness: Brave men such as Colonel Sherburn could be used for the public good as much as for its antagonism. Twain suggested, "Station a brave man in each affected community to encourage, support, and bring to light the deep disapproval of lynching hidden in the secret places of its heart—for it is there, beyond question. Then these communities will find something better to imitate—of course, being human, they must imitate something." The only problem was that there were so few truly brave men. Twain agreed with Marryat (see Chapter 18, note 17) that *physical* courage is not the same thing as *moral* courage; and so, "upon reflection, the scheme will not work. There are not enough morally brave men in stock. We are out of moral-courage material; we are in a condition of profound poverty."

11 *I had my twenty-dollar gold piece.* Further proof that Huck gave to Jim the other twenty-dollar gold piece the slave-hunters gave the boy in Chapter 16.

12 *a dead head.* One who is admitted to a show without paying.

13 *It was the splendidest sight that ever was.* George Mayberry in "Reading and Writing" (*The New Republic*, May 1, 1944, p. 608) has praised Huck's description of the circus riders' performance as "prose that superbly fulfills its function; here of rendering the color, pageantry, and above all the movement of a circus performance as it works upon a boy's imagination." To Mayberry, the cadences of the next two paragraphs "enforce the description of the several phases of the action": "The preliminary easy riding is suggested by the balanced construction ('two and two, and gentleman and lady, side by side . . . drawers and undershirts . . . no shoes nor stirrups . . . their hands on their thighs easy and comfortable . . .'). When the performers stand up on their horses, the phrases expand to a rolling tripartite gait ('so gentle and wavy and graceful . . . so tall and airy and straight . . . their heads bobbing and skimming along, away up there under the tent-roof, and every lady's rose-leafy dress flapping soft and silky around her hips . . .'). Then the action accelerates to a rousing climax and drops to a close while 'everybody clapped their hands and went just about wild'—in an appropriate spondiac terminal."

Although he did acknowledge that Huck's "the most loveliest parasol" is somewhat out of character, Mayberry argued that this passage was "a notable example of a kind of writing by no means American, but marked in modern American writing at its best."

14 *And by-and-by a drunk man tried to get into the ring—said he wanted to ride.* Twain describes one of the most common acts of backwoods circuses during the time. Huck's recollection is identical to that of E. W. Howe in *Plain People* (1929, pp. 46–47) who had been a boy in Missouri during the Civil War. William Dean Howells had seen the same trick during his childhood in the Ohio valley; and he described it in "Circuses and Shows" in Chapter 9 of *A Boy's Town:* "One of the most popular acts was that where a horse has been trained to misbehave, so that nobody can mount him; and after the actors have tried him, the ring-master turns to the audience, and asks if some gentleman among them wants to try it. Nobody stirs, till at last a tipsy country-jake is seen making his way down from one of the top-seats towards the ring. He can hardly walk, he is so drunk, and the clown has to help him across the ring-board, and even then he trips and rolls over on the sawdust, and has to be pulled to his feet. When they bring him up to the horse, he falls against it; and the little fellows think he will certainly get killed. . . . The ring-master and the clown manage to get the country-jake onto the broad platform on the horse's back, and then the ring-master cracks his whip, and the two supes who have been holding the horse's head let go, and the horse begins cantering round the ring. The little fellows are just sure the country-jake is going to fall off, he reels and totters so; . . . and pretty soon the country-jake begins to straighten up. He begins to unbutton his long gray overcoat, and then he takes it off and throws it into the ring, where one of the supes catches it. Then he sticks a short pipe into his mouth, and pulls on an old wool hat, and flourishes a stick that the supe throws to him, and you see that he is an Irishman just come across the sea; and then off goes another coat, and he comes out a British soldier in white duck trousers and red coat. That comes off, and he is an American sailor, with his hands on his hips, dancing a hornpipe. Suddenly away flash wig and beard and false-face, the pantaloons are stripped off with the same movement, the actor stoops for the reins lying on the horse's neck, and James Rivers, the greatest three-horse rider in the world nimbly capers on the broad pad, and kisses his hand to the shouting and cheering spectators as he dashes from the ring

HE SHED SEVENTEEN SUITS.

air, and altogether he shed seventeen suits. And then, there he was, slim and handsome, and dressed the gaudiest and prettiest you ever saw, and he lit into that horse with his whip and made him fairly hum—and finally skipped off, and made his bow and danced off to the dressing-room, and everybody just a-howling with pleasure and astonishment.

Then the ring-master he see how he had been fooled, and he *was* the sickest ring-master you ever see, I reckon. Why, it was one of his own men! He had got up that joke all out of his own head, and never let on to nobody. Well, I felt sheepish enough, to be took in so, but I wouldn't a been in that ring-master's place, not for a thousand dollars. I don't know; there may be bullier circuses than what that one was, but I never struck them yet. Anyways it was plenty good enough for *me*; and wherever I run across it, it can have all of *my* custom, every time.

Well, that night we had *our* show; but there warn't only about twelve people there; just enough to pay expenses. And **17** they laughed all the time, and that made the duke mad; and everybody left, anyway, before the show was over, but one boy which was asleep. So the duke said these Arkansaw lunkheads **18** couldn't come up to Shakspeare; what they wanted was low comedy—and maybe something ruther worse than low comedy, he reckoned. He said he could size their style. So next morning he got some big sheets of wrapping-paper and some black paint, and drawed off some handbills and stuck them up all over the village. The bills said:

The "drunk" rider. Illustration by Farny, *A Boy's Town* by William Dean Howells, *Harper's Young People*, June 3, 1890. *Courtesy the Library of Congress.*

past the braying and bellowing brass-band into the dressing-room!"

This famous circus trick was used elsewhere by American humorists, notably in "Great Attraction!" in Thompson's *Chronicles of Pineville* (pp. 11–38), and in "The Expensive Treat of Colonel Moses Grice" in Richard Malcolm Johnston's *Dukesborough Tales* (1871) which was reprinted in *Mark Twain's Library of Humor* (1888, pp. 206–222).

15 *like the very nation.* Like the Devil, from "damnation."

16 *It warn't funny to me, though.* What distinguishes Huck's recollection from other accounts of this famous circus act are the audience's reactions to the drunk's difficulties: They are upset, first by his disrupting the show and then by his angry words; they only laugh when it looks as if any minute he may fall off the horse.

17 *they laughed all the time . . .; and everybody left, anyway, before the show was over.* Obviously the "broad-sword conflict in Richard III" seemed rather tame after the shooting of Boggs by Sherburn.

Wecter in *Sam Clemens of Hannibal* (pp. 188–189) noted how similar the king and duke's Romeo and Juliet is to another account of a dreary backwoods performance, "The —— Troupe," published in Orion Clemens's *Hannibal Journal* (March 18, 1852): "All the little boys in town gazed on the groups of astonishing pictures which appeared on the . . . bills, and were thereby wrought up to an intense pitch of excitement. It was to be a real theatre, and the 'troupe' (which nobody had ever heard of before) was so 'celebrated.' Well, the momentous evening came.

Those who enjoyed the felicity of paying a quarter, to see the show, found a large man on the first story, who received the money, and a small man at the top of the second pair of steps, who received the tickets . . . the very persons who afterwards transformed into heros and soldiers by the power of paint. In the hall we found forty or fifty of our citizens, sitting in front of a striped curtain, behind which was all the mysterious paraphernalia of the theatre.

"When the curtain was pulled to one side, the first appearance on the stage was the large man. . . . He was evidently a novice, and acted his part about as you have seen boys, in a thespian society. He was intended to be a lover of the distinguished danseuse, who played the part of a miss in short dresses, though her apparent age would have justified her in wearing them longer, and we have seen spectacles on younger people. Then the small man . . . made up the third character in this burlesque of a farce, the dullness of which was not revealed even by the disgusting blackguardisms with which it was so profusely interlarded."

Surely this backwoods audience was as disappointed with this poor performance as were the Bricksville citizens by their celebrated company's presentation of the bombastic duke as "Romeo" and the old king as "Juliet."

18 *low comedy.* In the manuscript, Twain wrote that the duke "judged he could cater to their base instincts" (quoted by DeVoto, *Mark Twain at Work*, p. 84); but this phrase was dropped, evidently as being too suggestive of the nature of the subsequent performance of "David Garrick the Younger" and "Edmund Kean the Elder."

19 *THE KING'S CAMELOPARD*. A "camelopard," or "Cameleopard" is an archaic name for giraffe; even before this use, it described a mythical beast of the size of a camel and spotted like a leopard. Blair in *Mark Twain and Huck Finn* (pp. 319–320) has suggested that Twain knew Edgar Allan Poe's "Four Beasts in One; of the Homocameleopard" (first published in *Southern Literary Messenger*, March 1836, and reprinted in his *Tales of the Grotesque and Arabesque*, 1845). It describes a disgusting public exhibition by Antiochus Epiphanes, Antiochus the Illustrious, king of Syria, and the most potent of all the aristocrats of the East. To celebrate his having killed by his own hand one thousand Jews, the tyrant appears before his barbaric people, worshipers of a baboon god, "ensconced in the hide of a beast, and is doing his best to play the part of a cameleopard; but this is done for the better sustaining his dignity as king." "With how superior a dignity," Poe continued, "the monarch perambulates on all fours! His tail, you perceive, is held aloft by his two principal concubines . . . ; and his whole appearance would be infinitely prepossessing, were it not for the protuberance of his eyes, which will certainly start out of his head, and the queer color of his face, which has become nondescript from the quantity of wine he has swallowed." Certainly Twain would have been amused by Poe's mocking account of so bestial a monarch; and perhaps something of this performance inspired the king's "tragedy" in the subsequent chapter.

20 *THE ROYAL NONESUCH*. A "nonesuch" is something unmatched and unrivaled. Originally the title of the duke's "thrilling tragedy" was "The Burning Shame," but as it was a particularly scandalous show, Twain obviously thought it best to use another name. He acknowledged in Chapter 27 of his *Autobiography* that he had first heard it through his friend Jim Gillis up in the mining camp in Nevada; and as early as 1877, Twain intended to describe it, in a projected novel about his brother Orion. "I had to modify it considerably to make it proper for print," he admitted in his *Autobiography* of its use in *Huckleberry Finn*, "and this was a great damage. As Jim told it, inventing it as he went along, I think it was one of the most outrageously funny things I have ever listened to. How mild it is in the book and how pale; how extravagant and how gorgeous in its unprintable form!" See Chapter 23, note 1.

21 *Admission 50 cents*. Note the irony that the price of admission to this "low comedy" is twice that to the "Shaksperean Revival."

AT THE COURT HOUSE!

FOR 3 NIGHTS ONLY!

The World-Renowned Tragedians

DAVID GARRICK THE YOUNGER!

AND

EDMUND KEAN THE ELDER!

Of the London and Continental Theatres,

In their Thrilling Tragedy of

19 THE KING'S CAMELOPARD

OR

20 THE ROYAL NONESUCH!!!

21 *Admission 50 cents.*

Then at the bottom was the biggest line of all—which said:

LADIES AND CHILDREN NOT ADMITTED

"There," says he, "if that line don't fetch them, I don't know Arkansaw!"

Chapter XXIII

TRAGEDY.

Well, all day him and the king was hard at it, rigging up a stage, and a curtain, and a row of candles for foot-lights; and that night the house was jam full of men in no time. When the place couldn't hold no more, the duke he quit tending door and went around the back way and come on to the stage and stood up before the curtain, and made a little speech, and praised up this tragedy, and said it was the most thrillingest one that ever was; and so he went on a-bragging about the tragedy, and about Edmund Kean the Elder, which was to play the main principal part in it; and at last when he'd got everybody's expectations up high enough, he rolled up the curtain, and the next minute the king come a-prancing out on all fours, naked; and he was painted all over, ring-streaked-and-striped, all sorts of colors, as splendid as a rainbow. And— but never mind the rest of his outfit, it was just wild, but it **1** was awful funny. The people most killed themselves laughing;

1 *but never mind the rest of his outfit, it was just wild, but it was awful funny.* But what exactly was "The Burning Shame" (a.k.a. "The Royal Nonesuch")? Robert Bridges in his review of the novel in *Life* (February 26, 1885, p. 119) identified it as "a polite version of the 'Giascutus' story," a hoax which by the late nineteenth century had entered American comic lore. The tale was frequently reprinted in books, newspapers, and magazines throughout the century; an early appearance was in the Palmyra, Missouri, *Whig* on October 9, 1845, but Twain could have read it in countless other versions. The *Whig* account relates how two broke Yankee clock-peddlers, roaming through the South, are "determined to take advantage of the passion for shows which possessed our people"; and to get some quick cash, they decide that one should "personate a rare beast, for which they invented the name of 'Gyascutus,' while the other was to be keeper or showman." In the next town, they tack up playbills, advertising their prey as "captured . . . in the wilds of the Arostook . . . more ferocious and terrible than the gnu, the hyena, or ant-eater of the African desert! Admittance 25 cents, children and servants half price." An eager crowd pays to enter the hall and view beneath the curtain "four horrible feet, which to less excited fancies would have born a wonderful resemblance to the feet and hands of a live Yankee, with strips of coonskin sewed round his wrists and ankles." While the hidden creature growls, the keeper begins his lecture on the beast's ferocity all the while poking it behind the curtain with a stick. Suddenly, it gives out a tremendous roar, and the man cries out in terror, "Ladies and gentlemen—*save yourselves—the Gyascutus is loose!*" "Pell-mell, hurly-burly, screaming, leaping,

223

crowding, the terrified spectators roll out"; and the two Yankees escape with their loot out the rear exit. (See Wecter, *Sam Clemens of Hannibal*, pp. 187–188; and Blair, *Mark Twain and Huck Finn*, p. 318).

This hoax certainly has much in common with "The Royal Nonesuch," but there is nothing in it that Twain need have suppressed. Obviously, as suggested by his bestial appearance, the king performed some obscene tricks. Daniel P. Mannix, the author of *Step Right Up!* (1951), has described an act "for men only" that he saw while working with a sideshow during the Depression: "A man comes out and explains he is going to present a trained dog act. Maybe they aren't interested in trained dogs? Well, they'll be interested in this one. He then calls. Off stage come barks and whines. Finally, the man exits and returns dragging a naked girl who is on all fours. She is generally painted in some way as with spots to represent a Dalmatian. The man tells her to sit up and beg, roll over, play dead, etc. Whenever he stops to address the 'tip' (the crowd), the girl goes over and, raising one leg pretends to urinate on him whereupon he indignantly kicks her away. This is used as a running gag throughout the show: "The girl goes through the motions of defecating, afterwards scratching with her hind legs. The man tells her there's a rat in the corner and she goes after it, wiggling her backside as she scratches in the corner. As a climax, the man calls on another dog which is invisible. He says this one is female. The girl goes through the motions of sniffing the imaginary dog's backside and then gets excited and pretends to mount him, going through the motions of breeding. The man tells her that that isn't nice and tries to get the invisible dog away from her but the girl holds on. In his efforts, the man falls to his hands and knees whereupon the girl mounts him and starts to breed him. Still crawling, the man exits, yelling for help and carrying the girl with him." Such a role as the trained dog could be played easily by an old man as by a girl; and such a show is unquestionably "something ruther worse than low comedy."

Wallace Graves in "Mark Twain's 'Burning Shame'" (*Nineteenth-Century Fiction*, June 1968, p. 98) has recorded a less extravagant performance than the trained dog act, but the tale Graves first heard in the 1930s closely follows the account in *Huckleberry Finn*: "It was about two destitute traveling actors [in Sweden] who decided to raise some money by giving a performance in a small town. Women and children were not admitted; they rigged a stage with a curtain, and made sure that an escape door at the rear of the stage was open for a quick getaway after the show. One man collected money while the audience filed in, then came round and appeared before the curtain announcing that a great dramatic play called 'The Burning Shame' was about to be shown. The curtain was then raised, and his partner, naked, came out on his hands and knees. The other said, 'And now, gentlemen, you are about to see The Tragedy of the Burning Shame.' He inserted a candle in the naked man's posterior, and lit it. When nothing further happened, the audience shouted for something more; the man said the performance was over; the viewers shouted, 'You mean, that's all?' 'Yes,' the man said,

and when the king got done capering, and capered off behind the scenes, they roared and clapped and stormed and haw-hawed till he come back and done it over again; and after that, they made him do it another time. Well, it would a made a cow laugh to see the shines that old idiot cut.

Then the duke he lets the curtain down, and bows to the people, and says the great tragedy will be performed only two nights more, on accounts of pressing London engagements, where the seats is all sold aready for it in Drury Lane; and then he makes them another bow, and says if he has succeeded in pleasing them and instructing them, he will be deeply obleeged if they will mention it to their friends and get them to come and see it.

Twenty people sings out:

"What, is it over? Is that *all*?"

The duke says "yes." Then there was a fine time. Every-

2 body sings out "sold," and rose up mad, and was agoing for that stage and them tragedians. But a big, fine-looking man jumps up on a bench, and shouts:

"Hold on! Just a word, gentlemen." They stopped to listen. "We are sold—mighty badly sold. But we don't want to be the laughing-stock of this whole town, I reckon, and never hear the last of this thing as long as we live. *No*. What we want, is to go out of here quiet, and talk this show up, and sell the *rest* of the town! Then we'll all be in the same boat.

3 Ain't that sensible?" ("You bet it is!—the jedge is right!"

4 everybody sings out.) "All right, then—not a word about any sell. Go along home, and advise everybody to come and see the tragedy."

Next day you couldn't hear nothing around that town but how splendid that show was. House was jammed again, that night, and we sold this crowd the same way. When me and the king and the duke got home to the raft, we all had a supper; and by-and-by, about midnight, they made Jim and me back her out and float her down the middle of the river and fetch her in and hide her about two mile below town.

The third night the house was crammed again—and they warn't new-comers, this time, but people that was at the show the other two nights. I stood by the duke at the door, and I see that every man that went in had his pockets bulging, or something muffled up under his coat—and I see it warn't no perfumery neither, not by a long sight. I smelt sickly eggs by

5 the barrel, and rotten cabbages, and such things; and if I know the signs of a dead cat being around, and I bet I do, there was sixty-four of them went in. I shoved in there for a minute,

6 but it was too various for me, I couldn't stand it. Well, when the place couldn't hold no more people, the duke he give a fellow a quarter and told him to tend door for him a minute, and then he started around for the stage door, I after him; but the minute we turned the corner and was in the dark, he says:

"Walk fast, now, till you get away from the houses, and then shin for the raft like the dickens was after you!"

THEIR POCKETS BULGED.

I done it, and he done the same. We struck the raft at the same time, and in less than two seconds we was gliding down stream, all dark and still, and edging towards the middle of the river, nobody saying a word. I reckoned the poor king was in for a gaudy time of it with the audience; but nothing of the sort; pretty soon he crawls out from under the wigwam, and says:

"Well, how'd the old thing pan out this time, Duke?"

He hadn't been up town at all.

We never showed a light till we was about ten mile below that village. Then we lit up and had a supper, and the king and the duke fairly laughed their bones loose over the way they'd served them people. The duke says:

"Greenhorns, flatheads! *I* knew the first house would keep mum and let the rest of the town get roped in; and I knew they'd lay for us the third night, and consider it was *their* turn now. Well, it *is* their turn, and I'd give something to know how much they take for it. I *would* just like to know how they're putting in their opportunity. They can turn it into a picnic if they want to—they brought plenty provisions."

Them rapscallions took in four hundred and sixty-five dollars in that three nights. I never see money hauled in by the wagon-load like that, before.

By-and-by, when they was asleep and snoring, Jim says:

"Don't it 'sprise you, de way dem kings carries on, Huck?"

"No," I says, "it don't."

"Why don't it, Huck?"

"Well, it don't, because it's in the breed. I reckon they're all alike."

"But, Huck, dese kings o' ourn is regular rapscallions;

'have you ever seen a better example of a 'Burning Shame'?' Then the two dashed out of town, the audience in hot pursuit." However, Graves does not question if his version was that known to Twain, or whether it was inspired by the famous unrevealed scene in *Huckleberry Finn*.

2 *"sold."* Cheated, deceived, taken in. Evidently these rough backwoodsmen are so fired up for something even worse than the king's obscene performance that they feel that they have not received their money's worth of entertainment from which women and children are barred.

3 *the jedge.* Obviously even the most prominent gentlemen of this Arkansas town could not resist the biggest line of all, "LADIES AND CHILDREN NOT ADMITTED."

4 *All right, then—not a word about any sell.* The "sell" of the Bricksville loafers is similar to that of some other townspeople in one of Twain's earliest sketches, "Historical Exhibition—A No. 1 Ruse" by "W. Epaninondas Adrastus Blab" (Hannibal *Daily Journal*, September 16, 1852; reprinted in *Early Tales and Sketches*, Vol. 1, 1979, pp. 79–82): A store advertises a show of some kind called "Bonaparte crossing the Rhine" as "one dime per head, children half price"; but "everybody who saw the sight seemed seized with a sudden fit of melancholy immediately afterwards" and "the uninitiated could get nothing out of him on the subject; he was mum." Finally, a little boy named Jim views the spectacle: a hog's bone (the "Bony-part") across a bacon rind (the "Rhine"). "Young man," the entrepreneur addresses the boy, "I am anxious . . . that you should be entirely satisfied with the exhibition . . .; and if it has met with favor in your eyes, I shall hold myself under the greatest obligations (with a profound bow), if you will use your influence in forwarding the cause of learning and knowledge (another bow), by inviting your friends to step in when they pass this way. What, may I ask, is your opinion of the exhibition?" Slowly, Jim replies, "Sold!—cheap . . . as . . . dirt!"

5 *if I know the signs of a dead cat being around, and I bet I do.* Twain harkens back to the introduction of Huckleberry Finn in Chapter 6 of *Tom Sawyer* where the "juvenile pariah of the village" is seen dragging a dead cat with which to cure warts.

6 *too various.* Too many varieties of offensive odors; overwhelming. Richard Watson Gilder could not stand it either; he dropped the references to the "dead cats" and "too various" from "Royalty on the Mississippi" in *The Century*.

7 *Saxon heptarchies.* A "heptarchy" is a government of seven persons, or an alliance of seven kingdoms, each with its own ruler. Huck vaguely recalls the Anglo-Saxon heptarchy in England, 449–828 A.D.

8 *He used to marry a new wife every day, and chop off her head next morning.* Actually Henry VIII had only six wives (two of whom he had beheaded), certainly enough for any monarch, but Huck has garbled the English king's life with *The Arabian Nights' Entertainment* in which King Shahriyar daily marries a new wife who is executed the next morning.

9 *Nell Gwynn. . . . Jane Shore. . . . Fair Rosamun.* Although all of these ladies were mistresses of English kings, none of them was wife to Henry VIII, who reigned from 1509 to 1547. Nell Gwynne was the concubine of Charles II (reigned 1660–1685); Jane Shore that of Edward IV (1461–1470 and 1471–1483); and "Fair" Rosamund Clifford was said to be that of Henry II (1154–1189), whose jealous queen supposedly had her murdered.

Nell Gwynn. *Courtesy the Library of Congress.*

Jane Shore. *Courtesy the Picture Collection, The New York Public Library, Astor, Lenox, and Tilden Foundations.*

dat's jist what dey is; dey's reglar rapscallions."

"Well, that's what I'm a-saying; all kings is mostly rapscallions, as fur as I can make out."

"Is dat so?"

"You read about them once—you'll see. Look at Henry the Eight; this'n 's a Sunday-School Superintendent to *him*. And look at Charles Second, and Louis Fourteen, and Louis Fifteen, and James Second, and Edward Second, and Richard **7** Third, and forty more; besides all them Saxon heptarchies that used to rip around so in old times and raise Cain. My, you ought to seen old Henry the Eight when he was in **8** bloom. He *was* a blossom. He used to marry a new wife every day, and chop off her head next morning. And he would do it just as indifferent as if he was ordering up eggs. **9** 'Fetch up Nell Gwynn,' he says. They fetch her up. Next morning, 'Chop off her head!' And they chop it off. 'Fetch up Jane Shore,' he says; and up she comes. Next morning 'Chop off her head'—and they chop it off. 'Ring up Fair Rosamun.' Fair Rosamun answers the bell. Next morning, **10** 'Chop off her head.' And he made every one of them tell him a tale every night; and he kept that up till he had hogged a thousand and one tales that way, and then he put them all in a **11** book, and called it Domesday Book—which was a good name and stated the case. You don't know kings, Jim, but I know them; and this old rip of ourn is one of the cleanest I've struck in history. Well, Henry he takes a notion he wants to get up some trouble with this country. How does he go at it —give notice?—give the country a show? No. All of a

HENRY THE EIGHTH IN BOSTON HARBOUR.

sudden he heaves all the tea in Boston Harbor overboard, and whacks out a declaration of independence, and dares them to come on. That was *his* style—he never give anybody a chance. He had suspicions of his father, the Duke of Wellington. Well, **12** what did he do?—ask him to show up? No—drownded him in a butt of mamsey, like a cat. S'pose people left money laying around where he was—what did he do? He collared it. S'pose he contracted to do a thing; and you paid him, and didn't set down there and see that he done it—what did he do? He always done the other thing. S'pose he opened his mouth —what then? If he didn't shut it up powerful quick, he'd lose a lie, every time. That's the kind of a bug Henry was; and if we'd a had him along 'stead of our kings, he'd a fooled that town a heap worse than ourn done. I don't say that ourn is lambs, because they ain't, when you come right down to the cold facts; but they ain't nothing to *that* old ram, anyway. All I say is, kings is kings, and you got to make allowances. Take them all around, they're a mighty ornery lot. It's the way they're raised."

"But dis one do *smell* so like de nation, Huck."

"Well, they all do, Jim. We can't help the way a king smells; history don't tell no way."

"Now de duke, he's a tolerble likely man, in some ways."

"Yes, a duke's different. But not very different. This one's a middling hard lot for a duke. When he's drunk, there ain't no near-sighted man could tell him from a king."

"Well, anyways, I doan' hanker for no mo' un um, Huck. Dese is all I kin stan'."

"It's the way I feel, too, Jim. But we've got them on our hands, and we got to remember what they are, and make allowances. Sometimes I wish we could hear of a country that's out of kings."

What was the use to tell Jim these warn't real kings and dukes? It wouldn't a done no good; and besides, it was just as I said; you couldn't tell them from the real kind.

I went to sleep, and Jim didn't call me when it was my turn. He often done that. When I waked up, just at daybreak, he was setting there with his head down betwixt his knees, moaning and mourning to himself. I didn't take notice, nor let on. I knowed what it was about. He was thinking about his wife and his children, away up yonder, and he was low and homesick; because he hadn't ever been away from home before in his life; and I do believe he cared just as much for his people as white folks does for ther'n. It don't seem natural, but I reckon it's so. He was often moaning and mourning that way, nights, when he judged I was asleep, and saying, "Po' little 'Lizabeth! po' little Johnny! it's mighty hard; I spec' I ain't ever gwyne to see you no mo', no mo'!" He was a mighty good nigger, Jim was.

But this time I somehow got to talking to him about his wife and young ones; and by-and-by he says:

"Fair Rosamund" Clifford. *Courtesy the Picture Collection, The New York Public Library, Astor, Lenox, and Tilden Foundations.*

10 *And he made every one of them tell him a tale every night; and he kept that up till he had hogged a thousand and one tales that way, and then he put them all in a book, and called it Domesday Book.* A further misreading of *The Arabian Nights' Entertainment* (subtitled *One Thousand and One Nights*) in which the king makes each of his wives tell him before retiring to bed some diverting tale to save her life, but none succeeds until Scheherazade so enchants him with her stories for one thousand and one nights that he decides not to have her executed; the summer he completed *Huckleberry Finn*, Twain wrote a dull burlesque "1,002nd Arabian Night" which Howells advised he not publish (but it was included in *Mark Twain's Satires and Burlesques*, pp. 91–133). The Domesday Book is the record of the Great Inquest, a survey of lands ordered by William the Conqueror in 1086.

11 *which was a good name and stated the case.* Huck reads "Domesday" as "Doomsday," or the day of reckoning. In the manuscript, Twain had written, "and he kept that up till he had hogged a thousand and one tales that way, and then he got out a copyright and published them all in a book, and called it Domesday Book—which was a good name and stated the case. Of course most any publisher would do that, but you wouldn't think a king would. If you didn't know kings" (Ferguson, "Huck Finn Aborning," p. 174); but knowledge of copyright is out of character for this backwoods boy, so the observation was struck out in the galleys.

12 *He had suspicions of his father, the Duke of Wellington. . . . drownded him in a butt of mamsey, like a cat.* Huck confuses the Duke of Wellington (1769–1852), the hero of the Battle of Waterloo in 1812, with George Duke of Clarence (1449–1478), who was secretly killed in the Bowyer's Tower by being drowned in a butt of malmsey, a sweet, strong wine, on the orders of his brother Edward IV. Shakespeare somewhat jovially reconstructed the murder in *Richard III*, Act I, scene iv, lines 84–280.

13 *it mine me er de time I treat my little 'Lizabeth so ornery.* The source of Jim's abuse of his little girl was an anecdote Twain once jotted down: "L. A. punished her child several days for refusing to answer and inattention (5 year old) then while punishing discovered it was deaf and dumb! (from scarlet fever). It showed no reproachfulness for the whippings—kissed the punisher and showed non-comprehension of what it was all about" (quoted by DeVoto, *Mark Twain at Work*, p. 67). "L. A." has not been identified. On another occasion, Twain considered writing "some rhymes about the little child whose mother boxed its ears for inattention and presently when it did not notice the heavy slamming of a door, perceived that it was deaf" (in *Mark Twain's Notebooks and Journals*, Vol. II, 1975, p. 510). So expertly does Twain relate this potentially sentimental scene that Jim still earns the modern reader's sympathy.

14 *de Lord God Amighty.* Perhaps to divert Olivia or some pious proofreader, Twain wrote in the margin of the manuscript, "This expression shall not be changed" (quoted by DeVoto, *Mark Twain at Work*, p. 82).

" What makes me feel so bad dis time, 'uz bekase I hear sumpn over yonder on de bank like a whack, er a slam, while **13** ago, en it mine me er de time I treat my little 'Lizabeth so ornery. She warn't on'y 'bout fo' year ole, en she tuck de sk'yarlet-fever, en had a powful rough spell; but she got well, en one day she was a-stannin' aroun', en I says to her, I says:

" ' Shet de do'.'

" She never done it; jis' stood dah, kiner smilin' up at me. It make me mad; en I says agin, mighty loud, I says:

" ' Doan' you hear me?—shet de do'!'

" She jis' stood de same way, kiner smilin' up. I was a-bilin'! I says:

" ' I lay I *make* you mine!'

" En wid dat I fetch' her a slap side de head dat sont her a-sprawlin'. Den I went into de yuther room, en 'uz gone 'bout ten minutes; en when I come back, dah was dat do' a-stannin' open *yit*, en dat chile stannin' mos' right in it, a-lookin' down and mournin', en de tears runnin' down. My, but I *wuz* mad, I was agwyne for de chile, but jis' den—it was a do' dat open innerds—jis' den, 'long come de wind en slam it to, behine de chile, ker-*blam!*—en my lan', de chile never move'! My breff mos' hop outer me; en I feel so—so—I doan' know *how* I feel. I crope out, all a-tremblin', en crope aroun' en open de do' easy en slow, en poke my head in behine de chile, sof' en still, en all uv a sudden, I says *pow!* jis' as loud as I could yell. *She never budge!* Oh, Huck, I bust out a-cryin' en grab her up in my arms, en say, ' Oh, de po' little thing! **14** de Lord God Amighty fogive po' ole Jim, kaze he never gwyne to fogive hisself as long's he live!' Oh, she was plumb deef en dumb, Huck, plumb deef en dumb—en I'd ben a-treat'n her so!"

Chapter XXIV

Blk Arab — Wll harmless when not out of his Head

HARMLESS.

Next day, towards night, we laid up under a little willow tow-head out in the middle, where there **1** was a village on each side of the river, and the duke and the king begun to lay out a plan for working them towns. Jim he spoke to the duke, and said he hoped it wouldn't take but a few hours, because it got mighty heavy and tiresome to him when he had to lay all day in the wigwam tied with the rope. You see, when we left him all alone we had to tie him, because if anybody happened on him all by himself and not tied, it wouldn't look much like he was a runaway nigger, you know. So the duke said it *was* kind of **2** hard to have to lay roped all day, and he'd cipher out some way to get around it.

He was uncommon bright, the duke was, and he soon struck it. He dressed Jim up in King Lear's outfit—it was a long curtain-calico gown, and a white horse-hair wig and whiskers; and then he took his theatre-paint and painted Jim's face and hands and ears and neck all over a dead dull solid blue, like a man that's been drownded nine days. Blamed if he warn't the

1 *there was a village on each side of the river*. Apparently they have drifted so far down the river that Arkansas is now on one side and Mississippi on the other.

2 *the duke said it* was *kind of hard to have to lay roped all day*. Although a scoundrel, the duke still seems to be "a tolerable likely man, in some ways," as Jim said in the last chapter. But not so the king.

"Hop out of the wigwam and carry on a little."
Illustration by E. W. Kemble, New York *World*,
December 10, 1899.

3 *Sick Arab—but harmless when not out of his head.* The duke may be thinking of Othello, Shakespeare's Moor, who murders his wife in a jealous rage; he has already dressed Jim in the clothes of another mad nobleman, King Lear.

4 *he looked considerable more than that.* In the manuscript, Twain had written exactly what Huck meant: "He looked like he was mortified" (Ferguson, "Huck Finn Aborning," p. 179).

5 *white beaver.* A tall hat, made out of white beaver fur; Kemble missed this detail, for he gives the king a black hat.

6 *he looked that grand and good and pious that you'd say he had walked right out of the ark, and maybe was old Leviticus himself.* Because the king now looks like a minister to Huck, the boy struggles to find an appropriate biblical metaphor but only garbles the story of Noah and the Ark in Genesis 6:15–9:17 with the name of a later book of the Old Testament; the reference to the ark was an afterthought, because the manuscript reads, "He had walked right out of the Bible" (Ferguson, "Huck Finn Aborning," p. 179).

horriblest looking outrage I ever see.   Then the duke took and wrote out a sign on a shingle so—

3   *Sick Arab—but harmless when not out of his head.*

And he nailed that shingle to a lath, and stood the lath up four or five foot in front of the wigwam.   Jim was satisfied. He said it was a sight better than laying tied a couple of years every day and trembling all over every time there was a sound. The duke told him to make himself free and easy, and if anybody ever come meddling around, he must hop out of the wigwam, and carry on a little, and fetch a howl or two like a wild beast, and he reckoned they would light out and leave him alone.   Which was sound enough judgment; but you take the average man, and he wouldn't wait for him to howl.   Why, **4** he didn't only look like he was dead, he looked considerable more than that.

These rapscallions wanted to try the Nonesuch again, because there was so much money in it, but they judged it wouldn't be safe, because maybe the news might a worked along down by this time.   They couldn't hit no project that suited, exactly; so at last the duke said he reckoned he'd lay off and work his brains an hour or two and see if he couldn't put up something on the Arkansaw village; and the king he allowed he would drop over to t'other village, without any plan, but just trust in Providence to lead him the profitable way— meaning the devil, I reckon.   We had all bought store clothes where we stopped last; and now the king put his'n on, and he told me to put mine on.   I done it, of course.   The king's duds was all black, and he did look real swell and starchy.   I never knowed how clothes could change a body before.   Why, before, he looked like the orneriest old rip that ever was; but now, **5** when he'd take off his new white beaver and make a bow and **6** do a smile, he looked that grand and good and pious that you'd say he had walked right out of the ark, and maybe was old Leviticus himself.   Jim cleaned up the canoe, and I got my paddle ready.   There was a big steamboat laying at the shore away up under the point, about three mile above town— been there a couple of hours, taking on freight.   Says the king:

"Seein' how I'm dressed, I reckon maybe I better arrive down from St. Louis or Cincinnati, or some other big place. Go for the steamboat, Huckleberry; we'll come down to the village on her."

I didn't have to be ordered twice, to go and take a steamboat ride.   I fetched the shore a half a mile above the village, and then went scooting along the bluff bank in the easy water. Pretty soon we come to a nice innocent-looking young country jake setting on a log swabbing the sweat off of his face, for it was powerful warm weather; and he had a couple of big carpetbags by him.

"Run her nose in shore," says the king.   I done it.   "Wher' you bound for, young man?"

"For the steamboat; going to Orleans."

" Git aboard," says the king. " Hold on a minute, my servant 'll he'p you with them bags. Jump out and he'p the gentleman, Adolphus "—meaning me, I see.

ADOLPHUS.

I done so, and then we all three started on again. The
young chap was mighty thankful; said it was tough work
toting his baggage such weather. He asked the king where
he was going, and the king told him he'd come down the river
and landed at the other village this morning, and now he was
going up a few mile to see an old friend on a farm up there.
The young fellow says :

" When I first see you, I says to myself, ' It's Mr. Wilks,
sure, and he come mighty near getting here in time.' But
then I says again, ' No, I reckon it ain't him, or else he
wouldn't be paddling up the river.' You *ain't* him, are you ? "

" No, my name's Blodgett—Elexander Blodgett—*Reverend*
Elexander Blodgett, I s'pose I must say, as I'm one o' the
Lord's poor servants. But still I'm jist as able to be sorry
for Mr. Wilks for not arriving in time, all the same, if he's
missed anything by it—which I hope he hasn't."

" Well, he don't miss any property by it, because he'll get
that all right; but he's missed seeing his brother Peter die—
which he mayn't mind, nobody can tell as to that—but his
brother would a give anything in this world to see *him* before
he died; never talked about nothing else all these three weeks;
hadn't seen him since they was boys together—and hadn't ever
seen his brother William at all—that's the deef and dumb one
—William ain't more than thirty or thirty-five. Peter and
George was the only ones that come out here; George was the
married brother; him and his wife both died last year.
Harvey and William's the only ones that's left now; and, as I
was saying, they haven't got here in time."

" Did anybody send 'em word ? "

" Oh, yes; a month or two ago, when Peter was first took;
because Peter said then that he sorter felt like he warn't going
to get well this time. You see, he was pretty old, and George's
g'yirls was too young to be much company for him, except Mary

7 *I'm going in a ship, . . . for Ryo Janeero.* Here Twain was likely recalling his own youthful ambitions. "I had been reading Lieutenant Herndon's account of his explorations of the Amazon," he wrote in Chapter 20 of his *Autobiography*, "and had been mightily attracted by what he said of coca. I made up my mind that I would go to the headwaters of the Amazon and collect coca and trade in it and make a fortune. I left for New Orleans in the steamer *Paul Jones* with this great idea filling my mind." But he never made it to South America. "When I got to New Orleans," he continued, "I inquired about ships leaving for Pará and discovered that there weren't any and learned that there probably wouldn't be any during that century. It had not occurred to me to inquire about these particulars before leaving Cincinnati, so there I was. I couldn't get to the Amazon." Fortunately, he had met one of the pilots of the *Paul Jones* and arranged in New Orleans to learn the trade under him.

8 *Joanna's . . . the one that gives herself to good works and has a hare-lip.* A "hare-lip" is a congenitally deformed lip, usually the upper one, in which there is a vertical fissure causing it to resemble the cleft lip of a rabbit; it was once believed to be caused by the mother's being frightened by a hare while pregnant. The young man has reversed the cause and the effect: Because a hare-lip was considered unattractive, Joanna must devote her life to helping others, by visiting and praying with the sick and the unconverted, and by distributing tracts, medicines, and food.

9 *a dissentering minister.* An English Protestant minister (usually a Congregationalist, Baptist, or Presbyterian) who dissents from the Church of England.

10 *she's a big Orleans boat.* "The New Orleans steamboats are a very different description of vessels to any I had yet seen," wrote Thomas Hamilton in *Men and Manners in America* (Vol. 2, 1833, pp. 180–181). "They are of great size, and the object being to carry as large a cargo as possible, the whole vessel . . . is devoted to this purpose, and the cabins for the passengers are raised in successive tiers above the main deck. . . . These vessels have very much the appearance of three-deckers, and many of them are upwards of 500 tons burden."

A New Orleans steamboat. Illustration by A. Hervieu, *Domestic Manners of the Americans* by Mrs. Frances Trollope, 1832. *Courtesy the General Research and Humanities Division, The New York Public Library, Astor, Lenox, and Tilden Foundations.*

Jane the red-headed one; and so he was kinder lonesome after George and his wife died, and didn't seem to care much to live. He most desperately wanted to see Harvey—and William too, for that matter—because he was one of them kind that can't bear to make a will. He left a letter behind for Harvey, and said he'd told in it where his money was hid, and how he wanted the rest of the property divided up so George's g'yirls would be all right—for George didn't leave nothing. And that letter was all they could get him to put a pen to."

"Why do you reckon Harvey don't come? Wher' does he live?"

"Oh, he lives in England—Sheffield—preaches there—hasn't ever been in this country. He hasn't had any too much time—and besides he mightn't a got the letter at all, you know."

"Too bad, too bad he couldn't a lived to see his brothers, poor soul. You going to Orleans, you say?"

7   "Yes, but that ain't only a part of it. I'm going in a ship, next Wednesday, for Ryo Janeero, where my uncle lives."

"It's a pretty long journey. But it'll be lovely; I wisht I was agoing. Is Mary Jane the eldest? How old is the others?"

8   "Mary Jane's nineteen, Susan's fifteen, and Joanna's about fourteen—that's the one that gives herself to good works and has a hare-lip."

"Poor things! to be left alone in the cold world so."

"Well, they could be worse off. Old Peter had friends, and they ain't going to let them come to no harm. There's Hobson, the Babtis' preacher; and Deacon Lot Hovey, and Ben Rucker, and Abner Shackleford, and Levi Bell, the lawyer; and Dr. Robinson, and their wives, and the widow Bartley, and—well, there's a lot of them; but these are the ones that Peter was thickest with, and used to write about sometimes, when he wrote home; so Harvey 'll know where to look for friends when he get's here."

Well, the old man he went on asking questions till he just fairly emptied that young fellow. Blamed if he didn't inquire about everybody and everything in that blessed town, and all about all the Wilkses; and about Peter's business—which was a tanner; and about George's—which was a carpenter; and

9 about Harvey's—which was a dissentering minister; and so on, and so on. Then he says:

"What did you want to walk all the way up to the steamboat for?"

10   "Because she's a big Orleans boat, and I was afeard she mightn't stop there. When they're deep they won't stop for a hail. A Cincinnati boat will, but this is a St. Louis one."

"Was Peter Wilks well off?"

"Oh, yes, pretty well off. He had houses and land, and it's reckoned he left three or four thousand in cash hid up som'ers."

"When did you say he died?"

"I didn't say, but it was last night."

Hailing a steamboat. Illustration from *Every Saturday*, September 16, 1871. *Courtesy the Library of Congress.*

HE FAIRLY EMPTIED THAT YOUNG FELLOW.

"Funeral to-morrow, likely?"

"Yes, 'bout the middle of the day."

"Well, it's all terrible sad; but we've all got to go, one time or another. So what we want to do is to be prepared; then we're all right."

"Yes, sir, it's the best way. Ma used to always say that."

When we struck the boat, she was about done loading, and pretty soon she got off. The king never said nothing about going aboard, so I lost my ride, after all. When the boat was gone, the king made me paddle up another mile to a lonesome place, then he got ashore, and says:

"Now hustle back, right off, and fetch the duke up here, and the new carpet-bags. And if he's gone over to t'other side, go over there and git him. And tell him to git himself up regardless. Shove along, now."

I see what *he* was up to; but I never said nothing, of course. **11** When I got back with the duke, we hid the canoe and then they set down on a log, and the king told him everything, just like the young fellow had said it—every last word of it. And all the time he was a doing it, he tried to talk like an English- **12** man; and he done it pretty well too, for a slouch. I can't imitate him, and so I ain't agoing to try to; but he really done it pretty good. Then he says:

"How are you on the deef and dumb, Bilgewater?" **13**

The duke said, leave him alone for that; said he had played a deef and dumb person on the histrionic boards. So then they waited for a steamboat.

About the middle of the afternoon a couple of little boats come along, but they didn't come from high enough up the river; but at last there was a big one, and they hailed her. She sent out her yawl, and we went aboard, and she was from Cincinnati; and when they found we only wanted to go four or five mile, they was booming mad, and give us a cussing, and said they wouldn't land us. But the king was calm. He says:

11 *I see what* he *was up to.* Blair in *Mark Twain and Huck Finn* (p. 327) has suggested that the king's new fraud was inspired in part by Fuller's *Imposters and Adventurers:* The chapter "The Seven False Dauphins" describes the false claimant Mathurin Bruneau, who, on learning of his resemblance to a rich woman's missing son, "hastily acquired information in regard to the family, and at once presented himself to the widow as her returned son. Received with joy . . . he sustained for some time this deception, and then disappeared."

12 *he tried to talk like an Englishman.* One of the ironies of this deception is that it is not the duke with his Shakespearean training but rather the ignorant king who must imitate the speech of an Englishman.

13 *How are you on the deef and dumb, Bilgewater?* The impersonation of a deaf-mute, a relatively simple deception, was a common device in popular fiction and melodrama of the period; for example, Melville's *Confidence-Man* is first encountered on the steamboat as a deaf-mute. It was also a popular trick of Twain's imposters, such as the Spaniard in Chapter 26 of *Tom Sawyer;* Simon Wheeler, the amateur detective, in an unpublished play, 1877; Brace Dunlap in "Tom Sawyer, Detective"; and the false slave in "Tom Sawyer's Conspiracy," 1898.

This fraud seems especially cruel coming so soon after Jim's lamentations for his deaf and dumb daughter.

14 *It was enough to make a body ashamed of the human race.* One of the most famous sentences in the novel. Twain expressed the same sentiment in Chapter 24 of *Tom Sawyer*, in the pedestrian phrase: "Huck's confidence in the human race was well-nigh obliterated." Once he had found the right words, Twain frequently used it in his work (for example, by Hank Morgan in Chapter 20 of *A Connecticut Yankee in King Arthur's Court;* and by Huck again, in Chapter 12 of *Tom Sawyer Abroad*). However, the power of this sentiment is undercut by its being prefaced by the offensive statement, "Well, if I ever struck anything like it, I'm a nigger." One must confess being a bit ashamed of Huck Finn, too.

"If gentlemen kin afford to pay a dollar a mile apiece, to be took on and put off in a yawl, a steamboat kin afford to carry 'em, can't it?"

So they softened down and said it was all right; and when we got to the village, they yawled us ashore. About two dozen men flocked down, when they see the yawl a coming; and when the king says—

"Kin any of you gentlemen tell me wher Mr. Peter Wilks lives?" they give a glance at one another, and nodded their heads, as much as to say, "What d' I tell you?" Then one of them says, kind of soft and gentle:

"I'm sorry, sir, but the best we can do is to tell you where he *did* live yesterday evening."

Sudden as winking, the ornery old cretur went all to smash, and fell up against the man, and put his chin on his shoulder, and cried down his back, and says:

"ALAS! OUR POOR BROTHER."

"Alas, alas! our poor brother—gone, and we never got to see him; oh, it's too, *too* hard!"

Then he turns around, blubbering, and makes a lot of idiotic signs to the duke on his hands, and blamed if *he* didn't drop a carpet-bag and bust out a-crying. If they warn't the beatenest lot, them two frauds, that ever I struck.

Well, the men gethered around, and sympathised with them, and said all sorts of kind things to them, and carried their carpet-bags up the hill for them, and let them lean on them and cry, and told the king all about his brother's last moments, and the king he told it all over again on his hands to the duke, and both of them took on about that dead tanner like they'd lost the twelve disciples. Well, if ever I struck anything like **14** it, I'm a nigger. It was enough to make a body ashamed of the human race.

ChapterXXV

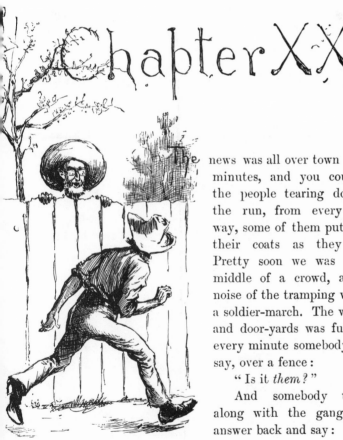

"YOU BET IT IS."

The news was all over town in two minutes, and you could see the people tearing down on the run, from every which way, some of them putting on their coats as they come. Pretty soon we was in the middle of a crowd, and the **1** noise of the tramping was like a soldier-march. The windows and door-yards was full; and every minute somebody would say, over a fence:

"Is it *them*?"

And somebody trotting along with the gang would answer back and say:

"You bet it is."

When we got to the house, the street in front of it was packed, and the three girls was standing in the door. Mary Jane *was* red-headed, but that **2** don't make no difference, she was most awful beautiful, and her face and her eyes was all lit up like glory, she was so glad her uncles was come. The king he spread his arms, and Mary **3** Jane she jumped for them, and the hare-lip jumped for the duke, and there they *had* it! Everybody most, leastways women, cried for joy to see them meet again at last and have such good times.

1 *the noise of the tramping was like a soldier-march*. Huck has adopted Colonel Sherburn's metaphor of Chapter 22 that a mob is an army.

2 *Mary Jane was red-headed, but that don't make no difference, she was most awful beautiful*. At this time, having red hair was not thought to be attractive. Typical of this attitude was a character's comment in Johnson Jones Hooper's *The Widow Rigby's Husband* (1851, p. 26) that "this feller married a red-headed widow for her money—no man ever married sech for anything else." Clemens, himself a redhead, facetiously attacked this prejudice in "Oh She Has a Red Head!" (Hannibal *Daily Journal*, May 13, 1853): "Turn your nose at red heads! What ignorance! I pity your lack of taste. Why, man, red is the natural color of beauty! What is there that is really beautiful or grand in Nature or Art, that is not tinted with this primordial color! . . . Most animals are fond of red—and *all children*, before their tastes are corrupted, and their judgements perverted, are fond of red. The Romans anciently regarded red hair as *necessary* to a beautiful lady!" (reprinted in *Early Tales and Sketches*, Vol. I, 1979, pp. 104–105).

3 *The king he spread his arms*. As Ferguson has pointed out in "Huck Finn Aborning" (p. 180), the king and the duke were considerably more lecherous in the manuscript than in the book: "Soon as he could, the duke shook the hare-lip, and sampled Susan, which was better looking. After the king had kissed Mary Jane fourteen or fifteen times, he give the duke a show, and tapered off on the others." See Chapter 28, notes 4 and 8.

4 *I never see anything so disgusting.* Blair in *Mark Twain and Huck Finn* (p. 329) has suggested a comparison of the king and the duke's blubbering with that of the swindler Simon Suggs when he is mistaken for General Thomas Witherspoon, "the rich hog-drover from Kentucky," and is "reunited" with the gentleman's nephew: "Young Mr. James Peyton and Captain Simon Suggs then embraced. Several of the bystanders laughed, but a large majority sympathized with the Captain. A few wept at the affecting sight, and one person expressed the opinion that nothing so soul-moving had ever before taken place in the city of Tuskaloosa. As for Simon, the tears rolled down his face, as naturally as if they had been called forth by real emotion, instead of being pumped up mechanically to give effect to the scene" (*Adventures of Captain Simon Suggs*, p. 62).

5 *the king . . . slobbers out a speech.* The king's pious rhetoric is the same as that used by another scoundrel, Senator Dilworthy, when he addresses the Cattleville Sunday School in Chapter 53 of *The Gilded Age*. Originally, in the manuscript, the king's speech was given in direct discourse: "Friends, good friends of the deceased, and ourn too, I trust—it's indeed a sore trial to lose him, and a sore trial to miss seeing him alive, after the wearisome long journey of four thousand mile; but it's a trial that's sweetened and sanctified to us by this dear sympathy and these holy tears; and so, out of our hearts we thank you, for out of our mouths we cannot, words being too weak and cold. May you find such friends and such sympathy yourselves, when your own time of trial comes, and may this affliction be softened to you as ourn is today, by the soothing ba'm of earthly love and the healing of heavenly grace. Amen."

"In this speech and its companion," Ferguson observed in "Huck Finn Aborning" (p. 175), "every phrase in the draft is carried over into the final text, but the indirect reporting, by implying compression from much greater length, immeasurably heightens the effect." Also, Huck's editorializing of this pious speech, "all full of tears and flapdoodle," increases its absurdity and hypocrisy and greatly sharpens its humor. However, one significant detail has been dropped: "Earthly love" is a term usually applied to carnal desire, another indication of the king's lechery.

Then the king he hunched the duke, private—I see him do it—and then he looked around and see the coffin, over in the corner on two chairs ; so then, him and the duke, with a hand across each other's shoulder, and t'other hand to their eyes, walked slow and solemn over there, everybody dropping back to give them room, and all the talk and noise stopping, people saying " Sh ! " and all the men taking their hats off and drooping their heads, so you could hear a pin fall. And when they got there, they bent over and looked in the coffin, and took one sight, and then they burst out a crying so you could a heard them to Orleans, most ; and then they put their arms around each other's necks, and hung their chins over each other's shoulders ; and then for three minutes, or maybe four, I never see two men leak the way they done. And mind you, everybody was doing the same ; and the place was that damp I never see anything like it. Then one of them got on one side of the coffin, and t'other on t'other side, and they kneeled down and rested their foreheads on the coffin, and let on to pray all to theirselves. Well, when it come to that, it worked the crowd like you never see anything like it, and so everybody broke down and went to sobbing right out loud—the poor girls, too ; and every woman, nearly, went up to the girls, without saying a word, and kissed them, solemn, on the forehead, and then put their hand on their head, and looked up towards the sky, with the tears running down, and then busted out and went **4** off sobbing and swabbing, and give the next woman a show. I never see anything so disgusting.

5 Well, by-and-by the king he gets up and comes forward a little, and works himself up and slobbers out a speech, all full of tears and flapdoodle about its being a sore trial for him and

LEAKING.

his poor brother to lose the diseased, and to miss seeing diseased alive, after the long journey of four thousand mile, but it's a trial that's sweetened and sanctified to us by this dear sympathy and these holy tears, and so he thanks them out of his heart and out of his brother's heart, because out of their mouths they can't, words being too weak and cold, and all that kind of rot and slush, till it was just sickening; and then he blubbers out a pious goody-goodly Amen, and turns himself loose and goes to crying fit to bust.

And the minute the words was out of his mouth somebody over in the crowd struck up the doxolojer, and everybody joined **6** in with all their might, and it just warmed you up and made you feel as good as church letting out. Music *is* a good thing; and after all that soul-butter and hogwash, I never see it **7** freshen up things so, and sound so honest and bully.

Then the king begins to work his jaw again, and says how him and his nieces would be glad if a few of the main principal friends of the family would take supper here with them this evening, and help set up with the ashes of the diseased; and **8** says if his poor brother laying yonder could speak, he knows who he would name, for they was names that was very dear to him, and mentioned often in his letters; and so he will name the same, to wit, as follows, viz.:—Rev. Mr. Hobson, and Deacon Lot Hovey, and Mr. Ben Rucker, and Abner Shackleford, and Levi Bell, and Dr. Robinson, and their wives, and the widow Bartley.

Rev. Hobson and Dr. Robinson was down to the end of the town, a-hunting together; that is, I mean the doctor was shipping a sick man to t'other world, and the preacher was pinting **9** him right. Lawyer Bell was away up to Louisville on some **10** business. But the rest was on hand, and so they all come and shook hands with the king and thanked him and talked to him; and then they shook hands with the duke, and didn't say nothing but just kept a-smiling and bobbing their heads like a **11** passel of sapheads whilst he made all sorts of signs with his hands and said "Goo-goo—goo-goo-goo," all the time, like a baby that can't talk.

So the king he blatted along, and managed to inquire about pretty much everybody and dog in town, by his name, and mentioned all sorts of little things that happened one time or another in the town, or to George's family, or to Peter; and he always let on that Peter wrote him the things, but that was a lie, he got every blessed one of them out of that young flathead that we canoed up to the steamboat.

Then Mary Jane she fetched the letter her father left behind, and the king he read it out loud and cried over it. It give the dwelling-house and three thousand dollars, gold, to the girls; and it give the tanyard (which was doing a good business), along with some other houses and land (worth about seven thousand), and three thousand dollars in gold to Harvey and William, and told where the six thousand cash was hid, down cellar. So these two frauds said they'd go and fetch it up, and

"All full of tears and flapdoodle." Illustration by E. W. Kemble, "Autograph Edition," 1899.

6 *the doxolojer.* The Doxology, "Old One Hundred," the familiar hymn by Thomas Ken (1637–1711):

> *Praise God, from whom all blessings flow,*
> *Praise Him, all creatures here below,*
> *Praise Him above, ye Heavenly Host,*
> *Praise Father, Son, and Holy Ghost. Amen.*

As shown in Chapter 17 of *Tom Sawyer*, it is usually sung, in unison, at the close of a service as the final blessing. Apparently whoever "struck up the doxolojer" here did so to cut short the king's sermon. See Chapter 20, note 6.

7 *soul-butter.* Unctuous pious flattery. The famous phrase was an afterthought, added in the proofs; the manuscript has instead the more prosaic "humbug and hogwash."

8 *set up with the ashes of the diseased.* As with that of Jesus Christ, the spirit of the dead is believed to tarry near the unburied body for at least three days in wait for resurrection, and the living must watch the corpse to keep away devils which lie in wait for the opportunity to capture the soul of the departed. It was also believed, in the South, that the body must be watched to keep cats from attacking the corpse.

9 *the doctor was shipping a sick man to t'other world.* In the nineteenth century, when doctors were not so universally venerated as they are today, they were often the brunt of jokes. For example, in Chapter 10 of *The Gilded Age*, Twain wrote, "He . . . has been a doctor a year now, and he has had two patients—no, three, I think, yes, it *was* three. I attended their funerals."

10 *Lawyer Bell was away up to Louisville*. Louisville, Kentucky, on the Ohio River, was about seven hundred miles away.

11 *a passel of sapheads*. Or "parcel of sapheads," a lot of fools.

12 *yaller-boys*. Or "yellow-jackets," gold coins of any denomination in United States currency.

13 *bein' . . . representatives of furrin heirs that's got left, is the line for you and me, Bilge*. Of course, this line of work is exactly what the two frauds tried to pull on Huck and Jim in claiming to be the Duke of Bridgewater and King Louis XVII; what they had previously used as a ruse to take advantage of a boy and his slave has now turned them a substantial profit.

14 *Thish-yer comes of trust'n to Providence*. The king's blasphemy is shared by Simon Suggs after he has pulled off a particularly profitable swindle: "Well! thar *is* a Providence that purvides; and ef a man will *only* stand squar' up to what's right, it *will* prosper his endeavors to make somethin' to feed his children on! Yes, thar *is* a Providence! . . . Ef a man says thar ain't no Providence, you may be sure thar's something wrong *here*," striking in the region of his vest pocket—"and *that* man will swindle you, ef he can—*certin!*" (Hooper, *Adventures of Captain Simon Suggs*, p. 81).

Twain increases the sarcasm in such an attitude by making his speaker a phony preacher. The writer was well aware of how all sorts of people, from king to thief, have twisted religious teachings to their own advantage. "The Christian's Bible is a drug-store," Twain explained in "Bible Teaching and Religious Practice," 1890 (in *What Is Man?*, 1973, p. 71). "Its contents remain the same; but the medical practice changes."

have everything square and above-board; and told me to come with a candle. We shut the cellar door behind us, and when they found the bag they spilt it out on the floor, and it was a **12** lovely sight, all them yaller-boys. My, the way the king's eyes did shine! He slaps the duke on the shoulder, and says:

"Oh, *this* ain't bully, nor noth'n! Oh, no, I reckon not! Why, Biljy, it beats the Nonesuch, *don't* it?"

The duke allowed it did. They pawed the yaller-boys, and sifted them through their fingers and let them jingle down on the floor; and the king says:

13 "It ain't no use talkin'; bein' brothers to a rich dead man, and representatives of furrin heirs that's got left, is the line **14** for you and me, Bilge. Thish-yer comes of trust'n to Providence. It's the best way, in the long run. I've tried 'em all, and ther' ain't no better way."

Most everybody would a been satisfied with the pile, and took it on trust; but no, they must count it. So they counts it, and it comes out four hundred and fifteen dollars short. Says the king:

"Dern him, I wonder what he done with that four hundred and fifteen dollars?"

They worried over that a while, and ransacked all around for it. Then the duke says:

"Well, he was a pretty sick man, and likely he made a mistake—I reckon that's the way of it. The best way's to let it go, and keep still about it. We can spare it."

"Oh, shucks, yes, we can *spare* it. I don't k'yer noth'n 'bout that—it's the *count* I'm thinkin' about. We want to be awful square and open and above-board, here, you know. We want to lug this h-yer money upstairs and count it before everybody—then ther' ain't noth'n suspicious. But when the dead man says ther's six thous'n dollars, you know, we don't wan't to——"

"Hold on," says the duke. "Less make up the deffisit" —and he begun to haul out yaller-boys out of his pocket.

"It's a most amaz'n' good idea, duke—you *have* got a rattlin' clever head on you," says the king. "Blest if the old Nonesuch ain't a heppin' us out agin"—and *he* begun to haul out yaller-jackets and stack them up.

It most busted them, but they made up the six thousand clean and clear.

"Say," says the duke, "I got another idea. Le's go upstairs and count this money, and then take and *give it to the girls*."

"Good land, duke, lemme hug you! It's the most dazzling idea 'at ever a man struck. You have cert'nly got the most astonishin' head I ever see. Oh, this is the boss dodge, ther' ain't no mistake 'bout it. Let 'em fetch along their suspicions now, if they want to—this'll lay 'em out."

When we got up stairs, everybody gethered around the table, and the king he counted it and stacked it up, three hun-

MAKING UP THE "DEFFISIT."

15 *the vale of sorrers.* "The Vale of Sorrows," a religious cliché for life on Earth which is said to be all transient and sorrowful.

16 *leather-headed.* Thick-headed, doltish.

dred dollars in a pile—twenty elegant little piles. Everybody looked hungry at it, and licked their chops. Then they raked it into the bag again, and I see the king begin to swell himself up for another speech. He says:

"Friends all, my poor brother that lays yonder has done generous by them that's left behind in the vale of sorrers. He **15** has done generous by these-yer poor little lambs that he loved and sheltered, and that's left fatherless and motherless. Yes, and we that knowed him, knows that he would a done *more* generous by 'em if he hadn't ben afeard o' woundin' his dear William and me. Now, *wouldn't* he? Ther' ain't no question 'bout it, in *my* mind. Well, then—what kind o' brothers would it be, that'd stand in his way at sech a time? And what kind o' uncles would it be that'd rob—yes, *rob*—sech poor sweet lambs as these 'at he loved so, at sech a time? If I know William—and I *think* I do—he—well, I'll jest ask him." He turns around and begins to make a lot of signs to the duke with his hands; and the duke he looks at him stupid and leather-headed a while, then all of a sudden he seems to catch **16** his meaning, and jumps for the king, goo-gooing with all his might for joy, and hugs him about fifteen times before he lets up. Then the king says, "I knowed it; I reckon *that* 'll convince anybody the way *he* feels about it. Here, Mary Jane, Susan, Joanner, take the money—take it *all*. It's the gift of him that lays yonder, cold but joyful."

Mary Jane she went for him, Susan and the hare-lip went for the duke, and then such another hugging and kissing I never see yet. And everybody crowded up with the tears in their eyes, and most shook the hands off of them frauds, saying all the time:

17 *it's fitten that his funeral orgies sh'd be public.* In the backwoods, one attended funerals even if one did not know the deceased well. It was common, when someone died, for a boy to be sent on horseback from house to house to tell the sad news; or an announcement might be published in the newspapers, inviting the public to the funeral. Eager to take advantage of any opportunity for socializing, all the men and women of a county might lay aside their work, no matter how important, to attend the funeral.

GOING FOR HIM.

" You *dear* good souls !—how *lovely !*—how *could* you ! "

Well, then, pretty soon all hands got to talking about the diseased again, and how good he was, and what a loss he was, and all that ; and before long a big iron-jawed man worked himself in there from outside, and stood a listening and looking, and not saying anything ; and nobody saying anything to him either, because the king was talking and they was all busy listening. The king was saying—in the middle of something he'd started in on—

"—they bein' partickler friends o' the diseased. That's why they're invited here this evenin' ; but to-morrow we want *all* to come—everybody ; for he respected everybody, he liked **17** everybody, and so it's fitten that his funeral orgies sh'd be public."

And so he went a-mooning on and on, liking to hear himself talk, and every little while he fetched in his funeral orgies again, till the duke he couldn't stand it no more ; so he writes on a little scrap of paper, " *obsequies*, you old fool," and folds it up and goes to goo-gooing and reaching it over people's heads to him. The king he reads it, and puts it in his pocket, and says :

"Poor William, afflicted as he is, his *heart's* aluz right. Asks me to invite everybody to come to the funeral—wants me to make 'em all welcome. But he needn't a worried—it was jest what I was at."

Then he weaves along again, perfectly calm, and goes to dropping in his funeral orgies again every now and then, just like he done before. And when he done it the third time, he says :

"I say orgies, not because it's the common term, because

it ain't—obsequies bein' the common term—but because orgies is the right term. Obsequies ain't used in England no more, now—it's gone out. We say orgies now, in England. Orgies is better, because it means the thing you're after, more exact. It's a word that's made up out'n the Greek *orgo*, outside, open, abroad; and the Hebrew *jeesum*, to plant, cover up; hence in*ter*. So, you see, funeral orgies is an open er public funeral." **18**

He was the *worst* I ever struck. Well, the iron-jawed man he laughed right in his face. Everybody was shocked. Everybody says, "Why *doctor!*" and Abner Shackleford says:

"Why, Robinson, hain't you heard the news? This is Harvey Wilks."

The king he smiled eager, and shoved out his flapper, and **19** says:

"*Is* it my poor brother's dear good friend and physician? I——"

"Keep your hands off of me!" says the doctor. "*You* talk like an Englishman—*don't* you? It's the worse imitation

THE DOCTOR.

I ever heard. *You* Peter Wilks' brother. You're a fraud, that's what you are!"

Well, how they all took on! They crowded around the doctor, and tried to quiet him down, and tried to explain to him, and tell him how Harvey'd showed in forty ways that he *was* Harvey, and knowed everybody by name, and the names of the very dogs, and begged and *begged* him not to hurt Harvey's feelings and the poor girls' feelings, and all that; but it warn't no use, he stormed right along, and said any man that pretended to be an Englishman and couldn't imitate the lingo no better than what he did, was a fraud and a liar. The poor

18 *So, you see, funeral orgies is an open er public funeral.* Actually, "orgies" is from the Greek, meaning "secret rites," referring particularly to the nocturnal festivities in honor of Bacchus, the god of wine; and in Latin, it means "secret frantic revels." The king's Freudian slip of the tongue reveals what sort of revels are on his lecherous mind. Twain repeated this joke by referring to "the funeral orgies of the dead King" of the Hawaiian Islands. "The term is coarse," he apologized in "Death of a Princess" (Sacramento, California, *Weekly Union*, July 21, 1866), "but perhaps it is a better one than a milder would be." Another misuse of the word appears in Chapter 33 of *Tom Sawyer* after the boys have found Injun Joe's gold in the cave and are getting ready to leave:

"'Now less fetch the guns and things,' said Huck.

"'No, Huck—leave them there. They're just the tricks to have when we go to robbing. We'll keep them there all the time, and we'll hold our orgies there, too. It's an awful snug place for orgies.'

"'What's orgies?'

"'*I* dono. But robbers always have orgies, and of course we've got to have them, too. . . .'"

Wecter in *Sam Clemens of Hannibal* (p. 195) described a possible source for the king's exercise in academic discourse: The leading divines of Hannibal once participated in a debate of religious topics, but the program soon digressed to being largely a discussion of a Greek derivative, in particular, that "the active transitive verb *bap* is always *dip*." Blair in *Mark Twain and Huck Finn* (p. 330) has suggested the model for the king's falsely erudite double-talk to be the discourse of Ephraim Jenkinson, "the greatest rascal under the canopy of heaven" who talks "a long string of learning about Greek and cosmogony, and the world," in Chapter 14 of Oliver Goldsmith's *The Vicar of Wakefield* (1766): "We talked upon several subjects. . . . 'Ay, Sir, the world is in its dotage, and yet the cosmogony or creation of the world has puzzled the philosophers of all ages. What a medley of opinions have they not broached upon the creation of the world? Sanconiathon, Manetho, Borosus, and Ocellus Lucanus, have all attempted it in vain. The latter has these words, *Anarchon ara kai atelutaion to pan*, which imply that all things have neither beginning nor end. Manetho also, who lived about the time of old NebuchadonAsser, Asser being a Syriac word usually applied as a surname to the kings of that country, as Teglat Phael-Asser, Nabon-Asser, he, I say, formed a conjecture equally absurd; for we as we usually say, *ek to biblion kubernetes*, which implies that books will never teach the world; so he attempted to investigate—But, Sir, I ask pardon, I am straying from the question.'—That he actually was; . . . but it was sufficient to shew me that he was a man of letters, and I now reverenced him the more."

Although in Chapter 62 of *Following the Equator* (1897) he viciously attacked *The Vicar of Wakefield* as "one long waste-pipe discharge of goody-goody puerilities and dreary moralities," Twain, nevertheless, must have been amused by the suggestion that "Asser" is usually applied as a surname to kings.

19 *his flapper.* His hand.

20 *his idiotic Greek and Hebrew.* Evidently, it was the king's explanation of the etymology of "orgies" that tipped the doctor off that the king and the duke are frauds; during the nineteenth century, physicians were usually schooled in the classical languages. Other townspeople who could have spotted the swindle might have been the Rev. Hobson and Levi Bell, a clergyman and a lawyer, for they too most likely knew Greek and Hebrew; but, conveniently, they both have been called away on other business.

21 *He is the thinnest kind of an impostor.* This speech originally read as follows: "He is the thinnest of thin imposters—has come here with a lot of empty names and facts which he picked up somewhere; and you weakly take them for proofs, and are assisted in deceiving yourselves by these thoughtless unreasoning friends here, who ought to know better. Mary Jane Wilks, you know me for your friend, and your honest and unselfish friend. Now listen to me: cast this paltry villain out—I beg you, I beseech you to do it. Will you?"

Wisely, Twain rewrote this passage. "As any reader of Victorian novels knows," Ferguson explained in "Huck Finn Aborning" (p. 175), "this was a natural literary idiom in the 1870s. But even if Dr. Robinson had really talked that way, it was not the natural idiom for Huck to report him in."

The doctor's loose grammar should not suggest ignorance. "This habit among educated men in the West is not universal," Twain explained in Chapter 26 of *Life on the Mississippi*, "but it is prevalent—prevalent in the towns, certainly, if not in the cities; and to a degree which one cannot help noticing, and marveling at."

22 *"All right, doctor,"* says the king, kinder mocking him, *"we'll try and get 'em to send for you."* The king's sarcasm increases when one speculates on the fate of the sick man whom the doctor and the preacher were visiting: Obviously the patient has died, for only the Rev. Hobson has stayed behind.

girls was hanging to the king and crying; and all of a sudden the doctor ups and turns on *them.* He says:

"I was your father's friend, and I'm your friend; and I warn you *as* a friend, and an honest one, that wants to protect you and keep you out of harm and trouble, to turn your backs

20 on that scoundrel, and have nothing to do with him, the ignorant tramp, with his idiotic Greek and Hebrew as he calls it.

21 He is the thinnest kind of an impostor—has come here with a lot of empty names and facts which he has picked up somewheres, and you take them for *proofs,* and are helped to fool yourselves by these foolish friends here, who ought to know better. Mary Jane Wilks, you know me for your friend, and for your unselfish friend, too. Now listen to me; turn this pitiful rascal out—I *beg* you to do it. Will you?"

Mary Jane straightened herself up, and my, but she was handsome! She says:

"*Here* is my answer." She hove up the bag of money and put it in the king's hands, and says, "Take this six thousand dollars, and invest for me and my sisters any way you want to and don't give us no receipt for it."

Then she put her arm around the king on one side, and Susan and the harelip done the same on the other. Everybody clapped their hands and stomped on the floor like a perfect storm, whilst the king held up his head and smiled proud. The doctor says:

"All right, I wash *my* hands of the matter. But I warn you all that a time's coming when you're going to feel sick whenever you think of this day"—and away he went.

22 "All right, doctor," says the king, kinder mocking him, "we'll try and get 'em to send for you "—which made them all laugh, and they said it was a prime good hit.

THE BAG OF MONEY.

Chapter XXVI

THE CUBBY.

Well when they was all gone, the king he asks Mary Jane how they was off for spare rooms, and she **1** said she had one spare room, which would do for Uncle William, and she'd give her own room to Uncle Harvey, which was a little bigger, and she would turn into the room with her sisters and sleep on a cot ; and up garret was a little cubby, with a pallet in it. The king said the cubby would do for his valley—meaning me.

So Mary Jane took us up, and she showed them their rooms, which was plain but nice. She said she'd have her frocks and a lot of other traps took out of her room if they was in Uncle Harvey's way, but he said they warn't. The frocks was hung along the wall, and before them was a curtain made out of calico that hung down to the floor. There was an old hair trunk in one corner, and a guitar box in another, and all sorts of little knick-knacks and jimcracks around, like girls brisken up a room with. The king **2** said it was all the more homely and more pleasanter for these

1 *she said she had one spare room*. Originally Twain arranged different sleeping accommodations for Mary Jane's guests: "Well, when they was all gone the king asked Mary Jane how they was off for spare rooms, and she said they had two; so he said they could put his valley in the same bed with him—meaning me. He said in England it warn't usual for a valley to sleep with his master, but in Rome he always done the way the Romans done, and besides he warn't proud, and reckoned he could stand Adolphus very well. Maybe he could; but I couldn't a stood him, only I was long used to sleeping with the other kind of hogs. So Mary Jane showed us all up, and they was plain rooms but nice."

This bit of sarcasm had to be scrapped when Twain determined the final course of the chapter; to give Huck some flexibility of movement, the boy had to be given his own room. See Ferguson, "Huck Finn Aborning" (p. 176). However, in revising the passage, Twain has dropped the explanation of what a "valley" is, as well as the boy's alias "Adolphus" given him by the king when they met the country jake in Chapter 24.

2 *brisken up*. Smarten up, trim.

3 *me and the hare-lip.* Although the young man in Chapter 24 said that Joanna was about fourteen, the same age as Huck, Kemble has portrayed her as several years older than the boy.

4 *William Fourth. . . . I knowed he was dead years ago.* William IV (1765–1837) was succeeded by Queen Victoria, the monarch of Great Britain during the time of the novel. Twain may have introduced this ruler here to continue his burlesque of royalty: William IV was quite a scoundrel and was said to have fathered eleven illegitimate children.

William IV. *Courtesy the Library of Congress.*

fixings, and so don't disturb them. The duke's room was pretty small, but plenty good enough, and so was my cubby.

That night they had a big supper, and all them men and women was there, and I stood behind the king and the duke's chairs and waited on them, and the niggers waited on the rest. Mary Jane she set at the head of the table, with Susan alongside of her, and said how bad the biscuits was, and how mean the preserves was, and how ornery and tough the fried chickens was—and all that kind of rot, the way women always do for to force out compliments; and the people all knowed everything was tip-top, and said so—said "How *do* you get biscuits to brown so nice?" and "Where, for the land's sake, *did* you get these amaz'n pickles?" and all that kind of humbug talky-talk, just the way people always does at a supper, you know.

3   And when it was all done, me and the hare-lip had supper in the kitchen off of the leavings, whilst the others was helping

SUPPER WITH THE HARE-LIP.

the niggers clean up the things. The hare-lip she got to pumping me about England, and blest if I didn't think the ice was getting mighty thin, sometimes. She says:

"Did you ever see the king?"

4   "Who? William Fourth? Well, I bet I have—he goes to our church." I knowed he was dead years ago, but I never let on. So when I says he goes to our church, she says:

"What—regular?"

"Yes—regular. His pew's right over opposite ourn—on t'other side the pulpit."

"I thought he lived in London?"

"Well, he does. Where *would* he live?"

"But I thought *you* lived in Sheffield?"   **5**

I see I was up a stump. I had to let on to get choked with a chicken bone, so as to get time to think how to get down again. Then I says:

"I mean he goes to our church regular when he's in Sheffield. That's only in the summer-time, when he comes **6** there to take the sea baths."

"Why, how you talk—Sheffield ain't on the sea."

"Well, who said it was?"

"Why, you did."

"I *didn't*, nuther."

"You did!"

"I didn't."

"You did."

"I never said nothing of the kind."

"Well, what *did* you say, then?"

"Said he come to take the sea *baths*—that's what I said."

"Well, then! how's he going to take the sea baths if it ain't on the sea?"

"Looky here," I says; "did you ever see any Congress water?"   **7**

"Yes."

"Well, did you have to go to Congress to get it?"

"Why, no."

"Well, neither does William Fourth have to go to the sea to get a sea bath."

"How does he get it, then?"

"Gets it the way people down here gets Congress water— in barrels. There in the palace at Sheffield they've got furnaces, and he wants his water hot. They can't bile that amount of water away off there at the sea. They haven't got no conveniences for it."

"Oh, I see, now. You might a said that in the first place and saved time."

When she said that, I see I was out of the woods again, and so I was comfortable and glad. Next, she says:

"Do you go to church, too?"

"Yes—regular."

"Where do you set?"

"Why, in our pew."

"*Whose* pew?"

"Why, *ourn*—your Uncle Harvey's."

"His'n? What does *he* want with a pew?"

"Wants it to set in. What did you *reckon* he wanted with it?"

"Why, I thought he'd be in the pulpit."

Rot him, I forgot he was a preacher. I see I was up a stump again, so I played another chicken bone and got another think. Then I says:

"Blame it, do you suppose there ain't but one preacher to a church?"

5 *Sheffield.* Located in South Yorkshire, about 158 miles northwest of London.

6 *he comes there to take the sea baths.* Huck is likely thinking of Bath where the wealthy came to take advantage of the mineral springs as a health cure.

7 *Congress water.* Mineral water from the Congress Spring at Saratoga, New York, now known as "Saratoga Vichy water"; it was known for its medicinal qualities, and as in Bath, people came to Saratoga Springs to convalesce.

Congress Spring, Saratoga Springs, New York. Illustration from *Every Saturday*, September 9, 1871. *Courtesy the Library of Congress.*

8 *Don't they give 'em holidays . . . Chistmas and New Year's week, and Fourth of July?* At this time, Christmas and New Year's were not yet British bank holidays; any day off was left to the discretion of the employer. And, of course, the English would not celebrate July 4th, the day of American Independence.

9 *nigger shows.* There was nothing in his childhood that Sam Clemens enjoyed more than the minstrel show. "The minstrels appeared with coal-black hands and faces," Twain recalled in Chapter 12 of his *Autobiography*, "and their clothing was a loud and extravagant burlesque of the clothing worn by the plantation slave of the time. . . . The minstrel used a very broad Negro dialect; he used it competently and with easy facility and it was funny—delightfully and satisfyingly funny. . . . 'Bones' and 'Banjo' were the prime jokers and whatever funniness was to be gotten out of paint and exaggerated clothing they utilized to the limit. . . . The minstrel troupes had good voices and both their solos and their choruses were a delight to me. . . . The minstrel show was born in the early forties and it had a prosperous career for about thirty-five years; then it degenerated into a variety show and was nearly all variety show with a Negro act or two thrown in incidentally."

A "nigger show." Illustration by True W. Williams, *The Adventures of Tom Sawyer*, 1876.

10 *I see it warn't nothing but a dictionary.* Blair in *Mark Twain and Huck Finn* (p. 415) has pointed out that Huck's pointless oath was probably inspired by something Twain had observed on his first trip to England: The American consulate required that, if one wanted to ship anything to America, he "must go there and swear to a great long rigamarole and *kiss the book* (years ago they found out it was a dictionary)."

11 *It ain't right nor kind for you to talk so to him.* And, remember, Joanna is the sister who has devoted her life to good works.

"Why, what do they want with more?"

"What!—to preach before a king! I never see such a girl as you. They don't have no less than seventeen."

"Seventeen! My land! Why, I wouldn't set out such a string as that, not if I *never* got to glory. It must take 'em a week."

"Shucks, they don't *all* of 'em preach the same day—only *one* of 'em."

"Well, then, what does the rest of 'em do?"

"Oh, nothing much. Loll around, pass the plate—and one thing or another. But mainly they don't do nothing."

"Well, then, what are they *for*?"

"Why, they're for *style*. Don't you know nothing?"

"Well, I don't *want* to know no such foolishness as that. How is servants treated in England? Do they treat 'em better 'n we treat our niggers?"

"*No!* A servant ain't nobody there. They treat them worse than dogs."

8   "Don't they give 'em holidays, the way we do, Christmas and New Year's week, and Fourth of July?"

"Oh, just listen! A body could tell *you* hain't ever been to England by that. Why, Hare-l—why, Joanna, they never see a holiday from year's end to year's end; never go to the

9   circus, nor theatre, nor nigger shows, nor nowheres."

"Nor church?"

"Nor church."

"But *you* always went to church?"

Well, I was gone up again. I forgot I was the old man's servant. But next minute I whirled in on a kind of an explanation how a valley was different from a common servant, and *had* to go to church whether he wanted to or not, and set with the family, on account of its being the law. But I didn't do it pretty good, and when I got done I see she warn't satisfied. She says:

"Honest Injun, now, hain't you been telling me a lot of lies?"

"Honest Injun," says I.

"None of it at all?"

"None of it at all. Not a lie in it," says I.

"Lay your hand on this book and say it."

10   I see it warn't nothing but a dictionary, so I laid my hand on it and said it. So then she looked a little better satisfied, and says:

"Well, then, I'll believe some of it; but I hope to gracious if I'll believe the rest."

"What is it you won't believe, Joe?" says Mary Jane,

11   stepping in with Susan behind her. "It ain't right nor kind for you to talk so to him, and him a stranger and so far from his people. How would you like to be treated so?"

"That's always your way, Maim—always sailing in to help somebody before they're hurt. I hain't done nothing to him. He's told some stretchers, I reckon; and I said I wouldn't

"HONEST INJUN."

12 *give . . . bark from the tomb.* A severe scolding, a shock; from the popular hymn "A Funeral Thought," No. 614, by Isaac Watts:

Hark! from the tombs a doleful sound,
My ears attend the cry:
"Ye living men, come view the ground
Where you must shortly lie!

"Princes, this clay must be your bed,
In spite of all your tow'rs;
The tall, the wise, the rev'red head,
Must lie as low as ours."

swallow it all; and that's every bit and grain I *did* say. I reckon he can stand a little thing like that, can't he?"

"I don't care whether it 'twas little or whether 'twas big, he's here in our house and a stranger, and it wasn't good of you to say it. If you was in his place, it would make you feel ashamed; and so you oughtn't to say a thing to another person that will make *them* feel ashamed."

"Why, Maim, he said——"

"It don't make no difference what he *said*—that ain't the thing. The thing is for you to treat him *kind*, and not be saying things to make him remember he ain't in his own country and amongst his own folks."

I says to myself, *this* is a girl that I'm letting that ole reptle rob her of her money!

Then Susan *she* waltzed in; and if you'll believe me, she did give Hare-lip hark from the tomb! **12**

Says I to myself, And this is *another* one that I'm letting him rob her of her money!

Then Mary Jane she took another inning, and went in sweet and lovely again—which was her way—but when she got done there warn't hardly anything left o' poor Hare-lip. So she hollered.

"All right, then," says the other girls, "you just ask his pardon."

She done it, too. And she done it beautiful. She done it so beautiful it was good to hear; and I wished I could tell her a thousand lies, so she could do it again.

I says to myself, this is *another* one that I'm letting him rob her of her money. And when she got through, they all jest laid themselves out to make me feel at home and know I was amongst friends. I felt so ornery and low down and mean, that I says to myself, My mind's made up; I'll hive that money for them or bust.

So then I lit out—for bed, I said, meaning some time or another. When I got by myself, I went to thinking the thing over. I says to myself, Shall I go to that doctor, private, and blow on these frauds? No—that won't do. He might tell who told him; then the king and the duke would make it warm for me. Shall I go, private, and tell Mary Jane? No—I dasn't do it. Her face would give them a hint, sure; they've got the money, and they'd slide right out and get away with it. If she was to fetch in help, I'd get mixed up in the business, before it was done with, I judge. No, there ain't no good way but one. I got to steal that money, somehow; and I got to steal it some way that they won't suspicion that I done it. They've got a good thing, here; and they ain't agoing to leave till they've played this family and this town for all they're worth, so I'll find a chance time enough. I'll steal it, and hide it; and by-and-by, when I'm away down the river, I'll write a letter and tell Mary Jane where it's hid. But I'd better hive it to-night, if I can, because the doctor maybe hasn't let up as much as he lets on he has; he might scare them out of here, yet.

So, thinks I, I'll go and search them rooms. Upstairs the hall was dark, but I found the duke's room, and started to paw around it with my hands; but I recollected it wouldn't be much like the king to let anybody else take care of that money but his own self; so then I went to his room and begun to paw around there. But I see I couldn't do nothing without a candle, and I dasn't light one, of course. So I judged I'd got to do the other thing—lay for them, and eavesdrop. About that time, I hears their footsteps coming, and was going to skip under the bed; I reached for it, but it wasn't where I thought it would be; but I touched the curtain that hid Mary Jane's frocks, so I jumped in behind that and snuggled in amongst the gowns, and stood there perfectly still.

They come in and shut the door; and the first thing the duke done was to get down and look under the bed. Then I was glad I hadn't found the bed when I wanted it. And yet, you know, it's kind of natural to hide under the bed when you are up to anything private. They sets down, then, and the king says:

"Well, what is it? and cut it middlin' short, because it's better for us to be down there a whoopin'-up the mournin', than up here givin' 'em a chance to talk us over."

"Well, this is it, Capet. I ain't easy; I ain't comfortable. That doctor lays on my mind. I wanted to know your plans. I've got a notion, and I think it's a sound one."

"What is it, duke?"

"That we better glide out of this, before three in the morning, and clip it down the river with what we've got.

THE DUKE LOOKS UNDER THE BED.

Specially, seeing we got it so easy—*given* back to us, flung at our heads, as you may say, when of course we allowed to have to steal it back. I'm for knocking off and lighting out."

That made me feel pretty bad. About an hour or two ago, it would a been a little different, but now it made me feel bad and disappointed. The king rips out and says:

"What! And not sell out the rest o' the property? March off like a passel o' fools and leave eight or nine thous'n' dollars' worth o' property layin' around jest sufferin' to be scooped in? —and all good saleable stuff, too."

The duke he grumbled; said the bag of gold was enough, and he didn't want to go no deeper—didn't want to rob a lot of orphans of *everything* they had.

"Why, how you talk!" says the king. "We shan't rob 'em of nothing at all but jest this money. The people that *buys* the property is the suff'rers; because as soon's it's found out 'at we didn't own it—which won't be long after we've slid—the sale won't be valid, and it'll all go back to the estate. These-yer orphans 'll git their house back agin, and that's enough for *them*; they're young and spry, and k'n easy earn a livin'. *They* ain't agoing to suffer. Why, jest think—there's thous'n's and thous'n's that ain't nigh so well off. Bless you, *they* ain't got noth'n to complain of."

"Well, the king he talked him blind; so at last he give in, and said all right, but said he believed it was blame foolishness to stay, and that doctor hanging over them. But the king says:

"Cuss the doctor! What do we k'yer for *him*? Hain't we got all the fools in town on our side? and ain't that a big enough majority in any town?"

So they got ready to go downstairs again. The duke says:

"I don't think we put that money in a good place."

That cheered me up. I'd begun to think I warn't going to get a hint of no kind to help me. The king says:

13 *Mary Jane'll be in mourning from this out; and first you know the nigger that does up the rooms will get an order to box these duds up and put 'em away.* For the funeral, Mary Jane will be going into "full mourning," meaning she must dress only in black for at least a year, and she will have no use for other clothes up in the king's room.

14 *do you reckon a nigger can run across money and not borrow some of it?* At the time, it was commonly assumed that any slave had the potential of becoming a thief. "They had an unfair show in the battle of life," Twain defended the slaves in Chapter 2 of *Pudd'nhead Wilson*, "and they held it no sin to take military advantage of the enemy—in a small way. . . . They would smouch provisions from the pantry whenever they got a chance; or a brass thimble, or a cake of wax, or an emery-bag, or a paper of needles, or a silver spoon, or a dollar bill, or small articles of clothing, or any other property of light value; and so far were they from considering such reprisals sinful, that they would go to church and shout and pray their loudest and sincerest with their plunder in their pockets. A farm smoke-house had to be kept heavily padlocked, for even the colored deacon himself could not resist a ham when Providence showed him in a dream, or otherwise, where such a thing hung . . . perfectly sure that in taking this trifle from the man who daily robbed him of an inestimable treasure—his liberty—he was not committing any sin that God would remember against him in the Last Great Day."

" Why ? "

13 " Because Mary Jane 'll be in mourning from this out ; and
14 first you know the nigger that does up the rooms will get an order to box these duds up and put 'em away ; and do you reckon a nigger can run across money and not borrow some of it ? "

" Your head's level agin, duke," says the king ; and he come a fumbling under the curtain two or three foot from where I was. I stuck tight to the wall, and kept mighty still, though quivery ; and I wondered what them fellows would say to me if they catched me ; and I tried to think what I'd better do if they did catch me. But the king he got the bag before I could think more than about a half a thought, and he never suspicioned I was around. They took and shoved the bag through a rip in the straw tick that was under the feather bed, and crammed it in a foot or two amongst the straw and said it was all right, now, because a nigger only makes up the feather bed, and don't turn over the straw tick only about twice a year, and so it warn't in no danger of getting stole, now.

But I knowed better. I had it out of there before they was

HUCK TAKES THE MONEY.

half-way downstairs. I groped along up to my cubby, and hid it there till I could get a chance to do better. I judged I better hide it outside of the house somewheres, because if they missed it they would give the house a good ransacking. I knowed that very well. Then I turned in, with my clothes all on ; but I couldn't a gone to sleep, if I'd a wanted to, I was in such a sweat to get through with the business. By-and-by I heard the king and the duke come up ; so I rolled off of my pallet and laid with my chin at the top of my ladder and waited to see if anything was going to happen. But nothing did.

So I held on till all the late sounds had quit and the early ones hadn't begun, yet ; and then I slipped down the ladder.

Chapter XXVII

A CRACK IN THE DINING-ROOM DOOR.

I CREPT to their doors and listened; they was snoring, so I tip-toed along, and got down-stairs all right. There warn't a sound any-wheres. I peeped through a crack of the dining-room door, and see the men that was watching the corpse all sound asleep on their chairs. The door was open into the parlor, where the corpse was laying, and there was a candle in both rooms. I passed along, and the parlor door was open; but I see there warn't nobody in there but the remainders of Peter; so I shoved on by; but the front door was locked, and the key wasn't there. Just then I heard somebody coming down the stairs, back behind me. I run in the parlor, and took a swift look around, and the only place I see to hide the bag was in the coffin. The lid was shoved along about a foot, showing the dead man's face down in there, with a wet cloth over it, and his shroud on. I tucked the money-bag in under the lid, just down beyond where his hands was crossed, which made me creep, they was so cold, and then I run back across the room and in behind the door.

1 *smouch*. Pilfer, a favorite word of Twain's.

2 *soothering*. Flattering, coaxing, affectionate, a colloquial word of Ireland and Cumberland.

The person coming was Mary Jane. She went to the coffin, very soft, and kneeled down and looked in; then she put up her handkerchief and I see she begun to cry, though I couldn't hear her, and her back was to me. I slid out, and as I passed the dining-room I thought I'd make sure them watchers hadn't seen me; so I looked through the crack and everything was all right. They hadn't stirred.

I slipped up to bed, feeling ruther blue, on accounts of the thing playing out that way after I had took so much trouble and run so much resk about it. Says I, if it could stay where it is, all right; because when we get down the river a hundred mile or two, I could write back to Mary Jane, and she could dig him up again and get it; but that ain't the thing that's going to happen; the thing that's going to happen is, the money 'll be found when they come to screw on the lid. Then the king ll get it again, and it 'll be a long day before he gives anybody **1** another chance to smouch it from him. Of course I *wanted* to slide down and get it out of there, but I dasn't try it. Every minute it was getting earlier, now, and pretty soon some of them watchers would begin to stir, and I might get catched—catched with six thousand dollars in my hands that nobody hadn't hired me to take care of. I don't wish to be mixed up in no such business as that, I says to myself.

When I got downstairs in the morning the parlour was shut up, and the watchers was gone. There warn't nobody around but the family and the widow Bartley and our tribe. I watched their faces to see if anything had been happening, but I couldn't tell.

Towards the middle of the day the undertaker come, with his man, and they set the coffin in the middle of the room on a couple of chairs, and then set all our chairs in rows, and borrowed more from the neighbours till the hall and the parlor and the dining-room was full. I see the coffin lid was the way it was before, but I dasn't go to look in under it, with folks around.

Then the people begun to flock in, and the beats and the girls took seats in the front row at the head of the coffin, and for a half an hour the people filed around slow, in single rank, and looked down at the dead man's face a minute, and some dropped in a tear, and it was all very still and solemn, only the girls and the beats holding handkerchiefs to their eyes and keeping their heads bent, and sobbing a little. There warn't no other sound but the scraping of the feet on the floor, and blowing noses—because people always blows them more at a funeral than they do at other places except church.

When the place was packed full, the undertaker he slid **2** around in his black gloves with his softy soothering ways, putting on the last touches, and getting people and things all shipshape and comfortable, and making no more sound than a cat. He never spoke; he moved people around, he squeezed in late ones, he opened up passage-ways, and done it all with nods and signs with his hands. Then he took his place over

THE UNDERTAKER.

3 *a melodeum*. Or "melodeon." An early form of the "American organ," a small wind-instrument with a keyboard, the bellows being worked by foot-pedals.

4 *it was only one dog*. Blair in *Mark Twain and Huck Finn* (p. 331) has noted the similarity between the ruckus at the Wilks funeral and that during a sermon delivered by Captain Duncan on the *Quaker City*, recorded by Twain in a journal of 1867: "In the midst of sermon, Capt. Duncan rushed madly out with one of those damned dogs, but didn't throw him overboard." In another entry in his notebook, Twain jotted only the enigmatic sentence, "He had a rat!" In Chapter 5 of *Tom Sawyer*, Twain described how just a pinch-bug and a stray poodle could so disrupt another church service: "The discourse was resumed presently, but it went lame and halting, all possibility of impressiveness being at an end; for even the gravest sentiments were constantly being received with a smothered burst of unholy mirth, under cover of some remote pew-back, as if the poor parson had said a rarely facetious thing."

against the wall. He was the softest, glidingest, stealthiest man I ever see; and there warn't no more smile to him than there is to a ham.

They had borrowed a melodeum—a sick one; and when **3** everything was ready, a young woman set down and worked it, and it was pretty skreeky and colicky, and everybody joined in and sung, and Peter was the only one that had a good thing, according to my notion. Then the Reverend Hobson opened up, slow and solemn, and begun to talk; and straight off the most outrageous row busted out in the cellar a body ever heard; it was only one dog, but he made a most powerful **4** racket, and he kept it up, right along; the parson he had to stand there, over the coffin, and wait—you couldn't hear yourself think. It was right down awkward, and nobody didn't seem to know what to do. But pretty soon they see that long-legged undertaker make a sign to the preacher as much as to say, "Dont you worry—just depend on me." Then he stooped down and begun to glide along the wall, just his shoulders showing over the people's heads. So he glided along, and the pow-wow and racket getting more and more outrageous all the time; and at last, when he had gone around two sides of the room, he disappears down cellar. Then, in about two seconds we heard a whack, and the dog he finished up with a most amazing howl or two, and then everything was dead still, and the parson begun his solemn talk where he left off. In a minute or two here comes this undertaker's back and shoulders gliding along the wall again; and so he glided, and glided, around three sides of the room, and then rose up, and shaded his mouth with his hands, and stretched his neck out towards the preacher, over the people's heads, and says, in a kind of

"HE HAD A RAT!"

a coarse whisper, "*He had a rat!*" Then he drooped down and glided along the wall again to his place. You could see it was a great satisfaction to the people, because naturally they wanted to know. A little thing like that don't cost nothing, and it's just the little things that makes a man to be looked up to and liked. There warn't no more popular man in town than what that undertaker was.

Well, the funeral sermon was very good, but pison long and tiresome; and then the king he shoved in and got off some of his usual rubbage, and at last the job was through, and the undertaker begun to sneak up on the coffin with his screw-driver. I was in a sweat then, and watched him pretty keen. But he never meddled at all; just slid the lid along, as soft as mush, and screwed it down tight and fast. So there I was! I didn't know whether the money was in there, or not. So, says I, s'pose somebody has hogged that bag on the sly?—now how do *I* know whether to write to Mary Jane or not? S'pose she dug him up and didn't find nothing—what would she think of me? Blame it, I says, I might get hunted up and jailed; I'd better lay low and keep dark, and not write at all; the thing's awful mixed, now; trying to better it, I've worsened it a hundred times, and I wish to goodness I'd just let it alone, dad fetch the whole business!

They buried him, and we come back home, and I went to watching faces again—I couldn't help it, and I couldn't rest easy. But nothing come of it; the faces didn't tell me nothing.

The king he visited around, in the evening, and sweetened everybody up, and made himself ever so friendly; and he give out the idea that his congregation over in England would be in a sweat about him, so he must hurry and settle up the estate right away, and leave for home. He was very sorry he was so pushed, and so was everybody; they wished he could stay longer, but they said they could see it couldn't be done. And he said of course him and William would take the girls home with them; and that pleased everybody too, because then the girls would be well fixed, and amongst their own relations; and it pleased the girls, too—tickled them so they clean forgot they ever had a trouble in the world; and told him to sell out as quick as he wanted to, they would be ready. Them poor things was that glad and happy it made my heart ache to see them getting fooled and lied to so, but I didn't see no safe way for me to chip in and change the general tune.

Well, blamed if the king didn't bill the house and the niggers and all the property for auction straight off—sale two days after the funeral; but anybody could buy private beforehand if they wanted to.

So the next day after the funeral, along about noontime, the girls' joy got the first jolt; a couple of nigger traders come along, and the king sold them the niggers reasonable, for three- **5** day drafts as they called it, and away they went, the two sons **6** up the river to Memphis, and their mother down the river to Orleans. I thought them poor girls and them niggers would **7** break their hearts for grief; they cried around each other, and took on so it most made me down sick to see it. The girls said they hadn't ever dreamed of seeing the family separated or sold away from the town. I can't ever get it out of my memory, the sight of them poor miserable girls and niggers hanging around each other's necks and crying; and I reckon I couldn't a stood it all but would a had to bust out and tell on our gang if I hadn't knowed the sale warn't no account and the niggers would be back home in a week or two.

The thing made a big stir in the town, too, and a good **8** many come out flat-footed and said it was scandalous to separate the mother and the children that way. It injured the frauds some; but the old fool he bulled right along, spite of all the duke could say or do, and I tell you the duke was powerful uneasy.

Next day was auction day. About broad-day in the morning, the king and the duke come up in the garret and woke me up, and I see by their look that there was trouble. The king says:

"Was you in my room night before last?"

"No, your majesty"—which was the way I always called him when nobody but our gang warn't around.

"Was you in there yisterday er last night?"

"No, your majesty."

"Honor bright, now—no lies."

"Honor bright, your majesty. I'm telling you the truth. I hain't been anear your room since Miss Mary Jane took you and the duke and showed it to you."

The duke says:

"Have you seen anybody else go in there?"

"No, your grace, not as I remember, I believe."

"Stop and think."

I studied a while, and see my chance, then I says:

"Well, I see the niggers go in there several times."

Both of them give a little jump; and looked like they

5 *three-day drafts as they called it.* The bill of exchange allows the purchaser three dates on which to pay the money owed; and if either party fails to fulfill the agreement at any point between the first and last payment, then the contract becomes invalid.

6 *the two sons up the river to Memphis, and their mother down the river to Orleans.* In "A True Story" *(The Atlantic Monthly*, November 1874, pp. 591–594), Twain recorded the grief suffered by a slave mother deprived of her children on the auction block, "repeated word for word" as he was told the story by Aunty Cord, a servant at Quarry Farm, near Elmira, New York, where the Clemenses spent their summers: "Dey put chains on us an' put us on a stan' as high as dis po'ch, . . . an' all de people stood aroun', crowds an' crowds. . . . An' dey sole my ole man, an' took him away, an' day begin to sell my chil'en an' take *dem* away, an' I begin to cry; an' de man say, 'Shet up yo' dam blubberin',' an' hit me on de mouf wid his han'. An' when de las' one was gone but my little Henry, I grab' *him* clost up to my breas' so, an' I ris up an' says, 'You shan't take him away,' I says; 'I'll kill de man dat tetches him!' I says. . . . But dey got him—dey got him, de men did; but I took an' tear de clo'es mos' off of 'em an' beat 'em over de head wid my chain; an' *dey* give it to *me*, too, but I didn't mine dat."

A slave mother deprived of her children. Illustration by George Cruikshank, *Uncle Tom's Cabin* by Harriet Beecher Stowe, 1853.

7 *I thought them poor girls and them niggers would break their hearts for grief.* The Wilks girls and their slaves are not expressing false sentimentality. Because they were generally raised by slaves and their playmates were slaves, the masters were often not only loyal to but even genuinely fond of their "niggers" and they of their owners. To Twain "house servant of ours" was synonymous with "playmate of mine; for I was playmate to all the niggers, preferring their society to that of the elect, I being a person of low-down tastes from the start, notwithstanding my high birth, and ever ready to forsake the communion of high souls if I could strike anything nearer my grade" (quoted by Wecter, *Sam Clemens of Hannibal*, pp. 75–76). Fortunately young Sam Clemens did not have to suffer what the Hawkinses did in Chapter 7 of *The Gilded*

Age when, due to a change in fortune, their property had to be sold off by the Sheriff: "The Hawkins hearts been torn to see Uncle Dan'l and his wife pass from the auction-block into the hands of a negro trader and depart for the remote South to be seen no more by the family. It had seemed like seeing their own flesh and blood sold into banishment."

8 *The thing made a big stir in the town, too, and a good many . . said it was scandalous to separate the mother and the children that way.* Twain is describing "the mild domestic slavery" of Hannibal, Missouri, and not that of Arkansas in the Deep South. He recalled in Chapter 7 of his *Autobiography*, "To separate and sell the members of a slave family to different masters was a thing not well liked by the people and so it was not often done, except in the settling of estates."

" WAS YOU IN MY ROOM ? "

hadn't ever expected it, and then like they *had*. Then the duke says :

" What, *all* of them ? "

" No—leastways not all at once. That is, I don't think I ever see them all come *out* at once but just one time."

" Hello—when was that ? "

" It was the day we had the funeral. In the morning. It warn't early, because I overslept. I was just starting down the ladder, and I see them."

" Well, go on, *go* on—what did they do ? How'd they act ? "

" They didn't do nothing. And they didn't act anyway, much, as fur as I see. They tip-toed away; so I seen, easy enough, that they'd shoved in there to do up your majesty's room, or something, s'posing you was up; and found you *warn't* up, and so they was hoping to slide out of the way of trouble without waking you up, if they hadn't already waked you up."

" Great guns, *this* is a go ! " says the king; and both of them looked pretty sick and tolerable silly. They stood there a thinking and scratching their heads a minute, and then the duke he bust into a kind of a little raspy chuckle, and says:

" It does beat all, how neat the niggers played their hand. They let on to be *sorry* they was going out of this region ! and I believed they *was* sorry. And so did you, and so did everybody. Don't ever tell *me* any more that a nigger ain't got any histrionic talent. Why, the way they played that thing, it would fool *anybody*. In my opinion there's a fortune in 'em. If I had capital and a theatre, I wouldn't want a better lay out than that—and here we've gone and sold 'em for a song. Yes, and ain't privileged to sing the song, yet.   Say, where *is* that song?—that draft?"

"In the bank for to be collected.   Where *would* it be?"

"Well, *that's* all right then, thank goodness."

Says I, kind of timid-like:

"Is something gone wrong?"

The king whirls on me and rips out:

"None o' your business!   You keep your head shet, and mind y'r own affairs—if you got any.   Long as you're in this town, don't you forgit *that*, you hear?"   Then he says to the duke: "We got to jest swaller it, and say noth'n: mum's the word for *us*."

As they was starting down the ladder, the duke he chuckles again, and says:

"Quick sales *and* small profits!   It's a good business— yes."

The king snarls around on him and says:

"I was trying to do for the best, in sellin' 'm out so quick. If the profits has turned out to be none, lackin' considable, and none to carry, is it my fault any more'n its yourn?"

"Well, *they'd* be in this house yet, and we *wouldn't* if I could a got my advice listened to."

The king sassed back, as much as was safe for him, and then swapped around and lit into *me* again.   He give me down **9** the banks for not coming and *telling* him I see the niggers come out of his room acting that way—said any fool would a *knowed* something was up.   And then waltzed in and cussed *himself* a while; and said it all come of him not laying late and taking his natural rest that morning, and he'd be blamed if he'd ever do it again.   So they went off a jawing; and I felt dreadful glad I'd worked it all off on to the niggers, and yet hadn't done the niggers no harm by it.

JAWING.   **10**

9 *He give me down the banks*. He gave me a scolding, a reprimand; an Irish expression.

10 *jawing*. Oddly, Gilder changed the illustration's caption "Jawing" to "A Coolness between friends" when it appeared in "Royalty on the Mississippi" in *The Century*.

Chapter XXVIII

IN TROUBLE.

By-and-by it was getting-up time; so I come down the ladder and started for downstairs, but as I come to the girls' room, the door was open, and I see Mary Jane setting by her old hair trunk, which was open and she'd been packing things in it—getting ready to go to England. But she had stopped now, with a folded gown in her lap, and had her face in her hands, crying. I felt awful bad to see it; of course anybody would. I went in there, and says:

"Miss Mary Jane, you can't abear to see people in trouble and I can't—most always. Tell me about it."

So she done it. And it was the niggers—I just expected it. She said the beautiful trip to England was most about spoiled for her; she didn't know *how* she was ever going to be happy there, knowing the mother and the children warn't ever going to see each other no more—and then busted out bitterer than ever, and flung up her hands, and says:

"Oh, dear, dear, to think they ain't *ever* going to see each other any more ! "

" But they *will*—and inside of two weeks—and I *know* it ! " says I.

Laws it was out before I could think !—and before I could budge, she throws her arms around my neck, and told me to say it *again*, say it *again*, say it *again!*

I see I had spoke too sudden, and said too much, and was in a close place. I asked her to let me think a minute ; and she set there, very impatient and excited, and handsome, but looking kind of happy and eased-up, like a person that's had a tooth pulled out. So I went to studying it out. I says to myself, I reckon a body that ups and tells the truth when he is in **1** a tight place, is taking considerable many resks, though I ain't had no experience, and can't say for certain ; but it looks so to me, anyway ; and yet here's a case where I'm blest if it don't look to me like the truth is better, and actually *safer*, than a lie. I must lay it by in my mind, and think it over some time or other, it's so kind of strange and unregular. I never see nothing like it. Well, I says to myself at last, I'm agoing to chance it ; I'll up and tell the truth this time, though it does seem most like setting down on a kag of powder and touching it off just to see where you'll go to. Then I says :

" Miss Mary Jane, is there any place out of town a little ways, where you could go and stay three or four days ? "

" Yes—Mr. Lothrop's. Why ? "

" Never mind why, yet. If I'll tell you how I know the niggers will see each other again—inside of two weeks—here in this house—and *prove* how I know it—will you go to Mr. Lothrop's and stay four days ? "

" Four days ! " she says ; " I'll stay a year ! "

" All right," I says, " I don't want nothing more out of *you* than just your word—I druther have it than another man's kiss- **2** the-Bible." She smiled, and reddened up very sweet, and I says, " If you don't mind it, I'll shut the door—and bolt it."

Then I come back and set down again, and says :

" Don't you holler. Just set still, and take it like a man. I got to tell the truth, and you want to brace up, Miss Mary, because it's a bad kind, and going to be hard to take, but there ain't no help for it. These uncles of yourn ain't no uncles at all—they're a couple of frauds—regular dead-beats. There, now we're over the worst of it—you can stand the rest middling easy."

It jolted her up like everything, of course ; but I was over **3** the shoal water now, so I went right along, her eyes a blazing higher and higher all the time, and told her every blame thing, from where we first struck that young fool going up to the steamboat, clear through to where she flung herself on to the king's breast at the front door, and he kissed her sixteen or **4** seventeen times—and then up she jumps, with her face afire like sunset, and says :

" The brute ! Come—don't waste a minute—not a *second*

1 *I reckon a body that ups and tells the truth when he is in a tight place, is taking considerable many resks.* Telling the truth is out of character for the boy. As Twain noted in his preface to the excerpt of "the Famous Grangerford-Shepherdson Feud" in *The Century* (December 1884, p. 268), "Readers who have met Huck Finn before (in *Tom Sawyer*) will not be surprised to note that whenever Huck is caught in a close place and is obliged to explain, the truth gets well crippled before he gets through."

2 *kiss-the-Bible.* Sacred oath.

3 *I was over the shoal water now.* Like a riverboat leaving port.

4 *he kissed her sixteen or seventeen times.* Twain has forgotten that earlier he deleted this detail. See Chapter 25, note 3, and note 8 here.

5 *we'll have them tarred and feathered, and flung in the river*. Redheads were believed to be especially fiery-tempered, but sweet Mary Jane takes the truth like any "man" in the novel would.

6 *I'd be all right, but there'd be another person that you don't know about who'd be in big trouble*. Even in the most dangerous situation, Huck always looks out for Jim's welfare.

INDIGNATION.

5 —we'll have them tarred and feathered, and flung in the river!'"

Says I:

"Cert'nly. But do you mean, *before* you go to Mr. Lothrop's, or——"

"Oh," she says, "what am I *thinking* about!" she says, and set right down again. "Don't mind what I said—please don't—you *won't*, now, *will* you?" Laying her silky hand on mine in that kind of a way that I said I would die first. "I never thought, I was so stirred up," she says; "now go on, and I won't do so any more. You tell me what to do, and whatever you say, I'll do it."

"Well," I says, "it's a rough gang, them two frauds, and I'm fixed so I got to travel with them a while longer, whether I want to or not—I druther not tell you why—and if you was to **6** blow on them this town would get me out of their claws, and *I'd* be all right, but there'd be another person that you don't know about who'd be in big trouble. Well, we got to save *him*, hain't we? Of course. Well, then, we won't blow on them."

Saying them words put a good idea in my head. I see how maybe I could get me and Jim rid of the frauds; get them jailed here, and then leave. But I didn't want to run the raft in day-time, without anybody aboard to answer questions but me; so I didn't want the plan to begin working till pretty late to-night. I says:

"Miss Mary Jane, I'll tell you what we'll do—and you won't have to stay at Mr. Lothrop's so long, nuther. How fur is it?"

"A little short of four miles—right out in the country, back here."

"Well, that'll answer. Now you go along out there, and lay low till nine or half-past, to-night, and then get them to fetch you home again—tell them you've thought of something. If you get here before eleven, put a candle in this window, and

if I don't turn up, wait *till* eleven, and *then* if I don't turn up
it means I'm gone, and out of the way, and safe. Then you
come out and spread the news around, and get these beats
jailed."

"Good," she says, "I'll do it."

"And if it just happens so that I don't get away, but get
took up along with them, you must up and say I told you the
whole thing beforehand, and you must stand by me all you can."

"Stand by you, indeed I will. They shan't touch a hair of
your head!" she says, and I see her nostrils spread and her eyes
snap when she said it, too.

"If I get away, I shan't be here," I says, " to prove these
rapscallions ain't your uncles, and I couldn't do it if I *was* here.
I could swear they was beats and bummers, that's all; though
that's worth something. Well, there's others can do that better
than what I can—and they're people that ain't going to be
doubted as quick as I'd be. I'll tell you how to find them.
Gimme a pencil and a piece of paper. There—' *Royal Nonesuch,
Bricksville.*' Put it away, and don't lose it. When the court

HOW TO FIND THEM.

wants to find out something about these two, let them send up
to Bricksville and say they've got the men that played the
Royal Nonesuch, and ask for some witnesses—why, you'll have
that entire town down here before you can hardly wink, Miss
Mary. And they'll come a-biling, too."

I judged we had got everything fixed about right, now. So
I says:

"Just let the auction go right along, and don't worry. Nobody don't have to pay for the things they buy till a whole day
after the auction, on accounts of the short notice, and they ain't
going out of this till they get that money—and the way we've
fixed it the sale ain't going to count, and they ain't going to
get no money. It's just like the way it was with the niggers—
it warn't no sale, and the niggers will be back before long.
Why, they can't collect the money for the *niggers*, yet—they're
in the worst kind of a fix, Miss Mary."

"Well," she says, " I'll run down to breakfast now, and then
I'll start straight for Mr. Lothrop's."

7 *leather-face.* Expressionless. Throughout this confession, even before she speaks, Huck has been able to read Mary Jane's emotions through the changes in her facial expressions.

8 *Do you reckon you can go and face your uncles, when they come to kiss you good-morning.* In the manuscript, Twain had written, "Do you reckon you can face your uncles, and take your regular three or four good-morning smacks?" (Ferguson, "Huck Finn Aborning," p. 180). But Twain made the change evidently when he decided to make the frauds less lecherous. See Chapter 25, note 3.

9 *it's the little things that smoothes people's roads the most, down here below.* Huck has oddly fallen into the idiom of a Sunday-school superintendent; according to church teachings, Heaven expects Mary Jane to love everyone, especially such "lost lambs" as the king and the duke. See Chapter 13, note 13.

" 'Deed, *that* ain't the ticket, Miss Mary Jane," I says, "by no manner of means; go *before* breakfast."

"Why?"

"What did you reckon I wanted you to go at all for, Miss Mary?"

"Well, I never thought—and come to think, I don't know. What was it?"

7   "Why, it's because you ain't one of these leather-face people. I don't want no better book than what your face is. A body can
8 set down and read it off like coarse print. Do you reckon you can go and face your uncles, when they come to kiss you good-morning, and never——"

"There, there, don't! Yes, I'll go before breakfast—I'll be glad to. And leave my sisters with them?"

"Yes—never mind about them. They've got to stand it yet a while. They might suspicion something if all of you was to go. I don't wan't you to see them, nor your sisters, nor nobody in this town—if a neighbour was to ask how is your uncles this morning, your face would tell something. No, you go right along, Miss Mary Jane, and I'll fix it with all of them. I'll tell Miss Susan to give your love to your uncles and say you've went away for a few hours for to get a little rest and change, or to see a friend, and you'll be back to-night or early in the morning."

"Gone to see a friend is all right, but I won't have my love given to them."

"Well, then, it shan't be." It was well enough to tell *her* so—no harm in it. It was only a little thing to do, and no
9 trouble; and it's the little things that smoothes people's roads the most, down here below; it would make Mary Jane comfortable, and it wouldn't cost nothing. Then I says: "There's one more thing—that bag of money."

"Well, they've got that; and it makes me feel pretty silly to think *how* they got it."

"No, you're out, there. They hain't got it."

"Why, who's got it?"

"I wish I knowed, but I don't. I *had* it, because I stole it from them: and I stole it to give to you; and I know where I hid it, but I'm afraid it ain't there no more. I'm awful sorry, Miss Mary Jane, I'm just as sorry as I can be; but I done the best I could; I did, honest. I come nigh getting caught, and I had to shove it into the first place I come to, and run—and it warn't a good place."

"Oh, stop blaming yourself—it's too bad to do it, and I won't allow it—you couldn't help it; it wasn't you fault. Where did you hide it?"

I didn't want to set her to thinking about her troubles again; and I couldn't seem to get my mouth to tell her what would make her see that corpse laying in the coffin with that bag of money on his stomach. So for a minute I didn't say nothing—then I says:

"I'd rather not *tell* you where I put it, Miss Mary Jane, if you don't mind letting me off; but I'll write it for you on a piece of paper, and you can read it along the road to Mr. Lothrop's, if you want to. Do you reckon that'll do?"

"Oh, yes."

So I wrote: "I put it in the coffin. It was in there when you was crying there, away in the night. I was behind the door, and I was mighty sorry for you, Miss Mary Jane."

HE WROTE.

It made my eyes water a little, to remember her crying there all by herself in the night, and them devils laying there right under her own roof, shaming her and robbing her; and when I folded it up and give it to her, I see the water come into her eyes, too; and she shook me by the hand, hard, and says:

"*Good*-bye—I'm going to do everything just as you've told me; and if I don't ever see you again I sha'n't ever forget you, and I'll think of you a many and a many a time, and I'll *pray* for you, too!"—and she was gone.

Pray for me! I reckoned if she knowed me she'd take a job that was more nearer her size. But I bet she done it, just the same—she was just that kind. She had the grit to pray **10** for Judus if she took the notion—there warn't no backdown to her, I judge. You may say what you want to, but in my opinion she had more sand in her than any girl I ever see; in **11** my opinion she was just full of sand. It sounds like flattery, but it ain't no flattery. And when it comes to beauty—and goodness too—she lays over them all. I hain't ever seen her since that time that I see her go out of that door; no, I hain't ever seen her since, but I reckon I've thought of her a many and a many a million times, and of her saying she would pray for me; and if ever I'd a thought it would do any good for me to pray for *her*, blamed if I wouldn't a done it or bust.

Well, Mary Jane she lit out the back way, I reckon; because nobody see her go. When I struck Susan and the hare-lip, I **12** says:

"What's the name of them people over on t'other side of the river that you all goes to see sometimes?"

They says:

"There's several; but it's the Proctors, mainly."

"That's the name," I says; "I most forgot it. Well, Miss Mary Jane she told me to tell you she's gone over there in a dreadful hurry—one of them's sick."

"Which one?"

"I don't know; leastways I kinder forget; but I think it's——"

"Sakes alive, I hope it ain't *Hanner*?"

10 *She had the grit to pray for Judus*. She had the pluck to pray for anyone, even the greatest villain in Christian history; Twain had originally written "Judas Iscariott," but it was perhaps too blasphemous (and not likely what Huck would say) and thus he changed it. In praising Mary Jane's courage, Huck somewhat apologetically accuses her of going against conventional Christian morality.

11 *she had more sand in her*. See Chapter 8, note 13.

12 *struck*. Met, ran into.

13 *erysipelas*. Erysipelas, or "Saint Anthony's fire," a severe skin disease.

14 *consumption*. The common nineteenth-century name for tuberculosis, one of the most dreaded diseases of the time.

15 *yaller janders*. Yellow jaundice, a liver ailment which discolors the skin.

16 *brain fever*. Specifically, equine encephalomyelitis, an inflammation of the brain or its members.

17 *"Why he stumped his* toe." Twain recorded a variant of the joke in the Buffalo *Express* (August 18, 1869): In Nevada, a man with consumption "took the smallpox from a negro, the cholera from a Chinaman, and the yellow fever and the erysipelas from other parties, and swallowed fifteen grains of strychnine, and fell out of the third story window and broke his neck. Verdict of the jury, 'Died by the visitation of God!'" (quoted by Duskis, *The Forgotten Works of Mark Twain*, p. 62).

"I'm sorry to say it," I says, "but Hanner's the very one."

"My goodness—and she so well only last week! Is she took bad?"

"It ain't no name for it. They set up with her all night, Miss Mary Jane said, and they don't think she'll last many hours."

"Only think of that, now! What's the matter with her?"

I couldn't think of anything reasonable, right off that way, so I says:

"Mumps."

HANNER WITH THE MUMPS.

"Mumps your granny! They don't set up with people that's got the mumps."

"They don't, don't they? You better bet they do with *these* mumps. These mumps is different. It's a new kind, Miss Mary Jane said."

"How's it a new kind?"

"Because it's mixed up with other things."

"What other things?"

13   "Well, measles, and whooping-cough, and erysipelas, and
14,15,16 consumption, and yaller janders, and brain fever, and I don't know what all."

"My land! And they call it the *mumps?*"

"That's what Miss Mary Jane said."

"Well, what in the nation do they call it the *mumps* for?"

"Why, because it *is* the mumps. That's what it starts with."

"Well, ther' ain't no sense in it. A body might stump his toe, and take pison, and fall down the well, and break his neck, and bust his brains out, and somebody come along and ask
17 what killed him, and some numskull up and say, 'Why, he stumped his *toe*.' Would ther' be any sense in that? *No*. And ther' ain't no sense in *this*, nuther. Is it ketching?"

"Is it *ketching?* Why, how you talk. Is a *harrow* catching?—in the dark? If you don't hitch on to one tooth, you're bound to on another, aint you ?   And you can't get away with that tooth without fetching the whole harrow along, can you ? Well, these kind of mumps is a kind of a harrow, as you may say—and it ain't no slouch of a harrow, nuther, you come to get it hitched on good."

" Well, it's awful, *I* think," says the hare-lip.   " I'll go to Uncle Harvey and——"

" Oh, yes," I says, " I *would*. Of *course* I would. I wouldn't lose no time."

" Well, why wouldn't you ? "

" Just look at it a minute, and maybe you can see.   Hain't your uncles obleeged to get along home to England as fast as they can ?   And do you reckon they'd be mean enough to go off and leave you to go all that journey by yourselves ? *You* know they'll wait for you.   So fur, so good.   Your uncle Harvey's a preacher, ain't he ?   Very well, then ; is a *preacher* going to deceive a steamboat clerk ? is he going to deceive a *ship-clerk ?*—so as to get them to let Miss Mary Jane go aboard ?   Now *you* know he ain't.   What *will* he do, then ? Why, he'll say, ' It's a great pity, but my church matters has got to get along the best way they can ; for my niece has been exposed to the dreadful pluribus-unum mumps, and **18** so it's my bounden duty to set down here and wait the three months it takes to show on her if she's got it.'   But never mind, if you think it's best to tell your Uncle Harvey——"

" Shucks, and stay fooling around here when we could all be having good times in England whilst we was waiting to find out whether Mary Jane's got it or not ?   Why, you talk like a **19** muggins."

" Well, anyway, maybe you better tell some of the neighbours."

" Listen at that, now.   You do beat all, for natural stupidness.   Can't you *see* that *they'd* go and tell ?   Ther' ain't no way but just to not tell anybody at *all*."

" Well, maybe you're right—yes, I judge you *are* right."

" But I reckon we ought to tell Uncle Harvey she's gone out a while, anyway, so he won't be uneasy about her ? "

" Yes, Miss Mary Jane she wanted you to do that.   She says, ' Tell them to give Uncle Harvey and William my love and a kiss, and say I've run over the river to see Mr.—Mr.—what *is* the name of that rich family your uncle Peter used to think so much of ?—I mean the one that——"

" Why, you must mean the Apthorps, ain't it ? "

" Of course ; bother them kind of names, a body can't ever seem to remember them, half the time, somehow. Yes, she said, say she has run over for to ask the Apthorps to be sure and come to the auction and buy this house, because she allowed her uncle Peter would ruther they had it than anybody else ; and she's going to stick to them till they say they'll come, and then, if she ain't too tired, she's coming home ; and if she is, she'll be home in the morning anyway.   She said, don't say nothing about the Proctors, but only about the Apthorps——
——which'll be perfectly true, because she *is* going there to speak

18 *the dreadful pluribus-unum mumps.* Huck is trying to recall the phrase "*E pluribus unum,*" one out of many, the motto of the United States of America; in trying to give an impressive name to this rare strain of "mumps," the boy garbles the only bit of Latin he has obviously ever learned. It is a particularly apt phrase not only because it is in character for such a preacher as him who uses a term like "funeral orgies" but also because it summarizes all of Hannah's afflictions as "one out of many."

19 *a muggins.* A fool, a simpleton.

20 *pisonest*. As both the manuscript and Kemble's illustration prove, this is a misprint for "piousest."

21 *two sets o' heirs to old Peter Wilks*. Blair in *Mark Twain and Huck Finn* (p. 328) has noted the similarity between the new development in the plot and the story of the false Martin Guerre as described in Fuller's *Imposters and Adventurers:* A man arrives in Normandy, claiming to be Martin Guerre who left his wife many years before; he is arrested, and his trial is interrupted when as the judges "were about to give the accused the benefit of the doubt, there arrived . . . a new Martin Guerre. . . . he recognized . . . his neighbors, his relatives, his friends, as the other had done before him. . . . The new-comer arrived just in time to drag the judges back into uncertainty."

about their buying the house; I know it, because she told me so, herself."

"All right," they said, and cleared out to lay for their uncles, and give them the love and the kisses, and tell them the message.

Everything was all right now. The girls wouldn't say nothing because they wanted to go to England; and the king and the duke would ruther Mary Jane was off working for the auction than around in reach of Doctor Robinson. I felt very good; I judged I had done it pretty neat—I reckoned Tom Sawyer couldn't a done it no neater himself. Of course he would a throwed more style into it, but I can't do that very handy, not being brung up to it.

Well, they held the auction in the public square, along towards the end of the afternoon, and it strung along and strung along, and the old man he was on hand and looking his level

20 pisonest, up there longside of the auctioneer, and chipping in a little Scripture, now and then, or a little goody-goody saying, of some kind, and the duke he was around goo-gooing for sympathy all he knowed how, and just spreading himself generly.

THE AUCTION.

But by-and-by the thing dragged through, and everything was sold. Everything but a little old trifling lot in the grave-yard. So they'd got to work *that* off—I never see such a girafft as the king was for wanting to swallow *everything*. Well, whilst they was at it, a steamboat landed, and in about two minutes up comes a crowd a whooping and yelling and laughing and carrying on, and singing out:

21 "*Here's* your opposition line! here's your two sets o' heirs to old Peter Wilks—and you pays your money and you takes your choice!"

Chapter XXIX

THE TRUE BROTHERS.

They was fetching a very nice-looking old gentleman along, and a nice-looking younger one, with his right arm in a sling. And my souls, how the people yelled, and laughed, and kept it up. But I didn't see no joke about it, and I judged it would strain the duke and the king some to see any. I reckoned they'd turn pale. But no, nary a pale did *they* turn. The duke he never let on he suspicioned what was up, but just went a goo-gooing around, happy and satisfied, like a jug that's googling out buttermilk; and as for the king, he just gazed and gazed down sorrowful on them new-comers like it give him the stomach-ache in his very heart to think there could be such frauds and rascals in the world. Oh, he done it admirable. Lots of the principal people gethered around the king, to let him see they was on his side. That old gentleman that had just come looked all puzzled to death. Pretty soon he begun to speak, and I see,

1 *I can't give the old gent's words, nor I can't imitate him.* And yet Huck was able to reproduce perfectly all the subtleties of the varying dialects of all the other characters, from the Missouri Negro speech of Jim to the duke's "histrionic" jargon to Colonel Sherburn's eloquence. W. Keith Kraus in "'Huckleberry Finn': A Final Irony" (*Mark Twain Journal*, Winter 1967–1968, pp. 18–19) has suggested that Huck has probably rather accurately recorded the "Englishman's" words, and that that is only one clue that the new "Harvey Wilks" and his "brother" are just another pair of frauds. There are perhaps too many convenient inconsistencies in their story; also they show no particular grief over the death of Peter Wilks. Not surprisingly then, the king and the duke do not betray any discomfort on the arrival of the second set of heirs; they see through the other pair as just another couple of frauds like themselves.

2 *dummy.* A common nineteenth-century term for a deaf-mute.

3 *Susan Powell.* Neither the ship nor the woman has been identified: There is no mention of such a boat in Lytle's *Merchant Steam Vessels of the United States 1807–1868*; and no "Susan Powell" is mentioned in Twain's autobiography, journals, or letters. Twain must just be recalling the custom of a riverboat being named after a lady, usually the captain's wife.

straight off, he pronounced *like* an Englishman, not the king's **1** way, though the king's *was* pretty good, for an imitation. I can't give the old gent's words, nor I can't imitate him; but he turned around to the crowd, and says, about like this:

"This is a surprise to me which I wasn't looking for; and I'll acknowledge, candid and frank, I ain't very well fixed to meet it and answer it; for my brother and me has had misfortunes, he's broke his arm, and our baggage got put off at a town above here, last night in the night by a mistake. I am Peter Wilks's brother Harvey, and this is his brother William, which can't hear nor speak—and can't even make signs to amount to much, now 't he's only got one hand to work them with. We are who we say we are; and in a day or two, when I get the baggage, I can prove it. But, up till then, I won't say nothing more, but go to the hotel and wait."

2   So him and the new dummy started off; and the king he laughs, and blethers out:

"Broke his arm—*very* likely *ain't* it?—and very convenient, too, for a fraud that's got to make signs, and hain't learnt how. Lost their baggage! That's *mighty* good!—and mighty ingenious—under the *circumstances!*"

So he laughed again; and so did everybody else, except three or four, or maybe half a dozen. One of these was that doctor; another one was a sharp-looking gentleman, with a carpet-bag of the old-fashioned kind made out of carpet-stuff, that had just come off of the steamboat and was talking to him in a low voice, and glancing towards the king now and then and nodding their heads—it was Levi Bell, the lawyer that was gone up to Louisville; and another one was a big rough husky that come along and listened to all the old gentleman said, and was listening to the king now. And when the king got done, this husky up and says:

"Say, looky here; if you are Harvey Wilks, when'd you come to this town?"

"The day before the funeral, friend," says the king.

"But what time o' day?"

"In the evenin'—'bout an hour er two before sundown."

"*How'd* you come?"

3   "I come down on the *Susan Powell*, from Cincinnati."

"Well, then, how'd you come to be up at the Pint in the *mornin'*—in a canoe?"

"I warn't up at the Pint in the mornin'."

"It's a lie."

Several of them jumped for him and begged him not to talk that way to an old man and a preacher.

"Preacher be hanged, he's a fraud and a liar. He was up at the Pint that mornin'. I live up there, don't I? Well, I was up there, and he was up there. I *see* him there. He come in a canoe, along with Tim Collins and a boy."

The doctor he up and says:

"Would you know the boy again if you was to see him, Hines?"

"I reckon I would, but I don't know. Why, yonder he is, now. I know him perfectly easy."

It was me he pointed at. The doctor says:

"Neighbours, I don't know whether the new couple is frauds or not; but if *these* two ain't frauds, I am an idiot, that's all. I think it's our duty to see that they don't get away from here till we've looked into this thing. Come along Hines; come along, the rest of you. We'll take these fellows to the tavern and affront them with t'other couple, and I reckon we'll find out *something* before we get through."

It was nuts for the crowd, though maybe not for the king's **4** friends; so we all started. It was about sundown. The doctor he led me along by the hand, and was plenty kind enough, but he never let *go* my hand.

We all got in a big room in the hotel, and lit up some

THE DOCTOR LEADS HUCK.

candles, and fetched in the new couple. First, the doctor says:

"I don't wish to be too hard on these two men, but *I* think they're frauds, and they may have 'complices that we don't know nothing about. If they have, won't the 'complices get away with that bag of gold Peter Wilks left? It ain't unlikely. If these men ain't frauds, they won't object to sending for that money and letting us keep it till they prove they're all right— ain't that so?"

Everybody agreed to that. So I judged they had our gang in a pretty tight place, right at the outstart. But the king he only looked sorrowful, and says:

"Gentlemen, I wish the money was there, for I ain't got no disposition to throw anything in the way of a fair, open,

4 *It was nuts for the crowd.* It was very agreeable to the crowd.

5 *a left-handed look*. A sinister look. The devil is said to linger on the left-side of the body. See Chapter 4, note 2.

6 *I reckon you ain't used to lying*. Actually Huck has been doing rather well for himself so far; but here is the first time he has had to lie to educated men.

out-and-out investigation o' this misable business; but alas! the money ain't there; you k'n send and see, if you want to."

"Where is it, then?"

"Well, when my niece give it to me to keep for her, I took and hid it inside o' the straw tick o' my bed, not wishin' to bank it for the few days we'd be here, and considerin' the bed a safe place, we not bein' used to niggers, and suppos'n' 'em honest, like servants in England. The niggers stole it the very next mornin' after I had went downstairs; and when I sold 'em I hadn't missed the money yit, so they got clean away with it. My servant here k'n tell you 'bout it, gentlemen."

The doctor and several said "Shucks!" and I see nobody didn't altogether believe him. One man asked me if I see the niggers steal it. I said "no," but I see them sneaking out of the room and hustling away, and I never thought nothing, only I reckoned they was afraid they had waked up my master and was trying to get away before he made trouble with them. That was all they asked me. Then the doctor whirls on me and says:

"Are *you* English too?"

I says "yes;" and him and some others laughed, and said, "Stuff!"

Well, then they sailed in on the general investigation, and there we had it, up and down, hour in, hour out, and nobody never said a word about supper, nor ever seemed to think about it—and so they kept it up, and kept it up; and it *was* the worst mixed-up thing you ever see. They made the king tell his yarn, and they made the old gentleman tell his'n; and anybody but a lot of prejudiced chuckleheads would a *seen* that the old gentleman was spinning truth and t'other one lies. And by-and-by they had me up to tell what I knowed. The king he give me a left-handed look out of the corner of his eye, and so I knowed enough to talk on the right side. I begun to tell about Sheffield, and how we lived there, and all about the English Wilkses, and so on; but I didn't get pretty fur till the doctor begun to laugh; and Levi Bell, the lawyer, says:

"Set down, my boy, I wouldn't strain myself, if I was you. I reckon you ain't used to lying, it don't seem to come handy; what you want is practice. You do it pretty awkward."

I didn't care nothing for the compliment, but I was glad to be let off, anyway.

The doctor he started to say something, and turns and says:

"If you'd been in town at first, Levi Bell——"

The king broke in and reached out his hand, and says:

"Why, is this my poor dead brother's old friend that he's wrote so often about?"

The lawyer and him shook hands, and the lawyer smiled and looked pleased, and they talked right along a while, and then got to one side and talked low; and at last the lawyer speaks up and says:

"That'll fix it. I'll take the order and send it, along with your brother's, and then they'll know it's all right."

So they got some paper and a pen, and the king he set down and twisted his head to one side, and chawed his tongue, and scrawled off something; and then they give the pen to the duke—and then for the first time, the duke looked sick. But he took the pen and wrote. So then the lawyer turns to the new old gentleman and says:

"You and your brother please write a line or two and sign your names."

THE DUKE WROTE.

Tho old gentleman wrote, but nobody couldn't read it. The lawyer looked powerful astonished, and says:

"Well, it beats *me*"—and snaked a lot of old letters out of his pocket, and examined them, and then examined the old man's writing, and then *them* again; and then says: "These old letters is from Harvey Wilks; and here's *these* two's handwritings, and anybody can see *they* didn't write them" (the king and the duke looked sold and foolish, I tell you, to see how the lawyer had took them in), "and here's *this* old gentleman's handwriting, and anybody can tell, easy enough, *he* didn't write them—fact is, the scratches he makes ain't properly *writing* at all. Now here's some letters from——"

The new old gentleman says:

"If you please, let me explain. Nobody can read my hand but my brother there—so he copies for me. It's *his* hand you've got there, not mine."

"*Well!*" says the lawyer, "this *is* a state of things. I've got some of William's letters too; so if you'll get him to write a line or so we can com——"

"He *can't* write with his left hand," says the old gentleman. "If he could use his right hand, you would see that he wrote his own letters and mine too. Look at both, please—they're by the same hand."

The lawyer done it, and says:

"I believe it's so—and if it ain't so, there's a heap stronger resemblance than I'd noticed before, anyway. Well, well, well! I thought we was right on the track of a slution, but it's gone **7** to grass, partly. But anyway, *one* thing is proved—*these* two ain't either of 'em Wilkses"—and he wagged his head towards the king and the duke.

Well, what do you think?—that muleheaded old fool

7 *it's gone to grass.* It's been knocked out, it's finished; prizefight slang, referring to the time when bare-knuckle bouts were staged in open fields. In Chapter 72 of *Roughing It*, Twain used the expression in writing of a Hawaiian king who went mad and challenged every man he met to box or wrestle: "Of course this pastime lost its novelty, inasmuch as it must necessarily have been the case when so powerful a deity sent a frail human opponent 'to grass' he never came back anymore."

8 *what was tattooed on his breast.* According to his notes for the novel (quoted by DeVoto, *Mark Twain at Work*, p. 76), Twain originally intended Peter Wilks's distinguishing characteristic mentioned in the letter to be the grotesque "glass eye with mark on the back of it."

9 *squshed.* Crushed, a vulgarism.

10 *to get fetched such a solid one.* To be struck with a powerful blow; appropriately, Huck describes this battle of wits in prizefight terms.

11 *he'll throw up the sponge.* Acknowledge defeat, like a fallen prizefighter.

12 *blister.* An objectionable person.

13 *pard.* Partner, pal.

14 *the whole* bilin' *of 'm.* The whole boiling of them, a seething mass, usually of people; the whole lot, omitting nothing, as in "the whole kit and caboodle."

15 *Le's duck 'em!* Let's tar and feather them! It is astonishing how quickly these previously hospitable people have turned from their affection for to hatred of these men.

wouldn't give in *then!* Indeed he wouldn't. Said it warn't no fair test. Said his brother William was the cussedest joker in the world, and hadn't *tried* to write—he see William was going to play one of his jokes the minute he put the pen to paper. And so he warmed up and went warbling and warbling right along, till he was actually beginning to believe what he was saying, *himself*—but pretty soon the new old gentleman broke in, and says:

"I've thought of something. Is there anybody here that helped to lay out my br—helped to lay out the late Peter Wilks for burying?"

"Yes," says somebody, "me and Ab Turner done it. We're both here."

Then the old man turns towards the king, and says:

8 "Per'aps this gentleman can tell me what was tattooed on his breast?"

Blamed if the king didn't have to brace up mighty quick,

9 or he'd a squshed down like a bluff bank that the river has cut under, it took him so sudden—and mind you, it was a thing

10 that was calculated to make most *anybody* sqush to get fetched such a solid one as that without any notice—because how was *he* going to know what was tattooed on the man? He whitened a little; he couldn't help it; and it was mighty still in there, and everybody bending a little forwards and gazing at him.

11 Says I to myself, *Now* he'll throw up the sponge—there ain't no more use. Well, did he? A body can't hardly believe it, but he didn't. I reckon he thought he'd keep the thing up till he tired them people out, so they'd thin out, and him and the duke could break loose and get away. Anyway, he set there, and pretty soon he begun to smile, and says:

"Mf! It's a *very* tough question, *ain't* it! *Yes*, sir, I k'n tell you what's tattooed on his breast. It's jest a small, thin, blue arrow—that's what it is; and if you don't look clost, you can't see it. *Now* what do you say—hey?"

12 Well *I* never see anything like that old blister for clean out-and-out cheek.

The new old gentleman turns brisk towards Ab Turner and

13 his pard, and his eye lights up like he judged he had got the king *this* time, and says:

"There—you've heard what he said! Was there any such mark on Peter Wilks's breast?"

Both of them spoke up and says:

"We didn't see no such mark."

"Good!" says the old gentleman. "Now, what you *did* see on his breast was a small dim P, and a B (which is an initial he dropped when he was young), and a W, with dashes between them, so: P—B—W"—and he marked them that way on a piece of paper. "Come—ain't that what you saw?"

Both of them spoke up again, and says:

"No, we *didn't.* We never seen any marks at all."

Well, everybody *was* in a state of mind now; and they sings out:

14, 15 "The whole *bilin'* of 'm 's frauds! Le's duck 'em! le's drown

"GENTLEMEN — GENTLEMEN!"

'em! le's ride 'em on a rail!" and everybody was whooping at once, and there was a rattling pow-wow. But the lawyer he jumps on the table and yells, and says:

"Gentlemen—gentle*men!* Hear me just a word—just a *single* word—if you PLEASE! There's one way yet—let's go and dig up the corpse and look."

That took them.

"Hooray!" they all shouted, and was starting right off; but the lawyer and the doctor sung out:

"Hold on, hold on! Collar all these four men and the boy, and fetch *them* along, too!"

"We'll do it!" they all shouted: "and if we don't find them marks we'll lynch the whole gang!"

I *was* scared, now, I tell you. But there warn't no getting away, you know. They gripped us all, and marched us right along, straight for the graveyard, which was a mile and a half down the river, and the whole town at our heels, for we made noise enough, and it was only nine in the evening.

As we went by our house I wished I hadn't sent Mary Jane out of town; because now if I could tip her the wink, she'd light out and save me, and blow on our dead-beats.

Well, we swarmed along down the river road, just carrying on like wild-cats; and to make it more scary, the sky was darking up, and the lightning beginning to wink and flitter, and the wind to shiver amongst the leaves. This was the most awful trouble and most dangersome I ever was in; and I was kinder stunned; everything was going so different from what I had allowed for; stead of being fixed so I could take my own time, if I wanted to, and see all the fun, and have Mary Jane at my back to save me and set me free when the close-fit come, here was nothing in the world betwixt me and sudden death but just them tattoo-marks. If they didn't find them—

16 *Goliar.* Goliath, the giant David slew (I Samuel 17).

17 *then such another crowding, . . . to scrouge in and get a sight, you never see.* Except in Chapter 21: This crowd acts just the way the Bricksville mob did when they tried to get a look at the dying Boggs.

18 *a perfect sluice of white glare.* A straight band of glaring light; from mining slang, referring to the jet of water in a trough used for washing out gold from clods of dirt.

19 *She* was *the best girl I ever see, and had the most sand.* In the manuscript, Twain had written, "She *was* the best girl that ever was! and you could depend on her like the everlasting sun and the stars, every time"; but it was changed in proof, because, as Ferguson argued in "Huck Finn Aborning" (p. 174), "The speech might have fitted the mouth of the Playboy of the Western World, but not Huck's." As it stands, the terse statement is a fitting conclusion to the boy's high admiration for Mary Jane.

I couldn't bear to think about it; and yet, somehow, I couldn't think about nothing else. It got darker and darker, and it was a beautiful time to give the crowd the slip; but that big husky had me by the wrist—Hines—and a body might as **16** well try to give Goliar the slip. He dragged me right along, he was so excited; and I had to run to keep up.

When they got there they swarmed into the graveyard and washed over it like an overflow. And when they got to the grave, they found they had about a hundred times as many shovels as they wanted, but nobody hadn't thought to fetch a lantern. But they sailed into digging, anyway, by the flicker of the lightning, and sent a man to the nearest house a half a mile off, to borrow one.

So they dug and dug, like everything; and it got awful dark, and the rain started, and the wind swished and swushed along, and the lightning come brisker and brisker, and the thunder boomed; but them people never took no notice of it, they was so full of this business; and one minute you could see everything and every face in that big crowd, and the shovelfuls of dirt sailing up out of the grave, and the next second the dark wiped it all out, and you couldn't see nothing at all.

At last they got out the coffin, and begun to unscrew the **17** lid, and then such another crowding, and shouldering, and shoving as there was, to scrouge in and get a sight, you never see; and in the dark, that way, it was awful. Hines he hurt my wrist dreadful, pulling and tugging so, and I reckon he clean forgot I was in the world, he was so excited and panting.

18   All of a sudden the lightning let go a perfect sluice of white glare, and somebody sings out:

"By the living jingo, here's the bag of gold on his breast!"

Hines let out a whoop, like everybody else, and dropped my wrist and give a big surge to bust his way in and get a look, and the way I lit out and shinned for the road in the dark, there ain't nobody can tell.

I had the road all to myself, and I fairly flew—leastways I had it all to myself except the solid dark, and the now-and-then glares, and the buzzing of the rain, and the thrashing of the wind, and the splitting of the thunder; and sure as you are born I did clip it along!

When I struck the town, I see there warn't nobody out in the storm, so I never hunted for no back streets, but humped it straight through the main one; and when I begun to get towards our house I aimed my eye and set it. No light there; the house all dark—which made me feel sorry and disappointed, I didn't know why. But at last, just as I was sailing by, *flash* comes the light in Mary Jane's window! and my heart swelled up sudden, like to bust; and the same second the house and all was behind me in the dark, and wasn't ever going to be **19** before me no more in this world. She *was* the best girl I ever see, and had the most sand.

The minute I was far enough above the town to see I could

make the tow-head, I begun to look sharp for a boat to borrow; and the first time the lightning showed me one that wasn't chained, I snatched it and shoved. It was a canoe, and warn't fastened with nothing but a rope. The tow-head was a rattling big distance off, away out there in the middle of the river, but I didn't lose no time; and when I struck the raft at last, I was so fagged I would a just laid down to blow and gasp if I could afforded it. But I didn't. As I sprung aboard I sung out:

"Out with you, Jim, and set her loose! Glory be to goodness, we're shut of them!"

Jim lit out, and was a coming for me with both arms spread,

"JIM LET OUT."

he was so full of joy; but when I glimpsed him in the lightning, my heart shot up in my mouth, and I went overboard backwards; for I forgot he was old King Lear and a drownded A-rab all in one, and it most scared the livers and lights out of me. But Jim fished me out, and was going to hug me and bless me, and so on, he was so glad I was back and we was shut of the king and the duke, but I says:

"Not now—have it for breakfast, have it for breakfast! **20** Cut loose and let her slide!"

So, in two seconds, away we went, a sliding down the river, and it *did* seem so good to be free again and all by ourselves on the big river and nobody to bother us. I had to skip around a bit, and jump up and crack my heels a few times, I couldn't help it; but about the third crack I noticed a sound that I knowed mighty well—and held my breath and listened and waited—and sure enough, when the next flash busted out over the water, here they come!—and just a laying to their oars and making their skiff hum! It was the king and the duke.

So I wilted right down on to the planks, then, and give up; and it was all I could do to keep from crying.

20 *have it for breakfast.* "Put a lid on it," wait until later.

Chapter XXX

1 *The man . . . kept saying he had a boy about as big as me that died last year*. Another instance of Huck's preoccupation with death.

THE KING SHAKES HUCK.

When they got aboard, the king went for me, and shook me by the collar, and says:

"Tryin' to give us the slip, was ye, you pup! Tired of our company—hey?"

I says:

"No, your majesty, we warn't—*please* don't, your majesty!"

"Quick, then, and tell us what *was* your idea, or I'll shake the insides out o' you!"

"Honest, I'll tell you everything, just as it happened, your ma-

1 jesty. The man that had aholt of me was very good to me, and kept saying he had a boy about as big as me that died last year, and he was sorry to see a boy in such a dangerous fix; and when they was all took by surprise by finding the gold, and made a rush for the coffin, he lets go of me and whispers, 'Heel it, now, or they'll hang ye, sure!' and I lit out. It didn't seem no good for *me* to stay—I couldn't do nothing, and I didn't want to be hung if I could get away. So I never stopped running till I found the canoe; and when I got here I told Jim to hurry, or they'd catch me and hang me yet, and

said I was afeard you and the duke wasn't alive, now, and I was awful sorry, and so was Jim, and was awful glad when we see you coming, you may ask Jim if I didn't."

Jim said it was so; and the king told him to shut up, and said, "Oh, yes, it's *mighty* likely!" and shook me up again, and said he reckoned he'd drownd me. But the duke says:

"Leggo the boy, you old idiot! Would *you* a done any different? Did you inquire around for *him*, when you got loose? *I* don't remember it."

So the king let go of me, and begun to cuss that town and everybody in it. But the duke says:

"You better a blame sight give *yourself* a good cussing, for you're the one that's entitled to it most. You hain't done a thing, from the start, that had any sense in it, except coming out so cool and cheeky with that imaginary blue-arrow mark. That *was* bright—it was right down bully; and it was the thing that saved us. For if it hadn't been for that, they'd a jailed us till them Englishmen's baggage come—and then—the penitentiary, you bet! But that trick took 'em to the graveyard, and the gold done us a still bigger kindness; for if the excited fools hadn't let go all holts and made that rush to get a look, we'd a **2** slept in our cravats to-night—cravats warranted to *wear*, too—longer than *we'd* need 'em."

They was still a minute—thinking—then the king says, kind of absent-minded like:

"Mf! And we reckoned the *niggers* stole it!"

That made me squirm!

"Yes," says the duke, kinder slow, and deliberate, and sarcastic, "*We* did."

After about a half a minute, the king drawls out:

"Leastways—*I* did."

The duke says, the same way:

"On the contrary—*I* did."

The king kind of ruffles up, and says:

"Looky here, Bilgewater, what'r you referrin' to?"

The duke says, pretty brisk:

"When it comes to that, maybe you'll let me ask, what was *you* referring to?"

"Shucks!" says the king, very sarcastic; "but *I* don't know—maybe you was asleep, and didn't know what you was about."

The duke bristles right up now, and says:

"Oh, let *up* on this cussed nonsense—do you take me for a blame' fool? Don't you reckon *I* know who hid that money in that coffin?"

"*Yes*, sir! I know you *do* know—because you done it yourself!"

"It's a lie!"—and the duke went for him. The king sings out:

"Take y'r hands off!—leggo my throat!—I take it all back!"

2 *we'd a slept in our cravats to-night—cravats warranted to wear, too—longer than* we'd *need 'em.* The duke, speaking in traveling salesman's lingo, is making a rather grisly joke about their escape from a "necktie party"—their being hanged by the mob. Perhaps he speaks in such a roundabout way, because it was considered bad luck to talk about getting hanged.

3 *to hook.* To steal cleverly.

4 *I never see such an old ostrich for wanting to gobble everything.* Supposedly ostriches will eat anything, even metal.

5 *you wanted to get what money I'd got out of the Nonesuch and one thing or another, and scoop it all!* In the manuscript the duke ended this accusation by calling the king "you unsatisfiable, tunnel-bellied old sewer!" (Ferguson, "Huck Finn Aborning," p. 180).

THE DUKE WENT FOR HIM.

The duke says:

"Well, you just own up, first, that you *did* hide that money there, intending to give me the slip one of these days, and come back and dig it up, and have it all to yourself."

"Wait jest a minute, duke—answer me this one question, honest and fair; if you didn't put the money there, say it, and I'll b'lieve you, and take back everything I said."

"You old scoundrel, I didn't, and you know I didn't. There, now!"

"Well, then, I b'lieve you. But answer me only jest this one more—now *don't* git mad; didn't you have it in your *mind*
3 to hook the money and hide it?"

The duke never said nothing for a little bit; then he says:

"Well—I don't care if I *did*, I didn't *do* it anyway. But you not only had it in mind to do it, but you *done* it."

"I wisht I may never die if I done it, duke, and that's honest. I won't say I warn't *goin'* to do it, because I *was*; but you—I mean somebody—got in ahead o' me."

"It's a lie! You done it, and you got to *say* you done it, or——"

The king begun to gurgle, and then he gasps out:

"'Nough!—*I own up!*"

I was very glad to hear him say that, it made me feel much more easier than what I was feeling before. So the duke took his hands off, and says:

"If you ever deny it again, I'll drown you. It's *well* for you to set there and blubber like a baby—it's fitten for you,
4 after the way you've acted. I never see such an old ostrich for wanting to gobble everything—and I a trusting you all the time, like you was my own father. You ought to been ashamed of yourself to stand by and hear it saddled on to a lot of poor niggers and you never say a word for 'em. It makes me feel ridiculous to think I was soft enough to *believe* that rubbage. Cuss you, I can see, now, why you was so anxious to make up
5 the deffesit—you wanted to get what money I'd got out of the Nonesuch, and one thing or another, and scoop it *all!*"

The king says, timid, and still a snuffling:

"Why, duke, it was you that said make up the deffersit, it warn't me."

"Dry up! I don't want to hear no more *out* of you!" says the duke. "And *now* you see what you *got* by it. They've got all their own money back, and all of *ourn* but a shekel or **6** two, *besides*. G'long to bed—and don't you deffersit *me* no more deffersits, long 's *you* live!"

So the king sneaked into the wigwam, and took to his bottle for comfort; and before long the duke tackled *his* bottle; and so in about a half an hour they was as thick as thieves again, **7** and the tighter they got, the lovinger they got; and went off a snoring in each other's arms. They both got powerful mellow, but I noticed the king didn't get mellow enough to forget to remember to not deny about hiding the money-bag again. That made me feel easy and satisfied. Of course when they got to snoring, we had a long gabble, and I told Jim everything. **8**

6 *a shekel*. A coin of ancient Babylon, metaphorically worth even less than a penny.

7 *as thick as thieves*. An appropriate metaphor, common to Southwestern humor.

8 *a long gabble*. A rapid, continuous, and intimate conversation.

1 *Spanish moss*. Also called "longbeard," native to the South; Mrs. Frances Trollope wrote in *Domestic Manners of the Americans* (1832, p. 8) that "it hangs gracefully from the boughs, converting the outline of all trees it hangs from into that of weeping willows." Although it grows on trees, it is not a parasite but an epiphyte; it takes no nourishment from the boughs from which it hangs. The appearance of Spanish moss suggests that the fugitives are now in the southeast corner of Arkansas, in Chicot County.

2 *they done a lecture on temperance; but they didn't make enough for them both to get drunk on*. This paragraph begins with a series of sarcastic puns.

3 *yellocution*. An onomatopoetic pun on elocution, a method of public speaking.

Chapter XXXI

SPANISH MOSS.

We dasn't stop again at any town, for days and days; kept right along down the river. We was down south in the warm weather, now, and a mighty long ways from home. We begun to come to trees with Spanish moss on them, hanging down from the limbs like long gray beards. It was the first I ever see it growing, and it made the woods look solemn and dismal. So now the frauds reckoned they was out of danger, and they begun to work the villages again.

First they done a lecture on temperance; but they didn't make enough for them both to get drunk on. Then in another village they started a dancing school; but they didn't know no more how to dance than a kangaroo does; so the first prance they made, the general public jumped in and pranced them out of town. Another time they tried a go at yellocution; but they didn't yellocute long till the audience got up and give them a solid good cussing and made them skip out. They tackled missionarying, and mesmerisering, and doctoring, and telling

280

fortunes, and a little of everything; but they couldn't seem to have no luck. So at last they got just about dead broke, and laid around the raft, as she floated along, thinking, and thinking, and never saying nothing, by the half a day at a time, and dreadful blue and desperate.

And at last they took a change, and begun to lay their heads together in the wigwam and talk low and confidential two or three hours at a time. Jim and me got uneasy. We didn't like the look of it. We judged they was studying up some kind of worse deviltry than ever. We turned it over and over, and at last we made up our minds they was going to break into somebody's house or store, or was going into the counterfeit-money business, or something. So then we was pretty scared, and made up an agreement that we wouldn't have nothing in the world to do with such actions, and if we ever got the least show we would give them the cold shake, and clear out and **4** leave them behind. Well, early one morning we hid the raft in a good safe place about two mile below a little bit of a shabby village, named Pikesville, and the king he went ashore, and **5** told us all to stay hid whilst he went up to town and smelt around to see if anybody had got any wind of the Royal Nonesuch there yet. ("House to rob, you *mean*," says I to myself; "and when you get through robbing it you'll come back here and wonder what's become of me and Jim and the raft—and you'll have to take it out in wondering.") And he said if he warn't back by midday, the duke and me would know it was all right, and we was to come along.

So we staid where we was. The duke he fretted and sweated around, and was in a mighty sour way. He scolded us for everything, and we couldn't seem to do nothing right; he found **6** fault with every little thing. Something was a-brewing sure. I was good and glad when midday come and no king; we could have a change, anyway—and maybe a chance for *the* change, on top of it. So me and the duke went up to the village, and hunted around there for the king, and by-and-by we found him in the back room of a little low doggery, very tight, and a lot **7** of loafers bullyragging him for sport, and he a cussing and threatening with all his might, and so tight he couldn't walk, and couldn't do nothing to them. The duke he begun to abuse him for an old fool, and the king begun to sass back; and the minute they was fairly at it, I lit out, and shook the reefs out **8** of my hind legs, and spun down the river road like a deer—for I see our chance; and I made up my mind that it would be a long day before they ever see me and Jim again. I got down there all out of breath but loaded up with joy, and sung out—

"Set her loose, Jim, we're all right, now!"

But there warn't no answer, and nobody come out of the wigwam. Jim was gone! I set up a shout—and then another —and then another one; and run this way and that in the woods, whooping and screeching; but it warn't no use—old Jim was gone. Then I set down and cried; I couldn't help it. But I couldn't set still long. Pretty soon I went out on the road,

4 *give them the cold shake*. Give them the slip.

5 *Pikesville*. Another backwoods town in the tradition of James M. Field's "Pokerville" and William Tappan Thompson's "Pineville."

6 *he found fault with every little thing*. In the manuscript, Twain had initially appended to this sentence, "and he even cussed Jim for being a fool and keeping his blue paint and King Lear clothes on, and made him take them off and wash himself off; and yet it warn't no fault of Jim's, for nobody ever told him he might do it"; but Twain crossed it out and noted in the margin, "This is lugged—shove it back yonder to where they escape lynching and regain raft" (Ferguson, "Huck Finn Aborning," pp. 177–178). However, Twain forgot to make the change, and so the novel never tells when or how Jim took off his "sick Arab" costume. Also, the deleted passage describes the duke's changing attitude toward Jim, a change of heart which allows the scoundrel's betrayal of the slave later in the chapter.

7 *doggery*. Groggery, a low drinking saloon.

8 *shook the reefs out of my hind legs*. Loosened himself up to go running off, from nautical slang.

9 *an old fellow . . . sold out his chance in him for forty dollars, becuz he's got to go up the river and can't wait.* Like Judge Clemens: Once Sam's father had to go down the river to settle a long-standing debt owed him, and because the man did not have the cash, he paid the judge with a slave named Charley; but to help him pay his way back up the river, he sold the slave for ten barrels of tar worth forty dollars. Years later, his son ashamedly recalled that his father then referred to the slave as no more than "an ox—and somebody else's ox. It makes a body homesick for Charley, even after fifty years" (quoted by Wecter, *Sam Clemens of Hannibal*, pp. 74–75). Although he never knew Charley, Twain's shame was nevertheless immense, and it obviously colored Huck's grief over the sale of his friend Jim.

trying to think what I better do, and I run across a boy walking, and asked him if he'd seen a strange nigger, dressed so and so, and he says:

"Yes."

"Wherebouts?" says I.

"Down to Silas Phelps' place, two mile below here. He's a runaway nigger, and they've got him. Was you looking for him?"

"You bet I ain't. I run across him in the woods about an hour or two ago, and he said if I hollered he'd cut my livers out—and told me to lay down and stay where I was; and I done it. Been there ever since; afeard to come out."

"Well," he says, "you needn't be afeard no more, becuz they've got him. He run off f'm down South, som'ers."

"It's a good job they got him."

"Well, I *reckon!* There's two hunderd dollars reward on him. It's like picking up money out'n the road."

"Yes, it is—and *I* could a had it if I'd been big enough; I see him *first.* Who nailed him?"

9 "It was an old fellow—a stranger—and he sold out his chance in him for forty dollars, becuz he's got to go up the river and can't wait. Think o' that, now! You bet *I'd* wait, if it was seven year."

"That's me, every time," says I. "But maybe his chance ain't worth no more than that, if he'll sell it so cheap. Maybe there's something ain't straight about it."

"But it *is*, though—straight as a string. I see the hand-

"WHO NAILED HIM?"

bill myself. It tells all about him, to a dot—paints him like a picture, and tells the plantation he's frum, below New*rleans*. No-sirree-*bob*, they ain't no trouble 'bout *that* speculation, you bet you. Say, gimme a chaw tobacker, won't ye?"

I didn't have none, so he left. I went to the raft, and set down in the wigwam to think. But I couldn't come to nothing. I thought till I wore my head sore, but I couldn't see no way out of the trouble. After all this long journey, and after all we'd done for them scoundrels, here was it all come to nothing, everything all busted up and ruined, because they could have the heart to serve Jim such a trick as that, and make him a slave again all his life, and amongst strangers, too, for forty dirty dollars.

Once I said to myself it would be a thousand times better for Jim to be a slave at home where his family was, as long as he'd *got* to be a slave, and so I'd better write a letter to Tom Sawyer, and tell him to tell Miss Watson where he was. But I soon give up that notion, for two things: she'd be mad and disgusted at his rascality and ungratefulness for leaving her, and so she'd sell him straight down the river again; and if she didn't, everybody naturally despises an ungrateful nigger, and they'd make Jim feel it all the time, and so he'd feel ornery and disgraced. And then think of *me!* It would get all around that Huck Finn helped a nigger to get his freedom; and if I was to ever see anybody from that town again, I'd be ready to get down and lick his boots for shame. That's just the way; a person does a low-down thing, and then he don't want to take no consequences of it. Thinks as long as he can hide it, it ain't no disgrace. That was my fix exactly. The more I studied about this, the more my conscience went to grinding me, and the more wicked and low-down and ornery I got to feeling. And at last, when it hit me all of a sudden that here was the plain hand of Providence slapping me in the face and letting me know my wickedness was being watched all the time from up there in heaven, whilst I was stealing a poor old woman's nigger that hadn't ever done me no harm, and now was showing me there's One that's always on the look-out, and ain't agoing to allow no such miserable doings to go only just so fur and no further, I most dropped in my tracks I was so scared. Well, I tried the best I could to kinder soften it up somehow for myself, by saying I was brung up wicked, and so I warn't so much to blame; but something inside of me kept saying, "There was the Sunday-school, you could a gone to it; and if you'd a done it they'd a learnt you, there, that people that acts as I'd been acting about that nigger goes to everlasting fire." **10**

It made me shiver. And I about made up my mind to pray; and see if I couldn't try to quit being the kind of a boy I was, and be better. So I kneeled down. But the words wouldn't come. Why wouldn't they? It warn't no use to try and hide it from Him. Nor from *me*, neither. I knowed very well why they wouldn't come. It was because my heart warn't right; it was because I warn't square; it was because I was playing

10 *everlasting fire.* Twain did not believe in the hellfire-and-damnation vision of the next world. "If I am appointed to live again," he wrote on the popular conception of Hell in the 1880s (in a statement published in *What Is Man?*, 1973, p. 57), "I feel sure it will be for some more sane and useful purpose than to flounder about for ages in a lake of fire and brimstone for having violated a confusion of ill-defined and contradictory rules said (but not evidenced) to be divine institution." Because he could not see how eternal punishment could serve any good, Twain did not believe it could exist. "To chasten a man in order to perfect him might be reasonable enough," he continued; "to annihilate him when he shall have proved incapable of reaching perfection might be reasonable enough: but to roast him forever for the mere satisfaction of seeing him roast would not be reasonable—even the atrocious God imagined by the Jews would tire of the spectacle eventually." However, unlike his creator, Huck is fully a product of the society in which he was raised; he can believe in (and fear) only what he has been taught to be reality.

double. I was letting *on* to give up sin, but away inside of me I was holding on to the biggest one of all. I was trying to make my mouth *say* I would do the right thing and the clean thing, and go and write to that nigger's owner and tell where he was; but deep down in me I knowed it was a lie—and He knowed it. You can't pray a lie—I found that out.

So I was full of trouble, full as I could be; and didn't know what to do. At last I had an idea; and I says, I'll go and write the letter—and *then* see if I can pray. Why, it was astonishing, the way I felt as light as a feather, right straight off, and my troubles all gone. So I got a piece of paper and a pencil, all glad and excited, and set down and wrote:

> Miss Watson your runaway nigger Jim is down here two mile below Pikesville and Mr. Phelps has got him and he will give him up for the reward if you send. HUCK FINN.

I felt good and all washed clean of sin for the first time I had ever felt so in my life, and I knowed I could pray now. But I didn't do it straight off, but laid the paper down and set

THINKING.

there thinking—thinking how good it was all this happened so, and how near I come to being lost and going to hell. And went on thinking. And got to thinking over our trip down the river; and I see Jim before me, all the time, in the day, and in the night-time, sometimes moonlight, sometimes storms, and we a floating along, talking, and singing, and laughing. But somehow I couldn't seem to strike no places to harden me against him, but only the other kind. I'd see him standing my watch on top of his'n, stead of calling me, so I could go on sleeping; and see him how glad he was when I come back out of the fog; and when I come to him again in the swamp, up there where the feud was; and such-like times; and would

always call me honey, and pet me, and do everything he could
think of for me, and how good he always was; and at last I
struck the time I saved him by telling the men we had small-
pox aboard, and he was so grateful, and said I was the best
friend old Jim ever had in the world, and the *only* one he's
got now; and then I happened to look around, and see that
paper.

It was a close place. I took it up, and held it in my hand.
I was a trembling, because I'd got to decide, for ever, betwixt
two things, and I knowed it. I studied a minute, sort of holding my breath, and then says to myself:

"All right, then, I'll *go* to hell"—and tore it up. **11**

It was awful thoughts, and awful words, but they was said.
And I let them stay said; and never thought no more about
reforming. I shoved the whole thing out of my head; and
said I would take up wickedness again, which was in my line, **12**
being brung up to it, and the other warn't. And for a starter,
I would go to work and steal Jim out of slavery again; and if **13**
I could think up anything worse, I would do that, too; because
as long as I was in, and in for good, I might as well go the
whole hog.

Then I set to thinking over how to get at it, and turned
over considerable many ways in my mind; and at last fixed up
a plan that suited me. So then I took the bearings of a woody
island that was down the river a piece, and as soon as it was
fairly dark I crept out with my raft and went for it, and hid it
there, and then turned in. I slept the night through, and got
up before it was light, and had my breakfast, and put on my **14**
store clothes, and tied up some others and one thing or another
in a bundle, and took the canoe and cleared for shore. I landed
below where I judged was Phelps' place, and hid my bundle in
the woods, and then filled up the canoe with water, and loaded
rocks into her and sunk her where I could find her again when
I wanted her, about a quarter of a mile below a little steam
sawmill that was on the bank.

Then I struck up the road, and when I passed the mill I
see a sign on it, "Phelps' Sawmill," and when I come to the
farm-houses, two or three hundred yards further along, I kept
my eyes peeled, but didn't see nobody around, though it was
good daylight, now. But I didn't mind, because I didn't want
to see nobody just yet—I only wanted to get the lay of the
land. According to my plan, I was going to turn up there
from the village, not from below. So I just took a look, and
shoved along, straight for town. Well, the very first man I see,
when I got there, was the duke. He was sticking up a bill
for the Royal Nonesuch—three-night performance—like that
other time. *They* had the cheek, them frauds! I was right
on him, before I could shirk. He looked astonished, and says:

"Hel-*lo*! Wher'd *you* come from?" Then he says, kind
of glad and eager, "Where's the raft?—got her in a good
place?"

I says:

11 "*All right, then, I'll go to hell.*" Finally, in this
famous crisis of conscience, Huck resolves the eternal
battle between temperament and training; and if in
following his instincts he defies society, then the
public be damned. There is indeed a morality which
is greater than that of social approval. Huck has
grown tremendously in character since he fled from
Pap's shanty to Jackson's Island; and now that he has
condemned himself, there is no turning back.

This decision is the climax of the novel; and as is
generally acknowledged, now begins the slow decline
of the narrative. There are indeed certain lapses in
Huck's character in the subsequent chapters; but
never does the boy regret his having aided the
runaway in his flight, and never does he weaken in
his determination to set his friend free for once and
all. Leo Marx in his notes to the 1967 Bobbs-Merrill
edition has pointed out that in pushing Huck the
"wrong way" in his tug of war between his conscience and temptation, Twain has inverted a standard method of Christian rhetoric that goes back
as far as the fourth century, to Saint Augustine's
Confessions.

12 *I would take up wickedness again, which was in my
line, being brung up to it.* Blair in *Mark Twain and Huck
Finn* (p. 353) has explained how Twain made extensive changes in this passage in the first revision of his
manuscript, by enlarging it by almost one hundred
and fifty words and making it more serious and more
earnest. The earlier draft included such a facetious
comment as, "What I had been getting ready for, and
longing for and pining for; always, day and night and
Sundays, was a career of crime. And just that thing
was the thing I was a-starting in on, now, for good
and all." So originally Twain intended this section in
part to be a return to the tone of the opening of the
novel, to the discussion of Tom Sawyer's Gang; but
in its final version, it became the classic argument
against conventional morality in nineteenth-century
American fiction.

13 *if I could think up anything worse, I would do that,
too.* Twain expressed the same sentiments in his
speech on "Theoretical and Practical Morals" (in
Mark Twain's Speeches, 1910, p. 132). "As by the fires
of experience, so by commission of crime," he slyly
argued, "you learn real morals. Commit all the
crimes, familiarize yourself with all sins, take them in
rotation (there are only two or three thousand of
them), stick to it, commit two or three every day, and
by-and-by you will be proof against them. When you
are through you will be proof against all sins and
morally perfect." Although he never did anything so
socially offensive as "nigger stealing," Twain admitted to his having stolen a watermelon when a boy;
but he was punished—the watermelon was green.

14 *my store clothes.* In the manuscript, Huck put on
"some old rough clothes" (Ferguson, "Huck Finn
Aborning," p. 178); but they would not have been
convincing for the mistaken identity of the following
chapter.

15 *matched half dollars*. A common gambling game in which the loser is determined by tossing coins.

16 *pegged along*. Worked on persistently.

17 *dry as a powder-horn*. He has not had a drop of liquor all this time; gunpowder was kept in a powderhorn to protect it from moisture.

" Why, that's just what I was agoing to ask your grace."

Then he didn't look so joyful—and says :

" What was your idea for asking *me?*" he says.

" Well," I says, " when I see the king in that doggery yesterday, I says to myself, we can't get him home for hours, till he's soberer ; so I went a loafing around town to put in the time, and wait. A man up and offered me ten cents to help him pull a skiff over the river and back to fetch a sheep, and so I went along ; but when we was dragging him to the boat, and the man left me aholt of the rope and went behind him to shove him along, he was too strong for me, and jerked loose and run, and we after him. We didn't have no dog, and so we had to chase him all over the country till we tired him out. We never got him till dark, then we fetched him over, and I started down for the raft. When I got there and see it was gone, I says to myself, ' they've got into trouble and had to leave ; and they've took my nigger, which is the only nigger I've got in the world, and now I'm in a strange country, and ain't got no property no more, nor nothing, and no way to make my living ;' so I set down and cried. I slept in the woods all night. But what *did* become of the raft then ?—and Jim, poor Jim ! "

" Blamed if *I* know—that is, what's become of the raft. That old fool had made a trade and got forty dollars, and when **15** we found him in the doggery the loafers had matched half dollars with him and got every cent but what he'd spent for whisky ; and when I got him home late last night and found the raft gone, we said, ' That little rascal has stole our raft and shook us, and run off down the river.' "

" I wouldn't shake my *nigger*, would I ?—the only nigger I had in the world, and the only property."

" We never thought of that. Fact is, I reckon we'd come to consider him *our* nigger ; yes, we did consider him so —goodness knows we had trouble enough for him. So when we see the raft was gone, and we flat broke, there warn't anything for it but to try the Royal Nonesuch another shake. And **16,17** I've pegged along ever since, dry as a powder-horn. Where's that ten cents ? Give it here."

I had considerable money, so I give him ten cents, but begged him to spend it for something to eat, and give me some, because it was all the money I had, and I hadn't had nothing to eat since yesterday. He never said nothing. The next minute he whirls on me and says :

" Do you reckon that nigger would blow on us ? We'd skin him if he done that ! "

" How can he blow ? Hain't he run off ? "

" No ! That old fool sold him, and never divided with me, and the money's gone."

" *Sold* him ? " I says, and begun to cry ; " why, he was *my* nigger, and that was my money. Where is he ?—I want my nigger."

" Well, you can't *get* your nigger, that's all—so dry up your blubbering. Looky here—do you think *you'd* venture to blow

18 *He looked kinder bothered.* And well he might, for he and the king could be arrested for "nigger stealing." But, of course, Huck does not dare "blow" on them.

HE GAVE HIM TEN CENTS.

on us? Blamed if I think I'd trust you. Why, if you *was* to blow on us—"

He stopped, but I never see the duke look so ugly out of his eyes before. I went on a-whimpering, and says:

"I don't want to blow on nobody; and I ain't got no time to blow, nohow. I got to turn out and find my nigger."

He looked kinder bothered, and stood there with his bills **18** fluttering on his arm, thinking, and wrinkling up his forehead. At last he says:

"I'll tell you something. We got to be here three days. If you'll promise you won't blow, and won't let the nigger blow, I'll tell you where to find him."

So I promised, and he says:

"A farmer by the name of Silas Ph——" and then he stopped. You see he started to tell me the truth; but when he stopped, that way, and begun to study and think again, I reckoned he was changing his mind. And so he was. He wouldn't trust me; he wanted to make sure of having me out of the way the whole three days. So pretty soon he says: "The man that bought him is named Abram Foster—Abram G. Foster—and he lives forty mile back here in the country, on the road to Lafayette."

"All right," I says, "I can walk it in three days. And I'll start this very afternoon."

"No you won't, you'll start *now*; and don't you lose any time about it, neither, nor do any gabbling by the way. Just keep a tight tongue in your head and move right along, and then you won't get into trouble with *us*, d'ye hear?"

That was the order I wanted, and that was the one I played for. I wanted to be left free to work my plans.

19 *some idiots don't require documents . . . down South here*. Apparently, because any "person of color" who traveled through Arkansas then was concluded to be a slave; after March 1843, no freed slave could emigrate to the state.

20 *the back country*. The interior and sparsely populated district.

"So clear out," he says; "and you can tell Mr. Foster whatever you want to. Maybe you can get him to believe that **19** Jim *is* your nigger—some idiots don't require documents—leastways I've heard there's such down South here. And when you tell him the handbill and the reward's bogus, maybe he'll believe you when you explain to him what the idea was for getting 'em out. Go 'long, now, and tell him anything you want to; but mind you don't work your jaw any *between* here and there."

20   So I left, and struck for the back country. I didn't look around, but I kinder felt like he was watching me. But I knowed I could tire him out at that. I went straight out in the country as much as a mile, before I stopped; then I doubled back through the woods towards Phelps'. I reckoned I better start in on my plan straight off, without fooling around, because I wanted to stop Jim's mouth till these fellows could get away. I didn't want no trouble with their kind. I'd seen all I wanted to of them, and wanted to get entirely shut of them.

STRIKING FOR THE BACK COUNTRY.

Chapter XXXII

STILL AND SUNDAY-LIKE.

When I got there it was all still and Sunday-like, and hot and sunshiny—the hands was gone to the fields; and there was them kind of faint dronings of bugs and flies in the air that makes it seem so lonesome and like everybody's dead and gone; and if a breeze fans along and quivers the leaves, it makes you feel mournful, because you feel like it's spirits whispering—spirits that's been dead ever so many years—and you always think they're talking about *you*. As a general **1** thing it makes a body wish *he* was dead, too, and done with it all.

Phelps' was one of these little one-horse cotton plantations; **2** and they all look alike. A rail fence round a two-acre yard; a stile, made out of logs sawed off and up-ended, in steps, like barrels of a different length, to climb over the fence with, and for the women to stand on when they are going to jump on to a horse; some sickly grass-patches in the big yard, but mostly it was bare and smooth, like an old hat with the nap rubbed off; big double log house for the white folks—hewed logs, with the

1 *As a general thing it makes a body wish he was dead, too, and done with it all.* Here Huck suffers from the same melancholy he described at the opening of the novel. "But it is right," T. S. Eliot noted in his introduction to a 1950 edition, "that the mood of the end of the book should bring us back to that of the beginning." Although the boy as yet is unaware of it, Twain has aptly returned his hero to the society that he had fled so many miles up the river. Huck again suffers the same sentiments (which he describes in almost the identical phrasing) in the opening of "Tom Sawyer, Detective."

2 *Phelps' was one of these little one-horse . . . plantations; and they all look alike.* And this one looks like that of Sam Clemens's uncle, John A. Quarles, in Monroe County, Missouri, recalled in Chapter 2 of the *Autobiography*: "It was a heavenly place for a boy. . . . The house was a double log one, with a spacious floor (roofed in) connecting it with the kitchen. . . . The farmhouse stood in the middle of a very large yard and the yard was fenced on three sides with rails and on the rear side with high palings; against these stood the smokehouse; beyond the palings was the orchard; beyond the orchard was the Negro quarters and the tobacco fields. The front yard was entered over a stile made of sawed-off logs of graduated heights. . . . Down a piece, abreast the house, stood a little log cabin against the rail fence; and there the woody hill fell sharply away, past the barns, the corncrib, the stables and the tobacco-curing house, to a limpid brook."

But the resemblance ended with the farm; Twain said that he never consciously used either Uncle John or his aunt in a book. The Phelps farm reappears as the locale of "Tom Sawyer, Detective."

3 *smoke-house*. Most Southern plantations, in these days before refrigeration, had small huts where tobacco, fish, or meat was smoked for preservation.

4 *ash-hopper*. A lye cask, resembling a hopper in a mill and containing ashes, in which the people made their soap.

5 *I heard the dim hum of a spinning-wheel wailing along up and sinking along down again . . . that is the lonesomest sound in the whole world.* Here Twain is recalling the spinning wheel at his uncle's farm, which he described in Chapter 3 of his *Autobiography* as "a wheel whose rising and falling wail, heard from a distance, was the mournfulest of all sounds to me and made me homesick and low spirited and filled my atmosphere with the wandering spirits of the dead."

6 *There ain't no harm in a hound, nohow.* "There ain't any dog that's got a lovelier disposition than a bloodhound," Huck admits in Chapter 9 of "Tom Sawyer, Detective." However, this breed was popularly believed to be savage, apparently due to nineteenth-century touring companies of *Uncle Tom's Cabin* which advertised "real live bloodhounds," tearing at Liza's flesh as she crosses the ice. On the contrary, bloodhounds are not vicious and do not attack their quarry.

"They peeped out from behind her." Illustration by E. W. Kemble, "Autograph Edition," 1899.

chinks stopped up with mud or mortar, and these mud-stripes been whitewashed some time or another; round-log kitchen, with a big broad, open but roofed passage joining it to the **3** house; log smoke-house back of the kitchen; three little log nigger-cabins in a row t'other side the smoke-house; one little hut all by itself away down against the back fence, and some **4** outbuildings down a piece the other side; ash-hopper, and big kettle to bile soap in, by the little hut; bench by the kitchen door, with bucket of water and a gourd; hound asleep there, in the sun; more hounds asleep, round about; about three shade-trees away off in a corner; some currant bushes and gooseberry bushes in one place by the fence; outside of the fence a garden and a water-melon patch; then the cotton fields begins; and after the fields, the woods.

I went around and clumb over the back stile by the ash-hopper, and started for the kitchen. When I got a little ways, **5** I heard the dim hum of a spinning-wheel wailing along up and sinking along down again; and then I knowed for certain I wished I was dead—for that *is* the lonesomest sound in the whole world.

I went right along, not fixing up any particular plan, but just trusting to Providence to put the right words in my mouth when the time come; for I'd noticed that Providence always did put the right words in my mouth, if I left it alone.

When I got half-way, first one hound and then another got up and went for me, and of course I stopped and faced them, and kept still. And such another pow-wow as they made! In a quarter of a minute I was a kind of a hub of a wheel, as you may say—spokes made out of dogs—circle of fifteen of them packed together around me, with their necks and noses stretched up towards me, a barking and howling; and more a coming; you could see them sailing over fences and around corners from everywheres.

A nigger woman come tearing out of the kichen with a rolling-pin in her hand, singing out, "Begone! *you* Tige! you Spot! begone, sah!" and she fetched first one and then another of them a clip and sent him howling, and then the rest followed; and the next second, half of them come back, wagging their **6** tails around me and making friends with me. There ain't no harm in a hound, nohow.

7 And behind the woman comes a little nigger girl and two little nigger boys, without anything on but tow-linen shirts, and they hung on to their mother's gown, and peeped out from behind her at me, bashful, the way they always do. And here comes the white woman running from the house, about forty-five or fifty year old, bareheaded, and her spinning-stick in her **8** hand; and behind her comes her little white children, acting the same way the little niggers was doing. She was smiling all over so she could hardly stand—and says:

"It's *you*, at last!—*ain't* it?"

I out with a "Yes'm," before I thought.

She grabbed me and hugged me tight; and then gripped

SHE HUGGED HIM TIGHT.

me by both hands and shook and shook; and the tears come in her eyes, and run down over; and she couldn't seem to hug and shake enough, and kept saying, "You don't look as much like your mother as I reckoned you would, but law sakes, I don't care for that, I'm *so* glad to see you! Dear, dear, it does seem like I could eat you up! Childern, it's your Cousin Tom!—tell him howdy."

But they ducked their heads, and put their fingers in their mouths, and hid behind her. So she run on:

"Lize, hurry up and get him a hot breakfast, right away— or did you get your breakfast on the boat?"

I said I had got it on the boat. So then she started for the house, leading me by the hand, and the children tagging after. When we got there, she set me down in a split-bottomed **9** chair, and set herself down on a little low stool in front of me, holding both of my hands, and says:

"Now I can have a *good* look at you; and laws-a-me, I've **10** been hungry for it a many and a many a time, all these long years, and it's come at last! We been expecting you a couple of days and more. What's kep' you?—boat get aground?"

"Yes'm—she——"

"Don't say yes'm—say Aunt Sally. Where'd she get aground?"

I didn't rightly know what to say, because I didn't know whether the boat would be coming up the river or down. But I go a good deal on instinct; and my instinct said she would be coming up—from down towards Orleans. That didn't help me much, though; for I didn't know the names of bars down **11** that way. I see I'd got to invent a bar, or forget the name of the one we got aground on—or— Now I struck an idea, and fetched it out:

7 *a little nigger girl and two little nigger boys, without anything on but tow-linen shirts.* Twain noted in Chapter 20 of Vol. II of *The Innocents Abroad* that, during his travels through the Holy Land, the Arabs had "nothing on but a long coarse shirt like the 'tow-linen' shirts which used to form the only summer garment of little negro boys on Southern plantations."

8 *her little white children.* The manuscript introduced two of these children, named Mat and Phil and both about Huck's age; but he soon dropped them to avoid further complicating his plot. "But," Ferguson explained in "Huck Finn Aborning" (p. 173), "he neglected to revise downward the ages of Silas and Sally (at first called Ruth) Phelps, who therefore appear in the book somewhat elderly for the parents of so young a family." Kemble apparently followed the manuscript description for his picture. But no matter: Twain introduced another Phelps girl, eighteen-year-old Benny, as a central character in "Tom Sawyer, Detective."

9 *she set me down . . ., and set herself down . . . in front of me, holding both of my hands, and says.* Aunt Sally's questions and Huck's forced answers have much in common with another embarrassing interview, that between Twain and a lady in Lucerne (mentioned in Chapter 11, note 7). Huck experiences the same discomfort Twain did ("It appeared to me that the ice was getting pretty thin here," "I sat still and let the cold sweat run down") as he was plied with questions that he had not the faintest idea of how to answer honestly.

10 *laws-a-me.* A mild version of "Lord help me."

11 *the names of bars.* Because bars are dangerous deposits of sand, gravel, or earth which form shallow places or islands in the river, steamboat pilots named them (often only with numbers) to help in the navigation around them.

12 *Well, it's lucky; because sometimes people do get hurt.* Aunt Sally's callous statement is perhaps Twain's bitterest comment on how good Christian men and women considered slaves as less than human and thus undeserving of the compassion due any other people. Her attitude is that of Jane Clemens. "Yet, kind-hearted and compassionate as she was," Twain wrote of his mother in Chapter 7 of his *Autobiography*, "she was not conscious that slavery was a bald, grotesque, and unwarrantable usurpation. She had never heard it assailed in any pulpit but had heard it defended and sanctified in a thousand; her ears were familiar with Bible texts that approved it but if there were any that disapproved it they had not been quoted by her pastors; as far as her experience went, the wise and the good and the holy were unanimous in the conviction that slavery was right, righteous, sacred, the peculiar pet of the Deity and a condition which the slave himself ought to be daily and nightly thankful for. Manifestly, training and association can accomplish strange miracles."

An ironic reversal of this response to a shipboard accident is recorded by John Habermehl in "Human Life is Cheap" in his *Life on the Western Rivers* (1901, p. 88): "Right here all of a sudden we hear an 'Oh,' and the next thing a splash; 'a man overboard, a man overboard.' The news of the accident soon reaches the ears of the owners of the boat and causes a palpitation of the hearts, until the anxious inquiry, 'Was it a nigger, a nigger?' is answered by 'No, he was white, one of the Dutch roustabouts tumbled in with a load on his back.' The assurance that it was a Dutchman and no nigger to pay for stopped the fluttering of the heart, leaving it as calm as a summer morning, with a deep sigh, 'Poor fellow!'"

13 *the old* Lally Rook. According to Lytle in *Merchant Steam Vessels of the United States 1807–1868*, a side-wheeler named *Lalla Rookh* traveled from its home port of Mobile, Alabama, from 1838 until it was "abandoned" in 1847. It was named for the heroine (literally "Lilly Cheek") of the sentimental Near Eastern epic by Thomas Moore, written in imitation of Sir Walter Scott's medieval narrative poems; and just as Scott did not know the Middle Ages first hand, Moore had never been to the East.

14 *she blowed out a cylinder-head and crippled a man.* "Their engines are generally constructed on the high-pressure principle," Hamilton described the large New Orleans boats in *Men and Manners in America* (Vol. 2, p. 181), "and one or two generally blow up every season, sending a score or two of parboiled passengers to an inconvenient altitude in the atmosphere."

15 *the wharf-boat.* "On the Western rivers," Bartlett explained in his *Dictionary of Americanisms*, "the height of the water is so variable that a fixed wharf would be useless. In its place is used a rectangular float, in part covered, for the reception of goods, or for a dram-shop. It is generally on the shore side, and is entered by a plank or movable platform."

"It warn't the grounding—that didn't keep us back but a little. We blowed out a cylinder-head."

"Good gracious! anybody hurt?"

"No'm. Killed a nigger."

12 "Well, it's lucky; because sometimes people do get hurt. Two years ago last Christmas, your Uncle Silas was coming up **13, 14** from Newrleans on the old *Lally Rook,* and she blowed out a cylinder-head and crippled a man. And I think he died afterwards. He was a Babtist. Your Uncle Silas knowed a family in Baton Rouge that knowed his people very well. Yes, I remember, now he *did* die. Mortification set in, and they had to amputate him. But it didn't save him. Yes, it was mortification—that was it. He turned blue all over, and died in the hope of a glorious resurrection. They say he was a sight to look at. Your uncle's been up to the town every day to fetch you. And he's gone again, not more'n an hour ago: he'll be back any minute, now. You must a met him on the road, didn't you?—oldish man, with a——"

"No, I didn't see nobody, Aunt Sally. The boat landed **15** just at daylight, and I left my baggage on the wharf-boat and went looking around the town and out a piece in the country, to put in the time and not get here too soon; and so I come down the back way."

"Who'd you give the baggage to?"

"Nobody.'

"Why, child, it'll be stole!"

"Not where *I* hid it I reckon it won't," I says.

"How'd you get your breakfast so early on the boat?"

It was kinder thin ice, but I says:

"The captain see me standing around, and told me I better have something to eat before I went ashore; so he took me in **16** the texas to the officers' lunch, and give me all I wanted."

I was getting so uneasy I couldn't listen good. I had my mind on the children all the time; I wanted to get them out to one side, and pump them a little, and find out who I was. But I couldn't get no show, Mrs. Phelps kept it up and run on so. Pretty soon she made the cold chills streak all down my back, because she says:

"But here we're a running on this way, and you hain't told me a word about Sis, nor any of them. Now I'll rest my works a little, and you start up yourn; just tell me *everything*—tell me all about 'm all—every one of 'm; and how they are, and what they're doing, and what they told you to tell me; and every last thing you can think of."

Well, I see I was up a stump—and up it good. Providence had stood by me this fur, all right, but I was hard and tight aground, now. I see it warn't a bit of use to try to go ahead **17** —I'd *got* to throw up my hand. So I says to myself, here's another place where I got to resk the truth. I opened my mouth to begin; but she grabbed me and hustled me in behind the bed, and says:

"Here he comes! stick your head down lower—there,

that'll do; you can't be seen, now. Don't you let on you're here. I'll play a joke on him. Childern, don't you say a word."

I see I was in a fix, now. But it warn't no use to worry; there warn't nothing to do but just hold still, and try and be ready to stand from under when the lightning struck.

I had just one little glimpse of the old gentleman when he come in, then the bed hid him. Mrs. Phelps she jumps for him and says:

"Has he come?"

"No," says her husband.

"Good-*ness* gracious!" she says, "what in the world *can* have become of him?"

"I can't imagine," says the old gentleman; "and I must say, it makes me dreadful uneasy."

"Uneasy!" she says, "I'm ready to go distracted! He *must* a come; and you've missed him along the road. I *know* it's so—something *tells* me so."

"Why Sally, I *couldn't* miss him along the road—*you* know that."

"But oh, dear, dear, what *will* Sis say! He must a come! You must a missed him. He——"

"Oh, don't distress me any more'n I'm already distressed. I don't know what in the world to make of it. I'm at my wit's end, and I don't mind acknowledging 't I'm right down scared. But there's no hope that's he come! for he *couldn't* come and me miss him. Sally, it's terrible—just terrible—something's happened to the boat, sure!"

"Why, Silas! Look yonder!—up the road!—ain't that somebody coming?"

He sprung to the window at the head of the bed, and that give Mrs. Phelps the chance she wanted. She stooped down quick, at the foot of the bed, and give me a pull, and out I come; and when he turned back from the window, there she stood, a-beaming and a-smiling like a house afire, and I standing pretty meek and sweaty alongside. The old gentleman stared, and says:

"Why, who's that?"

"Who do you reckon 't is?"

"I hain't no idea. Who *is* it?"

"It's *Tom Sawyer!*"

By jings, I most slumped though the floor. But there warn't no time to swap knives; the old man grabbed me by the **18** hand and shook, and kept on shaking; and all the time, how the woman did dance around and laugh and cry; and then how they both did fire off questions about Sid, and Mary, and the rest of the tribe.

But if they was joyful, it warn't nothing to what I was; for it was like being born again, I was so glad to find out who I **19** was. Well, they froze to me for two hours; and at last when my chin was so tired it couldn't hardly go, any more, I had told them more about my family—I mean the Sawyer family—than

A wharf-boat. Illustration from *Emerson's Magazine and Putnam's Monthly*, October 1857. *Courtesy the Library of Congress.*

16 *the officers' lunch.* The place where the officers were served their meals, now generally called "the officer's mess."

17 *throw up my hand.* Put down my cards and drop out, as in a poker game.

18 *swap knives.* Change tactics.

19 *it was like being born again.* Another of Huck's "resurrections."

The suppressed obscene version of "Who do you reckon it is?"

20

" WHO DO YOU RECKON 'T IS ? "

20 *"Who do you reckon 't is?"* While the book was in the press, this illustration was maliciously altered, perhaps by a printer's devil, to show an unusual shape emerging from Uncle Silas's pants like an erect penis. The salesmen were already canvassing the new novel when Charles L. Webster was shown the obscene plate. He immediately offered a reward of $500 for the apprehension and conviction of the person who so altered the engraving as "to make it obscene." Fortunately, although some of the salesman's "dummies" did contain the altered plate, most of the final copies were recalled, and in the first printing the offensive page had to be removed, and a corrected leaf tipped in. Unfortunately, the original publication date was postponed and so the book missed the important Christmas sales; but even this setback was better than to suffer the estimated $25,000 loss had the mistake not been discovered when it was.

21 *White River.* Apparently the tributary of the Mississippi River, running from Missouri through Arkansas.

ever happened to any six Sawyer families. And I explained all about how we blowed out a cylinder-head at the mouth of White River and it took us three days to fix it. Which was all right, and worked first rate; because *they* didn't know but what it would take three days to fix it. If I'd a called it a bolt-head it would a done just as well.

Now I was feeling pretty comfortable all down one side, and pretty uncomfortable all up the other. Being Tom Sawyer was easy and comfortable; and it stayed easy and comfortable till by-and-by I hear a steamboat coughing along down the river—then I says to myself, s'pose Tom Sawyer come down on that boat?—and s'pose he steps in here, any minute, and sings out my name before I can throw him a wink to keep quiet? Well, I couldn't *have* it that way—it wouldn't do at all. I must go up the road and waylay him. So I told the folks I reckoned I would go up to the town and fetch down my baggage. The old gentleman was for going along with me, but I said no, I could drive the horse myself, and I druther he wouldn't take no trouble about me.

Chapter XXXIII

"IT WAS TOM SAWYER."

So I started for town, in the wagon, and when I was half-way I see a wagon coming, and sure enough it was Tom Sawyer, and I stopped and waited till he come along. I says, "Hold on!" and it stopped alongside, and his mouth opened like a trunk, and staid so; and he swallowed two or three times like a person that's got a dry throat, and then says:

"I hain't ever done **1** you no harm. You know that. So, then, what you wan't to come back and ha'nt *me* for?"

I says:

"I hain't come back—I hain't been *gone*."

When he heard my voice, it righted him up some, but he warn't quite satisfied yet. He says:

"Don't you play nothing on me, because I wouldn't on you. Honest injun, now, you ain't a ghost?"

"Honest injun, I ain't," I says.

"Well—I—I—well, that ought to settle it, of course; but

1 *I hain't ever done you no harm. . . . what you wan't to . . . ha'nt* me *for?* Doubting Tom Sawyer says almost the same words as Jim when he first encountered Huck on Jackson's Island in Chapter 8; here Tom expresses the popular belief that ghosts haunt only those who did them harm in life.

2 *it hit him where he lived.* "Smote him sore with fear and dread," Hank Morgan explains this expression in Chapter 14 of *A Connecticut Yankee in King Arthur's Court.*

3 *Tom Sawyer fell, considerable, in my estimation.* Romantic Tom finally has a chance to play at robbery, but practical Huck recognizes the seriousness of the situation. Although he has reconciled himself to his "going to Hell," Huck is troubled because his training tells him that Tom Sawyer of the "respectable" middle-class has lowered himself to Huck's caste, that of "poor white trash," in agreeing to help free a slave.

I can't somehow seem to understand it, no way. Looky here, warn't you ever murdered *at all?*"

"No. I warn't ever murdered at all—I played it on them. You come in here and feel of me if you don't believe me."

So he done it, and it satisfied him; and he was that glad to see me again, he didn't know what to do. And he wanted to know all about it right off; because it was a grand adventure, **2** and mysterious, and so it hit him where he lived. But I said, leave it alone till by-and-by; and told his driver to wait, and we drove off a little piece, and I told him the kind of a fix I was in, and what did he reckon we better do? He said, let him alone a minute, and don't disturb him. So he thought and thought, and pretty soon he says:

"It's all right, I've got it. Take my trunk in your wagon, and let on it's your'n; and you turn back and fool along slow, so as to get to the house about the time you ought to; and I'll go towards town a piece, and take a fresh start, and get there a quarter or a half an hour after you; and you needn't let on to know me, at first."

I says:

"All right; but wait a minute. There's one more thing—a thing that *nobody* don't know but me. And that is, there's a nigger here that I'm a trying to steal out of slavery—and his name is *Jim*—old Miss Watson's Jim."

He says:

"What! Why Jim is——"

He stopped, and went to studying. I says:

"*I* know what you'll say. You'll say it's dirty low-down business; but what if it is?—*I'm* low down; and I'm agoing to steal him, and I want you to keep mum and not let on. Will you?"

His eye lit up, and he says:

"I'll *help* you steal him!"

Well, I let go all holts then, like I was shot. It was the most astonishing speech I ever heard—and I'm bound to say **3** Tom Sawyer fell, considerable, in my estimation. Only I couldn't believe it. Tom Sawyer a *nigger stealer!*

"Oh, shucks," I says, "you're joking."

"I ain't joking, either."

"Well, then," I says, "joking or no joking, if you hear anything said about a runaway nigger, don't forget to remember that *you* don't know nothing about him, and *I* don't know nothing about him."

Then we took the trunk and put it in my wagon, and he drove off his way, and I drove mine. But of course I forgot all about driving slow, on accounts of being glad and full of thinking; so I got home a heap too quick for that length of a trip. The old gentleman was at the door, and he says:

"Why, this is wonderful. Who ever would have thought it was in that mare to do it. I wish we'd a timed her. And she hain't sweated a hair—not a hair. It's wonderful. Why, I wouldn't take a hunderd dollars for that horse now; I wouldn't, honest ; and yet I'd a sold her for fifteen before, and thought t'was all she was worth."

That's all he said. He was the innocentest, best old soul I ever see. But it warn't surprising ; because he warn't only just a farmer, he was a preacher, too, and had a little one-horse log church down back of the plantation, which he built it himself at his own expense, for a church and school-house, and never charged nothing for his preaching, and it was worth it, too. There was plenty other farmer-preachers like that, and done the same way, down South.

In about half an hour Tom's wagon drove up to the front stile, and Aunt Sally she see it through the window because it was only about fifty yards, and says :

"Why, there's somebody come ! I wonder who 'tis ? Why, I do believe it's a stranger. Jimmy " (that's one of the children), " run and tell Lize to put on another plate for dinner."

Everybody made a rush for the front door, because, of course, a stranger don't come *every* year, and so he lays over the yaller **4** fever, for interest, when he does come. Tom was over the stile and starting for the house ; the wagon was spinning up the road for the village, and we was all bunched in the front door. Tom had his store clothes on, and an audience—and that was always nuts for Tom Sawyer. In them circumstances it warn't no trouble to him to throw in an amount of style that was suitable. He warn't a boy to meeky along up that yard like a **5** sheep ; no, he come calm and important, like the ram. When he got afront of us, he lifts his hat ever so gracious and dainty, like it was the lid of a box that had butterflies asleep in it, and he didn't want to disturb them, and says :

" Mr. Archibald Nichols, I presume ? "

" No, my boy," says the old gentleman, " I'm sorry to say

4 *a stranger . . . lays over the yaller fever, for interest.* High praise indeed: Yellow fever was a constant threat to the settlers of the Mississippi valley. The swamps during the summer were especially conducive to the breeding of mosquitoes, and the sickness was quickly spread from town to town along the river. In Chapter 29 of *Life on the Mississippi*, Twain quoted an account of an epidemic in Memphis: "In August the yellow fever had reached its extremest height. Daily, hundreds fell a sacrifice to the terrible epidemic. The city was becoming a mighty grave-yard, two-thirds of the population had deserted the place, and only the poor, the aged and the sick, remained behind, a sure prey for the insidious enemy. . . . On the street corners, and in the squares, lay sick men, suddenly overtaken by the disease; and even corpses, distorted and rigid. Food failed. Meat spoiled in a few hours in the fetid and pestiferous air, and turned black. . . . In the night stillness reigns. Only the physicians and the hearses hurry through the street; and out of the distance, at intervals, comes the muffled thunder of the railway train, which with the speed of the wind, and as if hunted by furies, flies by the pest-ridden city without halting."

5 *to meeky along.* To skulk, sneak along.

" MR. ARCHIBALD NICHOLS, I PRESUME ? "

6 *it wouldn't be Southern hospitality to do it.* By this time, "Southern hospitality" was already legendary. Hundley in *Social Relations in Our Southern States* (p. 57) expressed the then current opinion that nowhere could one find "a much heartier welcome, a warmer shake of the hand, a greater desire to please, and less frigidity of deportment" than in the American South.

7 *Hicksville, Ohio.* Then a lumbering district, founded in 1836 as a trading-post.

't your driver has deceived you; Nichols's place is down a matter of three mile more. Come in, come in."

Tom he took a look back over his shoulder, and says, "Too late—he's out of sight."

"Yes, he's gone, my son, and you must come in and eat your dinner with us; and then we'll hitch up and take you down to Nichols's."

"Oh, I *can't* make you so much trouble, I couldn't think of it. I'll walk—I don't mind the distance."

6 "But we won't *let* you walk—it wouldn't be Southern hospitality to do it. Come right in."

"Oh, *do*," says Aunt Sally; "it ain't a bit of trouble to us, not a bit in the world. You *must* stay. It's a long, dusty three mile, and we *can't* let you walk. And besides, I've already told 'em to put on another plate, when I see you coming; so you mustn't disappoint us. Come right in, and make yourself at home."

So Tom he thanked them very hearty and handsome, and let himself be persuaded, and come in; and when he was in, he **7** said he was a stranger from Hicksville, Ohio, and his name was William Thompson—and he made another bow.

Well, he run on, and on, and on, making up stuff about Hicksville and everybody in it he could invent, and I getting a little nervous, and wondering how this was going to help me out of my scrape; and at last, still talking along, he reached over and kissed Aunt Sally right on the mouth, and then settled back again in his chair, comfortable, and was going on talking; but she jumped up and wiped it off with the back of her hand, and says:

"You owdacious puppy!"

He looked kind of hurt, and says:

"I'm surprised at you, m'am."

"You're s'rp— Why, what do you reckon *I* am? I've a good notion to take and—say, what do you mean by kissing me?"

He looked kind of humble, and says:

"I didn't mean nothing, m'am. I didn't mean no harm. I—I—thought you'd like it."

"Why, you born fool!" She took up the spinning-stick, and it looked like it was all she could do to keep from giving him a crack with it. "What made you think I'd like it?"

"Well, I don't know. Only, they—they—told me you would."

"*They* told you I would. Whoever told you 's *another* lunatic. I never heard the beat of it. Who's *they?*"

"Why—everybody. They all said so, m'am."

It was all she could do to hold in; and her eyes snapped, and her fingers worked like she wanted to scratch him; and she says:

"Who's 'everybody?' Out with their names—or ther'll be an idiot short."

He got up and looked distressed, and fumbled his hat, and says :

"I'm sorry, and I warn't expecting it. They told me to. They all told me to. They all said kiss her; and said she'll like it. They all said it—every one of them. But I'm sorry, ma'm, and I won't do it no more—I won't, honest."

"You won't, won't you? Well, I sh'd *reckon* you won't !"

"No'm, I'm honest about it; I won't ever do it again. Till you ask me."

"Till I *ask* you! Well, I never see the beat of it in my born days ! I lay you'll be the Methusalem-numskull of crea- **8** tion before ever *I* ask you—or the likes of you."

"Well," he says, "it does surprise me so. I can't make it out, somehow. They said you would, and I thought you would. But—" He stopped and looked around slow, like he wished he could run across a friendly eye, somewhere's; and fetched up on the old gentleman's, and says, "Didn't *you* think she'd like me to kiss her, sir ? "

"Why, no, I—I—well, no, I b'lieve I didn't."

Then he looks on around, the same way, to me—and says :

"Tom, didn't *you* think Aunt Sally 'd open out her arms and say, ' Sid Sawyer——' '

"My land ! " she says, breaking in and jumping for him, " you impudent young rascal, to fool a body so—" and was going to hug him, but he fended her off, and says :

"No, not till you've asked me, first."

So she didn't lose no time, but asked him; and hugged him and kissed him, over and over again, and then turned him over to the old man, and he took what was left. And after they got a little quiet again, she says :

"Why, dear me, I never see such a surprise. We warn't looking for *you*, at all, but only Tom. Sis never wrote to me about anybody coming but him."

"It's because it warn't *intended* for any of us to come but Tom," he says; "but I begged and begged, and at the last minute she let me come, too; so, coming down the river, me and Tom thought it would be a first-rate surprise for him to come here to the house first, and for me to by-and-by tag along and drop in and let on to be a stranger. But it was a mistake, Aunt Sally. This ain't no healthy place for a stranger to come."

"No—not impudent whelps, Sid. You ought to had your jaws boxed ; I hain't been so put out since I don't know when. But I don't care, I don't mind the terms—I'd be willing to stand a thousand such jokes to have you here. Well, to think of that performance ! I don't deny it, I was most putrified with astonishment when you give me that smack."

We had dinner out in that broad open passage betwixt the house and the kitchen ; and there was things enough on that **9** table for seven families—and all hot, too; none of your flabby tough meat that's laid in a cupboard in a damp cellar all night and tastes like a hunk of old cold cannibal in the morning. Uncle **10**

8 *the Methusalem-numskull of creation.* The oldest fool who ever lived; according to Genesis 5:27, Methuselah lived 969 years, the greatest age of anyone in the Bible.

9 *there was things enough on that table for seven families—and all hot, too.* Twain is recalling the board of his Uncle John's farm as described in Chapter 2 of his *Autobiography:* "In the summer the table was set in the middle of the shady and breezy floor, and the sumptuous meals—well, it makes me cry to think of them. Fried chicken, roast pig; wild and tame turkeys, ducks and geese; venison just killed; squirrels, rabbits, pheasants, partridges, prairie-chickens; biscuits, hot batter cakes, hot buckwheat cakes, hot 'wheat bread,' hot rolls, hot corn-pone; fresh corn boiled on the ear, succotash, butter beans, string beans, tomatoes, peas, Irish potatoes, sweet potatoes; buttermilk, sweet milk, 'clabber'; watermelons, muskmelons, cantaloupes—all fresh from the garden; apple pie, peach pie, pumpkin pie, apple dumplings, peach cobbler—I can't remember the rest. The way that the things were cooked was perhaps the main splendor."

The Phelpses treat Huck as hospitably as the Grangerfords did in Chapter 17; by now Huck should, but does not, recognize that in this part of the country things are rarely as pleasant as they first appear.

10 *like a hunk of old cold cannibal.* In the manuscript, Twain had used an uglier simile, "like a hunk of your old cold grandfather" (Ferguson, "Huck Finn Aborning," p. 179); but the change is hardly an improvement.

11 *the king and the duke . . . looked like a couple of monstrous big soldier-plumes.* By describing the tarred-and-feathered scoundrels as waving above the crowd like the plumes on the hats or helmets of soldiers, Twain repeats the running metaphor that a mob is an army.

A PRETTY LONG BLESSING.

Silas he asked a pretty long blessing over it, but it was worth it; and it didn't cool it a bit, neither, the way I've seen them kind of interruptions do, lots of times.

There was a considerable good deal of talk, all the afternoon, and me and Tom was on the look-out all the time, but it warn't no use, they didn't happen to say nothing about any runaway nigger, and we was afraid to try to work up to it. But at supper, at night, one of the little boys says:

"Pa, mayn't Tom and Sid and me go to the show?"

"No," says the old man, "I reckon there ain't going to be any; and you couldn't go if there was; because the runaway nigger told Burton and me all about that scandalous show, and Burton said he would tell the people; so I reckon they've drove the owdacious loafers out of town before this time."

So there it was!—but *I* couldn't help it. Tom and me was to sleep in the same room and bed; so, being tired, we bid good-night and went up to bed, right after supper, and clumb out of the window and down the lightning-rod, and shoved for the town; for I didn't believe anybody was going to give the king and the duke a hint, and so, if I didn't hurry up and give them one they'd get into trouble sure.

On the road Tom he told me all about how it was reckoned I was murdered, and how pap disappeared, pretty soon, and didn't come back no more, and what a stir there was when Jim run away; and I told Tom all about our Royal Nonesuch rapscallions, and as much of the raft-voyage as I had time to; and as we struck into the town and up through the middle of it—it was as much as half-after eight, then—here comes a raging rush of people, with torches, and an awful whooping and yelling, and banging tin pans and blowing horns; and we jumped to one side to let them go by; and as they went by, I see they had the king and the duke astraddle of a rail—that is, I knowed

11 it *was* the king and the duke, though they was all over tar and feathers, and didn't look like nothing in the world that was human—just looked like a couple of monstrous big soldier-

12 *Human beings* can *be awful cruel to one another*. Although it has been threatened persistently throughout the novel, this is the first instance of a successful lynching. Throughout this chapter, Twain has been building up to a paradox in the Southern character: Although the Phelpses and their neighbors are God-fearing, hospitable men and women, at any moment they are capable of irrational cruelty.

13 *all the rest of a person's insides*. In the manuscript, Huck was more contemptuous of his conscience by saying "more room than a person's bowels" (Ferguson, "Huck Finn Aborning," p. 179).

TRAVELING BY RAIL.

plumes. Well, it made me sick to see it; and I was sorry for them poor pitiful rascals, it seemed like I couldn't ever feel any hardness against them any more in the world. It was a dreadful thing to see. Human beings *can* be awful cruel to **12** one another.

We see we was too late—couldn't do no good. We asked some stragglers about it, and they said everybody went to the show looking very innocent; and laid low and kept dark till the poor old king was in the middle of his cavortings on the stage; then somebody give a signal, and the house rose up and went

So we poked along back home, and I warn't feeling so brash as I was before, but kind of ornery, and humble, and to blame, somehow—though *I* hadn't done nothing. But that's always the way; it don't make no difference whether you do right or wrong, a person's conscience ain't got no sense, and just goes for him *anyway*. If I had a yaller dog that didn't know no more than a person's conscience does, I would pison him. It takes up more room than all the rest of a person's insides, and **13** yet ain't no good, nohow. Tom Sawyer he says the same.

Chap. XXXIV

VITTLES.

We stopped talking, and got to thinking. By-and-by Tom says:

"Looky here, Huck, what fools we are, to not think of it before! I bet I know where Jim is."

"No! Where?"

"In that hut down by the ash-hopper. Why, looky here. When we was at dinner, didn't you see a nigger man go in there with some vittles?"

"Yes."

"What did you think the vittles was for?"

"For a dog."

"So'd I. Well, it wasn't for a dog."

"Why?"

"Because part of it was watermelon."

"So it was—I noticed it. Well, it does beat all, that I never thought about a dog not eating watermelon. It shows how a body can see and don't see at the same time."

"Well, the nigger unlocked the padlock when he went in, and he locked it again when he come out. He fetched uncle a key, about the time we got up from table—same key, I bet. Watermelon shows man, lock shows prisoner; and it ain't likely there's two prisoners on such a little plantation, and where the people's all so kind and good. Jim's the prisoner: All right— I'm glad we found it out detective fashion; I wouldn't give **1** shucks for any other way. Now you work your mind and study out a plan to steal Jim, and I will study out one, too; and we'll take the one we like the best."

What a head for just a boy to have! If I had Tom Sawyer's head, I wouldn't trade it off to be a duke, nor mate of a steamboat, nor clown in a circus, nor nothing I can think of. I went to thinking out a plan, but only just to be doing something; I knowed very well where the right plan was going to come from. Pretty soon, Tom says:

"Ready?"

"Yes," I says.

"All right—bring it out."

"My plan is this," I says. "We can easy find out if it's Jim in there. Then get up my canoe to-morrow night, and fetch my raft over from the island. Then the first dark night that comes, steal the key out of the old man's britches, after he goes to bed, and shove off down the river on the raft, with Jim, hiding day-times and running nights, the way me and Jim used to do before. Wouldn't that plan work?"

"*Work?* Why cert'nly, it would work, like rats a fighting. But it's too blame' simple; there ain't nothing *to* it. What's the good of a plan that ain't no more trouble than that? It's as mild as goose-milk. Why, Huck, it wouldn't make no more **2** talk than breaking into a soap factory."

I never said nothing, because I warn't expecting nothing different; but I knowed mighty well that whenever he got *his* plan ready it wouldn't have none of them objections to it.

And it didn't. He told me what it was, and I see in a minute it was worth fifteen of mine, for style, and would make Jim just as free a man as mine would, and maybe get us all killed besides. So I was satisfied, and said we would waltz in on it. I needn't tell what it was, here, because I knowed it **3** wouldn't stay the way it was. I knowed he would be changing it around, every which way, as we went along, and heaving in new bullinesses wherever he got a chance. And that is what he done.

Well, one thing was dead sure; and that was, that Tom Sawyer was in earnest and was actuly going to help steal that nigger out of slavery. That was the thing that was too many for me. Here was a boy that was respectable, and well brung up; and had a character to lose; and folks at home that had characters; and he was bright and not leather-headed; and knowing and not ignorant; and not mean, but kind; and yet here he was, without any more pride, or rightness, or feeling, than to stoop to this business, and make himself a shame, and his family a shame, before everybody. I *couldn't* understand it, no way at all. It was outrageous, and I knowed I ought to

1 *detective fashion.* Only in passing does Twain mention another source of Tom's romanticism—detective stories. Twain had as little respect for this genre as for other romantic fiction. "What a curious thing a 'detective story' is," Twain wrote in his diary in 1896 (quoted in *Mark Twain's Hannibal, Huck and Tom*, 1969, p. 158). "And was there ever one that the author needn't be ashamed of, except 'The Murder in the Rue Morgue'?" Nevertheless, he did write "Tom Sawyer, Detective" and began "Tom Sawyer's Conspiracy"; but this latter, aborted project was as much a parody of private eye fiction as the last part of *Huckleberry Finn* is a burlesque of popular prison romance. In "Tom Sawyer's Conspiracy," Tom is as irrational as in his plan to steal Jim from the Phelpses: "What's common sense got to do with detecting, you leatherhead?" he tells Huck (p. 206). "It ain't got *anything* to do with it. What is wanted is genius and penetration and marvelousness. A detective that had common sense couldn't ever make a reputation— couldn't even make a living."

2 *mild as goose-milk.* Twain had written in the manuscript, "mild as Sunday School" (Ferguson, "Huck Finn Aborning," p. 179), certainly a more apt simile than the published one, because it brings the tone of Tom's new plan to that of the attack of his gang on the Sunday-school class in Chapter 3; but apparently it was thought too blasphemous and was changed.

3 *I needn't tell what it was, here, because I knowed it wouldn't stay the way it was. I knowed he would be changing it around, every which way, as we went along, and heaving in new bullinesses wherever he got a chance.* Huck is speaking as much about the author as about Tom: Obviously, at this point in the story, Twain did not have a clue exactly where the novel was heading.

just up and tell him so ; and so be his true friend, and let him quit the thing right where he was, and save himself. And I *did* start to tell him ; but he shut me up, and says :

"Don't you reckon I know what I'm about? Don't I generly know what I'm about?"

"Yes."

"Didn't I *say* I was going to help steal the nigger?"

"Yes."

"*Well*, then."

That's all he said, and that's all I said. It warn't no use to say any more ; because when he said he'd do a thing, he always done it. But *I* couldn't make out how he was willing to go into this thing ; so I just let it go, and never bothered no more about it. If he was bound to have it so, *I* couldn't help it.

When we got home, the house was all dark and still ; so we went on down to the hut by the ash-hopper, for to examine it. We went through the yard, so as to see what the hounds would do. They knowed us, and didn't make no more noise than country dogs is always doing when anything comes by in the night. When we got to the cabin, we took a look at the front and the two sides ; and on the side I warn't acquainted with—which was the north side—we found a square window-hole, up tolerable high, with just one stout board nailed across it. I says :

"Here's the ticket. This hole's big enough for Jim to get through, if we wrench off the board."

Tom says :

"It's as simple as tit-tat-toe, three-in-a-row, and as easy as

A SIMPLE JOB.

playing hooky.   I should *hope* we can find a way that's a little more complicated than *that*, Huck Finn."

"Well, then," I says, "how'll it do to saw him out, the way I done before I was murdered, that time?"

"That's more *like*," he says.   "It's real mysterious, and troublesome, and good," he says; "but I bet we can find a way that's twice as long.   There ain't no hurry; le's keep on looking around."

Betwixt the hut and the fence, on the back side, was a lean-to, that joined the hut at the eaves, and was made out of plank. It was as long as the hut, but narrow—only about six foot wide. The door to it was at the south end, and was padlocked.   Tom he went to the soap kettle, and searched around and fetched back the iron thing they lift the lid with; so he took it and prized out one of the staples.   The chain fell down, and we opened the door and went in, and shut it, and struck a match, and see the shed was only built against the cabin and hadn't no connection with it; and there warn't no floor to the shed, nor nothing in it but some old rusty played-out hoes, and spades, and picks, and a crippled plow.   The match went out, and so did we, and shoved in the staple again, and the door was locked as good as ever.   Tom was joyful.   He says:

"Now we're all right.   We'll *dig* him out.   It'll take about a week!"

Then we started for the house, and I went in the back door —you only have to pull a buckskin latch-string, they don't **4** fasten the doors—but that warn't romantical enough for Tom Sawyer: no way would do him but he must climb up the lightning-rod.   But after he got up half-way about three times, and missed fire and fell every time, and the last time most busted his brains out, he thought he'd got to give it up; but after he was rested, he allowed he would give her one more turn for luck, and this time he made the trip.

In the morning we was up at break of day, and down to the nigger cabins to pet the dogs and make friends with the nigger that fed Jim—if it *was* Jim that was being fed.   The niggers was just getting through breakfast and starting for the fields; and Jim's nigger was piling up a tin pan with bread and meat and things; and whilst the others was leaving, the key come from the house.

This nigger had a good-natured, chuckle-headed face, and his wool was all tied up in little bunches with thread.   That **5** was to keep witches off.   He said the witches was pestering him awful, these nights, and making him see all kinds of strange things, and hear all kinds of strange words and noises, and he didn't believe he was ever witched so long, before, in his life.   He got so worked up, and got to running on so about his troubles, he forgot all about what he'd been agoing to do. So Tom says:

"What's the vittles for?   Going to feed the dogs?"

The nigger kind of smiled around gradually over his face, like when you heave a brickbat in a mud puddle, and he says: **6**

4 *you only have to pull a buckskin latch-string, they don't fasten the doors.* See Chapter 21, note 13.

5 *his wool was all tied up . . . with thread.* See Chapter 1, note 23.

6 *brickbat.* A piece of brick.

7 *"Yes, Mars Sid, a dog. Cur'us dog, too. Does you want to go en look at 'im?"* This slave uses much the same trick as does Huck's "nigger" at the Grangerfords. See Chapter 18, note 27.

7   " Yes, Mars Sid, *a* dog. Cur'us dog, too. Does you want to go en look at 'im ? "

" Yes."

I hunched Tom, and whispers :

" You going, right here in the day-break ? *That* warn't the plan."

" No, it warn't—but it's the plan *now*."

So, drat him, we went along, but I didn't like it much. When we got in, we couldn't hardly see anything, it was so dark ; but Jim was there, sure enough, and could see us ; and he sings out :

" Why *Huck !* En good *lan' ! * ain' dat Misto Tom ? "

I just knowed how it would be ; I just expected it. *I* didn't know nothing to do ; and if I had, I couldn't a done it ; because that nigger busted in and says :

" Why, de gracious sakes ! do he know you genlmen ? "

We could see pretty well, now. Tom he looked at the nigger, steady and kind of wondering, and says :

" Does *who* know us ? "

" Why, dish-yer runaway nigger."

" I don't reckon he does ; but what put that into your head ? "

" What *put* it dar ? Didn' he jis' dis minute sing out like he knowed you ? "

Tom says, in a puzzled-up kind of way :

" Well, that's mighty curious. *Who* sung out ? *When* did he sing out ? *What* did he sing out ? " And turns to me, perfectly calm, and says, " Did *you* hear anybody sing out ? "

Of course there warn't nothing to be said but the one thing ; so I says :

" No ; *I* ain't heard nobody say nothing."

Then he turns to Jim, and looks him over like he never see him before ; and says :

" Did you sing out ? "

" No, sah," says Jim ; " *I* hain't said nothing, sah."

" Not a word ? "

" No, sah, I hain't said a word."

" Did you ever see us before ? "

" No, sah ; not as *I* knows on."

So Tom turns to the nigger, which was looking wild and distressed, and says, kind of severe :

" What do you reckon's the matter with you, anyway ? What made you think somebody sung out ? "

" Oh, it's de dad-blame' witches, sah, en I wisht I was dead, I do. Dey's awluz at it, sah, en dey do mos' kill me, dey sk'yers me so. Please to don't tell nobody 'bout it sah, er ole Mars Silas he'll scole me ; 'kase he says dey *ain't* no witches. I jis' wish to goodness he was heah now—*den* what would he say ! I jis' bet he couldn' fine no way to git aroun' it *dis* time. But it's awluz jis' so ; people dat's *sot*, stays sot ; dey won't look into nothn' en fine it out f'r deyselves, en when *you* fine it out en tell um 'bout it, dey doan' b'lieve you."

WITCHES.

Tom give him a dime, and said we wouldn't tell nobody ; and told him to buy some more thread to tie up his wool with ; and then looks at Jim, and says :

" I wonder if Uncle Silas is going to hang this nigger. If I was to catch a nigger that was ungrateful enough to run away, *I* wouldn't give him up, I'd hang him." And whilst the nigger stepped to the door to look at the dime and bite it to see if it was good, he whispers to Jim, and says :

" Don't ever let on to know us. And if you hear any digging going on nights, it's us : we're going to set you free."

Jim only had time to grab us by the hand and squeeze it, then the nigger come back, and we said we'd come again some time if the nigger wanted us to ; and he said he would, more particular if it was dark, because the witches went for him mostly in the dark, and it was good to have folks around then.

Chap. XXXV

1 *fox-fire.* The phosphorescent glow emitted by decaying wood.

It would be most an hour, yet, till breakfast, so we left, and struck down into the woods; because Tom said we got to have *some* light to see how to dig by, and a lantern makes too much, and might get us into trouble; what we must have was a lot of them rotten chunks that's called fox-fire and just makes a soft kind of a glow when you lay them in a dark place. We fetched an armful and hid it in the weeds, and set down to rest, and Tom says, kind of dissatisfied:

GETTING WOOD.

"Blame it, this whole thing is just as easy and awkard as it can be. And so it makes it so rotten difficult to get up a difficult plan. There ain't no watchman to be drugged—now there *ought* to be a watchman. There ain't even a dog to give a sleeping-mixture to. And there's Jim chained by one leg, with a ten-foot chain, to the leg of his bed: why, all you got to do is to lift up the bedstead and slip off the chain. And Uncle Silas he trusts everybody; sends the key to the punkinheaded nigger, and don't send nobody to watch the nigger. Jim could a got out of that window hole before this, only there wouldn't be no use trying to travel with a ten-foot chain on his leg. Why, drat it, Huck, it's the stupidest arrangement I ever see. You got to invent *all* the difficulties. Well, we can't help it, we got to do the best we can with the materials we've got. Anyhow, there's one thing—there's more honor in getting him out through a lot of difficulties and dangers, where there warn't one of them furnished to you by the people who it was their duty to furnish them, and you had to contrive them all out of your own head. Now look at just that one thing of the lantern. When you come down to the cold facts, we simply got to *let on* that a lantern's resky. Why, we could work with a torchlight procession if we wanted to, *I* believe. Now, whilst I think of it, we got to hunt up something to make a saw out of, the first chance we get."

"What do we want of a saw?"

"What do we *want* of it? Hain't we got to saw the leg of Jim's bed off, so as to get the chain loose?"

"Why, you just said a body could lift up the bedstead and slip the chain off."

"Well, if that ain't just like you, Huck Finn. You *can* get up the infant-schooliest ways of going at a thing. Why, **2** hain't you ever read any books at all?—Baron Trenck, nor **3** Casanova, nor Benvenuto Chelleeny, nor Henri IV., nor none of them heroes? Whoever heard of getting a prisoner loose in such an old-maidy way as that? No; the way all the best authorities does, is to saw the bed-leg in two, and leave it just so, and swallow the sawdust, so it can't be found, and put some dirt and grease around the sawed place so the very keenest **4** seneskal can't see no sign of it's being sawed, and thinks the bed-leg is perfectly sound. Then, the night you're ready, fetch the leg a kick, down she goes; slip off your chain, and there you are. Nothing to do but hitch your rope-ladder to the **5** battlements, shin down it, break your leg in the moat—because a rope-ladder is nineteen foot too short, you know—and there's your horses and your trusty vassles, and they scoop you up and fling you across a saddle and away you go, to your native Lan- **6** gudoc, or Navarre, or wherever it is. It's gaudy, Huck. I **7** wish there was a moat to this cabin. If we get time, the night of the escape, we'll dig one."

I says:

"What do we want of a moat, when we're going to snake him out from under the cabin?"

Bnt he never heard me. He had forgot me and everything else. He had his chin in his hand, thinking. Pretty soon, he sighs, and shakes his head; then sighs again, and says:

"No, it wouldn't do—there ain't necessity enough for it."

"For what?" I says:

"Why, to saw Jim's leg off," he says.

"Good land!" I says, "why, there ain't *no* necessity for it. And what would you want to saw his leg off for, anyway?"

2 *infant-schooliest ways.* "Sunday-schooliest ways" in the manuscript (Ferguson, "Huck Finn Aborning," p. 179); much of the sarcasm of the original was lost in the final, tame adjective.

3 *Baron Trenck . . . Casanova . . . Benvenuto Chelleeny . . . Henri IV.* Each of Tom's heroes made daring prison escapes; and as each was a notorious roué, their reputations were as scandalous as those of the mistresses of the various kings of England, mentioned in Chapter 23 (see note 9). The stories of their lives hardly made proper reading for children of the period.

Baron Frederich von Trenck (1726–1794), a Prussian adventurer, was an officer in Frederick the Great's army; but he was imprisoned for his alleged liaison with the emperor's sister. He escaped from

Baron Frederick von Trenck. *Courtesy the Library of Congress.*

prison several times, and described these exploits in memoirs, published in 1787. The book was an enormous success: Women of Paris, Belgium, and Vienna wore rings, necklaces, bonnets, and gowns à la Trenck; and at least seven dramatizations of his life were staged. He went to France during the Revolution and was guillotined as a spy in 1794.

Giovanni Jacopo Casanova (1725–1798), an Italian

Giovanni Jacopo Casanova and a conquest. *Courtesy the Picture Collection, The New York Public Library, Astor, Lenox, and Tilden Foundations.*

adventurer at the courts of Europe, wrote an infamous memoir (published posthumously in a trun-
cated version), detailing his affairs, imprisonments,
and escapes. "The supremest charm in Casanova's
Memoire," Twain wrote his brother Orion, February
26, 1880, "is, that he frankly, flowingly, and felicitously tells the dirtiest and vilest and most contempt-
ible things on himself, without ever suspecting that
they are other than things which the reader will admire and applaud" (quoted by Webster, *Mark Twain,
Business Man*, pp. 143–144).

Benvenuto Cellini (1500–1571), "that rough-hewn
saint" (as Hank Morgan calls him in Chapter 17 of *A
Connecticut Yankee in King Arthur's Court*), was one of
the greatest goldsmiths and sculptors of the Renais-
sance; however, he is perhaps best remembered for

Benvenuto Cellini. *Courtesy the Library
of Congress.*

his *Autobiography* which he began in 1558, and which
describes his legendary escape from the prison at San
Angelo in Rome. "That most entertaining of books,"
Twain wrote of Cellini's autobiography in his *Notebook* (1935, p. 144). "It will last as long as his beautiful Perseus."

Henry IV (1553–1610), the first Bourbon king of
France, succeeded to the throne in 1589 upon the

Henry IV of France. *Courtesy the
Library of Congress.*

ONE OF THE BEST AUTHORITIES.

"Well, some of the best authorities has done it. They
couldn't get the chain off, so they just cut their hand off, and
shoved. And a leg would be better still. But we got to let
that go. There ain't necessity enough in this case; and besides,
Jim's a nigger and wouldn't understand the reasons for it, and
how it's the custom in Europe; so we'll let it go. But there's
8 one thing—he can have a rope-ladder; we can tear up our
sheets and make him a rope-ladder easy enough. And we can
send it to him in a pie; it's mostly done that way. And I've
et worse pies."

"Why, Tom Sawyer, how you talk," I says; "Jim ain't got
no use for a rope-ladder."

"He *has* got use for it." How *you* talk; you better say
you don't know nothing about it. He's *got* to have a rope-
ladder; they all do."

"What in the nation can he *do* with it?"

"*Do* with it? He can hide it in his bed, can't he? That's
what they all do; and *he's* got to, too. Huck, you don't ever
seem to want to do anything that's regular; you want to be
starting something fresh all the time. S'pose he *don't* do
nothing with it? ain't it there in his bed, for a clew, after he's
gone? and don't you reckon they'll want clews? Of course
they will. And you wouldn't leave them any? That would be
a *pretty* howdy-do, *wouldn't* it! I never heard of such a
thing."

"Well," I says, "if it's in the regulations, and he's got to
have it, all right, let him have it; because I don't wish to go
back on no regulations; but there's one thing, Tom Sawyer—
if we go to tearing up our sheets to make Jim a rope-ladder,
we're going to get into trouble with Aunt Sally, just as sure as
you're born. Now, the way I look at it, a hickry-bark ladder
don't cost nothing, and don't waste nothing, and is just as good

to load up a pie with, and hide in a straw tick, as any rag ladder you can start; and as for Jim, he ain't had no experience, and so *he* don't care what kind of a——"

"Oh, shucks, Huck Finn, if I was as ignorant as you, I'd keep still—that's what *I'd* do. Who ever heard of a state prisoner escaping by a hickry-bark ladder? Why, it's perfectly ridiculous."

"Well, all right, Tom, fix it your own way; but if you'll take my advice, you'll let me borrow a sheet off of the clothes-line."

He said that would do. And that give him another idea, and he says:

"Borrow a shirt, too."   **9**

"What do we want of a shirt, Tom?"

"Want it for Jim to keep a journal on."

"Journal your granny—*Jim* can't write."   **10**

"S'pose he *can't* write—he can make marks on the shirt, can't he, if we make him a pen out of an old pewter spoon or a piece of an old·iron barrel-hoop?"

"Why, Tom, we can pull a feather out of a goose and make him a better one; and quicker, too."

"*Prisoners* don't have geese running around the donjon-keep to pull pens out of, you muggins. They *always* make their pens out of the hardest, toughest, troublesomest piece of   **11** old brass candlestick or something like that they can get their hands on; and it takes them weeks and weeks, and months and months to file it out, too, because they've got to do it by rubbing it on the wall. *They* wouldn't use a goose-quill if they had it. It ain't regular."

"Well, then, what'll we make him the ink out of?"

"Many makes it out of iron-rust and tears; but that's the   **12** common sort and women; the best authorities uses their own   **13** blood. Jim can do that; and when he wants to send any little common ordinary mysterious message to let the world know where's he's captivated, he can write it on the bottom of a tin plate with a fork and throw it out of the window. The Iron   **14** Mask always done that, and it's a blame' good way, too."

"Jim ain't got no tin plates. They feed him in a pan."

"That ain't anything; we can get him some."

"Can't nobody *read* his plates?"

"That ain't got nothing to *do* with it, Huck Finn. All *he's* got to do is to write on the plate and throw it out. You don't *have* to be able to read it. Why, half the time you can't read anything a prisoner writes on a tin plate, or anywhere else."

"Well, then, what's the sense in wasting the plates?"

"Why, blame it all, it ain't the *prisoner's* plates."

"But it's *somebody's* plates, ain't it?"

"Well, spos'n it is? What does the *prisoner* care whose——"

He broke off there, because we heard the breakfast-horn blowing. So we cleared out for the house.

Along during that morning I borrowed a sheet and a white

assassination of Henry III. He converted to Catholicism in 1589; he himself was assassinated in 1610.

4 *seneskal*. Tom has a bit muddled the word "seneschal," the powerful steward to a medieval lord.

5 *Nothing to do but hitch your rope-ladder to the battlements, shin down it, break your leg in the moat—because a rope-ladder is nineteen foot too short, you know.* Tom is likely remembering that Cellini's rope-ladder was too short, and he fell into the moat of Castel San Angelo and broke his leg.

6 *Langudoc*. Tom's mispronunciation of "Languedoc," a southern province of medieval France.

7 *Navarre*. The ancient kingdom on the Pyrenees, where Henry IV fled after his escape.

8 *we can tear up our sheets and make him a rope-ladder easy enough.* Tom describes perhaps the most common means of escape employed by prisoners both in fact (such as Baron von Trenck, Casanova, and Cellini) and in fiction (such as Abbé Faria in *The Count of Monte Cristo*; see note 19).

9 *Borrow a shirt. . . . for Jim to keep a journal on.* Prisoners were not always given books, paper, pens, or ink. Abbé Faria wrote a *Traité sur la possibilité d'une monarchie genérale en Italie* on two shirts; the Man in the Iron Mask (see note 14) wrote letters on his shirts; and Count de Charney of J. X. Boniface's *Picciola* (see Chapter 38, note 31) wrote on handkerchiefs.

10 Jim *can't write*. According to a Missouri law of 1847, no Negro or mulatto was to be taught to read or write. When Little Eva asks in Chapter 22 of *Uncle Tom's Cabin* why the slaves have not been taught to read and write, her mother replies in the rhetoric of the time: "Because it is no use for them to read. It don't help them to work any better, and they are not made for anything else." Missourians were particularly insistent on this point: Harriet Martineau described in *Retrospect of Western Travel* (Vol. II, 1838, pp. 209–211) how two students of Marion College were "lynched" in Palmyra just for having taught some slaves to read and write; the mob gave them the choice of either taking twenty lashes each or leaving the state forever, and they took the second option.

11 *pens out of . . . something . . . they can get their hands on.* Casanova made a pen by gnawing a splinter off of the door with his teeth; Abbé Faria made his out of the cartilage of the heads of hake; Count de Charney made a crowquill out of a toothpick. However, Tom is probably recalling that Abbé Faria made a knife, "my masterpiece," from an old iron candlestick.

12 *iron-rust and tears*. "Iron-rust and spit" in the manuscript (in DeVoto, *Mark Twain at Work*, p. 83).

13 *the best authorities uses their own blood.* Such as Baron von Trenck, and Abbé Faria (see note 19).

14 *The Iron Mask.* Tom has read *The Man in the Iron*

Mask, Vol. 6 in the series known as the "D'Artagnon Romances," *Le Vicomte de Bragelonne* (1848–1850) by Alexandre Dumas the Elder. It concerns that legend of the notorious prisoner of the Bastille whose face was always covered by an iron mask. The riddle of who this man was has never been solved. In his novel, Dumas followed the legend that he was the twin brother of Louis XV; in Chapter 31, "The Silver Dish," he described how the prisoner scratched his name on the back of a plate with a knife and threw it out the window of his cell. During the *Quaker City* excursion, Twain visited where the man was imprisoned in the Castle d'If (see note 19) and described the place in Chapter 11 of Vol. I of *The Innocents Abroad*: "They showed us the noisome cell where the celebrated 'Iron Mask'—that ill-starred brother of a hard-hearted king of France—was confined for a season, before he was sent to hide the strange mystery of his life from the curious in the dungeons of St. Marguerite. The place had a far greater interest for us than it could have had if we had known beyond all question who the Iron Mask was, and what his history had been, and why this most unusual punishment had been meted out to him. Mystery! That was the charm. That speechless tongue, those prisoned features, that heart so freighted with unspoken troubles, and that breast so oppressed with its piteous secret, had been here. These dank walls had known the man whose dolorous story is a sealed book forever! There was fascination in the spot."

The Man in the Iron Mask. *Courtesy the Library of Congress.*

THE BREAKFAST-HORN.

shirt off of the clothes-line; and I found an old sack and put them in it, and we went down and got the fox-fire, and put that in too. I called it borrowing, because that was what pap always called it; but Tom said it warn't borrowing, it was stealing. He said we was representing prisoners; and prisoners don't care how they get a thing so they get it, and nobody don't blame them for it, either. It ain't no crime in a prisoner to steal the thing he needs to get away with, Tom said; it's his right; and so, as long as we was representing a prisoner, we had a perfect right to steal anything on this place we had the least use for, to get ourselves out of prison with. He said if we warn't prisoners it would be a very different thing, and nobody but a mean ornery person would steal when he warn't a prisoner. So we allowed we would steal everything there was that come handy. And yet he made a mighty fuss, one

15 day, after that, when I stole a watermelon out of the nigger patch and eat it; and he made me go and give the niggers a

16 dime, without telling them what it was for. Tom said that what he meant was, we could steal anything we *needed*. Well, I says, I needed the watermelon. But he said I didn't need it to get out of prison with, there's where the difference was. He said if I'd a wanted it to hide a knife in, and smuggle it to Jim to kill the seneskal with, it would a been all right. So I let it go at that, though I couldn't see no advantage in my representing a prisoner, if I got to set down and chaw over a

17 lot of gold-leaf distinctions like that, every time I see a chance to hog a watermelon.

Well, as I was saying, we waited that morning till everybody was settled down to business, and nobody in sight around the yard; then Tom he carried the sack into the lean-to whilst I stood off a piece to keep watch. By-and-by he come out, and we went and set down on the wood-pile, to talk. He says:

"Everything's all right, now, except tools; and that's easy fixed."

"Tools?" I says.

"Yes."

"Tools for what?"

"Why, to dig with. We ain't agoing to *gnaw* him out, are we?"

"Ain't them old crippled picks and things in there good enough to dig a nigger out with?" I says.

He turns on me looking pitying enough to make a body cry, and says:

"Huck Finn, did you *ever* hear of a prisoner having picks and shovels, and all the modern conveniences in his wardrobe to dig himself out with? Now I want to ask you—if you got any reasonableness in you at all—what kind of a show would *that* give him to be a hero? Why, they might as well lend him the key, and done with it. Picks and shovels—why they wouldn't furnish 'em to a king."

"Well, then," I says, "if we don't want the picks and shovels, what do we want?"

"A couple of case-knives." **18**

"To dig the foundations out from under that cabin, with?"

"Yes."

"Confound it, it's foolish, Tom."

"It don't make no difference how foolish it is, it's the *right* way—and it's the regular way. And there ain't no *other* way, that ever *I* heard of, and I've read all the books that gives any information about these things. They always dig out with a case-knife—and not through dirt, mind you; generly it's through solid rock. And it takes them weeks and weeks and weeks, and for ever and ever. Why, look at one of them prisoners **19** in the bottom dungeon of the Castle Deef, in the harbor of Marseilles, that dug himself out that way; how long was *he* at it, you reckon?"

"I don't know."

"Well, guess."

"I don't know. A month and a half?"

"*Thirty-seven year*—and he come out in China. *That's* **20** the kind. I wish the bottom of *this* fortress was solid rock."

"*Jim* don't know nobody in China."

"What's *that* got to do with it? Neither did that other fellow. But you're always a-wandering off on a side issue. Why can't you stick to the main point?"

"All right—*I* don't care where he comes out, so he *comes* out; and Jim don't, either, I reckon. But there's one thing, anyway—Jim's too old to be dug out with a case-knife. He won't last."

"Yes he will *last*, too. You don't reckon it's going to take

15 *the nigger patch*. Slaves were generally allowed a certain amount of ground to grow food to supplement what their masters gave them, and whatever else they produced, could be sold at market to pay for clothes and other luxuries. These gardens benefitted both the slave and the master, the latter by his not feeling obligated to provide anything beyond the simple necessities.

16 *Tom said that what he meant was, we could steal anything we needed*. This argument over "borrowing" and "stealing" is a rephrasing of Huck and Jim's discussion over the morality of taking whatever provisions they needed for their escape. See Chapter 12, note 8.

17 *gold-leaf distinctions*. Superciliously fine distinctions; but these fancy arguments are just for "style" and can be as deceptive as gilding.

18 *case-knives*. Large kitchen or table knives.

19 *one of them prisoners in the bottom dungeon of the Castle Deef, in the harbor of Marseilles*. Abbé Faria, a priest who was imprisoned for conspiracy to unite Italy, is one of the principal characters of Dumas' famous novel *Le Comte de Monte Cristo* (1844). He was incarcerated in the cell next to that of Edmond Dantès in the infamous Chateau d'If off Marseilles. "We hired a sailboat and a guide," Twain recounted in Chapter 11 of Vol. I of *The Innocents Abroad*, "and

Abbé Faria and Edmund Dantes. *Courtesy the Library of Congress.*

made an excursion to one of the small islands to visit the Castle d'If. This ancient fortress has a melancholy history. It has been used as a prison for political prisoners for two or three hundred years. . . . The walls of these dungeons are as thick as some bedchambers at home are wide—fifteen feet. We saw the damp, dismal cells in which two of Dumas' heroes passed their confinement—heroes of *Monte Cristo*. It was here that the brave Abbé wrote a book with his own blood; with a pen made of a piece of iron hoop, and by the lamp made out of shreds of cloth soaked in grease obtained from his food; and then dug through the thick wall with some trifling instrument which he wrought himself out of a stray piece of iron or table cutlery, and freed Dantès from his chains. It was a pity that so many weeks of dreary labor should have come to naught at last."

Much of Tom's plan to rescue Jim is a parody of *The Count of Monte Cristo*, a particularly appropriate inspiration for, like *Huckleberry Finn*, it describes the history of someone (like Huck himself), thought to be dead, who returns under a new identity to steal back what is rightfully his.

20 *Thirty-seven year.* As usual, Tom exaggerates; Abbé Faria was incarcerated in the Castle d'If for only about ten years.

21 *Then his next move will be to advertise Jim, or something like that.* Tom and Huck only have about a year in which to release Jim. See Chapter 42, note 4.

thirty-seven years to dig out through a *dirt* foundation, do you?"

"How long will it take, Tom?"

21 "Well, we can't resk being as long as we ought to, because it mayn't take very long for Uncle Silas to hear from down there by New Orleans. He'll hear Jim ain't from there. Then his next move will be to advertise Jim, or something like that. So we can't resk being as long digging him out as we ought to. By rights I reckon we ought to be a couple of years; but we can't. Things being so uncertain, what I recommend is this: that we really dig right in, as quick as we can; and after that, we can *let on*, to ourselves, that we was at it thirty-seven years. Then we can snatch him out and rush him away the first time there's an alarm. Yes, I reckon that'll be the best way."

"Now, there's *sense* in that," I says. "Letting on don't cost nothing; letting on ain't no trouble; and if it's any object, I don't mind letting on we was at it a hundred and fifty year. It wouldn't strain me none, after I got my hand in. So I'll mosey along now, and smouch a couple of case-knives."

"Smouch three," he says; "we want one to make a saw out of."

"Tom, if it ain't unregular and irreligious to sejest it," I says, "there's an old rusty saw-blade around yonder sticking under the weatherboarding behind the smoke-house."

He looked kind of weary and discouraged-like, and says:

"It ain't no use to try to learn you nothing, Huck. Run along and smouch the knives—three of them." So I done it.

SMOUCHING THE KNIVES.

Chapter XXXVI

GOING DOWN THE LIGHTNING-ROD.

As soon as we reckoned everybody was asleep, that night, we went down the lightning-rod, and shut ourselves up in the lean-to, and got out our pile of fox-fire, and went to work. We cleared everything out of the way, about four or five foot along the middle of the bottom log. Tom said he was right behind Jim's bed now, and we'd dig in under it, and when we got through there couldn't nobody in the cabin ever know there was any hole there, because Jim's counterpin hung down [1] most to the ground, and you'd have to raise it up and look under to see the hole. So we dug and dug, with the case-knives, till most midnight; and then we was dog-tired, and our hands was blistered, and yet you couldn't see we'd done anything, hardly. At last I says:

"This ain't no thirty-seven year job, this is a thirty-eight year job, Tom Sawyer."

He never said nothing. But he sighed, and pretty soon he stopped digging, and then for a good little while I knowed he

1 *counterpin*. Counterpane, bedspread.

was thinking. Then he says:

"It ain't no use, Huck, it ain't agoing to work. If we was prisoners it would, because then we'd have as many years as we wanted, and no hurry; and we wouldn't get but a few minutes to dig, every day, while they was changing watches, and so our hands wouldn't get blistered, and we could keep it up right along, year in and year out, and do it right, and the way it ought to be done. But *we* can't fool along, we got to rush; we ain't got no time to spare. If we was to put in another night this way, we'd have to knock off for a week to let our hands get well—couldn't touch a case-knife with them sooner."

"Well, then, what we going to do, Tom?"

"I'll tell you. It ain't right, and it ain't moral, and I wouldn't like it to get out—but there ain't only just the one way; we got to dig him out with the picks, and *let on* it's case-knives."

"*Now* you're *talking!*" I says; "your head gets leveller and leveller all the time, Tom Sawyer," I says. "Picks is the thing, moral or no moral; and as for me, I don't care shucks for the morality of it, nohow. When I start in to steal a nigger, or a watermelon, or a Sunday-school book, I ain't no ways particular how it's done so it's done. What I want is my nigger; or what I want is my watermelon; or what I want is my Sunday-school book; and if a pick's the handiest thing, that's the thing I'm agoing to dig that nigger or that watermelon or that Sunday-school book out with; and I don't give a dead rat what the authorities thinks about it nuther."

"Well," he says, "there's excuse for picks and letting-on in a case like this; if it warn't so, I wouldn't approve of it, nor I wouldn't stand by and see the rules broke—because right is right, and wrong is wrong, and a body ain't got no business doing wrong when he ain't ignorant and knows better. It might answer for *you* to dig Jim out with a pick, *without* any letting-on, because you don't know no better; but it wouldn't for me, because I do know better. Gimme a case-knife."

He had his own by him, but I handed him mine. He flung it down, and says:

"Gimme a *case-knife.*"

I didn't know just what to do—but then I thought. I scratched around amongst the old tools, and got a pick-axe and give it to him, and he took it and went to work, and never said a word.

He was always just that particular. Full of principle.

So then I got a shovel, and then we picked and shoveled, turn about, and made the fur fly. We stuck to it about a half an hour, which was as long as we could stand up; but we had a good deal of a hole to show for it. When I got upstairs, I looked out at the window and see Tom doing his level best with the lightning-rod, but he couldn't come it, his hands was so sore. At last he says:

"It ain't no use, it can't be done. What you reckon I better do? Can't you think up no way?"

2 *dog-fennel*. Or "stinking camomile," so-called for its odor. Both dog-fennel and jimpson weeds are particularly miserable plants.

STEALING SPOONS.

"Yes," I says, "but I reckon it ain't regular.   Come up the stairs, and let on it's a lightning-rod."

So he done it.

Next day Tom stole a pewter spoon and a brass candlestick in the house, for to make some pens for Jim out of, and six tallow candles; and I hung around the nigger cabins, and laid for a chance, and stole three tin plates.   Tom said it wasn't enough; but I said nobody wouldn't ever see the plates that Jim throwed out, because they'd fall in the dog-fennel and **2** jimpson weeds under the window-hole—then we could tote them back and he could use them over again.   So Tom was satisfied.   Then he says:

"Now, the thing to study out is, how to get the things to Jim."

"Take them in through the hole," I says, "when we get it done."

He only just looked scornful, and said something about nobody ever heard of such an idiotic idea, and then he went to studying.   By-and-by he said he had ciphered out two or three ways, but there warn't no need to decide on any of them yet. Said we'd got to post Jim first.

That night we went down the lightning-rod a little after ten, and took one of the candles along, and listened under the window-hole, and heard Jim snoring; so we pitched it in, and it didn't wake him.   Then we whirled in with the pick and shovel, and in about two hours and a half the job was done. We crept in under Jim's bed and into the cabin, and pawed around and found the candle and lit it, and stood over Jim a while, and found him looking hearty and healthy, and then we woke him up gentle and gradual.   He was so glad to see us he

3 *a cold chisel.* A strong, highly tempered iron or steel chisel which can cut through cold iron.

4 *Uncle Silas come in every day or two to pray with him.* In his notes, Twain had considered introducing a struggle between Uncle Silas and his conscience over what to do about Jim: The farmer-preacher "wishes he would escape—if it warn't wrong, he'd set him free—but it's a too gushy generosity with another man's property" (quoted by DeVoto, *Mark Twain at Work,* p. 77). However, in making good-natured Uncle Silas largely indifferent toward the slave's fate, Twain has heightened the paradox of a man who preaches on Sunday and is blind to his fellow man's suffering the rest of the week. "Tom Sawyer, Detective" reveals certain characteristics of Uncle Silas's personality not evident in *Huckleberry Finn:* Although he is described by Tom Sawyer as "gentle as mush," the old man is so enraged by Brace Dunlap's intentions toward his daughter, Benny, that he strikes his neighbor; and when Dunlap is found dead, Uncle Silas is arrested for the crime.

Uncle Silas strikes to kill. Illustration by A. B. Frost, "Tom Sawyer, Detective," *Harper's Monthly,* September 1896. *Courtesy the Library of Congress.*

most cried; and called us honey, and all the pet names he **3** could think of; and was for having us hunt up a cold chisel to cut the chain off of his leg with, right away, and clearing out without losing any time. But Tom he showed him how unregular it would be, and set down and told him all about our plans, and how we could alter them in a minute any time there was an alarm; and not to be the least afraid, because we would see he got away, *sure.* So Jim he said it was all right, and we set there and talked over old times a while, and then Tom **4** asked a lot of questions, and when Jim told him Uncle Silas come in every day or two to pray with him, and Aunt Sally come in to see if he was comfortable and had plenty to eat, and both of them was kind as they could be, Tom says:

"*Now* I know how to fix it. We'll send you some things by them."

I said, "Don't do nothing of the kind; it's one of the most jackass ideas I ever struck;" but he never paid no attention to me; went right on. It was his way when he'd got his plans set.

So he told Jim how we'd have to smuggle in the rope-ladder pie, and other large things, by Nat, the nigger that fed him, and he must be on the look-out, and not be surprised, and not let Nat see him open them; and we would put small things in uncle's coat pockets and he must steal them out; and we would tie things to aunt's apron strings or put them in her apron pocket, if we got a chance; and told him what they would be and what they was for. And told him how to keep a journal on the shirt with his blood, and all that. He told him everything. Jim he couldn't see no sense in the most of it, but he allowed we was white folks and knowed better than him; so he was satisfied, and said he would do it all just as Tom said.

Jim had plenty corn-cob pipes and tobacco; so we had a right down good sociable time; then we crawled out through the hole, and so home to bed, with hands that looked like they'd been chawed. Tom was in high spirits. He said it was the best fun he ever had in his life, and the most intellectural; and said if he only could see his way to it we would keep it up all the rest of our lives and leave Jim to our children to get out; for he believed Jim would come to like it better and better the more he got used to it. He said that in that way it could be strung out to as much as eighty year, and would be the best time on record. And he said it would make us all celebrated that had a hand in it.

In the morning we went out to the wood-pile and chopped up the brass candlestick into handy sizes, and Tom put them and the pewter spoon in his pocket. Then we went to the nigger cabins, and while I got Nat's notice off, Tom shoved a piece of candlestick into the middle of a corn-pone that was in Jim's pan, and we went along with Nat to see how it would work, and it just worked noble; when Jim bit into it it most mashed all his teeth out; and there warn't ever anything could a worked better. Tom said so himself. Jim he never let on but what it was only just a piece of rock or something like that

that's always getting into bread, you know; but after that he never bit into nothing but what he jabbed his fork into it in three or four places, first.

And whilst we was a standing there in the dimmish light, here comes a couple of the hounds bulging in, from under Jim's bed; and they kept on piling in till there was eleven of them, and there warn't hardly room in there to get your breath. By jings, we forgot to fasten that lean-to door. The nigger Nat he only just hollered " witches!" once, and keeled over on to the floor amongst the dogs, and begun to groan like he was dying. Tom jerked the door open and flung out a slab of Jim's meat, and the dogs went for it, and in two seconds he was out himself and back again and shut the door, and I knowed he'd fixed the other door too. Then he went to work on the nigger, coaxing him and petting him, and asking him if he'd been imagining he saw something again. He raised up, and blinked his eyes around, and says:

" Mars Sid, you'll say I's a fool, but if I didn't b'lieve I see most a million dogs, er devils, er some'n, I wisht I may die right heah in dese tracks. I did, mos' sholy. Mars Sid, I *felt* um— I *felt* um, sah; dey was all over me. Dad fetch it, I jis' wisht I could git my han's on one er dem witches jis' wunst—on'y jis' wunst—it's all *I*'d ast. But mos'ly I wisht dey'd lemme 'lone, I does."

Tom says:

" Well, I tell you what *I* think. What makes them come here just at this runaway nigger's breakfast-time? It's because they're hungry; that's the reason. You make them a witch pie; that's the thing for *you* to do."

TOM ADVISES A WITCH PIE.

"But my lan', Mars Sid, how's *I* gwyne to make 'm a witch pie? I doan' know how to make it. I hain't ever hearn er sich a thing b'fo'."

"Well, then, I'll have to make it myself."

"Will you do it, honey?---will you? I'll wusshup de groun' und' yo' foot, I will!"

"All right, I'll do it, seeing it's you, and you've been good to us and showed us the runaway nigger. But you got to be mighty careful. When we come around, you turn your back; and then whatever we've put in the pan, don't you let on you see it at all. And don't you look, when Jim unloads the pan— something might happen, I don't know what. And above all, don't you *handle* the witch-things."

"*Hannel* 'm Mars Sid? What *is* you a talkin' 'bout? I wouldn' lay de weight er my finger on um, not f'r ten hund'd thous'n' billion dollars, I wouldn't."

Chap. XXXVII

THE RUBBAGE-PILE.

That was all fixed. So then we went away and went to the rubbage-pile in the back yard where they keep the old boots, and rags, and pieces of bottles, and wore-out tin things, and all such truck, and scratched around and found an old tin wash-pan and stopped up the holes as well as we could, to bake the pie in, and took it down cellar and stole it full of flour, and started for breakfast and found a couple of shingle-nails that Tom said would be handy for a prisoner to scrabble his name and sorrows on the dungeon walls with, and dropped one of them in Aunt Sally's apron pocket which was hanging on a chair, and t'other we stuck in the band of Uncle Silas's hat, which was on the bureau, because we heard the children say their pa and ma was going to the runaway nigger's house this morning, and then went to breakfast, and Tom dropped the pewter spoon in Uncle Silas's coat pocket, and Aunt Sally wasn't come yet, so we had to wait a little while.

And when she come she was hot, and red, and cross, and couldn't hardly wait for the blessing; and then she went to

1 *we . . . found a couple of shingle-nails that Tom said would be handy for a prisoner to scrabble his name and sorrows on the dungeon walls with.* Twain is again recalling Castle d'If whose walls, he wrote in Chapter 11 of Vol. I of *The Innocents Abroad*, "are scarred with the rudely-carved names of many and many a captive who fretted his life away here, and left no record of himself but these sad epitaphs wrought with his own hands. How thick the names were! . . . Names everywhere!—some plebian, some noble, some even

Inscriptions on the walls of the dungeon in the Castle d'If. Illustration by True W. Williams, *the Innocents Abroad*, 1869.

princely. Plebian, prince, and noble, had one solici-
tude in common—they would not be forgotten! They
could suffer solitude, inactivity, and the horrors of a
silence that no sound ever disturbed; but they could
not bear the thought of being utterly forgotten by the
world. Hence the carved names."

2 *sluicing out*. Pouring out quickly in a straight jet of
liquid; mining slang. See Chapter 29, note 18.

3 *Tom he turned kinder blue around the gills*. He turned
pale with fright.

2 sluicing out coffee with one hand and cracking the handiest
child's head with her thimble with the other, and says :

"I've hunted high, and I've hunted low, and it does beat
all, what *has* become of your other shirt."

My heart fell down amongst my lungs and livers and things,
and a hard piece of corn-crust started down my throat after it
and got met on the road with a cough and was shot across the
table and took one of the children in the eye and curled him
up like a fishing-worm, and let a cry out of him the size of a
3 war-whoop, and Tom he turned kinder blue around the gills,
and it all amounted to a considerable state of things for about
a quarter of a minute or as much as that, and I would as old
out for half price if there was a bidder.   But after that we was
all right again—it was the sudden surprise of it that knocked
us so kind of cold.   Uncle Silas he says :

"I's most uncommon curious, I can't understand it.   I
know perfectly well I took it *off*, because——"

"Because you hain't got but one *on*.   Just *listen* at the
man !   *I* know you took it off, and know it by a better way
than your wool-gethering memory, too, because it was on the
clo'es-line yesterday—I see it there myself.   But it's gone—
that's the long and the short of it, and you'll just have to change
to a red flann'l one till I can get time to make a new one.   And
it'll be the third I've made in two years ; it just keeps a body on
the jump to keep you in shirts ; and whatever you do manage to
do with 'm all, is more'n *I* can make out.   A body'd think you
would learn to take some sort of care of 'em, at your time of
life."

"I know it, Sally, and I do try all I can.   But it oughtn't
to be altogether my fault, because you know I don't see them
nor have nothing to do with them except when they're on me ;
and I don't believe I've ever lost one of them *off* of me."

"Well, it ain't *your* fault if you haven't, Silas—you'd a
done it if you could, I reckon.   And the shirt ain't all that's
gone, nuther.   Ther's a spoon gone ; and *that* ain't all.   There
was ten, and now ther's only nine.   The calf got the shirt I
reckon, but the calf never took the spoon, *that's* certain."

"Why, what else is gone, Sally ? "

"Ther's six *candles* gone—that's what.   The rats could a
got the candles, and I reckon they did ; I wonder they don't
walk off with the whole place, the way you're always going to
stop their holes and don't do it ; and if they warn't fools they'd
sleep in your hair, Silas—*you'd* never find it out ; but you
can't lay the *spoon* on the rats, and that I *know*."

"Well, Sally, I'm in fault, and I acknowledge it ; I've been
remiss ; but I won't let to-morrow go by without stopping up
them holes."

"Oh, I wouldn't hurry, next year'll do.   Matilda Angelina
Araminta *Phelps !* "

Whack comes the thimble, and the child snatches her claws
out of the sugar-bowl without fooling around any.   Just then,
the nigger woman steps on to the passage, and says :

4 *a young yaller wench.* A young mulatto woman; light-skinned female slaves were usually the domestic servants who attended the mistress and her children.

5 *I wished I was in Jerusalem or somewheres.* Huck is trying to think of Jericho; see Chapter 3, note 24.

"MISSUS, DEY'S A SHEET GONE."

"Missus, dey's a sheet gone."

"A *sheet* gone! Well, for the land's sake!"

"I'll stop up them holes *to-day*," says Uncle Silas, looking sorrowful.

"Oh, *do* shet up!— s'pose the rats took the *sheet?* Where's it gone, Lize?"

"Clah to goodness I hain't no notion, Miss Sally. She wuz on de clo's-line yistiddy, but she done gone; she ain' dah no mo', now."

"I reckon the world *is* coming to an end. I *never* see the beat of it, in all my born days. A shirt, and a sheet, and a spoon, and six can——"

"Missus," comes a young yaller wench, "dey's a brass **4** cannelstick miss'n."

"Cler out from here, you hussy, er I'll take a skillet to ye!"

Well, she was just a biling. I begun to lay for a chance; I reckoned I would sneak out and go for the woods till the weather moderated. She kept a raging right along, running her insurrection all by herself, and everybody else mighty meek and quiet; and at last Uncle Silas, looking kind of foolish, fishes up that spoon out of his pocket. She stopped, with her mouth open and her hands up; and as for me, I wished I was **5** in Jeruslem or somewheres. But not long; because she says:

"It's *just* as I expected. So you had it in your pocket all the time; and like as not you've got the other things there, too. How'd it get there?"

"I reely don't know, Sally," he says, kind of apologising,

6 *Acts Seventeen*. The Arkansas preacher has been reading about his biblical namesake, Silas, who accompanied Paul to the Thessalonians; but Uncle Silas remains unmoved by either the previous chapter which described the other Silas' imprisonment or by Paul's teaching in Acts 17:24–26: "God that made the world and all things therein . . . hath made of one blood all nations of men for to dwell on all the face of the earth." In Chapter 5 of Vol. II of *The Innocents Abroad*, Twain recounted his visit to Mars Hill, in Athens, "where St. Paul defined his position, and below was the market-place where he 'disputed daily' with the gossip-loving Athenians. We climbed the stone steps St. Paul ascended, and stood in the square-cut place he stood in." After this pilgrimage to the spot of Acts 17, he and his fellow pilgrims tried to steal some grapes, but were thwarted by Greek farmers with guns; perhaps this incident in part inspired the uproar Tom and Huck cause in Chapter 40.

7 *He went a mooning around*. He wandered around stupidly, as if in a dream.

" or you know I would tell. I was a-studying over my text in **6** Acts Seventeen, before breakfast, and I reckon I put it in there, not noticing, meaning to put my Testament in, and it must be so, because my Testament ain't in, but I'll go and see, and if the Testament is where I had it, I'll know I didn't put it in, and that will show that I laid the Testament down and took up the spoon, and——"

"Oh, for the land's sake! Give a body a rest! Go 'long now, the whole kit and biling of ye; and don't come nigh me again till I've got back my peace of mind."

I'd a heard her, if she'd a said it to herself, let alone speaking it out; and I'd a got up and obeyed her, if I'd a been dead. As we was passing through the setting-room, the old man he took up his hat, and the shingle-nail fell out on the floor, and he just merely picked it up and laid it on the mantel-shelf, and never said nothing, and went out. Tom see him do it, and remembered about the spoon, and says:

"Well, it ain't no use to send things by *him* no more, he ain't reliable." Then he says: "But he done us a good turn with the spoon, anyway, without knowing it, and so we'll go and do him one without *him* knowing it—stop up his rat-holes."

There was a noble good lot of them, down cellar, and it took us a whole hour, but we done the job tight and good, and ship-shape. Then we heard steps on the stairs, and blowed out our light, and hid; and here comes the old man, with a candle in one hand and a bundle of stuff in t'other, looking as absent-**7** minded as year before last. He went a mooning around, first to one rat-hole and then another, till he'd been to them all. Then he stood about five minutes, picking tallow-drip off of his candle and thinking. Then he turns off slow and dreamy towards the stairs, saying:

"Well, for the life of me I can't remember when I done it. I could show her now that I warn't to blame on account of the rats. But never mind—let it go. I reckon it wouldn't do no good."

And so he went on a mumbling upstairs, and then we left. He was a mighty nice old man. And always is.

Tom was a good deal bothered about what to do for a spoon, but he said we'd got to have it; so he took a think. When he had ciphered it out, he told me how we was to do; then we went and waited around the spoon-basket till we see Aunt Sally coming, and then Tom went to counting the spoons and laying them out to one side, and I slid one of them up my sleeve, and Tom says:

"Why, Aunt Sally, there ain't but nine spoons, *yet*."

She says:

"Go 'long to your play, and don't bother me. I know better, I counted 'm myself."

"Well, I've counted them twice, Aunty, and *I* can't make but nine."

She looked out of all patience, but of course she come to count—anybody would.

"I declare to gracious ther' *ain't* but nine!" she says. "Why, what in the world—plague *take* the things, I'll count 'm again."

So I slipped back the one I had, and when she got done counting, she says:

"Hang the troublesome rubbage, ther's *ten*, now!" and she looked huffy and bothered both. But Tom says:

"Why, Aunty, *I* don't think there's ten."

"You numskull, didn't you see me *count* 'm?"

"I know, but——"

"Well, I'll count 'm *again*."

So I smouched one, and they come out nine same as the other time. Well, she *was* in a tearing way—just a trembling

"IN A TEARING WAY."

all over, she was so mad. But she counted and counted, till she got that addled she'd start to count-in the *basket* for a spoon, sometimes; and so, three times they come out right, and three times they come out wrong. Then she grabbed up the basket **8** and slammed it across the house and knocked the cat galley-west; and she said cle'r out and let her have some peace, and if we come bothering around her again betwixt that and dinner, she'd skin us. So we had the odd spoon; and dropped it in her apron pocket whilst she was a giving us our sailing-orders, **9** and Jim got it all right, along with her shingle-nail, before noon. We was very well satisfied with this business, and Tom allowed it was worth twice the trouble it took, because he said *now* she couldn't ever count them spoons twice alike again to save her life; and wouldn't believe she'd counted them right, if she *did*; and said that after she'd about counted her head off, for the next three days, he judged she'd give it up and offer to kill anybody that wanted her to ever count them any more.

So we put the sheet back on the line, that night, and stole

8 *she . . . knocked the cat galley-west.* She knocked the cat head over heels; from "collyweston," dialectical English for "awry, askew, confused." Twain introduced this expression in an amusing exchange in "Schoolhouse Hill," 1898 (an early draft of *The Mysterious Stranger*, 1969, pp. 186–187), in which Tom struggles to get a strange new boy in town to understand him:

"Galley west? . . .

"It's just a word, you know. Means you've knocked his props from under him.

"Knocked his props out from under him?

"Yes—trumped his ace.

"Trumped his—

"Ace. That's it—pulled his leg.

"I assure you this is in error. I have not pulled his leg.

"But you don't understand. Don't you see? You've graveled him, and he's disgruntled.

. . . The new boy hesitated, passed his hand over his forehead, and began haltingly—

"It is still a little vague. It was but a poor dictionary—that French-English—and over-rich in omissions. Do you perhaps mean that he is jealous?

"Score *one!* That's it. Jealous—the very word. . . ."

9 *she was a giving us our sailing-orders.* She was telling them to get out.

10 *a noble brass warming-pan.* Before the introduction of central heating, to keep oneself warm at night, coals would be put in the bowl of the warming pan which once heated would be wrapped up and put at the foot of the bed to warm it when one went to sleep.

11 *it belonged to one of his ancestors with a long wooden handle.* Kemble has extended Twain's joke by literally interpreting Huck's misplaced modifier and giving Uncle Silas' ancestor a wooden leg.

12 *from England with William the Conqueror in the* Mayflower *or one of them early ships.* Twain is poking fun at American ancestor worship; when they are not claiming descent from European royalty like the king and the duke, Americans boast of having descended from the earliest settlers of the United States. Traditions are overvalued even in a young country. But once again Huck has garbled his history: William the Conqueror crossed the English Channel into Britain in 1066, and the Pilgrims came over from Holland on the *Mayflower* to Massachusetts in 1621; Huck may be trying to recall William Bradford, the first governor of the Plymouth colony.

13 *she come up smiling.* She succeeded admirably; from prizefight slang, usually applied to a boxer who, although badly beaten, comes out of defeat not only without complaining but also still good-humored.

14 *cramp him down to business.* Put him in his place; originally riverboat slang, meaning to force a steamboat in a desired direction.

one out of her closet: and kept on putting it back and stealing it again, for a couple of days, till she didn't know how many sheets she had, any more, and said she didn't *care*, and warn't agoing to bullyrag the rest of her soul out about it, and wouldn't count them again not to save her life, she druther die first.

So we was all right now, as to the shirt and the sheet and the spoon and the candles, by the help of the calf and the rats and the mixed-up counting; and as to the candlestick, it warn't no consequence, it would blow over by-and-by.

But that pie was a job; we had no end of trouble with that pie. We fixed it up away down in the woods, and cooked it there; and we got it done at last, and very satisfactory, too; but not all in one day; and we had to use up three wash-pans full of flour, before we got through, and we got burnt pretty much all over, in places, and eyes put out with the smoke; because, you see, we didn't want nothing but a crust, and we couldn't prop it up right, and she would always cave in. But of course we thought of the right way at last; which was to cook the ladder, too, in the pie. So then we laid in with Jim, the second night, and tore up the sheet all in little strings, and twisted them together, and long before daylight we had a lovely rope, that you could a hung a person with. We let on it took nine months to make it.

And in the forenoon we took it down to the woods, but it wouldn't go in the pie. Being made of a whole sheet, that way, there was rope enough for forty pies, if we'd a wanted them, and plenty left over for soup, or sausage, or anything you choose. We could a had a whole dinner.

But we didn't need it. All we needed was just enough for the pie, and so we throwed the rest away. We didn't cook none of the pies in the washpan, afraid the solder would melt; **10** but Uncle Silas he had a noble brass warming-pan which he **11** thought considerable of, because it belonged to one of his **12** ancestors with a long wooden handle that come over from England with William the Conqueror in the *Mayflower* or one of them early ships and was hid away up garret with a lot of other old pots and things that was valuable, not on account of being any account because they warn't, but on account of them being relicts, you know, and we snaked her out, private, and took her down there, but she failed on the first pies, because **13** we didn't know how, but she come up smiling on the last one. We took and lined her with dough, and set her in the coals, and loaded her up with rag-rope, and put on a dough roof, and shut down the lid, and put hot embers on top, and stood off five foot, with the long handle, cool and comfortable, and in fifteen minutes she turned out a pie that was a satisfaction to look at. But the person that et it would want to fetch a couple of kags of toothpicks along, for if that rope-ladder **14** wouldn't cramp him down to business, I don't know nothing what I'm talking about, and lay him in enough stomach-ache to last him till next time, too.

ONE OF HIS ANCESTORS.

Nat didn't look, when we put the witch-pie in Jim's pan; and we put the three tin plates in the bottom of the pan under the vittles; and so Jim got everything all right, and as soon as he was by himself he busted into the pie and hid the rope-ladder inside of his straw tick, and scratched some marks on a tin plate and threw it out of the window-hole.

Chap. XXXVIII

1 *Lady Jane Grey . . . Gilford Dudley . . . old Northumberland.* Tom has apparently been reading William Harrison Ainsworth's popular romance *The Tower of London* (1840): Through treachery, the Duke of Northumberland (1502–1553) persuaded young King Edward VI to break his father's will to change the line of succession in favor of the duke's Protestant daughter-in-law, Lady Jane Grey (1537–1554), instead of the king's Catholic sister, Mary Tudor. Upon Edward's death, the sixteen-year-old girl ruled England for nine days before she was arrested with the duke and his son, her husband Lord Guildford Dudley; they were imprisoned in the Tower of London before each died on the scaffold. Twain, however, sympathetically portrays the doomed Lady Jane Grey in *The Prince and the Pauper.*

Lady Jane Grey, with Lord Guildford Dudley on her left and the Duke of Northumberland on her right. *Courtesy the Picture Collection, The New York Public Library, Astor, Lenox, and Tilden Foundations.*

JIM'S COAT OF ARMS.

Making them pens was a distressid-tough job, and so was the saw; and Jim allowed the inscription was going to be the toughest of all. That's the one which the prisoner has to scrabble on the wall. But we had to have it; Tom said we'd *got* to: there warn't no case of a state prisoner not scrabbling his inscription to leave behind, and his coat of arms.

"Look at Lady Jane Grey," he says; "look at Gilford Dudley; look at old Northumberland! Why, Huck, s'pose it *is* considerble trouble?—what you going to do?—how you going to get around it? **2** Jim's *got* to do his inscription and coat of arms. They all do."

Jim says:

"Why, Mars Tom, I hain't got no coat o' arms; I hain't got nuffn but dish-yer ole shirt, en you knows I got to keep de journal on dat."

"Oh, you don't understand, Jim; a coat of arms is very different."

"Well," I says, "Jim's right, anyway, when he says he hain't got no coat of arms, because he hain't."

"I reckon *I* knowed that," Tom says, "but you bet he'll have one before he goes out of this—because he's going out *right,* and there ain't going to be no flaws in his record."

So whilst me and Jim filed away at the pens on a brickbat apiece, Jim a making his'n out of the brass and I making mine out of the spoon, Tom set to work to think out the coat of arms. By-and-by he said he'd struck so many good ones he didn't hardly know which to take, but there was one which he reckoned he'd decide on. He says:

"On the scutcheon we'll have a bend *or* in the dexter base, **3** a saltire *murrey* in the fess, with a dog, couchant, for common charge, and under his foot a chain embattled, for slavery, with a chevron *vert* in a chief engrailed, and three invected lines on a field *azure,* with the nombril points rampant on a dancette indented ; crest, a runaway nigger, *sable,* with his bundle over his shoulder on a bar sinister : and a couple of gules for supporters, which is you and me ; motto, *Maggiore fretta, minore atto.* **4** Got it out of a book—means, the more haste, the less speed."

"Geewhillikins," I says, "but what does the rest of it mean ? "

"We ain't got no time to bother over that," he says, "we got to dig in like all git-out."

"Well, anyway," I says, "what's *some* of it ? What's a fess ? "

"A fess—a fess is—*you* don't need to know what a fess is. I'll show him how to make it when he gets to it."

"Shucks, Tom," I says, "I think you might tell a person. What's a bar sinister ? " **5**

"Oh, *I* don't know. But he's got to have it. All the nobility does."

That was just his way. If it didn't suit him to explain a **6** thing to you, he wouldn't do it. You might pump at him a week, it wouldn't make no difference.

He'd got all that coat of arms business fixed, so now he started in to finish up the rest of that part of the work, which was to plan out a mournful inscription—said Jim got to have one, like they all done. He made up a lot, and wrote them out on a paper, and read them off, so:

1. *Here a captive heart busted.*

2. *Here a poor prisoner, forsook by the world and friends, fretted out his sorrowful life.*

3. *Here a lonely heart broke, and a worn spirit went to its rest, after thirty-seven years of solitary captivity.*

4. *Here, homeless and friendless, after thirty-seven years of bitter captivity, perished a noble stranger, natural son of* **7** *Louis XIV.*

Tom's voice trembled, whilst he was reading them, and he most broke down. When he got done, he couldn't no way make

2 *Jim's got to do his inscription and coat of arms. They all do.* "Every room, from roof to vault," Ainsworth described the Beauchamp Tower in Chapter 4 of Book II of *The Tower of London,* "is covered with melancholy memorials of its illustrious and unfortunate occupants. . . . In general, they are beautifully carved, ample time being allowed the writers for their melancholy employment." It was in a cell here that the Duke of Northumberland carved his coat of arms. "Allowed, as a matter of indulgence, to remain within the large room," Ainsworth wrote in Chapter 7 of Book II, the duke "occupied himself in putting the finishing touches to a carving on the wall, which he had commenced on his first imprisonment, and had wrought at intervals. This curious sculpture may still be seen on the right hand of the fire-place of the mess-room in the Beauchamp Tower, and contains his cognizance, a bear and a lion supporting a ragged staff surrounded by a border of roses, acorns, and flowers intermingled with foliage. Northumberland was employed upon the third line of the quatrain below his name, which remains unfinished to the present day, when he was interrupted by the entrance of a priest. . . ."

Again Twain is attacking the growth of ancestor-worship in the United States. "Distinctions of wealth and family, and those, too, well defined and strongly marked, have already appeared," Charles Augustus Murray wrote of American social republicanism in Vol. I, Chapter 12 of *Travels in North America,* "accompanied by a criterion apparently trifling, but . . . bearing strong evidence, namely, 'coats of arms,' and other heraldic anti-republican signs, which are daily gaining ground." Twain was writing as much for his time as about the past: The American mania for European titles and coats of arms had increased steadily during the Gilded Age.

Northumberland's inscription in the Tower of London. *Courtesy the Library of Congress.*

3 *scutcheon . . . supporters.* As James Birchfield has discussed in "Jim's Coat of Arms" (*Mark Twain Journal*, Summer 1969, pp. 15–16), Tom generally uses the correct heraldic terms here.

scutcheon. Escutcheon, the surface, usually shaped like a shield, on which the armorial emblems are depicted.

a bend. A horizontal band from top left to bottom right side across the shield from the top left to the bottom right.

the dexter base. An error: The dexter baston, which extends across the shield, could not be confined to the right-hand side of the bottom third.

a saltire murrey in the fess. A mulberry-colored diagonal cross on its side, within a horizontal band across the shield.

a dog, couchant. A dog lying down but with its head erect.

common charge. Whatever is on the base of the shield.

a chain embattled. A chain across the shield representing a row of battlements.

a chevron vert in a chief engrailed. A green band like an inverted "V," usually at the base of the shield, but here within its top third, which has scalloped edges, with the points downward.

invected lines on a field azure. Scalloped lines with the points downward and thus fitting within the engrailed edge, on a bright blue field.

the nombril points rampant. Generally the point situated between the fess point and the base of the shield, here pointing upward.

a dancette indented. A zigzag band with edges notched toward the middle of the shield.

crest . . . sable. A black figure.

bar sinister. Actually "bend sinister," a band, generally smaller than the fess, which runs across the shield from the bottom left to the top right.

a couple of gules. Apparently a pun, for "gules" merely means red.

supporters. Figures placed at each side of the shield, usually applied to animals.

Missouri State coat of arms. *Courtesy the Library of Congress.*

up his mind which one for Jim to scrabble on to the wall, they was all so good; but at last he allowed he would let him scrabble them all on. Jim said it would take him a year to scrabble such a lot of truck on to the logs with a nail, and he didn't know how to make letters, besides; but Tom said he would block them out for him, and then he wouldn't have nothing to do but just follow the lines. Then pretty soon he says:

"Come to think, the logs ain't agoing to do; they don't have log walls in a dungeon: we got to dig the inscriptions into a rock. We'll fetch a rock."

Jim said the rock was worse than the logs; he said it would take him such a pison long time to dig them into a rock, he wouldn't ever get out. But Tom said he would let me help him do it. Then he took a look to see how me and Jim was getting along with the pens. It was most pesky tedious hard work and slow, and didn't give my hands no show to get well of the sores, and we didn't seem to make no headway, hardly. So Tom says:

"I know how to fix it. We got to have a rock for the coat of arms and mournful inscriptions, and we can kill two birds with that same rock. There's a gaudy big grindstone down at the mill, and we'll smouch it, and carve the things on it, and file out the pens and the saw on it, too."

It warn't no slouch of an idea; and it warn't no slouch of a grindstone nuther; but we allowed we'd tackle it. It warn't quite midnight, yet, so we cleared out for the mill, leaving Jim at work. We smouched the grindstone, and set out to roll her home, but it was a most nation tough job. Sometimes, do what we could, we couldn't keep her from falling over, and she come mighty near mashing us, every time. Tom said she was going to get one of us, sure, before we got through. We got

A TOUGH JOB.

her half way; and then we was plumb played out, and most drownded with sweat. We see it warn't no use, we got to go and fetch Jim. So he raised up his bed and slid the chain off of the bed-leg, and wrapt it round and round his neck, and we crawled out through our hole and down there, and Jim and me laid into that grindstone and walked her along like nothing; and Tom superintended. He could out-superintend any boy I ever see. He knowed how to do everything.

Our hole was pretty big, but it warn't big enough to get the grindstone through; but Jim he took the pick and soon made it big enough. Then Tom marked out them things on it with the nail, and set Jim to work on them, with the nail for a chisel and an iron bolt from the rubbage in the lean-to for a hammer, and told him to work till the rest of his candle quit on him, and then he could go to bed, and hide the grindstone under his straw tick and sleep on it. Then we helped him fix his chain back on the bed-leg, and was ready for bed ourselves. But Tom thought of something, and says:

"You got any spiders in here, Jim?"

"No, sah, thanks to goodness I hain't, Mars Tom."

"All right, we'll get you some."

"But bless you, honey, I doan' *want* none. I's afeard un um. I jis' 's soon have rattlesnakes aroun'."

Tom thought a minute or two, and says:

"It's a good idea. And I reckon it's been done. It *must* a been done; it stands to reason. Yes, it's a prime good idea. Where could you keep it?"

"Keep what, Mars Tom?"

"Why, a rattlesnake."

"De goodness gracious alive, Mars Tom! Why, if dey was a rattlesnake to come in heah, I'd take en bust right out thoo dat log wall, I would, wid my head."

"Why, Jim, you wouldn't be afraid of it, after a little. You could tame it."

"*Tame* it!"

"Yes—easy enough. Every animal is grateful for kindness and petting, and they wouldn't *think* of hurting a person that pets them. Any book will tell you that. You try—that's all I ask; just try for two or three days. Why, you can get him so, in a little while, that he'll love you; and sleep with you; and won't stay away from you a minute; and will let you wrap him round your neck and put his head in your mouth."

"*Please*, Mars Tom—*doan'* talk so! I can't *stan'* it! He'd *let* me shove his head in my mouf—fer a favor, hain't it? I lay he'd wait a pow'ful long time 'fo' I *ast* him. En mo' en dat, I doan' *want* him to sleep wid me."

"Jim, don't act so foolish. A prisoner's *got* to have some **8** kind of a dumb pet, and if a rattlesnake hain't ever been tried, why, ther's more glory to be gained in your being the first to ever try it than any other way you could ever think of to save your life."

"Why, Mars Tom, I doan' *want* no sich glory. Snake

4 Maggiore fretta, minore atto. . . . *the more haste, the less speed.* Actually "the more haste, the less action," an appropriate motto for Tom's cavalier attitude toward Jim's plight. This was a maxim common to schoolbooks of the day.

5 *a bar sinister. . . . he's got to have it. All the nobility does.* Twain is making a sarcastic remark about aristocracy: A bar sinister is the mark of a bastard.

6 *If it didn't suit him to explain a thing to you, he wouldn't do it.* With his head so full of empty romantic traditions, Tom may be well acquainted with symbols and rituals, but he is ignorant of their meanings.

7 *a noble stranger, natural son of Louis XIV.* A "natural son" is a bastard; one of the theories of the Man in the Iron Mask was that he was the illegitimate child of Louis XIV and Mademoiselle de la Vallière.

8 *A prisoner's got to have some kind of a dumb pet.* Count de Charney made pets of spiders; Baron von Trenck trained a mouse. So too did Byron's Prisoner of Chillon who admits:

> *With spiders I had friendship made,*
> *And watch'd them in their sullen trade,*
> *Had seen the mice by moonlight play,*
> *And why should I feel less than they?*

9 *We can get you some garter-snakes.* Twain is again recalling the Quarles farm. "Along outside of the front fence ran the country road," he wrote in Chapter 3 of his *Autobiography*, "dusty in the summertime and a good place for snakes—they liked to lie in it and sun themselves; when they were rattlesnakes . . . we killed them . . .; when they were 'house snakes' or 'garters' we carried them home and put them in Aunt Patsy's work basket for a surprise; for she was prejudiced against snakes, and always when she took the basket in her lap and they began to climb out of it, it disordered her mind. She never could seem to get used to them; her opportunities went for nothing." As seen in the next chapter, Aunt Sally shares Aunt Patsy's "prejudice."

10 *you can tie some buttons on their tails, and let on they're rattlesnakes.* "Buttons" is a colloquial word for rattlesnake rattles.

11 *a coase comb en a piece o' paper.* A "coarse comb" is a large, wide-toothed comb which can be made into a musical instrument by covering it with a piece of tissue paper and blowing through it.

12 *a juice-harp.* A "Jew's harp" is made of an elastic metal tongue fastened at one end to a small lyre-shaped frame and is played between the teeth. Both this and the coarse comb are crude instruments then popular with slaves.

take 'n bite Jim's chin off, den *whah* is de glory? No, sah, I doan' want no sich doin's."

"Blame it, can't you *try?* I only *want* you to try—you needn't keep it up if it don't work."

"But de trouble all *done*, ef de snake bite me while I's a tryin' him. Mars Tom, I's willin' to tackle mos' anything 'at ain't onreasonable, but ef you en Huck fetches a rattlesnake in heah for me to tame, I's gwyne to *leave*, dat's *shore*."

"Well, then, let it go, let it go, if you're so bullheaded about **9, 10** it. We can get you some garter-snakes and you can tie some buttons on their tails, and let on they're rattlesnakes, and I reckon that'll have to do."

"I k'n stan' *dem*, Mars Tom, but blame' 'f I couldn' get

BUTTONS ON THEIR TAILS.

along widout um, I tell you dat. I never knowed b'fo', 't was so much bother and trouble to be a prisoner."

"Well, it *always* is, when it's done right. You got any rats around here?"

"No, sah, I hain't seed none."

"Well, we'll get you some rats."

"Why, Mars Tom, I doan' *want* no rats. Dey's de dad-blamedest creturs to 'sturb a body, en rustle roun' over 'im, en bite his feet, when he's tryin' to sleep, I ever see. No, sah, gimme g'yarter-snakes 'f I's got to have 'm, but doan' gimme no rats, I ain' got no use f'r um, skasely."

"But Jim, you *got* to have 'em—they all do. So don't make no more fuss about it. Prisoners ain't ever without rats. There ain't no instance of it. And they train them, and pet them, and learn them tricks, and they get to be as sociable as flies. But you got to play music to them. You got anything to play music on?"

11   "I ain' got nuffn but a coase comb en a piece o' paper, en **12** a juice-harp; but I reck'n dey wouldn' take no stock in a juice-harp."

"Yes they would. *They* don't care what kind of music 'tis. A jew-sharp's plenty good enough for a rat. All animals likes music—in a prison they dote on it. Specially, painful music;

and you can't get no other kind out of a jews-harp. It always interests them; they come out to see what's the matter with you. Yes, you're all right; you're fixed very well. You want to set on your bed, nights, before you go to sleep, and early in the mornings, and play your jews-harp; play The Last Link is **13** Broken—that's the thing that'll scoop a rat, quicker'n anything **14** else; and when you've played about two minutes, you'll see all the rats, and the snakes, and spiders, and things begin to feel worried about you, and come. And they'll just fairly swarm over you, and have a noble good time."

" Yes, *dey* will, I reck'n, Mars Tom, but what kine er time is *Jim* havin'? Blest if I kin see de pint. But I'll do it ef I got to. I reck'n I better keep de animals satisfied, en not have no trouble in de house."

Tom waited to think over, and see if there wasn't nothing else; and pretty soon he says:

" Oh—there's one thing I forgot. Could you raise a flower here, do you reckon ? "

" I doan' know but maybe I could, Mars Tom; but it's tolable dark in heah, en I ain' got no use fr no flower, nohow, en she'd be a pow'ful sight o' trouble."

" Well, you try it, anyway. Some other prisoners has done it."

" One er dem big cat-tail-lookin' mullen-stalks would grow in **15** heah, Mars Tom, I reck'n, but she wouldn' be wuth half de trouble she'd coss."

" Don't you believe it. We'll fetch you a little one, and you plant it in the corner, over there, and raise it. And don't call it mullen, call it Pitchiola—that's its right name, when it's in **16** a prison. And you want to water it with your tears."

IRRIGATION.

" Why, I got plenty spring water, Mars Tom."

" You don't *want* spring water; you want to water it with your tears. It's the way they always do."

" Why, Mars Tom, I lay I kin raise one er dem mullen-stalks twyste wid spring water whiles another man's a *start'n* one wid tears."

13 *The Last Link is Broken*. See Chapter 17, note 45.

14 *scoop*. Take, fetch.

15 *mullen-stalks*. Or "mullein"; a large wild plant with coarse leaves and yellow tubular flowers, of the same family as the North American foxglove.

16 *Pitchiola*. Tom has been reading the popular romance *Picciola, or Captivity Captive* (1836) by "M. D. Saintine," Joseph Xavier Boniface. When the Count de Charney is imprisoned by Napoleon for treason, the only thing which makes his life worth living is a plant growing in his cell that the jailor calls "le picciola" (the stalk).

"That ain't the idea.   You *got* to do it with tears."

"She'll die on my han's, Mars Tom, she sholy will; kase I doan' skasely ever cry."

So Tom was stumped.   But he studied it over, and then said Jim would have to worry along the best he could with an onion.   He promised he would go to the nigger cabins and drop one, private, in Jim's coffee pot, in the morning.   Jim said he would "jis' 's soon have tobacker in his coffee;" and found so much fault with it, and with the work and bother of raising the mullen, and jews-harping the rats, and petting and flattering up the snakes and spiders and things, on top of all the other work he had to do on pens, and inscriptions, and journals, and things, which made it more trouble and worry and responsibility to be a prisoner than anything he ever undertook, that Tom most lost all patience with him; and said he was just loadened down with more gaudier chances than a prisoner ever had in the world to make a name for himself, and yet he didn't know enough to appreciate them, and they was just about wasted on him.   So Jim he was sorry, and said he wouldn't behave so no more, and then me and Tom shoved for bed.

Chapter XXXIX

IN the morning we went up to the village and bought a wire rat trap and fetched it down, and unstopped the best rat hole, and in about an hour we had fifteen of the bulliest kind of ones ; and then we took it and put it in a safe place under Aunt Sally's bed. But while we was gone for spiders, little Thomas Franklin Benjamin **1** Jefferson Elexander Phelps found it there, and opened the door of it to see if the rats would come out, and they did ; and Aunt Sally she come in, and when we got back she was a standing on top of the bed raising Cain, and the rats was doing what they could to keep off the dull times for her. So she took and dusted us both with the hickry, and we was as much as two hours catching another fifteen or sixteen, drat that meddlesome cub, and they warn't the likeliest, nuther, because the first haul was the pick of the flock. I never see a likelier lot of rats than what that first haul was.

KEEPING OFF DULL TIMES.

We got a splendid stock of sorted spiders, and bugs, and frogs, and caterpillars, and one thing or another ; and we like-to

1 *Thomas Franklin Benjamin Jefferson Elexander Phelps.* "In those old days," Twain explained in a note to Chapter 11 of *The Gilded Age*, "the average man called his children after his most revered literary and historical idols; consequently there was hardly a family, at least in the West, but had a Washington in it—and also a Lafayette, a Franklin, and six or eight sounding names from Byron, Scott, and the Bible, if the offspring held out." Eggleston burlesqued the same custom in *The Hoosier School-Boy* by naming a little boy Christopher Columbus George Washington Marquis de Lafayette Risdale, "a victim of that mania which some people have for 'naming after' great men."

2 *allycumpain*. Elecampane, a large coarse and bitter
herb with yellow flowers, whose root was formerly
used as a remedy in pulmonary diseases.

got a hornet's nest, but we didn't.   The family was at home.
We didn't give it right up, but staid with them as long as we
could ; because we allowed we'd tire them out or they'd got to
tire us out, and they done it.   Then we got allycumpain and
rubbed on the places, and was pretty near all right again, but
couldn't set down convenient.   And so we went for the snakes,
and grabbed a couple of dozen garters and house-snakes, and
put them in a bag, and put it in our room, and by that time it
was supper time, and a rattling good honest day's work ; and
hungry ?—oh, no, I reckon not !   And there warn't a blessed
snake up there, when we went back—we didn't half tie the
sack, and they worked out, somehow, and left.   But it didn't
matter much, because they was still on the premises somewheres.   So we judged we could get some of them again.   No,
there warn't no real scarcity of snakes about the house for a
considerble spell.   You'd see them dripping from the rafters
and places, every now and then ; and they generly landed in
your plate, or down the back of your neck, and most of the time
where you didn't want them.   Well, they was handsome, and
striped, and there warn't no harm in a million of them ; but
that never made no difference to Aunt Sally, she despised
snakes, be the breed what they might, and she couldn't stand
them no way you could fix it ; and every time one of them
flopped down on her, it didn't make no difference what she was
doing, she would just lay that work down and light out.   I
never see such a woman.   And you could hear her whoop to
Jericho.   You couldn't get her to take aholt of one of them
with the tongs.   And if she turned over and found one in bed,
she would scramble out and lift a howl that you would think
the house was afire.   She disturbed the old man so, that he
said he could most wish there hadn't ever been no snakes
created.   Why, after every last snake had been gone clear out
of the house for as much as a week, Aunt Sally warn't over it
yet ; she warn't near over it ; when she was setting thinking
about something, you could touch her on the back of her neck
with a feather and she would jump right out of her stockings.
It was very curious.   But Tom said all women was just so.
He said they was made that way ; for some reason or other.

We got a licking every time one of our snakes come in her
way ; and she allowed these lickings warn't nothing to what
she would do if we ever loaded up the place again with them.
I didn't mind the lickings, because they didn't amount to
nothing ; but I minded the trouble we had, to lay in another
lot.   But we got them laid in, and all the other things ; and
you never see a cabin as blithesome as Jim's was when they'd all
swarm out for music and go for him.   Jim didn't like the
spiders, and the spiders didn't like Jim ; and so they'd lay for
him and make it mighty warm for him.   And he said that
between the rats, and the snakes, and the grindstone, there
warn't no room in bed for him, skasely ; and when there was, a
body couldn't sleep, it was so lively, and it was always lively,
he said, because *they* never all slept at one time, but took turn
about, so when the snakes was asleep the rats was on deck, and

when the rats turned in the snakes come on watch, so he always had one gang under him, in his way, and t'other gang having a circus over him, and if he got up to hunt a new place, the spiders would take a chance at him as he crossed over. He said if he ever got out, this time, he wouldn't ever be a prisoner again, not for a salary.

Well, by the end of three weeks, everything was in pretty good shape. The shirt was sent in early, in a pie, and every time a rat bit Jim he would get up and write a little in his journal whilst the ink was fresh; the pens was made, the inscriptions and so on was all carved on the grindstone; the bedleg was sawed in two, and we had et up the sawdust, and it

3 *When Louis XVI. was going to light out of the Tooleries, a servant girl done it.* The Tuileries was the royal palace of France; in 1871, it burned down and is now the site of a park near the Louvre. In "Varennes: Count Fersen" of *The French Revolution* (1838), Thomas Carlyle described how "a certain false Chambermaid of the Palace" betrayed Louis XVI to his enemies when the king tried to flee the Tuileries.

SAWDUST DIET.

give us a most amazing stomach-ache. We reckoned we was all going to die, but didn't. It was the most undigestible sawdust I ever see; and Tom said the same. But as I was saying, we'd got all the work done, now, at last; and we was all pretty much fagged out, too, but mainly Jim. The old man had wrote a couple of times to the plantation below Orleans to come and get their runaway nigger, but hadn't got no answer, because there warn't no such plantation; so he allowed he would advertise Jim in the St. Louis and New Orleans papers; and when he mentioned the St. Louis ones, it give me the cold shivers, and I see we hadn't no time to lose. So Tom said, now for the nonnamous letters.

"What's them?" I says.

"Warnings to the people that something is up. Sometimes it's done one way, sometimes another. But there's always somebody spying around, that gives notice to the governor of the castle. When Louis XVI. was going to light out of the **3** Tooleries, a servant girl done it. It's a very good way, and so is the nonnamous letters. We'll use them both. And it's usual for the prisoner's mother to change clothes with him, and

4 *confiding and mullet-headed.* Trusting and stupid.

5 *Jim'll take the . . . gown off of me and wear it.* In his notes for the novel (in DeVoto, *Mark Twain at Work,* p. 77), Twain explained why he must escape in a dress: "Men won't shoot at women."

6 *the nigger woman's gown.* An error: Tom means Aunt Sally's gown.

7 *an evasion.* A corruption of the French word *évasion,* or escape, as in Dumas' *L'évasion du duc de Beaufort.*

she stays in, and he slides out in her clothes. We'll do that too."

" But looky here, Tom, what do we want to *warn* anybody for, that's something's up? Let them find it out for themselves —it's their look-out."

" Yes, I know; but you can't depend on them. It's the way they've acted from the very start—left us to do *everything.*
4 They're so confiding and mullet-headed they don't take notice of nothing at all. So if we don't *give* them notice, there won't be nobody nor nothing to interfere with us, and so after all our hard work and trouble this escape 'll go off perfectly flat: won't amount to nothing—won't be nothing *to* it."

" Well, as for me, Tom, that's the way I'd like."

" Shucks," he says, and looked disgusted. So I says:

" But I ain't going to make no complaint. Anyway that suits you suits me. What you going to do about the servant-girl?"

" You'll be her. You slide in, in the middle of the night, and hook that yaller girl's frock."

" Why, Tom, that'll make trouble next morning; because of course she prob'ly hain't got any but that one."

" I know; but you don't want it but fifteen minutes, to carry the nonnamous letter and shove it under the front door."

" All right, then, I'll do it; but I could carry it just as handy in my own togs."

" You wouldn't look like a servant-girl, *then,* would you? "

" No, but there won't be nobody to see what I look like, *anyway.*"

" That ain't got nothing to do with it. The thing for us to do, is just to do our *duty,* and not worry about whether anybody *sees* us do it or not. Hain't you got no principle at all? "

" All right, I ain't saying nothing; I'm the servant-girl. Who's Jim's mother? "

" I'm his mother. I'll hook a gown from Aunt Sally."

" Well, then, you'll have to stay in the cabin when me and Jim leaves."

" Not much. I'll stuff Jim's clothes full of straw and lay
5 it on his bed to represent his mother in disguise, and Jim 'll
6 take the nigger woman's gown off of me and wear it, and we'll all evade together. When a prisoner of style escapes, it's called
7 an evasion. It's always called so when a king escapes, f'rinstance. And the same with a king's son; it don't make no difference whether he's a natural one or an unnatural one."

So Tom he wrote the nonnamous letter, and I smouched the yaller wench's frock, that night, and put it on, and shoved it under the front door, the way Tom told me to. It said:

Beware. Trouble is brewing. Keep a sharp look-out. UNKNOWN FRIEND.

Next night we stuck a picture which Tom drawed in blood, of a skull and crossbones, on the front door; and next night another one of a coffin, on the back door. I never see a family in such a sweat. They couldn't a been worse scared if the place had a been full of ghosts laying for them behind every-

TROUBLE IS BREWING.

8 *bulge.* Scheme.

9 *a desprate gang of cutthroats from over in the Ingean Territory going to steal your runaway nigger.* The Indian federal land grant of what is now Oklahoma; it was then a refuge for outlaws. Tom again seems to be emulating John Murrell, the land pirate, who, in addition to robbing, horse-stealing, counterfeiting, and murder, stole slaves and projected a Negro insurrection; but he was betrayed by someone (like the "Unknown Friend") who infiltrated his gang and informed on their plans. See Chapter 2, note 12.

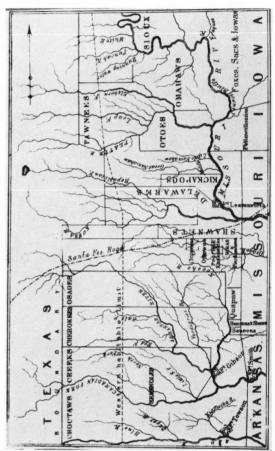

Map of the Indian Territory. Illustration from *Democratic Review*, February 1844. *Courtesy the Map Division, The New York Public Library, Astor, Lenox, and Tilden Foundations.*

thing and under the beds and shivering through the air. If a door banged, Aunt Sally she jumped, and said " ouch ! " if anything fell, she jumped, and said " ouch ! " if you happened to touch her, when she warn't noticing, she done the same; she couldn't face noway and be satisfied, because she allowed there was something behind her every time—so she was always a whirling around, sudden, and saying " ouch," and before she'd get two-thirds around, she'd whirl back again, and say it again; and she was afraid to go to bed, but she dasn't set up. So the thing was working very well, Tom said; he said he never see a thing work more satisfactory. He said it showed it was done right.

So he said, now for the grand bulge ! So the very next **8** morning at the streak of dawn we got another letter ready, and was wondering what we better do with it, because we heard them say at supper they was going to have a nigger on watch at both doors all night. Tom he went down the lightning-rod to spy around; and the nigger at the back door was asleep, and he stuck it in the back of his neck and come back. This letter said :

> *Don't betray me, I wish to be your friend. There is a desprate gang of cut-* **9** *throats from over in the Ingean Territory going to steal your runaway nigger to-night, and they have been trying to scare you so as you will stay in the house and not bother them. I am one of the gang, but have got religion and wish to quit it and lead a honest life again, and will betray the helish design. They will sneak down from northards, along the fence, at midnight exact, with a* **10** *false key, and go in the nigger's cabin to get him. I am to be off a piece and blow a tin horn if I see any danger; but stead of that, I will BA like a sheep soon as they get in and not blow at all; then whilst they are getting his chains loose, you slip there and lock them in, and can kill them at your leasure. Don't do anything but just the way I am telling you, if you do they will suspicion something and raise whoopjamboreehoo. I do not wish any reward but to know* **11** *I have done the right thing.*
>
> UNKNOWN FRIEND.

10 *a false key.* A copy of the real key, usually made from a wax mold of the original.

11 *whoopjamboreehoo.* A noisy carousal.

Chapter XL

FISHING.

We was feeling pretty good, after breakfast, and took my canoe and went over the river a fishing, with a lunch, and had a good time, and took a look at the raft and found her all right, and got home late to supper, and found them in such a sweat and worry they didn't know which end they was standing on, and made us go right off to bed the minute we was done supper, and wouldn't tell us what the trouble was, and never let on a word about the new letter, but didn't need to, because we knowed as much about it as anybody did, and as soon as we was half upstairs and her back was turned, we slid for the cellar cubboard and loaded up a good lunch and took it up to our room and went to bed, and got up about half-past eleven, and Tom put on Aunt Sally's dress that he stole and was going to start with the lunch, but says:

"Where's the butter?"

"I laid out a hunk of it," I says, "on a piece of a corn-pone."

"Well, you *left* it laid out, then—it ain't here."

"We can get along without it," I says.

"We can get along *with* it, too," he says; "just you slide down cellar and fetch it. And then mosey right down the lightning-rod and come along. I'll go and stuff the straw into Jim's clothes to represent his mother in disguise, and be ready to *ba* like a sheep and shove soon as you get there."

So out he went, and down cellar went I. The hunk of butter, big as a person's fist, was where I had left it, so I took up the slab of corn-pone with it on, and blowed out my light, and started upstairs, very stealthy, and got up to the main floor all right, but here comes Aunt Sally with a candle, and I clapped the truck in my hat, and clapped my hat on my head, and the next second she see me; and she says:

"You been down cellar?"

"Yes'm."

"What you been doing down there?"

"Noth'n."

"*Noth'n!*"

"No'm."

"Well, then, what possessed you to go down there, this time of night?"

"I don't know'm."

"You don't *know?* Don't answer me that way, Tom, I want to know what you been *doing* down there?"

"I hain't been doing a single thing, Aunt Sally, I hope to gracious if I have."

I reckoned she'd let me go, now, and as a generl thing she would; but I s'pose there was so many strange things going on she was just in a sweat about every little thing that warn't yard-stick straight; so she says, very decided:

"You just march into that setting-room and stay there till I come. You been up to something you no business to, and I lay I'll find out what it is before *I'm* done with you."

So she went away as I opened the door and walked into the setting-room. My, but there was a crowd there! Fifteen **1** farmers, and every one of them had a gun. I was most powerful sick, and slunk to a chair and set down. They was setting around, some of them talking a little, in a low voice, and all of them fidgety and uneasy, but trying to look like they warn't; but I knowed they was, because they was always taking off their hats, and putting them on, and scratching their heads, and changing their seats, and fumbling with their buttons. I warn't easy myself, but I didn't take my hat off, all the same.

I did wish Aunt Sally would come, and get done with me, and lick me, if she wanted to, and let me get away and tell Tom how we'd overdone this thing, and what a thundering hornet's nest we'd got ourselves into, so we could stop fooling around, straight off, and clear out with Jim before these rips got out of patience and come for us.

At last she come, and begun to ask me questions, but I *couldn't* answer them straight, I didn't know which end of me was up; because these men was in such a fidget now, that some was wanting to start right *now* and lay for them desperadoes,

1 *Fifteen farmers, and every one of them had a gun.* In Arkansas, it was considered every man's business and duty to apprehend fugitive slaves and "nigger stealers." "Every crime increases in magnitude in proportion as it affects the welfare and interest of the community," Marryat explained in "Lynch Law" in his 1839 diary. "Of punishments, it will be observed that society has awarded the most severe for crimes committed against itself, rather than those that offend God. Upon this principle, in the Southern and Western States, you may murder *ten* white men and no one will arraign you or trouble himself about the matter; but *steal one nigger*, and the whole community are in arms, and express the most virtuous indignation against the sin of theft, although that of murder will be disregarded."

EVERY ONE HAD A GUN.

and saying it warn't but a few minutes to midnight; and others was trying to get them to hold on and wait for the sheep-signal; and here was aunty pegging away at the questions, and me a shaking all over and ready to sink down in my tracks I was that scared; and the place getting hotter and hotter, and the butter beginning to melt and run down my neck and behind my ears; and pretty soon, when one of them says, " *I'm* for going and getting in the cabin *first*, and right *now*, and catching them when they come," I most dropped; and a streak of butter come a trickling down my forehead, and Aunt Sally she see it, and turns white as a sheet, and says:

"For the land's sake what *is* the matter with the child!— he's got the brain fever as shore as you're born, and they're oozing out!"

And everybody runs to see, and she snatches off my hat, and out comes the bread, and what was left of the butter, and she grabbed me, and hugged me, and says:

"Oh, what a turn you did give me! and how glad and grateful I am it ain't no worse; for luck's against us, and it never rains but it pours, and when I see that truck I thought we'd lost you, for I knowed by the color and all, it was just like your brains would be if— Dear, dear, whydn't you *tell* me that was what you'd been down there for, I wouldn't a cared. Now cler out to bed, and don't lemme see no more of you till morning!"

I was upstairs in a second, and down the lightning-rod in another one, and shinning through the dark for the lean-to. I couldn't hardly get my words out, I was so anxious; but I told Tom as quick as I could, we must jump for it, now, and not a minute to lose—the house full of men, yonder, with guns!

His eyes just blazed; and he says:

" No!—is that so? *Ain't* it bully! Why, Huck, if it was to do over again, I bet I could fetch two hundred! If we could put it off till——"

"Hurry! *hurry!*" I says. "Where's Jim?"

"Right at your elbow; if you reach out your arm you can touch him. He's dressed, and everything's ready. Now we'll slide out and give the sheep-signal."

But then we heard the tramp of men, coming to the door, and heard them begin to fumble with the padlock; and heard a man say:

"I *told* you we'd be too soon; they haven't come—the door is locked. Here, I'll lock some of you into the cabin and you lay for 'em in the dark and kill 'em when they come; and the rest scatter around a piece, and listen if you can hear 'em coming."

So in they come, but couldn't see us in the dark, and most trod on us whilst we was hustling to get under the bed. But we got under all right, and out through the hole, swift but soft—Jim first, me next, and Tom last, which was according to Tom's orders. Now we was in the lean-to, and heard trampings close by outside. So we crept to the door, and Tom stopped us there and put his eye to the crack, but couldn't make out nothing, it was so dark; and whispered and said he would listen for the steps to get further, and when he nudged us Jim must glide out first, and him last. So he set his ear to the crack and listened, and listened, and listened, and the steps a scraping around, out there, all the time; and at last he nudged us, and we slid out, and stooped down, not breathing, and not making the least noise, and slipped stealthy towards the fence, in Injun **2** file, and got to it, all right, and me and Jim over it; but Tom's britches catched fast on a splinter on the top rail, and then he hear the steps coming, so he had to pull loose, which snapped the splinter and made a noise; and as he dropped in our tracks and started, somebody sings out:

"Who's that? Answer, or I'll shoot!"

But we didn't answer; we just unfurled our heels and **3** shoved. Then there was a rush, and a *bang, bang, bang!* and the bullets fairly whizzed around us! We heard them sing out:

"Here they are! They've broke for the river! after 'em, boys! And turn loose the dogs!"

So here they come, full tilt. We could hear them, because they wore boots, and yelled, but we didn't wear no boots, and didn't yell. We was in the path to the mill; and when they got pretty close on to us, we dodged into the bush and let them go by, and then dropped in behind them. They'd had all the dogs shut up, so they wouldn't scare off the robbers; but by this time somebody had let them loose, and here they come, making pow-wow enough for a million; but they was our dogs; so we stopped in our tracks till they catched up; and when they see it warn't nobody but us, and no excitement to offer them, they only just said howdy, and tore right ahead towards **4** the shouting and clattering; and then we up steam again and whizzed along after them till we was nearly to the mill, and then struck up through the bush to where my canoe was tied,

2 *Injun file.* Single file; North American Indians generally traveled on a hunt or into battle, one following the other by treading in the footsteps of the man before him.

3 *unfurled our heels and shoved.* Or "showed our heels," to be off quickly.

4 *they only just said howdy, and tore right ahead towards the shouting and clattering.* Fortunately Twain avoided inserting into the novel a bit of forced slapstick between Huck and the hounds that he jotted in his notebook: "I fetched away a dog, part of the way—I had him by the teeth in my britches, behind" (quoted by DeVoto, *Mark Twain at Work*, p. 77).

5 '*Son of Saint Louis, ascend to heaven!*' Said to be the last words heard by Louis XVI before his execution. In "Regicide: Place de la Révolution" of *The French Revolution*, Carlyle described the scene: "The drums are beating: '*Taisez-vous*, Silence!' he cries 'in a terrible voice, *d'une vois terrible.*' He mounts the scaffold, not without delay. . . . He strips off the coat; stands disclosed in a sleeve-waistcoat of white flannel. The Executioners approach to bind him; he spurns, resists; Abbé Edgeworth [the father confessor] has to remind him how the Saviour, in whom men trust, submitted to be bound. His hands are tied, his head bare; the fatal moment is come. He advances to the edge of the Scaffold, 'his face very red,' and says: 'Frenchmen, I die innocent; it is from the Scaffold and near appearing before God that I tell you so. I pardon my enemies; I desire that France—' A General on horseback . . . prances out, with uplifted hand; '*Tambours!*' The drums drown the voice. 'Executioners, do your duty!' The Executioners, desperate lest they be murdered, . . . seize the hapless Louis: six of them desperate, him singly desperate, struggling there; and bind him to their plank. Abbé Edgeworth, stooping, bespeaks him: 'Son of Saint Louis, ascend to Heaven.' The Axe clanks down; a King's life is shorn away. It is Monday the 21st of January 1793. He was aged Thirty-eight years four months and twenty-eight days."

"Son of Saint Louis, ascend to Heaven." 18th century French print. *Courtesy the Library of Congress.*

TOM CAUGHT ON A SPLINTER.

and hopped in and pulled for dear life towards the middle of the river, but didn't make no more noise than we was obleeged to. Then we struck out, easy and comfortable, for the island where my raft was; and we could hear them yelling and barking at each other all up and down the bank, till we was so far away the sounds got dim and died out. And when we stepped on to the raft, I says:

"*Now*, old Jim, you're a free man *again*, and I bet you won't ever be a slave no more."

"En a mighty good job it wuz, too, Huck. It 'uz planned beautiful, en it 'uz *done* beautiful; en dey ain't *nobody* kin git up a plan dat's mo' mixed-up en splendid den what dat one wuz."

We was all as glad as we could be, but Tom was the gladdest of all, because he had a bullet in the calf of his leg.

When me and Jim heard that, we didn't feel so brash as what we did before. It was hurting him considerble, and bleeding; so we laid him in the wigwam and tore up one of the duke's shirts for to bandage him, but he says:

"Gimme the rags, I can do it myself. Don't stop, now; don't fool around here, and the evasion booming along so handsome; man the sweeps, and set her loose! Boys, we done it elegant!—'deed we did. I wish *we'd* a had the handling of **5** Louis XVI., there wouldn't a been no 'Son of Saint Louis, ascend to heaven!' wrote down in *his* biography: no, sir, we'd a whooped him over the *border*—that's what we'd a done with *him*—and done it just as slick as nothing at all, too. Man the sweeps—man the sweeps!"

But me and Jim was consulting—and thinking. And after we'd thought a minute, I says:

"Say, it Jim."

So he says:

"Well, den, dis is de way it look to me, Huck. Ef it wuz *him* dat 'uz bein' sot free, en one er de boys wuz to git shot, would he say, 'Go on en save me, nemmine 'bout a doctor f'r to save dis one?' Is dat like Mars Tom Sawyer? Would he say dat? You *bet* he wouldn't! *Well,* den, is *Jim* gwyne to say it? No, sah—I doan' budge a step out'n dis place, 'dout a *doctor;* not if it's forty year!"

JIM ADVISES A DOCTOR.

I knowed he was white inside, and I reckoned he'd say what **6** he did say—so it was all right, now, and I told Tom I was agoing for a doctor. He raised considerble row about it, but me and Jim stuck to it and wouldn't budge; so he was for crawling out and setting the raft loose himself; but we wouldn't let him. Then he give us a piece of his mind—but it didn't do no good.

So when he sees me getting the canoe ready, he says:

"Well, then, if you're bound to go, I'll tell you the way to do, when you get to the village. Shut the door, and blindfold the doctor tight and fast, and make him swear to be silent as the grave, and put a purse full of gold in his hand, and then take and lead him all around the back alleys and everywheres, in the dark, and then fetch him here in the canoe, in a roundabout way amongst the islands, and search him, and take his chalk away from him, and don't give it back to him till you get him back to the village, or else he will chalk this raft so he can find it again. It's the way they all do." **7**

So I said I would, and left, and Jim was to hide in the woods when he see the doctor coming, till he was gone again.

6 *I knowed he was white inside.* Surely the highest compliment a poor white of the South at this time could have paid a slave. By his unselfish devotion to the wounded Tom, Jim has demonstrated another aspect of his humanity to Huck Finn.

7 *It's the way they all do.* Tom is recalling the Arabian Nights tale of "Ali Baba and the Forty Thieves." On discovering the drawn and quartered body of his brother Cassim strung up in the thieves' den, Ali Baba cuts the pieces down and returns home. To prepare the remains for proper burial, he sends a servant girl to fetch a cobbler to sew the parts together. She engages one named Mustapha by placing some gold in his palm; but to protect her master from discovery by his enemies, she blindfolds the cobbler before leading him to the house. Meanwhile, the thieves have sent a spy to find out who has Cassim's body; and on interviewing Mustapha, he too blindfolds the cobbler, so he can lead the thief to Ali Baba's door, which he marks an "X" with a piece of chalk. Fortunately, the servant sees the mark; and when the thieves arrive to search for the house, they come upon door after door chalked with X's. Hans Christian Andersen included a similar incident in "The Tinder Box": When the giant dog spirits away the princess to the soldier's room, her lady-in-waiting follows them and makes a mark on the soldier's door; however, the dog has seen her do it, and so he goes from house to house, similarly marking their doors.

"Ali Baba and the Forty Thieves" was one of Twain's favorite children's stories, and he suggested that Harper & Brothers include it in their *Favorite Fairy Tales.* In Tom's recalling the famous Arabian Nights tale, the novel has returned to the storybook atmosphere of its opening.

Chapter XLI

THE DOCTOR.

The doctor was an old man; a very nice, kind-looking old man, when I got him up. I told him me and my brother was over on Spanish Island hunting, yesterday afternoon, and camped on a piece of a raft we found, and about midnight he must a kicked his gun in his dreams, for it went off and shot him in the leg, and we wanted him to go over there and fix it and not say nothing about it, nor let anybody know, because we wanted to come home this evening, and surprise the folks.

"Who is your folks?" he says.

"The Phelpses, down yonder."

"Oh," he says. And after a minute, he says: "How'd you say he got shot?"

"He had a dream," I says, "and it shot him."

"Singular dream," he says.

So he lit up his lantern, and got his saddle-bags, and we started. But when he see the canoe, he didn't like the look of her—said she was big enough for one, but didn't look pretty safe for two. I says:

"Oh, you needn't be afeard, sir, she carried the three of us, easy enough."

"What three?"

"Why, me and Sid, and—and—and *the guns;* that's what I mean."

"Oh," he says.

But he put his foot on the gunnel, and rocked her; and shook his head, and said he reckoned he'd look around for a bigger one. But they was all locked and chained; so he took my canoe, and said for me to wait till he come back, or I could hunt around further, or maybe I better go down home and get them ready for the surprise, if I wanted to. But I said I didn't; so I told him just how to find the raft, and then he started.

I struck an idea, pretty soon. I says to myself, spos'n he can't fix that leg just in three shakes of a sheep's tail, as the saying is? spos'n it takes him three or four days? What are we going to do?—lay around there till he lets the cat out of the bag? No, sir, I know what *I'll* do. I'll wait, and when he comes back, if he says he's got to go any more, I'll get down there, too, if I swim; and we'll take and tie him, and keep him, and shove out down the river; and when Tom's done with him, we'll give him what it's worth, or all we got, and then let him get ashore.

So then I crept into a lumber pile to get some sleep; and next time I waked up the sun was away up over my head! I shot out and went for the doctor's house, but they told me he'd gone away in the night, some time or other, and warn't back yet. Well, thinks I, that looks powerful bad for Tom, and I'll dig out for the island, right off. So away I shoved, and turned the corner, and nearly rammed my head into Uncle Silas's stomach! He says:

UNCLE SILAS IN DANGER.

2 *Sid's at the post-office to see what he can hear*. At this time, the local post office was often a major social center of a backwoods community. The arrival of the mail was an event, not so much for the letters (which were often few) but rather for the postman's news from other towns. "Presently the United States mail arrived, on horseback," Twain in Chapter 1 of *The Gilded Age* described a typical scene of a frontier town. "There was but one letter, and it was for the postmaster. The long-legged youth who carried the mail tarried an hour to talk, for there was no hurry; and in a little while the male population of the village had assembled to help."

3 *And the place was plumb full of farmers and farmers' wives, to dinner*. The dinner conversation at the Phelpses is a revision of a scene Twain jotted in his notes (quoted by DeVoto, *Mark Twain at Work*, p. 76): "He must hear some Arkansas women, over their pipes and knitting (spitting from between teeth), swap reminiscences of Sister this and Brother that, and 'what become of so and so?—what his first wife's name?' Very religious people. Ride 10 or 15 miles to church and tie the horses to trees. Let 'em drop in ignorant remarks about monarchs in Europe, and mix them up with Biblical monarchs." DeVoto praised this note for containing "a great deal of Mark Twain" as well as "a great deal of the American novel which, as a new embodiment of experience, he and his contemporaries were forging" (p. 80). This observation is also true of the final discussion finally incorporated into the book.

4 *clack*. Loud talk or chat.

5 *Hotchkiss. . . . Dunlap*. Twain made further use of the names in later stories about Tom Sawyer and Huckleberry Finn: For example, Mrs. Hotchkiss becomes "Hannah Hotchkiss" in "Schoolhouse Hill," an early draft of *The Mysterious Stranger*; and a "Brace Dunlap" appears in "Tom Sawyer, Detective."

6 *Sister. . . . Brer*. "'Sister' in the Methodist, or Presbyterian, or Baptist, or Campellite Church— nothing more," Twain explained in a note to Chapter 3 of "Schoolhouse Hill" (in *The Mysterious Stranger*, 1969, p. 191). "A common form, in those days." "Every man was expected to join one or another of the seventeen religious denominations," Twain recalled the old days in a suppressed passage of *Life on the Mississippi* (published in the 1944 Limited Editions Club edition, p. 407). "In the West and the South, and in portions of the East, people did not call each other Mr. Smith, and Mrs. Jones—no, it was 'Brother' Smith, and 'Sister' Jones—a phrase which survives in Uncle Remus's 'Ole Brer Fox' and 'Ole Brer Rabbit.'"

" Why, *Tom!* Where you been, all this time, you rascal?"

" *I* hain't been nowheres," I says, "only just hunting for the runaway nigger—me and Sid."

" Why, where ever did you go?" he says. " Your aunt's been mighty uneasy."

" She needn't," I says, "because we was all right. We followed the men and the dogs, but they outrun us, and we lost them; but we thought we heard them on the water, so we got a canoe and took out after them, and crossed over but couldn't find nothing of them; so we cruised along up-shore till we got kind of tired and beat out; and tied up the canoe and went to sleep, and never waked up till about an hour ago,
2 then we paddled over here to hear the news, and Sid's at the post-office to see what he can hear, and I'm a branching out to get something to eat for us, and then we're going home."

So then we went to the post-office to get " Sid "; but just as I suspicioned, he warn't there; so the old man he got a letter out of the office, and we waited a while longer but Sid didn't come; so the old man said come along, let Sid foot it home, or canoe-it, when he got done fooling around—but we would ride. I couldn't get him to let me stay and wait for Sid; and he said there warn't no use in it, and I must come along, and let Aunt Sally see we was all right.

When we got home, Aunt Sally was that glad to see me she laughed and cried both, and hugged me, and give me one of them lickings of hern that don't amount to shucks, and said she'd serve Sid the same when he come.

3 And the place was plumb full of farmers and farmers' wives,
4 to dinner; and such another clack a body never heard. Old
5 Mrs. Hotchkiss was the worst; her tongue was agoing all the time. She says:
6 " Well, Sister Phelps, I've ransacked that-air cabin over an' I b'lieve the nigger was crazy. I says so to Sister Damrell— didn't I, Sister Damrell?—s'I, he's crazy, s'I—them's the very words I said. You all hearn me: he's crazy, s'I; everything shows it, s'I. Look at that-air grindstone, s'I; want to tell *me* 't any cretur 'ts in his right mind 's agoin' to scrabble all

OLD MRS. HOTCHKISS.

them crazy things on to a grindstone, s'I?   Here sich 'n' sich a person busted his heart; 'n' here so 'n' so pegged along for thirty-seven year, 'n' all that—natcherl son o' Louis somebody, 'n' sich everlast'n rubbage.   He's plumb crazy, s'I; it's what I says in the fust place, it's what I says in the middle, 'n' it's what I says last 'n' all the time—the nigger's crazy—crazy 's **7** Nebokoodneezer, s'I."

"An' look at that-air ladder made out'n rags, Sister Hotchkiss," says old Mrs. Damrell, " what in the name o' goodness *could* he ever want of——"

"The very words I was a-sayin' no longer ago th'n this minute to Sister Utterback, 'n' she'll tell you so herself.   Sh-she, look at that-air rag ladder, sh-she; 'n' s'I, yes, *look* at it, s'I—what *could* he a wanted of it, s'I?   Sh-she, Sister Hotchkiss, sh-she——"

"But how in the nation'd they ever *git* that grindstone *in* there, *any*-way? 'n' who dug that-air *hole*? 'n' who——"

"My very *words*, Brer Penrod!   I was a-sayin'—pass that-air sasser o' m'lasses, won't ye?—I was a-sayin' to Sister Dunlap, jist this minute, how *did* they git that grindstone in there, s'I.   Without *help*, mind you—'thout *help*! *Thar's* wher' 'tis.   Don't tell *me*, s'I; there *wuz* help, s'I; 'n' ther' wuz a *plenty* help, too, s'I; ther's ben a *dozen* a-helpin' that nigger, 'n' I lay I'd skin every last nigger on this place, but *I'd* find out who done it, s'I; 'n' moreover, s'I——"

"A *dozen* says you!—*forty* couldn't a done everything that's been done.   Look at them case-knife saws and things, how tedious they've been made; look at that bed-leg sawed off with 'm, a week's work for six men; look at that nigger made out'n straw on the bed; and look at——"

"You may *well* say it, Brer Hightower!   It's jist as I was a-sayin' to Brer Phelps, his own self.   S'e, what do *you* think of it, Sister Hotchkiss, s'e? think o' what, Brer Phelps, s'I? think o' that bed-leg sawed off that a way, s'e? *think* of it, s'I?   I lay it never sawed *itself* off, s'I—somebody *sawed* it, s'I; that's my opinion, take it or leave it, it mayn't be no 'count, s'I, but sich as 't is, it's my opinion, s'I, 'n' if anybody k'n start a better one, s'I, let him *do* it, s'I, that's all.   I says to Sister Dunlap, s'I——"

"Why, dog my cats, they must a ben a house-full o' niggers in there every night for four weeks, to a done all that work, Sister Phelps.   Look at that shirt—every last inch of it kivered over with secret African writ'n done with blood!   Must a ben a raft uv 'm at it right along, all the time, amost.   Why, I'd give two dollars to have it read to me; 'n' as for the niggers that wrote it, I 'low I'd take 'n' lash 'm t'll——"

"People to *help* him, Brother Marples!   Well, I reckon you'd *think* so, if you'd a been in this house for a while back.   Why, they've stole everything they could lay their hands on— and we a watching, all the time, mind you.   They stole that shirt right off o' the line! and as for that sheet they made the rag ladder out of ther' ain't no telling how many times they

7 *crazy's Nebokoodneezer*. Nebuchadnezzar was the heathen king of Babylon who (in Daniel 4:1–37) was made mad by God for seven years until he acknowledged the god of the Israelites: "He was driven from men, and did eat grass as oxen, and his body was wet with the dew of heaven, till his hairs were grown like eagle's feathers, and his nails like birds' claws."

didn't steal that ; and flour, and candles, and candlesticks, and spoons, and the old warming-pan, and most a thousand things that I disremember, now, and my new calico dress ; and me, and Silas, and my Sid and Tom on the constant watch day *and* night, as I was a telling you, and not a one of us could catch hide nor hair, nor sight nor sound of them ; and here at the last minute, lo and behold you, they slides right in under our noses, and fools us, and not only fools *us* but the Injun Territory robbers too, and actuly gets *away* with that nigger, safe and sound, and that with sixteen men and twenty-two dogs right on their very heels at that very time ! I tell you, it just bangs anything I ever *heard* of. Why, *sperits* couldn't a done better, and been no smarter. And I reckon they must a *been* sperits— because, *you* know our dogs, and ther' ain't no better ; well, them dogs never even got on the *track* of 'm, once ! You explain *that* to me, if you can !—*any* of you ! "

" Well, it does beat ——"

" Laws alive, I never——"

" So help me, I wouldn't a be——"

" *House*-thieves as well as——"

" Goodnessgracioussakes, I'd a ben afeard to *live* in sich a——"

" 'Fraid to *live !*—why, I was that scared I dasn't hardly go to bed, or get up, or lay down, or *set* down, Sister Ridgeway. Why, they'd steal the very—why, goodness sakes, you can guess what kind of a fluster *I* was in by the time midnight come, last night. I hope to gracious if I warn't afraid they'd steal some o' the family ! I was just to that pass, I didn't have no reasoning faculties no more. It looks foolish enough, *now*, in the day-time ; but I says to myself, there's my two poor boys asleep, 'way upstairs in that lonesome room, and I declare to goodness I was that uneasy 't I crep' up there and locked 'em in ! I *did.* And anybody would. Because, you know, when you get scared, that way, and it keeps running on, and getting worse and worse, all the time, and your wits gets to addling, and you get to doing all sorts o' wild things, and by-and-by you think to yourself, spos'n *I* was a boy, and was away up there, and the door ain't locked, and you——" She stopped, looking kind of wondering, and then she turned her head around slow, and when her eye lit on me—I got up and took a walk.

Says I to myself, I can explain better how we come to not be in that room this morning, if I go out to one side and study over it a little. So I done it. But I dasn't go fur, or she'd a sent for me. And when it was late in the day, the people all went, and then I come in and told her the noise and shooting waked up me and " Sid," and the door was locked, and we wanted to see the fun, so we went down the lightning-rod, and both of us got hurt a little, and we didn't never want to try *that* no more. And then I went on and told her all what I told Uncle Silas before ; and then she said she'd forgive us, and maybe it was all right enough anyway, and about what a **8** body might expect of boys, for all boys was a pretty harum-

scarum lot, as fur as she could see; and so, as long as no harm
hadn't come of it, she judged she better put in her time being
grateful we was alive and well and she had us still, stead of
fretting over what was past and done. So then she kissed me,
and patted me on the head, and dropped into a kind of a brown **9**
study; and pretty soon jumps up, and says:

"Why, lawsamercy, it's most night, and Sid not come yet!
What *has* become of that boy?"

I see my chance; so I skips up and says:

"I'll run right up to town and get him," I says.

"No you won't," she says. "You'll stay right wher' you
are; *one's* enough to be lost at a time. If he ain't here to
supper, your uncle 'll go."

Well, he warn't there to supper; so right after supper
uncle went.

He come back about ten, a little bit uneasy; hadn't run
across Tom's track. Aunt Sally was a good *deal* uneasy; but
Uncle Silas he said there warn't no occasion to be—boys will be
boys, he said, and you'll see this one turn up in the morning,
all sound and right. So she had to be satisfied. But she said
she'd set up for him a while, anyway, and keep a light
burning, so he could see it.

And then when I went up to bed she come up with me and
fetched her candle, and tucked me in, and mothered me so
good I felt mean, and like I couldn't look her in the face; and
she set down on the bed and talked with me a long time, and

AUNT SALLY TALKS TO HUCK.

said what a splendid boy Sid was, and didn't seem to want to
ever stop talking about him; and kept asking me every now
and then, if I reckoned he could a got lost, or hurt, or maybe
drownded, and might be laying at this minute, somewheres,
suffering or dead, and she not by him to help him, and so the

9 *a brown study*. Gloomy meditations; "miles and
miles away," Huck explains in Chapter 11 of "Tom
Sawyer, Detective."

10 *not for kingdoms*. Not for "Kingdom-Come," Heaven, not for anything.

tears would drip down, silent, and I would tell her that Sid was all right, and would be home in the morning, sure ; and she would squeeze my hand, or maybe kiss me, and tell me to say it again, and keep on saying it, because it done her good, and she was in so much trouble. And when she was going away, she looked down in my eyes, so steady and gentle, and says :

"The door ain't going to be locked, Tom ; and there's the window and the rod ; but you'll be good, *won't* you ? And you won't go ? For *my* sake."

Laws knows I *wanted* to go, bad enough, to see about Tom, and was all intending to go ; but after that, I wouldn't a went, **10** not for kingdoms.

But she was on my mind, and Tom was on my mind ; so I slept very restless. And twice I went down the rod, away in the night, and slipped around front, and see her setting there by her candle in the window with her eyes towards the road and the tears in them ; and I wished I could do something for her, but I couldn't, only to swear that I wouldn't never do nothing to grieve her any more. And the third time, I waked up at dawn, and slid down, and she was there yet, and her candle was most out, and her old gray head was resting on her hand, and she was asleep.

Chapter XLII

TOM SAWYER WOUNDED.

The old man was up town again, before breakfast, but couldn't get no track of Tom; and both of them set at the table, thinking, and not saying nothing, and looking mournful, and their coffee getting cold, and not eat anything. And by-and-by the old man says:

"Did I give you the letter?"

"What letter?"

"The one I got yesterday out of the post-office."

"No, you didn't give me no letter."

"Well, I must a forgot it."

So he rummaged his pockets, and then went off somewheres where he had laid it down, and fetched it, and give it to her. She says:

"Why it's from St. Petersburg—it's from Sis."

I allowed another walk would do me good; but I couldn't stir. But before she could break it open, she dropped it and run—for she see something. And so did I. It was Tom Saw-

1 *some of them wanted to hang Jim, for an example to all the other niggers around there, so they wouldn't be trying to run away.* "Why has lynching, with various barbaric accompaniments," demanded Twain in "The United States of Lyncherdom" (*A Pen Warmed-up in Hell*, p. 182), "become a favorite regulator . . . in several parts of the country? Is it because men think a lurid terrible punishment a more forcible object lesson and a more effective deterrent than sober and colorless hanging done privately in jail would be? Surely sane men do not think that. Even the average child should know better. It should know that any strange and much-talked-of event is always followed by imitations, the world being so well supplied with excitable people who only need a little stirring up to make them lose what is left of their heads and do mad things which they would not have thought of ordinarily."

The lynching of a fugitive slave. Illustration from *Archy Moore, the White Slave* by Richard Hildreth, 1855. *Courtesy the Rare Book Room, the Library of Congress.*

2 *a raft of trouble.* A great deal of trouble, used disparagingly.

3 *the people that's always the most anxious for to hang a nigger . . . is always the very ones that ain't the most anxious to pay for him when they've got their satisfaction out of him.* A particularly cynical observation: The crowd backs down not for any moral reason; their cowardice results purely from economics. Because Jim is merely chattel, his murderer would have had to compensate his master for any harm done to his property. The young Sam Clemens shared this fear when he and another boy rolled a rock down a hill and just missed killing a slave in its path; he confessed to an old childhood friend on his return to Hannibal in 1902, "If we had killed that man we'd have had a dead nigger on our hands without a cent to pay for him" (quoted by Paine, *Mark Twain: A Biography*, Vol. 3, p. 1170). Perhaps Twain had in mind here another incident in his childhood in Hannibal, described in Chapter 7 of his *Autobiography*: "When a white man killed a Negro man for a trifling little offence everybody seemed indifferent about it—as regarded the slave—though considerable sympathy was felt for the slave's owner, who had been bereft of valuable property by a worthless person who was not able to pay for it."

4 *till his owner come or he was sold at auction, because he didn't come in a certain length of time.* Twain has confused Missouri and Arkansas law. In Missouri, a

yer on a mattress; and that old doctor; and Jim, in *her* calico dress, with his hands tied behind him; and a lot of people. I hid the letter behind the first thing that come handy, and rushed. She flung herself at Tom, crying, and says:

"Oh, he's dead, he's dead, I know he's dead!"

And Tom he turned his head a little, and muttered something or other, which showed he warn't in his right mind; then she flung up her hands, and says:

"He's alive, thank God! And that's enough!" and she snatched a kiss of him, and flew for the house to get the bed ready, and scattering orders right and left at the niggers and everybody else, as fast as her tongue could go, every jump of the way.

I followed the men to see what they was going to do with Jim; and the old doctor and uncle Silas followed after Tom **1** into the house. The men was very huffy, and some of them wanted to hang Jim, for an example to all the other niggers around there, so they wouldn't be trying to run away, like Jim **2** done, and making such a raft of trouble, and keeping a whole family scared most to death for days and nights. But the others said, don't do it, it wouldn't answer at all, he ain't our nigger, and his owner would turn up and make us pay for him, **3** sure. So that cooled them down a little, because the people that's always the most anxious for to hang a nigger that hain't done just right, is always the very ones that ain't the most anxious to pay for him when they've got their satisfaction out of him.

They cussed Jim considerble, though, and give him a cuff or two, side the head, once in a while, but Jim never said nothing, and he never let on to know me, and they took him to the same cabin, and put his own clothes on him, and chained him again, and not to no bed-leg, this time, but to a big staple drove into the bottom log, and chained his hands, too, and both legs, and said he warn't to have nothing but bread and **4** water to eat, after this, till his owner come or he was sold at auction, because he didn't come in a certain length of time, and filled up our hole, and said a couple of farmers with guns **5** must stand watch around about the cabin every night, and a bull-dog tied to the door in the day-time; and about this time they was through with the job and was tapering off with a kind of generl good-bye cussing, and then the old doctor comes and takes a look, and says:

"Don't be no rougher on him than you're obleeged to, because he ain't a bad nigger. When I got to where I found the boy, I see I couldn't cut the bullet out without some help, and he warn't in no condition for me to leave, to go and get help; and he got a little worse and a little worse, and after a long time he went out of his head, and wouldn't let me come anigh him, any more, and said if I chalked his raft he'd kill me, and no end of wild foolishness like that, and I see I couldn't do anything at all with him; so I says, I got to have *help*, somehow; and the minute I says it, out crawls this nigger from

somewheres, and says he'll help, and he done it, too, and done
it very well. Of course I judged he must be a runaway nigger,
and there I *was !* and there I had to stick, right straight along
all the rest of the day, and all night. It was a fix, I tell you !
I had a couple of patients with the chills, and of course I'd of
liked to run up to town and see them, but I dasn't, because the **6**
nigger might get away, and then I'd be to blame ; and yet
never a skiff come close enough for me to hail. So there I had
to stick, plumb till daylight this morning ; and I never see a
nigger that was a better nuss or faithfuller, and yet he was
resking his freedom to do it, and was all tired out, too, and I
see plain enough he'd been worked main hard, lately. I liked
the nigger for that ; I tell you, gentlemen, a nigger like that **7**
is worth a thousand dollars—and kind treatment, too. I had
everything I needed, and the boy was doing as well there as he
would a done at home—better, maybe, because it was so quiet ;
but there I *was*, with both of 'm on my hands ; and there I
had to stick, till about dawn this morning ; then some men in
a skiff come by, and as good luck would have it, the nigger
was setting by the pallet with his head propped on his knees,
sound asleep ; so I motioned them in, quiet, and they slipped
up on him and grabbed him and tied him before he knowed
what he was about, and we never had no trouble. And the boy
being in a kind of a flighty sleep, too, we muffled the oars and **8**
hitched the raft on, and towed her over very nice and quiet, and
the nigger never made the least row nor said a word, from the
start. He ain't no bad nigger, gentlemen ; that's what I think
about him."

Somebody says :

"Well, it sounds very good, doctor, I'm obleeged to say."

Then the others softened up a little, too, and I was mighty
thankful to that old doctor for doing Jim that good turn ; and

captured slave had to be committed to the local jail
and then advertised on the courthouse door and later
in the papers; if unclaimed after a year, he then was
sold at auction. But, in Arkansas, the fugitive had to
be kept in jail for six months, during which his
capture had to be advertised in the papers; then he
was transferred to the penitentiary for another six
months, and if his owner still did not answer the
announcements, the prisoner became the property of
the state for life. It was not until 1861 that, in
Arkansas, a runaway slave could be sold at auction,
and then only after two years in the penitentiary and
after the sale was advertised for six weeks.

5 *a bull-dog tied to the door in the day-time.* Bull dogs
are more vicious than hound dogs (see Chapter 32,
note 6); Jim's captors are making sure that there is no
way that he will escape again.

6 *the nigger might get away, and then I'd be to blame.* In
the slave states, anyone who failed to report seeing a
runaway, could be immediately arrested for aiding
and abetting the flight of the fugitive.

7 *a nigger like that is worth a thousand dollars.* This is
not much of a compliment when one recalls that Miss
Watson was willing to sell Jim for eight hundred
dollars. Although Jim has proven his humanity, the
good doctor still views him only as another man's
property.

8 *muffled the oars.* Covered the oars to deaden the
sound.

THE DOCTOR SPEAKS FOR JIM.

9 *but they didn't think of it.* Despite their kind words, Jim's captors have not really changed in their attitudes toward the runaway.

10 *I'd got through the breakers that was laying just ahead of me.* River metaphor for overcoming anticipated difficulties.

11 *we could put up a yarn for the family that would wash.* We could make up a story that the family would believe.

I was glad it was according to my judgment of him, too ; because I thought he had a good heart in him and was a good man, the first time I see him. Then they all agreed that Jim had acted very well, and was deserving to have some notice took of it, and reward. So every one of them promised, right out and hearty, that they wouldn't cuss him no more.

Then they come out and locked him up. I hoped they was going to say he could have one or two of the chains took off, because they was rotten heavy, or could have meat and greens

9 with his bread and water, but they didn't think of it, and I reckoned it warn't best for me to mix in, but I judged I'd get the doctor's yarn to Aunt Sally, somehow or other, as soon as

10 I'd got through the breakers that was laying just ahead of me. Explanations, I mean, of how I forgot to mention about Sid being shot, when I was telling how him and me put in that dratted night paddling around hunting the runaway nigger.

But I had plenty time. Aunt Sally she stuck to the sick-room all day and all night ; and every time I see Uncle Silas mooning around, I dodged him.

Next morning I heard Tom was a good deal better, and they said Aunt Sally was gone to get a nap. So I slips to the

11 sick-room, and if I found him awake I reckoned we could put up a yarn for the family that would wash. But he was sleeping, and sleeping very peaceful, too ; and pale, not fire-faced the way he was when he come. So I set down and laid for him to wake. In about a half an hour, Aunt Sally comes gliding in, and there I was, up a stump again ! She motioned me to be still, and set down by me, and begun to whisper, and said we could all be joyful now, because all the symptoms was first rate, and he'd been sleeping like that for ever so long, and looking better and peacefuller all the time, and ten to one he'd wake up in his right mind.

So we set there watching, and by-and-by he stirs a bit, and opened his eyes very natural, and takes a look, and says :

" Hello, why I'm at *home !* How's that ? Where's the raft ? "

" It's all right," I says.

" And *Jim ?* "

" The same," I says, but couldn't say it pretty brash. But he never noticed, but says :

" Good ! Splendid ! *Now* we're all right and safe ! Did you tell aunty ? "

I was going to say yes ; but she chipped in and says :

" About what, Sid ? "

" Why, about the way the whole thing was done."

" What whole thing ? "

" Why, *the* whole thing. There ain't but one ; how we set the runaway nigger free—me and Tom."

" Good land ! Set the run— What *is* the child talking about ! Dear, dear, out of his head again ! "

" *No,* I ain't out of my HEAD ; I know all what I'm talking about. We *did* set him free—me and Tom. We laid out to do it, and we *done* it. And we done it elegant, too." He'd got a start, and she never checked him up, just set and stared and stared, and let him clip along, and I see it warn't no use for *me* to put in. "Why, Aunty, it cost us a power of work—weeks of it—hours and hours, every night, whilst you was all asleep. And we had to steal candles, and the sheet, and the shirt, and your dress, and spoons, and tin plates, and case-knives, and the warming-pan, and the grindstone, and flour, and just no end of things, and you can't think what work it was to make the saws, and pens, and inscriptions, and one thing or another, and you can't think *half* the fun it was. And we had to make up the pictures of coffins and things, and nonnamous letters from the robbers, and get up and down the lightning-rod, and dig the hole into the cabin, and make the rope-ladder and send it in cooked up in a pie, and send in spoons and things to work with, in your apron pocket "——

"Mercy sakes!"

——"and load up the cabin with rats and snakes and so on, for company for Jim; and then you kept Tom here so long with the butter in his hat that you come near spiling the whole business, because the men come before we was out of the cabin, and we had to rush, and they heard us and let drive at us, and I got my share, and we dodged out of the path and let them go by, and when the dogs come they warn't interested in us, but went for the most noise, and we got our canoe, and made for the raft, and was all safe, and Jim was a free man, and we done it all by ourselves, and *wasn't* it bully, Aunty!"

"Well, I never heard the likes of it in all my born days! So it was *you*, you little rapscallions, that's been making all this trouble, and turned everybody's wits clean inside out and scared us all most to death. I've as good a notion as ever I had in my life, to take it out o' you this very minute. To think, here I've been, night after night, a—*you* just get well once, you young scamp, and I lay I'll tan the Old Harry out o' both o' ye!" **12**

But Tom, he *was* so proud and joyful, he just *couldn't* hold in, and his tongue just *went* it—she a-chipping in, and spitting fire all along, and both of them going it at once, like a cat-convention; and she says:

"*Well*, you get all the enjoyment you can out of it *now*, for mind I tell you if I catch you meddling with him again——"

"Meddling with *who*?" Tom says, dropping his smile, and looking surprised.

"With *who*? Why, the runaway nigger, of course. Who'd you reckon?"

Tom looks at me very grave, and says:

"Tom, didn't you just tell me he was all right? Hasn't he got away?"

"*Him?*" says Aunt Sally; "the runaway nigger? 'Deed he hasn't. They've got him back, safe and sound, and he's in that cabin again, on bread and water, and loaded down with chains, till he's claimed or sold!"

Tom rose square up in bed, with his eye hot, and his nostrils

12 *the Old Harry*. The Devil; like Miss Watson, Aunt Sally is such a good Christian that she cannot even say the devil's name.

13 *Old Miss Watson . . . set him free in her will.*
Manumission, or the setting free of slaves, particularly on the death of the owner, was common to
Miss Watson's class (for example, Roxy is set free in
Chapter 4 of *Pudd'nhead Wilson* at the death of her
master). Missouri laws were more liberal on this
point than those of other slave states, but, after 1845,
it could occur only with a written will; an oral
promise was held invalid. Miss Watson, however,
did not suffer a great change of heart toward Jim: It
was already considered déclassé to think of selling a
slave down the river, and to absolve this social sin,
she had no other choice than to set Jim free in her
will.

TOM ROSE SQUARE UP IN BED.

opening and shutting like gills, and sings out to me:

"They hain't no *right* to shut him up! *Shove!*—and don't
you lose a minute. Turn him loose! he ain't no slave; he's as
free as any cretur that walks this earth!"

"What *does* the child mean?"

"I mean every word I *say*, Aunt Sally, and if somebody don't
go, *I'*ll go. I've knowed him all his life, and so has Tom, there.

13 Old Miss Watson died two months ago, and she was ashamed
she ever was going to sell him down the river, and *said* so;
and she set him free in her will."

"Then what on earth did *you* want to set him free for,
seeing he was already free?"

"Well, that *is* a question, I must say; and *just* like
women! Why, I wanted the *adventure* of it; and I'd
a waded neck-deep in blood to—goodness alive—AUNT
POLLY!"

If she warn't standing right there, just inside the door, looking as sweet and contented as an angel half-full of pie, I wish
I may never!

Aunt Sally jumped for her, and most hugged the head off
of her, and cried over her, and I found a good enough place for
me under the bed, for it was getting pretty sultry for *us*, seemed
to me. And I peeped out, and in a little while Tom's Aunt Polly
shook herself loose and stood there looking across at Tom over
her spectacles--kind of grinding him into the earth, you know.
And then she says:

"Yes, you *better* turn y'r head away—I would if I was you,
Tom."

"Oh, deary me!" says Aunt Sally; "*is* he changed so?
Why, that ain't *Tom* it's Sid; Tom's—Tom's—why, where is
Tom? He was here a minute ago."

"You mean where's Huck *Finn*—that's what you mean! I
reckon I hain't raised such a scamp as my Tom all these years,

not to know him when I *see* him.   That *would* be a pretty howdy-do.   Come out from under that bed, Huck Finn."

So I done it.   But not feeling brash.

Aunt Sally she was one of the mixed-upest looking persons I ever see; except one, and that was Uncle Silas, when he come in, and they told it all to him.   It kind of made him drunk, as you may say, and he didn't know nothing at all the rest of the day, and preached a prayer-meeting sermon that night that give him a rattling ruputation, because the oldest **14** man in the world couldn't a understood it.   So Tom's Aunt Polly, she told all about who I was, and what; and I had to up and tell how I was in such a tight place that when Mrs. Phelps took me for Tom Sawyer—she chipped in and says, "Oh, go on and call me Aunt Sally, I'm used to it, now, and 'tain't no need to change"—that when Aunt Sally took me for Tom Sawyer, I had to stand it—there warn't no other way, and I knowed he wouldn't mind, because it would be nuts for him, being a mystery, and he'd make an adventure out of it and be perfectly satisfied.   And so it turned out, and he let on to be Sid, and made things as soft as he could for me.

And his Aunt Polly she said Tom was right about old Miss Watson setting Jim free in her will; and so, sure enough, Tom Sawyer had gone and took all that trouble and bother to set a free nigger free! and I couldn't ever understand, before, until that minute and that talk, how he *could* help a body set a nigger free, with his bringing-up.

Well, Aunt Polly she said that when Aunt Sally wrote to her that Tom and *Sid* had come, all right and safe, she says to herself:

"Look at that, now!   I might have expected it, letting him go off that way without anybody to watch him.   So now I got to go and trapse all the way down the river, eleven hundred **15** mile, and find out what that creetur's up to, *this* time; as long as I couldn't seem to get any answer out of you about it."

"Why, I never heard nothing from you," says Aunt Sally.

"Well, I wonder!   Why, I wrote to you twice, to ask you what you could mean by Sid being here."

"Well, I never got 'em, Sis."

Aunt Polly, she turns around slow and severe, and says:

"You, Tom!"

"Well—*what?*" he says, kind of pettish.

"Don't you what *me*, you impudent thing—hand out them letters."

"What letters?"

"*Them* letters.   I be bound, if I have to take aholt of you I'll——"

"They're in the trunk.   There, now.   And they're just the same as they was when I got them out of the office.   I hain't looked into them, I hain't touched them.   But I knowed they'd make trouble, and I thought if you warn't in no hurry, I'd——"

"Well, you *do* need skinning, there ain't no mistake about

14 *the oldest man in the world couldn't a understood it*. In times past, when age was venerated, it was commonly believed that the older a man got, the wiser he became.

15 *all the way down the river, eleven hundred mile*. This distance between Hannibal and the Phelps farm is confirmed in Chapter 2 of "Tom Sawyer, Detective" when Huck and Tom take a steamboat that was going "all the way down the Upper Mississippi and all the way down the Lower Mississippi to that farm in Arkansaw without having to change steamboats at St. Louis: not so very much short of a thousand miles at one pull." However, that would put Uncle Silas' place in northern Louisiana. Perhaps Aunt Polly is referring to the round-trip here: In speaking of his Uncle John Quarles's farm in Chapter 2 of his *Autobiography*, Twain admitted, "In *Huck Finn* and 'Tom Sawyer, Detective' I moved it to Arkansas. It was all of six hundred miles, but it was no trouble."

"HAND OUT THEM LETTERS"

it. And I wrote another one to tell you I was coming; and I s'pose he——"

"No, it come yesterday; I hain't read it yet, but *it's* all right, I've got that one."

I wanted to offer to bet two dollars she hadn't, but I reckoned maybe it was just as safe to not to. So I never said nothing.

Chapter the Last.

OUT OF BONDAGE.

The first time I catched Tom, private, I asked him what was his idea, time of the evasion?—what it was he'd planned to do if the evasion worked all right and he managed to set a nigger free that was already free before? And he said, what he had planned in his head, from the start, if we got Jim out all safe, was for us to run him down the river, on the raft, and have adventures plumb to the mouth of the river, and then tell him about his being free, and take him back up home on a steamboat, in style, and pay him for his lost time, and write word ahead and get out all the niggers around, and have them waltz him into town with a torchlight procession and a brass band, and then he would be a hero, and so would we. But I reckoned it was **1** about as well the way it was.

1 *But I reckoned it was about as well the way it was.* But it does happen just as Tom had hoped, if one is to believe the opening of *Tom Sawyer Abroad:* "You see, when we three come back up the river in glory, as you might say, from that long travel, and the village received us with a torchlight procession and speeches, and everybody hurrah'd and shouted, and some got drunk, it made us heroes, and that was what Tom Sawyer had always been hankerin' to be." But why would the entire town of St. Petersburg come out to greet a pair of phony "nigger stealers" and the former runaway? Perhaps, in composing *Tom Sawyer Abroad*, Twain just glanced over the last chapter of *Huckleberry Finn* and misread what Tom had wished for as what actually happened.

2 *le's all three . . . go for howling adventures amongst the Injuns.* In Chapter 13 of *A Boy's Town*, Howells described exactly what the allure of the Indians was to smalltown boys of the time: Theirs was "a world where people spent their lives in hunting and fishing and ranging the woods, and never grew up into the toils and cares that can alone make men of boys. They wished to escape these, as many foolish persons do among civilized nations, and they thought if they could only escape them they would be happy; they did not know that they would be merely savage."

Twain did not share this admiration for the "noble savage." Soon after he completed *Huckleberry Finn*, Twain began "Huck Finn and Tom Sawyer among the Indians"; and the new novel tried to debunk the James Fenimore Cooper concept of the Indian just as the earlier book had attacked the influence of Sir Walter Scott's chivalry on the South. The new story relates how Tom, Huck, and Jim escape to the Great Plains, and they quickly learn how vindictive the Sioux can be when they massacre a family who befriended the three whites from Missouri, for the killing of an Indian by a white man; the tale was never completed, because (as Walter Blair suggested in *Life*, December 20, 1968, p. 50A) Twain did not know how to handle the inevitable fate of a woman who has been abducted by the band, that of being tied to four pegs, and abused to the point of death.

3 *I ain't got no money for to buy the outfit.* And it could be a considerable expense, because the inventory of the outfit as given in "Huck Finn and Tom Sawyer among the Indians" consisted of five pack-mules, lucifer matches, an almanac, a flask or two of liquor, "skillets and coffee pots and tin cups, and blankets, and three sacks of flour, and bacon and sugar and coffee, and fish hooks, and pipes and tobacco, and ammunition, and pistols, and three guns, and glass beads, and all such things" (*Mark Twain's Hannibal, Huck and Tom*, p. 97).

We had Jim out of the chains in no time, and when Aunt Polly and Uncle Silas and Aunt Sally found out how good he helped the doctor nurse Tom, they made a heap of fuss over him, and fixed him up prime, and give him all he wanted to eat, and a good time, and nothing to do. And we had him up to the sick-room; and had a high talk; and Tom give Jim forty dollars for being prisoner for us so patient, and doing it up so good, and Jim was pleased most to death, and busted out, and says:

"*Dah*, now, Huck, what I tell you?—what I tell you up dah on Jackson islan'? I *tole* you I got a hairy breas', en what's de sign un it; en I *tole* you I ben rich wunst, en gwineter to be rich *agin*; en it's come true; en heah she *is*! *Dah*, now! doan' talk to *me*—signs is *signs*, mine I tell you; en I knowed jis' 's well 'at I 'uz gwineter be rich agin as I's a stannin' heah dis minute!"

And then Tom he talked along, and talked along, and says,
2 le's all three slide out of here, one of these nights, and get an outfit, and go for howling adventures amongst the Injuns, over in the Territory, for a couple of weeks or so; and I says, all
3 right, that suits me, but I ain't got no money for to buy the outfit, and I reckon I couldn't get none from home, because it's likely pap's been back before now, and got it all away from Judge Thatcher and drunk it up.

"No he hain't," Tom says; "it's all there, yet—six thousand dollars and more; and your pap hain't ever been back since. Hadn't when I come away, anyhow."

Jim says, kind of solemn:

"He ain't a comin' back no mo', Huck."

I says:

"Why, Jim?"

"Nemmine why, Huck—but he ain't comin' back no mo'."

But I kept at him; so at last he says:

"Doan' you 'member de house dat was float'n down de river,

TOM'S LIBERALITY.

en dey wuz a man in dah, kivered up, en I went in en un-kivered him and didn' let you come in? Well, den, you k'n git yo' money when you wants it; kase dat wuz him."

Tom's most well, now, and got his bullet around his neck on a watch-guard for a watch, and is always seeing what time it is, and so there ain't nothing more to write about, and I am rotten glad of it, because if I'd a knowed what a trouble it was to make a book I wouldn't a tackled it and ain't agoing to no more. But I reckon I got to light out for the Territory ahead of the rest, because Aunt Sally she's going to adopt me and sivilize **4, 5** me, and I can't stand it.   I been there before.

THE END.   YOURS TRULY, HUCK FINN.

4 *Aunt Sally she's going to adopt me*. But what about the Widow Douglas? Twain never fully resolves his plot: It was Miss Watson, not Huck's guardian, who died, so the boy should return to Hannibal to live with the widow. Twain did get the sisters confused: In his notes he had to ask himself, "Widow Douglas—then who is 'Miss Watson'? Ah, she's WD's *sister*" (quoted by DeVoto, *Mark Twain at Work*, p. 71); and inexplicably he raised Miss Watson from the dead in the unpublished "Tom Sawyer's Conspiracy."

5 *and sivilize me, and I can't stand it*. With the coming of the railroads, frontiersmen such as the legendary Mike Fink and Mike Shuck kept moving farther and farther West in search of complete freedom; thus the Territory was quickly becoming the last refuge from civilization in all of the country. Twain shared Huck's scorn for "sivilization" as mostly sham and a nuisance. But one should not make too much of Huck's declaration of independence; because, as Eugene McNamara in "Huck Lights Out for the Territory" (*The University of Windsor Review*, Fall 1966, pp. 68–74) has argued, it may only be a device to leave open the possibility of more adventures, such as "Huck Finn and Tom Sawyer among the Indians."

Autograph of "Mark Twain"/Samuel L. Clemens.

APPENDIX

The "Raft Chapter" from *Life on the Mississippi*, 1883

The following passage was originally a part of the manuscript of Huckleberry Finn, *appearing after the second paragraph of Chapter 16 (see Note 4 of that chapter). However, having put aside that novel, "a book I have been working at, by fits and starts, during the past five or six years, and may possibly finish in the course of five or six more," Twain inserted it into Chapter 3 of* Life on the Mississippi *to illustrate (he explained in that book) "keelboat talk and manners, and that now departed and hardly-remembered raft-life" on the western river before the Civil War. When he finally completed* Huckleberry Finn *the following year, the author intended to return this episode to its original place in the novel; he was particularly fond of this adventure of Huck Finn and considered including it in the program of his public readings with George W. Cable. But when the publisher objected to enlarging the new book with this "old Mississippi matter," Twain left it out of the published work.*

Some critics (such as DeVoto in the 1944 Limited Editions Club edition) have restored the "Raft Chapter" to Huckleberry Finn; *nevertheless, being a lengthy, highly detailed account of a particular phase of long-lost American life, it is perhaps more suited to* Life on the Mississippi *than to* Huckleberry Finn. *The passage may, as its defenders have argued, enlarge on themes established earlier in the story; but it suffers from what Howells said of portions of* Tom Sawyer *in "Mark Twain"* (The Century, *September 1882, p. 782), "an excess of reality in portraying the characters and conditions" of the Southwest before the Civil War.*

1 *they would talk about Cairo*. Huck and Jim suspect that they have passed Cairo, Illinois, where the slave was to escape to the free states.

But you know a young person can't wait very well when he is impatient to find a thing out. We talked it over, and by and by Jim said it was such a black night, now, that it wouldn't be no risk to swim down to the big raft and crawl aboard and listen—

1 they would talk about Cairo, because they would be calculating to go ashore there for a spree, maybe, or anyway they would send boats ashore to buy whiskey or fresh meat or something. Jim had a wonderful level head, for a nigger: he could most always start a good plan when you wanted one.

I stood up and shook my rags off and jumped into the river, and struck out for the raft's light. By and by, when I got down nearly to her, I eased up and went slow and cautious. But everything was all right—nobody at the sweeps. So I swum down along the raft till I was most abreast the camp fire in the middle, then I crawled aboard and inched along and got in amongst some bundles of shingles on the weather side of the fire. **2** There was thirteen men there—they was the watch on deck of course. And a mighty rough-looking lot, too. They had a jug, and tin cups, and they kept the jug moving. One man was singing—roaring, you may say; and it wasn't a nice song—for a parlor anyway. He roared through his nose, and strung out the last word of every line very long. When he was done they all fetched a kind of Injun war-whoop, and then another was sung. It begun:

'There was a woman in our towdn,   **3**
    In our towdn did dwed'l (dwell,)
She loved her husband dear-i-lee,
    But another man twyste as wed'l.   **4**

Singing too, riloo, riloo, riloo,
    Ri-too, riloo, rilay - - - e,
She loved her husband dear-i-lee,
    But another man twyste as wed'l.'

And so on—fourteen verses. It was kind of poor, and when he was going to start on the next verse one of them said it was the **5** tune the old cow died on; and another one said, 'Oh, give us a rest.' And another one told him to take a walk. They made fun of him till he got mad and jumped up and begun to cuss the crowd, and said he could lame any thief in the lot.

They was all about to make a break for him, but the biggest man there jumped up and says—

'Set whar you are, gentlemen. Leave him to me; he's my **6** meat.'

Then he jumped up in the air three times and cracked his heels together every time. He flung off a buckskin coat that was all hung with fringes, and says, 'You lay thar tell the chawin-up's done;' and flung his hat down, which was all over ribbons, and says, 'You lay thar tell his sufferins is over.'

Then he jumped up in the air and cracked his heels together again and shouted out—

'Whoo-oop! I'm the old original iron-jawed, brass-mounted, **7** copper-bellied corpse-maker from the wilds of Arkansaw!—Look at me! I'm the man they call Sudden Death and General Desolation! Sired by a hurricane, dam'd by an earthquake, half-brother to the cholera, nearly related to the small-pox on the mother's side! Look at me! I take nineteen alligators and a bar'l of whiskey for breakfast when I'm in robust health, and a bushel of rattlesnakes and a dead body when I'm ailing! I split the everlasting rocks with my glance, and I squench the thunder **8** when I speak! Whoo-oop! Stand back and give me room according to my strength! Blood's my natural drink, and the wails of the dying is music to my ear! Cast your eye on me, gentlemen!—and lay low and hold your breath, for I'm bout to turn myself loose!'

All the time he was getting this off, he was shaking his head and looking fierce, and kind of swelling around in a little circle, tucking up his wrist-bands, and now and then straightening up and beating his breast with his fist, saying, 'Look at me, gentlemen!' When he got through, he jumped up and cracked his heels together three times, and let off a roaring 'whoo-oop! I'm the bloodiest son of a wildcat that lives!'

2 *on the weather side of the fire.* On the side from which the wind is blowing, so the boy is out of the path of the smoke and the light of the fire.

3 *There was a woman in our towdn.* Twain quotes the first verse of a variant of a popular folk song. In Scotland, it is known as "The Wily Auld Carle" and "The Wife of Kelso"; in Maine as "Old Woman of Dover"; in Kentucky as "Old Woman of London"; in Ohio as "Old Woman of Slapsadam"; in North Carolina as "The Old Woman's Blind Husband"; and in Missouri as "There was an Old Woman":

There was an old woman in our town,
    In our town did dwell.
She loved her husband dearly,
    But another man twice as well.

She went down to the doctor's shop
    To see what she could find
To see if she could find anything
    To make her old man blind.

She found six dozen old beef bones
    And made him chew them all.
He says, "Old woman, I am so blind
    I can't see you at all."

He says, "Old woman, I'll drown myself
    If I could find the way."
She says, "My dearest husband,
    I'll go show you the way."

She took him by the hand
    And led him to the brim.
He says, "Old Woman, I'll drown myself
    If you will push me in."

The old woman stepped a little one side
    To give a sounding spring.
The old man stepped a little one side,
    And she went bounding in.

Then she bawled out, she squawled out,
    As loud as she could bawl.
He says, "Old woman, I am so blind
    I can't see you at all."

The old man being good-natured
    And thought that she might swim,
He goes and gets a good long pole
    And pushed her further in.

Some versions add the following:

Now my song is ended,
    I'll sing you no more.
Wasn't she an old fool?
    And he was seventy-four.

Or,

Now my song is ended,
    I'll sing you no more.
Wasn't she an old fool
    To trust her husband so?

This slightly improper ballad was one of Twain's favorite songs; for example, in Chapter 13 of *The Prince and the Pauper*, he had Miles Hendon sing a few lines while sewing some clothes for Edward Tudor.

4 *But another man twyste as wed'l.* While reading the proofs of *The Prince and the Pauper*, Howells objected to this line as being "rather strong milk for babes"; and Twain softened it in that book. However, when the author himself took the role of Miles Hendon in a performance of the story, presented by his daughters and their friends at Christmas in 1884, Twain sang it unexpurgated. See *Mark Twain–Howells Letters*, pp. 375 and 874.

5 *the tune the old cow died on.* In *Hoosier Folklore* (December 1948, pp. 105–106), Ruth Ann Musick published this Missouri folk song "The Tune the Old Cow Died On":

> *Farmer John from his work came home*
> *One summer's afternoon,*
> *And sat himself down by the maple grove*
> *And sang himself this tune*
>
> Chorus
> *Ri fol de ol, Di ri fol dal di*
> *Tune the old cow died on.*
>
> *The farmer's cows came running home*
> *And round him formed a ring;*
> *For they never heard good Farmer John*
> *Before attempt to sing.*
>
> *The oldest cow in the farmer's herd*
> *Tried hard to join the song;*
> *But she couldn't strike that melody—*
> *Her voice was loud and strong.*
>
> *The farmer laughed till the tears rolled down*
> *His cheeks like apples red;*
> *The cow got mad and tried to sing*
> *Until she dropped down dead.*
>
> *The farmer had an inquest held*
> *To see what killed the cow.*
> *The verdict of the jury was*
> *What I mean to tell you now.*
>
> *They said that the cow would be living yet*
> *To chew her cud with glee*
> *If good Farmer John hadn't sung that song*
> *Beneath the maple tree.*

6 *my meat.* My quarry, my prey.

7 *I'm the old original iron-jawed, brass-mounted, copper-bellied corpse-maker from the wilds of Arkansaw!* Fighting was a common diversion of riverboatmen of the period. "The incredible strength of their pectoral muscles, growing out of their peculiar labor and manner of life," explained T. B. Thorpe in "Remembrances of the Mississippi" (*Harper's Monthly*, December 1855, p. 30), "made fights with them a direful necessity—it was an appetite, and, like pressing hunger, had to be appeased. The keel-boatman who boasted that he had never been whipped, stood upon

Then the man that had started the row tilted his old slouch hat down over his right eye; then he bent stooping forward, with his back sagged and his south end sticking out far, and his fists a-shoving out and drawing in in front of him, and so went around in a little circle about three times, swelling himself up and breathing hard. Then he straightened, and jumped up and cracked his heels together three times, before he lit again (that made them cheer), and he begun to shout like this—

'Whoo-oop! bow your neck and spread, for the kingdom of sorrow's a-coming! Hold me down to the earth, for I feel my powers a-working! whoo-oop! I'm a child of sin, *don't* let me get a start! Smoked glass, here, for all! Don't attempt to look at me with the naked eye, gentlemen! When I'm playful I use the meridians of longitude and parallels of latitude for a seine, and drag the Atlantic Ocean for whales! I scratch my head with the lightning, and purr myself to sleep with the thunder! When I'm cold, I bile the Gulf of Mexico and bathe in it; when I'm hot I fan myself with an equinoctial storm; when I'm thirsty I reach up and suck a cloud dry like a sponge; when I range the earth hungry, famine follows in my tracks! Whoo-oop! Bow your neck and spread! I put my hand on the sun's face and make it night in the earth; I bite a piece out of the moon and hurry the seasons; I shake myself and crumble the mountains! Contemplate me through leather—*don't* use the naked eye! I'm the man with a petrified heart and biler-iron bowels! The massacre of isolated communities is the pastime of my idle moments, the destruction of nationalities the serious business of my life! The boundless vastness of the great American desert is my enclosed property, and I bury my dead on my own premises!' He jumped up and cracked his heels together three times before he lit (they cheered him again), and as he come down he shouted out: 'Whoo-oop! bow your neck and spread, for the pet child of calamity's a-coming!'

Then the other one went to swelling around and blowing again—the first one—the one they called Bob; next, the Child of Calamity chipped in again, bigger than ever; then they both got at it at the same time, swelling round and round each other and punching their fists most into each other's faces, and whooping and jawing like Injuns; then Bob called the Child names, and the Child called him names back again; next, Bob called him a heap rougher names and the Child come back at him with the very worst kind of language; next, Bob knocked the Child's hat off, and the Child picked it up and kicked Bob's ribbony hat about six foot; Bob went and got it and said never mind, this warn't going to be the last of this thing, because he was a man that never forgot and never forgive, and so the Child better look out, for there was a time a-coming, just as sure as he was a living man, that he would have to answer to him with the best blood in his body. The Child said no man was willinger than he was for that time to come, and he would give Bob fair warning, *now*, never to cross his path again, for he could never rest till he had waded in his blood, for such was his nature, though he was sparing him now on account of his family, if he had one.

Both of them was edging away in different directions, growling and shaking their heads and going on about what they was going to do; but a little black-whiskered chap skipped up and says—

'Come back here, you couple of chicken-livered cowards, and I'll thrash the two of ye!'

And he done it, too. He snatched them, he jerked them this

way and that, he booted them around, he knocked them sprawling faster than they could get up. Why, it warn't two minutes till they begged like dogs—and how the other lot did yell and laugh and clap their hands all the way through, and shout 'Sail in, Corpse-Maker!' 'Hi! at him again, Child of Calamity!' 'Bully for you, little Davy!' Well, it was a perfect pow-wow for a while. Bob and the Child had red noses and black eyes when they got through. Little Davy made them own up that they were sneaks and cowards and not fit to eat with a dog or drink with a nigger; **12** then Bob and the Child shook hands with each other, very solemn, and said they had always respected each other and was willing to let bygones be bygones. So then they washed their faces in the river; and just then there was a loud order to stand by for a crossing, and some of them went forward to man the sweeps there, and the rest went aft to handle the after-sweeps.

I laid still and waited for fifteen minutes, and had a smoke out of a pipe that one of them left in reach; then the crossing was finished, and they stumped back and had a drink around and went to talking and singing again. Next they got out an old fiddle, and one played and another patted juba, and the rest **13** turned themselves loose on a regular old-fashioned keel-boat **14** breakdown. They couldn't keep that up very long without **15** getting winded, so by and by they settled around the jug again.

They sung 'jolly, jolly raftman's the life for me,' with a **16** rousing chorus, and then they got to talking about differences betwixt hogs, and their different kind of habits; and next about women and their different ways: and next about the best ways to put out houses that was afire; and next about what ought to be done with the Injuns; and next about what a king had to do, and how much he got; and next about how to make cats fight; and next about what to do when a man has fits; and next about differences betwixt clear-water rivers and muddy-water ones. The man they called Ed said the muddy Mississippi water was **17** wholesomer to drink than the clear water of the Ohio; he said if you let a pint of this yaller Mississippi water settle, you would have about a half to three quarters of an inch of mud in the bottom, according to the stage of the river, and then it warn't no better than Ohio water—what you wanted to do was to keep it stirred up—and when the river was low, keep mud on hand to put in and thicken the water up the way it ought to be.

The Child of Calamity said that was so; he said there was nutritiousness in the mud, and a man that drunk Mississippi water could grow corn in his stomach if he wanted to. He says—

'You look at the graveyards; that tells the tale. Trees won't grow worth shucks in a Cincinnati graveyard, but in a Sent Louis graveyard they grow upwards of eight hundred foot high. It's all on account of the water the people drunk before they laid up. A Cincinnati corpse don't richen a soil any.'

And they talked about how Ohio water didn't like to mix with Mississippi water. Ed said if you take the Mississippi on a rise when the Ohio is low, you'll find a wide band of clear water all the way down the east side of the Mississippi for a hundred mile or more, and the minute you get out a quarter of a mile from shore and pass the line, it is all thick and yaller the rest of the way across. Then they talked about how to keep tobacco from getting moldy, and from that they went into ghosts and told **18** about a lot that other folks had seen; but Ed says—

'Why don't you tell something that you've seen yourselves? Now let me have a say. Five years ago I was on a raft as big as this, and right along here it was a bright moonshiny night, and I

a dangerous eminence, for every aspirant for fame was bound to dispute his claim to such distinction." Whenever two such "ring-tailed squealers" or "salt-water roarers," of the "half-alligator" variety, met, they would roll up their sleeves, crow like gaming-cocks, and try to outboast each other. "I'm from the Lightning Forks of Roaring River. I'm *all* man, save what is wild cat and extra lightning. I'm as hard to run against as a cypress snag—I never back water. . . . Cock-a-doodle-doo! I did hold down a bufferlo bull, and tar off his scalp with my teeth. . . . I'm the man that, single-handed, towed the broadhorn over a sandbar—the identical infant who girdled a hickory by smiling at the bark, and if any one denies it, let him make his will and pay the expenses of a funeral. I'm the genuine article, tough as bull's hide, keen as a rifle. . . . I'm painfully ferochus—I'm spiling for some one to whip me—if there's a creeter in this diggin' that wants to be disappointed in trying to do it, let him yell—whoop-hurra!"

And the most famous of these riverboatmen was Mike Fink who challenged all comers with, "Hurray for me, you scapegoats! I'm a land-screamer—I'm a water-dog—I'm a snapping turkle—I can lick five times my own weight in wild-cats. . . . I can out-run, out-dance, out-jump, out-dive, out-drink, out-holler, and out-lick any white thing in the shape o' human that's ever put foot within two thousand miles o' the big Mississip! Whoop!" (*Mike Fink, A Legend of the Ohio*, by Emerson Bennett, 1852, p. 28).

Such larger-than-life characters soon passed into American folklore; and their form of extravagant brag survives in the taunts of Muhammad Ali. Soon, however, humorists came to recognize such frontier bullies as being more talk than action. Other examples of this comic type in American literature before the Civil War include Captain Roaring Ralph Stackpole and Bloody Ned in Robert Montgomery Bird's *Nick of the Woods*; Ned Jones in William Pauper Thompson's *Chronicles of Pineville*; Chunkey in William T. Porter's *The Big Bear of Arkansas*; but the combatants perhaps most like Twain's Child of Calamity and Big Bob are Mike Hooter and Arch Coony in Thomas Chandler Haliburton's *Traits of American Character* (1852, pp. 296–301) who exchange more cusses than cuffs.

8 *squench.* Suppress, quell.

9 *Smoked glass.* Used to protect the eyes when looking directly into the sun, as in an eclipse. In this battle of wits, by suggesting that he himself is a god who can alter the cosmos, Child of Calamity upstages Big Bob who by comparison is merely a mortal with superhuman strength.

10 *I put my hand on the sun's face and make it night in the earth.* As in an eclipse; however, when the moon covers the sun in such an occurrence, it actually remains day even when the light is blocked out.

11 *I bite a piece out of the moon and hurry the seasons.* It was once believed that the phases of the moon altered the seasons, and not that they actually follow the course of the earth's rotation around the sun.

12 *drink with a nigger.* At the time, considered a habit of only the lowest of the low. In discussing his relationship with the slave, Uncle Jake, in Chapter 28 of *Tom Sawyer*, Huck confesses, "Sometimes, I've set right down and eat *with* him. But you needn't tell that. A body's got to do things when he's awful hungry he wouldn't want to do as a steady thing."

13 *patted juba.* Or "patting Juby, or jubilee," a lively tap dance, accompanied by clapping hands and slapping knees, while singing,

> *Juba up and Juba down,*
> *Juba all around the town,*
> *Juba this and Juba that,*
> *And Juba round the 'simmon vat.*
> *Hoe corn and hill tobacco,*
> *Get over double trouble, Juba, boys.*
> *Juba!*

This slave jig is said to be of African origin, Juba being an evil spirit. Despite their disdain for "niggers," these men nevertheless enjoy the slaves' entertainments.

14 *keel-boat.* A large, long, slender, and light flatboat, propelled by either oars or sails, used in America primarily in low water on the Upper Mississippi and Ohio rivers.

15 *breakdown.* Any wild, boisterous, or riotous dance, a shuffling dance in rapid motions; it may even be a juba, as in Chapter 16 of *The Gilded Age* where "they saw two negroes . . . 'breaking down' in approved style, amid the 'hi, hi's' of the spectators."

16 *"jolly, jolly raftsman's the life for me."* Twain may be referring to a variant of a song quoted by John Habermehl in *Life on the Western Rivers* (1901):

> *The boatman is a lucky man,*
> *No one can do as the boatman can,*
> *The boatman dance and the boatman sing*
> *The man is up to everything.*
>
> Chorus
> *Hi-O, the way we go*
> *Floating down the river on the Ohio.*
>
> *When the boatman gets on shore*
> *He spends his money and works for more.*
> *When the boatman goes on shore,*
> *Look, old man, your sheep is gone,*
> *He steals your sheep and steals your shote,*
> *He puts 'em in a bag and totes 'em to the boat.*
>
> *Dance, the boatman, dance all night*
> *Till broad daylight,*
> *And go home with the girls in the morning.*
> *I never saw a pretty girl in all my life,*
> *But what she would be a boatman's wife.*

17 *the muddy Mississippi water was wholesomer to drink than the clear water of the Ohio.* Charles Dickens tested this belief on his first American tour. "We drank the muddy water of this river while we were upon it," he recalled in Chapter 12 of *American Notes*. "It is

was on watch and boss of the stabboard oar forrard, and one of my pards was a man named Dick Allbright, and he come along to where I was sitting, forrard—gaping and stretching, he was—and stooped down on the edge of the raft and washed his face in the river, and come and set down by me and got out his pipe, and had just got it filled, when he looks up and says—

"'Why looky-here,' he says, 'ain't that Buck Miller's place, over yander in the bend?'

"'Yes,' says I, 'it is—why?' He laid his pipe down and leant his head on his hand, and says—

"'I thought we'd be furder down.' I says—

"'I thought it too, when I went off watch'—we was standing six hours on and six off—'but the boys told me,' I says, 'that the raft didn't seem to hardly move, for the last hour,' says I, 'though she's a slipping along all right, now,' says I. He give a kind of a groan, and says—

"'I've seed a raft act so before, along here,' he says, "'pears to me the current has most quit above the head of this bend durin' the last two years,' he says.

'Well, he raised up two or three times, and looked away off and around on the water. That started me at it, too. A body is always doing what he sees somebody else doing, though there mayn't be no sense in it. Pretty soon I see a black something floating on the water away off to stabboard and quartering behind us. I see he was looking at it, too. I says—

"'What's that?' He says, sort of pettish,—

"'Tain't nothing but an old empty bar'l.'

"'An empty bar'l!' says I, 'why,' says I, 'a spy-glass is a fool to *your* eyes. How can you tell it's an empty bar'l?' He says—

"'I don't know; I reckon it ain't a bar'l, but I thought it might be,' says he.

"'Yes,' I says, 'so it might be, and it might be anything else, too; a body can't tell nothing about it, such a distance as that,' I says.

'We hadn't nothing else to do, so we kept on watching it. By and by I says—

"'Why looky-here, Dick Allbright, that thing's a-gaining on us, I believe.'

'He never said nothing. The thing gained and gained, and I judged it must be a dog that was about tired out. Well, we swung down into the crossing, and the thing floated across the bright streak of the moonshine, and, by George, it *was* a bar'l. Says I—

"'Dick Allbright, what made you think that thing was a bar'l, when it was a half a mile off,' says I. Says he—

"'I don't know.' Says I—

"'You tell me, Dick Allbright.' He says—

"'Well, I knowed it was a bar'l; I've seen it before; lots has seen it; they says it's a haunted bar'l.'

'I called the rest of the watch, and they come and stood there, and I told them what Dick said. It floated right along abreast, now, and didn't gain any more. It was about twenty foot off. Some was for having it aboard, but the rest didn't want to. Dick Allbright said rafts that had fooled with it had got bad luck by it. The captain of the watch said he didn't believe in it. He said he reckoned the bar'l gained on us because it was in a little better current than what we was. He said it would leave by and by.

'So then we went to talking about other things, and we had a song, and then a breakdown; and after that the captain of the watch called for another song; but it was clouding up, now, and the bar'l stuck right thar in the same place, and the song didn't seem to have much warm-up to it, somehow, and so they didn't finish it, and there warn't any cheers, but it sort of dropped flat, and nobody said anything for a minute. Then everybody tried to talk at once, and one chap got off a joke, but it warn't no use, they didn't laugh, and even the chap that made the joke didn't laugh at it, which ain't usual. We all just settled down glum, and watched the bar'l, and was oneasy and oncomfortable. Well, sir, it shut down black and still, and then the wind begin to moan around, and next the lightning begin to play and the thunder to grumble. And pretty soon there was a regular storm, and in the middle of it a man that was running aft stumbled and fell and sprained his ankle so that he had to lay up. This made the boys **19** shake their heads. And every time the lightning come, there was that bar'l with the blue lights winking around it. We was always on the look-out for it. But by and by, towards dawn, she was gone. When the day come we couldn't see her anywhere, and we warn't sorry, neither.

'But next night about half-past nine, when there was songs and high jinks going on, here she comes again, and took her old roost on the stabboard side. There warn't no more high jinks. Everybody got solemn; nobody talked; you couldn't get anybody to do anything but set around moody and look at the bar'l. It begun to cloud up again. When the watch changed, the off watch stayed up, 'stead of turning in. The storm ripped and roared around all night, and in the middle of it another man tripped and sprained his ankle, and had to knock off. The bar'l left towards day, and nobody see it go.

'Everybody was sober and down in the mouth all day. I don't mean the kind of sober that comes of leaving liquor alone—not that. They was quiet, but they all drunk more than usual—not together—but each man sidled off and took it private, by himself.

'After dark the off watch didn't turn in; nobody sung, nobody talked; the boys didn't scatter around, neither; they sort of huddled together, forrard; and for two hours they set there, perfectly still, looking steady in the one direction, and heaving a sigh once in a while. And then, here comes the bar'l again. She took up her old place. She staid there all night; nobody turned in. The storm come on again, after midnight. It got awful dark; the rain poured down, hail, too; the thunder boomed and roared and bellowed; the wind blowed a hurricane; and the lightning spread over everything in big sheets of glare, and showed the whole raft as plain as day; and the river lashed up white as milk as far as you could see for miles, and there was that bar'l jiggering along, same as ever. The captain ordered the watch to **20** man the after sweeps for a crossing, and nobody would go—no more sprained ankles for them, they said. They wouldn't even *walk* aft. Well then, just then the sky split wide open, with a crash, and the lightning killed two men of the after watch, and crippled two more. Crippled them how, says you? Why, *sprained their ankles!*

'The bar'l left in the dark betwixt lightnings, towards dawn. Well, not a body eat a bite at breakfast that morning. After that the men loafed around, in twos and threes, and talked low together. But none of them herded with Dick Allbright. They all give him the cold shake. If he come around where any of the men was, they split up and sidled away. They wouldn't man the sweeps with him. The captain had all the skiffs hauled up on the raft, alongside of his wigwam, and wouldn't let the dead men be took ashore to be planted; he didn't believe a man that got ashore

considered wholesome by the natives, and is something more opaque than gruel."

18 *they went into ghosts*. Riverboatmen were particularly fearful of ghosts. See also Chapter 8, p. 15.

19 *he had to lay up*. He had to take to his bed.

20 *jiggering*. Moving in a succession of rapid jerks, fidgeting, as when attacked by chiggers.

21 *dogging.* Following closely, persistently, as in tracking with dogs.

22 *without a jint started.* Without moving a single joint, effortlessly.

23 *one night he choked his child, which was crying, not intending to kill it.* Dick Allbright's "owning up" to his killing of the baby foreshadows a similar confession, that of Jim's abuse of his deaf-and-dumb daughter in Chapter 23.

24 *Edward. . . . Edmund. . . . Edwin.* Twain recognizes that "Ed" is a nickname for numerous proper names; in a sense, the shortened form is as much an alias as "Charles William Allbright," "Aleck James Hopkins," or "Mark Twain."

would come back; and he was right.

'After night come, you could see pretty plain that there was going to be trouble if that bar'l come again; there was such a muttering going on. A good many wanted to kill Dick Allbright, because he'd seen the bar'l on other trips, and that had an ugly look. Some wanted to put him ashore. Some said, let's all go ashore in a pile, if the bar'l comes again.

'This kind of whispers was still going on, the men being bunched together forrard watching for the bar'l, when, lo and behold you, here she comes again. Down she comes, slow and steady, and settles into her old tracks. You could a heard a pin drop. Then up comes the captain, and says:—

21 "'Boys, don't be a pack of children and fools; I don't want this bar'l to be dogging us all the way to Orleans, and *you* don't; well, then, how's the best way to stop it? Burn it up,—that's the way. I'm going to fetch it aboard," he says. And before anybody could say a word, in he went.

'He swum to it, and as he come pushing it to the raft, the men spread to one side. But the old man got it aboard and busted in the head, and there was a baby in it! Yes, sir, a stark naked baby. It was Dick Allbright's baby; he owned up and said so.

'"Yes," he says, a-leaning over it, "yes, it is my own lamented darling, my poor lost Charles William Allbright deceased," says he,—for he could curl his tongue around the bulliest words in the language when he was a mind to, and lay them before you
22 without a jint started, anywheres. Yes, he said he used to live up
23 at the head of this bend, and one night he choked his child, which was crying, not intending to kill it,—which was prob'ly a lie,—and then he was scared, and buried it in a bar'l, before his wife got home, and off he went, and struck the northern trail and went to rafting; and this was the third year that the bar'l had chased him. He said the bad luck always begun light, and lasted till four men was killed, and then the bar'l didn't come come any more after that. He said if the men would stand it one more night,—and was a-going on like that,—but the men had got enough. They started to get out a boat to take him ashore and lynch him, but he grabbed the little child all of a sudden and jumped overboard with it hugged up to his breast and shedding tears, and we never see him again in this life, poor old suffering soul, nor Charles William neither.'

'*Who* was shedding tears?' says Bob; 'was it Allbright or the baby?'

'Why, Allbright, of course; didn't I tell you the baby was dead? Been dead three years—how could it cry?'

'Well, never mind how it could cry—how could it *keep* all that time?' says Davy. 'You answer me that.'

'I don't know how it done it,' says Ed. 'It done it though—that's all I know about it.'

'Say—what did they do with the bar'l?' says the Child of Calamity.

'Why, they hove it overboard, and it sunk like a chunk of lead.'

24 'Edward, did the child look like it was choked?' says one.

'Did it have its hair parted?' says another.

'What was the brand on that bar'l, Eddy?' says a fellow they called Bill.

'Have you got the papers for them statistics, Edmund?' says Jimmy.

'Say, Edwin, was you one of the men that was killed by the lightning?' says Davy.

'Him? O, no, he was both of 'em,' says Bob. Then they all haw-hawed.

'Say, Edward, don't you reckon you'd better take a pill? You look bad—don't you feel pale?' says the Child of Calamity.

'O, come, now, Eddy,' says Jimmy, 'show up; you must a kept **25** part of that bar'l to prove the thing by. Show us the bunghole— **26** *do*—and we'll all believe you.'

'Say, boys,' says Bill, 'less divide it up. Thar's thirteen of us. I can swaller a thirteenth of the yarn, if you can worry down the **27** rest.'

Ed got up mad and said they could all go to some place which he ripped out pretty savage, and then walked off aft cussing to himself, and they yelling and jeering at him, and roaring and laughing so you could hear them a mile.

'Boys, we'll split a watermelon on that,' says the Child of Calamity; and he come rummaging around in the dark amongst the shingle bundles where I was, and put his hand on me. I was warm and soft and naked; so he says 'Ouch!' and jumped back.

'Fetch a lantern or a chunk of fire here, boys—there's a snake here as big as a cow!'

So they run there with a lantern and crowded up and looked in on me.

'Come out of that, you beggar!' says one.

'Who are you?' says another.

'What are you after here? Speak up prompt, or overboard you go.'

'Snake him out, boys. Snatch him out by the heels.'

I began to beg, and crept out amongst them trembling. They looked me over, wondering, and the Child of Calamity says—

'A cussed thief! Lend a hand and less heave him overboard!'

'No,' says Big Bob, 'less get out the paint-pot and paint him a sky blue all over from head to heel, and *then* heave him over!'

'Good! that's it. Go for the paint, Jimmy.'

When the paint come, and Bob took the brush and was just going to begin, the others laughing and rubbing their hands, I begun to cry, and that sort of worked on Davy, and he says—

''Vast there! He's nothing but a cub. I'll paint the man that **28** tetches him!'

So I looked around on them, and some of them grumbled and growled, and Bob put down the paint, and the others didn't take it up.

'Come here to the fire, and less see what you're up to here,' says Davy. 'Now set down there and give an account of yourself. How long have you been aboard here?'

'Not over a quarter of a minute, sir,' says I.

'How did you get dry so quick?'

'I don't know, sir. I'm always that way, mostly.'

'Oh, you are, are you? What's your name?'

I warn't going to tell my name. I didn't know what to say, so I just says—

'Charles William Allbright, sir.' **29**

Then they roared—the whole crowd; and I was mighty glad I said that, because maybe laughing would get them in a better humor.

When they got done laughing, Davy says—

'It won't hardly do, Charles William. You couldn't have growed this much in five year, and you was a baby when you come out of the bar'l, you know, and dead at that. Come, now, tell a straight story, and nobody'll hurt you, if you ain't up to anything wrong. What *is* your name?'

25 *show up*. Put up; provide the evidence.

26 *the bunghole*. The place in the barrel where the water or other liquid is poured out.

27 *worry down the rest*. Force down the rest by dogged effort.

28 *'Vast*. Avast, stop.

29 *Charles William Allbright*. Ironically, "dead" Huck Finn here is resurrected as the murdered baby. It is another example of child death along the river.

30 *Yes, sir, in a trading scow. . . . It's our first trip.* In Chapter 16 Huck intended to stick to this "stretcher" by telling whomever he might meet on the shore that "pap was behind, coming along with a trading scow, and was a green hand at the business, and wanted to know how far it was to Cairo." He abandons the tale when he encounters the slave hunters.

'Aleck Hopkins, sir. Aleck James Hopkins.'

'Well, Aleck, where did you come from, here?'

'From a trading scow. She lays up the bend yonder. I was born on her. Pap has traded up and down here all his life; and he told me to swim off here, because when you went by he said he would like to get some of you to speak to a Mr. Jonas Turner, in Cairo, and tell him——'

'Oh, come!'

'Yes, sir, it's as true as the world; Pap he says——'

'Oh, your grandmother!'

They all laughed, and I tried again to talk, but they broke in on me and stopped me.

'Now, looky-here,' says Davy; 'you're scared, and so you talk wild. Honest, now, do you live in a scow, or is it a lie?'

30   'Yes, sir, in a trading scow. She lays up at the head of the bend. But I warn't born in her. It's our first trip.'

'Now you're talking! What did you come aboard here, for? To steal?'

'No, sir, I didn't.—It was only to get a ride on the raft. All boys does that.'

'Well, I know that. But what did you hide for?'

'Sometimes they drive the boys off.'

'So they do. They might steal. Looky-here; if we let you off this time, will you keep out of these kind of scrapes hereafter?'

''Deed I will, boss. You try me.'

'All right, then. You ain't but little ways from shore. Overboard with you, and don't you make a fool of yourself another time this way.—Blast it, boy, some raftsmen would rawhide you till you were black and blue!'

I didn't wait to kiss good-bye, but went overboard and broke for shore. When Jim come along by and by, the big raft was away out of sight around the point. I swum out and got aboard, and was mighty glad to see home again.

BIBLIOGRAPHY

By Mark Twain

"The Dandy Frightening the Squatter," *The Carpet-Bag*, May 1, 1852.

"Historical Exhibition—A No. 1 Ruse," Hannibal *Journal*, September 16, 1852.

"Love Concealed: To Miss Katie of H———l," Hannibal *Daily Journal*, May 6, 1853.

"'Oh, She Has a Red Head!'" Hannibal *Daily Journal*, May 13, 1853.

"Reflections on the Sabbath," San Francisco *Golden Era*, March 18, 1866.

"Story of the Bad Boy Who Didn't Come to Grief," San Francisco *Californian*, December 23, 1865.

"A Complaint about Correspondents," San Francisco *Californian*, March 24, 1866.

"Morality and Huckleberries," San Francisco *Alta California*, September 6, 1868.

The Innocents Abroad. Illustrated by True W. Williams and others. Hartford, Connecticut: American Publishing Co., 1869.

"Post-Mortem Poetry," *The Galaxy*, June 1870, pp. 864–865.

"The Indignity put upon the Remains of George Holland by the Rev. Mr. Sabine," *The Galaxy*, February 1871, pp. 320–321.

Mark Twain's (Burlesque) Autobiography, and First Romance. Illustrated by H. L. Stephens. New York: Sheldon & Co., 1871.

Roughing It. Illustrated by True W. Williams and others. Hartford, Connecticut: American Publishing Co., 1872.

The Gilded Age. By Mark Twain and Charles Dudley Warner. Illustrated by Augustus Hoppin, H. L. Stephens, True W. Williams, and others. Hartford, Connecticut: American Publishing Co., 1874.

"A True Story Repeated Word for Word as I Heard It," *The Atlantic Monthly*, November 1874, pp. 591–594.

Mark Twain's Sketches, New and Old. Illustrated by True W. Williams. Hartford, Connecticut: American Publishing Co., 1875.

The Adventures of Tom Sawyer. Illustrated by True W. Williams. Hartford, Connecticut: American Publishing Co., 1876.

"The Facts Concerning the Recent Carnival of Crime in Connecticut," *The Atlantic Monthly*, June 1876, pp. 641–650.

"Contributor's Club: The Boston Girl," *The Atlantic Monthly*, June 1880, pp. 851–860.

A Tramp Abroad. Illustrated by W. Fr. Brown, True W. Williams, B. Day, W. W. Denslow, and others. Hartford, Connecticut: American Publishing Co., 1880.

Date 1601. West Point, New York: Academie Presse, 1882.

The Prince and the Pauper. Illustrated by Frank T. Merrill. Boston: James R. Osgood and Co., 1882.

Life on the Mississippi. Illustrated by E. H. Garrett, Harley, A. B. Shute, and others. Boston: James R. Osgood and Co., 1883.

"An Adventure of Huckleberry Finn: With an Account of the Famous Grangerford-Shepherdson Feud," illustrated by E. W. Kemble, *The Century*, December 1884, pp. 268–278.

"Jim's Investments, and King Sollermun," illustrated by E. W. Kemble, *The Century*, January 1885, pp. 456–458.

"Royalty on the Mississippi: As Chronicled by Huckleberry Finn," illustrated by E. W. Kemble, *The Century*, February 1885, pp. 544–567.

Adventures of Huckleberry Finn. Illustrated by E. W. Kemble. New York: Charles L. Webster and Co., 1885.

"The Private History of a Campaign That Failed," illustrated by E. W. Kemble, *The Century*, December 1885, pp. 193–204.

"International Copyright," *The Century*, February 1886, p. 634.

Mark Twain's Library of Humor. Edited by Mark Twain, William Dean Howells, and Charles Hopkins Clark. Illustrated by E. W. Kemble. New York: Charles L. Webster and Co., 1888.

A Connecticut Yankee in King Arthur's Court. Illustrated by Dan Beard. New York: Charles L. Webster and Co., 1889.

The American Claimant. Illustrated by Dan Beard. New York: Charles L. Webster and Co., 1892.

"Tom Sawyer Abroad," illustrated by Dan Beard, *St. Nicholas*, November 1893 through April 1894.

Tom Sawyer Abroad. Illustrated by Dan Beard. New York: Charles L. Webster and Co., 1894.

The Tragedy of Pudd'nhead Wilson and the Comedy of Those Two Extraordinary Twins. Illustrated. Hartford, Connecticut: American Publishing Co., 1894.

"Fenimore Cooper's Literary Offenses," *North American Review*, July 1895, pp. 1–12.

"Tom Sawyer, Detective," illustrated by A. B. Frost, *Harper's Monthly*, August and September 1896.

Tom Sawyer Abroad; Tom Sawyer, Detective; and Other Stories. Illustrated by Dan Beard and A. B. Frost. New York and London: Harper & Bros., 1896.

Following the Equator. Illustrated by Dan Beard, A. B. Frost, Peter Newell, and others, and with photographs. Hartford, Connecticut: American Publishing Co., 1897.

"John Hay and the Ballads," *Harper's Weekly*, October 21, 1905, p. 1530.

Extract from Captain Stormfield's Visit to Heaven. Frontispiece by Albert Levering. New York and London: Harper & Bros., 1909.

Is Shakespeare Dead? New York and London: Harper & Bros., 1909.

Mark Twain's Speeches. Introduction by William Dean Howells. New York and London: Harper & Bros., 1910.

The Mysterious Stranger. Edited by Albert Bigelow Paine. Illustrated by N. C. Wyeth. New York and London: Harper & Bros., 1916.

Mark Twain's Letters. 2 vols. Edited by Albert Bigelow Paine. New York and London: Harper & Bros., 1917.

Mark Twain's Speeches. Introduction by Albert Bigelow Paine, and an appreciation by William Dean Howells. New York and London: Harper & Bros., 1923.

Mark Twain's Notebook. Edited by Albert Bigelow Paine. New York and London: Harper & Bros., 1935.

Mark Twain's Letters to Will Bowen. Edited by Theodore Hornberger. Austin: University of Texas Press, 1941.

Life on the Mississippi. Introduction by Edward Wagenknecht, with suppressed passages edited by Willis Wager. Illustrated by Thomas Hart Benton. New York: The Limited Editions Club, 1944.

The Portable Mark Twain. Edited by Bernard DeVoto. New York: Viking, 1946.

The Love Letters of Mark Twain. Edited by Dixon Wecter. New York and London: Harper & Bros., 1949.

The Autobiography of Mark Twain. Edited by Charles Neider. New York: Harper & Row, 1959.

Mark Twain–Howells Letters. 2 vols. Edited by Henry Nash Smith, William M. Gibson, and Frederick Anderson. Cambridge, Massachusetts: Harvard University Press, 1960.

Mark Twain's Letters to His Publishers. Edited by Hamlin Hill. Berkeley and Los Angeles: University of California Press, 1967.

Mark Twain's Which Was the Dream? and Other Symbolic Writings of Later Years. Edited by John S. Tuckey. Berkeley and Los Angeles: University of California Press, 1967.

Mark Twain's Satires and Burlesques. Edited by Franklin R. Rogers. Berkeley and Los

Angeles: University of California Press, 1968.

Mark Twain's Hannibal, Huck and Tom. Edited by Walter Blair. Berkeley and Los Angeles: University of California Press, 1969.

The Mysterious Stranger. Edited by William M. Gibson. Berkeley and Los Angeles: University of California Press, 1969.

Mark Twain's Fables of Men. Edited by John S. Tuckey. Berkeley and Los Angeles: University of California Press, 1972.

What Is Man? and Other Philosophical Writings. Edited by Paul Baender. Berkeley and Los Angeles: University of California Press, 1973.

A Pen Warmed-up in Hell. Edited by Frederick Anderson. New York: Harper & Row, 1972.

Mark Twain's Notebooks and Journals, Vol. I. Edited by Frederick Anderson, Michael B. Frank, and Kenneth M. Sanderson. Berkeley and Los Angeles: University of California Press, 1975.

Mark Twain's Notebooks and Journals, Vol. II. Edited by Frederick Anderson, Lin Salamo, and Berend L. Stein. Berkeley and Los Angeles: University of California Press, 1975.

Life As I See It. Edited by Charles Neider. New York: Harper & Row, 1977.

Early Tales and Sketches, Vol. I, *1851–1864.*

Edited by Edgar Marquess Branch, Robert H. Hirst, and Harriet Elinor Smith. Berkeley and Los Angeles: University of California Press, 1979.

Mark Twain's Notebooks and Journals, Vol. III. Edited by Robert Park Browning, Michael B. Frank, and Lin Salamo. Berkeley and Los Angeles: University of California Press, 1979.

The Adventures of Tom Sawyer; Tom Sawyer Abroad; Tom Sawyer, Detective. Edited by John C. Gerber, Paul Baender, and Terry Firkins. Berkeley and Los Angeles: University of California Press, 1980.

Notable Editions of *Huckleberry Finn*

According to the title page of the manuscript and the first American edition, the correct title of the novel is Adventures of Huckleberry Finn. *By error, "The" was added by the publishers to the running heads and by Kemble to his opening illustration; consequently the cover and title page of the first British edition, set by Chatto & Windus from American sheets, reads "The Adventures of Huckleberry Finn." Most subsequent editions retain the incorrect* The Adventures of Huckleberry Finn *to conform with* The Adventures of Tom Sawyer.

The Adventures of Huckleberry Finn (Tom Sawyer's Comrade). Illustrated by E. W. Kemble. London: Chatto & Windus, 1884.

Adventures of Huckleberry Finn (Tom Sawyer's Comrade). Illustrated by E. W. Kemble. New York: Charles L. Webster & Co., 1885.

Adventures of Huckleberry Finn (Tom Sawyer's Comrade). Illustrated by E. W. Kemble. Montreal: Dawson, 1885.

The Adventures of Huckleberry Finn (Tom Sawyer's Comrade). Leipzig: B. Tauchnitz, 1885.

The Adventures of Huckleberry Finn. Illustrated by E. W. Kemble. New York and London: Harper & Bros., 1896.

The Adventures of Huckleberry Finn. "Autograph Edition." With four new halftone plates by E. W. Kemble. New York and London: Harper & Bros., 1899.

The Adventures of Huckleberry Finn. Introduction by Brander Matthews. New York and London: Harper & Bros., 1918.

The Adventures of Huckleberry Finn. Illustrated by Worth Brehm. New York and London: Harper & Bros., 1923.

The Adventures of Huckleberry Finn. Illustrated with stills from the 1920 Paramount motion picture. London: Eveleigh Nash & Grayson, 1923.

The Adventures of Huckleberry Finn. Introduction and notes by Eizo Ohashi. Tokyo: Kenkyusha, 1923.

The Adventures of Huckleberry Finn. Edited by Emily Fanning Barry and Herbert B. Bruner. New York and London: Harper & Bros., 1931.

The Adventures of Huckleberry Finn. Introduction by Booth Tarkington. Illustrated by E. W. Kemble. New York: The Limited Editions Club, 1933.

The Adventures of Huckleberry Finn. Illustrated by A. S. Forrest. London: T. Nelson & Sons, 1935.

The Adventures of Huckleberry Finn. Introduction by John T. Winterich. Illustrated by Norman Rockwell. New York: Heritage Press, 1940.

The Adventures of Tom Sawyer and The Adventures of Huckleberry Finn. "A Modern Library Giant Edition." New York: Random House, 1940.

Adventures of Huckleberry Finn. Edited with an introduction by Bernard DeVoto. Illustrated by Thomas Hart Benton. New York: The Limited Editions Club, 1942.

Tom Sawyer and Huckleberry Finn. Everyman's Library. Introduction by Christopher Morley. London: Dent; New York: E. P. Dutton, 1943.

The Adventures of Huckleberry Finn. Introduction by May Lamberton Becker. Illustrated by Baldwin Hawes. Cleveland: World Publishing Co., 1947.

The Adventures of Huckleberry Finn. Illustrated by Edward Burra. London: Paul Elek, 1948.

The Adventures of Huckleberry Finn. Illustrated by Donald McKay. New York: Grosset & Dunlap, 1948.

The Adventures of Huckleberry Finn. Introductions by Brander Matthews and Dixon Wecter. New York and London: Harper & Bros., 1948.

The Adventures of Huckleberry Finn. Introduction by Lionel Trilling. New York: Holt, Rinehart, and Winston, 1948.

The Adventures of Tom Sawyer and The Adventures of Huckleberry Finn. Moscow: Foreign Publishing House, 1948.

The Adventures of Huckleberry Finn. Introduction by T. S. Eliot. London: Cresset Press; New York: Chanticleer Press, 1950.

The Adventures of Huckleberry Finn. Illustrated by Richard M. Powers. Garden City, New York: Doubleday, 1954.

The Adventures of Huckleberry Finn. Illustrated by C. Walter Hodges. London: Dent; New York: E. P. Dutton, 1955.

Adventures of Huckleberry Finn. Edited with an introduction and notes by Henry Nash Smith. Boston: Houghton Mifflin, 1958.

Huckleberry Finn. Illustrated by Geoffrey Whittam. London: Weidenfeld & Nicolson, 1958.

The Adventures of Huckleberry Finn. Illustrated by Logan McFarland. London: Collins, 1960.

The Adventures of Huckleberry Finn. Illustrated by W. Mitchell Ireland. London: Collins, 1960.

The Adventures of Tom Sawyer and The Adventures of Huckleberry Finn. Preface by Clara Clemens. New York: Platt & Munk, 1960.

The Adventures of Huckleberry Finn. Illustrated by Edward Ardizzone. London: Heinemann, 1961.

Adventures of Huckleberry Finn. Introduction by Kenneth S. Lynn. Edited by Francis Dunham. Boston: Houghton Mifflin Co., 1962.

Adventures of Huckleberry Finn. Introduction and bibliography by Hamlin Hall. San Francisco: Chandler Publishing Co., 1962.

The Adventures of Huckleberry Finn. Afterword by Clifton Fadiman. Illustrated by John Falter. New York and London: Macmillan, 1962.

Huck Finn and His Critics. Edited by Richard Lettes, Robert F. McDonnell, and William E. Morris. New York: Macmillan, 1962.

The Adventures of Huckleberry Finn: Illustrated by Raymond Sheppard. London and Glasgow: Blackie, 1965.

The Adventures of Huckleberry Finn. Edited with an introduction and notes by Peter Coveney. Harmondsworth, England: Penguin, 1966.

The Adventures of Huckleberry Finn. Illustrated by Kamil Lhotak. London: Hamlyn, 1966.

Adventures of Huckleberry Finn. Edited with an introduction and notes by Leo Marx. Indianapolis: Bobbs-Merrill, 1967.

The Art of Huckleberry Finn. Edited by Hamlin Hill and Walter Blair. San Francisco: Chandler Publishing Co., 1969.

Adventures of Huckleberry Finn. Introduction by Edgar M. Branch. Edited by James K. Bowen and Richard Vanderbeets. Glenview, Illinois: Scott, Foresman, 1970.

Adventures of Huckleberry Finn. Edited by Sculley Bradley, Richmond Croom Beatty, E. Hudson Long, and Thomas Cooley. New York: Norton, 1977.

The Complete Adventures of Tom Sawyer and Huckleberry Finn. Illustrated by Warren Chappell. New York: Harper & Row, 1978.

The Adventures of Tom Sawyer and The Adventures of Huckleberry Finn. Introduction by James Dickey. New York and London: New American Library, 1979.

About Mark Twain

Aldrich, Mrs. Thomas Bailey. *Crowding Memories.* Boston and New York: Houghton Mifflin, 1916.

Babcock, C. Merton. "Mark Twain, Mencken and 'The Higher Goofyism,'" *American Quarterly,* Winter 1964, pp. 587–594.

Bennett, Arnold. "Arnold Bennett Considers Twain Was Divine Amateur," *The* (London) *Bookman,* June 1910, p. 118.

Brack, Jr., O. M. "Mark Twain in Knee Pants: The Expurgation of *Tom Sawyer Abroad,*" *Proof 2,* 1972, pp. 145–151.

Brooks, Van Wyck. *The Ordeal of Mark Twain.* New York: E. P. Dutton, 1920.

Catalogue of the Library and Manuscripts of Samuel L. Clemens (Mark Twain). New York: Anderson Auction Co., 1911.

Covici, Pascal, Jr. "Dear Master Wattie: The Mark Twain–David Watt Bowser Letters," *Southwest Review,* Spring 1960, pp. 105–121.

DeVoto, Bernard. *Mark Twain's America.* Boston and New York: Houghton Mifflin, 1932.

Dreiser, Theodore. "Mark the Double Twain," *The English Journal,* October 1935, pp. 615–627.

Duskis, Henry, ed. *The Forgotten Writings of Mark Twain.* New York: Philosophical Library, 1963.

English, Thomas H. *Mark Twain to Uncle Remus.* Atlanta, Georgia: Emory University Library, 1953.

Faulkner, William. "The Art of Fiction," *The Paris Review,* Spring 1956, pp. 46–47.

Gilder, Rosamund. *Letters of Richard Watson Gilder.* Boston and New York: Houghton Mifflin, 1916.

Gribben, Alan. "Mark Twain, Phrenology, and the 'Temperaments,'" *American Quarterly,* March 1972, pp. 45–68.

Harnsberger, Caroline Thomas. *Mark Twain's View of Religion.* Evanston, Illinois: Schiori Press, 1961.

Howells, William Dean. "Mark Twain," *The Century,* September 1882, pp. 780–783.

———. "Mark Twain: An Inquiry," *North American Review,* February 1901, pp. 308–321.

———. *My Mark Twain: Reminiscences and Criticism.* New York and London: Harper & Bros., 1910.

———. "Recent Literature," *The Atlantic Monthly,* May 1876, pp. 621–622.

Johnson, Merle. *A Bibliography of the Works of Mark Twain.* New York and London: Harper & Bros., 1935.

Johnson, Clifton. *Highways and Byways of the Mississippi Valley.* New York: Macmillan, 1906, pp. 162, 181.

Kaplan, Justin. *Mark Twain and His World.* New York: Simon and Schuster, 1974.

———. *Mr. Clemens and Mark Twain.* New York: Simon and Schuster, 1966.

Macdonald, Dwight. "Mark Twain: An Unsentimental Journey," *The New Yorker,* April 9, 1960, pp. 160–196.

"Mark Twain Talks," Portland *Sunday Oregonian,* August 11, 1895, p. 10.

Masters, Edgar Lee. *Mark Twain: A Portrait.* New York and London: Scribners, 1938.

Matthews, Brander. "Memories of Mark Twain," *The Tocsin of Revolt and Other Essays.* New York: Scribners, 1922.

Meltzer, Milton. *Mark Twain Himself.* New York: Thomas Y. Crowell Co., 1960.

Mumford, Lewis. *The Golden Day.* New York: Boni and Liveright, 1926.

Orians, G. Harrison. "Walter Scott, Mark Twain, and the Civil War," *The South Atlantic Quarterly,* October 1941, pp. 342–359.

Paine, Albert Bigelow. *Mark Twain: A Biography.* 3 vols. New York and London: Harper & Bros., 1912.

Park, Edwin J. "A Day with Mark Twain," Chicago *Tribune,* September 19, 1886.

Pattee, Fred Lewis. *A History of American Literature Since 1870.* New York: Century Co., 1915.

Pettit, Arthur Gordon. *Mark Twain and the South.* Lexington: University Press of Kentucky, 1974.

———. "Mark Twain and the Negro, 1867–1869," *The Journal of Negro History,* April 1871, pp. 88–96.

Ramsay, Robert L., and Emberson, Frances Guthrie. "A Mark Twain Lexicon," *University of Missouri Studies,* January 1, 1938, pp. 1–278.

Rubin, Louis D., Jr. *George W. Cable.* New York: Pegasus, 1969.

Sanderlin, George. *Mark Twain: As Others Saw Him.* New York: Coward, McCann & Geoghegan, 1978.

Sinclair, Upton. *Mammonart.* Pasadena, California: privately printed for the author, 1925.

Sosey, Frank S. "Palmyra and Its Historical Environment," *The Missouri Historical Review,* April 1929, pp. 361–362.

Turner, Arlin. *Mark Twain and G. W. Cable.* East Lansing: Michigan State University Press, 1960.

Webster, Samuel Charles. *Mark Twain, Business Man.* Boston: Little, Brown, 1946.

Wecter, Dixon. *Sam Clemens of Hannibal.* Boston: Houghton Mifflin, 1952.

Welsh, Donald H. "Sam Clemens' Hannibal, 1836–1838," *Midcontinent American Studies Journal,* Spring 1962, pp. 28–43.

About *Huckleberry Finn*

Adams, Lucille. *Huckleberry Finn: A Descriptive Bibliography of the Huckleberry Finn Collection at the Buffalo Public Library.* Buffalo, New York: Buffalo Public Library, 1950.

Ashmead, John. "A Possible Hannibal Source for Mark Twain's Dauphin," *American Literature,* March 1962, pp. 105–107.

Bailey, Roger. "Twain's *Adventures of Huckleberry Finn,* Chapters 1 and 2," *The Explicator,* September 1967, No. 2.

Baldanza, Frank. "The Structure of *Huckleberry Finn,*" *American Literature,* November 1955, pp. 347–355.

Belden, H. M. "Scyld Scefing and Huck Finn," *Modern Language Notes,* May 1918, p. 315.

Besant, Walter. "My Favorite Novelist and His Best Book," *Munsey's Magazine*, February 1898, pp. 659–664.

Birchfield, James. "Jim's Coat of Arms," *Mark Twain Journal*, Summer 1969, pp. 15–16.

Blair, Walter. "The French Revolution and *Huckleberry Finn*," *Modern Philology*, August 1957, pp. 21–35.

———. *Mark Twain and Huck Finn*. Berkeley and Los Angeles: University of California Press, 1960.

———. "The Reasons Mark Twain did not finish his story," *Life*, December 20, 1968, p. 50A.

Branch, Edgar M. "The Two Providences: Thematic Form in *Huckleberry Finn*," *College English*, January 1950, pp. 188–195.

Bridges, Robert. "Mark Twain's Blood-Curdling Humor," *Life*, February 26, 1885, p. 119.

Byers, John R., Jr. "Miss Emmeline Grangerford's Hymn Book," *American Literature*, May 1971, pp. 259–263.

———. "The Pokeville Preacher's Invitation in *Huckleberry Finn*," *Mark Twain Journal*, Summer 1977, pp. 15–16.

Carkeet, David. "The Dialects in *Huckleberry Finn*," *American Literature*, November 1979, pp. 315–332.

DeVoto, Bernard. *Mark Twain at Work*. Cambridge, Massachusetts: Harvard University Press, 1942.

Eby, Cecil D., Jr. "Mark Twain's 'Plug' and 'Chaw': An Anecdotal Parallel," *Mark Twain Journal*, Summer 1960, pp. 11, 25.

Ellison, Ralph. "The Negro Writer in America," *Partisan Review*, Spring 1958, p. 215.

Evans, Elizabeth. "Thomas Wolfe: Some Echoes from Mark Twain," *Mark Twain Journal*, Summer 1976, pp. 5–6.

Farrell, James T. "Mark Twain's Huckleberry Finn and Tom Sawyer," *The League of Frightened Philistines and Other Papers*. New York: Vanguard Press, 1945, pp. 25–30.

Ferguson, DeLancey. "Clemens' *Huckleberry Finn*," *The Explicator*, April 1946, No. 42.

———. "Huck Finn Aborning," *The Colophon*, Spring 1938, pp. 171–180.

Fiedler, Leslie A. "Come Back to the Raft Ag'in, Huck Honey," *An End to Innocence*. Boston: Beacon Press, 1955, pp. 142–151.

Flory, Claude R. "Huck, Sam and the Small-Pox," *Mark Twain Journal*, Winter 1964–1965, pp. 1–2, 8.

Foner, Philip S. *Mark Twain: Social Critic*. New York: International Publishers, 1958.

Gaffney, W. G. "Mark Twain's 'Duke' and 'Dauphin,'" *Names*, September 1966, pp. 175–178.

Graves, Wallace. "Mark Twain's 'Burning Shame,'" *Nineteenth-Century Fiction*, June 1968, pp. 93–98.

Hansen, Chadwick. "The Character of Jim in the Ending of *Huckleberry Finn*," *The Massachusetts Review*, Autumn 1963, pp. 45–66.

Hemingway, Ernest. *Green Hills of Africa*. New York: Scribners, 1935, p. 22.

———. *Ernest Hemingway Selected Letters*. Edited by Carlos Baker. New York: Scribners, 1981, p. 188.

Highfill, Phillip H., Jr. "Incident in *Huckleberry Finn*," *American Literature*, November 1941, p. 6.

Hinz, Joseph. "Huck and Pluck: 'Bad' Boys in American Fiction," *The South Atlantic Quarterly*, January 1952, pp. 120–129.

Hoffman, Daniel G. *Form and Fable in American Fiction*. New York: Oxford University Press, 1961.

Housman, A. E. A letter of February 2, 1927, *Mark Twain Quarterly*, Winter 1936, p. 8.

Jones, Joseph. "The 'Duke's' Tooth-Powder Racket: A Note on *Huckleberry Finn*," *Modern Language Notes*, November 1946, pp. 468–469.

Joyce, James. *Selected Joyce Letters*. Edited by Richard Ellmann. New York: Viking, 1975, p. 1940.

Kirkham, E. Bruce. "Huck and Hamlet," *Mark Twain Journal*, Summer 1969, pp. 17–18.

Kraus, W. Kenneth. "*Huckleberry Finn*: A Final Irony," *Mark Twain Journal*, Winter 1967–1968, pp. 18–19.

Kruse, Horst H. "Annie and Huck: A Note on *The Adventures of Huckleberry Finn*," *American Literature*, May 1967, pp. 207–214.

Lorch, Fred W. "A Note on Tom Blankenship (Huckleberry Finn)," *American Literature*, November 1941, pp. 351–353.

McNamara, Eugene. "Huck Lights Out for the Territory; Mark Twain's Unfinished Sequel," *The University of Windsor Review*, Fall 1966, pp. 67–74.

Marx, Leo. "Mr. Eliot, Mr. Trilling, and *Huckleberry Finn*," *American Scholar*, Autumn 1953, pp. 423–440.

———. "The Pilot and the Passenger: Landscape Conventions and the Style of *Huckleberry Finn*," *American Literature*, May 1956, pp. 129–146.

Matthews, Brander. "*Huckleberry Finn*," *The* (London) *Saturday Review*, January 31, 1885, pp. 153–154.

May, Charles E. "Literary Masters and Masturbators: Sexuality, Fantasy, and Reality in *Huckleberry Finn*," *Literature and Psychology*, No. 2, 1978, pp. 85–92.

Mayberry, George. "Reading and Writing," *The New Republic*, May 1, 1944, p. 608.

Metzger, Charles E. "*The Adventures of Huckleberry Finn* as Picaresque," *The Midwest Quarterly*, Spring 1964, pp. 249–256.

Moore, O. H. "Mark Twain and Don Quixote," *Publications of the Modern Language Association*, June 1922, pp. 324–326.

Pritchett, V. S. "Current Literature," *The New Statesman*, August 2, 1941, p. 113.

Rogers, Franklin R. *Mark Twain's Burlesque Patterns*. Dallas, Texas: Southern Methodist University Press, 1960.

Seelye, John. *The True Adventures of Huckleberry Finn*. Evanston, Illinois: Northwestern University Press, 1970.

Slater, Joseph. "Notes and Queries: Music at Col. Grangerford's: A Footnote to *Huckleberry Finn*," *American Literature*, March 1949, pp. 108–111.

Stone, Albert E., Jr. *The Innocent Eye*. New Haven, Connecticut: Yale University Press, 1961.

Trilling, Lionel. "*Huckleberry Finn*," *The Liberal Imagination*. New York: Viking, 1950, pp. 104–117.

Weeks, Robert P. "The Captain, the Prophet, and the King," *Mark Twain Journal*, Winter 1975–1976, pp. 9–12.

Wiley, B. J. "Guyuscutus, Royal Nonesuch, and Other Hoaxes," *Southern Folklore Quarterly*, December 1944, pp. 251–275.

Wood, Clement. *More Adventures of Huckleberry Finn*. New York and Cleveland: World, 1940.

Wood, Grant. "My Debt to Mark Twain," *Mark Twain Quarterly*, Fall 1937, pp. 6, 14, 24.

About E. W. Kemble

David, Beverly R. "The Pictorial *Huckleberry Finn*: Mark Twain and His Illustrator E. W. Kemble," *American Quarterly*, October 1979, pp. 331–351.

———. "Visions of the South: Joel Chandler Harris and His Illustrators," *American Literary Realism*, Summer 1976, pp. 189–206.

Kemble, E. W. "Illustrating *Huckleberry Finn*," *The Colophon*, February 1930, pp. 45–52.

Morris, Courtland. "The Model for Huck Finn," *Mark Twain Quarterly*, Fall 1938, pp. 22–23.

Obituary, *New York Times*, September 20, 1933.

INDEX

Page numbers in italics indicate illustrations.